BUSINESS PROCESS MODELING, SIMULATION, AND DESIGN

Manuel Laguna

Leeds School of Business
University of Colorado at Boulder

Johan Marklund

Leeds School of Business
University of Colorado at Boulder

PEARSON
Prentice
Hall

Upper Saddle River, New Jersey 07458

Library of Congress Cataloging-in-Publication Data

Laguna, Manuel.
    Business process modeling, simulation, and design / Manuel Laguna, Johan
      Marklund. p. cm.
    Includes bibliographical references and index.
    ISBN 0-13-091519-X (pbk.)
        1. Industrial management—Mathematical models—Textbooks. 2. Business
        planning—Textbooks. 3. Reengineering (Management)—Textbooks. I. Marklund,
        Johan. II. Title.

HD62.17.L34 2004
658.4'0352—dc22

                                                    2003064793

Executive Editor: Tom Tucker
Editorial Assistant: Dawn Stapleton
Media Project Manager: Nancy Welcher
Executive Marketing Manager: Debbie Clare
Marketing Assistant: Amanda Fisher
Managing Editor (Production): John Roberts
Production Editor: Maureen Wilson
Manufacturing Buyer: Michelle Klein
Cover Design: Bruce Kenselaar
Composition: Integra Software Services Pvt. Ltd.
Full-Service Project Management: Jennifer Welsch, BookMasters, Inc.
Printer/Binder: Hamilton Printing Co.

Credits and acknowledgments borrowed from other sources and reproduced, with per-
mission, in this textbook appear on appropriate page within text.

Pearson Education LTD.
Pearson Education Singapore, Pte. Ltd
Pearson Education, Canada, Ltd
Pearson Education–Japan

Pearson Education Australia PTY, Limited
Pearson Education North Asia Ltd
Pearson Educación de Mexico, S.A. de C.V.
Pearson Education Malaysia, Pte. Ltd

10 9 8 7 6 5 4 3 2 1
ISBN 0-13-091519-X

To Our Parents

Brief Contents

Contents

Preface

As the title suggests, this book is about analytical business process modeling and design. It is the result of several years of teaching a business process design and simulation course at the undergraduate and the MBA levels in the Leeds School of Business at the University of Colorado at Boulder. We have also drawn from one of the author's experiences delivering a simulation course in the Industrial Engineering and Management program at Lund University in Sweden.

The main motivation for writing this textbook stems from our struggle to find a book that approaches business process design from a broad, quantitative modeling perspective. The main objective with this book is thus to provide students with a comprehensive understanding of the multitude of analytical tools that can be used to model, analyze, understand, and ultimately design business processes. We believe that the most flexible and powerful of these tools, although not always the most appropriate, is discrete event simulation.

The wide range of approaches covered in this book include graphical flowcharting tools, deterministic models for cycle time analysis and capacity decisions, and analytical queuing methods, as well as the use of data envelopment analysis (DEA) for benchmarking purposes. What distinguishes this textbook from general operations management (OM) books, most of which cover many of the same topics, is its focus on business processes as opposed to just manufacturing processes or general OM problems, and its emphasis on simulation modeling using state-of-the-art commercial simulation software. Essentially, *Business Process Modeling, Simulation, and Design* can be thought of as a hybrid between traditional books on process management, operations management, and simulation. Although it would be desirable for all students in operations management to take several courses in each of these topics, the reality is that few business school curricula today allow that. In our experience, simulation especially tends to be shoved to the side simply because it is perceived to be too technical. However, our firm belief, manifested by our writing of this book, is that this need not and should not be the case. The rapid development of user-friendly simulation software with graphical interfaces has made the use of simulation accessible even to those lacking computer programming skills, and it provides a great medium for illustrating and understanding implications of capacity restrictions and random variation on process performance. Furthermore, the growing interest in simulation-based tools in industry suggests that an understanding of simulation modeling, its potential as well as its limitations for analyzing and designing processes, is of key importance for students looking for a future career in operations management.

Before proceeding with a discussion of how we picture this book being used, it is worthwhile to summarize what the book is *not*. It is not a traditional, qualitatively oriented book on process management, although we dedicate one chapter to these important issues. It is not a traditional book on operations management, although it covers some of the traditional tools found in most OM books. Furthermore, it is not a traditional book on simulation, although discrete event simulation is used extensively. It is a book that attempts to bring these topics together by placing an analytical modeling perspective on process design and particularly emphasizing the power of simulation modeling as a vehicle for analyzing and designing business processes.

This textbook is ideal for a one-semester undergraduate or MBA course within an operations management business school curriculum. The MBA course typically would cover some of the more advanced topics in greater depth, such as DEA (which does not require that students have some previous exposure to linear programming, but it is helpful) simulation optimization, and queuing. The MBA course also could include a more involved simulation project. In addition, we envision this book being used for an undergraduate course in industrial engineering or within an engineering management program. In terms of requirements, the textbook assumes that students have taken a basic course in business statistics. However, if students have been exposed to a basic course in operations management and have some prior knowledge of quantitative techniques, this gives an additional opportunity to explore some of the topics covered in this textbook in more detail. In terms of how to cover the material, we recommend following the chapter sequence.

The text is organized as follows.

- Chapter 1 sets the stage by defining what we mean by a business process and business process design. It also points to the importance of these issues for overall business performance and the organization's strategic positioning.
- Chapter 2 explains some fundamental principles for successful process management and also takes a closer look at two of the more influential, process-oriented improvement programs in recent years: Six Sigma and Business Process Reengineering. The rationale is that although the focus of the book is on analytical modeling and design rather than implementation and change management, even the best possible design is of little use if it is not implemented and managed properly.
- Chapter 3 presents a simulation-based methodology for business process design projects. The approach identifies a number of steps or issues that typically need to be dealt with during a process design project from initialization to implementation. The approach can be seen as a road map to the remainder of the book in the sense that the tools and methods discussed in the following chapters can be used to address some of the specified issues.
- Chapter 4 deals with a range of basic tools for analyzing and designing processes that display limited variability in demand and activity times (i.e., deterministic as opposed to stochastic models). The first part of the chapter discusses several graphical tools for charting and describing processes. These tools are particularly useful for understanding existing processes. The second part of the chapter investigates seven fundamental process design principles and associated methods of analysis.
- Chapter 5 focuses on how to manage process flows, particularly with regard to cycle time and capacity analysis. As in Chapter 4, we consider only deterministic situations with perfect information regarding demand, resource availability, and activity times.
- Chapter 6 introduces queuing and simulation as means for explicitly incorporating randomness and variability into the process analysis. The queuing sections discuss queuing strategies, properties of the exponential distribution, the Poisson process, traditional birth and death processes, and the corresponding queuing models including single and multiple servers with and without restrictions on the queuing population and/or the queue lengths. We also discuss waiting/shortage costs and applications to process design situations. The simulation sections introduce the concept of simulation and illustrate it by a simple spreadsheet model of a single-server queuing model.
- Chapter 7 provides an introduction to the simulation software Extend that is used for simulation modeling. The focus is on how to get a model up and running, including working with simple animation, modeling random processing times, and limited labor resources. The chapter also discusses how to collect data and use the built-in tools for statistical analysis.
- Chapter 8 continues exploring how to use Extend to model more complex business processes and capture features like prioritization, attribute assignment, blocking, balking and reneging queues, routing through multiple and parallel paths, batching, resource allocation, activity-based costing, and cycle time analysis.
- Chapter 9 deals with the important issue of statistical analysis of input and output data. Topics covered include determination of input data distributions, random number generation, and how to analyze output data. Of particular importance is how to compare the performance of alternative process designs.
- Chapter 10 discusses state-of-the-art methods for optimizing design parameters using simulation.
- Chapter 11 shows how to use data envelopment analysis (DEA) for benchmarking purposes. The chapter is accompanied by an Excel add-in tool for solving the underlying linear programming models.

The simulation modeling is done entirely with the Extend software, enabling the students to work hands-on with models of their own. A potential criticism associated with this software-integrated approach is that the acquired knowledge may be thought of as being software dependent. However, our experience is that after initially investing some time in understanding the software, the main challenge and learning lie in creating abstract models of processes, a conceptual framework that is software independent. Furthermore, because the functionality of most modern simulation software is very similar, exposure to one product promotes a valuable understanding of the potential and limitations of simulation modeling in general.

The textbook includes a CD with a student version of Extend OR V6 and the Excel add-in for solving DEA problems. For instructors, an additional CD is available that includes solutions to end-of-chapter problems, prebuilt Extend models, and some additional simulation exercises/projects with suggested solutions.

There are many individuals among our colleagues, families, and friends who have contributed to this book as sources of inspiration, encouragement, and support. Our deepest gratitude goes to all of you. Others have had a more direct influence on this book, and we take this opportunity to express our appreciation for their valuable help. Special thanks go to Pat Diamond and others at Imagine That Inc., who worked with us on the simulation models and allowed us to distribute the student version of Extend LT with our text. We would also like to thank the following reviewers, who provided many valuable suggestions in shaping this textbook:

George E. Monahan, University of Illinois
Charles Munson, Washington State University
C. Surrender Reddy, Saginaw Valley State University
Joseph Sarkis, Clark University
Shane J. Schvaneveldt, Weber State University

Our gratitude also goes to past and present students in the undergraduate and graduate programs at the Leeds School of Business who have helped shape this book into what it is today. Special thanks go to Marco Better for helping us put together the instructor's manual. We are indebted to our Leeds School of Business colleagues Thomas Vossen, Cathleen S. Burns, and David E. Monarchi for providing helpful criticism and feedback on earlier drafts.

And thank you to Tom Tucker at Prentice Hall who encouraged us to pursue this project and provided help and advice along the way. Finally, our thanks to Maureen Wilson and Dawn Stapleton at Prentice Hall, and Jennifer Welsch at BookMasters, who capably guided our manuscript through production. Thank you for making this book a reality!

Introduction to Business Process Design

Booming competition in an increasingly global marketplace leaves no room for successful companies to harbor internal inefficiencies. Even more importantly, customers are becoming more demanding; if one product or service does not live up to their expectations, there are many more from which to choose. The stakes are high, and so is the penalty for not satisfying the right customers with the right products and services. The quest for internal efficiency and external effectiveness means that organizations must align their internal activities and resources with the external requirements, or to put it differently, business processes must be designed appropriately. To that end, the main objective of this book is to provide the reader with a comprehensive understanding of the wide range of analytical tools that can be used for modeling, analyzing, and ultimately designing business processes. Particular emphasis is placed on discrete event simulation, as it represents one of the most flexible and powerful tools available for these purposes.

However, before investigating the different analytical tools in Chapters 4 through 11, we need to understand what business processes and process design are all about. This first chapter is devoted to a detailed definition of business processes and business process design, including the concepts of process hierarchies, process architecture, and incremental process improvement as opposed to process design. An important distinction made in this respect is between the activities of designing a process and implementing the design; the former is the focus of this book.

This introductory chapter also discusses the importance of business process design for the overall business performance and the organization's business strategy. The last section of this chapter explores why inefficient and ineffective business processes come to exist in the first place.

Chapter 2 deals with the important issues of managing and improving processes, including issues of implementation and change management. Chapter 3 then discusses a simulation-based methodology for business process design projects. This can be construed as a road map for the remaining eight chapters of this book, which focus on tools and modeling.

1.1 What Is a Business Process?

From a pragmatic point of view, a business process describes how something is done in an organization. However, the in-depth analysis and design of business processes, the theme of this book, require further examination.

Let us start by dissecting the words *business* and *process*. Most people probably would contest that they have a clear notion about what a business is. In broad terms, we will define a business as "an organizational entity that deploys resources to provide customers with desired products or services." This definition serves our purposes because it encompasses profit-maximizing firms and supply chains, as well as nonprofit organizations and governmental agencies.

A process is a somewhat more ambiguous concept with different meanings, depending on the context in which it is used. For example, a biologist or medical doctor refers to breathing as a life-sustaining *process*. In mathematics or engineering, the concept of random or deterministic *processes* describes event occurrences. In politics, the importance of election *processes* is obvious, in education a key concept is the learning *process*, and so on. *Merriam Webster's Dictionary*, online 11th edition, defines *process* as (i) a natural phenomenon marked by gradual changes that lead to a particular result, (ii) a natural continuing activity or function, or (iii) a series of actions or operations conducing to an end. The last of these definitions is of particular interest for our understanding of business processes, because it leads into the traditional high-level definition of a process used in the operations management literature: *a process specifies the transformation of inputs to outputs*. The transformations typically are classified as follows.

- *Physical*, for instance, the transformation of raw materials to a finished product.
- *Locational*, for instance, the transportation service provided by an airline.
- *Transactional*, for instance, banking and transformation of cash into stocks by a brokerage firm.
- *Informational*, for instance, the transformation of financial data into information in the form of financial statements.

The simple transformation perspective forms the basis for the so-called process view of an organization. (See Figure 1.1.) According to this perspective, any organizational entity or business can be characterized as a process or a network of processes.

The process view makes no assumptions of the types of processes constituting the organization. However, often a process is automatically thought of as a manufacturing or production process. We employ the term *business process* to emphasize that this book is not focusing on the analysis and design of manufacturing processes per se, although they will be an important subset of the entire set of business processes that define an organization. Table 1.1 provides some examples of generic processes other than traditional production/manufacturing processes that one might expect to find in many businesses. For the remainder of this book, the terms *process* and *business process* will be used interchangeably.

The simple transformation model of a process depicted in Figure 1.1 is a powerful starting point for understanding the importance of business processes. However, for purposes of detailed analysis and design of the transformation process itself, we need to go further and look behind the scenes, inside the "black box" model so to speak, at process types, process hierarchies, and determinants of process architecture.

Inputs **Process** Outputs

FIGURE 1.1 The Transformation Model of a Process

TABLE 1.1 Examples of Generic Business Processes Other Than Traditional Production and Manufacturing Processes

Accounts payable	Inventory management
Accounts receivable	Order fulfillment
Admissions (e.g., hospitals and universities)	New employee training
Auditing	Performance appraisal
Billing	Product approval (e.g., pharmaceuticals)
Budget planning	Product development
Business planning	Purchasing
Client acquisition	Receiving
Continuous improvement	Shipping
Credit approval	Vendor certification
Human resources planning and hiring	Warranty and claims processing

1.1.1 PROCESS TYPES AND HIERARCHIES

Based on their scope within an organization, processes can be characterized into three different types: *individual processes*, which are carried out by separate individuals; *vertical* or *functional processes*, which are contained within a certain functional unit or department; and *horizontal* or *cross-functional processes*, which cut across several functional units (or, in terms of supply chains, even across different companies). See Figure 1.2 for illustration.

FIGURE 1.2 Illustration of Individual, Vertical, and Horizontal Processes

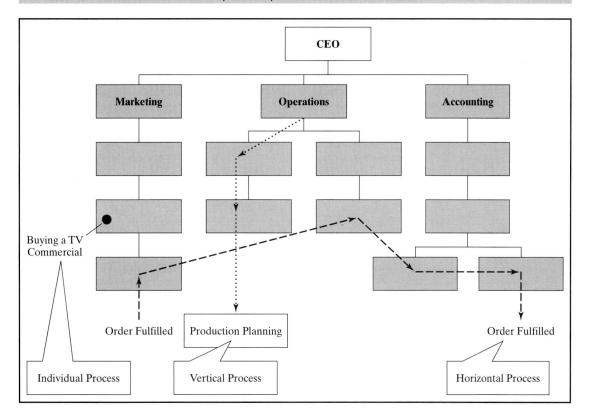

It follows that a hierarchy exists between the three process types in the sense that a cross-functional process typically can be decomposed into a number of connected functional processes or subprocesses, which consist of a number of individual processes. Moving down even further in detail, any process can be broken down into one or more activities that are comprised of a number of tasks. As an illustration, consider the order-fulfillment process in Figure 1.2, which in its entirety is cross functional. However, it consists of functional subprocesses (e.g., in the sales and marketing departments) that receive the order request by phone, process the request, and place a production order with the operations department. The order receiving itself is an activity comprised of the tasks of answering the phone, talking to the customer, and verifying that all necessary information is available to process the order. If we assume that the order-receiving activity is performed by a single employee, this constitutes an example of an individual process.

In terms of process design, cross-functional business processes that are core to the organization and include a significant amount of nonmanufacturing-related activities often offer the greatest potential for improvement. Core processes are defined by Cross et al. (1994) as all the functions and the sequence of activities (regardless of where they reside in the organization), policies and procedures, and supporting systems required to meet a marketplace need through a specific strategy. A core process includes all the functions involved in the development, production, and provision of specific products or services to particular customers. An underlying reason why cross-functional processes often offer high improvement potential compared to functional processes in general, and production/manufacturing processes in particular, is that they are more difficult to coordinate and often suffer from suboptimization[1]. An important reason for this tendency toward suboptimization is the strong departmental interests inherent in the functional[2] organization's management structure.

Roberts (1994) provides some additional explanations for the high improvement potential of cross-functional business processes.

- Improvements in cross-functional business processes have not kept up with improvements in manufacturing processes over the years. In other words, the current margin for improvement is greater in nonmanufacturing-related business processes.
- Waste and inefficiency are more difficult to detect in cross-functional processes than in functional processes due to increased complexity.
- Cross-functional business processes often devote as little as 5 percent or less of the available process time to activities that deliver value to the customers.
- Customers are five times more likely to take their business elsewhere because of poor service-related business processes than because of poor products.

---

[1]The term *suboptimization* refers to situations in which optimizing a subsystem according to its local objectives leads to an inferior solution for the overall system. For example, a production manager under budgetary pressure might decide not to allow any more overtime. As a consequence, the orders accepted by the sales staff cannot be met on time, which leads to order cancellations. For profit-maximizing firms, this implies revenue reductions due to lost sales and also long-term effects in terms of loss of goodwill and reputation.

[2]Traditionally, companies have developed organizational structures based on the type of work performed. This type of organization is commonly known as a *functional organization* because work is organized on the basis of the function it serves. A restaurant that classifies its workers as cooks, dishwashers, bartenders, and so on has classified them on the basis of the function they serve or the type of work they perform. Likewise, a manufacturer of consumer goods with accounting, finance, sales, and engineering departments has organized its employees on the basis of the tasks they perform.

1.1.2 DETERMINANTS OF THE PROCESS ARCHITECTURE

The process architecture or process structure can be characterized in terms of five main components or elements (see, for example, Anupindi et al. [1999]): the inputs and outputs, the flow units, the network of activities and buffers, the resources, and the information structure, some of which we have touched upon briefly already. To a large extent, process design and analysis has to do with understanding the restrictions and opportunities these elements offer in a particular situation. We will deal with this extensively in Chapters 2 through 9.

Inputs and Outputs

The first step in understanding and modeling a process is to identify its boundaries; that is, its entry and exit points. When that is done, identifying the input needed from the environment in order for the process to produce the desired output is usually fairly straightforward. It is important to recognize that inputs and outputs can be tangible (raw materials, cash, and customers) or intangible (information, energy, and time). To illustrate, consider a manufacturing process where inputs in terms of raw materials and energy enter the process and are transformed into desired products. Another example would be a transportation process where customers enter a bus station in New York as inputs and exit as outputs in Washington. In order to perform the desired transformation, the bus will consume gasoline as input and produce pollution as output. Similarly, a barbershop takes hairy customers as input and produces less hairy customers as output. An example in which inputs and outputs are information or data is an accounting process where unstructured financial data enter as input and a well-structured financial statement is the output. To summarize, the inputs and outputs establish the interaction between the process and its environment.

Flow Units

A unit of flow or *flow unit* can be defined as a "transient entity[3] that proceeds through various activities and finally exits the process as finished output." This implies that depending on the context, the flow unit can be a unit of input (e.g., a customer or raw material), a unit of one or several intermediate products or components (e.g., the frame in a bicycle-assembly process), or a unit of output (e.g., a serviced customer or finished product). The characteristics and identity of flow units in a system, as well as the points of entry and departure, can vary significantly from process to process. Typical types of flow units include materials, orders, files or documents, requests, customers, patients, products, paper forms, cash, and transactions. A clear understanding and definition of flow units is important when modeling and designing processes because of their immediate impact on capacity and investment levels.

It is customary to refer to the generic unit of flow as a *job*, and we will use this connotation extensively in Chapters 3 through 9. Moreover, an important measure of flow dynamics is the flow rate, which is the number of jobs that flow through the process per unit of time. Typically, flow rates vary over time and from point to point in the process. We will examine these issues in more detail in Chapter 5.

---

[3]In the field of discrete event simulation, the term *transient entity* is given to jobs that enter the simulated system, where activities are performed to complete such jobs before exiting. Therefore, in that context, transient entities and flows are synonymous. In simulation, there is also the notion of resident entities, which are the resources needed to perform activities.

The Network of Activities and Buffers

From our discussion of process hierarchies, we know that a process is composed of activities. In fact, an accurate way to describe a process would be as a network of activities and buffers through which the flow units or jobs have to pass in order to be transformed from inputs to outputs. Consequently, for in-depth analysis and design of processes, we must identify all relevant activities that define the process and their precedence relationships; that is, the sequence in which the jobs will go through them. To complicate matters, many processes accommodate different types of jobs that will have different paths through the network, implying that the precedence relationships typically are different for different types of jobs. As an example, consider an emergency room, where a patient in cardiac arrest clearly has a different path through the ER process than a walk-in patient with a headache. Moreover, most processes also include buffers between activities, allowing storage of jobs between them. Real-world examples of buffers are waiting rooms at a hospital, finished goods inventory, and lines at an airport security checkpoint. A common goal in business process design is to try to reduce the time jobs spend waiting in buffers and thereby achieve a higher flow rate for the overall process.

Activities can be thought of as micro processes consisting of a collection of tasks. Finding an appropriate level of detail to define an activity is crucial in process analysis. A tradeoff exists between activity and process complexity. Increasing the complexity of the individual activities by letting them include more tasks decreases the complexity of the process description. (See Figure 1.3.) The extreme is when the entire process is defined as one activity and we are back to the simple "black box" input/output transformation model.

Several classifications of process activities have been offered in the literature. Two basic approaches are depicted in Figure 1.4.

Both approaches classify the activities essential for the process to meet the customers' expectations as value-adding activities. The difference is in the classification of control, and policy and regulatory compliance activities. One approach is based on the belief that although control activities do not directly add value to the customer, they are essential to conducting business. Therefore, these activities should be classified as *business-value-adding* (also known as control) activities. The contrasting view is a classification based on the belief that anything that does not add value to the customer

FIGURE 1.3 Process Complexity Versus Individual Activity Complexity

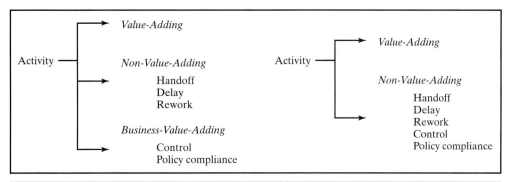

FIGURE 1.4 Classification of Activities

should be classified as a *non-value-adding* activity. This classification can be determined by asking the following question: Would your customer be willing to pay for this activity? If the answer is no, then the activity does not add value. It is then believed that control activities, such as checking the credit history of a customer in a credit-approval process, would fall into the category of non-value-adding activities because the customer (in this case, the applicant) would not be willing to pay for such an activity.

To understand the value-adding classification, the concept of value must be addressed. Although this is an elusive concept, for our purposes it is sufficient to recognize that it involves doing the right things and doing things right. Doing the right things means providing the customers with what they want (i.e., being effective). Activities that contribute to transforming the product or service to better conform to the customer's requirements have the potential to add value. For example, installing the hard drive in a new personal computer brings the product closer to being complete and is, therefore, value adding. However, to be truly value–added, the activity also must be carried out efficiently using a minimum of resources; that is, it must be done right. If this were not the case, waste would occur that could not be eliminated without compromising the process effectiveness. If the hard drive installation were not done properly, resulting in damaged and scrapped hard drives or the need for rework, the installation activity would not be value adding in its true sense. Even though the right activity was performed, it was not done correctly, resulting in more than the minimum amount of resources being consumed. Clearly, this extra resource consumption is something for which the customer would not be willing to pay.

The task of classifying activities should not be taken lightly, because the elimination of non-value-adding activities in a process is one of the cornerstones of designing or redesigning efficient processes. One of the most common and straightforward strategies for eliminating non-value-adding and control activities is the integration of tasks. Task consolidation typically eliminates wasteful activities, because handoffs account for a large percentage of non-value-adding time in many processes. Also, controls (or control activities) are generally in place to make sure that the work performed upstream in the process complies with policies and regulations. Task aggregation tends to eliminate handoffs and controls; therefore, it increases the ratio of value-adding activities to non-value-adding activities (and/or business-value-adding activities).

To illustrate the process of classifying activities, let us consider the famous IBM Credit example, first introduced by Hammer and Champy (1993). IBM Credit is in the business of financing computers, software, and services that the IBM Corporation sells. This is an important business for IBM, because financing customers' purchases is extremely profitable. The process formerly used consisted of the following sequence of activities.

1. Field sales personnel called in requests for financing to a group of 14 people.
2. The person taking the call logged information on a piece of paper.
3. The paper was taken upstairs to the credit department.
4. A specialist (a) entered the information into a computer system and (b) did a credit check.
5. The results of the credit check (a) were written on a piece of paper and (b) sent to the business practices department.
6. Standard loan contracts were modified to meet customer requirements.
7. The request was (a) sent to a "pricer," where (b) an interest rate was determined.
8. The interest rate (a) was written on a piece of paper and (b) sent to a clerical group.
9. A quote was developed.
10. The quote was sent to field sales via FedEx.

A possible classification of these activities into the categories of value-adding, non-value-adding, and business-value-adding appears in Table 1.2.

Note that only a small fraction of the activities are considered to add value to the customer (i.e., the sales field agent). Arguably, the only activity that adds value might be number 9; however, we also have included activity 1 because the customer triggers the process with this activity and activity 6 because the customization of the contract is forced by the peculiarities of each specific request. Handoffs account for a considerable percentage of the non-value-adding activities (3, 5(b), 8(b), and 10). This description does not include all the delays that are likely to occur between handoffs, because in practice, agents in this process did not start working on a request immediately upon receipt. In fact, although the actual work took in total only 90 minutes to perform, the entire process consumed 6 days on average and sometimes took as long as 2 weeks. In Section 3.6.2 of Chapter 3, we will discuss how the process was redesigned to achieve turnaround times of 4 hours on the average.

Resources

Resources are tangible assets that are necessary to perform activities within a process. Examples of resources include the machinery in a job shop, the aircraft of an airline, and the faculty at an educational institution. As these examples imply, resources often are divided into two categories: capital assets (e.g., real estate, machinery, equipment, and computer systems) and labor (i.e., the organization's employees and the knowledge they possess). As opposed to inputs, which flow through the process and leave, resources are utilized rather than consumed. For example, an airline utilizes resources such as aircraft and personnel to perform the transportation process day after day. At the same time, the jet fuel, which is an input to the process, is not only used but consumed.

TABLE 1.2 Activity Classifications for IBM Credit

Category	Activities
Value-Adding	1, 6, 9
Non-Value-Adding	2, 3, 4(a), 5, 7(a), 8, 10
Business-Value-Adding	4(b), 7(b)

Information Structure

The last element needed in order to describe the process architecture is the information structure. The information structure specifies which information is required and which is available in order to make the decisions necessary for performing the activities in a process. For example, consider the inventory replenishment process at a central warehouse; the information structure specifies the information needed in order to implement important operational policies, such as placing an order when the stock level falls below a specified reorder point.

Based on our definition of a business and the exploration of process hierarchies and architecture, a more comprehensive and adequate definition of a business process emerges.

A business process is a network of connected activities and buffers with well-defined boundaries and precedence relationships, which utilize resources to transform inputs into outputs for the purpose of satisfying customer requirements. (See Figure 1.5.)

1.1.3 WORKFLOW MANAGEMENT SYSTEMS

The term *workflow* often is used in connection with process management and process analysis, particularly in the field of information systems. It refers to how a job flows through the process, the activities that are performed on it, the people involved, and the information needed for its completion. The workflow is, therefore, defined by the flow units along with the network of activities and buffers, the resources, and the information structure discussed previously. Management of administrative processes often is referred to as workflow management, and information systems that support workflow management are called workflow management systems. For our purposes, we can think of workflow management as synonymous with process management.

Document processing has a fundamental place in workflow management, as business documents are the common medium for information processes (such as data flow analysis, database storage and retrieval, transaction processing, and network

FIGURE 1.5 **A Process Defined as a Network of Activities and Buffers with Well-Defined Boundaries Transforming Inputs to Customer Required Outputs Using a Collection of Resources**

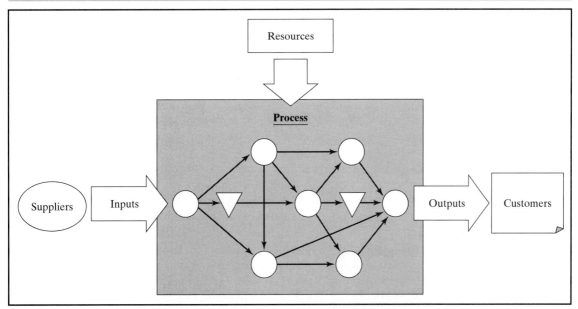

communications) and business processes. Workflow management controls the actions taken on documents moving through a business process. Specifically, workflow management software is used to determine and control who can access which document, what operations employees can perform on a given document, and the sequence of operations that are performed on documents by the workers in the process.

Workers have access to documents (e.g., purchase orders and travel authorizations) in a workflow management system. These individuals perform operations, such as filling and modifying fields, on the documents. For example, an employee who is planning to take a business trip typically must fill out a travel authorization form to provide information such as destination, dates of travel, and tentative budget. The document might go to a travel office where additional information is added. Then, the form probably goes to a manager, who might approve it as is, ask for additional information, or approve a modified version (for instance, by reducing the proposed travel budget). Finally, the form goes back to the individual requesting the travel funds. This simple example illustrates the control activities that are performed before the request to travel is granted. The activities are performed in sequence to guarantee that the approved budget is not changed at a later stage. Although the sequence is well established and ensures a desired level of control, workflow management software should be capable of handling exceptions (e.g., when the manager determines that it is in the best interest of the company to bypass the normal workflow sequence), reworking loops (e.g., when more information is requested from the originator of the request), and obtaining permissions to modify and update the request before the manager makes a final decision. Workflow management software developers are constantly incorporating additional flexibility into their products so buyers can deal with the increasing complexity of modern business processes without the need for additional computer programming.

1.2 The Essence of Business Process Design

The essence of business process design can be described as how to do things in a good way. *Good* in this context refers to process efficiency and process effectiveness. The last statement is important; process design is about satisfying customer requirements in an efficient way. An efficient process that does not deliver customer value is useless. A well-designed process does the right things in the right way.

From a more formal perspective, business process design is concerned with configuring the process architecture (i.e., the inputs and outputs, the flow units, the network of activities and buffers, the resources, and the information structure; see Figure 1.5), in a way that satisfies customer requirements in an efficient way. It should be noted that process customers can be internal and external to the organization. However, it is important that the requirements of the internal customers are aligned with the overall business goals, which ultimately means satisfying the desires of the external customers targeted in the business strategy.

Although business process design concerns all types of processes, we have already indicated that for reasons of coordination and suboptimization, it is often most valuable when dealing with complex horizontal processes that cut across the functional or departmental lines of the organization and reach all the way to the end customer. An example is the order-fulfillment process illustrated in Figure 1.2.

The roots of the functional organization date back to the late 1700s, when Adam Smith proposed the concept of the division of labor in *An Inquiry into the Nature and Causes of the Wealth of Nations* (1776). Referring to the 17 operations required to produce a pin, Smith argued that assigning one task to each of 17 workers would be more efficient and would produce more pins than having 17 workers each autonomously perform all 17 tasks. According to Smith, dividing work into discrete tasks provides the following benefits.

- Each worker's skill increases by repeatedly performing the same task.
- No time is lost due to switching workers from one task to another.
- Workers are well positioned to develop improved tools and techniques as a result of focusing on a single task.

What Smith's model does not address is that as products and services become more complex and customers require more varieties of them, the need for many more activities and the coordination of the resulting basic tasks comprising these activities becomes extremely difficult. The division of labor has the goal of creating highly specialized workers who can complete basic tasks efficiently. Even if the workers become highly efficient at their tasks, the process as a whole can be inefficient. Inefficiencies in a process design with the division of labor paradigm are primarily related to the need for handing off work from one station to the next and for coordinating the flow of the jobs in the process. Perhaps the most significant drawbacks associated with handing off work are the delays and errors introduced when a job is passed from worker to worker.

Consider, for example, the traditional approach to designing new products illustrated by Shafer and Meredith (1998). The process typically begins when the marketing department collects information about customers' needs and desires. This information is then relayed to a research and development (R&D) department, which is responsible for designing the product to meet the customers' requirements. After the design is completed, it is up to the manufacturing department to produce the product exactly as specified in the design. After the product is produced, it is the responsibility of the sales department to sell it. Finally, after a consumer purchases the product, the customer service department must provide after-sales services such as help with installation and warranty repairs. This process, although involving several departments, appears to have a logical structure, but in reality it is not uncommon that the engineers in R&D design a feature that manufacturing cannot produce or one that can be produced only at a high cost. In this sequential approach (commonly known as "over-the-wall design"), the production problem would not be discovered until after the design is finalized and handed off to manufacturing. Upon discovering the problem, manufacturing would have to send the design back to R&D for modifications. Clearly, each time a design has to go back and forth between R&D and manufacturing, it involves yet another handoff and increases the delay in introducing the new product.

This example illustrates an essential issue often addressed in process design—namely, that completing a set of activities sequentially, one at a time, tends to increase the time required to complete the entire process. In addition, significant delays can occur in the discovery of important information that would have influenced the quality of the output from activities already completed; this tends to extend the completion time even further. The solution is to try to do as many activities as possible in parallel. Sophisticated product development teams use the concept of concurrent engineering[4] to avoid the "over-the-wall design" problem and shorten the process time.

---

[4]Concurrent engineering is one of the most effective strategies designed to shorten product development cycle times and increase the likelihood of designing robust and manufacturable products. In simple terms, the strategy consists of overlapping various phases of the design and development process, allowing for downstream work to begin before the prior phase of work has been completed. Implementing concurrent engineering is not a trivial matter, due to the increased need for information to flow between the different phases of the process.

As just indicated, the road to a good process design starts with a profound understanding of what the customers want and thereby what the process is supposed to deliver. Although understanding customer preferences and purchasing behavior is a field of study in its own right, for process design purposes, four dimensions of customer requirements are particularly important: cost, quality, response time, and variety. Arriving at a good process design also requires a thorough understanding of the current process (if one exists) and any new enablers that change the rules of the game, such as IT developments, breakthrough technologies, or changes in legislation. A first approach, particularly in redesign situations, is to try to eliminate waste, waiting times, and non-value-adding activities to speed up the process. However, it is important not to get stuck in the old ways of doing things and leverage the power of process design by challenging rooted perceptions of how to do things.

Throughout the book, we will use the terms *design* and *redesign* interchangeably because from an analytical point of view, no major difference can be distinguished between designing a new process and redesigning an existing one. This statement hinges on the fact that in this book, we make a clear distinction between designing a process and implementing the design. The latter is a tremendously challenging task that requires good skills in change management and in knowing how to motivate and inspire an organization to change. Ultimately, success will depend on the buy-in from people at all levels of the organization. In implementing a new design, a big difference is evident between making changes to an existing process and establishing a process in a "greenfield organization" (or an organization that does not have any processes in place), the former usually being the more difficult situation to handle. Because the focus of this book is on the analytical modeling, analysis, and design of processes, from our perspective the analytical approach for design and redesign is the same. We will touch briefly upon the important issues of process and change management in Chapter 2. However, for a more in-depth treatment of this important area, we refer to books solely devoted to the subject of how to achieve and sustain organizational changes; these can be found in the management and human resource literature.

1.2.1 INCREMENTAL PROCESS IMPROVEMENT AND PROCESS DESIGN

In our quest to define the essence of what we refer to as business process design, it is valuable to discuss the relationship between incremental improvement and design. Clearly, both are about how to do things in a good way, and most of the tools for analyzing process that are covered in this book are just as useful in an incremental improvement project as in a design project. However, a subtle but important difference can be detected in terms of the objectives and the degrees of freedom available to a process design team compared to an incremental improvement team. The scope for the former usually far exceeds that of the latter.

The difference between incremental process improvement and process design parallels the difference between systems improvement and systems design that John P. Van Gigch so eloquently described more than 25 years ago (Van Gigch, 1978). Van Gigch's book championed the notion of a systems approach to problem solving, a field from which process design and reengineering[5] have borrowed many concepts. In the

---

[5]Reengineering or business process reengineering (BPR) is an improvement program, based on the ideas of Hammer, Champy, and Davenport published in the early 1990s, that advocates radical redesign and revolutionary change of core business processes as a recipe for success. The principles of BPR will be discussed further in Chapter 2.

following, we adapt Van Gigch's descriptions to the context of process design, acknowledging that if a system is defined as an assembly or set of related elements, a process is nothing else but an instance of a system.

Many of the problems arising in the practice of designing business processes stem from the inability of managers, planners, analysts, administrators, and the like to differentiate between incremental process improvement and process redesign. Incremental improvement refers to the transformation or change that brings a system closer to standard or normal operating conditions. The concept of incremental improvement carries the connotation that the design of the process is set and that norms for its operation have been established. In this context, improving a process refers to tracing the causes of departures from established operating norms, or investigating how the process can be made to yield better results—results that come closer to meeting the original design objectives. Because the design concept is not questioned, the main problems to be solved are as follows.

1. The process does not meet its established goals.
2. The process does not yield predicted results.
3. The process does not operate as initially intended.

The incremental improvement process starts with a problem definition, and through analysis, we search for elements of components or subprocesses that might provide possible answers to our questions. We then proceed by deduction to draw certain tentative conclusions.

Design also involves transformation and change. However, design is a creative process that questions the assumptions on which old forms have been built. It demands a completely new outlook in order to generate innovative solutions with the capability of increasing process performance significantly. Process design is by nature inductive. (See Chapter 3 for a further discussion of inductive versus deductive thinking.)

1.2.2 AN ILLUSTRATIVE EXAMPLE

To illustrate the power of process design in improving the efficiency and effectiveness of business processes, we will look at an example from the insurance industry, adapted from Roberts (1994).

Consider the claims-handling process of a large insurance company. Sensing competitive pressure coupled with the need to be more responsive to its customers, the company decided to overhaul its process for handling claims related to the replacement of automobile glass. The CEO thought that if her plan was successful, she would be able to use any expertise acquired from this relatively low-risk endeavor as a springboard for undertaking even more ambitious redesign projects later. Furthermore, the project would give the company an important head start on the learning curve associated with redesign activities.

The CEO immediately appointed an executive sponsor to shepherd the project. Following some preliminary analysis of the potential payoff and impact, the CEO and the executive sponsor developed a charter for a process design team and collaborated to handpick its members.

Early on, the team created a chart of the existing process to aid in their understanding of things as they were. This chart is depicted in simplified form in Figure 1.6. (In Chapter 4, we will introduce methods and tools for creating several charts for process analysis.) This figure summarizes the following sequence of events for processing claims under the existing configuration.

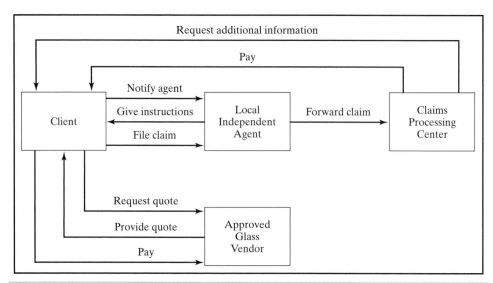

FIGURE 1.6 Existing Claims-Handling Process

1. The client notifies a local independent agent that she wishes to file a claim for damaged glass. The client is given a claim form and is told to obtain a replacement estimate from a local glass vendor.
2. After the client has obtained the estimate and completed the claim form, the independent agent verifies the accuracy of the information and then forwards the claim to one of the regional processing centers.
3. The processing center receives the claim and logs its date and time of arrival. A data entry clerk enters the contents of the claim into a computer (mainly for archiving purposes). Then, the form is placed in a hard-copy file and routed, along with the estimate, to a claims representative.
4. If the representative is satisfied with the claim, it is passed along to several others in the processing chain, and a check eventually is issued to the client. However, if any problems are associated with the claim, the representative attaches a form and mails a letter back to the client for the necessary corrections.
5. Upon receiving the check, the client can go to the local glass vendor and have the glass replaced.

Using the existing process, a client might have to wait one to two weeks before being able to replace his or her automobile glass. If the glass happens to break on a weekend, the process could take even longer.

Given the goal to come up with a radical overhaul of the process, the team recommended the solution depicted in Figure 1.7. The team accomplished this after evaluating a number of process configurations. The evaluation was done in terms of the cost versus the benefits resulting from each configuration.

Structural as well as procedural changes were put into place. Some of these, especially the procedural changes, are not entirely evident simply by contrasting Figures 1.6 and 1.7. The changes in procedures involved the following.

- The claims representative was given final authority to approve the claim.
- A long-term relationship was established with a select number of glass vendors, enabling the company to leverage its purchasing power and to pay the vendor directly. Furthermore, because the prices are now prenegotiated, it is no longer necessary to obtain an estimate from the vendor. (Note that this procedural

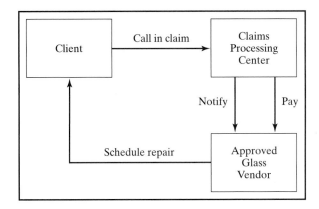

FIGURE 1.7 Redesigned Claims-Handling Process

change is similar to the well-established total quality management [TQM] notion of *vendor certification.*)
- Rather than going through a local agent, obtaining an estimate, and filling out a form, the client now simply contacts the processing center directly by phone to register a claim.

The structural changes are manifested in the following sequence of events, which describe the flow of the process.

1. Using a newly installed, 24-hour hot line, the client speaks directly with a claims representative at one of the company's regional processing centers.
2. The claims representative gathers the pertinent information over the phone, enters the data into the computer, and resolves any problems related to the claim on the spot. The representative then tells the client to expect a call from a certain glass vendor, who will make arrangements to repair the glass at the client's convenience.
3. Because the claim now exists as an electronic file that can be shared through a local area network (LAN), the accounting department can immediately begin processing a check that will be sent directly to the local glass vendor.

A number of significant benefits—some more quantifiable than others—resulted from changing the process to introduce a new design.

- The client can now have the glass repaired in as little as 24 hours versus 10 days. This represents a 90 percent improvement in the process cycle time (i.e., the elapsed time from when the claim is called in until the glass is replaced).
- The client has less work to do because a single phone call sets the process in motion. Also, the client is no longer required to obtain a repair estimate.
- Problems are handled when the call is initiated, thus preventing further delays in the process.
- Problems with lost or mishandled claims virtually disappear.
- The claim now passes through fewer hands, resulting in lower costs. By establishing a long-term relationship with a select number of glass vendors, the company is able to leverage its purchasing power to obtain a 30 percent to 40 percent savings on a paid claim.
- Because fewer glass vendors are involved, a consolidated monthly payment can be made to each approved vendor, resulting in additional savings in handling costs. The company now issues 98 percent fewer checks.

- By dealing with preapproved glass vendors, the company can be assured of consistent and reliable service.
- The claims representatives feel a greater sense of ownership in the process, because they have broader responsibilities and expanded approval authority.

It is evident that the new process was designed by framing the situation in these terms: How do we settle claims in a manner that will cause the least impact on the client while minimizing processing costs? If instead they had asked How can we streamline the existing process to make it more efficient? their inquiry might not have removed the independent agent from the processing chain. The fundamental difference between these two questions is that the first one is likely to lead to a radical change in the process design because it goes to the core issue of how to best satisfy the customer requirements, and the second one is likely to lead to the introduction of technology without process change (i.e., automation without redesign). Could further efficiencies still be realized in this process? Without a doubt! This is where an incremental and continuous improvement approach should take over.

1.3 Business Process Design, Overall Business Performance, and Strategy

To put process design into a larger context, we point out some links among process design, overall business performance, and strategy.

1.3.1 BUSINESS PROCESS DESIGN AND OVERALL BUSINESS PERFORMANCE

What is overall business performance and how is it measured? A detailed answer to this question is to a large extent company specific. However, in general terms we can assert that the performance of a business should be measured against its stated goals and objectives.

For a profit-maximizing firm, the overarching objective is usually to maximize long-term profits or shareholder value. In simple terms, this is achieved by consistently, over time, maximizing revenues and minimizing costs, which implies satisfying customer requirements in an efficient way. For nonprofit organizations, it is more difficult to articulate a common goal. However, on a basic level, presumably one objective is to survive and grow while providing customers with the best possible service or products. Consider, for example, a relief organization with the mission of providing shelter and food for people in need. In order to fulfill this mission, the organization must first of all survive, which means that it must maintain a balanced cash flow by raising funds and keeping operational costs at a minimum. Still, to effectively help as many people as possible in the best possible way requires more than just capital and labor resources; it requires a clear understanding of exactly what kind of aid their "customers" need the most. Furthermore, the ability to raise funds in the long run most likely will be related directly to how effectively the organization meets its goals; that is, how well it performs.

To summarize, a fundamental component in overall business performance regardless of the explicitly stated objectives is to satisfy customer requirements in an efficient way. In the long term, this requires well-designed business processes.

1.3.2 BUSINESS PROCESS DESIGN AND STRATEGY

Strategy guides businesses toward their stated objectives and overall performance excellence. In general terms, *strategy* can be defined as "the unifying theme that aligns all individual decisions made within an organization."

In principle, profit-maximizing firms address their fundamental objective of earning a return on their investment that exceeds the cost of capital in two ways. Either the firm establishes itself in an industry with above-average returns, or it leverages its competitive advantage over the other firms within an industry to earn a return that exceeds the industry average. These two approaches define two strategy levels that are distinguishable in most large enterprises. The corporate strategy answers the question Which industries should we be in? The business strategy answers the question How should we compete within a given industry?

Although both strategies are of utmost importance, the intensified competition in today's global economy requires that no matter what industry one operates in, one must be highly competitive. Consequently, a prerequisite for success is an effective business strategy. In fact, nonprofit organizations need to be competitive, as well. For example, the relief organization mentioned previously most likely has to compete against other organizations of the same type for funding. Similarly, a university competes against other universities for students, faculty, and funding.

Developing a business strategy is, therefore, a crucial undertaking in any business. Many different approaches deal with this issue in a structured, step-by-step fashion. However, developing a sound business strategy requires a profound understanding of the organization's external and internal environment combined with a set of clearly defined, long-term goals. The external environment includes all external factors (e.g., social, political, economical, and technological) that influence the organization's decisions. Still, in most instances the core external environment is comprised of the firm's industry or market, defined by its relationship with customers, suppliers, and competitors. The internal environment refers to the organization itself, its goals and values, its resources, its organizational structure, and its systems. This means that understanding the internal environment to a large extent has to do with understanding the hierarchy and structure of all business processes.

A clear understanding of the internal environment promotes an understanding of the organization's internal *strengths* and *weaknesses*. Similarly, in-depth knowledge of the external environment provides insights into the *opportunities* and *threats* the organization is facing. Ideally, the business strategy is designed to take advantage of the opportunities by leveraging the internal strengths while avoiding the threats and protecting its weaknesses. This basic approach is referred to as a *SWOT* analysis.

The link between business process design and the business strategy is obvious when it comes to the internal environment; the internal strengths and weaknesses are to a large extent embodied in the form of well-designed and poorly designed business processes. By carefully redesigning processes, weaknesses can be turned into strengths, and strengths can be further reinforced to assure a competitive advantage. The link to the external environment might be less obvious, but remember that a prerequisite for achieving an effective process design is to understand the customer requirements. Furthermore, to be an efficient design, the process input has to be considered, which implies an understanding of what the suppliers can offer. In order for the business strategy to be successful, the organization must be able to satisfy the requirements of the targeted customers in an efficient, competitive way.

Our discussion so far can be synthesized through the concept of strategic fit. Strategic fit refers to a match between the strategic or competitive position the organization wants to achieve in the external market, and the internal capabilities necessary to take it there. Another way of looking at this is to realize that strategic fit can by attained by a market-driven strategy or a process-driven strategy, or most commonly a combination of the two. In a market-driven strategy, the starting point is the key competitive priorities, meaning the strategic position the firm wants to reach. The organization then has to design and implement the necessary processes to support this position. In a process-driven strategy, the starting point is the available set of process capabilities. The organization then identifies a strategic position that is supported by these processes. This perspective illustrates that business process design is an important tool for linking the organization's internal capabilities to the external environment so that the preferred business strategy can be realized.

1.4 Why Do Inefficient and Ineffective Business Processes Exist?

Throughout most of this chapter, we have been praising business process design and advocating the importance of well-designed processes. So, if businesses acknowledge this, then why were inefficient and ineffective (i.e., broken) processes designed in the first place? Hammer (1990), one of the founding fathers of the reengineering movement (discussed in Chapter 2), provided an insightful answer: Most of the processes and procedures seen in a business were not designed at all—they just happened. The following examples of this phenomenon are adapted from Hammer's article.

Consider a company whose founder one day recognizes that she doesn't have time to handle a chore, so she delegates it to Smith. Smith improvises. Time passes, the business grows, and Smith hires an entire staff to help him cope with the work volume. Most likely, they all improvise. Each day brings new challenges and special cases, and the staff adjusts its work accordingly. The potpourri of special cases and quick fixes is passed from one generation of workers to the next. This example illustrates what commonly occurs in many organizations; the ad hoc has been institutionalized and the temporary has been made permanent.

In another company, a new employee inquires: "Why do we send foreign accounts to the corner desk?" No one knew the answer until a company veteran explained that 20 years ago, an employee named Mary spoke French and Mary sat at the corner desk. Today, Mary is long gone and the company does not even do business in French-speaking countries, but foreign accounts are still sent to the corner desk.

An electronics company spends $10 million per year to manage a field inventory worth $20 million. Why? Once upon a time, the inventory was worth $200 million and the cost of managing it was $5 million. Since then, warehousing costs have escalated, components have become less expensive, and better forecasting techniques have minimized the number of units in inventory. The only thing that remains unchanged is the inventory management system.

Finally, consider the purchasing process of a company in which initially, the only employees are the original founders. Because the cofounders trust each other's judgment with respect to purchases, the process consists of placing an order, waiting for the order to arrive, receiving the order, and verifying its contents (see "Original Purchasing Process" in Figure 1.8). When the company grows, the cofounders believe that they cannot afford to have the same level of trust with other employees in the company. Control mechanisms are installed to guarantee the legitimacy of the purchase orders. The process grows, but the number of value-adding activities (i.e., Ordering and Receiving) remains the same. (See "Evolved Purchasing Process" in Figure 1.8.)

Hammer introduced the notion of "information poverty" to explain the need for introducing activities that make existing processes inefficient. Many business processes originated before the advent of modern computer and telecommunications technology, and therefore they contain mechanisms designed to compensate for information poverty. Although companies today are information affluent, they still use the same old mechanisms and embed them in automated systems. Large inventories are excellent examples of a mechanism to deal with information poverty, which in this case means

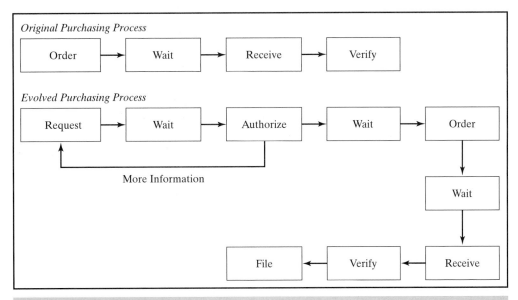

FIGURE 1.8 Process Evolution

lack of knowledge with respect to demand. Information technology enables most operations to obtain point-of-sales data in real time that can be used to drastically reduce or virtually eliminate the need for inventories in many settings. Consequently, inefficient or ineffective processes can be the result of an organization's inability to take advantage of changes in the external and internal environments that have produced new design enablers such as information technology.

Another reason for the existence of inefficient process structures is the local adjustments made to deal with changes in the external and internal environments. When these incremental changes accumulate over time, they create inconsistent structures. Adjustments often are made to cope with new situations, but seldom does anyone ever question whether an established procedure is necessary.

In other words, inefficient and ineffective processes usually are not designed; they emerge as a consequence of uncoordinated incremental change or the inability to take advantage of new design enablers.

1.5 Summary

Business processes describe how things are done in a business and encompass all activities taking place in an organization including manufacturing processes, as well as service and administrative processes. A more precise definition useful for purposes of modeling and analysis is that a business process is "a network of connected activities with well-defined boundaries and precedence relationships that utilizes resources to transform inputs to outputs with the purpose of satisfying customer requirements." Depending on the organizational scope, a business process can be categorized hierarchically as cross functional, functional, or individual; typically, the cross-functional processes offer the greatest potential for improvement.

The essence of business process design is to determine how to do things in an efficient and effective way. More formally, business process design can be described as a configuration of the process architecture, (i.e., the inputs and outputs, the flow units, the network of activities and buffers, the resources, and the information structure), so as to satisfy external and internal customer requirements in an efficient way. In this context, it is important that the requirements of the internal customers are aligned with the overall business goals, which ultimately boils down to satisfying the desires of the external customers targeted in the business strategy.

A linkage between overall business performance and business process design can be made through the fundamental need of any business, profit maximizing or not, to satisfy and thereby attract customers while maintaining an efficient use of resources. For a nonprofit organization, this is a necessity for survival because it enables the company to continue fulfilling its purpose. For profit-maximizing organizations, the ability to reach the overarching objective of generating long-term profits and returns above the cost of capital is contingent upon the firm's long-term ability to maximize revenues and minimize costs. In the long run, this requires well-designed business processes. Similarly, in developing a business strategy, business process design is an important vehicle for linking the internal capabilities with the external opportunities. This allows the company to achieve a strategic fit between the firm's desired competitive position in the external market and the internal capabilities necessary to reach and sustain this position.

Finally, in this chapter, we also illustrated the fact that the emergence of inefficient and ineffective processes is inherent to most organizations simply because they must adjust to changes in their internal and external environments. These incremental adjustments, which usually make good sense when they are introduced, at least locally, tend to accumulate with time and create inefficient structures. On the other hand, another common reason for inefficiencies is the inability to take advantage of new design enablers such as information technology and automating old work processes instead of using the new technology to do things in a more efficient way. This is why we have emphasized that inefficient and ineffective processes usually are not designed; they emerge as a consequence of uncoordinated incremental change or inability to take advantage of new design enablers.

1.6 References

Anupindi, R., S. Chopra, S. D. Deshmukh, J. A. Van Mieghem, and E. Zemel. 1999. *Managing business process flows.* Upper Saddle River, NJ: Prentice Hall.

Cross, K. F., J. J. Feather, and R. L. Lynch. 1994. *Corporate renaissance: The art of reengineering.* Cambridge, MA: Blackwell Business.

Davenport, T. 1993. *Process innovation: Reengineering work through information technology.* Boston: Harvard Business School Press.

Davenport, T., and J. Short. 1990. The new industrial engineering: Information technology and business process redesign. *Sloan Management Review* 31, 4 (Summer): 11–27.

Gabor, A. 1990. *The man who discovered quality.* New York: Penguin Books.

Goldsborough, R. 1998. PCs and the productivity paradox. *ComputorEdge* 16, 43 (October 26): 23–24.

Grant, R. M. 1995. *Contemporary strategy analysis.* Cambridge, MA: Blackwell Publishers.

Grover, V., and M. J. Malhotra. 1997. Business process reengineering: A tutorial on the concept, evolution, method, technology, and application. *Journal of Operations Management* 15: 193–213.

Hammer, M. 1990. Reengineering work: Don't automate, obliterate. *Harvard Business Review* 71(6): 119–131.

Hammer, M., and J. Champy. 1993. *Reengineering the corporation: A manifesto for business revolution.* New York: Harper Business.

Harbour, J. L. 1994. *The process reengineering workbook.* New York: Quality Resources.

Lowenthal, J. N. 1994. *Reengineering the organization: A step-by-step approach to corporate revitalization.* Milwaukee, WI: ASQC Quality Press.

Manganelli, R. L., and M. M. Klein. 1994. A framework for reengineering. *Management Review* (June): American Management Association, 10–16.

Petrozzo, D. P., and J. C. Stepper. 1994. *Successful reengineering.* New York: John Wiley and Sons.

Roberts, L. 1994. *Process reengineering: A key to achieving breakthrough success.* Milwaukee, WI: ASQC Quality Press.

Shafer, S. M., and J. R. Meredith. 1998. *Operations management: A process approach with spreadsheets.* New York: John Wiley and Sons.

Van Gigch, John P. 1978. *Applied general systems theory.* New York: Harper and Row Publishers.

1.7 Discussion Questions and Exercises

1. *Requisition Process* (adapted from Harbour, 1994)—A large company is having trouble processing requisition forms for supplies and materials. Just getting through the initial approval process seems to take forever. Then, the order must be placed, and the supplies and materials must be received and delivered to the correct location. These delays usually cause only minor inconveniences. However, a lack of supplies and materials sometimes stops an entire operation. After one such instance, a senior manager has had enough. The manager wants to know the reason for the excessive delays. The manager also wants to know where to place blame for the problem!

   A process analysis is done at the manager's request. The requisition process is broken down into three subprocesses: (1) requisition form completion and authorization, (2) ordering, and (3) receiving and delivery. The process analysis also reveals that the first subprocess consists of the steps shown in Table 1.3.

   TABLE 1.3 Steps in the Requisition Process

Step	Time (minutes)
1. Requisition form initiated	10
2. Form mailed to procurement	720
3. Form sits in IN basket	75
4. Requisition form completed	18
5. Form sits in OUT basket	75
6. Form mailed for authorization	720
7. Form sits in IN basket	45
8. Form reviewed and authorized	12
9. Form sits in OUT basket	90
10. Form mailed to ordering	720

   a. Classify the activities in this process.
   b. Who is the customer?
   c. Translate what you think the customer wants into measures of process performance.
   d. How is the process performing under the measures defined in part (c)?
   e. Comment on the manager's attitude.

2. *Receiving and Delivery Process* (adapted from Harbour, 1994)—The company in exercise 1 has a large manufacturing complex that is spread over a large area. You are assigned to study the receiving-and-delivery subprocess in order to make recommendations to the senior manager for streamlining the process. The subprocess begins with receiving goods on the warehouse loading dock, and it ends with the goods being delivered to the correct location. Before you were assigned to this project, the senior manager had a student intern do a simple process analysis. The manager instructed the student to observe the process and describe the various steps. Also, the student was told to find average processing times for each step in the process. The information collected by the student is summarized in Table 1.4.

   a. Classify the activities in this process.
   b. Who is the customer?
   c. Translate what you think the customer wants into measures of process performance.
   d. How is the process performing under the measures defined in part (c)?
   e. Comment on the instructions given to the intern by the senior manager in reference to the process analysis.

3. *Hospital Administrative Processes* (adapted from Harbour, 1994)—A director of administration for a large hospital complex receives some disturbing news. A recent auditor's report states that 28 percent of all hospital costs are related to administrative costs. The director is determined to lower this figure. She has read some magazine and newspaper articles about

TABLE 1.4 Steps in the Receiving-and-Delivery Process

No.	Step	Time (minutes)
1	Received goods temporarily sit on loading dock.	120
2	Goods are visually inspected for damage.	3
3	Goods are carried to the warehouse.	10
4	Goods are stored in the warehouse.	1,440
5	Goods are removed from the warehouse and carried to the loading dock.	10
6	Goods sit on the loading dock awaiting loading.	60
7	Goods are carried to a truck.	10
8	Goods are trucked to a satellite storage area.	20
9	Goods are carried from the truck to a satellite storage area.	10
10	Goods are stored in the satellite storage area.	320
11	Goods are inspected for damage.	2
12	Goods are carried to a truck.	10
13	Goods are trucked to the required location.	15
14	Goods are carried to the required location.	10

business process design and has decided to try it to see if it works. She calls a special off-site meeting. The meeting is held at a luxury hotel, and only senior-level managers are invited. At the meeting, she presents her concerns. She then states that the purpose of the meeting is to redesign the various administrative processes. A brainstorming session is conducted to identify potential problems. The problems are then prioritized. The meeting breaks for lunch.

After lunch, everyone works on developing some solutions. A number of high-level process maps are taped to the wall, and the director discusses each of the identified problems. One suggested solution is reorganization. Everyone loves the idea. Instead of 12 major divisions, it is suggested to reorganize into 10. After the meeting is over, the director spends 4 hours hammering out the details of the reorganization. She returns to work the next day and announces the reorganization plan. Sitting in her office, she reflects on her first process redesigning efforts. She is pleased.

a. How would you rate the director's redesign project? Would you give her a pay raise?

b. How would you conduct this process redesigning effort?

4. *Environmental Computer Models* (adapted from Harbour, 1994)—An environmental company specializes in developing computer models. The models display the direction of groundwater flow, and they are used to predict the movement of pollutants. The company's major customers are state and federal agencies. The development of the computer models is a fairly complex process. First, numerous water wells are drilled in an area. Then probes are lowered into each well at various depths. From instruments attached to the probes, a number of recordings are made. Field technicians, who record the data on paper forms, do this. The data consist mostly of long lists of numbers. Back in the office, a data-entry clerk enters the numbers into a computer. The clerk typically enters hundreds of numbers at a time. The entered data are then used to develop the computer models.

Recently, the company has experienced numerous problems with data quality. Numerous data entry errors have resulted in the generation of inaccurate models. When this happens, someone must carefully review the entered data. When incorrect numbers are identified, they are reentered and another computer model is generated. This rework process often must be repeated more than once. Because it takes a long time to generate the models, such errors add considerable cost and time to a project. However, these additional costs cannot be passed on to the customer. Prices for the computer models are based on fixed bids, so the company must pay all rework costs. Alarmingly, rework costs have skyrocketed. On the last two jobs, such additional costs eliminated almost all profits. The company has decided to fix the problem. The company's first step has been to hire an expert in data quality.

The consultant makes a series of random inspections. First, the consultant checks the original numbers recorded by the field technicians. They all seem correct. Next, the consultant examines the data entered by the data entry clerks. Numerous transposition errors are identified. Some of the errors are huge. For example, one error changed 1,927 to 9,127; another changed 1,898 to 8,198. The consultant proposes some process changes, including adding an inspection step after the computer data entry step. The consultant suggests that someone other than the data entry clerk should perform this inspection. Because each model has hundreds of numbers, the additional inspection step will take some time. However, the consultant can think of no other way to prevent the data entry errors. The proposed process is outlined in Table 1.5.

The consultant was paid and left for what he described as a "well-deserved vacation" in Hawaii. The company currently is hiring people to staff the third step in the process.

TABLE 1.5 Proposed Process for Environmental Computer Models

Step	Description
1	Field technicians record data on paper forms.
2	Data entry clerks then enter the data into a computer.
3	A printout of the database is made, and a second group of employees cross-checks the data and the original forms.
4	Any necessary corrections are made.
5	The computer model is generated.

   a. What measures should be used to assess the performance of this process?
   b. How would the consultant's proposed process perform according to the measures defined in part (a)?
   c. Do you agree with the consultant's methodology and improvement strategies?
   d. Would you propose a different process?

5. On June 3, 2000, Toronto Pearson Airport implemented a new process to connect international flights (for example, those arriving from Europe) and United States–bound flights. The new process was described on Connection Information Cards that were made available to arriving passengers. The card outlined the following nine steps for an "easy and worry-free connection":
   1. Complete Canadian and U.S. forms during the flight.
   2. Proceed through Canada Immigration/Customs.
   3. Follow signage upstairs to Baggage Claim and pick up your bags.
   4. Hand Canada customs card to the customs officer; follow sign for connecting customers.
   5. Proceed to the connecting baggage drop-off belt and place your bags on the belt.
   6. A frequent shuttle bus to Terminal 2 leaves from the departure level (upstairs).
   7. Disembark at U.S. Departures; proceed to the carousel behind U.S. check-in counters ("Connecting to U.S.A.") and pick up your bags.
   8. Proceed through U.S. Customs and Immigration.
   9. Leave your bags on the baggage belt before going through security to your gate.
   Construct a list of activities and include all non-value-adding activities associated with waiting (e.g., waiting for luggage, waiting for an immigration officer, waiting for a shuttle). Estimate the percentage of time passengers spend on value-adding activities versus the time spent on non-value-adding activities. Identify potential sources of errors or additional delays that can result in a hassle to the passengers. Do you expect this process to deliver on the promise of an "easy and worry-free connection"?

6. A city council hires a consultant to help redesign the building permit process of the city. After gaining an understanding of the current process, the consultant suggests that the best solution is to create a one-size-fits-all process to handle all building-related applications. What is your opinion about the consultant's solution?

Process Management and Process-Oriented Improvement Programs

Although the focus of this book is on analytical process modeling, evaluation, and design rather than implementation and change management, it is clear that the best design in the world is of little interest unless it can be implemented and managed successfully. Therefore, this chapter will look at the governing principles behind successful process management, which is at the core of all the process-oriented improvement programs that have surfaced over the last couple of decades. We also will take a closer look at the basic ideas behind two of the most influential programs of this sort in recent years.

The list of candidate approaches can be made long and covers many of the buzz-words that have appeared in the management arena in recent times: JIT, TQM, TQC, Lean Manufacturing, Quick Response, BPR, ABM/ABC, and Six Sigma. The ones we will examine are Six Sigma, which is a state-of-the-art quality-improvement program, and business process reengineering (BPR), which has its roots in strategic management. The rationale for choosing these approaches is, first of all, that they appeared on the managerial radar screen fairly recently. Second, they stem from different business disciplines, illustrating the wide impact of the process view. Third, they do not have a clear manufacturing focus but rather an emphasis on business processes in general.

It should be noted that sometimes process management in itself is considered a specific improvement program developed at IBM during the 1980s. Without diminishing the importance of the work performed at IBM, we will use the term *process management* in a generic sense to mean a collection of basic principles, guidelines, and insights for how to manage processes. The last part of the chapter contrasts the revolutionary change tactic for implementing a new process design advocated by the BPR movement with a more evolutionary approach used successfully by many companies.

2.1 Process Management and the Power of Adopting a Process View

Process management, as defined in this chapter, deals with the issues of managing, controlling, and improving processes. Process design is an important element in successfully managing a process; however, so are the implementation of the design and the continuous improvement and control systems necessary to reach a desirable level of process performance. Another important aspect is managing the people involved in the process.

Process management originated in the field of modern quality management. The focus on processes and process control is a fundamental component of quality management today and an integral part of the ideas put forward by its founders: Deming, Juran, Crosby, Feigenbaum, and Ishikawa. The power of adopting a process focus was made all too obvious by the Japanese during the 1970s and 1980s when they expanded the notions of quality and productivity to completely new levels.

The strength of adopting a process view and the importance of process management uncover the weaknesses of functional organizations. Although the functional structure has many virtues, not least of which is achieving economies of scale and scope, it has the inherent weakness of fostering a focus on skills and resource utilization rather than work output. As mentioned in Chapter 1, this tends to lead to suboptimization of resources due to insufficient coordination and transparency of the overall process. According to Melan (1993), this tendency can be further explained by the following conditions that are usually built into the functional structure.

- Reward systems that promote the values and support the objectives of the functional department rather than the business in its entirety. For example, the performance of an employee in the manufacturing department might be based on his or her output quantity. However, the quality of the output is deemed more important for the firm, which must satisfy customer requirements.
- Group behavior, which encourages a strong loyalty within the department and an "us versus them" attitude toward other departments within the firm.
- Strong cultural and behavioral patterns within a function. These patterns can differ across departments, reinforcing the "us versus them" mentality.
- A high degree of decentralization, creating "firms within the firm," each with its own agenda.

The deficiency of the functional organization in terms of suboptimization due to lack of coordination also has been discussed extensively in the organizational literature. To quote Mintzberg (1979), "The functional structure lacks a built-in mechanism for coordinating the workflow" and has given rise to concepts such as matrix and project organizations.

A process focus remedies the issues of coordination and transparency by creating a clear emphasis on work output and the fact that this output must meet the customers' requirements. In terms of people management, adopting a process view means that the process structure needs to be made clear to everyone involved. This increased transparency tends to improve the employees' understanding of how their efforts fit into the big picture and why their contribution matters. This, in turn, is usually a good way to make people feel proud of what they do. Pride encourages involvement and participation, a cornerstone in modern quality management and a stepping-stone for successfully empowering the workforce. Another effect of adopting a process orientation is that it helps break down barriers among departments and hampers the "us versus them" attitude by creating a sense of loyalty to the process and everyone involved.

Historically, quality management has focused largely on the manufacturing sector. It was not until the broader concept of Total Quality Management (TQM) got wide recognition in the mid to late 1980s that the principles of quality management and process thinking were applied to a significant degree in the service sector. The principles of process management, therefore, have been drawn primarily from managing manufacturing processes. However, time has proven them equally valuable in managing service processes. The explanation is that the main challenges with process management lie in the focus on workflow; that is, how a job moves through an organization.

Whether the job is a product or a service is inconsequential, at least as far as the basic principles of process management are concerned.

Having acquired a general understanding about the purpose of process management and why process orientation is a powerful approach, the next step in understanding what successful process management entails is to identify the characteristics of well-managed processes. According to Melan (1993), the core principles for successful process management involve the following.

1. Establishing process ownership.
2. Analyzing boundaries and interfaces.
3. Defining the process by documenting its workflow.
4. Identifying control points and measurements.
5. Monitoring the process for control purposes by implementing the measures.
6. Taking corrective action and providing feedback if deviations indicate that the process is no longer in control.

Based on these core principles, the road to successful process management of an existing process can be divided into three phases: Phase I, *initialization;* Phase II, *definition;* and Phase III, *control.* (See Figure 2.1.)

Subsections 2.1.1 through 2.1.3 are devoted to an in-depth investigation of what these phases entail. Section 2.1.4 provides an illustrative example of a document distribution process. The exposition in these subsections is largely based on the work of Melan (1993).

2.1.1 PHASE I: INITIALIZATION

The purpose of the initialization phase is to appoint a process owner or process manager and to define the boundaries and interfaces for the process; that is, its entry and exit points. In other words, the objectives of the initialization phase are to clarify the scope of the process and to determine who will take responsibility for it. (See Figure 2.2.)

Process Ownership

In order to make things happen in any organizational structure, someone must be in charge. Processes are no exceptions. Lack of accountability tends to paralyze the decision-making process and at best leads to uncoordinated actions pulling the process in different directions. Comments like "It's not my responsibility" and "Don't blame me, it's their fault" are symptomatic of a process without an established process owner.

FIGURE 2.1 The Basic Principles of Process Management

FIGURE 2.2 The Initialization Phase

The difficulty in assigning process ownership is essentially a function of process complexity, culture, organizational structure, and management attitudes. Typically, cross-functional processes in decentralized organizations with uninterested management pose the greatest challenge.

Ownership in general implies possession; consider, for example, ownership of a factory. However, process ownership usually does not imply possession of the resources used by the process. It refers to the responsibility and accountability for the work performed within the process and for the process output. More precisely, the critical duties facing the process owner include the following.

- Be accountable and have authority for sustaining process performance and, when necessary, for implementing changes.
- Facilitate problem resolutions and make sure action is taken.
- Mediate jurisdictional issues among functional managers with authority over different activities or resources in the process. For example, in order to meet the delivery dates, the sales manager wants the employees in the paint shop to work overtime. For budgetary reasons, the paint shop manager opposes this. The owner of the delivery process needs to step in and mediate the issue.

Because of differences in culture, organizational structure, operating environment, and personal relationships, no definite rules can establish how to identify and assign process ownership in an effective way. It needs to be done on an individual, case-by-case basis. However, some general guidelines suggest that the process owner can be the manager with the most resources invested in the process, the manager who is most affected if the process does not work as intended, or simply the manager who does the most work directly related to the process. In any case, it is important that the process owner has a high enough position in the organization to see how the process fits into the larger scope of the entire business.

For processes contained within a work group, a department, or a function, it is usually fairly easy to find a suitable process owner. The logical choice is the manager who is already responsible for a majority of the activities and resources involved in the process. Matters generally become more intricate in situations where the process transcends different geographical locations or functional, organizational, or national boundaries. For these types of processes, the process owner often has to come from the top management layer in order to muster enough clout to fulfill the process owner responsibilities mentioned previously. For example, it is not unusual that corporate vice presidents are assigned ownership of core business processes. It should be emphasized that although assigning ownership is a requirement for successful process management and process improvement, it also requires process owner commitment and involvement. The process owner is not just for show; that person needs to be engaged and take charge.

Establishing process ownership is closely related to determining the scope of the process, meaning its boundaries and interfaces. In some cases, it might even be better to clarify these issues prior to appointing a process owner.

Analyzing Process Boundaries and Interfaces

As discussed in Chapter 1, process boundaries define the entry and exit points; that is, the points where input flows into and output flows out of the process. The boundaries provide a clear picture of the process scope. For example, an order delivery process might begin with the receipt of a customer order via fax and end with a truck delivery to the customer's doorstep. In this case, the receipt of the fax constitutes the input boundary or entry point, and the output boundary or exit point is when the product is left on the customer's doorstep. Defining boundaries is necessary in order to assign process ownership properly and to identify the process's external interfaces: the input interface with the suppliers and the output interface with the customers.

Internal interfaces, on the other hand, represent handoff points within the process boundaries. Typically, the most critical internal interfaces are where the process crosses organizational or functional boundaries with different managers (i.e., when the job or workflow is handed off from one department or business unit to the next). However, any handoff between activities, individuals, work groups, or other resources does represent an interface. Because most workflow problems are caused by insufficient interface communication (i.e., lack of coordination), it is important to identify critical interfaces early.

A useful approach to deal with interface-related workflow problems is the customer-producer-supplier (CPS) model, which is based on the simple premise that a producer's output should satisfy the customer's requirements. Notice that this is closely related to the definition of a business process provided in Chapter 1. The CPS model has three agents: the supplier who provides the inputs, the producer who transforms the input into value-added output, and the customers who are the recipients of the output. The interactions among these agents can be divided into three phases: the output requirement phase, the production capability phase, and the input requirement phase. (See Figure 2.3.) A fundamental principle in the CPS approach is that all requirements must be mutually agreed upon by the parties involved: the producer and the customer, and the supplier and the producer, respectively.

The output requirement phase is the first step in the CPS approach and involves defining and reaching an agreement on the customer requirements for the final process output. To avoid misunderstandings and costly rework procedures, the customer requirements should be documented carefully. Methods for analyzing and documenting requirements include the following.

- Word descriptions of a qualitative or quantitative nature; for example, "The service should be timely, respectful, error free, and not cost more than $50."
- Graphical and quantitative specifications; for example, blueprints or pictures shown to a hairdresser.
- Attribute lists of qualitative or quantitative characteristics; for example, the service experience at a barbershop can be described by the following list: comfortable chairs, short waiting time, maximum cutting time of 30 minutes, fashionable hairstyles to choose from, and price less than $20.

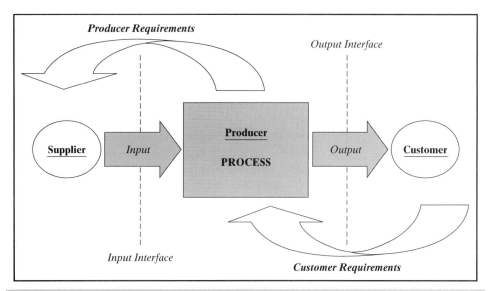

FIGURE 2.3 The Customer-Producer-Supplier (CPS) Model

- Information flow charts, which are particularly useful in software development and data processing, specify data types, frequencies, and so on.
- Deployment matrices, which represent basic variants of the well-established quality function deployment method (QFD), widely used in product and service design for translating customer requirements into product and service characteristics. See, for example, Hauser and Clausing (1988) and Mizuno and Akao (1994).

Having acquired a good understanding of the customer requirements, the next step in the CPS approach is the *production capability phase,* during which the producer assesses the process capabilities to see if it can meet the customer requirements. If the process is unable to match the requirements, the producer has to renegotiate the requirements with the customer or change the process. For example, Joe in accounting is required to present a budget report on the 25th of every month. To complete the report, Joe needs data from several sources within the company 1 week before the report is due. At the moment, these inputs are often late and incomplete, preventing Joe from completing his report on time. To resolve the situation, Joe must renegotiate the output due date with his customers, renegotiate the input data due dates with the suppliers, or change the process to shorten its lead time.

The final step in the CPS approach is the *input requirement phase,* during which the producer negotiates with the suppliers to agree on the input requirements necessary to satisfy the producer's needs. The input requirements usually revolve around cost, timeliness, quantity, and quality characteristics. It is not unusual for the customer to be one of the suppliers also; for example, a customer might provide information in terms of a blueprint for a specified product to be produced.

The three phases of the CPS model are interrelated and although conceptually described as a sequential process, they usually have to be performed iteratively in order to result in a well-coordinated process. By applying the CPS model to all critical interfaces, we adopt a view of the process as a chain of customers where coordination across interfaces is the result of a thorough understanding of internal and external customer requirements.

2.1.2 PHASE II: DEFINITION

After assigning process ownership and defining the process scope, the next step to successful process management is to acquire a thorough understanding of the process workflow, the activities, and their precedence relationships (see Figure 2.4). More precisely, the objective of the definition phase is to document the activities and workflow that constitute the process and thereby facilitate communication and understanding regarding operational details for everyone involved in the process. Also, understanding how things are working currently provides a baseline against which to evaluate process improvement.

A simple but important rule in order to manage and improve a process is that one must first understand it. Often just defining and documenting a process will reveal some obvious inefficiency, such as the existence of redundant or non-value-adding activities. In fact, many redesign projects never go beyond this rudimentary level of analysis.

The question that remains is how to document the process in a way that leads to understanding and communication. Most commonly, word descriptions are used to detail the documentation of the work content in activities and tasks. These descriptions are referred to as operating procedures or standard operating procedures. Unfortunately, these documents tend to be fairly lengthy and not overly reader-friendly; on the other hand, they usually contain detailed information (which may or may not be up-to-date).

The preferred way to document entire processes regarding how the work flows between activities is to use some type of flowchart-based method, meaning a combination of graphical and verbal description. A wide range of different graphical tools for describing processes and workflow is discussed in Chapter 4, including general process charts, process activity charts, process flow diagrams, and general flowcharts. The first step toward having something to document is to gather information about the process. Common information-gathering techniques include the following.

- Individual or group interviews with people working in the process.
- Analytical observation (i.e., following people around and documenting what they do).
- Review of relevant documentation (e.g., existing operating procedures).

It is worth emphasizing that although information gathering and documentation appear to be disjointed activities, they often are hard to separate. For instance, an

FIGURE 2.4 The Definition Phase

efficient technique in interviewing employees about what they do is to draw simple flowcharts together with them. The graphical picture helps them sort out what tasks they really perform.

To summarize, defining a process is a two-step procedure.

1. Identify the process boundaries, input, and output.
2. Collect information about the work performed in the process, define activities, and describe the workflow (i.e., the network of activities and the path a job follows) using some type of graphical tool.

2.1.3 PHASE III: CONTROL

After assigning ownership, setting boundaries, aligning interfaces, and defining activities and work flows, the last phase of successful process management is to establish a system for controlling the process and providing feedback to the people involved. As shown in Figure 2.5, the process control phase can be divided into three steps: establishing control points, developing and implementing measurements, and obtaining feedback and exercising control.

Establishing Control Points

Control points are activities such as inspection, verification, auditing, measuring, checking, or counting. In Chapter 1, we saw that these activities often are referred to as business-value-adding, meaning activities that are essential for the business but not something for which the customer is willing to pay.

Control systems are essential to any operation or organization. Without them, managers have no way of assessing the effects of their decisions, and therefore no way of knowing whether the organization or process is heading in the right direction. If no control points are established within the process, the only means of assessing the process performance is to rely on customer feedback. Although extremely important, the purpose of the process is to satisfy the customer requirements; therefore, sole reliance on customer feedback leaves the process in a reactive rather than proactive mode. Poor quality is discovered too late when the work has already reached the customer and jeopardized future business because customers are unsatisfied and annoyed. Handling rework and returns at this stage also is costly. In service industries,

FIGURE 2.5 The Control Phase

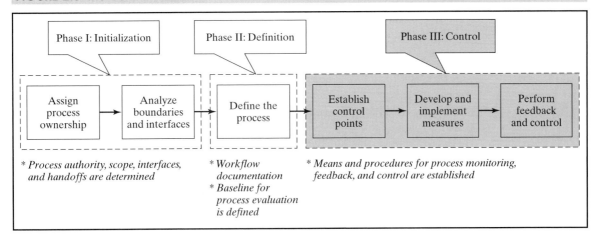

the situation is even more sensitive because only limited opportunities are available to correct a service after the fact. For example, the barber cannot put the hair back and start over if the customer is not satisfied. The only way to assure quality is to correct and control the process itself, which requires in-process control points. To avoid unhappy customers, the barber should verify that a customer wants to have his or her hair no longer than half an inch *before* it is cut off.

The location of control points within a process depends on two factors: how critical it is for the customer satisfaction that a certain activity is performed as intended, and feasibility, meaning how physically and economically feasible it is to install a control point at a specific point in the process.

Developing and Implementing Measurements

Having established the control points, the next question is what to measure. For proper control, the measurements should be meaningful, accurate, timely, and useful. Collecting the measurements may involve complete inspection or sampling techniques. In either case, the measurements can be categorized into the following five types.

1. *Measures of conformance,* which imply verification that the work conforms to a given specification or requirement.
2. *Measures of response time,* which focus on the time it takes to complete a sequence of activities. Response time is often referred to as lead time or cycle time.
3. *Measures of service levels*, which focus on the degree to which a service or resource is available to a user or customer. For example, the service level at a storage facility is often measured as the fraction of customer orders in a replenishment cycle that can be filled upon request.
4. *Measures of repetition*, which refer to the frequency of recurring events, such as the number of times a job needs to be reworked before it is approved.
5. *Measures of cost,* which for control purposes often include the "cost of quality." This cost refers to the cost of waste, which traditionally is divided into three major components: *prevention costs* associated with preventing future nonconformance, *appraisal costs* associated with detecting nonconformities, and *failure costs,* which are the costs of dealing with nonconformities including scrap and rework warranties. A distinction also can be made between internal and external failure costs. The internal failure costs are due to rework within the organization, so only internal customers are affected by the defects. External failure costs occur when the nonconformities affect external customers. These costs are usually more severe because they involve warranties and the potential loss of future business in addition to the immediate rework costs.

The broader issue of measurement implementation typically involves answering the following questions.

1. What is to be controlled and measured? What are the critical factors or the most important customer requirements? For example, a critical factor for FedEx is response or cycle time.
2. What is currently being measured? Are recent data available that can be used to determine the measure?
3. If no measurement data are readily available, can a business case be made for installing a new measurement system?
4. Given the chosen measurement, what is the appropriate sampling method? What sample sizes should be used, and what should the measurement frequency be?

In order to leverage the full potential of any measurement data for identifying problems and changes in process performance, the data need to be analyzed statistically and then displayed graphically. In other words, the data must be converted into useful information. Examples of the most common types of statistical charts are bar charts, pie charts, histograms, Pareto charts, box plots, and scatter plots. However, the predominant tool for process control is the well-known process control chart, also called as the Shewhart chart.

Feedback and Control

It is critically important to provide feedback and take corrective action in response to detected process deviations in order to stabilize and improve the process. The objectives of corrective actions are either regulation or improvement. Regulation, or control, aims at maintaining the process performance at a certain level; improvement is intended to reduce variability so the process is more predictable or to raise the average performance level. If mechanisms for regulation and improvement are lacking, the process could become unstable and degrade over time.

An important enabler for corrective action is feedback. The people in the process need to be aware of how the quality of their work affects the overall process performance, and how errors in their work impact the downstream activities (i.e., internal customers) and ultimately the external customer. However, it is extremely important that the process owner is sensitive to how feedback is provided. When it is given in a constructive manner, employees usually perceive feedback as a positive action and will display interest and concern for the information, as well as for the process. This tends to make people feel that they matter and encourages them to get more involved. In some cases, employees will suggest ways to improve their work and the process performance. Getting everyone involved and committed to their work and the process is one of the keys to successful process management. On the other hand, if feedback is given in a punitive manner, it will alienate employees and can do more harm than good.

2.1.4 AN ILLUSTRATIVE EXAMPLE: MANAGING A DOCUMENT DISTRIBUTION PROCESS

The following example adapted from Melan (1993) illustrates the basic principles of process management discussed in this chapter thus far.

Joe recently started his new position as associate manager of the business development department, with special responsibility for strategic planning. In January and in June, Joe is now responsible for formulating and issuing copies of the company's strategic plan to the firm's key managers. In fact, this is one of his more important functions. The managers then have to respond to Joe within 2 weeks regarding a wide range of strategic issues before the plan can be finalized. The importance and visibility of this document mean that any kind of problems with the process will reflect badly on Joe personally and on his department.

In early January, copies of the document were delivered from the print shop. Joe's staff then sorted the documents, put them in envelopes addressed to the designated managers, and left them to be picked up by internal mailing services. The address to each manager eligible to receive a copy was easily available from a distribution list kept by the departmental secretary. No mailing problems were reported to Joe. By mid-January, only four managers had responded to Joe, who was disappointed and embarrassed to report to his manager that he would not be able to finalize the strategic plan before the agreed deadline. He then immediately began making phone calls to the 24 managers who had not responded and was astonished by their responses.

- Three had not yet received the document.
- Two had just received the document at their new location.
- Seven complained about missing pages.
- Four reported pages out of sequence.
- Five said they could not respond in only 1 week.
- Three had left the organization.

The following day, Joe received a message from his manager to be in his office the next morning with an analysis of the problem and an action plan for how to avoid this type of debacle in the future.

Clearly, this process was not well managed. The following pages will discuss how the basic principles of process management can be used to improve it.

Assign Process Ownership

It is clear that Joe is the manager responsible for formulating and distributing the strategic plan document. Although he has no managerial control over the print shop or the mailing services, he is perceived as the owner of the entire process by his managers and is held accountable for its failure. Neither the print shop nor the mailing service is aware of its role in the process and that Joe is the owner of the process; they just perform an operation without understanding its impact. This is why it is important to clarify to all parties involved who the process owner is.

Analyze Boundaries and Interfaces

With the process ownership in place, Joe needs to analyze the process boundaries and interfaces. Based on the detected problems, he decides to focus his attention on the document distribution process starting when the print shop receives the original document to be copied and ending when the mailing services deliver the mailed copy to the managers. Joe also defines two critical internal interfaces: the first one when the job (i.e., the copies) leaves the print shop and is handed off to his staff and the second one when the addressed envelopes are handed off to the mailing service. The external interfaces coincide with the boundaries. Furthermore, it should be noted that for the document distribution process, the input to the print shop is the original master document, and the supplier is Joe's department. The customers at the other end are the managers who are to receive a copy of the document. A high-level flowchart describing the process along with its boundaries and interfaces is given in Figure 2.6.

From the telephone conversations Joe had with the managers, he can conclude that many of the problems are related to the critical interfaces and lack of communication and coordination across them. Delivery delays and poor quality of the document copies appear to be the main issues. To approach the interface problems, Joe decides to use the customer-producer-supplier (CPS) model, starting with the requirements of the final customers and working his way back through the process. The phone conversations with the managers who received the copied document (i.e., the final customers) revealed that they have two main requirements: a perfect copy of the document and 2 weeks to prepare a reply. Following the CPS model, Joe now focuses on the production capabilities of the mailing services. A manager at mailing services informs Joe that in order for mail to be distributed the next day, the sender must take it directly to the mail room. If it is left at the department to be picked up by mailing services, it takes an additional day before the envelopes are

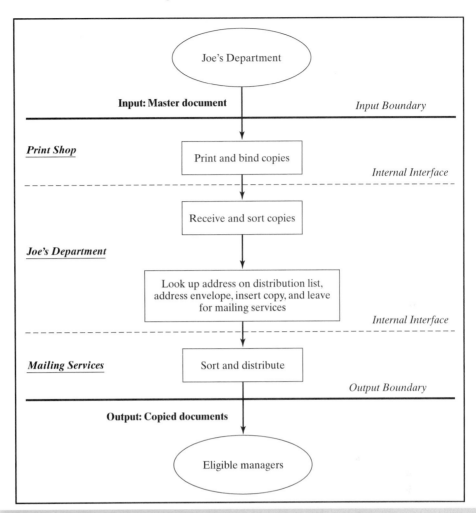

FIGURE 2.6 High-Level Flowchart of the Document Distribution Process

delivered to their recipients. Furthermore, if the mail is going to one of the company's satellite locations, which is the case for several managers on Joe's distribution list, it might take up to 4 days until the envelopes are delivered, assuming they are brought straight to the mail room. In the current process, the envelopes were left at Joe's department and the assumption was next-day delivery.

The input to mailing services is the addressed envelopes supplied by Joe's department. Consequently, following the CPS model and assuming Joe intends to continue using internal mailing services, the supplier requirements indicate that Joe needs to deliver the copied documents to the mail room 4 days earlier than what was done this time in order to satisfy the customer requirements. Another option would be to use an external courier, but Joe has no room in his budget for that. He also could change the mailing services process to shorten the delivery time, but Joe has no managerial jurisdiction over mailing services, so this is not a viable option either.

The next interface of interest is that between Joe's department and the print shop, where the former is the internal customer to the latter. The requirements posed by Joe's department are linked directly to the end-customer requirements: The copies should be of good quality and be delivered promptly. The manager of the print shop informs Joe that for a large size document such as the strategic plan, a 2-day lead-time is to be expected. A rush job increases the risk of receiving bad-quality copies. When the last job was done, Joe's secretary, not understanding the production capabilities, requested "same-day service" but received the copies 2 days later. Also, the print shop staff noticed a reversed sequence of page numbers but assumed this was desired because that was how the original master document was arranged. The print shop just copies the master document as is. Assuming that Joe will continue using the print shop, understanding the print shop's capabilities renders some clear requirements on the supplier of the master document, which is Joe's department: The document must be in perfect shape and be delivered to the print shop 2 days before it needs to be sorted, addressed, and put in envelopes.

To summarize, applying the CPS model has revealed some important requirements that Joe's department must take into account in order to get the copied documents out on a certain day. Basically, the print shop needs the master document delivered in the morning of day 1, and the master document must at this point be in perfect shape because it is copied as is. The print shop delivers the copied documents to Joe's department in the morning of day 3; then Joe's staff has half a day to sort, address, and deliver the sealed envelopes to the mail room. Internal mailing services guarantees delivery to all locations during day 7. In addition to the timing issues that Joe must consider, his department also must pay special attention to the quality of the master document and the correctness of the distribution list.

Define the Process

Having determined the scope of the process, Joe is in a position to define the activities and workflow that are within the boundaries. The most common approach is to start with a high-level flowchart, like the one in Figure 2.6, and then create a hierarchy of successively more detailed flowcharts over the different subprocesses and activities until the right level of detail is obtained in the description. The right level is found when additional details no longer appear to offer further opportunities for improvement. In this particular case, Joe decides not to proceed beyond the high level or macro flowchart in Figure 2.6.

Establish Control Points

The current process does not contain any internal control points; as a result, Joe might not realize that something is wrong with the process until it is too late. This situation represents a high "failure cost" for Joe in terms of lost credibility within the firm. Based on the customer feedback and the analysis so far, Joe finds three instances where control points appear to make sense.

1. Inspection of the master document before it is delivered to the print shop to assure that what goes to the print shop is flawless. This responsibility falls on Joe's secretary and his other staff members.

2. Inspection of the copies received from the print shop by Joe's staff before they are put into envelopes and mailed. This is done to assure that pages are not missing and that pictures are not blurred due to quality problems in the print shop. Applying the CPS model, Joe should negotiate with the print shop and require them to change their process to avoid quality problems of this sort. This would make the inspection of the final copies redundant and save Joe some resources. However, even if Joe has enough clout to make this happen, it makes sense in the short run to install the control point to make sure the print

shop process performs as intended, simply because the outcome is so important to Joe.

3. Verification that the distribution list is accurate (the right people are on it and their addresses are correct). This job is appropriate for Joe's staff. The purpose is to avoid sending copies to those who are no longer with the company or sending copies to the wrong address. The problem is magnified by the confidentiality of the strategy document.

As the quality of the process improves, these inspections will become redundant. Installing inspection points is not an efficient way to achieve quality output in the long run. However, it allows one to gather data in order to track down the root causes of problems that are occurring in dysfunctional processes.

Develop and Implement Measures

After determining the control points, the next step for Joe is to specify what to measure. Starting with the inspection of the master document at control point 1, it is important to record not just that a mistake occurred but what the mistake is. This assures that the data can be used to facilitate root cause analysis and improve the process that produces the original master document. Based on the customer feedback, it appears that the frequency of missing pages and pages out of sequence should be tracked. In addition, it seems wise to look for typographical errors, the types of mistakes, and their frequency.

Control point 2, dealing with the quality of the copies coming out of the print shop, will focus again on document quality, so the same measures should be used (i.e., frequency of missing pages; pages out of sequence; and a range of typographical errors including blurred figures, text alignment, and so on.)

For the third control point, verification of distribution list accuracy, interesting measures to track are number of address changes and the turnover of managers on the list. Joe decides to use these categorized frequency measures to track the copying and address quality.

In addition to the three internal control points, Joe also decides to solicit regular feedback from the end customers regarding copy quality and delivery time. To track the performance of the last step in the distribution process, the mail delivery, Joe also decides to record the time when the envelopes are delivered to the mailroom and then ask the final recipients in their response to the strategic plan document to specify when they received the envelope. This way, Joe will have a means to track the total distribution time because he will know when the master document was delivered to the print shop. Joe also intends to ask the managers to comment on the copying quality.

Perform Feedback and Control

An important issue for Joe is to try to improve process efficiency without compromising its effectiveness. In the proposed setup, inspection time decreases efficiency. By tracking the measurements discussed previously and using them to provide feedback to the people working in the process, he hopes to stimulate employee involvement and also put pressure on the managers of the print shop and internal mailing services by showing them data on their performance. Joe anticipates that this will stimulate them to take corrective action to improve their internal processes and eliminate the demand for inspection. In order to present the data in a pedagogical and convincing way, Joe has a wide range of charts and statistical tools at his disposal. To keep things simple, he has decided to start with basic histograms, and bar and pie charts. The data gathering will be initiated the next time the distribution process is activated in about 6 months.

Summary and Final Remarks

To complete the picture, let us review what Joe, based on the basic principles of process management, has come up with in terms of an action plan to improve process performance and achieve a well-managed document distribution process.

First, Joe will make sure that the master document is finished at least 7 working days before it should be delivered to the designated managers. He will allow them at least 2 weeks to prepare a response. Furthermore, Joe's staff is instructed to inspect the master copy of the strategic plan, searching especially for any missing pages, pages that are out of sequence, or apparent typographical mistakes. These mistakes should be categorized and counted. The staff also needs to make sure the two-day production lead-time is taken into consideration.

Second, Joe's staff is instructed to inspect each copy of the strategic plan for missing pages, pages that are out of sequence, and typographical errors and record the mistakes found. If enough mistakes are found and the time line permits it, the whole batch should be returned to the print shop to be redone. If there is not enough time to return the whole batch, the faulty documents will be reworked at Joe's department and the time for this should be recorded. This rework time can easily be translated into costs and will provide Joe with some convincing arguments when providing feedback to the print shop manager. An important issue in this respect is to explain the effect of the print shop quality problems on the document distribution process and the overall strategy development process.

Third, the distribution list should be updated shortly before the envelopes are addressed. The number of changes to the list should be recorded; tracking the changes over time will help Joe decide how often the list needs to be updated. For now, updates will be done prior to every distribution round.

Fourth, the date and time that the envelopes are taken to the mail room should be recorded as a means of tracking how long they spend in the internal mailing system. To obtain the arrival times, Joe will ask that the managers disclose in their response to the strategic plan exactly when the document was delivered. He also will ask them to comment on the document copying quality.

By implementing these changes, Joe takes a huge step toward proactive process management, so he can avoid situations in which the process problems are not discovered until it is too late to correct them. Joe is also in a good position to explain to his boss at their meeting the next day what caused the problems with the document distribution process and what he plans to do to prevent future mishaps of this kind. Apart from the immediate actions to assure the effectiveness of the process in the near future, Joe also can point to the necessary long-term improvements. If the print shop and mailing services improve their internal efficiency, Joe can eliminate the inspection activities and thereby improve the overall efficiency of the document distribution process. Most likely, drastic improvements could be made to the process performances in the print shop and the mailing services if their managers were willing to rethink their entire design.

2.2 Six Sigma Quality Programs

Launched in 1987, Six Sigma was the name of a companywide, process-oriented initiative at Motorola for achieving breakthrough improvement in quality and productivity. It represented Motorola's customized approach to quality management and was heavily influenced by the principles of modern quality thinking. The novelty with the Six Sigma approach was how these basic principles were combined into an integrated program for process and quality improvement. Because of the tremendous success of the

Six Sigma approach at Motorola, rendering them the first Malcolm Baldrige National Quality Award in 1988 (the most prestigious U.S. quality award), other companies around the world—including IBM, ABB, Kodak, Allied Signal, and GE—embarked on Six Sigma initiatives of their own during the early to mid-1990s. The ongoing success of these programs has led to exponential growth in the number of prestigious global firms in a wide range of industries to adopt the Six Sigma approach. Recent examples include Ford, Compaq, American Express, Honeywell, Nokia, Ericsson, Phillips, Samsung, Johnson & Johnson, J.P. Morgan, Maytag, Sony, and Dupont. See, for example, Magnusson et al. (2000). In the meantime, the original Motorola concept has undergone some changes and evolved into what today is one of the most renowned and rapidly spreading quality improvement programs.

2.2.1 SIX SIGMA DEFINITIONS

Six Sigma can be defined as "an improvement program aimed at reducing variability and achieving near elimination of defects from every product, process, and transaction." See, for example, Tomkins (1997). However, this somewhat narrow definition does not capture the strategic implications of Six Sigma initiatives. In a broader sense, a Six Sigma program can be described as a companywide strategic initiative for process improvement in manufacturing and service organizations. Six Sigma has the clear objective of reducing costs and increasing revenues; that is, increasing process efficiency and process effectiveness.

The Six Sigma approach is built around a project and a result-oriented, quantitative, and disciplined improvement methodology. This methodology focuses on variance reduction but also emphasizes cycle time reduction and yield improvement. The methodology usually is divided into five steps: define, measure, analyze, improve, and control (DMAIC). (Sometimes the define step is omitted and presumed to have been performed before the methodology is applied.) This methodology is embedded in a corporate framework based on top management commitment, stakeholder involvement, training programs, and measurement systems. We will look more closely at these issues, including the improvement methodology, in Section 2.2.4. However, it is worth noting the similarity between the DMAIC methodology and phases II and III in the process management framework discussed in Section 2.1.

The goal of the Six Sigma program, as it was conceived at Motorola, is to reduce the variation of the individual processes so that they render no more than 3.4 defects per million opportunities. To explain this further, we need to recognize that any product or process characteristic that is measured has some desired target value, T, and some upper and/or lower specification limits, USL and LSL, respectively. If the measured characteristic falls outside these limits, the product or service is considered defective. Furthermore, there is variation in any process output, so the measured characteristic will not be the same for every unit of output. Assuming that the distribution of process output follows a normal distribution with population mean, μ, and standard deviation, σ, Six Sigma Quality refers to a situation in which the distance between the target value and the closest of the specification limits is at least 6σ. See Figure 2.7. The number 3.4 defects per million opportunities is obtained as a one-sided integration under the normal distribution curve beyond 4.5σ from the process mean, μ. The explanation for this construct is that the process mean, μ, is allowed to shift over time and deviate from the target value by as much as 1.5σ. It is worth emphasizing that not all companies using Six Sigma programs choose to adhere to these particular numerical goals. An overarching Six Sigma objective is to achieve near elimination of defects, but ultimately it is up to each individual company to define what they consider "near elimination."

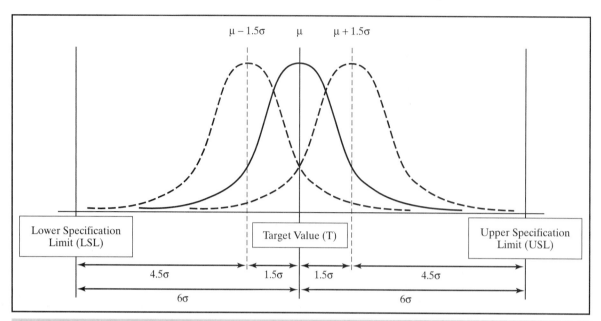

FIGURE 2.7 The Technical Definition of Six Sigma Quality as Achieved When the Distance Between the Process Target Value and the Closest Specification Limit Is at Least Six Standard Deviations (sigma), and the Process Mean Does Not Deviate More Than 1.5 Sigma from the Target Value, T

2.2.2 THE SIX SIGMA COST AND REVENUE RATIONALE

A characterizing feature of Six Sigma that distinguishes it from most other quality management initiatives is its fierce focus on bottom line results. The top priorities and explicit objectives in every Six Sigma project are to decrease costs by improving process efficiency and to increase revenues by improving process effectiveness. The success of Six Sigma and the reason it is heralded in corporate boardrooms is its ability to achieve these goals. To acquire a better understanding of Six Sigma, we need to take a closer look at how its process improvement program is related to the underlying cost and revenue rationale.

The Cost or Efficiency Rationale

In simple terms, a firm's profit or bottom line is given by its revenues minus its costs during a specified accounting period. Consequently, by decreasing costs, a firm experiences an immediate positive effect on the bottom line. Clearly this is the logic behind all efficiency improvement programs and cannot be attributed to Six Sigma alone. However, Six Sigma does bring an aggressive and focused approach to the table, based on attacking all types of costs, including labor costs. However, to assure cooperation and involvement from employees, Six Sigma ensures that the labor cost reductions are realized through increased productivity instead of layoffs.

A fundamental principle is that every improvement project must render measurable cost savings and every training course must include cost-cutting projects. To further understand the Six Sigma approach to cost reduction and improved process performance, it is helpful to consider the dimensions of variation, cycle time, and yield. This ultimately will lead to the efficiency or loop summarizing the cost rationale.

Variation is embedded in any process through the input used and the actual work or transformation being performed. A key operative objective in Six Sigma (see the technical definition in Section 2.2.1) is to decrease process variation and thereby increase quality and reduce costs. The first step to achieving this is to measure and gather data on important process, product, and/or service characteristics. In order to quantify and track the variation in these characteristics, the data need to be statistically analyzed and visualized graphically. After the measuring system is in place, the focus is placed on identifying the sources of variation.

Based on what is causing it, the variation usually is divided into two types: common cause variation and special cause variation. The latter, also referred to as nonrandom variation, typically is due to relatively few identifiable causes but tends to produce large, unpredictable contributions to the overall variation. Some recurrent special causes of variation are differences in the quality of input material from different suppliers, faulty equipment, and process tampering due to bad measurement systems or inadequate training of employees. The first step in reducing the overall variation is to eliminate the special cause variation by attacking its roots. The random or common cause variation, on the other hand, is typically the result of many contributing sources such that it is considered inherent in the process and can be affected only by implementing a radically new design.

Three important concepts in understanding the impact of variation on process performance are dispersion, predictability, and centering. In general terms, large dispersion refers to large variation or variability in the measured process characteristics. Predictability implies that the process characteristics over time belong to the same statistical distributions. In other words, a predictable process is considered to be in statistical control, meaning that over time the measured characteristic belongs to the same statistical distribution; that is, with the same mean and dispersion (often measured in terms of standard deviation). Given a process in statistical control, the dispersion refers to the width of the distribution; high dispersion implies that it is more likely to end up far away from the process mean. Centering refers to how well the mean of the process distribution is aligned with the target value. Ideally, we would like the process to be predictable, and the corresponding distribution should have a low dispersion and be well centered.

The standard approach for variability reduction in Six Sigma is as follows.

1. Eliminate special cause variation to reduce the overall dispersion and bring the process into statistical control (i.e., improve the predictability).
2. Reduce the dispersion of the predictable process.
3. Center the process to target.

The Six Sigma philosophy is well in line with Deming's mantra of striving for continuous improvements, as well as Taguchi's perception that any deviation from the process target value will cause excess costs.

The tools used in Six Sigma approaches to reduce variation are the same as in traditional quality and process control: the 7QC tools and factorial experiments. These tools will not be explored further in this book. The interested reader can turn to any basic textbook about quality control or quality management, such as Foster (2001) or Evans and Lindsay (2002).

Cycle time and *yield* are important characteristics of any process. The cycle time is the time a job spends in the process, sometimes also referred to as process or production lead time. The process yield or productivity is the amount of output per unit of input or per unit of time. Consequently, cycle time and yield can be used to describe a variety of process performance aspects including input material, equipment utilization, setup times, lead times, capacity, and productivity.

Six Sigma improvement projects that focus on cycle times and yield follow the same approach as for variation, namely to gain predictability, reduce dispersion, and center with target. However, when it comes to centering, the target is usually more broadly defined in order to minimize cycle time and maximize yield improvement. For example, consider the operations of a regional distribution center (DC) where trucks arrive with incoming goods. At the DC, the trucks are unloaded and then reloaded with outgoing goods before they depart. For scheduling purposes, it is desirable to have trucks stay the same amount of time at the depot. The cycle time—the time a truck spends at the DC—is currently 2 ± 0.5 hours. Improving the performance in terms of predictability and reduced dispersion means that the trucks would depart more consistently in 2-hour intervals. To improve the centering, we would like to reduce the average cycle time without increasing the dispersion. Tentatively, by changing the unloading and loading process, perhaps by acquiring more or better forklift trucks, the average cycle time could be reduced to 1.5 hours, increasing the number of trucks and the tonnage handled by the DC on a daily basis. In Six Sigma companies, this type of improvement would be recorded in terms of the cost savings due to the increased capacity and in terms of the reduced variability.

The focus on cycle time and yield is not unique to Six Sigma; it has been emphasized by many business improvement programs including Lean Manufacturing, Time Based Management, Business Process Reengineering, and Activity Based Management. However, Six Sigma adds the important requirement that improvements in average cycle time or yield must not be made at the expense of increased process variability.

The Six Sigma cost rationale can be summarized by the *efficiency loop* (sometimes called the bottom line loop) illustrated in Figure 2.8. Improvement projects lead to cost savings by targeting the dimensions of variation, cycle time, and yield. Moreover, lower costs lead to increased profits. To complete the loop and achieve long-term effects, the last component is commitment to the Six Sigma initiative and to individual improvement projects. Without commitment from top management and other stakeholders, the Six Sigma initiative will not survive. Therefore, a core concern in Six Sigma is to generate this commitment and attention. An efficient Six Sigma strategy in this respect is to report the cost savings of every individual improvement project directly to top management.

FIGURE 2.8 The Six Sigma Efficiency Loop

The Revenue or Effectiveness Rationale

Determinants of a company's revenues are its sales volume, closely related to its market share, together with the prices it can charge for its products and services; both are highly dependent on the level of customer satisfaction. To put it differently, the firm's ability to generate revenues is contingent on how well it can satisfy the external customers' requirements and desires. According to Motorola, GE, and other Six Sigma companies, the Six Sigma recipe of improved process performance in terms of predictability, small dispersion, and good centering of characteristics important to the customers has been successful in this respect. The key to success is the focus in every improvement project on identifying and meeting the customer requirements, internal as well as external. An important concept in this respect is the CPS model discussed in Section 2.1. A critical insight is that the measured characteristics must be important not only for the process internally but also for its external customers.

To identify customer requirements and translate them into product and service characteristics, Six Sigma advocates the use of Quality Function Deployment (QFD). The customers are then asked not only about their critical requirements but also about the desired target values and specification limits for these requirements. The same approach is used whether the customers are external or internal. However, as discussed in Section 2.1, the internal customer requirements must be aligned with those of the external customers, who ultimately generate the revenues. A rigorous measurement system to make sure the processes consistently match the defined characteristics—produce few defects in the eyes of the customer—is another important ingredient in the Six Sigma pursuit of increased revenues.

The revenue rationale can be summarized by the effectiveness loop (sometimes referred to as the top line loop): *Improved customer satisfaction leads to increased market share and larger sales volumes as well as a potential to charge higher prices, together implying increased revenues.* Combining the effectiveness loop with the efficiency loop, as shown in Figure 2.9, summarizes the Six Sigma Cost and Revenue Rationale.

2.2.3 SIX SIGMA IN PRODUCT AND PROCESS DESIGN

Six Sigma has proven to be a successful strategic initiative for improving process performance when considering the dimensions of variation, cycle time, and yield by eliminating special cause variation. However, improvement projects eventually will arise for which it is not possible to reach the desired levels of performance simply by eliminating the special cause variation. In these situations, it is necessary to question the very design of the process. Six Sigma prescribes applying the same DMAIC methodology and the same statistical tools for improving the process or product design as for improving the performance of a process with a given design. In addition, prototyping and simulation are typical Six Sigma activities in designing products. Experience shows that using the Six Sigma program for design and implementation of new processes is considerably more complex than using it within an existing design. At the same time, it offers tremendous bottom line potential.

The Six Sigma approach to product and process design has three complimentary objectives or design steps.

1. System design: To design the product/process to satisfy and delight the customers.
2. Parameter design: To make the design less sensitive to variation by determining appropriate values for the design parameters.
3. Tolerance design: To reduce the process variability by narrowing tolerances on input material and work performed.

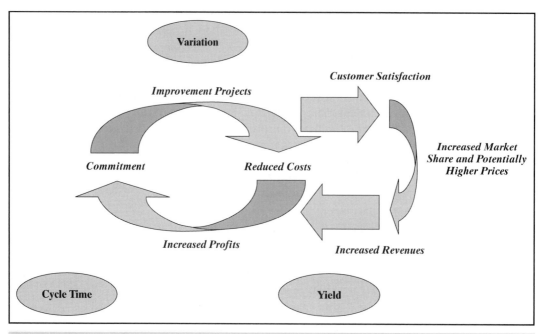

FIGURE 2.9 The Six Sigma Rationale Combining the Efficiency and Effectiveness Loops

2.2.4 THE SIX SIGMA FRAMEWORK

As mentioned earlier, the Six Sigma framework, which is the vehicle used to attain the stated objectives and fulfill the Six Sigma rationale, encompasses five major components: top management commitment; stakeholder involvement; training; measurement system; and at the very core, the five-step improvement methodology DMAIC. (See Figure 2.10.) The formalized framework, with its disciplined and quantitatively oriented improvement methodology, is what sets Six Sigma apart from many other management programs. Therefore, this section is devoted to taking a closer look at each of these framework components.

FIGURE 2.10 The Six Sigma Framework

Top Management Commitment

To leverage the full potential of Six Sigma, it must be an integral part of the firm's business strategy. This requires long-term management commitment. In a sense, the entire Six Sigma framework is relying on top management commitment to materialize. Without it, the ambitious Six Sigma program will not survive. The commitment must go beyond lip service and manifest itself in pragmatic and involved management, to push the Six Sigma concept out to every part of the organization. However, this does not imply that top management should be engaged in the daily improvement activities; their role is as owners of the Six Sigma initiative and project sponsors. A strength of Six Sigma, compared to many other improvement programs, is its bottom line focus, which tends to help keep top management's motivation and commitment at a high level.

Stakeholder Involvement

A successful Six Sigma program needs active support and involvement from all its important stakeholders, with particular emphasis on the employees, the suppliers, and the customers. Other stakeholders are owners and in a broad sense, society.

The most important stakeholder group with respect to Six Sigma is the people in the organization. Without their active support and involvement, the initiative will never take off. Six Sigma tries to ensure this involvement through attractive training programs, the formalized improvement methodology, and frequent feedback on process performance and rates of improvement. Constructive union involvement is in many cases also a necessary prerequisite for workforce involvement.

The suppliers are another critical stakeholder group because wide variations in the quality and characteristics of the input immediately affect the firm's processes and their output. Therefore, key suppliers are often encouraged and supported in launching their own Six Sigma initiatives. Furthermore, a common Six Sigma strategy for involving suppliers is to share the performance data on the input they deliver.

As recognized in the Six Sigma revenue rationale, the importance of the customers and their perceptions cannot be overestimated. Six Sigma cannot reach its full potential without understanding and involving the organization's customers. Ways for involving the firm's customers include identifying their requirements and desires, having customers participate in internal Six Sigma training courses, and actively helping customers improve their processes using the Six Sigma methodology.

Training

One important, characterizing feature of Six Sigma is a comprehensive and formalized training program. The training is largely focused on understanding the statistical tools used for the data analysis, which is a cornerstone in the Six Sigma improvement methodology. However, the courses also cover topics such as process performance, the DMAIC improvement methodology, project management, quality function deployment, and the Six Sigma framework. In order for Six Sigma to succeed, this knowledge has to be diffused throughout the entire organization.

Although the structure might vary, the Six Sigma strategy includes three fairly standardized training course levels: basic, medium, and comprehensive. They differ in scope, detail, and practical application. Comprehensive training is reserved for those employees who will devote a majority of their time to running Six Sigma improvement projects throughout the organization. The basic training is offered to all employees to prepare them for participating in improvement projects at their own workplace. As more and more projects are being performed, an increasing number of people are exposed to the Six Sigma approach, which raises the level of understanding even further. A distinguishing and appreciated feature of the Six Sigma training programs is that they go beyond classroom teaching and require the participants to apply their knowledge in hands-on improvement projects.

A common way to denote the hierarchical roles in the Six Sigma program is to use a martial arts–inspired belt rank system. Typically, the belt levels are White Belts, Green Belts, Black Belts, Master Black Belts, and Champions in increasing order of training and responsibility. Sometimes Yellow Belts are included between the White and Green Belts. Relating the training program to these different roles, the White Belt course is typically a 1-day course that provides a basic introduction to Six Sigma. It is offered to all or most of the workforce. The Green Belt course usually targets foremen and middle management. It teaches the participants to apply the DMAIC methodology, including the necessary statistical tools, in a real project. The Black Belt course is a comprehensive course for full-time improvement experts. Although it has no formal prerequisites, it is beneficial if the participants on this level have a basic understanding of mathematics, statistics, and the firm's core processes. The Black Belt training lasts for about 6 months, and it consists of several weeks of seminars between which the participants are required to work on different improvement projects with specified cost-savings requirements. The Black Belts represent the force that drives the operational process improvement activities. They typically are handpicked from the ranks of the most promising young leaders in the organization. The Master Black Belt is a qualified Black Belt who works full-time teaching Six Sigma courses. The Champion is a senior executive whose primary duties are to drive the improvement work forward, to be an advocate for the Six Sigma program in the top management circle, and to serve as a source of knowledge and experience. In addition, the Champion often participates in the selection of improvement projects.

Apart from the three courses mentioned, the standardized Six Sigma training program also includes a course in Six Sigma engineering and one in Six Sigma management. The former is a Black Belt course that focuses on the design of products and processes, and the latter deals with Six Sigma rollout issues and how to create the necessary momentum to keep the program moving.

Measurement System

A central issue in Six Sigma is to base decisions on factual data and to quantify the effects of implemented improvements. Therefore, a measurement system that collects the relevant data is of critical importance. As discussed previously, the preferred measurement in Six Sigma is variation because it can be used to measure dispersion and centering of any characteristic of interest, including those categorized as cycle time or yield. In deciding which characteristics to monitor, the focus should be on what is important to the customers. The universal variation metric used in Six Sigma is defects per million opportunities (dpmo), and the goal is to achieve fewer than 3.4 dpmo for all products and processes. Because all individual characteristics are measured using the same metric, it is easy to track performance over time; to compare different processes; and to consolidate individual measures for larger processes, projects, classes of products and services, and even for the entire company. The measurement system helps emphasize the process performance issues throughout the entire organization. A keyword in this respect is *simplicity*—a single metric that is easy to understand and easy to remember.

The Improvement Methodology

At the core of every Six Sigma project is the same formalized improvement methodology consisting of the five phases: define, measure, analyze, improve, and control. See Figure 2.11. As mentioned earlier, the methodology is based on a quantitative

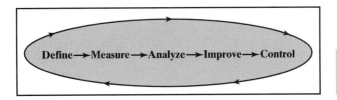

FIGURE 2.11 The Six Sigma Improvement Methodology DMAIC

philosophy, emphasizing that decisions must be based on factual data, not guesses. The Six Sigma training, therefore, focuses on applying appropriate statistical tools in each of the five phases.

The *define* phase deals with the selection of appropriate improvement projects. Valuable sources of information in identifying candidate projects and areas of improvement include the aforementioned measurement system, customer complaints, customer satisfaction surveys, nonconformity reports, returns and warranty claims, and employee suggestions. After identifying a potential area of improvement, the next step is to define the project scope and the processes involved. In some cases, the scope might be limited to improving the performance of just one characteristic, but other projects might involve a complete redesign of entire processes or products. Having identified a number of candidate projects, the question is which project to pursue. Commonly used selection criteria include customer and company benefits, complexity, cost savings potential, and likelihood of success.

After a project has been selected, it is assigned to an improvement team consisting of an appropriate mix of Black, Green, and White Belts. Larger projects also include a top management sponsor or champion.

The *measure* phase involves deciding exactly which characteristics to improve and what needs to be measured in more detail. The general measurement system might not be detailed enough for the project in question, implying the need for additional control and measure points. Apart from identifying the characteristics or result variables to be improved, it is also important at this stage to identify and measure the critical input variables affecting the output. The input variables are classified as either control factors or noise factors. Control factors are input variables that can be affected and controlled in the short term, and noise factors are outside the direct control of the improvement team. The control factors typically have an immediate impact on the special cause variation in the output variables; this is the natural starting point for improvement. Another important issue in the measure phase is to define what constitutes unacceptable performance or a defect. Finally, enough data need to be collected to assess the current performance of the process and provide the foundation for improving it.

The *analyze* phase uses the preliminary data gathered in the measure phase to document the current performance and create a baseline against which to gauge the improvement efforts. The analysis typically involves calculations of means, standard deviations, and defects per million opportunities for the targeted characteristics and control factors. Moreover, control charts are often used to assess whether the process can be considered to be in statistical control. To better assess the relative performance and set appropriate improvement goals, it is also common to benchmark against other similar processes or products internally or externally.

Based on the analyzed data, the *improve* phase focuses on how to achieve the necessary improvements in predictability, dispersion, and centering. A core activity is to identify and eliminate root causes for nonrandom variability by going for the simplest improvement opportunities first. The 7QC tools are used extensively for these purposes. Advanced statistical tools including experimental design are applied when no special cause variation can be detected easily from the gathered data. At this point, if no special causes can be identified the project focus shifts to improving the design of the process or product and thereby reducing the random variation.

After the desired improvements have been achieved, the *control* phase is initialized to verify and institutionalize the change. Important activities include process monitoring using control charts, and documentation of changes that are made using, for example, flowcharts and formalized reporting of estimated cost savings. The experiences and results from the improvement project also need to be made available to the rest of the organization. An important lesson from Six Sigma companies is that projects breed projects, and sharing experiences has the twofold effect of transferring knowledge and spurring interest in the program.

2.2.5 CONCLUDING REMARKS: KEY REASONS FOR THE SUCCESS OF SIX SIGMA

To conclude our discussion on Six Sigma, we will summarize some of the acknowledged reasons for its ongoing success.

The bottom line focus and big dollar impact encourages and maintains top management commitment and support, which is a necessity for the program to succeed in the long term.

The emphasis and consistent use of a unified and quantitative approach to process improvement facilitates communication and real results. The disciplined application of the DMAIC methodology creates a common language through which people from different business units can share experiences and learn from each other's successes and failures with regards to process improvement efforts. It also creates awareness throughout the organization that successful process improvement must be based on factual data and not guesswork. Vague statements such as "We believe that the cycle time has been significantly reduced" are no longer acceptable. The standard answer to this is "Show me the data."

The emphasis placed on understanding and satisfying customer needs assures that the process improvements focus not only on the efficiency aspects (to do things right), but also on the effectiveness issues (to do the right things). This assures that the Six Sigma revenue rationale is fully leveraged. The focus on quantitative metrics forces Six Sigma companies to quantify and document customer needs and the current ability to satisfy them. Anecdotal information is replaced by reliable factual data gathered through formal customer interactions and evaluations.

The combination of the right projects, the right people, and the right tools is probably the most notable strength of the Six Sigma approach. By carefully selecting important projects and training the most talented people to apply the appropriate statistical tools on these projects, Six Sigma companies have achieved remarkable synergies. In the past, tools-oriented approaches have had mixed results because of the inherent risk of focusing on finding applications for the tools rather than finding appropriate tools for the most important problems. The tools used in Six Sigma are not new; the novelty is in the way the Six Sigma approach manages to integrate them into the improvement process. A key success factor is the rigorous Six Sigma training program and its focus on hands-on application of the course material to real projects.

2.3 Business Process Reengineering

Reengineering, or business process reengineering (BPR) as it is commonly known, became a buzzword in the 1990s, spurring a tremendous interest in process design. The essence of the reengineering philosophy is to achieve drastic improvements by completely redesigning core business processes; that is, by rethinking the way business is conducted. To relate this to the distinction between process design and implementation, reengineering advocates radical design changes and fast revolutionary implementation to achieve drastic improvements. Numerous articles and books addressing this topic have been written since the publication of Michael Hammer's seminal manuscript "Reengineering Work: Don't Automate, Obliterate" (1990) and the contemporaneous work by Thomas Davenport and James Short, "The New Industrial Engineering" (1990). The popular press also actively reported on success stories as well as implementation failures of BPR. Some of the success stories are familiar, as reported in a BPR tutorial article by Grover and Malhotra (1997).

- "Ford cuts accounts payable headcount by 75 percent"
- "Mutual Benefit Life (MBL) improves insurance underwriting efficiency by 40 percent"
- "Xerox redesigns its order-fulfillment process and improves service levels by 75 percent to 97 percent and cycle times by 70 percent with inventory savings of $500 million"
- "Detroit Edison reduces payment cycles for work orders by 80 percent"

On the other side of the coin, estimates suggest that approximately 50 percent to 70 percent of reengineering projects have failed to achieve the dramatic results anticipated in their objectives (Hammer and Champy, 1993). Moreover, even the so-called successful projects, such as the reengineering of Ford Motor Company's accounts payable process, sometimes have taken 5 years or longer to implement and yield positive results (Petrozzo and Stepper, 1994). Several issues have been cited as reasons for these failures and long delays.

- Lack of top-management support and leadership (a champion) for the project.
- Poor understanding of the organization and infrastructure needed to support the new design.
- Inability to deliver the necessary advances in technology.
- Lack of expert guidance and motivation.

Hammer and Champy's reasons for failure are more detailed and include a number of observations gathered during business process reengineering efforts in which they have participated.

- Attempting to fix a process instead of changing it.
- Lack of focus on business processes.
- Neglecting people values and beliefs.
- Willingness to settle for minor results.
- Quitting too early.
- Placing prior constraints on the definition of the problem and the scope of the redesign effort.
- Allowing existing corporate cultures and management attitudes to prevent the reengineering effort from getting started.

- Trying to make business process design changes happen from the bottom up.
- Selecting a project leader who does not understand the key issues associated with reengineering business processes.
- Skimping on the resources devoted to the reengineering effort.
- Burying reengineering efforts in the middle of the corporate agenda.
- Dissipating energy across too many reengineering projects.
- Attempting to change core business processes when the chief executive officer is 2 years from retirement.
- Failing to distinguish process reengineering from other business improvement programs.
- Concentrating exclusively on design (and hence ignoring everything except process redesign).
- Trying to change business processes without making anybody unhappy.
- Pulling back when people resist making design changes.
- Dragging out the effort.

Hammer and Champy believe that the common thread that runs through all of these pitfalls can be traced to the role of senior management. It is interesting to note that for many years, W. Edwards Deming advocated the same notion in reference to failures when implementing total quality programs (Gabor, 1990). Furthermore, it falls in line with the focus on top management commitment in Six Sigma discussed in Section 2.2. Although the frequency of failure is considerable, organizations that approach the design of business processes with understanding, commitment, and strong executive leadership are likely to reap large benefits. This implies that companies must be absolutely clear about what they are trying to accomplish when designing effective business processes and how they will go about doing it. Many experts believe that a considerable number of failures associated with the reengineering of business processes can be attributed directly to misunderstanding the underlying philosophy behind BPR.

Just as the experts have identified reasons for failure, they also point to several reasons for the success of projects that change processes with the goal of radically improving their efficiency. For example, Cross et al. (1994) mention that some common themes appear in many highly successful reengineering efforts. The following similarities can be found in successful implementations.

1. Companies use process design to grow the business rather than retrench.
2. Companies place emphasis on serving the customer and on aggressively competing with quantity and quality of products and services.
3. Companies emphasize getting more customers, more work, and more revenues, and not simply concentrating on cutting back through cost reductions and downsizing.

2.3.1 REENGINEERING AND ITS RELATIONSHIP WITH OTHER EARLIER PROGRAMS

In order to better understand the basis for the reengineering movement and its importance for business process design, we must trace its origins and links to earlier process improvement programs. The term *reengineering* has been used loosely to describe almost every sort of management improvement program (Manganelli and Klein, 1994). Therefore, it is not surprising that ill-named programs fail to deliver on the advertised promise of reengineering. The following definitions of *reengineering* help sort out what this program is and what it is not.

- Reengineering is the fundamental rethinking and radical change of business processes to achieve dramatic improvements in critical, contemporary measures of performance, such as cost, quality, service, and speed (Hammer and Champy, 1993).
- Reengineering is the rapid and radical redesign and change of strategic, value-added business processes—and the systems, policies, and organizational structures that support them—to optimize the work flows and productivity in an organization (Manganelli and Klein, 1994).
- Reengineering is the fundamental rethinking and redesign of operating processes and organizational structure; it focuses on the organization's core competencies to achieve dramatic improvements in organizational performance (Lowenthal, 1994).

These definitions have common themes, which point out the characteristics of this program. In particular, the definitions explain that reengineering focuses on core competencies or value-added business processes. They also indicate that the goal is to achieve dramatic improvement by rapid and radical redesign and change. Given these definitions, it becomes clear why projects that yield only marginal improvements in measures such as cost, service, and speed are generally considered failures. The element of rapid change also indicates that reengineering efforts that drag out might be labeled failures.

In addition to examining the descriptive elements embedded in these definitions, it is useful to compare the attributes of reengineering with those of other change programs. Table 2.1 provides a summary of key dimensions used to differentiate among several change programs. Bear in mind that Table 2.1 tends in some cases to oversimplify the differences among programs.

Rightsizing and restructuring typically refer to adjustments in staffing requirements and changes in formal structural relationships, respectively. Neither approach focuses on business processes. Automation refers to typical application of technologies (including information technology, or IT), where the application focuses mainly on automating existing procedures without questioning their appropriateness or legitimacy. That is, automation does not question whether the procedures should be changed or some activities should be eliminated; it simply adds technology with the hope of improving the current process efficiency.

Total quality management (TQM) and reengineering focus on processes. However, TQM emphasizes continuous improvement and bottom-up participation, usually within

TABLE 2.1 Reengineering and Other Change Programs

	Rightsizing	*Restructuring*	*Automation*	*TQM*	*Reengineering*
Assumptions questioned	Staffing	Reporting relationships	Technology applications	Customer needs	Fundamental
Focus of change	Staffing, job responsibilities	Organization	Systems	Bottom-up improvements	Radical changes
Orientation	Functional	Functional	Procedures	Processes	Processes
Role of Information Technology	Often blamed	Occasionally emphasized	To speed up existing systems	Incidental	Key
Improvement goals	Usually incremetal	Usually incremental	Incremental	Incremental	Dramatic and significant
Frequency	Usually one time	Usually one time	Periodic	Continuous	Usually one time

Source: Adapted from Grover and Malhotra, 1997.

each business function, as well as continuous evaluation of current practices resulting in incremental changes in work design. Reengineering, on the other hand, typically is initiated from the top down, focuses on broad cross-functional processes, questions the logic of existing designs, and is usually a one-shot attempt at achieving quantum improvements. IT, which is only incidental to TQM, is often a key enabler of process reengineering. Six Sigma, which is not included in Table 2.1 because it emerged in parallel with BPR, can in many respects be construed as an extension of TQM complemented with elements of BPR. As we have seen, Six Sigma focuses on important processes and how they deliver customer value. Moreover, the objectives of drastic bottom line impact are achieved through a combination of aggressive and recurring improvement projects to get breakthrough results, and continuous improvement and process control for institutionalizing the change through incremental improvements.

The relationship between radical or discontinuous improvement (typical of successful process reengineering projects) and incremental improvement (typical of TQM programs) can be seen in Figure 2.12.

TQM and Six Sigma provide the performance measurement and problem-solving data to alert management when it is time to completely change a process. A key element in this determination is given by the inability of marginal improvements to provide the change necessary to remain competitive. Incremental improvement usually results in diminishing returns, whereby it becomes economically impractical to implement additional minor changes to a process.

In Figure 2.12, we assume that a successful process reengineering project results in a radical improvement, where the theoretical capability might not be reached immediately. A powerful approach to use to monitor the performance of the process according to the measures established during the design effort is statistical process control[1] (SPC) with process control charts (or Shewhart charts) as one of its main tools. SPC is also instrumental during the continuous improvement phase, which has the goal of

FIGURE 2.12 Radical Versus Incremental Improvement

Source: Adapted from Cross et al. 1994.

---

[1]The principles of statistical process control and the use of control charts are covered in any basic textbook on quality control or quality management. See, for example, Foster (2001) and Evans and Lindsay, (2002). For a more advanced treatment of the technical aspects see, for example, Duncan (1986).

making the process reach its theoretical capability. W. Edwards Deming referred to the cycle of continuous/radical/continuous improvement as *continual improvement*.

2.3.2 A BRIEF HISTORY OF REENGINEERING

Most publications in reengineering give Michael Hammer credit for laying much of the foundation for this approach. However, the history of this process improvement methodology involves much more than Hammer's seminal work. The article by Grover and Malhotra (1997) is one of the few published materials that attempts to provide an answer to the question of how everything got started. They note that their answer is based on speculating about the effect of a number of converging occurrences on the mobilization and subsequent popularity of reengineering as a program for radical change. The following is an adaptation from Grover and Malhotra (1997).

The origins of the movement can be traced to projects undertaken by management consulting firms. Around the mid-1980s, the idea of redesigning business processes was being advanced by large consulting units such as Peat Marwick and McKinsey & Co. Index Group and Michael Hammer directed programs on a cross-functional system in which several firms were studied (including Mutual Benefit Life and Ford). These firms used many of the components of reengineering, particularly the notion of applying information technology, to make radical changes in cross-functional processes.

For a number of years, even before the birth of reengineering, TQM brought the notion of a process focus onto the management agenda. The idea of improving business processes also was discussed at high management levels. At the core of these discussions was the concept of process performance as it relates to quality, service, and time-based competition. The TQM movement attempted to increase process performance by concentrating its efforts on continuous improvement (i.e., the Japanese *kaizen*) and employing tools such as statistical process control. It became evident later that reengineering followed a different path.

Another factor that influenced the reengineering movement was the economy. The recession through the late 1980s and early 1990s stimulated managers to think of new ways to increase process efficiency. Global competition further squeezed profits and led to reactive approaches and cost cutting/downsizing programs. The increasingly loose middle-management levels that focus on white-collar processes came under particular pressure in these programs, which also were aimed at increasing a company's ability to be flexible and responsive.

The general belief is that investments in technology should result in productivity improvement. Yet this was not happening for many firms, leading to the phenomenon generally referred to as the *productivity paradox*. Stephen Roach coined this term to refer to the fact that despite the powerful market and service innovations created by computers in the 1980s, no evidence was showing that investment in IT had any effect on overall productivity. U.S. firms invested $100 billion in IT in the 1980s, and productivity essentially remained the same.

One explanation for this phenomenon is that the organizations were not taking advantage of the capabilities the new technologies offered. Rather, companies were simply using technology to speed up and automate existing practices. Clearly, if an activity or a set of activities is not effective to begin with, performing it faster and with less human intervention does not automatically make it effective.

For instance, one major financial institution reported that more than 90 steps were required for an office worker to get office supplies. These steps mostly involved filling out forms and getting the required signatures. Given the capabilities of information technology, it is certainly true that these steps could be automated and speeded up. For example, a computer system could be developed to generate all the forms automatically and then automatically e-mail them to the appropriate person for authorization. However, is automating all these steps the best solution? Clearly, some consideration must be given to eliminating some or most of these forms of control. Hammer later coined the phrase "paving cow paths" to describe organizations that simply adopt a new technology without considering the capabilities it offers to perform work in entirely new and better ways (Shafer and Meredith, 1998).

In response to the attention generated by the productivity paradox, companies that had spent (and were spending) vast amounts of money on newer and more powerful information technologies attempted to leverage these investments by tying them to programs focused on process changes.

Although the reengineering movement was gaining momentum, there were still some doubts concerning its legitimacy. The articles by Davenport and Short (1990) and Hammer (1990) helped legitimize the movement, mainly because they appeared in journals with audiences that include academics and practitioners. The books by Hammer and Champy (1993) and Davenport (1993) followed these articles. Both of these books gained immediate popularity and spurred a lot of reengineering activity in practice and academia.

Some of the early aggressive adopters of reengineering like Cigna, MBL, Xerox, and IBM were highly publicized in the popular press. Consulting firms and vendors (with their own vested interests) began to repackage their products and market proprietary solutions for reengineering. The rhetoric of reengineering transcended the original concept and was often used to describe any change or system initiative. This practice eventually gave reengineering a bad name, and many companies that are currently engaging in process change do not label such efforts as reengineering projects. Regardless of the label, the foundations and tools used in designing or redesigning business processes are solid and remain relevant.

It can be said that the notion of reengineering came to the right place at the right time when it was first introduced. Pushed by consultants at a time when businesses were looking for answers on how to compete effectively in the changing marketplace, the concept was embraced. However, since its original conception, various realities of accomplishing radical change and minimizing the pain have set in.

2.3.3 WHEN SHOULD A PROCESS BE REENGINEERED?

To provide an answer to the question of when processes should be reengineered, it is important to first discuss the three forces that Hammer and Champy (1993) believe "are driving today's companies deeper and deeper into a territory that most of their executives and managers find frighteningly unfamiliar." They call these forces the three C's: customers, competition, and change.

Customers have increasingly become more educated (in the broadest sense of the word) and therefore more demanding. Customers do not settle for high quality in products and services, because they take that attribute as a given. Customer expectations have soared and now include the ability to select products and services that uniquely fit their needs. As Hammer and Champy put it: "The mass market has broken into pieces, some as small as a single customer." Some Pizza Hut stores, for example, keep track of the orders placed by their customers and mail discount coupons with offerings customized to individual tastes. Some call centers record the name of the customer representative to whom the customer spoke last time and automatically route a new call to the same representative to create the sense of a personal relationship. Customers are likely to get used to this superior level of service and will not be easily satisfied with less.

The competition has also changed, in the sense that there is more of it, and it sometimes comes from unexpected sources. Each market segment where goods and services are sold establishes the basis for competition. The same product, for example, may be sold in different markets by emphasizing price in one, quality in another, functionality (attributes) at yet another, and reliability or service elsewhere. Free trade agreements among countries, such as the North Atlantic Free Trade Agreement (NAFTA), or within the European Union (EU) compound the complexity and the intensity of competition because governments are less willing to implement policies designed to protect the local industry. The good news for consumers is that this intense competition tends to drive quality up and prices down. The challenge for companies is that the level of efficiency in their operations must increase (to various degrees, depending on the status quo), because companies must be able to compete with the world's best.

The conventional wisdom that if it ain't broke, don't fix it no longer applies to a rapidly changing business environment. Change is forced upon companies in many different ways, including the need to develop new products and services constantly. This need induces change in processes and organizational structures. For example, it is not enough for a company to introduce a new product that customers are going to love; the company must be sure that its order-fulfillment process is not going to irritate retailers that will in turn make decisions about shelf space and promotions. Changes in technology also have forced companies to be more adaptive and responsive, because customers expect to be able to utilize technological advances to their full potential. For example, suppose the owner of a bed and breakfast in a secluded, attractive part of the world decides to advertise its business on the World Wide Web. If the Web page does a good job of selling this vacation spot but fails to provide an electronic reservation system, potential guests might be lost.

With the three C's in mind, consider the following questions that Cross et al. (1994) have found useful in determining when to redesign and reengineer a process.

- Are your customers demanding more for less?
- Are your competitors likely to provide more for less?
- Can you hand-carry work through the process five times faster than your normal cycle time?
- Have your incremental quality-improvement efforts been stalled or been a disappointment?
- Have investments in technology not panned out?
- Are you planning to introduce radically new products and services or serve new markets?
- Are you in danger of becoming unprofitable?
- Have your downsizing and cost-cutting efforts failed to turn the ship around?
- Are you merging or consolidating operations?
- Are your core business processes fragmented and disintegrated?

Consider the third question and the IBM Credit example in Section 1.1.2. Two senior managers walked a request through this process, asking personnel in each step to put aside whatever they were doing and to process the request as they normally would. They learned from this experiment that performing the actual work took in total only 90 minutes. The rest of the time (up to an average of 6 days) was attributed to non-value-adding activities such as waiting and rework. Clearly, the two senior managers were able to hand-carry a financing request more than five times faster than the average cycle time. In fact, assuming working days of 8 hours, they were able to hand-carry the request 32 times faster than the average cycle time!

One of the main reasons for launching a process redesign effort is the realization that continuous improvement activities have stopped yielding results. As depicted in

Figure 2.12, the continuous improvement programs exhibit a profile of diminishing returns, making additional contributions to higher performance levels increasingly more expensive. This is due to the theoretical capability of the process. We use the term *capability* loosely to describe the ability of a process to achieve a desired level of performance; performance in this case can be measured by quality, service, speed, or cost. Once continuous improvement efforts lead a process to operate at or near its theoretical capability, the only way to significantly increase the level of performance is to change the process by completely redesigning it.

2.3.4 WHAT SHOULD BE REENGINEERED?

Processes, not organizations, are redesigned and reengineered. The confusion between organizational units and processes as objects of reengineering projects arises because departments, divisions, and groups are entities that are familiar to people in business but processes are not. Organizational lines are visible and can be plainly drawn in organizational charts, but processes are not visible. Organizational units have names; processes often do not.

Roberts (1994) makes the distinction between *formal* and *informal* business processes. Formal processes are typically guided by a set of written policies and procedures; informal processes are not. Formal processes are often prime candidates for reengineering for the following reasons.

1. Formal processes typically involve multiple departments and a relatively large number of employees. As a result of their scope and complexity, such processes usually have the most to offer in terms of net benefits realized from improvement.
2. Because formal processes operate under a set of rigid policies and procedures, they are more likely to be bound by assumptions and realities that are no longer valid. Informal processes also can become slaves of tradition, but such processes are more likely to be improved as the need for improvement becomes apparent—especially if the organization supports change and does not discourage risk taking.
3. Informal processes tend to be contained within a unit in the organizational structure (e.g., a department or division). Therefore, issues of process ownership, control, and information sharing tend to be minimal.

Because it is not possible or even desirable to radically reengineer every formal business process at the same time, careful thought should be given to a starting point. Provided the executive management level is truly committed to the reengineering philosophy, Roberts (1994) suggests the following sequential screening criteria for choosing which process to reengineer first.

1. A process that has a high likelihood of being reengineered successfully.
2. A process for which the reengineering effort can produce rapid results.
3. A process that, when reengineered, will result in significant benefits to the customer and the organization.

Note the similarity among the criteria used in Six Sigma for prioritizing improvement projects and the ones suggested by Hammer and Champy (1993) and Roberts.

1. *Dysfunction:* Which processes are in deepest trouble?
2. *Importance:* Which processes have the greatest impact on the company's customers?
3. *Feasibility:* Which of the company's processes are currently most susceptible to successful reengineering?

Let us now examine each of these characteristics in more detail.

Dysfunction.   As a general rule, dysfunctional or broken processes are hard to miss, because people inside the company are clear about their inefficiencies. Consider a process that uses the World Wide Web to create sales leads. Prospective customers enter information in an electronic form that sends an e-mail message to a central location. A clerk in the central location prints the e-mail messages and types the information into another electronic form that feeds a database that sales representatives can access. This process is broken, because data move from electronic form to paper and back to an electronic file. Clearly, a direct link should be provided to avoid retyping data.

Many educational institutions ask instructors to hand in final grades using forms that are machine-readable. Typically, these forms (also known as "bubble sheets") consist of small circles arranged in rows where instructors can code the correct grade for each student by filling in the right combination of circles using a pencil. The forms are processed mechanically to create an electronic file of the grades. The electronic file is used to update the records of each student in the appropriate database of the institution. This process was appropriate when instructors kept records of the performance of each student in grade books. Today, however, grade books are replaced with electronic workbooks or spreadsheets, and the process is forcing grades to be moved from electronic media to paper so that a mechanical device can transform them back to an electronic form. This process is broken, because it adds unnecessary steps and increases the probability of introducing errors when the grades are coded in the bubble sheets using a printout of the instructor's records. The process could be simplified considerably if a direct link between the instructors' files and the institution databases is established with the proper level of security.

Hammer and Champy compiled a list of symptoms that help identify broken processes. Each symptom is associated with a disease, as summarized in Table 2.2.

Be aware that symptoms do not always show up where the disease resides. In other words, in some situations symptoms might be terribly misleading. An organization that Hammer and Champy studied had an order-fulfillment process that was "badly flawed," but the customers didn't think that was the case. In fact, the customers were satisfied because they received exactly what they ordered when they wanted it. As a result, superficially the process appeared healthy. However, the company's sales were lagging. Was the sales process broken? No, the order-fulfillment process was in such bad condition that customers received their products on time only because salespeople went to the warehouse, picked up the orders, and delivered them themselves. That pleased the customers, but salespeople were making deliveries instead of selling; as a result, sales suffered.

TABLE 2.2   Symptoms and Diseases of Broken Processes

	Symptom	*Disease*
1	Extensive information exchange, data redundancy and rekeying	Arbitrary fragmentation of a natural process
2	Inventory, buffers, and other assets	System slack to cope with uncertainty
3	High ratio of checking and control to value-adding	Fragmentation
4	Rework and iteration	Inadequate feedback along chains
5	Complexity, exceptions, and special cases	Accretion onto a simple base

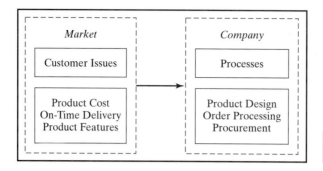

FIGURE 2.13 Mapping of Customer Issues to Processes

Importance.   Companies cannot ask their customers which processes are most important to them. However, as depicted in Figure 2.13, companies can determine what issues their customers care strongly about and can correlate those issues with the processes that most influence them. For example, if customers care about product cost, the company might consider the product development and design process as being of high importance, given that a large percentage of the product cost is committed in the design stage.

Customers of a Web-based, computer-part supplier care about accuracy and the speed of delivery of ordered parts. These customers depend on receiving the right parts (e.g., memory chips of desired capacity) on time. The supplier should consider the order-fulfillment process the core of the business.

Feasibility.   The feasibility of reengineering a process is linked to the scale of the associated project: The larger a process is, the broader its scope is. A greater payoff is possible when a large process is reengineered, but the likelihood of project success decreases. Also, a project that requires a large investment will encounter more hurdles than one that does not. Hence, the forces that play a role in determining the feasibility of a process as a prospect for reengineering are, as depicted in Figure 2.14: process scope, project cost, process owner commitment, and the strength of the team in charge of reengineering the selected process.

Mutual Benefit reduced the time to issue a policy from 3 weeks to 3 hours. Then it fell into insolvency and was taken by regulators a few months after Hammer's 1990

FIGURE 2.14 Forces Affecting Process Feasibility

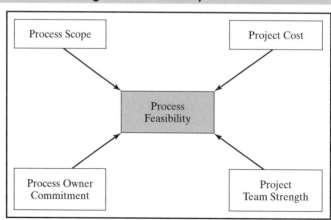

article was published. This is an example of the *process paradox,* which refers to the decline and failure of businesses that have achieved dramatic improvements through process reforms. To avoid the process paradox, companies must not only get a "process right" but get the "right process right."

It should be noted that neither Roberts nor Hammer and Champy suggest that the method to select a process to redesign and reengineer is a formal one. That is, determining what to redesign is not a purely analytical exercise, whereby with a given number of inputs the output is fully determined. In fact, many aspects of process design—and if we include the implementation phase, reengineering—are closer to art than to science. In the chapters ahead, we will look at a number of principles and tools that can be used to guide and assist the process design effort with the goal of exploiting the best aspects of art and science.

2.3.5 SUGGESTED REENGINEERING FRAMEWORKS

As we have discussed, the principles of reengineering have emerged from experiences at many different companies, and no one manual or distinct framework exists for how to go about a reengineering project. This differs from a program such as Six Sigma, which has its origins in one company (Motorola) and is anchored in a well-defined methodology. As a result of the heterogeneity of the reengineering concept, a variety of suggested frameworks have been proposed by practitioners and researchers. In the next few pages, we will look closer at three such frameworks suggested by Roberts (1994), Lowenthal (1994), and Cross et al. (1994). The purpose is to illustrate the fact that the reengineering concept, although it has some distinctive trademarks, is not one uniquely defined program but rather a family of approaches with some common traits and an explicit focus on radical design and rapid, revolutionary implementation.

Roberts (1994) offers the reengineering framework depicted in Figure 2.15 that starts with a gap analysis and ends with a transition to continuous improvement. The gap analysis technique attempts to determine three kinds of information: (1) the way things should be, (2) the way things are, and (3) how best to reconcile the difference between the two. An interesting feature of his framework is a feedback loop that goes from a pilot test to the process design stage. This indicates that some design modifications might be needed following a risk and impact analysis and the pilot test.

The model by Lowenthal (1994), on the other hand, consists of four phases: (1) preparing for change, (2) planning for change, (3) designing for change, and (4) evaluating change. See Figure 2.16. The first phase sets the foundation for future activity by achieving the following goals.

- Building understanding and support in management and increasing management awareness of the need for change.
- Preparing for a cultural shift and buy-in by the organization's employees (including informing the employees of their role in the upcoming reengineering project).

The second phase operates under the assumption that organizations need to plan their future due to the constantly changing marketplace. The first two phases are performed in parallel, because neither one of them should be viewed as a prerequisite of the other.

The third phase provides a method to identify, assess, map, and ultimately design business processes. It offers the necessary framework for translating insights about the process being explored into quantum leaps of change.

The fourth phase provides a means to evaluate the improvement during a predetermined time frame, usually a year, and to develop priorities for the coming years.

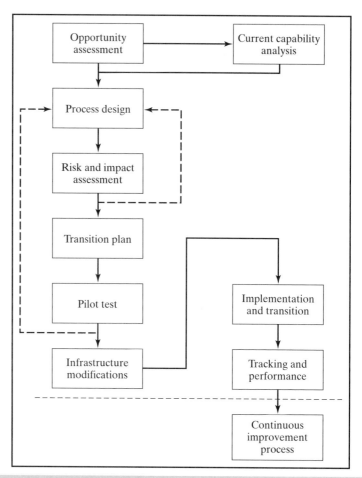

FIGURE 2.15 Robert's Framework for Process Reengineering

Specifically, this phase helps determine whether the reengineering effort has been successful and where future efforts should be concentrated.

The framework suggested by Cross et al. (1994) in a sense shows the building blocks of process reengineering. The approach is divided into three phases, as depicted in Figure 2.17.

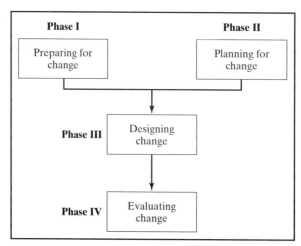

FIGURE 2.16 Lowenthal's Framework for Process Reengineering

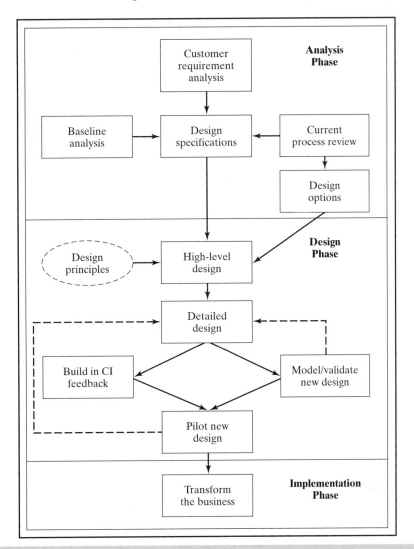

FIGURE 2.17 Cross and Associates Framework for Process Reengineering

In the first phase, an in-depth understanding of the markets and customer requirements is developed. Also, research is directed toward a detailed understanding of how the work currently is being done. This is compared with the performance levels required to meet and beat the competition. In some cases, it is useful at this stage to benchmark best industry practices. Chapter 11 discusses how data envelopment analysis (DEA) can be used for this purpose.

During the analysis phase, some immediate opportunities for improvement might become apparent. For example, at one company, a simple review of the process convinced management to eliminate numerous approval and sign-off steps. This eliminated nearly 30 percent of the cycle time and 10 percent of the effort to get the work through the process. It took only 1 week from reviewing the process and discussing the findings to make the changes.

The design phase relies on design principles that fall into six categories: (1) service quality, (2) workflow, (3) workspace, (4) continuous improvement, (5) workforce, and (6) information technology. Service quality principles provide guidance regarding the design of processes as they relate to customer contacts. Workflow principles relate to the basic nature of managing the flow of work through a series of steps.

Workspace principles address the ergonomic factors and layout options. Continuous improvement principles help ensure that a process can be self-sustaining by incorporating continuous improvement and learning. Workforce principles are based on the premise that any workflow requires people and people are an integral part of the process design and implementation, and not an afterthought.

The design phase also includes the development of detailed maps, procedures, and operating policies and the design of supporting infrastructure (e.g., performance measures, job and organizational design, and compensation systems). The design is confirmed by validation through interviews and business models at the same time as key performance measures are defined. The design phase concludes with a pilot test, whose results may trigger changes to the blueprinted design.

Finally, the implementation phase involves the institutionalization of the new design into the day-to-day operations. The planning for implementation typically begins in parallel with the pilot, and in some cases in parallel with the earlier analysis and design work.

2.4 Revolutionary Versus Evolutionary Change

The traditional definition of *reengineering* emphasizes radical redesign and rapid implementation leading to revolutionary change. However, in reality constraining factors often arise, such as union concerns, training and IT needs, strong culture, and cemented organizational boundaries that make a rapid implementation at best very costly. In fact, this is one of the main reasons many reengineering projects have taken a lengthy amount of time and thereby have been considered failures. A revolutionary change that turns the whole organization on its head has the potential to achieve vast improvements, but it is also risky, and if it fails it might cause more harm than good.

As a consequence, many companies end up pursuing a successful strategy for breakthrough improvements based on radical redesign combined with a more evolutionary change process, implementing the plans they can, given the current restrictions. See, for example, Cooper and Markus (1995), Stoddard and Jarvenpaa (1995), and Jarvenpaa and Stoddard (1998). The radical redesign constitutes the blueprint for change and provides motivation as well as a clear goal for the organization. As the implementation proceeds, the original design usually has to be revised to accommodate the organizational constraints and the changing market conditions faced by the company. The process design that is finally fully implemented is therefore usually a compromise between the blueprinted "ideal" design and the original process. This implies that the improvements might not be as drastic as advocated by the reengineering movement, but at the same time the risk of failure is considerably lower.

In the following section, we will clarify what characterizes the concepts of evolutionary and revolutionary change, discuss their pros and cons, and note when it might make more sense to pursue one or the other to implement a new process design.

The evolutionary change model is based on the assumption that the people directly affected by and involved in a change process also must take an active part in the design and implementation of that change. See, for example, Jick (1993), Cooper and Markus (1995), Jarvenpaa and Stoddard (1998), and references therein. In other words, the evolutionary change theory advocates that change should come from within the organization itself, managed by the current leadership and carried out by the current employees. The communication should be broad and open, and the pace of change should be adapted to the available capabilities and resources, meaning that milestones and yardsticks are flexible.

The motivation for change arises from internal feelings of dissatisfaction with the current situation and a desire to do better. Moreover, new processes and procedures are piloted and implemented before they are cemented by the introduction of new IT systems. Inherently, the evolutionary model assumes that real change is best achieved through incremental improvements over time.

The advantages with evolutionary change are that it is less disruptive and risky than the revolutionary counterpart, but also that it tends to increase the organization's general capacity for change. The disadvantage is that it takes a long time to achieve the desired vision, and it must be kept alive and adjusted over time as market conditions change. It is worth noting that the continuous improvement and empowerment focus in quality management is closely related to the evolutionary change philosophy.

The revolutionary change model is based on the so-called punctuated equilibrium paradigm. See, for example, Gersick (1991), which views radical change as occurring at certain instances in time with long periods of incremental change in between. Revolutionary change unfolds quickly and alters the very structure of the organization, the business practices, and the culture. Together with this type of change comes disorder, uncertainty, and identity crises.

The radical change needs to be top driven, typically by the CEO, and externally imposed on the organization. It requires external resources and an outside viewpoint. The change is driven by senior management, and these individuals need to provide the right vision, create the right culture, and build the necessary political alliances. See, for example, Nadler et al. (1995), Gersick (1991), Jarvenpaa and Stoddard (1998).

Outsiders in terms of consultants or new executives are brought in to lead and participate in the change process because they are not afraid to challenge the status quo. The change team is typically small and secluded from the rest of the organization so that they are not unduly influenced by the current way of doing things. Communication regarding what is about to happen is minimal and on a need-to-know basis.

The motivation for change is a crisis, financial or otherwise, and the milestones are firm to clearly mark that a new order is in place. As part of the change process, every member of the organization needs to be qualified for the new organization; if a person doesn't measure up, he or she has no place.

Revolutionary change is also characterized by tough decisions including relentless cost cutting and conflict resolution. The advantage with the revolutionary approach is that drastic results can be achieved quickly. However, the enormous strain put on the organization also makes the project risky, and the probability of failure is not to be discarded lightly. The personal involvement required from top management also might divert their attention from the external marketplace, implying increased risk of lost market opportunities and possibly misaligned strategies. Another disadvantage is that the nature of revolutionary change goes against the core values that most organizations want to instill—namely empowerment, bottom-up involvement, and innovation. The secrecy and exclusion of employees from the change process also creates insecurity about their roles, leading them to resist rather than embrace change, not just for the moment but also in the long run. Table 2.3 summarizes some important elements of the evolutionary and revolutionary change models.

Clearly, the descriptions of the evolutionary and revolutionary change models constitute the extreme points on a continuum of different change strategies, and no definite answers clarify when to use a certain approach. However, based on empirical research,

TABLE 2.3 Elements of Evolutionary and Revolutionary Change Theories

Element	Evolutionary Change Model	Revolutionary Change Model
Leadership	Insiders	Outsiders
Outside resources	Few, if any, consultants	Consultant-led initiative
Physical separation	No, part-time team members	Yes, greenfield site
Crisis	None	Poor performance
Milestones	Flexible	Firm
Reward system	Unchanged	New
IT/process change	Process first	Simultaneous process and IT change

Source: Adapted from Jarvenpaa and Stoddard, 1998.

Jarvenpaa and Stoddard (1998) conclude that revolutionary implementation tends to be appropriate under special conditions, such as when the following situations are true.

1. A true performance crisis exists.
2. The change concerns a smaller, self-contained unit.
3. The organization has deep pockets; for example, in terms of a rich parent company.
4. The organization is free from the "not-invented-here" syndrome and can freely import solutions from outside the company or other parts of the company, such as using purchased software packages.

However, if not facing an immediate crisis, which leaves little choice but to pursue a risky revolutionary change tactic or go broke, many companies tend to use a more cautious evolutionary implementation strategy.

The critical element is time. If management is in a reactive mode and must respond to an immediate threat, a revolutionary change tactic might be the only sound choice. On the other hand, if management is in a proactive mode and initiates the change process in anticipation of a future need, there might be time to implement the radical design through an evolutionary approach with less risk. Although the vast improvements advocated in the reengineering movement might not be attained in this case, empirical evidence shows that a well-managed organization can accomplish breakthrough results using a combination of radical redesign and evolutionary implementation. By deploying an evolutionary tactic, the organization also learns how to change. This means it will be in a better position to implement future designs faster.

2.5 Summary

This chapter has looked at the governing principles of successful process management and discussed why it is important to adopt a process view. We also have described the basis for Six Sigma and business process reengineering, two of the most influential improvement programs developed in recent years. Both have a process orientation and to various degrees center on the principles for process management. The importance of distinguishing between process design and implementation, as well as between evolutionary and revolutionary change tactics as means to carry out the implementation, has also been explored.

The importance and power of adopting a process view points directly to the weaknesses of the functional organization in terms of coordination and transparency across functional areas. The lack of coordination and the tendency to focus on internal functional goals, in less-than-perfect alignment with the overall organizational objectives, makes the functional organization prone to suboptimization. As a remedy, the process view, with its focus on horizontal workflows, emphasizes coordination and customer needs. In terms of people management, adopting a process view means that the process structure needs to be made clear to everyone involved. Creating a better understanding of how each individual's contribution fits into the big picture encourages involvement and participation, which are cornerstones in modern quality management and stepping-stones for successfully empowering the workforce.

The core principles for successful process management can be grouped into the following activities.

- Establishing process ownership.
- Analyzing boundaries and interfaces.
- Defining the process by documenting its workflow.
- Identifying control points and measurements.
- Monitoring the process for control purposes by implementing measures.
- Taking corrective action and providing feedback if deviations indicate that the process is no longer in control.

The road to successful process management of an already-designed process can be divided into three phases comprising the activities previously listed: initialization, definition, and control. In terms of attacking the difficult coordination issues across functional boundaries and interfaces, a useful concept is the customer-producer-supplier (CPS) model. Applying this model to every critical interface in the process is an effective way of aligning internal and external customer needs, and it fosters a view of the process as a chain of customers that need to be satisfied.

In a broad sense, Six Sigma can be described as a companywide strategic initiative for process improvement in manufacturing and service organizations. Its clear objective is to improve bottom-line results by reducing costs and increasing revenues. The goal of the Six Sigma program as it was originally conceived at Motorola is to reduce the variation of the individual processes to render no more than 3.4 defects per million opportunities.

At the core of the Six Sigma approach is a project- and result-oriented, quantitative and disciplined improvement methodology focused on reducing variability but also improving cycle times and yield. The methodology consists of five steps: *define, measure, analyze, improve,* and *control.* In many ways, these steps relate to the basic principles of process management. The methodology is embedded in a corporate framework based on top-management commitment, stakeholder involvement, training programs, and measurement systems. Although Six Sigma was originally Motorola's customized approach to quality management and process improvement, its ongoing success has brought it into the boardrooms of some of the world's most successful companies. Six Sigma's success is often attributed to a strong bottom-line focus and big dollar impact; the emphasis and consistent use of a unified and quantitative approach to process improvement; the emphasis placed on understanding and satisfying customer needs; and the combination of the right projects, the right people, and the right tools.

The reengineering philosophy of achieving drastic performance improvements by a complete redesign of core business processes, combined with rapid implementation of the new design, created a tremendous interest in the 1990s. However, quickly achieving revolutionary change is connected with high risks as well as potentially high returns. The large number of failed initiatives caused more harm than good and has given reengineering a mixed reputation. Several reasons for these failures have been cited, including lack of top-management support and project leadership, poor understanding of the current organization and operations, inability to obtain and adapt the necessary technology, neglecting people's values and beliefs, placing prior constraints on the scope and problem definition of the design effort, and quitting too early when people resist making changes. Most of these issues relate to the rapid implementation of the radically new design and the compressed time perspective that is inherent in the traditional reengineering definition. The soundness of the general principles for business process design advocated by the reengineering movement is unabated, including the principles for deciding when and what to redesign.

The difficulty and high risk of using a revolutionary change tactic for implementation has led some companies to embark on a successful strategy for breakthrough improvements based on radical process design combined with a more evolutionary implementation tactic. The advantages include lower risk of failure and improved long-term organizational ability to accept change. A disadvantage is that the final implementation might not give the order-of-magnitude improvements that a revolutionary change might be capable of. The approach also requires more time; therefore, in order to use this strategy, management must be proactive. If a company is facing an immediate crisis, a revolutionary change tactic might be the only hope.

2.6 References

Cooper, R., and M. L. Markus. 1995. Human reengineering. *Sloan Management Review* 36 (Summer): 39–50.

Cross, K. F., J. J. Feather, and R. L. Lynch. 1994. *Corporate renaissance: The art of reengineering.* Cambridge, MA: Blackwell Business.

Davenport, T. 1993. *Process innovation: Reengineering work through information technology.* Boston: Harvard Business School Press.

Davenport, T., and J. Short. 1990. The new industrial engineering: Information technology and business process redesign. *Sloan Management Review* (Summer): 11–27.

Duncan A. J. 1986. *Quality control and industrial statistics,* 5th edition. Homewood, IL: D. Irwin.

Evans, J. R., and W. M. Lindsay. 2002. *The management and control of quality,* 5th edition. Cincinnati, OH: South-Western, Thomson Learning.

Foster, T. S. 2001. *Managing quality: An integrative approach.* Upper Saddle River, NJ: Prentice Hall.

Gabor, A. 1990. *The man who discovered quality.* New York: Penguin Books.

Gersick, C. J. G. 1991. Revolutionary change theories: A multilevel exploration of the punctuated equilibrium paradigm. *Academy of Management Review* 16 (January): 10–36.

Goldsborough, R. 1998. PCs and the productivity paradox. *ComputorEdge* (October 26): 23–24.

Grover, V., and M. J. Malhotra. 1997. Business process reengineering: A tutorial on the concept, evolution, method, technology, and application. *Journal of Operations Management* 15: 193–213.

Hammer, M. 1990. Reengineering work: Don't automate, obliterate. *Harvard Business Review* 71(6): 119–131.

Hammer, M., and J. Champy. 1993. *Reengineering the corporation: A manifesto for business revolution.* New York: Harper Business.

Harbour, J. L. 1994. *The process reengineering workbook.* New York: Quality Resources.

Harrington, H. J. 1991. *Business process improvement: The breakthrough strategy for total quality, productivity, and competitiveness.* New York: McGraw-Hill.

Harry, M. J. 1998. *The vision of Six Sigma,* 8 volumes. Pheonix, AZ: Tri Star Publishing.

Harry, M. J., and R. Schroeder. 2000. *Six Sigma: The breakthrough management strategy revolutionizing the world's top corporations.* New York: Doubleday.

Hauser, J., and D. Clausing. 1988. The house of quality. *Harvard Business Review* (May-June): 63–73.

Hoerl, R. W. 1998. Six Sigma and the future of the quality profession. *Quality Progress* 31(6).

Jarvenpaa, S. L., and D. B. Stoddard. 1998. Business process redesign: Radical and revolutionary change. *Journal of Business Research* 41: 15–27.

Jick, T. D. 1993. *Managing change: Cases and concepts.* Burr Ridge, IL: Irwin.

Lowenthal, J. N. 1994. *Reengineering the organization: A step-by-step approach to corporate revitalization.* Milwaukee, WI: ASQC Quality Press.

Magnusson, K., Korslid, D., and B. Bergman. 2000. *Six Sigma: The pragmatic approach.* Lund, Sweden: Studentlitteratur.

Manganelli, R. L., and M. M. Klein. 1994. A framework for reengineering. *Sloan Management Review* (June): 10–16.

Melan, E. H. 1993. *Process management: Methods for improving products and services.* New York: McGraw-Hill.

Mintzberg, H. 1979. *The structuring of organizations.* Upper Saddle River, NJ: Prentice Hall.

Mizuno S., and Y. Akao. 1994. *QFD: The customer-driven approach to quality planning and development.* Tokyo, Japan: Asian Productivity Organization.

Munro, R. A. 2000. Linking Six Sigma with QS-9000: Auto industry adds new tools for quality improvement. *Quality Progress* 33(5).

Nadler, D. A., R. B. Shaw, and A. W. Walton. 1995. *Discontinuous change.* San Francisco: Jossey-Bass Publishers.

Petrozzo, D. P., and J. C. Stepper. 1994. *Successful reengineering.* New York: John Wiley and Sons.

Robbins, S. P. 1990. *Organization theory: Structure designs and applications,* 3rd edition. New Jersey: Prentice-Hall International Inc.

Roberts, L. 1994. *Process reengineering: A key to achieving breakthrough success.* Milwaukee, WI: ASQC Quality Press.

Shafer, S. M., and J. R. Meredith. 1998. *Operations management: A process approach with spreadsheets.* New York: John Wiley and Sons.

Stoddard D. B., and S. L. Jarvenpaa. 1995. Business process redesign: Tactics for managing radical change. *Journal of Management Information Systems* 12 (Summer): 81–107.

Tomkins, R. 1997. GE beats expected 13% rise. *Financial Times*, October 10, 1997.

2.7 Discussion Questions and Exercises

1. What are some of the main advantages and challenges of adopting a process-oriented view of the organization? How are these related to the traditional functional structure?

2. What are the purposes of and challenges with each of the six main principles or activities that define successful process management? Does it make sense to group the activities into the three phases initialization, definition, and control? Why or why not?

3. How is the Six Sigma improvement methodology related to the basic principles of process management and the three phases of initialization, definition, and control?

4. Explain the CPS model and the "chain of customers" concept. How does this help facilitate an effective process orientation?

5. Considering the document distribution example in Section 2.1.4:
   • What would you say are the main problems with the management of this process?
   • Do you agree with Joe's approach for arriving at a better managed process?
   • Is there anything you would do differently?
   • Do you see any potential for radical redesign of the entire process? What do you suggest?

6. What is the technical definition of Six Sigma quality, and how is this definition related to the measure of 3.4 dpmo?

7. How would you define or describe a Six Sigma initiative to a friend who has never heard about this before? What is new with Six Sigma compared to other quality-management programs?

8. What are the components of the Six Sigma framework? Are there any similarities with issues emphasized in reengineering and general process management? What is the importance of each individual component for the overall approach? What are the implications if a certain element is not in place?

9. Do the Six Sigma cost and revenue rationale and the combined effect of the efficiency and effectiveness loops make sense? How would you interpret this in a situation where Six Sigma is applied at a hospital or an educational institution like a university?

10. What is the standard approach in Six Sigma for reducing variability? How does it relate to improvements in cycle time and yield?

11. What are the traditional roles in a Six Sigma improvement project, and how are they related to the training scheme? Does this approach make sense to you? Can you see any potential drawbacks, for example, in light of the theories for evolutionary and revolutionary change?

12. At the core of Six Sigma programs lies the improvement methodology DMAIC. Discuss how each of its five steps relates to the other components of the Six Sigma framework.

13. What are some of the reasons often mentioned for the success of Six Sigma? What are the rationales? Do you think they make sense?

14. What are some of the often-cited reasons for reengineering failures? Can you see any connections to the Six Sigma framework or the general principles for process management?

15. How would you position Six Sigma in relation to reengineering and TQM?

16. What is the meaning of the *process paradox*? How can it be avoided?

17. What are some of the criteria often used to determine when a process should be redesigned? What forces drive the need for process redesign?

18. Discuss the principles commonly used in reengineering for deciding which processes to redesign? How do these criteria relate to those used in Six Sigma for prioritizing among improvement projects?

19. Discuss the similarities and differences among the reengineering frameworks suggested by Roberts, Lowenthal, and Cross et al., described in Section 2.3.5. Also, what connections can be seen with the Six Sigma framework?

20. Explain how total quality management and business process redesign can support one another in the context of the methodology outlined in Figure 2.15.

21. How can the general revolutionary change model help explain the many reengineering failures? What is the pragmatic strategy many companies tend to use in order to lower the risk of failure and the cost of change but still leverage the potential of business process design? What are its main advantages and disadvantages? What is the prerequisite for this strategy to be a viable option?

22. *PCs and the Productivity Paradox* (adapted from Goldsborough, 1998)—Despite the riotous instability of stock prices lately, some prognosticators are advising us not to worry. Sure, the stock market has experienced unprecedented growth without significant downslide for 7 straight years. And sure the market has always been cyclical in the past. But we're in the midst of a revolution, say the pundits, an information revolution. Spurred by personal computers and the Internet, the economy has morphed in a fundamental way. Information technology has ushered in a paradigm-smashing leap in productivity that might have made recession passé.

    Not so fast, say those who've studied these issues. It's not even clear that personal computers have affected productivity appreciably, let alone leading to the kind of improvements that would allow us to sail off with our mutual fund investments into a tranquil prosperity. Bureau of Labor Statistics figures show that despite the personal computer "revolution" and the billions invested in technology, productivity gains measured in output per hour have remained at a feeble annual rate of 1 percent for the past 30 years, which pales in comparison to the brawny productivity growth of 3 percent annually experienced during the 1950s and 1960s.

    Common sense indicates that personal computers should increase productivity. They let individuals plan and budget far more effectively than a calculator or a table. They make it possible to keep track of people and things far more easily than a roster or a list. They help people communicate far more efficiently than a typewriter or a telephone. They can tap far more research sources than the largest collection of periodicals or books. Even though some studies have shown that PCs have had a positive impact on productivity, and even though some experts contend that such intangibles as convenience and service don't show up in the statistics, the fact remains that the productivity figures haven't budged. This anomaly has been called the "productivity paradox," and if you look at your own habits and those of people around you, you'll see some of the reasons why.
    - Those memos with their fancy fonts and elaborate formatting take longer to create than the simple typewritten memos of the past.
    - Likewise with those presentations adorned with graphics, sound effects, and animation.
    - E-mail makes it easy to stay in the loop, but wading through scores of nonessential messages each day is definitely a time sink.
    - The Web can be an invaluable informational resource, but the temptation is great to jump from one site to another, each in turn less relevant to your work needs. Not to mention using the Web to shop, check out sports scores, and engage in chitchat.
    - Then there is the equipment maintenance. Whereas in the past only specialists got silicon under their fingernails, today everybody has to deal with software bugs, hardware conflicts, and system crashes. And when the machine is not cooperating, it lures you to tinker endlessly in pursuit of PC perfection.
    - A few years ago, a survey by SBT Accounting Systems of San Rafael, California, showed that the typical computer user in a business setting wastes 5.1 hours each week on PCs.
    - Another study by Forrester Research of Cambridge, Massachusetts, showed that 20 percent of employees' time spent on the Internet at work doesn't involve their jobs.

This is not to say that you should trade your Pentium III machine for a typewriter or prevent workers from having access to the Internet. It's not the technology that's the villain. It's how we use it. Because the machines are so dumb—all they really do is add and subtract zeros and ones—we have to be smart in managing them.

a. What policies can a company establish to remedy some of the causes for the productivity paradox?

b. Should the productivity paradox be a factor when considering the application of information technology to business process design?

A Simulation-Based Framework for Business Processes Design Projects

Chapters 1 and 2 defined the concepts of business processes, process design, process management, and evolutionary as opposed to revolutionary implementation tactics. We also looked closely at the basic principles of Six Sigma and business process reengineering as representatives of recent process-oriented improvement programs. This chapter introduces a framework for structuring business process design projects. The framework is expressed as a number of important issues or steps that typically need to be addressed in these types of projects. It also puts special emphasis on the usefulness of simulation. Because the general purpose of the analytical tools investigated in Chapters 4 through 11 is to support process design projects, the framework also can be viewed as a road map for the remaining chapters of this book. This also means that many of the design principles and issues touched upon in this chapter will be revisited in subsequent chapters for a more thorough analysis.

The scope of a design project as defined in this chapter ranges from the strategic vision of what needs to be done to the final blueprint of the new design. Important intermediate issues include defining and selecting the right process to address, evaluating potential design enablers, and acquiring an understanding of the current process if one exists. In adherence to our distinction between process design and implementation, we do not consider *detailed* implementation issues to be part of the design project. Consequently, the framework does not deal explicitly with how to implement the design or how to manage organizational change and make it stick. At the same time, we cannot completely separate the design project from the implementation issues. First, it is pointless to design processes that will never be implemented. Therefore, in selecting which processes to design or redesign, we need to consider the expected implementation challenges and corresponding costs. Second, as discussed in Section 2.4, an evolutionary implementation implies sequential adjustments of the original blueprinted design due to emerging implementation restrictions and changes in market demands. To that end, high-level implementation issues are included in our framework (see Figure 3.1).

As will be apparent, many of the ideas and principles underlying the framework have sprung from the reengineering movement with its focus on radical business process redesign. However, it is important to remember that our focus is on business

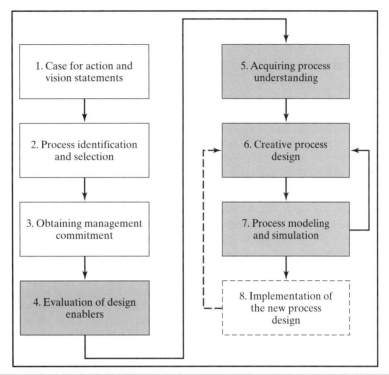

FIGURE 3.1 A Framework for Business Process Design Projects. Aspects of the Shaded Steps Are the Focus of Chapters 4–11 and Can Be Considered as the Core Activities Relating to Analytical Process Modeling and Design.

process design (or synonymously, redesign) per se, which in our connotation refers to developing the blueprint for a new process. This does not prescribe the strategy for how the design is going to be implemented. Reengineering, on the other hand, refers to radical process design and revolutionary implementation. Consequently, in the following sections, we will draw on the sound principles for process design stemming from the process improvement and reengineering literature, but we do not make any assumptions regarding how the design ultimately is implemented.

The framework is influenced by an approach in Chase et al. (1998) that explicitly advocates the use of computer simulation for the modeling and testing of proposed process designs. However, there are also similarities with the frameworks suggested by Lowenthal, Roberts, and Cross et al. discussed in Section 2.3.5, as well as with the Six Sigma framework covered in Section 2.2.4. Our framework consists of the following eight steps, also depicted in Figure 3.1:

1. Case for action and vision statements.
2. Process identification and selection.
3. Obtaining management commitment.
4. Evaluation of design enablers.
5. Acquiring process understanding.
6. Creative process design.
7. Process modeling and simulation.
8. Implementation of the new process design.

The first seven steps correspond directly to our definition of a design project. The eighth step refers to the high-level implementation concerns mentioned previously and will be discussed only briefly. The shaded steps 4 through 7 in Figure 3.1 refer to the core design activities, carried out by the design team. They will be analyzed further using the modeling approaches and tools explored in Chapters 4 through 11.

The first issue in a business process design project is the formulation of a case for action and vision statements. This step communicates a clear message regarding the need for change and a vision of where to go. This is followed by the identification and selection of the process to be designed or redesigned. This step stresses the fact that not all processes can (or should) be redesigned at once, and the selection should be based on a cost/benefit analysis. This step also includes appointing a design team appropriate for the selected process. The third step, obtaining management commitment, is crucial not just for the design project itself but even more so when considering the likelihood of successful implementation. The importance of top-management involvement increases with the scope of the design and implementation.

The fourth step initiates the actual process design activities by encouraging the design team to evaluate possible enablers of a new process design. The most important design enabler in most cases is new technology. Following an understanding of relevant design enablers, the design team needs to clarify the process to be designed. Important means for acquiring this understanding based on existing processes include process charts and flowcharts, described in Chapter 4. However, it also involves an understanding of customer requirements and the overall purpose of the process and its deliverables.

Step 6 refers to the creative activity of coming up with a new conceptual design for the process. This is where team members use their imagination and general design principles to create a process capable of achieving the level of performance demanded by the marketplace. Business process benchmarking is often used to obtain ideas and stimulate creativity, as well as for gaining process understanding. The seventh step in the framework emphasizes the use of modeling and simulation as a means for testing and predicting the performance of the proposed design. Note the feedback loop from step 7 to step 6 (see Figure 3.1), because process modeling and simulation should be used interactively by the design team to test ideas and to stimulate creativity. The advantage with simulation compared to pilot tests performed on the real system is that it is a cheaper and faster alternative. The drawback is that issues related to human behavior that affect the implementation of the design might go undetected. Consequently, for larger processes a pilot test is still recommended as a first step toward full-blown implementation.

When the team is satisfied with the predicted performance of the proposed process, the implementation phase is initiated, possibly with a pilot test. The feedback loop from step 8 to step 6 indicates that the design might have to be modified due to unexpected implementation issues detected in a pilot test or as an integral part of an evolutionary change tactic.

The remainder of this chapter is devoted to describing the methodological steps in more detail, completing our suggested framework for business process design projects.

3.1 Step 1: Case for Action and Vision Statements

It has been documented that the companies that are the most successful in selling change to their employees are those that develop the clearest message about the need for change. Hammer and Champy (1993), among others, emphasize that this communication should include two key messages:

1. *A case for action statement:* This shows where the company is as an organization and why it can't stay there.
2. *A vision statement:* This is what the organization needs to become and the objectives that need to be fulfilled in order to get there.

Clearly, the focus and importance of the case for action and the vision statements depend on the scope of the business process design project in question. If the project has a large scope and focuses on processes that are core to the organization, the action and vision statements involve the strategic position of the entire company as indicated in the aforementioned steps 1 and 2. When the design project has a more modest scope, the need for action and vision statements is still important for determining the direction of the design project, but they typically refer to a business unit or department rather than the entire company.

The *case for action* should be brief. Hammer and Champy (1993) illustrate the formulation of an effective case for action with the one in Figure 3.2, which shows the documents that senior management of a pharmaceutical company prepared to convince employees that the research and development process was in dire need of change. This case for action contains five major elements that make it effective: (1) business context, (2) business problem, (3) marketplace demands, (4) diagnostics, and (5) cost of inaction.

The *business context* means describing what is currently happening, what is changing, and what is important in the environment in which the company operates. The leading competitors, according to the case for action in Figure 3.2, are operating with much shorter development cycles. The *business problem* is the source of the company's concerns. The company admits that it is taking too long to develop and register new drugs. The *marketplace demands* are the conditions that have established performance standards that the company cannot meet. The *diagnostics* section establishes why the company is unable to meet the marketplace demands. In this case, the company realizes that having globally integrated R&D organizations means a competitive advantage. Finally, the cost of inaction spells out the consequences of not changing. The pharmaceutical company estimates the cost of every week of delay in the development and registration process.

The *vision statement* should state the objectives for the new process in qualitative and quantitative terms. These objectives can include goals for cost reduction, shorter

---

FIGURE 3.2 Case for Action (pharmaceutical company)

We are disappointed by the length of time we require to develop and register drugs in the United States and in major international markets.

Our leading competitors achieve significantly shorter development cycles because they have established larger-scale, highly flexible, globally integrated R&D organizations that operate with a uniform set of work practices and information systems.

The competitive trend goes against our family of smaller, independent R&D organizations, which are housed in several decentralized operating companies around the world.

We have strong competitive and economic incentives to move as quickly as possible toward a globally integrated model of operation. Each week we save in the development and registration process extends the commercial life of our patent protection and represents, at mininmum, an additional $1 million in annual pretax profit—for each drug in our portfolio.

time-to-market, improved quality and customer satisfaction levels, and specific values for financial indicators. With these objectives in place, a meaningful reference is established against which to measure progress. It also defines what the new process design should be able to achieve and thereby provides guidance to the design team regarding where to aim. Moreover, having a clear set of goals in place helps spur ongoing action during implementation. Remember that this is one of the cornerstones in the Six Sigma motivation for focusing on one unifying measure and the goal of 3.4 defects per million opportunities.

Vision statements do not need to be long, but they should have solid content and not be too simplistic. For example, the statement "We want to be number one in our industry" provides no clue as to what the company needs to do in order to achieve this vision. Compare this statement with the one expressed by Federal Express in its early years: "We will deliver the package by 10:30 the next morning." This statement is about operations (we will get the package delivered); it has measurable objectives (we will deliver it by 10:30 A.M.); and it changed the basis for competition in an entire industry (from long, unpredictable delivery times to guaranteed overnight delivery). Figure 3.3 shows a longer vision statement, corresponding to the case for action of the pharmaceutical company in Figure 3.2.

The Federal Express vision statement and the one in Figure 3.3 are effective, because they contain three key elements: (1) They focus on operations, (2) they include measurable objectives and metrics, and (3) they define a desired situation that will provide a competitive advantage for the organization when it is reached.

3.2 Step 2: Process Identification and Selection

Process selection is critical to the success of a design project and the subsequent implementation of the designed process. In Sections 2.2.4 and 2.3.4, we addressed the question of how to prioritize improvement projects in Six Sigma and reengineering programs, respectively. Initially, all business processes of an organization should be considered candidates for redesign. Of particular interest are those processes that are core to the organization, because changing these offers the highest potential to impact the organization's overall performance. On the other hand,

---

FIGURE 3.3 Vision Statement (pharmaceutical company)

We are a worldwide leader in drug development.

1. We have shortened drug development and registration by an average of 6 months.
2. We are acknowledged leaders in the quality of registration submissions.
3. We have maximized the profit potential of our development portfolio.

We have created, across our operating companies, a worldwide R&D organization with management structures and systems that let us mobilize our collective development resources responsibly and flexibly.

1. We have established uniform and more disciplined drug development, planning, decision-making, and operational processes across all sites.
2. We employ innovative technology-based tools to support our work and management practices at all levels and between all R&D sites.
3. We have developed and implemented common information technology architecture worldwide.

they also represent the largest commitment financially and the greatest challenge to change successfully (i.e., successful design *and* implementation). As the reengineering movement has proven, the risk of failure is high but so are the rewards of success.

Regardless of the scope, prioritizing is an important activity because restrictions in budget and resources prevent engaging in too many design projects simultaneously. The criteria of *dysfunction*, *importance*, and *feasibility* can be used to screen the candidate processes and determine which process to redesign first. These criteria were discussed in Section 2.3.4 and can be summarized by the following questions.

- Which process is currently in most trouble?
- Which process is most critical to accomplishing the firm's business strategy and has the greatest impact on the company's customers?
- Which process is most likely to be designed and implemented successfully?

Other relevant questions that can help management narrow down the choices include the following.

- What is the project scope, and what are the costs involved in the design project and in the subsequent implementation?
- Can a strong team be formed to redesign and possibly also implement the chosen process effectively?
- Is it likely that management will have a strong commitment to change the process?
- Does the process need a new design, or could a continuous incremental improvement approach deliver the desired results?
- Is the process obsolete or the technology used outdated?

When selecting the appropriate design project, implementation must be considered. The cost associated with the change tactic must be recognized and compared with the limits of the available budget. As discussed in Section 2.4, a revolutionary implementation tactic is usually costly but much faster than an evolutionary strategy. It is pointless to design a new process that can never be implemented due to resource limitations. Another important aspect to consider is the likelihood of configuring a design team with the right attributes to handle the task of redesigning the chosen process, and in some cases to play a major part in its implementation. Another consideration is how likely it is that management commitment will be maintained throughout the design and implementation effort for a certain process.

When selecting processes to be redesigned, it is helpful to recognize that not all processes that perform below expectations do so because of a bad design. As discussed in Section 2.2 on Six Sigma, if the improvement goals can be reached by eliminating the sources of special cause variation (i.e., by applying a continuous improvement methodology), the process under consideration might not be the best candidate for redesign. In general, this means that the process is currently operating below its potential, as defined by its design, and therefore continuous improvement techniques can be effective in closing the gap between actual performance and the theoretical capability (see also Figure 2.12 and the related discussion in Sections 2.2 and 2.3). Other important issues to consider before selecting a certain process for a design project are whether the process is obsolete or the technology it uses is outdated. If replacing the technology is sufficient to achieve the desired performance results, then the process does not need to be redesigned at this time.

After a process is selected, a design team is configured and assigned to the task of conceiving a new process design. The team usually is comprised of a mix of insiders and outsiders with respect to the process in question. The inside individuals can provide profound insight into current operations. The outsiders have no stake in the current way of doing things, and they bring a fresh perspective and possibly some unique new expertise to the table.

3.3 Step 3: Obtaining Management Commitment

The organization's top management must set the stage for the design project itself and for the subsequent implementation process. Evidence shows that if top management does not buy into the proposed change, the improvement effort is bound for failure. This is reflected by the fact that top-management support is emphasized in all significant improvement programs including Six Sigma and business process reengineering. In fact, the more profound and strategic the change is, the more crucial top-management involvement becomes. If the scope and importance of the process to be designed and implemented are more modest and primarily tactical in nature, involving the top management of the entire corporation might be less crucial. It might suffice to engage only the top executives of the business unit or functional units directly involved in the process.

Securing management commitment, though important, is not simple. Some argue that commitment cannot be achieved without education; that is, management will not commit to something it does not fully understand. True commitment can occur only after management has gained enough understanding of the design and implementation processes and has recognized the need for change. See, for example, Phase I of Lowenthal's model discussed in Section 2.3.5.

Recall that many failures associated with reengineering core business processes have been attributed to the change-resistant attitude of the organization's middle managers and the lack of top-management commitment. These two issues are closely related because people, including middle managers, are more likely to be fearful of change when direction is lacking. If top management commits and establishes a sense of where the whole organization is heading, people can get excited about these changes and the meaning of their work within the new process design. Furthermore, as discussed in Section 2.4, revolutionary change tactics put a tremendous strain on the organization by forcing it through a rapid change. Consequently, clear direction and commitment become particularly important when utilizing rapid implementation approaches. A more evolutionary change tactic with its slower progression has in general fewer problems with change-resistant attitudes.

3.4 Step 4: Evaluation of Design Enablers

New technology in general and information technology in particular are considered essential enablers for new business process designs. However, inappropriate use of technology can block attempts to do things in new ways by reinforcing old ways of thinking and old behavioral patterns. Other enablers could be changes in legislature or changes in the market structure on the customer side, the supply side, or among the competition. However, because it is the most prominent process design enabler, we will focus our attention on new technology.

A design team should follow two important principles when evaluating the potential of new technology for enabling new process designs.

1. Do not equate technology with automation. It will prevent creative process design.
2. Do not look for problems first and then seek technology solutions to fix them.

In other words, embedding an existing business process in a new information system does not qualify as a new process design. Consider, for example, what automation might have accomplished at the insurance company in Section 1.2.2. The company could have tried to implement an electronic transfer of claims from the local independent agent to the claims-processing center and within the processing center. Such a system would have simplified the old process by eliminating the data entry step at the processing center and possibly replacing office mail with electronic mail. The automation, however, would have done nothing to eliminate the requests for additional information from the processing center to the customer, which not only adds time to the process but also tends to annoy the customer.

Breakthrough improvements are usually not possible with automation alone. In these situations, the technology is used to accelerate the existing process but not to do the necessary work in new ways. Doing things the wrong way faster does not lead to radical improvements.

How can a redesigning team avoid getting caught in the automation trap? A key rule is that the team should not make the mistake of evaluating technology using an existing process as the only point of reference. Consider the following two questions that a team might ask (Hammer and Champy, 1993).

- How can new technology be used to enhance, streamline, or improve what we are currently doing?
- How can new technology allow us to do new things that we are currently not doing?

Note that the first question does involve an element of automation, but the second question has a clear focus on innovation. That is, the second question focuses on exploiting state-of-the-art technology to achieve entirely new goals. The team must keep in mind that the true potential of new technology lies in breaking compromises that were made to accommodate limitations in the old technology. Table 3.1 summarizes the ability of some disruptive technologies to break old rules and compromises (Hammer and Champy, 1993).

Successful application of modern technology within the context of process design requires *inductive* rather than *deductive* thinking. In general terms, inductive reasoning means working with observed data or facts to identify structures or patterns, and using these observations to reach a general conclusion. Deductive reasoning, on the other hand, starts with general conclusions in terms of hypotheses, theories, or accepted beliefs and uses these to explain or solve a specific problem through logical arguments.

Many executives and senior managers tend to feel more comfortable with deductive thinking. This means they are good at defining a particular problem associated with a managerial situation. They then seek alternative solutions to the problem based on accepted beliefs and theories, and they evaluate the impact of adopting a particular solution. A major challenge for the design team is to adopt an inductive approach and develop the ability to evaluate current and emerging technologies without getting trapped in conventional beliefs about how things should be done. They are then in a position to identify creative applications that enable new breakthrough process designs. In essence, inductive thinking requires the ability to recognize that modern

TABLE 3.1 Technology as a Mechanism to Break Rules

Old Rule	Disruptive Technology	New Rule
Information can appear in only one place at a time.	Shared databases	Information can appear simultaneously in as many places as needed.
Only experts can perform complex work.	Expert systems	A generalist might be able to do the work of an expert.
Businesses must choose between centralization and decentralization.	Telecommunication networks (including intranets)	Businesses can simultaneously reap the benefits of centralization and decentralization.
Managers make all decisions.	Decision support tools (database access and modeling tools)	Decision making is part of everyone's job.
Field personnel need offices where they can receive, store, retrieve, and transmit information.	Wireless data communication and portable computers	Field personnel can send and receive information wherever they are.
The best contact with a potential buyer is personal contact.	Interactive videodisk and Web pages	The best contact with a potential buyer is effective contact.
People must find where things are.	Automatic identification and tracking technology	Things tell you where they are.
Plans get revised periodically.	High-performance computers	Plans get revised instantaneously.

technology could be an effective solution to a problem that the company is not yet aware it has.

To make our discussion on new technology as an enabler for change more concrete, the following two sections will look at how (information) technology has enabled new process designs in the banking and grocery store industries.

3.4.1 EXAMPLE: THE INTERNET-ENABLING CHANGE AT CHASE MANHATTAN BANK

The tremendous advances in information technology (IT) in recent years, in particular those related to the Internet, have triggered numerous initiatives in e-commerce–related areas. Some businesses have expanded their electronic linkages with their partners and suppliers, and others have added electronic services to their customers. This section will look at how e-commerce has enabled change at Chase Manhattan Bank[1].

Traditionally, the financial engineers at Chase compared the efficiency of delivering services using alternative channels and their impact on the bottom line. With the availability of new information technology, it was time for them to understand the effectiveness of e-business compared to other existing channels such as physical branches and ATMs. From a unit cost perspective, e-commerce allows Chase to deliver services more economically and in a more timely fashion.

---

[1]"Chase-ing e-business," *IIE Transactions* 32:6 (June 2000): 25.

The move to electronic commerce cannot be achieved without redesigning processes that were historically paper based. The business process unit at Chase managed a project with the operations and legal departments to redesign the processing of money judgment documents, such as restraining notices and account levies. This was a purely paper-based process. So, Chase worked with other banks, government agencies, and creditor rights attorneys to transform the paper-based process into an e-process. The change involved modifying the laws that govern levies and subpoenas to allow electronic service of these legal documents. Other important projects at Chase include e-business changes in retail banking and e-commerce work in the global and institutional banking areas. These projects will allow large corporate customers to have Web access to their account data and to perform transactions online.

For Chase and other companies, electronic business offers tremendous opportunities to break compromises and improve efficiency and effectiveness in the service offering. However, in order to realize this potential, many of their business processes need to be completely redesigned to support the new business environment. When business managers decide they want to initiate a Web presence, it usually means a dramatic change in several business processes. Redesign projects in these companies focus on establishing high-level process strategies that increase efficiency, productivity, and coordination among groups as opposed to concentrating on small pieces of key business processes.

3.4.2 EXAMPLE: NEW TECHNOLOGY AS A CHANGE ENABLER IN THE GROCERY INDUSTRY

After a brief look at how new technology has impacted the banking industry, we now turn our attention to the traditional and well-known retail and grocery store industry. Steven L. Cohen (2000) predicts that this industry will undergo significant change in the next 25 years. He argues that the supermarket of the future will rely heavily on technology as well as process engineering tools and techniques to compete. The following is a description of the changes that Cohen predicts in the supermarket industry and that are enabled by new technology.

The typical supermarket today has scanners at the front checkout area that read the price and description of items from their universal product code. About 85 percent of all items can be scanned from either manufacturer or in-store UPC labels applied to packaging. On-hand shelf inventory is set, ordered, and maintained by personnel with the experience and knowledge to know how fast a particular item sells in that store location. Items are replenished periodically.

Orders are placed by handwritten communication, telephone, fax, and by using a handheld ordering machine that records the warehouse code number. This information is transmitted to each supplier as appropriate. The orders are printed out at the warehouse, and each item is picked from the warehouse's inventory. Typically, as each case of product is pulled from the storage area at the warehouse, it is brought to a central staging area. The cases are built as a block onto a pallet, and the pallet is wrapped in plastic film for stability and marked for delivery to a particular store location.

After the order is filled, the pallets are loaded onto trucks and shipped to the store. The pallets are off-loaded at the store into the receiving area; broken down; and separated onto large, flat-wheeled carts by the grocery store workers according to the aisle or area of the store to be restocked. These wheeled carts are brought onto the sales floor. The grocery store worker checks each case against the shelf and restocks the item. If a case is damaged or contains the wrong products, these items are set aside. The grocery store manager then calls in a report to the warehouse's customer service department at the next opportunity. The overstock of items is repacked, condensed onto as few pallets as possible, and placed in store inventory to be put on the sales floor at a later time.

The billing information is printed on paper and is sent with the order to the store. In most cases, but not always, the UPC information is on the bill of sale from the suppliers. The personnel working in scanning check each bill line by line and item by item to compare it to existing information in the store's computer system. If an adjustment to the item description, a change in UPC code, or a change in price information occurs, the scanning operator makes the change in the computer, prints a temporary tag, and later walks the store to find these changed items and put up the new shelf tag.

Many of the problems and challenges with the processes described are related to lack of communication and the application of new methods and technologies. Technology can play an important role in driving the change in how manufacturers, warehouses, and retailers communicate with each other. Consider, for example, the following.

- Communication networks can be established to allow lower inventory levels and just-in-time delivery from the manufacturer to the retailer.
- On-hand shelf inventory in the retail store can be linked to the store's main computer.
- Automatic computer reordering can be established to maintain stock on hand.
- Increases in demand due to seasonal or market changes can be flagged for store management.
- Manufacturers can develop more efficient packaging methods, allowing for more flexible units sizes, which would minimize the number of backorders at the warehouse and retail levels.
- Aisles in the store can be divided into aisle, aisle side, and section (e.g., Aisle 1, Side A, Section 14). This would facilitate restocking of products and mapping of the store and its products, and allow the manufacturer, warehouse, and retailer to apply simulation techniques to plan store and product layouts.
- Orders at the warehouse can be picked and palletized according to aisles and sometimes aisle side.
- When the truck arrives from the warehouse to the store, the pallets can be brought directly onto the sales floor for restocking without time-consuming breakdown of pallets and sorting of stock onto carts for the appropriate aisle.

To implement process changes enabled by the appropriate application of new technology, employees would have to be better trained and computer literate. Some of the changes in employees' roles and responsibilities might include the following.

- Employees who are restocking the shelves in the store would carry small, handheld computer/printers. To find out what section of the aisle a product is in, the employee would scan the UPC tag on a case of product, which would eliminate time wasted searching for shelf location.
- In case an item is damaged or if it is simply the wrong product, employees would be able to enter that information into the handheld computer for credit or return to the warehouse.
- Updated pricing information would be forwarded to the store mainframe via the billing department so that all appropriate price changes and percentage calculations could be completed before the order arrives at the store.
- The people putting up the order would check the shelf tag and compare the item they are stocking to the posted retail information. If necessary, they would print a new tag to update the price change, thus eliminating discrepancies between shelf and register pricing.

On the customer side, information technology also could produce some changes, for example, in shopping habits. Paper coupons could be a thing of the past, because retailers and manufacturers could offer virtual coupons as customers develop electronic shopping lists. Information tracking and customer shopping cards could supply manufacturers and store owners with useful data. The store would be able to tailor its on-shelf inventory and perform better shelf management by tracking consumers' purchasing habits, and thus increase the rate of inventory turnover.

To summarize, information and increased computer capability would enable manufacturers, warehouses, retailers, and customers to communicate more effectively. As a result, members of the supply chain would be able to voice their desires and needs more effectively.

3.5 Step 5: Acquiring Process Understanding

Understanding the process to be designed is a key element of any design effort. In terms of process understanding, only a subtle difference exists between redesigning an existing process in an organization and creating a design for a currently nonexisting process. In both cases, we must understand what the new process is supposed to do, and particularly what customers desire from it. In the former case, it is also important to understand what the existing process is doing and why it is currently unsatisfactory. However, even if the process to be designed is the only one of its kind within the organization, similar processes usually can be found elsewhere. Business process benchmarking, further discussed in Section 3.6.1, is a tool that is often used to gain process understanding and inspire creative new designs by studying related processes with recognized excellent performance. In the following section, we will look first at some important issues related to gaining understanding about an existing process. Then we will consider aspects of process understanding related to customers and their requirements.

3.5.1 UNDERSTANDING THE EXISTING PROCESS

To acquire the necessary understanding of an existing process, whether it is internal to the organization or an external benchmark, the design team needs to seek the answers to the following general questions.

- What does the existing process do?
- How well (or poorly) does the existing process perform?
- What are the critical issues that govern the process performance?

These questions can be answered at various levels of detail. Hammer and Champy (1993) argue that the goal of a design team must be to understand the process and not to analyze it. The difference is that understanding can be achieved at a high level, but analysis implies documenting every detail of the existing process. In other words, the team can gain enough understanding of the process to have the intuition and insight to redesign it without analyzing the process in "agonizing detail."

Analyzing to an extreme generally is considered a mistake. It is easy to fall into this trap, because the analysis activity tends to give a false impression of progress. However, process analysis should not be ignored or considered a negative activity either, because in many situations it helps persuade others that a new design is necessary. Conventional process analysis is also a useful tool in the implementation or post-implementation steps. At this stage, a continuous improvement approach is used to close the gap between the theoretical capabilities of the new process and its actual performance. Further investigation of several tools associated with conventional process analysis can be found in Chapters 4 and 5.

The rationale for emphasizing understanding over analyzing is fairly straightforward: The team must avoid what is referred to as "analysis paralysis." This phrase is used to describe the phenomenon of becoming so familiar with a process that it becomes virtually impossible to think of new ways in which to produce the same output. Analysis is then considered an inhibitor of creativity, which is one of the main assets that the design team must possess in order to be successful. Note that understanding a process is not less difficult than analyzing it; on the contrary, in many ways understanding can be considered harder. It is also hard to know when the team has gained enough understanding to be able to move to the creative design and modeling phase without neglecting important pieces of information regarding the process in question. This issue has no simple answers.

We conclude this section with a discussion regarding concrete issues that are important to consider when gaining understanding of an existing process. The essential issues and activities we consider are the configuration of the design team, building a high-level process map or flowchart, testing the original scope and scale, and identifying the process owner (Lester, 1994).

The Configuration of the Design Team.   The design team performs most of the work in the process-understanding and new-process-design phases. As mentioned in Section 3.2, the team is made up of business insiders (those performing the current processes, including managers and workers) and outsiders (those not directly involved in the current process, such as consultants, human resource experts, and customers). A ratio that works well is three insiders for each outsider.

Building a High-Level Process Map.   The map should focus on the customer and be business oriented; that is, instead of consisting of names of organizations (such as marketing and distribution), the map should depict the interactions between connected business processes and how they support the customer's processes. The goal of this map is as follows.

1. To build a common understanding among the team and other stakeholders.
2. To encourage a common vocabulary that cuts across functional boundaries.
3. To highlight the subprocesses that are critical to achieving customer demands.
4. To test the boundaries established by the initial scope and scale.
5. To identify key interface points.
6. To pinpoint redundancies and other forms of wasted effort.

The map should have about 6 and certainly no more than 15 subprocesses from start to finish. An example of a high-level process map for a telecommunications company is depicted in Figure 3.4. Note that the map is neither a detailed flowchart[2] nor an organizational chart. It shows the interactions between subprocesses and not the flow of work or data. (Later, in Chapter 4, several charts will be introduced including service systems maps, which contain a higher level of detail because they focus on activities and flows.)

Testing the Original Scope and Scale.   The design team should reassess the initial scope and scale based on the new information available through self-examination, benchmarking, and customer visits. This activity is iterative in the sense that the team might have to revisit the scope and scale issue more than once.

---

[2]A flowchart is a graphical description of the process flow. This tool is thoroughly explained in Chapter 4.

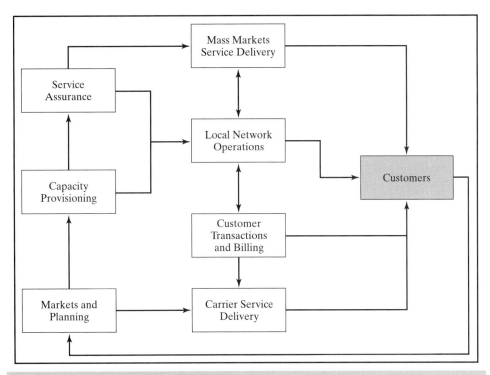

FIGURE 3.4 High-Level Process Map for a Telecommunications Company

Identifying the Process Owner.   The process owner, as discussed in Section 2.1, is the person who will take responsibility for the new business process and will be held accountable for the results of the process. The more the process owner is involved in the design of the new process, the smoother the transition to the subsequent implementation phase will be. Therefore, identifying this individual and involving him or her in the process design project will allow for valuable early interaction and input throughout the design phase.

3.5.2 UNDERSTANDING THE CUSTOMER

A crucial element in understanding a process is to understand its customers and their current and future needs. Customers demand basically two things from any provider of products and services: (1) They want products and services that meet their needs and requirements, and (2) they want to obtain those products and services efficiently and effectively. Understanding these requirements is fundamental to arriving at a good process design. This is why most experts agree that the best place for a team to begin to understand a process is at the customer end (see, for example, the CPS model discussed in Section 2.1.1). To gain an understanding of the customers' needs, the following questions would be useful for the design team to consider (Hammer and Champy, 1993).

- What are the customers' real requirements?
- What do they say they want and what do they really need if the two are different?
- What problems do they have?
- What processes do they perform with the output?

Because the ultimate goal of designing a new process is to create one that satisfies customer demands, it is critical for the design team to truly understand these needs and desires. Also note that to gain this understanding, it is not sufficient to simply ask customers what they need, because in most cases the answer is based on what they *think* they need. There is an important difference between stated and real (or hidden) needs. For example, a customer might state the need for a clothes dryer, but the real need is to remove moisture from clothes. Identifying the real or hidden need opens the door for new, creative ways to satisfy this need other than via the conventional dryer. Another example would be customers of a residential construction contractor who state that they need an efficient heating system. Their real need is a warm home and low heating costs. This real need is best fulfilled if the contractor pays attention to the insulation of the house and uses energy-conserving, three-pane windows instead of the standard single-pane windows. Focusing on the stated need would mean installing the best heating system available at great cost. However, in a poorly insulated house with single-pane windows, it would most likely not make much of a difference. As a result, although the stated need was addressed, the customers will be unhappy because their real need was not satisfied by the building process.

3.6 Step 6: Creative Process Design

Process design is just as much a creative art as it is a science, and maybe even more so. Consequently, there exists no cookbook solution or uniform stepwise method for arriving at a good process design. Process designers need to use creative thinking and put aside current rules, procedures, and values in order to find new ways of doing the necessary work. Existing processes tend to be complicated and inefficient because they have evolved over time. As discussed in Section 1.4, most processes were not designed; they just emerged as new parts of the process were added to satisfy some immediate need. Because the process is expanded incrementally, the intermediate decisions of how to incorporate new elements into the process affect the final design and its efficiency.

Suboptimal solutions and inefficient systems are created when local incremental methods are used to find answers for decision or design problems. At each intermediate stage, the arrangement of information might be right, but this does not ensure that the final arrangement will be entirely correct (or optimal). Consider an experiment designed by Dr. Edward de Bono, founder of the Cognitive Research Trust in Cambridge, England. When two pieces of plastic are given to someone with instructions to arrange them in a shape that can be described easily, the pieces are always arranged into a rectangle as shown in Figure 3.5.

If these pieces represent two elements of a process, then the person was given the task of designing the simplest process that incorporates the given elements. We assume that the simplest process is the one that can be described most easily. The person has used the available information to find a design that maximizes simplicity. Then a square piece is added, as shown in Figure 3.6. The task is still to arrange the pieces in a shape that is easy to describe, so the result is usually another rectangle, as shown in Figure 3.6.

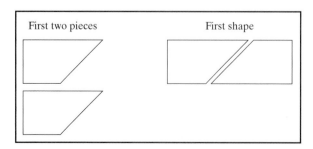

FIGURE 3.5 Arrangement of the First Two Pieces

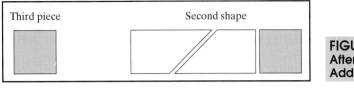

FIGURE 3.6 Arrangement After the Third Piece Is Added

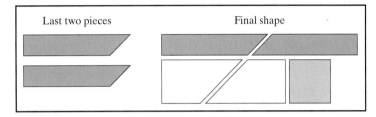

FIGURE 3.7 Arrangement After the Last Two Pieces Are Added

Then two additional pieces are added as shown in Figure 3.7. Few people are able to incorporate these two final pieces effectively; that is, in a way such that the final shape is easy to describe. For example, the configuration in Figure 3.7 might be obtained.

The difficulty stems from the tendency to add the new pieces without redesigning the existing structure. This makes the construction of the second rectangle almost inevitable after the first one has been made. Yet, considering the pieces independently of the sequence in which they appeared, the square pattern is just as good an arrangement for the second step. From the square pattern, the final arrangement, shown in Figure 3.8, is obvious, but if one starts at the rectangle, it is nearly impossible to conceive.

This example illustrates how a particular arrangement of information might make the best possible sense at the time and in the sequence it is presented, and yet it can represent a block to further development. Extending the analogy, when a design team encounters an inefficient and ineffective design based on a "rectangle," the team must break away from this configuration to introduce the "square" as an entirely different way to think about the process.

3.6.1 BENCHMARKING

Benchmarking essentially refers to the efforts of comparing the organization's activities and performance in certain areas with what others in the same industry or in other disciplines are doing. Every benchmarking relationship involves two parties: the target firm, or the benchmark that is being observed, and the initiator firm

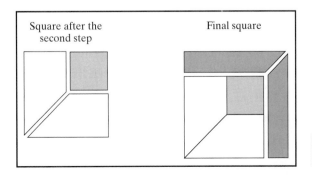

FIGURE 3.8 A More Effective Design

that requests contact and observes. It is important to recognize that these roles are usually not static over time. The target firm often enters into a reciprocal agreement to study some aspects of the initiator firm's operations. Without offering something in return, it is often difficult for the initiator firm to gain access to all the desired information.

Embarking on a benchmarking effort has two basic purposes.

1. To assess the firm's or the process's current performance relative to the competition and thereby identify performance gaps and set performance goals.
2. To stimulate creativity and inspire ideas for how to improve on current process performance.

Based on which objective is the most important and on what is being benchmarked, it is possible to identify a number of different types of benchmarking and an infinite number of ways to execute the benchmarking activities. However, the second objective of learning how to improve process performance typically requires a more involved approach with close interaction between the initiator firm and the target firm, often including on-site visits. This type of benchmarking often is referred to as business process benchmarking and is what will be examined in this section. The type of benchmarking that focuses on identifying performance gaps and goals in certain metrics, whether measures of productivity, time, quality, or finance, will be explored further in Chapter 11. In that chapter, we show how data envelopment analysis (DEA) can be a useful tool to analyze this type of benchmarking data and define relevant performance goals.

In the context of a process design project, both objectives are relevant. The design team must be able to determine relevant performance goals to know what to aim for in creating the new design. Even more importantly, business process benchmarking can be used to stimulate the design team's creativity and to generate ideas for how to do things in a new way. In order for this to happen, it is important that the target firms are chosen carefully. The idea is to learn and be inspired by the best. This could refer to the best in an industry (best-in-class benchmarks) or the best across all industries (often called best-of-the-best or best-in-the world benchmarks). Generally, the further away a design team goes from its own industry, the greater the potential is of getting break-through design ideas. However, at the same time, it is more challenging to identify and translate similarities between processes. A famous example of successful out-of-industry or best-of-the-best benchmarking is Xerox, which in order to improve their warehousing operations turned to the mail order company L.L. Bean.

After identifying an appropriate target firm, a good starting point for a business process benchmarking effort is the 5w2h framework developed by Robinson (1991). This framework specifies seven questions that should be answered through the business process benchmarking effort. Five of these questions begin with the letter *w* (*who, what, when, where,* and *why*), and the remaining two start with the letter *h* (*how* and *how much*). See Table 3.2. If the initiator's design team can answer these questions after the benchmarking effort is completed, it has acquired a good understanding of the process under study. In considering the 5w2h questions, it is important to recognize that they should be viewed in the context of a process.

The 5w2h framework also can be used to acquire an in-depth understanding of an existing process that is about to be redesigned. Therefore, it complements the discussion in Section 3.5.1 about how to gain understanding of an existing process.

Even though the 5w2h framework seems simple enough, finding answers to these questions for a complex cross-functional process is not easy. Effectively managing a large-scale business process benchmarking effort is a difficult matter associated with high costs. In the context of our process design project, the benefits must be weighed

TABLE 3.2 The 5w2h Framework

Classification	5w2h Questions	Description
People	Who?	Who is performing the activity? Why is this person doing it? Could/Should someone else perform the activity?
Subject matter	What?	What is being done in this activity? Can the activity in question be eliminated?
Sequence	When?	When is the best time to perform this activity? Does it have to be done at a certain time?
Location	Where?	Where is this activity carried out? Does it have to be done at this location?
Purpose	Why?	Why is this activity needed? Clarify its purpose.
Method	How?	How is the activity carried out? Is this the best way or are alternatives possible?
Cost	How much?	How much does it currently cost? What would be the tentative cost after improvement?

Source: Adapted from Robinson, 1991.

against these costs. As indicated before, there exists no cookbook approach to process design. Process benchmarking is sometimes useful to generate ideas for new designs, but in other cases it can cost more than it is worth. This is why the scope of the benchmarking effort must be controlled carefully.

A more in-depth discussion of issues related to management of benchmarking projects falls beyond the scope of this book but can be found in Camp (1995).

3.6.2 DESIGN PRINCIPLES

The creative nature of the design phase makes it impossible to specify any definite rules for how to proceed and how to succeed. However, it is possible to point to a number of general design principles that can help guide the design team and inspire its creativity. See, for example, Hammer (1990), Chase et al. (1998), and Hyer and Wemmerlöv (2002). In broad terms, these design principles relate to who does the work and where, when, and why it is done. However, they also involve the information and level of integration necessary to coordinate the process. In this section, we will take a closer look at 10 general design principles from a qualitative perspective. We will refer to them as people-oriented and conceptual because many of them are related directly to horizontal and vertical work integration contingent on the workforce's capabilities. Furthermore, their focus is to inspire the creativity of the design team in its efforts to come up with a new conceptual process design.

At the end of this section, we also will mention briefly seven somewhat more technical and flow-oriented workflow design principles. These principles have a long tradition in industrial engineering where they have been used successfully for improving the efficiency of manufacturing processes. Chapter 4 provides a detailed investigation of these principles together with modeling approaches and analytical tools. It is also worth noting that all the quantitative tools and modeling approaches explored in Chapters 5 through 11 have the purpose of facilitating analysis and evaluation of several aspects of a given process design. They represent ways to quantitatively investigate the effects of applying the design principles discussed in this section to specific real-world situations.

The people-oriented and conceptual design principles that we will discuss are summarized in Figure 3.9. In reviewing Figure 3.9 and for our discussion of these design

1. Organize work around outcomes, not individual tasks	6. Treat geographically dispersed resources as though they were centralized
2. Let those who use the process output perform the process	7. Link parallel activities instead of just integrating their output
3. Merge information processing and data-gathering activities	8. Design the process for the dominant flow, not the exceptions
4. Capture the information once—at the source	9. Look for ways to mistake-proof the process
5. Put the decision point where the work is performed and build control into the process	10. Examine process interactions to avoid suboptimization

FIGURE 3.9 People-Oriented and Conceptual Design Principles

principles, it is important to keep in mind that they are guiding principles and not absolute rules. Every design instance is unique and needs to be treated as such. Trying to apply these design principles without discretion is more likely a road to disaster than one to success in business process design.

1. Organize work around outcomes, not individual tasks. The idea behind this principle is to move away from highly specialized and fractionalized task assignments and more toward horizontally integrated activities. Process complexity is reduced and activity complexity is increased, as illustrated in Figure 1.3. The rationale for moving in this direction is that it leads to fewer activities in the process that need formal coordination. It also reduces the number of handoffs and eliminates the related control steps, all of which represent some of the major causes of process inefficiencies. It also increases the work content for individual workers, which encourages them to take responsibility for their work and to take pride in what they do. These are important people issues that attempt to empower the workforce and lead to high-quality output.

Applying the principle implies that several specialized tasks previously performed by different people should be combined into a single activity. This activity can then be performed by an individual "case worker" or by a "case team" consisting of a limited number of individuals with complementary skills. The choice between the two includes considerations regarding the scope of work, the capacity needs, how critical it is to avoid handoffs, the importance of a single point of contact for customers, the required ability to handle exceptions, cultural issues, training costs, and so on. It should be mentioned that an important enabler for horizontal integration is cross-functional training, which means that each individual is trained to perform several different tasks.

The principle has spawned the integration of the labor approach known as case management (Davenport and Nohria, 1994). The case manager's role represents a break with the conventional approach to the division of labor. Davenport and Nohria have observed four common components of a successful case manager's role. The case manager:

- Completes or manages a "closed-loop" work process to deliver an entire product or service to the customer.
- Is located where the customer and various other functions or matrix dimensions intersect.
- Has the authority to make decisions and address customer issues.
- Easily accesses information from around the organization and uses information technology in decision making.

Case management is an appropriate design for work that is performed along process lines rather than in business functions. Unlike the business functions, processes are designed around the completion of a significant product or service. Furthermore, case management is particularly useful in processes that deal with customers and therefore involve managing the entire cycle of activities from customer order to product or service delivery, billing, and payment. In many ways, case management parallels the governing ideas for process management discussed in Section 2.1, with the case manager playing the role of the process owner.

In Section 1.1.2, we described the process at IBM Credit Corporation, which was documented in an attempt to improve performance. The entire process consumed 6 days on average, and sometimes it took as long as 2 weeks, although the actual work could be completed in an average of 90 minutes. IBM tried several fixes with the goal of improving this process. For example, they installed a control desk that could answer questions from field salespersons. The control desk helped find the status of each request but also added more turnaround time.

After some brainstroming, IBM Credit realized that the problem did not lie in the tasks and the people performing them but in the structure of the process, which forced work to be handed from one office to another. The existing process was designed under the assumption that each request was unique and difficult to process, therefore requiring the intervention of four highly trained specialists. The reality was that most requests were simple and straightforward. So in the end, IBM Credit replaced its specialists with generalists supported by an easy-to-use computer system that provided access to the databases and tools that specialist would use. The generalists became case workers in charge of the transaction from the beginning to the end. They would get help from a small pool of specialists when requests were indeed unique and difficult to handle.

2.   Let those who use the process output perform the process. Another way of expressing this is that work should be carried out where it makes most sense to do it. By avoiding excessive delegation of responsibilities, the risk of coordination inefficiencies and "laissez faire" mentality decreases. If you are using the output you produced yourself, there is no one to blame or point a finger at if that output does not meet your expectations. This idea is closely related to the principle of horizontal integration of specialized tasks discussed previously. The objective is again to avoid handoffs and coordination inefficiencies.

A typical example of the application of this principle is allowing employees to make some of their own purchases without going through a purchasing department. The purchases can be limited to a given dollar amount in order to maintain a certain amount of control over expenses. Another example is the various sorts of so-called vendor managed inventory (VMI) initiatives whereby a company asks its suppliers to manage its incoming goods or parts inventory. Wal-Mart has successfully implemented this principle, using information technology to transfer point-of-sale data to suppliers, who use the data to monitor inventory levels and assume the responsibility of telling Wal-Mart when to reorder.

3. **Merge information processing and data-gathering activities.** This principle is based on having the people who collect the data also analyze it and turn it into useful information. This idea is closely related to the previous principle of having those who use the output of the process perform the process. The difference is the particular focus on information processing, which is often a major issue in administrative business processes. Having the same people collect the data and process it into information eliminates the need for an additional group to process and when necessary, reconcile data that they did not collect. This reduces the risk of introducing errors and presenting inaccurate information. An example is the traditional accounts payable department that receives and reconciles purchase orders and supplier invoices. Through electronic order and information processing, the need for invoices is eliminated. This increases the accuracy of the submitted information and renders much of the traditional reconciling work obsolete.

4. **Capture the information once—at the source.** Information should not be reentered several times into different computerized systems or have to move back and forth between electronic and paper format. To avoid errors and costly reentries, it should be collected and captured by the company's computerized information system only once—at the source (i.e., where it was created). This idea is closely connected to principle 3 of merging information processing into the activity that gathers the data. The objectives in both cases are to speed up the process, avoid mistakes, and assure high information quality at a lower cost. A typical example that violates this principle of capturing the data at the source is given by the original claims processing process of the insurance company in Section 1.2.2. Information gathered by the independent agent is later rekeyed at the claims-processing center. Furthermore, the information was typically incomplete, forcing additional contact with the customer.

5. **Put the decision point where the work is performed, and build control into the process.** Case management compresses processes horizontally in the same way that employee empowerment compresses the organization vertically. Vertical compression occurs when workers make decisions in instances where they used to go up the managerial hierarchy for an answer. This principle encourages decision making to become part of the process instead of keeping it separate. An effective way to achieve this is to let workers assume some of the responsibilities previously assigned to management. Under the mass-production division of labor paradigm, the assumption is that workers have neither the time nor the inclination to monitor and control the work they are doing, and furthermore that they lack the knowledge to make decisions about it. Today, this assumption can be discarded, due to a more educated and knowledgeable workforce and the advent of decision support systems. Controls are made part of the process, reinforcing a vertical integration that results in flatter, more responsive organizations.

6. **Treat geographically dispersed resources as though they were centralized.** Modern information technology makes it possible to break spatial compromises through virtual colocation of individuals and work teams. This means that although they are sitting at different locations, employees can have on-line access to the same information and multiple media to support instantaneous communication. As a result, geographically disbursed resources should not constrain the design team to consider only decentralized approaches. This does not imply that a centralized structure is always the best alternative, but it leaves that door open for the design team despite potential spatial restrictions. Concrete examples of enabling technologies include GroupWare software, which facilitates parallel processing of jobs performed by geographically dispersed

organizational units, intranets, and videoconferencing. The latter technology enables people at different locations to see the reactions and the body language of those with whom they communicate.

7.   Link parallel activities instead of just integrating their output. An important cause of costly rework and delays in processes is related to situations where outcomes of parallel sequences of activities are being integrated or assembled. If any discrepancies or errors are detected in either of the outputs to be combined, the job is delayed and requires at least partial rework. The problem is compounded if detection of the problem is delayed.

The heart of the problem is that most processes that perform activities in parallel let these activities operate independently. Therefore, operational errors are not found before the integration activity is performed, resulting in the need for an excessive amount of additional resources for rework. Parallel activities should be linked and coordinated frequently to minimize the risk of realizing that major rework must be done at the integration step. To illustrate, consider the simultaneous construction of a tunnel through both sides of a mountain. Without continuous linking of the two parallel approaches, the risk is high that they will not meet in the middle as intended. The result is a costly rework project or two parallel tunnels through the mountain at twice the cost.

8.   Design the process for the dominant flow, not for the exceptions. By focusing too much on the exceptions and special cases that could arise, the process design tends to be overly complicated. For example, some jobs might be so expensive or performed for such important customers that higher-level management believes it is necessary to inspect them. However, these exceptional cases do not imply that all jobs should be subject to management approval. An approval step should not be designed into the process unless it is needed for all jobs. An excellent example of a process suffering from too much focus on exceptional cases is the original process at IBM Credit Corporation discussed previously and in Section 1.1.2.

9.   Look for ways to mistake-proof the process. To mistake-proof or fail-safe the process means designing it so that it becomes virtually impossible for certain mistakes or errors to occur. Due to its Japanese origins, mistake-proofing is also referred to as *Poka-Yoke*, a well-known strategy for waste reduction and improvement in product and process design. Countless examples of this conceptually simple but somewhat elusive design principle can be cited: ATMs that start buzzing if you do not remove your card, self-flushing public toilets, templates that guide correct insertions of components, order-entry systems that will not accept incorrect part numbers, color-coded fields for data entry, on-line process documentation guiding work execution in real time, and personal digital organizers with sound reminders for important appointments.

A tenth principle, derived from the systems design theory (Van Gigch, 1978), can be added to the nine aforementioned principles.

10. Examine process interactions to avoid suboptimization. A process improvement developed in isolation for a distinct part of the overall process might seem effective in light of the particular subprocess in question. However, by neglecting interactions with other subprocesses and the effects on the overall process, an isolated improvement could easily result in a suboptimal design in the context of an enlarged horizon. Looking for improvements by analyzing only portions of the total process leads to what is known in general systems theory as *disjointed incrementalism*. To illustrate, consider the following example of suboptimization adapted from Hammer and Champy (1993).

A plane belonging to a major airline is grounded one afternoon for repairs at Springfield Airport. The nearest mechanic qualified to perform the repair works at Jamestown Airport. Joe, the maintenance manager at Jamestown, refuses to send the mechanic to Springfield that afternoon. The reason is that after completing the repairs, the mechanic would have to stay overnight at a hotel and the hotel bill would come out of Joe's budget. Therefore, the mechanic is not dispatched to the Springfield site until the following morning, enabling him to fix the plane and return home the same day. This means that Joe's budget is not burdened with the $100 hotel bill. Instead, a multi-million dollar aircraft sits idle, and the airline stands to lose hundreds of thousands of dollars in revenue. Joe is not foolish or careless; he is doing what he is supposed to do—namely, to control and minimize his expenses. Minimizing labor costs might be a worthwhile goal for the maintenance subsystem viewed in isolation, but it disregards the goals of the larger system—the airline, for which earning revenue is the overriding objective.

To conclude our discussion on the people-oriented and conceptual design principles, let us look at Figure 3.10, which summarizes the principles and some of the recurring themes and objectives that characterize them. Particularly, principles 1 through 4 have a common focus on horizontal integration of tasks into augmented activities, thereby eliminating handoffs, control points, and sources of errors. Horizontal integration also implies fewer activities to coordinate within the process at the price of increased task complexity within each activity. A key issue is then to have cross-trained personnel who can perform the tasks in an activity without formal coordination.

FIGURE 3.10 Summary of the Considered People-Oriented and Conceptual Design Principles

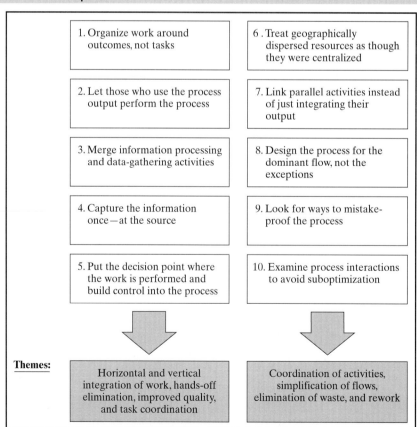

```
┌─────────────────────────────────────┐
│  ┌───────────────────────────────┐  │
│  │ Focus:  Efficient process flows,│  │
│  │        managing resource capacity,│  │
│  │        throughput, and cycle times│  │
│  └───────────────────────────────┘  │
│  ┌───────────────────────────────┐  │
│  │ ✓ Establish product orientation│  │
│  │   in the process               │  │
│  │                                │  │
│  │ ✓ Eliminate buffers            │  │
│  │                                │  │
│  │ ✓ Establish one-at-a-time      │  │
│  │   processing                   │  │
│  │                                │  │
│  │ ✓ Balance the flow to the      │  │
│  │   bottleneck                   │  │
│  │                                │  │
│  │ ✓ Minimize sequential          │  │
│  │   processing and handsoffs     │  │
│  │                                │  │
│  │ ✓ Schedule work based on its   │  │
│  │   critical characteristics     │  │
│  │                                │  │
│  │ ✓ Minimize multiple paths due  │  │
│  │   to specialized operations    │  │
│  │   for exception handling       │  │
│  └───────────────────────────────┘  │
└─────────────────────────────────────┘
```

FIGURE 3.11 Summary of the Traditional Workflow Design Principles

Principle 5 complements the horizontal integration by focusing on the importance of vertical work integration and delegation of responsibility. Empowering workers eliminates formal control points and facilitates easier coordination through decentralization. Moreover, principles 6 through 10 focus on aspects of coordinating activities so that waste, rework, and other inefficiencies are avoided.

The aforementioned people-oriented and conceptual design principles can be complemented with seven somewhat more technical or flow-oriented design principles. These stem from the field of industrial engineering and are often referred to as *work flow design principles*. The principles are to: (1) establish a product orientation in the process, (2) eliminate buffers, (3) establish one-at-a-time processing, (4) balance the flow to the bottleneck[3], (5) minimize sequential processing and handoffs, (6) schedule work based on its critical characteristics, and (7) minimize multiple paths due to specialized operations for exception handling. See Figure 3.11. Industrial engineers have applied these principles successfully to design of manufacturing systems for decades. In broad terms, they focus on achieving efficient process flows, managing resource capacities, maximizing throughput, and reducing cycle times. (See also Figure 3.11.) Detailed discussions of these important design principles are included in Chapter 4, where each will be investigated thoroughly together with relevant tools for implementation, quantitative modeling, and evaluation.

3.7 Step 7: Process Modeling and Simulation

Conceptual process designs must be tested before they are implemented. It is possible for the design to be flawed or to simply not deliver the intended outcomes. The design team uses test results to decide whether to proceed with the implementation phase or go back to the drawing board to revise the design. The iteration between

---

[3]A bottleneck is the resource that through its capacity restriction limits the output of the entire process. (See Chapter 4.)

design modifications and testing continues until the team is satisfied with the predicted performance of the new process.

The testing can be done through implementation of pilot projects as suggested by Roberts (1994). See Section 2.3.5. However, this is generally an expensive way to perform an initial assessment of the process performance. It also takes quite some time before enough data are available from the pilot to make a sound judgment of the effects of the new design. As a result, the design team is fairly restricted about how much testing can be done. Therefore, an attractive alternative is to use process modeling and quantitative tools for the initial testing. Among the available modeling tools, the most flexible and in many respects most powerful (although not always the most appropriate) is simulation. The advantage of using quantitative models to test the design is that it is much cheaper and faster than the pilot implementation approach. This means that the design team has much greater freedom in testing new ideas, which stimulates creativity and allows the team to arrive at better process designs. The drawback is that any model, by definition, is an approximation of reality, although it can never capture all aspects of it. Particularly hard to model are behavioral issues, which have to do with attitudes, resistance to change, and worker behavior—all factors that to a large extent are unknown before the implementation. Therefore, process modeling and simulation can never completely replace pilot testing, and vice versa. Rather, the two approaches complement each other. In terms of supporting the design team in developing a good blueprint for a process design, process modeling and simulation is a powerful approach. To finalize the design and explore behavioral issues, pilot testing is often a worthwhile step before moving on to a full-blown implementation.

The remainder of this section is devoted to a conceptual discussion regarding the usefulness of simulation, or more specifically, discrete event simulation for process modeling and evaluation. The technical aspects of discrete event process simulation and simulation modeling are thoroughly treated in Chapters 6 through 10.

In general terms, *simulation* means "to mimic reality in some way." This can be done through physical models like wind tunnels or through computer-based models. Flight simulation is a well-known example of a computer-based model. Simulation in the context of process modeling actually refers to discrete computer event simulation. This is a technique that allows the representation of processes, people, and technology in a dynamic computer model. Process modeling and simulation as a concept consist of the following basic steps.

1. Building a simulation model of the process.
2. Running the simulation model.
3. Analyzing the performance measures.
4. Evaluating alternative scenarios.

The simulation model mimics the operations of a business process, including customer arrivals, truck deliveries, people missing work, and machines breaking down. This is accomplished by stepping through the events in compressed time, often while displaying an animated picture of the flow. While stepping through the events, the simulation software accumulates data related to the model elements, including capacity utilization of resources, number of jobs, and waiting times in buffers. The performance of the process can then be evaluated through statistical analysis of the collected output data. Although conceptually straightforward, successfully using simulation for process modeling and design requires some technical skills. We will examine these technical issues regarding process modeling and simulation in detail in Chapters 6 through 10.

One of the major strengths of simulation modeling as a tool for business process design is that it can help reduce the risks inherent in any type of change. The use of scenario-based what-if analyses enables the design team to test various alternatives and choose the best one. The result is that goals can be met in an efficient manner (Avni 1999). With regards to what-if analyses, the main advantages of simulation modeling over tests performed on the real system are that (1) it is done "off-line" without disturbing current operations, and (2) time is compressed in a simulation run. In a redesign effort, an existing process is observed and strategies are developed to change it to enhance performance. Testing such strategies on the real system would disturb daily operations and negatively impact results. In a simulation model, any strategy can be tested safely without upsetting the environment. Time compression can be used because in a simulation model, events are accelerated. By only considering the *discrete events* when something happens in the system, simulation can compress time and "advance the clock" much faster than it would occur in real time, enabling the analyst to examine longer time horizons. Depending on the size of the model and the computer's capabilities, several years can be simulated in minutes or even seconds.

Another risk that simulation can help mitigate is that of suboptimization. As the simulation model encompasses various processes, analysts can study how these processes interact and how changing one process impacts the others. For example, in a manufacturing facility, maximization of the output of a group of machines can increase inventory in the assembly area. However, a simulation model containing machining and assembly information can be used to optimize the overall output and inventory.

As mentioned, simulation modeling also promotes creativity and thereby leads to better designs. With the low cost of testing a new design at virtually no risk, people are less reluctant to participate in the design process and to pitch in new ideas. The flow of ideas gains momentum, and soon a brainstorm session produces a much-needed shower of creativity.

In relation to other quantitative tools, a major strength of simulation modeling is its ability to *capture system dynamics*. Random events such as equipment breakdowns and customer arrivals are modeled by using probability distributions. As the simulation advances in time, the embedded distributions are sampled through the use of random-number generators. Hence, the dynamic interaction among system elements is captured. For example, two workstations in a sequential flow might break down at the same time and cause no inventory accumulation between them; however, the occurrence of stoppages at different times might cause significant blockage or idle time and reduce output. In other words, *when* something happens can be as important as *what* happens.

Another interesting aspect of simulation that is directly related to the simulation software available today is its ability to provide animation to help visualize the process operations. Through the use of animation, ideas come alive. Equally important are the multitude of other graphical tools enabling dynamic reporting of results and trends. Time series, histograms, and pie charts are some of the dynamic reporting features of most simulation software packages today. These features help simulation modeling enhance communication. At the same time, the quantitative nature of simulation reporting brings objectivity into the picture. Improvement initiatives can be compared and prioritized. Subjective statements such as "That idea will never work" or "We don't know how much improvement we will obtain" can be put to rest.

To conclude this discussion on the usefulness of simulation modeling, consider as an example a team in charge of redesigning the customer service process of a call center. A simulation model could help the design team capture the dynamics of the system. This is done by incorporating into the model the random nature of calls arriving at the center and the time it takes to serve each of these calls. The model also can capture the process structure, including the interdependencies among customer representatives and the alternative routing schemes. With the model in place, it is easy for the design team to test different scenarios and new ideas for improving the process performance. Particularly, it can assist in determining staffing levels, telecommunications technology requirements, and operational policies.

3.8 Step 8: Implementation of the New Process Design

As indicated in the introduction to this chapter, a detailed discussion of implementation issues and challenges is beyond the scope of our framework for business process design projects. However, the design project cannot be considered in complete isolation from the subsequent implementation step. When selecting the process to be designed (or redesigned), the implementation strategy is an important factor, because clearly, designing a process that will never be implemented is pointless. Crucial criteria in this respect are time, cost, improvement potential, and likelihood of success. In this section, we discuss some high-level implementation issues that can have a direct bearing on these issues and thereby on the process design project as a whole.

As discussed in Chapter 2, the implementation strategy or change tactic can be identified conceptually as revolutionary, evolutionary, or on a continuum in between. For a more detailed discussion of the characteristics of revolutionary and evolutionary change, see Section 2.4. However, in broad terms, a revolutionary implementation approach means rapid change with high costs, primarily caused by the need for external resources. It also implies a high potential for quick, dramatic improvements, as well as a high potential for failure. It requires a committed and decisive CEO and management team that can make harsh decisions to force the change through the organization.

An evolutionary change tactic typically requires a longer time horizon and does not offer the same potential for dramatic improvements in the short run. On the other hand, the costs are lower because the change is achieved primarily by using internal resources. An evolutionary approach also gives the organization time to adapt and embrace the change gradually. This reduces the risk of organizational collapse and destructive behavior, making it more likely that the introduced changes will last. The extended time horizon requires long-term management commitment to keep the vision alive. It also implies that the original blueprinted design probably will need to be revised as market conditions change. In other words, the original design is viewed as an ideal that typically needs to be modified in accordance with restrictions identified during implementation and considered too expensive to remove.

Regardless of the chosen implementation strategy, leadership is critical for success. Any form of significant change necessitates continued engagement on the part of senior executives and senior management. (See, for example, Sections 2.2 through 2.5.) Often, the design team, or part of it, also has the responsibility for implementing the new designs. This is particularly true in reengineering projects. However, support and buy-in from line managers are crucial pieces for successful implementation, given that these managers are accountable for delivering the expected improved performance. Training employees in supplemental skills needed in the new process is also important for successful implementation. Recall that many of the conceptual design principles discussed in Section 3.6.2 involve horizontal and vertical compression of work and responsibilities, which are contingent on workforce capabilities.

As a final note related to the discussion of the importance of measuring progress in Sections 2.1 and 2.2, after the implementation is completed, it is important to assess the effects of the change. When measuring the overall effects, the performance of the new process can be compared to that of the old process before the change. However, the new design also can be compared to the objectives specified in the beginning of the design project, many of which should be included in the mission statement. (See Section 3.1.) A comparison with the performance of the old process shows the effects compared to the status quo, and a comparison against the stated objectives gauges the performance against the specified goals.

It is also important to reflect on what can be learned from the process design and the implementation of projects. What worked, what did not, and why? What were the main challenges? What design ideas did not work out in practice and why not? If the implemented design is different than the original blueprinted design, simulation can be used to assess how far from the performance objectives this ideal design is. It is also important to ask why the blueprinted process design was not fully implemented. Was it because of flaws in the blueprinted design, which made it impossible to implement, or because of mistakes made in the implementation phase? This feedback is invaluable information for improving the activities related to designing and implementing a new process. Recall from Section 2.2 that an important activity in Six Sigma is for the improvement teams to share their experiences and success with the rest of the company, thereby transferring knowledge and maintaining momentum for change.

3.9 Summary

This chapter introduced a framework for structuring business process design projects, particularly emphasizing the usefulness of process modeling and simulation for analysis and evaluation of new process designs. The framework consists of eight major steps or issues that typically need to be addressed in process design projects. They range from the strategic vision of what needs to be done to the final blueprint of the new process design. (See Figure 3.12.) The framework also includes high-level implementation concerns. However, the detailed implementation issues are outside the scope of the framework and the process design project as defined here.

FIGURE 3.12 Summary of the Simulation-Based Framework for Business Process Design Projects

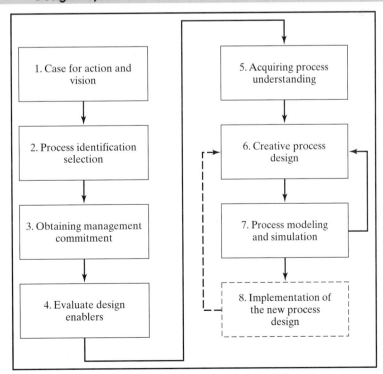

The framework starts at a strategic level with the case for action and vision statements. The former explains why it is necessary to change, and the latter specifies where to go and includes concrete, measurable objectives. These objectives provide a direction for the entire design project and in many cases also for the subsequent implementation project. After the overall objectives are in place, the next steps are to identify and select the process that needs a new design, and to obtain management commitment for the design project as well as for the subsequent implementation. Having chosen the process and secured management support, the actual design activities can begin with investigating potential design enablers and acquiring an understanding of the process to be designed. The most common enabler for new process designs is new (information) technology. Process understanding has two main elements: understanding what the process is supposed to do as defined by customer needs and desires, and understanding what the process is currently doing, if a process exists. A potential source of information for gaining process understanding as well as for generating design ideas and stimulating creativity is business process benchmarking.

With a profound understanding of available design enablers and the process to be designed, the design team must leverage its creativity to develop a new conceptual design. Ten general design principles were outlined that can help stimulate the team's creativity and provide some guidance, but these are not set rules or a recipe for success. Common themes through the conceptual design principles are horizontal and vertical work integration and the use of information technology to improve coordination and avoid suboptimization of the process. This chapter also looked briefly at seven more technical and flow-oriented design principles to be investigated further in Chapter 4.

Having conceived a new conceptual design, the design team needs to test it to see if it will perform as intended and meet the stated objectives. Process modeling and simulation represent powerful methods for numerical evaluation of a given design. With them, it is easy to perform what-if analyses and test new ideas. Advantages compared to testing on the real-world system include low cost, no disturbance of current operations, and speed. It is important to recognize that to leverage the full potential of process modeling and simulation, it needs to be used interactively by the design team to test new ideas and to stimulate creativity.

3.10 References

Avni, T. 1999. Simulation modeling primer. *IIE Solutions* 31(9): 39–41.

Camp, R. 1995. *Business process benchmarking.* Milwaukee, WI: ASQ Quality Press.

Champy, J. 1996. *Reengineering management—The mandate for new leadership.* New York: Harper Business.

Chase, R. B., N. J. Aquilano, and F. J. Jacobs. 1998. *Production and operations management: Manufacturing and services,* 8th edition. New York: McGraw-Hill/Irwin.

Cohen, S. L. 2000. The supermarket in 2010. *IIE Solutions* 32(4): 38–41.

Cross, K. F., J. J. Feather, and R. L. Lynch. 1994. *Corporate renaissance: The art of reengineering.* Cambridge, MA: Blackwell Business.

Davenport, T., and N. Nohria. 1994. Case management and the integration of labor. *Sloan Management Review* (Winter): 11–23.

Hammer, M. 1990. Reengineering work: Don't automate, obliterate. *Harvard Business Review* 71(6): 119–131.

Hammer, M., and J. Champy. 1993. *Reengineering the corporation: A manifesto for business revolution.* New York: Harper Business.

Hyer, N., and U. Wemmerlöv. 2002. *Reorganizing the factory: Competing through cellular manufacturing.* Portland, OR: Productivity Press.

Lester, D. 1994. Reengineering methodology and case study. In *Beyond the basics of reengineering: Survival tactics for the 90's.* Norcross, GA: Industrial Engineering and Management Press.

Lowenthal, J. N. 1994. *Reengineering the organization: A step-by-step approach to corporate revitalization.* Milwaukee, WI: ASQC Quality Press.

Roberts, L. 1994. *Process reengineering: A key to achieving breakthrough success.* Milwaukee, WI: ASQC Quality Press.

Robinson, A. 1991. *Continuous improvement in operations: A systematic approach to waste reduction.* Cambridge, MA: Productivity Press.

Tumay, K. 1995. Business process simulation. In *Proceedings of the 1995 Winter Simulation Conference,* www.informs-cs.org/wscpapers.html, editors C. Alexopoulos, K. Kang, W. R. Lilegdon, and D. Goldsman, 55–60.

Van Gigch, J. P. 1978. *Applied general systems theory,* 2d edition. New York: Harper and Row.

3.11 Discussion Questions and Exercises

1. Telsol, a telecommunications company, faces new competition in the local telephone service industry due to deregulation. The company operated as a monopoly for many years, but now it has to compete for customers in the local market. Cable TV companies have started to offer telephone services using their existing coaxial cable and are quickly gaining market share. Telsol can no longer afford to irritate customers, because these customers are now able to obtain telephone services from other companies. Executives at Telsol believe that the quality of service must increase drastically to avoid losing many of Telsol's customers. Customers have identified two critical service areas: (1) response to repair calls, and (2) response to requests for new lines. Currently, repair calls take an average of 4 days (from the time the call is received until the repair job is completed) to satisfy. Requests for new lines are currently taking an average of 7 days to fulfill. This is the average elapsed time from when the request is made until the new line is operational.

   Telsol would like to redesign its processes and dramatically improve its efficiency (especially in the aforementioned service areas). Write a vision statement and a case for action that Telsol could use to launch a redesign project.

2. Customer relationship management (CRM) has emerged as one of the hottest applications in business software. It has been defined as a "horizontal business strategy that focuses on customer-facing portions of business processes." CRM software is designed to integrate a company's sales, marketing, and customer support functions in order to serve the customer better, while at the same time making the information available throughout the organization. Search the Web for an application of CRM software that enabled a company to achieve higher levels of customer service and improve profitability while redesigning key business processes.

3. What are some of the important considerations when selecting a process for a design project? How might the scope of the process influence the relative importance of the criteria used? Are all processes with poor performance top candidates for redesign? How does this relate to the discussions regarding differences between incremental continuous improvement and process design in Chapters 1 and 2?

4. In most improvement programs, top-management commitment is emphasized as a key success factor. Why do you think this is? Is the role of top management different in a situation with a revolutionary implementation strategy than it would be under an evolutionary change tactic? How?

5. What is the difference between process design or redesign and automation?

6. Explain in your own words the difference between inductive and deductive thinking.

7. Give an example of the application of the following disruptive technologies in a setting familiar to you.
   a. Shared databases
   b. Wireless communications
   c. Handheld computing

8. What are the main issues in understanding a process? Are there any differences between a design project and a redesign project? How does the concept of "analysis paralysis" fit in?

9. Discuss how benchmarking can be a useful tool in business process design projects.

10. Discuss the difference between stated and real (or hidden) customer needs. Why is this distinction important in the context of business process design? Give an example.

11. Identify similarities and differences among the 10 conceptual design principles discussed in Section 3.6.2. How would you summarize the underlying ideas or themes? Do the principles make sense? Why or why not?

12. Describe a potential application of case management in the following organizations:
    a. Dell Computers
    b. A telecommunications company
    c. A community hospital
13. Discuss the advantages and disadvantages of using quantitative process modeling and simulation for testing new designs. How would you relate process modeling and simulation to pilot tests on the real system?

4

Basic Tools
for Process Design

Modeling business processes with the goal of creating effective designs requires more than word processors and spreadsheets. Electronic spreadsheets are useful for mathematical models, but they are less practical in the context of modeling business processes. The tools that are introduced in this chapter help designers check for feasibility, completeness, and effectiveness of a proposed design. These tools facilitate a better understanding of the processes under consideration and the design issues associated with them. The tools are associated with specific design principles, as shown in Table 4.1.

Section 4.2 discusses additional design principles not shown in Table 4.1, such as the elimination of buffers, the establishment of a product orientation, one-at-a-time processing, and the elimination of multiple paths through operations. The specific tools for these design principles are not identified, but they are discussed because it is important to keep them in mind when designing business processes.

Most of the tools presented here assume the availability of key data, such as processing times and the steps required to complete a process. Therefore, we will first address the issue of collecting relevant data that are needed for the application of the basic tools described here. In manufacturing, *tagging* of parts is a method that often is used to collect data associated with a process. Tagging is the process of documenting every activity that occurs during a process. The main data collected by tagging methods are processing times. Tagging is done with two data collection instruments, known in the context of business processes as a job tagging sheet and a workstation log sheet.

A job tagging sheet is a document that is used to gather activity information. If performed correctly, tagging gives an accurate snapshot of how a process is completed within an organization. The information that is gathered can give the company many insights to what is happening in a process, including the steps necessary to complete a job as well as the processing and delay times associated with each activity. The data collected in the job tagging sheets can be used as the input to several design tools that are discussed in this and subsequent chapters. An example of a job tagging sheet is shown in Figure 4.1. The job tagging sheet accompanies a job from the beginning to the end.

Workstation log sheets are used to document the activities that occur at each workstation. This information can be used to determine the utilization and potential capacity of a workstation. However, management must assure employees that the information collected is part of a continuous improvement or process design effort and

TABLE 4.1 Tools and Design Principles

Design Principle	*Tool*
Eliminating non-value-added activities and measuring process improvement	General process chart
Understanding process flow and its relationship to infrastructure configuration	Process flow diagram and load-distance analysis
Understanding work flow	Flowcharting, data flow diagrams, and integrated definition modeling
Balancing flow and capacity	Line balancing
Minimizing sequential processing and handoffs	Case management
Processing work based on its characteristics	Scheduling

not a "witch hunt." A commitment must be made to improving processes and not individual efficiencies. Figure 4.2 shows an example of a workstation log sheet.

Appendix L of *Reorganizing the Factory: Competing Through Cellular Manufacturing* by Nancy Hyer and Urban Wemmerlöv (2002) contains a detailed discussion on tagging in the context of manufacturing processes.

4.1 Process Flow Analysis

Four charts typically used for process flow analysis are the general process chart, the process flow diagram, the process activity chart, and the flowchart (Melnyk and Swink, 2002). In general, these charts divide activities into five different categories: operation, transportation (physical and information), inspection, storage, and delay. Figure 4.3 shows a common set of symbols used to represent activities in charts for process flow analysis. The list of symbols is not exhaustive or universal. Special symbols are sometimes used to document or design a process in specific application areas. For instance, Ryerson Polytechnic University's School of Radio and Television Arts has developed a flowcharting system along with a set of specialized symbols for interactive multimedia. The system offers flowcharting functionality to multimedia writers, developers, and designers (www.rcc.ryerson.ca/rta/flowchart). Flowcharting is discussed further in Section 4.1.3.

In a variety of settings, operations are the only activities that truly add value to the process. Transportation generally is viewed as a handoff activity, and inspection is a control activity. Note, however, that in some situations transportation might be considered the main value-adding activity (or operation) in the process. Think, for example, about airlines, freight companies, postal services, and cab and bus companies.

The difference between storage and delay is that storage is a scheduled (or planned) delay. This occurs, for example, when jobs are processed in batches. If a process uses a batch size of two jobs, then the first job that arrives must wait for a second job before processing can continue. The time that the first job has to wait for the second to complete a batch is not a planned delay (or storage).

A delay, on the other hand, is unplanned waiting time. Delays normally occur when a job (or batch of jobs) must wait for resources to be freed before processing can continue. A delay is always a non-value-added activity, but under certain circumstances, storage might add value to the customer. For example, consider an order-fulfillment process that carries an inventory of finished goods to shorten the time it takes to fulfill an order. If customers are interested in rapid delivery of their orders, then the storage activity might be valuable to them.

FIGURE 4.1 Example of a Job Tagging Sheet

Shop Order Number: [ ]

Shop Order Qty: [ ] Part Number: [ ]

Shop Order Issue Date: [ ]

Part Tagging Sheet

Step #	Process Description	Op #	Machine ID	Shift	Lot Size In	Lot Size Out	Activity Start Date	Activity Start Time	Activity Stop Date	Activity Stop Time	Comments ex. 3 scrap, split qty
1							_/_/01		_/_/01		
2							_/_/01		_/_/01		
3							_/_/01		_/_/01		
4							_/_/01		_/_/01		
5							_/_/01		_/_/01		
6							_/_/01		_/_/01		
7							_/_/01		_/_/01		
8							_/_/01		_/_/01		
9							_/_/01		_/_/01		
10							_/_/01		_/_/01		
11							_/_/01		_/_/01		
12							_/_/01		_/_/01		
13							_/_/01		_/_/01		
14							_/_/01		_/_/01		

Purpose   To track exactly where parts/components travel througout it's manufacturing process and to find MCT(Manufacturing Cycle Time)

Directions   A   Person to give shop/job order to floor attaches tag sheet to paperwork and enters all fields   with a double lined border

B   The first Line should be filled out by SET-UP PERSON if set-up is required.   No Qty's are entered unless scrap is produced.

C   The next line is filled out by OPERATOR. Start time is first complete piece-stop is last piece before the qty is moved to the

The Sheet should be attached to parts and follow throughout.   Repeat process until last operation.   Pull tag off before ready to ship.

FIGURE 4.2 Example of a Workstation Log Sheet

Machine Log

Machine ID:

Activity					Part #	Shop / Job Order Number	Lot Size In	Lot Size Out	Shift	Activity Start		Activity Stop		Comments
Set-UP	Repair	PrevMai	Run	Other						Date	Time	Date	Time	
										__/__/01		__/__/01		
										__/__/01		__/__/01		
										__/__/01		__/__/01		
										__/__/01		__/__/01		
										__/__/01		__/__/01		
										__/__/01		__/__/01		
										__/__/01		__/__/01		
										__/__/01		__/__/01		
										__/__/01		__/__/01		
										__/__/01		__/__/01		
										__/__/01		__/__/01		
										__/__/01		__/__/01		
										__/__/01		__/__/01		

Purpose: To determine machine availibility

Directions: A All necessary Equip needs to have a Machine Log attached to Machine. Person who attaches Machine Log enters Machine ID at the top of the Sheet.

B Lines should be filled in whenever an activity is performed on the machine for longer than 1/2 hr. If several 20 min activities happen throughout the day-- add up the total time and enter as one line. Person who is performing activity is responsible for entering the information.

C Full sheets should be placed in the back of the plastic sleeve and a new log sheet should be brought to the front with the correct Machine ID filled in.

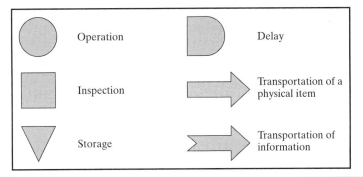

FIGURE 4.3 Activity Symbols

4.1.1 GENERAL PROCESS CHARTS

The general process chart summarizes the current process, the redesigned process, and the expected improvements from the proposed changes (Table 4.2). This chart characterizes the process by describing the number of activities by category, the amount of time activities in each category take overall, and the corresponding percentage of the process total.

   The information that is summarized in the general process chart indicates with a single glance major problems with the existing process, and how the proposed (redesigned) process will remedy some (or all) of these problems. These problems are measured by the time (and corresponding percentage of time) spent on value-added and non-value-added activities. A redesigned process should increase the percentage of time spent on value-added activities by reducing the number of non-value-added activities or the time spent on such activities. Note that the summary focuses on the time to perform the activities (labeled *Time*) and the frequency of occurrence (labeled *No.*) in each category.

   The example in Table 4.2 shows that although the number of value-added activities (i.e., the operations) did not change in the redesigned process, the percentage of time that the process performs operations increases from 10 percent to 37.5 percent. This is achieved by reducing the amount of time spent on non-value-added and control activities. The negative numbers in the columns labeled *Difference* indicate the reduction in the frequency of occurrence (*No.* column) and total time (*Time* column) corresponding to each category.

4.1.2 PROCESS FLOW DIAGRAMS

The most typical application of process flow diagrams has been the development of layouts for production facilities. These diagrams provide a view of the spatial relationships in a process. This is important, because most processes move something from

TABLE 4.2 An Example of a General Process Chart

Activities	*Current Process*			*Redesigned Process*			*Difference*	
	No.	**Time**	**%**	**No.**	**Time**	**%**	**No.**	**Time**
Operations	5	30	10	5	30	37.5	0	0
Inspections	3	60	20	1	20	25.0	–2	–40
Transportation	10	120	40	2	20	25.0	–8	–100
Storage	0	0	0	0	0	0	0	0
Delays	7	90	30	1	10	12.5	–6	–80
Total	25	300	100	9	80	100	–16	–220

activity to activity, so physical layouts determine the distance traveled and the handling requirements.

The process flow diagram is a tool that allows the analyst to draw movements of items from one activity or area to another on a picture of the facility. The resulting diagram measures process performance in units of time and distance. This fairly straightforward analysis must include all distances over which activities move work, including horizontal and vertical distance when the process occupies different floors or levels of a facility. The diagram assumes that moving items requires time in proportion to the distance and that this time affects overall performance. This is why accurate process flow diagrams are particularly helpful in the design of the order-picking process described at the end of the chapter.

The analyst can add labels to the different areas in the process flow diagrams. These labels are then used to indicate the area in which an activity is performed by adding a column in the process activity chart. Alternatively, the process flow diagram may include labels corresponding to an activity number in the process activity chart. This labeling system creates a strong, complementary relationship between the two tools. The process activity chart details the nature of process activities, and the process flow diagram maps out their physical flows. Together, they help the operations analyst better understand how a process operates.

A process flow diagram is a valuable tool for process design. Consider, for example, a process with six work teams, labeled A to F, and physically organized as depicted in Figure 4.4.

Clearly, unnecessary transportation occurs due to the current organization of the work groups within the facility. The sequence of activities is such that work is performed in

FIGURE 4.4 Example of a Process Flow Diagram

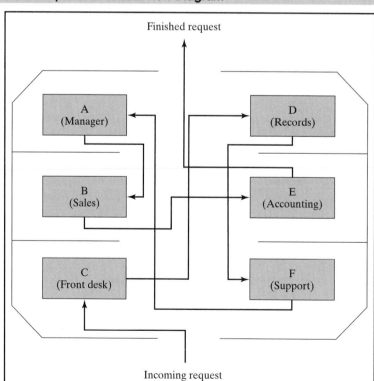

the following order: C, D, F, A, B, and E. Rearranging the work groups to modify the flow of work through the facility, as depicted in Figure 4.5, results in a more efficient layout.

The focus of an analysis of a process flow diagram is on excessive and unnecessary movements. These may be evident by long moves between activities, crisscrosses in paths, repeated movements between two activities, or other illogical or convoluted flows. An effective design eliminates crisscrosses and locates sequential, high-volume activities close together to minimize move times.

The physical arrangement of people, equipment, and space in a process raises four important questions.

1. What centers should the layout include?
2. How much space does each workstation (or center) need?
3. How should each center's space be configured?
4. Where should each center be located?

The process flow diagram is most helpful in answering question 4 regarding the location of each center. The diagram also can be complemented with a simple quantitative method to compare alternative designs. The method is based on calculating a load-distance score for each pair of work centers. The load-distance score (LD score) between work centers i and j is found as follows.

$$\text{LD score}(i,j) = \text{Load}(i,j) \times \text{Distance}(i,j)$$

The *load value* is a measure of "attraction" between two work centers. For example, the load can represent the volume of items flowing between the two work centers during a workday. Hence, the larger the volume of traffic is, the more attraction there is between the two centers. The goal is to find a design that will minimize the total load-distance score (that is, the sum over all pairs of work centers). Consider the load matrix in Table 4.3 associated with two alternative designs depicted in Figure 4.6.

FIGURE 4.5 Redesigned Process Flow Diagram

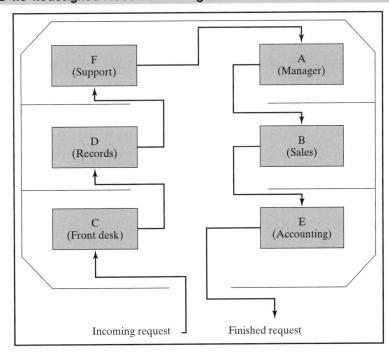

TABLE 4.3 Example of a Load Matrix

	A	B	C	D	E	F
A		20		20		80
B			10		75	
C				15		90
D					70	

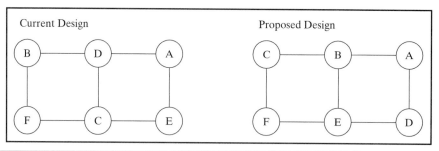

FIGURE 4.6 Location of Work Centers in Alternative Designs

The calculations in Table 4.4 compare the two designs in Figure 4.6. The comparison is in terms of the load-distance score. The distances in Table 4.4 are rectilinear. This means that the number of line segments (in the grid) between two centers determines the distance. For example, one needs to go through three lines in the grid to connect work centers A and F in both designs in Figure 4.6.

The total load-distance score for the proposed design is clearly better than the current design (570 vs. 790). However, the savings in operational costs derived from the new design must be compared with the corresponding relocation costs. It might be possible to find a solution where only a few work centers need to be moved and still achieve a significant improvement from the current design.

Distances typically are measured either as rectilinear or Euclidian for the purpose of calculating a load-distance score. In general, if center 1 is located in position (x_1, y_1) and center 2 is in position (x_2, y_2), the distance between the centers can be calculated as follows.

TABLE 4.4 Load-Distance Calculation for Two Designs

Centers	Load	Current Design Distance	Current Design LD score	Proposed Design Distance	Proposed Design LD score
(A,B)	20	2	40	1	20
(A,D)	20	1	20	1	20
(A,F)	80	3	240	3	240
(B,C)	10	2	20	1	10
(B,E)	75	3	225	1	75
(C,D)	15	1	15	3	45
(C,F)	90	1	90	1	90
(D,E)	70	2	140	1	70
		Total	790		570

$$\text{Rectilinear distance} = |x_1 - x_2| + |y_1 - y_2|$$

$$\text{Euclidian distance} = \sqrt{(x_1 - x_2)^2 + (y_1 - y_2)^2}$$

For instance, the rectilinear distance between a center located in position $(3, 7)$ and a center located in position $(4, 2)$ is $|3 - 4| + |7 - 2| = 1 + 5 = 6$. The corresponding Euclidian distance is $\sqrt{(3 - 4)^2 + (7 - 2)^2} = 5.1$. The Euclidian distance is the length of a straight line between the two points.

4.1.3 PROCESS ACTIVITY CHARTS

The general process chart does not place activities in sequence, which is important and necessary to gain a high-level understanding of the differences between two alternative processes. For example, two alternative processes with the same mix of activities would have identical summarized information in the general process chart, although one may place most of the control activities at the beginning of the process and the other one at the end.

The process activity chart complements the general process chart by providing details to gain an understanding of the sequence of activities in the process. (See Figure 4.7.) The analyst fills in the required information and identifies the appropriate symbol for each activity in one line of the chart and then connects the symbols to

FIGURE 4.7 Example of a Process Activity Chart

No.	Description	Time	Value code (V/N/C)	Symbol
1	Walk to lab	7	N	
2	Wait	10	N	
3	Fill insurance form	6	C	
4	Fill out lab form	5	C	
5	Wait	7	N	
6	Undressing	3	V	
7	Take X-ray	5	V	
8	Develop X-ray	12	V	
9	Check X-ray	3	C	
10	Transfer X-ray	10	N	
11	Walk back	7	N	

Process Activity Chart — Page: 1 of 1

Process: X-ray   Date: 5/1/03

Developed by: Boulder Community Hospital   Current Process ✔   Proposed Process ☐

For each activity, fill in the required information. Also, connect the symbols to show the flow through the process.
The value code indicates whether the activity adds value (V), does not add value (N), or controls (C).

show the flow of the process. The completed chart describes the exact sequence of activities along with the related information. The arrow ($\rightarrow$) in Figure 4.7 is used to represent the transportation of physical items or information.

Although a basic chart can be built with the activity category, the time requirement, and the activity description, more elaborate charts can be developed to include other pieces of information by adding more columns to the chart. For example, information about the number of people involved in each activity can give an indication of staffing needs and overall cost.

Note that the process activity chart considers average activity times only. An estimate of the total time to process a job can then be obtained by adding the activity times. However, this estimate ignores the variation associated with the time to perform each activity. Also note that the chart is not useful when the process includes several variants, because each variant needs its own chart. For example, a process where some requests might need the work of a group of specialists would require two charts: one with the flow of requests without the specialists and one with the flow of requests through the specialists. Finally, the process activity chart cannot show two or more simultaneous activities like those in processes organized in parallel. Flowcharts, described in the following subsection, overcome this limitation. Unlike the process activity chart, flowcharts are capable of depicting processes with multiple paths and parallel activities.

4.1.4 FLOWCHARTS

Flowcharts are a fundamental tool for designing and redesigning processes. They graphically depict activities, typically in a sidelong arrangement such that they follow the movement of a job from left to right through the process. A flowchart can help identify loops in a process (i.e., a series of activities that must be repeated because of problems such as lack of information or errors). A flowchart also can be used to show alternative paths in the process, decision points, and parallel activities. In addition to the symbols in Figure 4.3, a symbol for a decision point is required when creating flowcharts. The decision symbol is a diamond ($\blacklozenge$), as illustrated in Figure 4.8.

To illustrate the use of flowcharts, consider the ordering process in Figure 4.8, which begins with a telephone operator taking information over the phone. The operator then passes order information once a day to a supervisor who reviews it for accuracy and

FIGURE 4.8 Example of a Flowchart

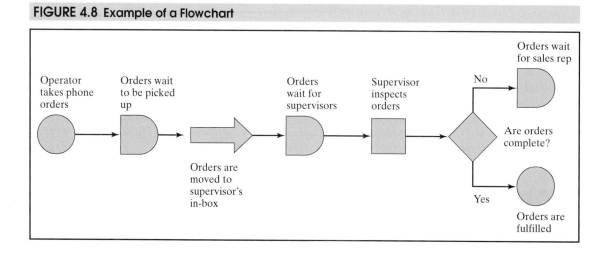

completeness. Accurate orders are fulfilled by customer service, and incomplete orders are set aside for a sales representative, who will contact the customer.

Due to the decision point after the inspection activity, the process in Figure 4.8 has two possible paths. Therefore, this process would generate two activity charts (one for each path) but only one flowchart.

Flowcharts can be used to convey additional information, going beyond the sequence of activities and the logical steps in the process. For instance, flowcharts also might include a time estimate associated with the execution of each activity. An estimate of the activity time can be obtained by using the following equation.

$$\text{Activity time} = \frac{\text{Unit processing time} \times \text{Batch size} + \text{Setup time}}{\text{Efficiency}}$$

Unit processing time = the time to process a single job.
Batch size = the number of jobs in a batch.
Setup time = the time necessary to get ready to process the next batch of jobs.
Efficiency = a measure that indicates the speed of processing with respect to a specified standard time.

This relationship assumes that the standard time to process one unit is known (or can be estimated). It also assumes that the standard time to set up the processing of an entire batch is known. Because the standard times correspond to a worker with 100 percent efficiency, the activity time will increase if the efficiency of the worker decreases.

Suppose it takes 2 minutes to inspect one order for completeness in an order-fulfillment process. Also suppose that the supervisor inspects orders in batches of 20 and that it takes 10 minutes to prepare the inspection of the batch. If the supervisor was recently hired and therefore her efficiency is currently 80 percent, the inspection time for 20 orders is given by the following equation.

$$\text{Activity time} = \frac{2 \times 20 + 10}{0.8} = 62.5 \text{ minutes}$$

If orders are not processed in batches and no preparation time (setup) is needed before the actual inspection, then the inspection time per order is:

$$\text{Activity time} = \frac{2 \times 1 + 0}{0.8} = 2.5 \text{ minutes}$$

Therefore, 20 orders could be processed in 50 minutes. These calculations assume that the mean or average values associated with unit processing and setup times are accurate estimates of the actual values. However, this assumption is not always valid. In many situations, the time values vary significantly, so a more accurate representation is a frequency (or probability) distribution. When probability distributions govern the activity times as well as the arrival time of the items to the process, a simple flowchart might not be sufficient to fully understand the process dynamics. Chapters 7 through 10 explore the use of an advanced tool for process design known as discrete event simulation, which follows the principles of a flowchart to create a dynamic representation of the process.

Other information that can be included in a flowchart includes frequency values for paths originating from a decision point. For example, in the processes shown in Figure 4.8, frequency information associated with the probability of a complete order could be displayed. If an order is complete approximately 90 percent of the time, then

90 percent would be placed next to the *Yes* path and 10 percent would be placed next to the *No* path. Chapter 5 will examine how to use a flowchart with activity times and frequency information in the context of managing process flows.

Flowcharting is often done with the aid of specialized software. For instance, Figure 4.9 shows a flowchart for a telephone order process created with a flowcharting software tool called SmartDraw. The symbols used in the flowchart in Figure 4.9 are specific to SmartDraw and vary from those depicted in Figure 4.3.

4.1.5 SERVICE SYSTEM MAPPING

Service system mapping (SSM) is an extension of traditional flowcharting. It documents how a business process interacts with its customers and the role they play in the delivery of service. The technique was created by Gray-Judson-Howard in Cambridge, Massachusetts, with the purpose of viewing activities in the context of how they add value to the customers. SSM has the following goals.

- To build shared and consistent perceptions of customers' experience with the entire core process.
- To identify all points of contact between the business process and its customers.
- To provide the basis for developing an economic model of the business.
- To identify opportunities for improving the effectiveness of the business process.
- To provide a framework for designing business processes.
- To aid in pinpointing control points and strategic performance measures.

According to Cross et al. (1994), benefits of using service system mapping for process design include the following.

- *Improved Communication:* By providing a graphic representation of the day-to-day processing, a map is usually a significant improvement over written descriptions (one picture is worth a thousand words). A map reduces the risk of varied and inaccurate representations of current operations and establishes a foundation for effective companywide collaboration on business process improvements. In other words, SSM helps employees move from the current to the desired state of operations.
- *Market Research Focus:* By providing an accurate, step-by-step portrayal of points of customer contact from the customer's perspective, a map enhances management's ability to target and focus on areas critical to customer satisfaction. The need to improve understanding of certain aspects of customer contact may suggest further targeted market research.
- *Operations Design and Process Management:* Upstream and downstream effects are easier to identify when additions, deletions, or alterations are made up on a map. A map also allows operations or back-room activity to be viewed in a broader context in relation to the customer.
- *Application of Information Technology:* Information systems can be designed from a more strategic perspective using SSM. Not only are the customer contact points, materials flows, and specific activities depicted, but the information flows required to perform key activities also are included. New information systems (or enhancements to existing systems) can be designed to link value-added activities in the core process.
- *Critical Performance Measures Focus:* Mapping facilitates the collection of key measures necessary in process redesign. SSM also fosters the development of effective policies, procedures, guidelines, and training programs that help set the context for performance management systems. With a map, a design team can pinpoint the critical measurement points. A broad pictorial perspective facilitates

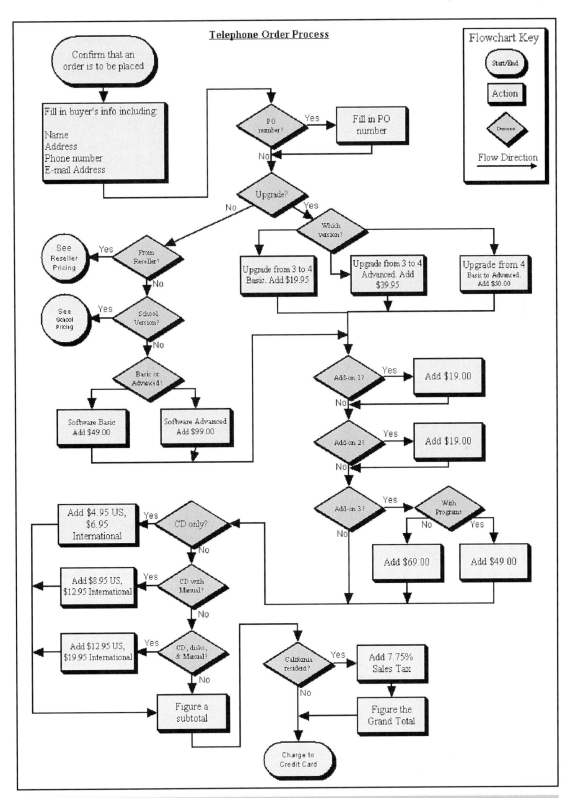

FIGURE 4.9 Flowchart of a Telephone Order Process Developed with SmartDraw

the design of measures to meet the best strategic balance between service quality, product quality, and profitability. Performance measures are most effective when controlling the horizontal flow of work as depicted by the map and when unconstrained by the vertical structure of the organization. The map provides this perspective by depicting all activities in a continuous flow rather than compartmentalizing them by their organizational function.

Although the particular characteristics of a map, including the level of detail, are specific to each application, a general template for service system mapping exists. This template consists of two main elements: horizontal bands and process segments.

The purpose of horizontal bands is to organize activities in terms of the different "players" in a process. (See Figure 4.10.) An SSM typically contains the following five bands.

- End-user or customer band.
- Frontline or distribution channel band.
- Backroom activity band.
- Centralized support or information systems (IS) band.
- Vendor or supplier band.

In Figure 4.10, the customer triggers the beginning of the process by performing activity A. For instance, activity A could be a phone call. A frontline employee performs activity B (e.g., answering the phone call and checking the status of an order). The backroom activity band could include warehouse activities in an order-fulfilment process or underwriting activities in a policy-issuing process of an insurance company. Activities E, F, and I are assigned to the information systems band, which could mean, for example, database queries. Activity H is performed 30 percent of the time; the other 70 percent of the time this activity is bypassed. The process finishes with a frontline employee (e.g., a customer or sales representative) contacting the customer (see activities J and K). The bands in an SSM can be customized to each situation; however, it is generally recommended not to have more than seven bands in one map.

Process segments are sets of activities that represent a subprocess; that is, a segment produces a well-defined output given some input. For example, an order-fulfillment process can be divided into receiving, filling, shipping, and billing. (See Figure 4.11.)

FIGURE 4.10 Example of an SSM with Horizontal Bands

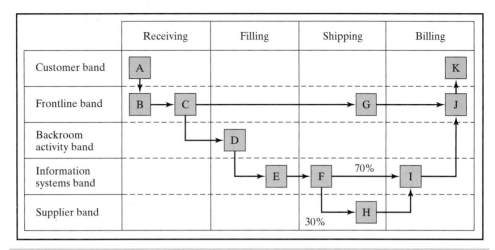

FIGURE 4.11 Example of an SSM with Horizontal Bands and Process Segments

Note that these segments (or subprocesses) are chronologically ordered from left to right in the map.

The process segments do not have to be similar in size as measured by the number of activities. It is more important that the process is partitioned into segments that produce meaningful output.

As originally proposed, service system maps use additional icons and conventions to convey information. For example, a computer icon can be placed next to an arrow to indicate that the communication occurs via e-mail or a file transfer. Similarly, a telephone icon indicates a phone call, or a fax machine icon indicates that a fax is sent. In addition to these icons, software companies have developed flowcharting packages with increased flexibility and functionality. The following software products are examples of flowcharting tools with service system map features.

Micrografx (www.igrafx.com)
PaceStar (www.pacestar.com/links/edgwin.htm)
RFFlow (www.rff.com/)
SmartDraw (www.smartdraw.com/drawing/flowcharts/coolex.htm)
TeamFlow (http://teamflow.com/)
Tension Software (www.tensionsoftware.com/flowchartmaker/index.html)
Visio 2000 (www.microsoft.com/office/visio/)
Visual Thought (www.bombshellstudios.com/samples/co/vt.html)

Most of these software tools follow the traditional flowchart notation represented by activity symbols similar to those depicted in Figure 4.3. An example of an SSM developed with SmartDraw is shown in Figure 4.12. The SSM depicted in Figure 4.12 is rotated 90 degrees with respect to Figure 4.10. In other words, instead of representing process participants as horizontal bands, they are represented as vertical bands. Because the process is small enough, no process segments are shown.

4.2 Workflow Design Principles and Tools

A set of workflow design principles was briefly introduced in Chapter 3. This section will expand the discussion of these principles and present appropriate tools for their implementation.

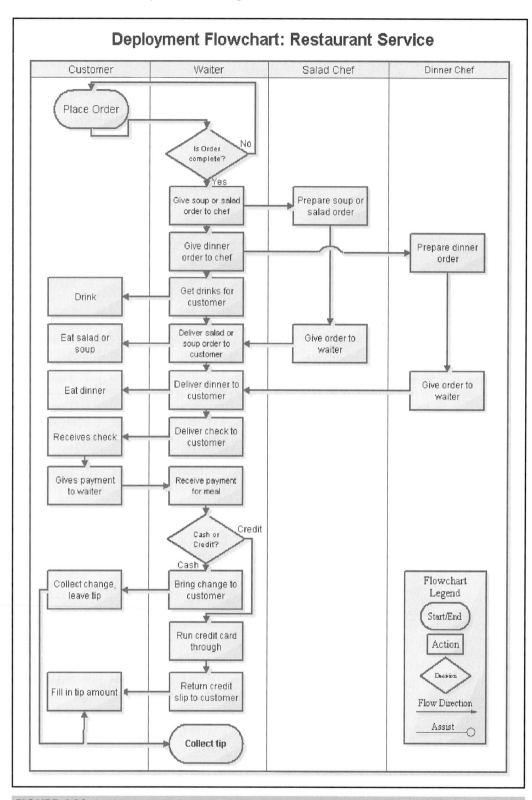

FIGURE 4.12 Example of an SSM Developed with SmartDraw

4.2.1 ESTABLISH A PRODUCT ORIENTATION IN THE PROCESS

A set of activities can be organized in two basic ways: by function or by product or service. In a functional (or process) orientation, workstations or departments are grouped according to their function. For example, all drilling equipment is located in one area of a machine shop, or all technical support personnel are located in one area of a computer software company. The functional (or process) orientation is most common when the same activity must serve many different customers. Because demand levels for these activities are generally low or unpredictable, management does not like to set aside human and capital resources exclusively for a particular product, service, or customer type. In a process orientation, utilization of equipment and labor tends to be high because the requirements for all products and services can be pooled. Also, employee supervision can be more specialized.

With a product orientation, all necessary activities required to complete a finished product or service are organized into an integrated sequence of work modules. This means that resources are dedicated to individual products or services. Consequently, activities are organized around the product's or service's route, rather than being shared among many products. The advantages of a product orientation are as follows.

- Faster processing rates.
- Lower work-in-process inventories.
- Less unproductive time lost to changeovers.
- Less transportation time.
- Fewer handoffs.

To understand the difference between functional and product orientation, consider a process with five activities and two types of customers, A and B. The routing for customer A (i.e., the sequence of activities necessary to complete the service associated with this type of customer) is 1, 2, 4, 5, and 3. The routing for customer B is 3, 1, 4, 2, and 5. In a function-oriented system, each resource that performs the corresponding activity is located in one area (as illustrated in Figure 4.13a), and customers must travel to each area to be served. A product-oriented system, on the other hand, has dedicated servers for each activity and customer type in order to streamline the processing of each customer (Figure 4.13b).

Note that a product orientation is a capital-intensive way of organizing activities, because the resources are not pooled. Therefore, the volume of customers A and B

FIGURE 4.13 Process Versus Product or Orientation

must be sufficient to justify a product-oriented organization and keep resource utilization at an acceptable level. Unfortunately, volumes are not always high enough to justify dedicating resources to a single product or service. In such situations, it might be possible to create a *hybrid* orientation in the process. One popular hybrid orientation in manufacturing is known as *group technology*. This technique groups parts or products with similar characteristics into families and sets aside groups of machines for their production. The equivalent in a business process is to group jobs (e.g., requests or customers) into families. Families may be based on demand or routing requirements. The next step is to organize the resources (e.g., equipment and people) needed to perform the basic activities into separate areas called *cells*. Each cell must be able, with minor adjustments, to deal with all the jobs in the same family.

Suppose two more customers are added to the previous example: customer C with routing 3, 2, 4, 5, and 1, and customer D with routing 1, 3, 4, 2, and 5. Because customer C shares the sequence of activities 2, 4, and 5 with customer A, the family AC can be formed within a group technology orientation. Similarly, a family BD can be created with customers B and D because they share the sequence of activities 4, 2, and 5. A cell AC would handle customers A and C, and a cell BD would handle customers B and D. (See Figure 4.14.)

The hybrid orientation based on group technology simplifies customer routings and reduces the time a job is in the process.

4.2.2 ELIMINATE BUFFERS

In the context of business processes, a buffer consists of jobs that are part of the work-in-process (WIP) inventory. The term *work-in-process* was coined in manufacturing environments to denote the inventory within the production system that is no longer raw material, but not a finished product either. In more general terms, WIP consists of all the jobs that are in queues, moving from one operation to the next, being delayed for any reason, being processed, or residing in buffers. Whether intentional or not, buffers cause logistical nightmares and create unnecessary work and communication problems. When buffers exist, tracking systems are needed to identify the jobs that are in each buffer. Effort is spent in finding orders, expediting work, and communicating status to customers.

Consider the following example from Cross et al. (1994).

> At a computer company, the processing of changes to maintenance contracts was taking 42 days as a result of a series of paperwork buffers

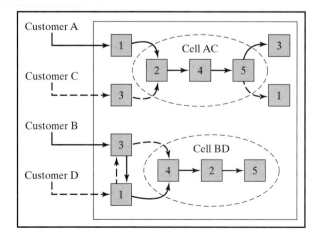

FIGURE 4.14 Hybrid Orientation

between functional areas in the process. Some areas were hiding many of the errors that appeared on customer bills. After establishing a product orientation and reorganizing into teams, the buffers disappeared. Processing errors were caught immediately and eliminated. The impact was an 80 percent reduction in backlog and a 60 percent reduction in cycle time. Cash flow also improved, reducing the need to borrow capital to finance operations.

Note that in this example, changing the system from a process to a product orientation eliminated buffers. However, a product orientation does not always guarantee a buffer-free operation. A product-oriented process must be well balanced in order to minimize buffers.

4.2.3 ESTABLISH ONE-AT-A-TIME PROCESSING

The goal of this principle is to eliminate batch processing, or in other words, to make the batch size equal to one. By doing so, the time that a job has to wait for other jobs in the same batch is minimized, before or after any given activity. Every process has two kinds of batches: *process batches* and *transfer batches*. The process batch consists of all the jobs of the same kind that a resource will process until the resource changes to process jobs of a different kind. For example, a scanner in a bank could be used to scan checks to create electronic files of the checks written by each customer and also to scan other documents. Then the process batch associated with the job of scanning checks is the number of checks processed until the scanner is configured to scan other documents.

Transfer batches refer to the movement of jobs between activities or workstations. Rather than waiting for the entire process batch to be finished, work that has been completed can be transferred to the next workstation. Consequently, transfer batches are typically equal to or smaller than process batches. The advantage of using transfer batches that are smaller than the process batch is that the total processing time is reduced; as a result, the amount of work in process in the system is decreased.

Figure 4.15 compares the total processing time of a process with three activities in sequence when the batch sizes are changed. In this example, it is assumed that each item requires one unit of processing time in activities 1 and 3 and 0.5 of a time unit in activity 2.

When the transfer batch is the same as the process batch, the total processing time for 100 items is 250 units of time. When the transfer batch is changed to a size of 20 items, then the total processing time for 100 items is 130 units of time. In this case, the first 20 units are transferred from activity 1 to 2 at time 20. Then at time 30, this batch is transferred from activity 2 to 3. Note that between time 30 and time 40, the resources associated with activity 2 are idle (or working on activities of a different process).

From the point of view of the utilization of resources, two values are important: setup time and processing run time. Larger batch sizes require fewer setups and, therefore, can generate more processing time and more output. This is why larger batch sizes are desirable for bottleneck resources[1] (i.e., those with the largest utilization). For non-bottleneck resources, smaller process batch sizes are desirable, because the use of existing idle times reduces work-in-process inventory.

---

[1]The bottleneck is the resource with lowest capacity in the process.

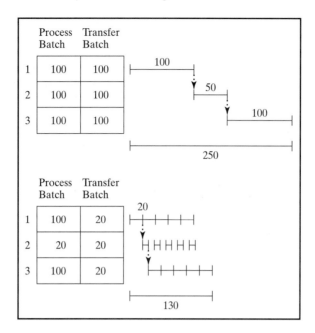

FIGURE 4.15 Effect of Changing Batch Sizes

4.2.4 BALANCE THE FLOW TO THE BOTTLENECK

The principle of balancing the flow to the bottleneck is linked to an operation management philosophy known as Theory of Constraints (TOC). Eliyahu M. Goldratt coined this term and popularized the associated concepts in his book *The Goal* (Goldratt and Cox, 1992). This book uses the Socratic method to challenge a number of assumptions that organizations make to manage operations. The novel narrates Alex Rogo's struggle to keep schedules, reduce inventory, improve quality, and cut costs in the manufacturing facility that he manages. Jonah, a physicist with a background that is "coincidentally" similar to Goldratt's, guides Alex through a successful turnaround of his plant by applying simple rules to the plant's operations. Jonah reveals the first rule in the following exchange (page 139 of *The Goal*).

> "There has to be some relationship between demand and capacity." Jonah says, "Yes, but as you already know, you should not balance capacity with demand. What you need to do instead is balance the *flow of product* through the plant with demand from the market. This, in fact, is the first of nine rules that express the relationships between bottlenecks and non-bottlenecks and how you should manage your plant. So let me repeat it for you: Balance flow, not capacity."

Balancing the flow and not the capacity challenges a long-standing assumption. Historically, manufacturers have tried to balance capacity across a sequence of processes in an attempt to match capacity with market demand. However, making all capacities the same might not have the desired effect. Such a balance would be possible (and desirable) only if the processing times of all stations were constant or had a small variance. Variation in processing times causes downstream workstations to have idle times when upstream workstations take longer to complete their assigned activities. Conversely, when upstream workstations' processing time is shorter, inventory builds up between stations. The effect of statistical variation is cumulative. The only way that this variation can be smoothed is by increasing work in process to absorb the variation (a bad choice because process managers should be trying to reduce WIP as explained in Section 4.2.2), or increasing capacities downstream to be able to compensate for the longer upstream times. The rule here is that capacities within the process sequence do not need to be balanced to the same levels. Rather, attempts should be made to balance the flow of product through the system (Chase et al., 1998).

When processing times do not show significant variability, the *line balancing* approach of manufacturing can be applied to create workstations in a process. The goal of line balancing is to balance capacity (instead of flow, as proposed by Goldratt); therefore, it should not be used when processing times vary significantly. The line balancing method is straightforward, as indicated in the following steps.

1. Specify the sequential relationships among activities using a precedence diagram. The diagram is a simplified flowchart with circles representing activities and arrows indicating immediate precedence requirements.
2. Use the market demand (in terms of an output rate) to determine the line's cycle time *(C)* (i.e., the maximum time allowed for work on a unit at each station).

$$C = \frac{\text{Process time per day}}{\text{Market demand per day (in units)}}$$

3. Determine the theoretical minimum number of stations (*TM*) required to satisfy the line's cycle time constraint using the following formula.

$$TM = \frac{\text{Sum of activity times}}{C}$$

4. Select a primary rule by which activities are to be assigned to workstations and a secondary rule to break ties.
5. Assign activities, one at a time, to the first workstation until the sum of the activity times is equal to the line's cycle time or until no other activity is feasible because of time or sequence restrictions. Repeat the process for the rest of the workstations until all the activities are assigned.
6. Evaluate the efficiency of the line as follows.

$$Efficiency = \frac{\text{Sum of activity times}}{C \times \text{Actual number of stations}}$$

7. If efficiency is unsatisfactory, rebalance using a different rule.

Example 4.1
Consider the activities in Table 4.5, a market demand of 25 requests per day, and a 420-minute working day. Find the balance that minimizes the number of workstations.

Solution
1. Draw a precedence diagram. Figure 4.16 illustrates the sequential relationships in Table 4.5.
2. The next step is to determine the cycle time (i.e., the value of *C*). Because the activity times and the working day are both given in minutes, no time conversion is necessary.

$$C = \frac{420 \text{ min/day}}{25 \text{ req/day}} = 16.8 \text{ min/req}$$

TABLE 4.5 Activity Times and Immediate Predecessors

Activity	Time (in minutes)	Immediate Predecessor
A	2	—
B	11	A
C	4	B
D	5	—
E	7	D
F	6	C
G	2	C
H	10	E
I	2	E
J	8	F, G, H, I
K	6	J

3. Calculate the theoretical minimum number of stations required (i.e., the value of *TM*).

$$TM = \frac{63 \text{ min}}{16.8 \text{ min}} = 3.75 \text{ stations} = 4 \text{ (rounded up)}$$

4. Select a rule to assign activities to stations. Research has demonstrated that some rules are better than others for certain problem structures (Chase et al., 1998). In general, the strategy is to use a rule that gives priority to activities that either have many followers or are of long duration, because they effectively constrain the final balance. In this example, our primary rule assigns activities in order of the largest number of followers, as shown in Table 4.6.

   The secondary rule, used for tie-breaking purposes, will be to assign activities in order of longest activity time. If two or more activities have the same activity time, then one is chosen arbitrarily.

5. The assignment process starts with activity A, which is assigned to workstation 1. Because activity A has a time of 2 minutes, there are 16.8 − 2 = 14.8 minutes of idle time remaining in workstation 1. We also know that after the assignment of activity A, the set of feasible activities consists of activities B and D. Because either one of these

FIGURE 4.16 Precedence Diagram

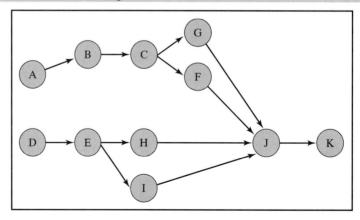

TABLE 4.6 Number of Followers

Activity	Number of Followers
A	6
B and D	5
C and E	4
F, G, H, and I	2
J	1
K	0

activities could be assigned to workstation 1 and both have the same number of followers, activity B is chosen, because it has the longer time of the two. Workstation 1 now consists of activities A and B with an idle time of $14.8 - 11 = 3.8$ minutes. Because activities C and D cannot feasibly be assigned to workstation 1, a new workstation must be created. The process continues until all activities are assigned to a workstation, as illustrated in Table 4.7.

6. Calculate the efficiency of the line.

$$Efficiency = \frac{63 \text{ min}}{16.8 \text{ min} \times 5} = 75\%$$

7. Evaluate the solution. An efficiency of 75 percent indicates an imbalance or idle time of 25 percent across the entire process. Is a better balance possible? The answer is yes. The balance depicted in Figure 4.17 is the result of using the longest activity time rule as the primary rule and the largest number of followers as the secondary rule.

   Note that it is possible for the longest activity time to be greater than the cycle time required for meeting the market demand. If activity H in the previous example had required 20 minutes instead of 10 minutes, then the maximum possible process output would have been $420/20 = 21$ requests per day. However, there are a few ways in which the cycle time can be reduced to satisfy the market demand.

   1. *Split the activity.* Is there a way of splitting activity H so that the work can be shared by two workstations?

TABLE 4.7 Results of Balancing with Largest Number of Followers Rule

Station	Activity	Station Idle Time (min.)	Feasible Activities	Activities with Most Followers	Activities with Longest Time
1	A	14.8	B, D	B, D	B
	B	3.8	None		
2	D	11.8	C, E	C, E	E
	E	4.8	C, I	C	
	C	0.8	None		
3	H	6.8	F, G, I	F, G, I	F
	F	0.8	None		
4	G*	14.8	I		
	I	12.8	J		
	J	4.8	None		
5	K	10.8			

* Denotes an activity arbitrarily assigned when a tie remains after applying the primary and secondary selection rules.

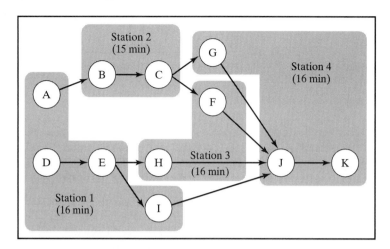

FIGURE 4.17 A More Efficient Solution

2. *Use parallel workstations.* The workstations are identical and requests would be sent to either one, depending on the current load.
3. *Train the worker.* Is it possible to train a worker so that activity H can be performed faster? Note that in this case the effect of the training should be such that the worker can become at least 19 percent faster (because the time for activity H exceeds the required cycle time by ([1 – 20/16.8] × 100 percent, or approximately 19 percent).
4. *Work overtime.* The output of activity H is 420/20 = 21 requests per day, 4 short of the required 25. Therefore, 80 minutes of overtime is needed per day.
5. *Redesign.* It might be possible to redesign the process in order to reduce the activity time and meet market demand.

4.2.5 MINIMIZE SEQUENTIAL PROCESSING AND HANDOFFS

Sequential processing can create two problems that lengthen total process time: (1) Operations are dependent on one another and therefore constrained or gated by the slowest step, and (2) no one person is responsible for the whole service encounter (Cross et al. 1994).

Example 4.2

This example illustrates the benefits of the design principle of minimizing sequential processing. Assume that a service requires 30 minutes to complete. Suppose that four activities of 10, 7, 8, and 5 minutes are assigned each to one of four individuals. In other words, the process is a line with four stations, as depicted in Figure 4.18a. According to the concepts in the previous section, the process has an output rate of six jobs per hour and an efficiency of $30/(10 \times 4) = 75$ percent.

Significant improvements can be achieved by replacing sequential processing with parallel processing (Figure 4.18b). For example, if each of the four workers performs the entire process (i.e., each performs the four steps in the process), output per hour theoretically could be increased by 33.3 percent to an output of eight jobs per hour. However, it might not be possible to achieve the theoretical output of the parallel process due to the differences in performance of each individual. Nevertheless, the parallel process will always produce more output than its sequential counterpart, as long as the total parallel time (in this case, $30 \times 4 = 120$) is less than the slowest station time multiplied by the square of the number of stations (in this case, $10 \times 4^2 = 160$).

If each worker in this example were to take 40 minutes to complete each job in the parallel process, then the total time in the parallel system would be 160 minutes and the output would be the same as in the sequential process. On the other hand, suppose that four workers require

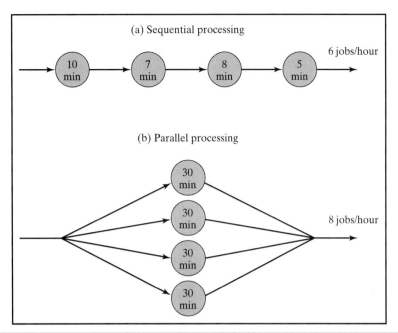

FIGURE 4.18 Sequential Versus Parallel Processing

30, 36, 40, and 32 minutes to complete a single job. Then the output of the parallel process would be as follows.

$$\frac{60}{30} + \frac{60}{36} + \frac{60}{40} + \frac{60}{32} = 7.04 \text{ jobs per hour,}$$

which represents a 17.4 percent improvement over the sequential process. Creating parallel servers capable of completing a set of activities that represent either an entire transaction or a segment of a larger process is related to the concept of case management introduced in Chapter 3. In Example 4.2, the process is transformed from employing specialized workers to employing case workers.

4.2.6 ESTABLISH AN EFFICIENT SYSTEM FOR PROCESSING WORK

Jobs typically are processed in the order in which they arrive at a workstation. This mode of operation is known as the first-in-first-out (FIFO) or first-come-first-served (FCFS) processing policy. As part of the design of a process, the analyst may consider alternative ways in which work is processed. The development and implementation of alternative processing policies belong to the general area of scheduling. Scheduling involves determining a processing order and assigning starting times to a number of jobs that tie up various resources for a period of time. Typically, the resources are in limited supply. Jobs are comprised of activities, and each activity requires a certain amount of specified resources for a given amount of time.

The importance of considering alternative scheduling schemes increases with the diversity of the jobs in the process. Consider, for example, a process that provides technical support for a popular software package. In such a process, e-mail, faxes, and telephone calls are received and tie up resources (i.e., support personnel). Some requests for technical assistance might take longer to complete due to their complexity. As a result, requests that can be processed faster might be delayed unnecessarily if the requests are simply answered in the order they are received and routed to the next available support person.

A simple scheduling approach is to classify work into "fast" and "slow" tracks, based on an estimation of the required processing time. At a major university, approximately 80 percent of the applications for admission to undergraduate programs are considered for a fast-track process, because the applicants are either an "easy accept" or an "easy reject." The remaining 20 percent are applicants whose files must be examined more thoroughly before a decision can be made. The same principle applies to supermarkets, where customers are routed (and implicitly scheduled for service) to regular and express cashiers.

Other characteristics that can be used to schedule jobs through a process include the following.

- Arrival time.
- Estimated processing time.
- Due date (i.e., when the customer expects the job to be completed).
- Importance (e.g., as given by monetary value).

A key element of a scheduling system is its ability to identify "good" schedules. Ideally, a numerical measure could be used to differentiate the good schedules from the bad ones. This numerical measure is generally known as the *objective function*, and its value is either minimized or maximized. Finding the "right" objective function for a scheduling situation, however, can be difficult. First, such important objectives as customer satisfaction with quality or promptness are difficult to quantify and are not immediately available from accounting information. Second, a process is likely to deal with three different objectives.

1. Maximize the process output over some period of time.
2. Satisfy customer desires for quality and promptness.
3. Minimize current out-of-pocket costs.

In practice, surrogate objectives are used to quantify the merit of a proposed schedule. For example, if the objective is to maximize utilization of resources, a surrogate objective might be to minimize the time it takes to complete the last job in a given set of jobs. (This time is also known as the *makespan*.) On the other hand, if customers tolerate some tardiness (i.e., the time elapsed after a promised delivery time) but become rapidly and progressively more upset when the tardiness time increases, minimizing maximum tardiness might be a good objective function. Some of the most common surrogate objective functions are:

- Minimize the makespan.
- Minimize the total (or average) tardiness.
- Minimize the total (or average) weighted tardiness.
- Minimize the maximum tardiness.
- Minimize the number of tardy jobs.
- Minimize the amount of time spent in the system (i.e., the processing plus the waiting time).

As mentioned previously, the makespan is the total time required to complete a set of jobs. The total tardiness is the sum of the tardiness associated with each job. Tardiness is when the completion time lasts beyond the due date. The weighted tardiness is calculated as the product of the tardiness value and the importance (or weight) of a job.

Example 4.3
In order to understand the effect that scheduling decisions have on these objective functions, consider a set of five jobs, characterized by the values given in Table 4.8, to be processed by a single server.

TABLE 4.8 Scheduling Example

Job	Arrival Time (min.)	Estimated Processing Time (min.)	Due Date	Importance (weight)
A	15	30	100	10
B	17	15	220	5
C	22	45	120	12
D	30	60	110	8
E	35	20	150	11

In this example, assume that the single server is allowed to process the jobs in any order he or she wishes. Note that if the objective is to minimize the makespan, all processing orderings give the same solutions—170 minutes (the sum of all the processing times). In other words, the server can process the jobs in any order and the makespan will remain the same. Also note that this is not the case when the service facility consists of more than one server.

Now suppose the server decides to process the jobs in the order they arrived; that is, the server uses the first-in-first-out (FIFO) scheduling rule. In this case, the processing order is A, B, C, D, and finally E. If no idle times between jobs are considered, then the starting and finishing times for this sequence are as shown in Table 4.9. (In this table, it is assumed that the server starts processing after the arrival of the last job; that is, at time 35.)

The calculations in Table 4.9 show that a large weighted tardiness penalty is incurred when the jobs are processed using the FIFO rule.

A rule that is particularly useful when jobs have specified due dates is known as *earliest-due-date-first* (EDD). Using EDD, the jobs are sequenced in increasing order of their due date values. The schedule that results from applying this rule to the example is A, D, C, E, and B. The corresponding calculations are shown in Table 4.10.

The EDD schedule is better than the FIFO schedule in terms of tardiness and weighted tardiness. However, the number of tardy jobs is the same for both schedules. Although the EDD schedule is better than the FIFO rule in terms of the tardiness measures that have been considered, the EDD schedule is not optimal. In other words, it is possible to find schedules that are better than the one produced by the EDD rule in terms of tardiness and weighted tardiness.

TABLE 4.9 FIFO Schedule

Job	Starting Time	Ending Time	Tardiness	Weighted Tardiness	Tardy Jobs
A	35	65	0	0	0
B	65	80	0	0	0
C	80	125	5	60	1
D	125	185	75	600	1
E	185	205	55	605	1
Total			135	1,265	3

TABLE 4.10 EDD Schedule

Job	Starting Time	Ending Time	Tardiness	Weighted Tardiness	Tardy Jobs
A	35	65	0	0	0
D	65	125	15	120	1
C	125	170	50	600	1
E	170	190	40	440	1
B	190	205	0	0	0
Total			105	1,160	3

An important characteristic of the EDD schedule is that it gives the optimal solution to the problem of minimizing the maximum tardiness. The maximum tardiness in the FIFO schedule is 75, due to job D. The maximum tardiness in the EDD schedule is 50, due to job C. Therefore, it can be stated with certainty that no other job sequence will result in a maximum tardiness of less than 50.

In addition to FIFO and EDD, researchers and practitioners have developed many other rules and algorithms (sets of steps) for sequencing and scheduling problems. For example, consider two related rules known as: (1) shortest-processing-time-first (SPT) and (2) weighted SPT (WSPT).

The SPT rule simply orders the jobs by their processing time, whereby the job with the shortest time is processed first, followed by the job with the next shortest time, and so on. The result of applying this rule to the example is given in Table 4.11. In terms of weighted tardiness, the SPT sequence is better than FIFO and EDD in this example.

The WSPT schedule can be obtained by first calculating the weight to processing time (WP) ratio for each job. The value of this ratio for job A is 10/30 = 0.333; that is, the weight of 10 is divided by the processing time of 30. After calculating all the ratio values, the WSPT sequence is obtained by ordering the jobs from the largest WP ratio to the smallest. It is easy to verify that the WSPT sequence for this example is E, A, B, C, and D. As a matter of coincidence, this sequence results in the same tardiness and weighted tardiness values as the ones corresponding to the SPT sequence. This, however, is not necessarily always the case.

Finally, an algorithm is described that will minimize the number of tardy jobs when the importance (or weight) of all the jobs is considered equal. The procedure is known as Moore's Algorithm and can be summarized by the following sequence of steps.

1. Order the jobs using the EDD rule.
2. If there are no tardy jobs, stop. The optimal solution has been found.
3. Find the first tardy job.
4. Suppose that the tardy job is the kth job in the sequence. Remove the job with the longest processing time in the set of jobs from the first one to the kth one. (The jobs that are removed in this step are inserted at the end of the sequence after the algorithm stops.)
5. Revise the completion times and return to step 2.

Example 4.4
Next, this algorithm is applied to the data in Example 4.3.

Step 1:	See Table 4.12.
Step 2:	There are three tardy jobs in the sequence.
Step 3:	Job D is the first tardy job.
Step 4:	Job D must be removed from the sequence, because its processing time of 60 is larger than the processing time of 30 corresponding to job A.
Step 5:	See Table 4.13.
Step 6:	No more tardy jobs remain in the sequence. The optimal solution has been found.

TABLE 4.11 SPT Schedule

Job	Starting Time	Ending Time	Tardiness	Weighted Tardiness	Tardy Jobs
B	35	50	0	0	0
E	50	70	0	0	0
A	70	100	0	0	0
C	100	145	25	300	1
D	145	205	95	760	1
Total			120	1,060	2

TABLE 4.12 Step 1 of Moore's Algorithm to Minimize Number of Tardy Jobs

Job	Processing Time	Due Date	Completion	Tardy Jobs
A	30	100	65	0
D	60	110	125	1
C	45	120	170	1
E	20	150	190	1
B	15	220	205	0

TABLE 4.13 Step 5 of Moore's Algorithm to Minimize Number of Tardy Jobs

Job	Processing Time	Due Date	Completion	Tardy Jobs
A	30	100	65	0
C	45	120	110	0
E	20	150	130	0
B	15	220	145	0

The optimal schedule, therefore, is A, C, E, B, and D. Job D is the only tardy job with a tardiness of $205 - 110 = 95$ and a weighted tardiness of 760. This schedule turns out to be superior to all the other ones examined so far in terms of multiple measures of performance (i.e., average tardiness, weighted tardiness, and number of tardy jobs). However, the application of Moore's Algorithm guarantees an optimal sequence only with respect to the number of tardy jobs when all the jobs have the same weight. In other words, Moore's Algorithm does not minimize values based on tardiness (such as total tardiness or weighted tardiness), so it is possible to find a different sequence with better tardiness measures.

4.2.7 MINIMIZE MULTIPLE PATHS THROUGH OPERATIONS

A process with multiple paths is confusing and, most likely, unnecessarily complex. Also, multiple paths result in a process in which resources are hard to manage and work is difficult to schedule. Paths originate from decision points that route jobs to departments or individuals. For example, a telephone call to a software company could be routed to customer service, sales, or technical support. If the call is classified correctly, then the agent in the appropriate department is able to assist the customer and complete the transaction. In this case, there are multiple paths for a job, but the paths are clearly defined and do not intersect.

Suppose now that a customer would like to order one of the software packages that the company offers, but before placing the order she would like to ask some technical questions. Her call is initially routed to a sales agent, who is not able to answer technical questions. The customer is then sent to a technical support agent and back to sales to complete the transaction.

These multiple paths can be avoided in a couple of ways. The obvious solution is to have sales personnel who also understand the technical aspects of the software they are selling. Because this might not be feasible, information technology (such as a database of frequently asked questions) can be made available to sales agents. If the question is not in the database, the sales agent could contact a technical specialist to obtain an answer and remain as the single point of contact with the customer.

Alternatively, the process can be organized in case teams (see Section 3.6.2 about design principles) that are capable of handling the three aspects of the operation: sales, customer service, and technical support. In this way, calls are simply sent to the next available team. A team can consist of one (a case manager) or more people (case team) capable of completing the entire transaction.

4.3 Additional Diagramming Tools

An important aspect of designing a business process is the supporting information infrastructure. The tools reviewed so far in this chapter focus on the flow of work in a business process. In addition to the flow of work (e.g., customers, requests, or applications) the process designer must address the issues associated with the flow of data. Although this book does not address topics related to the design and management of information systems, it is important to mention that data flow diagrams are one of the main tools used for the representation of information systems. Specifically, data flow diagramming is a means of representing an information system at any level of detail with a graphic network of symbols showing data flows, data stores, data processes, and data sources/destinations. The purpose of data flow diagrams is to provide a semantic bridge between users and information systems developers. The diagrams are graphical and logical representations of what a system does, rather than physical models showing how it does it. They are hierarchical, showing systems at any level of detail, and they are jargonless, allowing user understanding and reviewing. The goal of data flow diagramming is to have a commonly understood model of an information system. The diagrams are the basis of structured systems analysis. Figure 4.19 shows a data flow diagram for insurance claim software developed with SmartDraw.

Another flowcharting tool that was not mentioned in the previous section is the so-called integrated definition (IDEF) methodology. IDEF is a structured approach to enterprise modeling and analysis. The IDEF methodology consists of a family of methods that serve different purposes within the framework of enterprise modeling. For instance, IDEF0 is a standard for function modeling, IDEF1 is a method of information modeling, and IDEF1x is a data-modeling method.

IDEF0 is a method designed to model the decisions, actions, and activities of an organization or system; therefore, it is the most directly applicable in business process design. IDEF0 was derived from a well-established graphical language, the structured analysis and design technique (SADT). The U.S. Air Force commissioned the developers of SADT to develop a function-modeling method for analyzing and communicating the functional perspective of a system. Effective IDEF0 models help organize the analysis of a system and promote good communication between the analyst and the customer. IDEF0 is useful in establishing the scope of an analysis, especially for a functional analysis. As a communication tool, IDEF0 enhances domain expert involvement and consensus decision making through simplified graphical devices. As an analysis tool, IDEF0 assists the modeler in identifying what functions are performed, what is needed to perform those functions, what the current system does right, and what the current system does wrong. Thus, IDEF0 models are often created as one of the first tasks of a system development effort.

The "box and arrow" graphics of an IDEF0 diagram show the function as a box and the interfaces to or from the function as arrows entering or leaving the box. To express functions, boxes operate simultaneously with other boxes, with the interface arrows "constraining" when and how operations are triggered and controlled. The basic syntax for an IDEF0 model is shown in Figure 4.20.

A complete description of the family of IDEF methods can be found in www.idef.com.

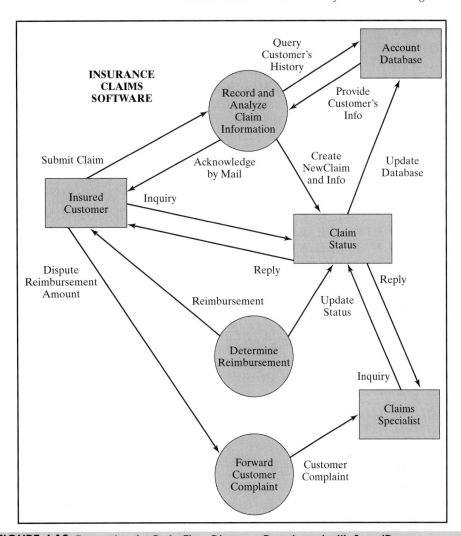

FIGURE 4.19 Example of a Data Flow Diagram Developed with SmartDraw

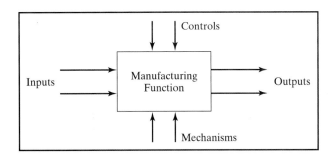

FIGURE 4.20 Basic Syntax for an IDEF0 Model

4.4 From Theory to Practice: Designing an Order-Picking Process

This chapter will conclude with a discussion of the use of some of the basic process design tools in the context of the operations at a warehouse (Saenz, 2000). The goal is to point out where some basic tools may be applied in the design of a real-world process. The situation deals with the redesign of the order-picking process at a warehouse of a company that has been affected by the advent of e-commerce and increased customer demands. It is assumed that this change in the environment has affected all functions of a traditional warehouse.

To keep the company competitive, management decided to improve the performance of their warehouse operations, starting with the order-picking process. Traditional warehouse functions include receiving products, storing products, replenishing products, order picking, packing, and shipping. Order picking is the heart of most warehouse operations and impacts inbound and outbound processes. Designing an effective picking process can lead to the overall success of a warehouse operation and business. Several key issues need to be considered when designing a picking process: order profiling, picking equipment, slotting strategy, replenishing, layout, and picking methods.

Customers are tending toward making smaller, more frequent orders, which makes order profiling for each product an essential ingredient in the design of a picking process. *Order profiling* refers to defining the product activity in terms of the number of "lines" ordered per product over some period of time—in other words, the number of times one travels to a location to pick an item. Based on this criterion, products are classified as fast-moving, medium-moving, slow-moving, or dead items. The cubic velocity of a product plays an equally important role in classifying activity. It helps determine if a product requires broken-case (each), case, or pallet-picking equipment. The cubic velocity is calculated by multiplying the quantity picked per item by the product's cubic dimensions. A product classified as slow moving might have a large cubic velocity. Similarly, a product classified as a fast mover might have a small cubic velocity. These two factors play a critical role when defining the picking equipment and potential product slotting.

Note that order profiling can be done by using simple calculations based on data collected for each product in the warehouse. Order profiling is an important input to the facility layout tool discussed in Section 4.1.2.

To select the most efficient picking equipment, the product activity, cubic velocity, and variety of products must be considered. The three basic types of picking are broken case, case, and pallet. The emergence of e-commerce has triggered the use of new technology in the picking process. Advanced picking technologies include radio frequency terminals, wireless speech technology, and pick- or put-to-light systems. In a radio frequency terminal system, the terminal is used to initiate and complete orders. The location and quantity of each product is displayed on the terminal screen. Wireless speech recognition terminals convert electronic text into voice commands that guide the operator during picking. The operator uses a laser or pen scanner to initiate and close orders. The information is received using the radio frequency terminal, which usually is secured around the operator's waist. In a pick- or put-to-light system, the operator uses a tethered scanner or a radio frequency scanner to initiate orders. Bay and location displays are illuminated to guide the operator through the picking process. The operator follows the lights and displays to complete orders. Typically, the right balance of technology and manual methods results in effective picking operations. Process flow diagrams (Section 4.1.2) and data flow diagrams (Section 4.3) are useful in this phase of the design.

Regardless of the picking equipment used, an effective slotting strategy is critical to an efficient picking process. The basic definition of *slotting* is "the assignment of a product to a location." The benefits of an effective slotting strategy include increased throughput, improved labor utilization, reduced injuries, better cube utilization, and reduced product damage. The art of effective slotting is assigning the fast-moving items to the most ergonomic levels, while balancing the volume across many aisles to reduce order and labor congestion. The most active items (top 20 percent) are placed on the middle picking level to improve picker productivity and reduce the risk of injury. The slotting assignment must be reviewed for its effectiveness monthly or as the activity of products fluctuates with seasonality. The general process chart (Section 4.1.1) can be used to compare the effectiveness of the assignment policies, because this chart shows a summary of the percentage of time that is spent in activities such as transportation and storage.

Replenishing the forward picking area is essential to the flow and effectiveness of the picking process. Picking locations are replenished when the pick location inventory reaches some defined inventory level. Replenishments usually are triggered visually or are generated by the system. Visually triggered replenishments involve an operator viewing the inventory level of each location to determine whether replenishments are required. System-generated replenishments are handled by defining a minimum inventory level in the system for each location. When the minimum inventory level is reached, the system triggers the replenishment task. Scheduling (Section 4.2.6) of the replenishment activities results in an improved overall performance of the process.

The picking area layout should be integrated with the inbound and outbound flow. An efficient layout minimizes handling, maximizes space utilization, and reduces backtracking. The distance to other areas in the warehouse, such as reserve storage, must be considered in the layout design. Two layout alternatives include *U*-shaped and straight-through flow. Facility layout tools typically are used in practice to address the issues associated with the physical configuration of the warehouse.

Finally, picking methods must be established to determine material flow and standard operating procedures. Picking methods are defined in terms of pickers per order (the number of pickers that work on a single order at one time), lines per pick (the number of orders a single item is picked for at one time), and periods per shift (the frequency of order scheduling during one shift). An accurate order profile is required to determine the most appropriate picking method. Flowcharting (Section 4.1.4) is the main tool used to design effective picking methods.

The design of a picking process illustrates where some of the tools that were introduced in this chapter can be used to design a fairly complex process associated with the operation of a warehouse.

4.5 Summary

The knowledge and understanding of basic analysis tools for business process design is fundamental. Before one is able to employ more powerful tools to deal with the complexities of real business processes, it is essential to understand and apply the basic tools presented in this chapter. In some cases, these basic tools may be all that are needed to design a process. For instance, a process may be studied and viable designs may be developed using only flowcharts. Even in the cases when basic tools are not enough and analysts must escalate the level of sophistication, the concepts reviewed in this chapter are always needed as the foundation for the analysis.

4.6 References

Chase, R. B., N. J. Aquilano, and F. J. Jacobs. 1998. *Production and operations management—Manufacturing and services,* 8th edition. New York: McGraw-Hill/Irwin.

Cross, K. F., J. J. Feather, and R. L. Lynch. 1994. *Corporate renaissance: T1he art of reengineering.* Cambridge, MA: Blackwell Business.

Goldratt, E. M., and J. Cox. 1992. *The goal,* 2d revised edition. Great Barrington, MA: North River Press, Inc.

Hyer, N., and U. Wemmerlöv. 2002. *Reorganizing the factory: Competing through cellular manufacturing.* Portland, OR: Productivity Press.

Melnyk, S. and M. Swink. 2002. *Value-driven operations management: An integrated modular approach.* New York: McGrawHill/Irwin.

Saenz, N. 2000. It's in the pick. *IIE Solutions* 32(7): 36–38.

4.7 Discussion Questions and Exercises

1. Develop a general process chart for the requisition process in Exercise 1 of Chapter 1.
2. Develop a general process chart for the receiving and delivering process in Exercise 2 of Chapter 1.
3. Develop a process activity chart for the IBM Credit example in Section 1.1.2 of Chapter 1.
4. Develop a flowchart for the claims-handling process in Section 1.2.2 of Chapter 1.
5. A department within an insurance company is considering the layout for a redesigned process. A computer simulation was built to estimate the traffic from each pair of offices. The load matrix in Table 4.14 summarizes the daily traffic.

TABLE 4.14 Load Matrix for Problem 5

From\To	B	C	E	F
A	10	75		140
B			95	
C			130	130
D			10	
E				95

   a. If other factors are equal, which two offices should be located closest to one another?

   b. Figure 4.21 shows one possible layout for the department. What is the total load-distance score for this plan using rectilinear distance? (*Hint*: The rectilinear distance between offices A and B is 3.)

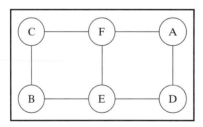

FIGURE 4.21 Possible Layout for Exercise 5

   c. Switching which two departments will most improve the total load-distance score?

6. A firm with four departments has the load matrix shown in Table 4.15 and the current layout shown in Figure 4.22.

TABLE 4.15 Load Matrix for Problem 6

From\To	B	C	D
A	12	10	8
B		20	6

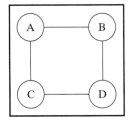

FIGURE 4.22 Current Layout for Exercise 6

   a. What is the load-distance score for the current layout? (Assume rectilinear distance.)

   b. Find a better layout. What is its total load-distance score?

7. A scientific journal uses the following process to handle submissions for publication.
  - The authors send the manuscript to the Journal Editorial Office (JEO).
  - The JEO sends a letter to the authors to acknowledge receipt of the manuscript. The JEO also sends a copy of the manuscript to the editor-in-chief (EIC).
  - The EIC selects an associate editor (AE) to be responsible for handling the manuscript and notifies the JEO.
  - The JEO sends a copy of the manuscript to the AE.
  - After reading the manuscript, the AE selects two referees who have agreed to review the paper. The AE then notifies the JEO.
  - The JEO sends copies of the manuscript to the referees.
  - The referees review the manuscript and send their reports to the JEO.
  - The JEO forwards the referee reports to the appropriate AE.
  - After reading the referee reviews, the AE decides whether the manuscript should be rejected, accepted, or revised. The decision is communicated to the JEO.
  - If the manuscript is rejected, the JEO sends a letter to the authors thanking them for the submission (and wishing them good luck getting the manuscript published somewhere else!).
  - If the manuscript is accepted, the JEO forwards the manuscript to production. The JEO also notifies the authors and the EIC.
  - If the manuscript needs revisions, the JEO forwards the referee reviews to the authors.
  - The authors revise the manuscript following the recommendations outlined in the referee reports. The authors then resubmit the manuscript to the JEO.
  - The JEO sends a resubmission directly to the responsible AE.
  - After reading a resubmitted manuscript, the AE decides whether the revised version can now be accepted or needs to be sent to the referees for further reviewing.
    - a. Construct a service system map for this process.
    - b. Identify opportunities for reengineering.

8. Calculate the efficiency of the line-balancing solution depicted in Figure 4.17.

9. Sola Communications has redesigned one of its core business processes. Processing times are not expected to vary significantly, so management wants to use the line-balancing approach to assign activities to workstations. The process has 11 activities, and the market demand is to process 4 jobs per 400-minute working day. Table 4.16 shows the standard time and immediate predecessors for each activity in the process.

   a. Construct a precedence diagram.

   b. Calculate the cycle time corresponding to a market demand of 4 jobs per day.

   c. What is the theoretical minimum number of workstations?

   d. Use the longest activity time rule as the primary rule to balance the line.

   e. What is the efficiency of the line? How does it compare with the theoretical maximum efficiency?

   f. Is it possible to improve the line's efficiency? Can you find a way of improving it?

10. A process consists of eight activities. The activity times and precedence relationships are given in Table 4.17. The process must be capable of satisfying a market demand of 50 jobs

TABLE 4.16 Data for Exercise 9

Activity	Time (in minutes)	Immediate Predecessor
A	70	—
B	15	A
C	8	—
D	32	—
E	47	C, D, G
F	25	B, E
G	61	—
H	52	—
I	29	G, H
J	42	I
K	50	F, J

TABLE 4.17 Data for Exercise 10

Activity	Time (in minutes)	Immediate Predecessor
A	5	—
B	4	—
C	2	A
D	3	A and B
E	2	B
F	6	D and E
G	3	C and F
H	2	F

per day in a 400-minute working day. Use the longest activity time rule to design a process line. Does the line achieve maximum efficiency?

11. A process manager wants to assign activities to workstations as efficiently as possible and achieve an hourly output rate of four jobs. The department uses a working time of 56 minutes per hour. Assign the activities shown in Table 4.18 (times are in minutes) to workstations using the "most followers" rule. Does the line of workstations achieve maximum efficiency?

TABLE 4.18 Data for Exercise 11

Activity	Time (in minutes)	Immediate Predecessor
A	3	—
B	2	A
C	4	B
D	7	—
E	4	D and G
F	5	—
G	6	F
H	9	C and E
I	5	H

12. A business process has a market demand of 35 jobs per day. A working day consists of 490 minutes, and the process activity times do not exhibit significant amounts of variation. A reengineering team would like to apply the line-balancing technique to assign activities to workstations. The activity times and the immediate predecessors of each activity are given in Table 4.19.
    a. Use the longest activity rule as the primary rule to assign activities to stations.
    b. Compare the efficiency of the line with the theoretical maximum efficiency. Is it possible to improve the line efficiency?

TABLE 4.19 Data for Exercise 12

Activity	Time (in minutes)	Immediate Predecessors
A	3	None
B	6	None
C	7	A
D	5	A, B
E	2	B
F	4	C
G	5	F
H	7	D, E
I	1	H
J	6	E
K	4	G, I, J

13. Longform Credit receives an average of 1,200 credit applications per day. Longform's advertising touts its efficiency in responding to all applications within hours. Daily application-processing activities, average times, and required preceding activities (activities that must be completed before the next activity) are listed in Table 4.20. Assuming an 8-hour day, find the best assignment of activities to workstations using the longest activity time rule. Calculate the efficiency of your design. Has your design achieved maximum efficiency?

TABLE 4.20 Data for Exercise 13

Activity	Description	Average Time (in minutes)	Immediately Preceding Activity
A	Open and stack applications	0.20	None
B	Process enclosed letter; make note of and handle any special requirements	0.37	A
C	Check off form 1 for page 1 of application	0.21	A
D	Check off form 2 for page 2 of application; file original copy of application	0.18	A
E	Calculate credit limit from standardized tables according to forms 1 and 2	0.19	C and D
F	Supervisor checks quotation in light of special processing of letter, notes type of form letter, address, and credit limit to return to applicant	0.39	B and D
G	Secretary types details on form letter and mails	0.36	E, F
	Total	1.90	

14. Suppose the jobs in Table 4.21 must be processed at a single facility. (All times are given in minutes.) Assume that processing starts after the last job arrives, that is at time 20. Compare

TABLE 4.21 Data for Exercise 14

Job	Arrival Time	Estimated Processing Time	Due Date	Importance
A	3	23	76	20
B	6	12	54	18
C	8	34	87	27
D	12	16	98	12
E	15	8	37	10
F	20	19	62	23

the performance of each of the following scheduling rules according to the average weighted tardiness, maximum tardiness, and number of tardy jobs.
a. FIFO
b. EDD
c. SPT

15. Consider the jobs in Table 4.22. Use Moore's Algorithm to find the sequence that minimizes the number of tardy jobs. Assume that processing can start at time zero.

TABLE 4.22 Data for Exercise 15

Job	A	B	C	D	E	F
Due Date	15	6	9	23	20	30
Processing time	10	3	4	8	10	6

16. Time commitments have been made to process seven jobs on a given day, starting at 9:00 A.M. The manager of the process would like to find a processing sequence that minimizes the number of tardy jobs. The processing times and due dates are given in Table 4.23.

TABLE 4.23 Data for Exercise 16

Jobs	A	B	C	D	E	F	G
Due Time	11:00	15:00	10:05	12:45	14:00	12:40	13:00
Processing Time	0:30	1:15	1:00	0:20	0:45	2:00	1:10

17. A telecommunications company needs to schedule five repair jobs on a particular day in five locations. The repair times (including processing, transportation, and breaks) for these jobs have been estimated as shown in Table 4.24. Also, the customer service representatives have made due date commitments as shown in the table. If a due date is missed, the repair needs to be rescheduled, so the company would like to minimize the number of missed due dates. Find the optimal sequence, assuming that the first repair starts at 8:00 A.M.

TABLE 4.24 Data for Exercise 17

Location	Repair Time	Due Date
Walnut	1:15	2 P.M.
Valmont	2:30	Noon
Topaz	1:45	10 A.M.
Wright	0:30	11 A.M.
Baseline	2:00	3 P.M.

CHAPTER 5

Managing Process Flows

A central idea in process dynamics is the notion of stocks and flows. Stocks are accumulations that are created due to the difference between the inflow to a process and its outflow. Everyone is familiar with stocks and flows. The finished goods inventory of a manufacturing firm is the stock of products in its warehouse. The number of people employed by a business also represents a stock—in this case, of resources. The balance in a checking account is a third example of a form of stock. Stocks are altered by inflows and outflows. For instance, a firm's inventory increases with the flow of production and decreases with the flow of shipments (and possibly other flows dues to spoilage and shrinkage). The workforce increases via a hiring rate and decreases via the rate of resignations, layoffs, and retirements. The balance of a bank account increases with deposits and decreases with withdrawals (Sterman, 2000).

This chapter uses the notion of stocks and flows in the context of business processes. Three operational variables typically are used to study processes in terms of their stocks and flows: *throughput, work-in-process,* and *cycle time*[1]. Also in this chapter, the relationship among these operational variables will be examined with what is known as Little's law. The chapter finishes with an application of *theory of constraints* to capacity analysis.

5.1 Business Processes and Flows

Any business process (i.e., manufacturing or service) can be characterized as a set of activities that transform inputs into outputs (see Chapter 1). There are two main methods for processing inputs. The first, *discrete processing*, is familiar to most people in manufacturing and service industries. It is the production of goods (e.g., cars, computers, television sets, and so on) or services (e.g., a haircut, a meal, a hotel night, and so on) that are sold in separate, identifiable units.

The second method is nondiscrete or *continuous processing*, where products are not distinct units and typically involve liquids, powders, or gases. Examples include such products as gasoline, pharmaceuticals, flour, paint, and such continuous processes as the production of textiles and the generation of electricity. Note that ultimately, almost all products from a continuous process become discrete at either the packing stage or the point of sale, as is the case with electrical power.

Most business processes are discrete, where a unit of flow being transformed is often referred to as a *flow unit* or a *job* (see Section 1.1.2). Typical jobs consist of customers, orders, bills, or information. Resources perform the transformation activities.

---

[1]Cycle time also is called production lead time or lead time in manufacturing environments..

139

As defined in Chapter 1, resources may be capital assets (e.g., real estate, machinery, equipment, or computer systems) or labor (i.e., the organization's employees and their expertise). A job follows a certain routing within a process, determining the temporal order in which activities are executed. Routing provides information about the activities to be performed, their sequence, the resources needed, and the time standards. Routings are job-dependent in most business processes. In general, a process (architecture) can be characterized in terms of its jobs, activities, resources, routings, and information structure (see also Chapter 1, Section 1.1.2).

Example 5.1[2]

Speedy Tax Services offers low-cost tax preparation services in many locations throughout New England. In order to expedite a client's tax return efficiently, Speedy's operations manager has established the following process. Upon entering a tax-preparation location, each client is greeted by a receptionist who asks a series of short questions to determine which type of tax service the client needs. This takes about 5 minutes. Clients are then referred to either a professional tax specialist if their tax return is complicated or a tax preparation associate if the return is relatively simple. The average time for a tax specialist to complete a return is 1 hour, and the average time for an associate to complete a return is 30 minutes. Typically, during the peak of the tax season, an office is staffed with six specialists and three associates, and it is open for 10 hours per day. After the tax returns have been completed, the clients are directed to see a cashier (each location has two cashiers) to pay for having their tax return prepared. This takes about 6 minutes per client to complete. During the peak of the tax season, an average of 100 clients per day come into a location, 70 percent of which require the services of a tax specialist.

This example includes four resource types: receptionist, tax specialists, tax preparation associates, and cashiers. The jobs to be processed are clients seeking help with their tax returns. The routing depends on whether the tax return is considered complicated. The routing also includes an estimate of the processing time at each activity.

As mentioned previously, the purpose of this chapter is to examine processes from a flow perspective. *Jobs* will be used here as the generic term for "units of flow." Jobs become process outflow after the completion of the activities in their specified routing. In manufacturing processes, industrial engineers are concerned with the flow of materials. In an order-fulfillment process, the flow of orders is the main focus. A process has three types of flows.

- *Divergent flows* refine or separate input into several outputs.
- *Convergent flows* bring several inputs together.
- *Linear flows* are the result of sequential steps.

One aspect of the process design is to determine the dominant flow in the process. For example, an order-fulfillment process can be designed to separate orders along product lines (or money value), creating separate linear flows. As an alternative, the process may perform a number of initial activities in sequence until the differences in the orders require branching, creating divergent flows.

In manufacturing, material flows have been given the following names based on the shape of the dominant flow (Finch and Luebbe, 1995).

- V-Plant: A process dominated by divergent flows.
- A-Plant: A process dominated by converging flows.
- I-Plant: A process dominated by linear flows.
- T-Plant: A hybrid process that yields a large number of end products in the last few stages.

---

[2]Adapted from *Fundamentals of Operations Management,* 4th edition, by M. M. Davis, N. J. Aquilano, and R. B. Chase, Boston: McGraw-Hill Irwin, 2003.

An important measure of flow dynamics is the *flow rate*, defined as "number of jobs per unit of time." Flow rates are not necessarily constant throughout a process over time. The notations $R_i(t)$ and $R_o(t)$ will be used to represent the inflow rates and the outflow rates at a particular time t. More precisely, we define the following.

$R_i(t) =$ rate of incoming jobs through all entry points into the process
$R_o(t) =$ rate of outgoing jobs through all exit points from the process

These definitions will be used to discuss key concepts that are used to model and manage flows.

5.1.1 THROUGHPUT RATE

Inflow rates and outflow rates vary over time, as indicated by the time-dependent notation of $R_i(t)$ and $R_o(t)$. Consider, for example, the inflow and outflow rates per time period t depicted in Figure 5.1.

The inflow rates during the first seven periods of time are larger than the outflow rates. However, during the eighth period (i.e., $t = 8$), the outflow rate is 10 jobs per unit of time, and the inflow rate is only 4. Using the notation, we have:

$$R_i(8) = 4$$
$$R_o(8) = 10$$

If we add all the $R_i(t)$ values and divide the sum by the number of time periods, we can calculate the average inflow rate R_i. Similarly, we can obtain the average outflow rate, denoted by R_o. In a stable process, $R_i = R_o$. Although the inflow and outflow rates of the process depicted in Figure 5.1 fluctuate considerably through time, the process can be considered stable over the time horizon of 30 periods because $R_i = R_o \approx$ five jobs per unit of time.

Process stability, however, is defined in terms of an infinite time horizon. In other words, in a stable process, the average inflow rate matches the average outflow rate as the number of periods tends to infinity. Hence, when analyzing stable processes, it is not necessary to differentiate between the average inflow rate and the average outflow

FIGURE 5.1 Inflow and Outflow Rates per Time Period

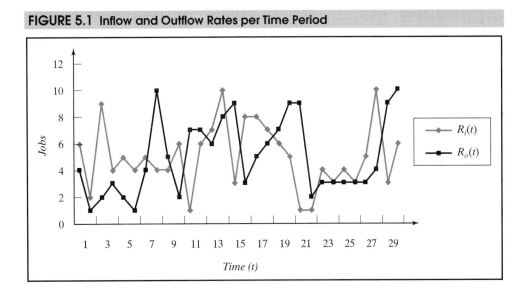

rate, because both of them simply represent the average flow rate through the process. The Greek letter λ (lambda) denotes the average flow rate or throughput rate of a stable process.

$$\lambda = R_i = R_O$$

In queuing theory, λ typically denotes the average effective arrival rate to the system; that is, the number of arrivals that eventually are served per unit of time (see Chapter 6, Section 6.2). In general, λ is often referred to as the process throughput (and is given in terms of jobs per unit of time).

5.1.2 WORK-IN-PROCESS

If a snapshot of a process is taken at any given point in time, it is likely that a certain number of jobs would be found within the confines of the process. These jobs have not reached any of the exit points of the process, because the transformation that represents the completion of these jobs has not been finished. As discussed in Section 4.2.2, the term *work-in-process* (WIP) originally was used to denote the inventory within a manufacturing system that is no longer raw material, but also not a finished product.

All jobs within the process boundaries are considered WIP, regardless of whether they are being processed or they are waiting to be processed. As discussed in Chapter 4, *batching* has significant impact on the amount of WIP in the process. To take advantage of a particular process configuration, managers often prefer to process a large number of jobs before changing the equipment to process something else or before passing the items to the next processing step. Insurance claims, for example, are sometimes processed in batches in the same way that catalog orders from mail order retailers are frequently batched. When an order is called in, the order is placed with a group of orders until the number of orders is considered sufficient to warrant sending them all to the warehouse to be filled and shipped. The accumulation of orders in some situations might increase the time that customers wait for a product because it might increase the amount of time the order spends in the process.

A trend in manufacturing has been to reduce the batch sizes in order to become more responsive to a market where customers expect shorter waiting times (see also Section 4.2.3). The just-in-time (JIT) manufacturing philosophy dictates that production batches should be as small as possible in order to decrease the time each job spends in the process. Thereby each job spends less time waiting for a batch to be completed before it is moved to the next step. However, the key to implementing this philosophy is to reduce the time required to make necessary changes to the equipment to process a different batch of jobs. This time is known as setup or changeover time. When setup time is lengthy, large batches are preferred because this implies fewer changeovers.

For instance, consider a bank that uses a machine to process checks, and suppose that the checks can be wallet size or book size. If changing the setup of the machine from one size to the other requires a considerable amount of time, then the manager in charge of the process might decide to run large batches of each job type to minimize the number of changeovers.

Companies have developed a variety of strategies to reduce changeover time. Better design of processes and parts has resulted in greater standardization of components, fewer components, and fewer changeovers. In addition, better organization and training of workers have made changeovers easier and faster. Improved design of equipment and fixtures also has made the reduction in changeover time possible (Finch and Luebbe, 1995).

For instance, one strategy that is commonly used to reduce setup time is to separate setup into preparation and actual setup. The idea is to do as much as possible (during the preparation) while the machine or process is still operating. Another strategy consists of moving the material closer to the equipment and improving the material handling in general.

Because the inflow rate and the outflow rate vary over time, the work-in-process also fluctuates. We refer to the work-in-process at time t as WIP(t). The up-and-down fluctuation of WIP(t) obeys the following rules:

- WIP(t) increases when $R_i(t) > R_o(t)$. The increase rate is $R_i(t) - R_o(t)$.
- WIP(t) decreases when $R_i(t) < R_o(t)$. The decrease rate is $R_o(t) - R_i(t)$.

Figure 5.2 shows the work-in-process level as observed over a period of time. From the beginning of the observation horizon to the time labeled as t_1, the outflow rate is larger than the inflow rate; therefore, the work-in-process is depleted at a rate that is the difference between the two flow rates. That is, the work-in-process decreases at a rate of $R_o(t) - R_i(t)$ during the beginning of the observation period until time t_1. During the time period from t_1 to t_2, the inflow rate is larger than the outflow rate; therefore, the work-in-process increases. The work-in-process stays constant from time t_2 to time t_3, indicating that the inflow and the outflow rates are equal during this period. In Figure 5.2, we consider that the inflow and outflow rates remain constant between any two consecutive time periods (e.g., between t_1 and t_2 or t_2 and t_3). For some processes, these time periods may be small. In the supermarket industry, for example, changes in the inflow and outflow rates are monitored every 15 minutes. These data are transformed into valuable information to make operational decisions, such as those related to labor scheduling.

The average work-in-process is also of interest. To calculate the average WIP, we add the number of jobs in the process during each period of time and divide the sum by the number of periods in the observed time horizon. We will use WIP to denote the

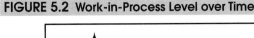

FIGURE 5.2 Work-in-Process Level over Time

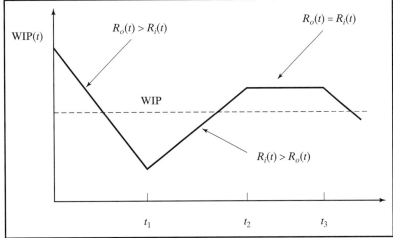

average (or expected) number of jobs in the process[3]. The dashed line in Figure 5.2 represents the average work-in-process during the observed period.

5.1.3 CYCLE TIME

Cycle time (also known as throughput time) is one of the most important measures of performance of a business process. This value is frequently the main focus when comparing the performance of alternative process designs. The cycle time is the time that it takes to complete an individual job from start to finish. In other words, it is the time that it takes for a job to go from the entry point to the exit point of a process. This is the time that a customer experiences. For example, the cycle time at a bank may be the time that elapses from the instant a customer enters the facility until the same customer leaves. In an Internet ordering process, cycle time may be the time elapsed from the time a customer places an order until the order is received at home. Because jobs follow different routings in a process, the cycle time can be considerably different from job to job. For example, some jobs might have a routing through a set of activities performed by resources with large capacity and, therefore, would not have to wait to be processed, resulting in shorter cycle times. On the other hand, long cycle times can be the result of jobs having to compete for scarce resources.

The cycle time of any given job is the difference between its departure time from the process and its arrival time to the process. If a customer joins a queue in the post office at 7:43 A.M. and leaves at 7:59 A.M., the customer's cycle time is 16 minutes. The average cycle time (CT) is the sum of the individual cycle times associated with a set of jobs divided by the total number of jobs[4]. The cycle time depends not only on the arrival rate of jobs in a given time period but also on the routing and the availability of resources.

Because the cycle time is the total time a job spends in the process, the cycle time includes the time associated with value-adding and non-value-adding activities. The cycle time typically includes:

- Processing time,
- Inspection time,
- Transportation time,
- Storage time,
- Waiting time (planned and unplanned delay time).

Processing time is often related to value-adding activities. However, in many cases, the processing time is only a small fraction of the cycle time. Cycle time analysis is a valuable tool for identifying opportunities to improve process performance. For example, if an insurance company finds out that it takes 100 days (on average) to process a new commercial account and that the actual processing time is only about 2 days, then there might be an opportunity for a significant process improvement with respect to cycle time.

5.1.4 LITTLE'S LAW

A fundamental relationship between throughput, work-in-process, and cycle time is known as Little's law. J. D. C. Little proposed a proof for this formula in connection with queuing theory (Little, 1961). The relationship, which has been shown to hold for a wide class of queuing situations, is:

$$\text{WIP} = \lambda \text{CT}$$

---

[3]In queuing theory, which will be introduced in Chapter 6, L is used to denote the expected number of jobs in the process.

[4]In queuing theory, the average cycle time is referred to as the expected time in the system and is denoted by W.

The formula states that the average number of jobs in the process is proportional to the average time that a job spends in the process, where the factor of proportionality is the average arrival rate. Little's law refers to the average (or expected) behavior of a process. The formula indicates that if two of the three operational measures can be managed (that is, their values are determined by conscious managerial decisions), the value of the third measure is also completely determined. Three basic relationships can be inferred from Little's law.

1. Work-in-process increases if the throughput rate or the cycle time increases.
2. The throughput rate increases if work-in-process increases or cycle time decreases.
3. Cycle time increases if work-in-process increases or the throughput rate decreases.

These relationships must be interpreted carefully. For example, is it true that in an order-fulfillment process, more work-in-process inventory results in an increase of cycle time? Most people would argue that higher levels of inventory (either of finished product or of work-in-process) should result in a shorter cycle time, because the order can be filled faster when the product is finished (or in the process to be finished) than when it has to be produced from scratch. Is Little's law contradicting common sense? The answer is no. A closer examination of the order-fulfillment process reveals that there are, in fact, two work-in-process inventories: one associated with purchasing orders and the other with products. In this case, Little's law applies only to the work-in-process inventory of orders and not to the inventory of products. Now it is reasonable to state that if the number of orders in the pipeline (i.e., the work-in-process inventory of orders) increases, the cycle time experienced by the customer also increases.

Finally, some companies use a performance measure known as *inventory turns* or *turnover ratio*. If WIP is the number of jobs in a process at any point in time, then the turnover ratio indicates how often the WIP is replaced in its entirety by a new set of jobs. The turnover ratio is simply the reciprocal of the cycle time; that is:

$$\text{Turnover ratio} = \frac{1}{\text{CT}}$$

Example 5.2

An insurance company processes an average of 12,000 claims per year. Management has found that on average, at any one time, 600 applications are at various stages of processing (e.g., waiting for additional information from the customer, in transit from the branch office to the main office, waiting for an authorization, and so on). If it is assumed that a year includes 50 working weeks, how many weeks (on the average) does processing a claim take?

$$\lambda = \frac{12,000}{50} = 240 \text{ claims/week}$$
$$\text{WIP} = 600 \text{ jobs}$$
$$\text{WIP} = \lambda\,\text{CT}$$
$$\text{CT} = \frac{\text{WIP}}{\lambda} = \frac{600}{240} = 2.5 \text{ weeks}$$

Little's law indicates that the average cycle time for this claim process is 2.5 weeks. Suppose management does not consider this cycle time acceptable (because customers have been complaining that the company takes too long to process their claims). What options does management have to reduce the cycle time to, say, 1 week? According to Little's law, in order to reduce the cycle time, either the work-in-process must be reduced or the throughput rate must be increased.

A process redesign project is conducted, and it is found that most claims experience long, unplanned delays (e.g., waiting for more information). The new process is able to minimize or eliminate most of the unplanned delays, reducing the average work-in-process by half. The cycle time for the redesigned process is then:

$$CT = \frac{WIP}{\lambda} = \frac{300}{240} = 1.25 \text{ weeks}$$

5.2 Cycle Time and Capacity Analysis

In this section, the concepts of cycle time, throughput, and work-in-process inventory are used along with Little's law to analyze the capacity of processes. A process is still viewed as a set of activities that transforms inputs into outputs. Jobs are routed through a process, and resources perform the activities. The routing of jobs and the possibility of rework affect cycle time, and the amount of resources and their capabilities affect process capacity.

5.2.1 CYCLE TIME ANALYSIS

Cycle time analysis refers to the task of calculating the average cycle time for an entire process or a process segment. The cycle time calculation assumes that the time to complete each activity is available. The activity times are average values and include waiting time (planned and unplanned delays). Flow diagrams are used to analyze cycle times, assuming that only one type of job is being processed. In the simplest case, a process may consist of a sequence of activities with a single path from an entry point to an exit point. In this case, the cycle time is simply the sum of the activity times. However, not all processes have such a trivial configuration. Therefore, the cycle time analysis needs to be considered in the presence of rework, multiple paths, and parallel activities.

Rework

An important consideration when analyzing cycle times relates to the possibility of rework. Many processes use control activities to monitor the quality of the work. These control activities (or inspection points) often use specified criteria to allow a job to continue processing. That is, the inspection points act as an accept/reject mechanism. The rejected jobs are sent back for further processing, affecting the average cycle time and ultimately the capacity of the process (as will be discussed in the next section).

Example 5.3

Figure 5.3 shows the effect of rework on the average cycle time of a process segment. In this example, it is assumed that each activity (i.e., receiving the request and filling out parts I and II of the order form) requires 10 minutes (as indicated by the number between parentheses) and that the inspection (the decision symbol labeled "Errors?") is done in 4 minutes on the average. The jobs are processed sequentially through the first three activities, and then the jobs are inspected for errors. The inspection rejects an average of 25 percent of the jobs. Rejected jobs must be reworked through the last two activities associated with filling in the information in the order form.

Without the rework, the cycle time of this process segment from the entry point (i.e., receiving the request) to the exit point (out of the inspection activity) is 34 minutes; that is, the sum of the activity times and the inspection time. Because 25 percent of the jobs are rejected and must be processed through the activities that fill out the order form as well as being inspected once more, the cycle time increases by 6 minutes (24×0.25) to a total of 40 minutes on the average. In this case, the assumption is that jobs are rejected only one time.

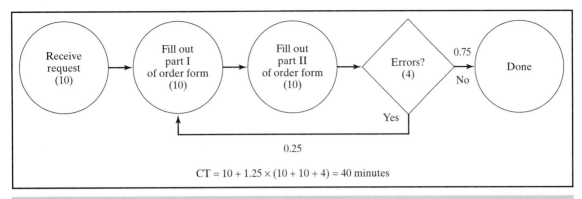

$$CT = 10 + 1.25 \times (10 + 10 + 4) = 40 \text{ minutes}$$

FIGURE 5.3 Cycle Time Calculation with a Rework Loop

If it is assumed that the rejection percentage after the inspection in a rework loop is given by r, and that the sum of the times of activities within the loop (including inspection) is given by T, then the following general formula can be used to calculate the cycle time from the entry point to the exit point of the rework loop.

$$CT = (1 + r) \times T$$

This formula assumes that the rework is done only once. That is, it assumes that the probability of an error after the first rejection goes down to zero. If the probability of making an error after an inspection remains the same, then the cycle time through the rework loop can be calculated as follows.

$$CT = \frac{T}{1 - r}$$

In Example 5.3, the average cycle time for the entire process would be calculated as follows, taking into consideration that the probability of an error remains at 25 percent regardless of the number of times the job has been inspected:

$$CT = 10 + \frac{(10 + 10 + 4)}{0.75} = 42 \text{ minutes}$$

Multiple Paths

In addition to rework, a process might include routings that create separate paths for jobs after specified decision points. For example, a process might have a decision point that splits jobs into "fast track" and "normal track." In this case, a percentage must be given to indicate the fraction of jobs that follow each path.

Example 5.4

Figure 5.4 shows a flowchart of the process for Speedy Tax Services described in Example 5.1. All clients are received by the receptionist, after which a decision is made to send a fraction of the clients to a professional tax specialist and the remaining clients to a tax preparation associate. On the average, 70 percent of the clients have complicated tax returns and need to work with a professional tax specialist. The remaining 30 percent of the clients have simple tax returns and can be helped by tax preparation associates. The numbers between parentheses associated with each activity indicate the activity time (in minutes). With this information, the average cycle time associated with this process can be calculated. In this case, the cycle time represents the average time that it takes for a client to complete his or her tax return and pay for the service.

The cycle time calculation in Figure 5.4 represents the sum of the contribution of each activity time to the total. All clients are received by a receptionist, so the contribution of this

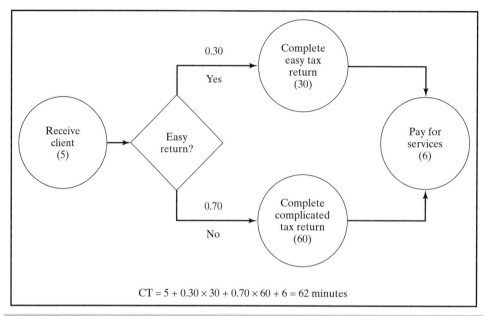

$$CT = 5 + 0.30 \times 30 + 0.70 \times 60 + 6 = 62 \text{ minutes}$$

FIGURE 5.4 Cycle Time Calculation with Multiple Paths

activity to the total cycle time is 5 minutes. Similarly, the contribution of the last activity to the cycle time is 6 minutes, given that all clients must pay before leaving the facility. The contribution of the other two activities in the process is weighted by the percentage of clients that are routed through each of the two paths.

A general formula can be derived for a process with multiple paths. Assume that m paths originate from a decision point. Also assume that the probability that a job follows path i is p_i and that the sum of activity times in path i is T_i. Then the average cycle time across all paths is given by:

$$CT = p_1 \times T_1 + p_2 \times T_2 + \ldots + p_m \times T_m$$

Parallel Activities

Cycle time analysis also should contemplate routings in which activities are performed in parallel. For example, a technician in a hospital can set up the X-ray machine for a particular type of shot (as required by a physician), while the patient prepares (e.g., undresses). These two activities occur in parallel, because it is not necessary for the technician to wait until the patient is ready before starting to set up the X-ray machine. Because one of these activities will require less time, the other has to wait for further processing. Typically, the patient will finish first and will wait to be called for the X ray. The contribution to the cycle time is then given by the maximum time from all the parallel activities.

Example 5.5

Figure 5.5 depicts a process with five activities. The first activity consists of opening an envelope and splitting its contents into three different items: application, references, and credit history. Each of these items is processed in parallel, and a decision is made regarding this request after the parallel activities have been completed. The numbers between parentheses in Figure 5.5 are activity times in minutes.

The cycle time calculation in Figure 5.5 results in a total of 40 minutes for the process under consideration. This is the sum of 5 minutes for the first activity, 20 minutes for checking the credit history (which is the parallel activity with the longest time), and 15 minutes for

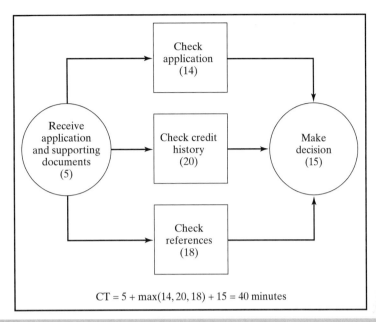

$$CT = 5 + \max(14, 20, 18) + 15 = 40 \text{ minutes}$$

FIGURE 5.5 Cycle Time Calculation with Parallel Activities

making a decision. Note that the flow diagram in Figure 5.5 has no decision point after the first activity, because all the jobs are split in the same way; that is, the routing of all the jobs is the same and includes the parallel processing of the "checking" activities. Note also that these are considered inspection activities, and therefore the square is used to represent them in the flow-chart in Figure 5.5.

The general formula for process segments with parallel activities is a simplification of the one associated with multiple paths. Because there is no decision point when the jobs are split, it is not necessary to account for probability values. It is assumed that T_i is the total time of the activities in path i (after the split) and that the process splits into m parallel paths. Then the cycle time for the process segment with parallel paths is given by:

$$CT = \max(T_1, T_2, \ldots, T_m)$$

Example 5.6

Before concluding this section, let us apply the aforementioned principles for cycle time analysis to a small process. Assume that a process has been described and that the flow diagram in Figure 5.6 was drawn appropriately from these descriptions. The numbers in paranthesis shown in Figure 5.6 are activity times in minutes. The process consists of nine activities. A decision point is included after activity A, because only 30 percent of the jobs are required to go through activity B. A rework loop sends jobs back from the inspection point I to activity D. This loop assumes that the reworked jobs are examined a second time and that they always pass the inspection; that is, jobs are reworked only one time. The process has two parallel activities, F and G, before the last activity is performed.

The cycle time calculation that corresponds to the process in Figure 5.6 starts with the time for activity A. Next, the contribution of 6 minutes (i.e., 0.3×20) from activity B is added. This is followed by the time of activity C (23 minutes) and the contribution of the activities in the rework loop. Note that the times within the rework loop are added, including the inspection time, and multiplied by 110 percent. This operation accounts for the 10 percent of jobs that are sent back after inspection. Finally, the contribution of the parallel activities is calculated as the maximum time between activity F and G, followed by the activity time for H. The average cycle time for this process is determined to be 92.5 minutes.

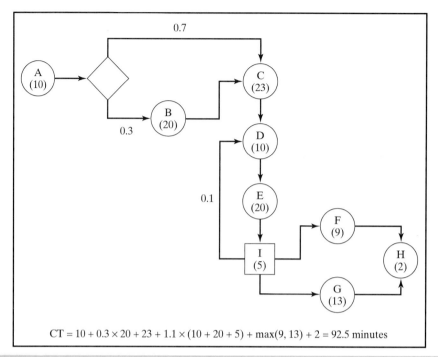

$$CT = 10 + 0.3 \times 20 + 23 + 1.1 \times (10 + 20 + 5) + \max(9, 13) + 2 = 92.5 \text{ minutes}$$

FIGURE 5.6 An Example of Cycle Time Analysis

After calculating the cycle time of a process, the analyst should calculate what is known as the *cycle time efficiency*. Assuming that all processing times are value adding, the cycle time efficiency indicates the percentage of time, from the actual cycle time, that is spent performing value-adding work. Mathematically, the cycle time efficiency is expressed as follows.

$$\text{Cycle time efficiency} = \frac{\text{Process time}}{\text{CT}}$$

Process time also is referred to as the *theoretical cycle time,* because theoretically a job can be completed in that time (that is, if no waiting would occur). To calculate the *process time*, replace activity time with the processing time (i.e., the activity time minus the waiting time). It should be recognized that the cycle time efficiency calculated here is conceptually the same as the efficiency calculation in Chapter 4, which was connected with line balancing.

Example 5.7

Table 5.1 shows the time values associated with the activities in Example 5.6. The time values are broken down into processing time and waiting time. The activity time is the sum of these two values.

Using the processing times in Table 5.1 and the flow diagram in Figure 5.6, the process time (or theoretical cycle time) can be calculated as follows.

$$\text{Process time} = 2 + 0.3 \times 5 + 8 + 1.1 \times (3 + 4 + 4) + \max(2, 4) + 2 = 29.6 \text{ minutes}$$

The cycle time efficiency can now be found as follows.

$$\text{Cycle time efficiency} = \frac{29.6}{92.5} = 0.32$$

This means that less than one third of the actual cycle time is spent in processing, and the rest of the time is spent waiting.

TABLE 5.1 Activity Times for Example 5.7

Activity	Processing Time (in min.)	Waiting Time (in min.)	Activity Time (in min.)
A	2	8	10
B	5	15	20
C	8	15	23
D	3	7	10
E	4	16	20
Inspection	4	1	5
F	2	7	9
G	4	9	13
H	2	0	2

Redesign projects in several industries (e.g., insurance, hospitals, and banking) indicate that it is not unusual to find cycle time efficiencies of less than 5 percent. This occurs, for example, in applications for a new insurance policy, where the process time is typically 7 minutes and the cycle time is normally 72 hours.

5.2.2 CAPACITY ANALYSIS

Capacity analysis complements the information obtained from a cycle time analysis when studying flows in a process. Flowcharts are important also for analyzing capacity, because the first step in the methodology consists of estimating the number of jobs that flow through each activity. This step is necessary because resources (or pools of resources) perform the activities in the process, and their availability limits the overall capacity. The number of jobs flowing through each activity is determined by the configuration of the process, which may include, as in the case of the cycle time analysis, rework, multiple paths, and parallel activities.

Rework

When a process or process segment has a rework loop, the number of jobs flowing through each activity varies according to the rejection rate.

Example 5.8

Figure 5.7 depicts a process with a rework loop. Requests are processed through three activities and then inspected for errors. Suppose 100 requests are received. Because an average of 25 percent of the requests are rejected, the second and third activities, which are inside the

FIGURE 5.7 Number of Requests Flowing Through Each Activity in a Process with Rework

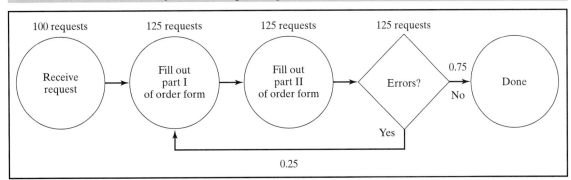

rework loop, end up processing 125 jobs in the long run. This is assuming that rejected requests always pass inspection the second time.

Next, a general formula is derived for calculating the number of jobs per activity in a rework loop. Assume that n jobs enter the rework loop and that the probability of rejecting a job at the inspection station is r. The number of jobs flowing through each activity in the loop, including the inspection station, is given by the following equation.

$$\text{Number of jobs} = (1 + r) \times n$$

When the rejection rate stays the same regardless of the number of times that a job has been reworked and inspected, then the number of jobs that are processed by activities inside the rework loop is given by the following equation.

$$\text{Number of jobs} = \frac{n}{1 - r}$$

According to this formula, the activities inside the rework loop in Example 5.8 (see Figure 5.7) process 133.33 requests on the average.

Multiple Paths

The job routings in a process may include decision points that create multiple paths. The flow through each path varies according to the frequency with which each path is selected (as indicated in the decision point).

Example 5.9

Figure 5.8 shows a flowchart of the process for Speedy Tax Services described in Example 5.1, which contains multiple paths. Assume that 100 clients enter the process, and we want to calculate the number of clients that are processed at each activity on the average.

Because 30 percent of the clients have simple tax returns, about 30 clients out of 100 are helped by tax preparation associates. On the average, the remaining 70 clients are helped by

FIGURE 5.8 Number of Clients Flowing Through Each Activity in a Process with Multiple Paths

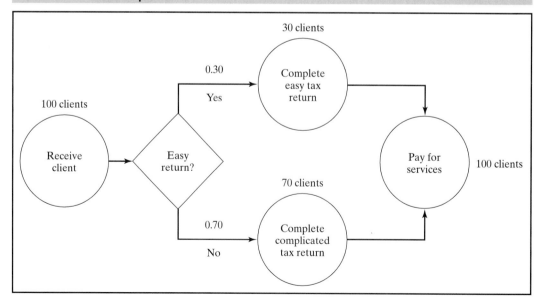

professional tax specialists. It is important to note that all 100 clients must pay for the services rendered, so they are routed through the cashiers.

To derive a general formula for the number of jobs in each path, assume that the probability that a job follows path i is p_i. Also assume that n jobs enter the decision point. Then, the number of jobs in path i is given by the following equation.

$$\text{Number of jobs in path } i = p_i \times n$$

Parallel Activities

When jobs split into parallel activities, the number of jobs flowing through each activity remains the same as the number of jobs that enter the process (or process segment).

Example 5.10

Figure 5.9 shows a process with five activities, three of which are performed in parallel. Assuming that 100 applications are received, all activities experience the same load of 100 applications, as shown in Figure 5.9.

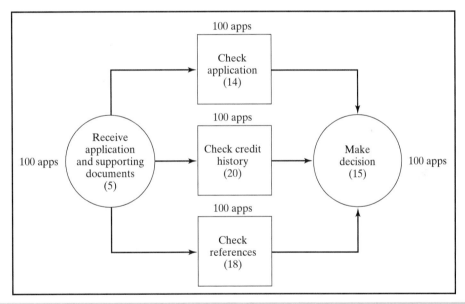

FIGURE 5.9 Number of Applications Flowing Through Each Activity in a Process with Parallel Activities

In this case, no general formula is necessary, because the number of jobs remains the same after a split into parallel activities or paths. The next step in analyzing capacity is to determine the capacity of each resource or pool of resources. This calculation is illustrated using the process of Example 5.6, whose flowchart is depicted in Figure 5.6.

Example 5.11

For each activity in the process, the processing time, the type of resource required, and the number of jobs processed through each activity must be known. This information is summarized in Table 5.2.

The available resources of each type also must be known. Table 5.2 indicates that there are three types of resources, labeled R1, R2, and R3. Assume that there are two units of resource R1, two units of resource R2, and one unit of resource R3.

TABLE 5.2 Resource Capacity Data for Example 5.11

Activity	Processing Time (in min.)	Resource Requirement	Number of Jobs
A	2	R1	1
B	5	R1	0.3
C	8	R2	1
D	3	R2	1.1
E	4	R2	1.1
Inspection	4	—	1.1
F	2	R1	1
G	4	R3	1
H	2	R3	1

TABLE 5.3 Pool Capacity Calculation for Example 5.11

Resource	Unit Load (min.)	Unit Capacity (jobs/min.)	Available Resources (units)	Pool Capacity (jobs/min.)
R1	$2 + 5 \times 0.3 + 2 = 5.5$	1/5.5	2	2/5.5 = 0.36
R2	$8 + 1.1 \times (3 + 4) = 15.7$	1/15.7	2	2/15.7 = 0.13
R3	$4 + 2 = 6$	1/6	1	1/6 = 0.17

The resource unit and pool capacity can now be calculated as follows. For each resource type, find the unit load. To calculate the *unit load* for a given resource, first multiply the processing time by the number of jobs for each activity for which the resource is required, and then add the products. This is illustrated in the second column of Table 5.3. The *unit capacity* for each resource is the reciprocal of the unit load and indicates the number of jobs that each unit of resource can complete per unit of time. This is shown in the third column of Table 5.3.

Finally, to find the *pool capacity* associated with each resource type, multiply the number of resource units (i.e., the resource availability) by the unit capacity. The values corresponding to resources R1, R2, and R3 are shown in column 5 of Table 5.3 (labeled Pool Capacity).

The pool capacities in Table 5.3 indicate that resource R2 is the bottleneck of the process, because this resource type has the smallest pool capacity. The pool capacity of R2 is 0.13 jobs per minute or 7.8 jobs per hour, compared to 0.36 jobs per minute or 21.6 jobs per hour for R1 and 0.17 jobs per minute or 10.2 jobs per hour for R3.

It is important to realize that the bottleneck of a process refers to a resource or resource pool and not to an activity. In other words, capacity is not associated with activities but with resources. Also note that because the slowest resource pool limits the throughput rate of the process, the *process capacity* is determined by the capacity of the bottleneck. Therefore, the capacity of the process depicted in Figure 5.6 is 7.8 jobs per hour.

The process capacity, as previously calculated, is based on processing times instead of activity times. Because processing times do not include waiting time, the process capacity calculation is a value that can be achieved only in theory. That is, if jobs are processed without any delays (either planned or unplanned), the process can achieve its theoretical capacity of 7.8 jobs per hour. In all likelihood, however, the process actual throughput rate (or actual capacity) will not match the theoretical process capacity; therefore, a measure of efficiency can be calculated. The measure in this case is known as the *capacity utilization*, and it is defined as follows.

$$\text{Capacity utilization} = \frac{\text{Throughput rate}}{\text{Process capacity}}$$

With this mathematical relationship, the capacity utilization can be calculated for each resource type in a process.

Example 5.12

Assume that the throughput rate of the process in Example 5.11 is six jobs per hour. This additional piece of information gives the following capacity utilization values for each resource in the process.

$$\text{Capacity utilization for R1} = \frac{6}{21.8} = 27.5\%$$

$$\text{Capacity utilization for R2} = \frac{6}{7.8} = 76.9\%$$

$$\text{Capacity utilization for R3} = \frac{6}{10.2} = 58.8\%$$

Similar to the way the capacity of the process is related to the capacity of the bottleneck resource, the capacity utilization of the process is related to the capacity utilization at the bottleneck. Thus, based on the calculations in Example 5.12 the capacity utilization of the process in Example 5.11 is 76.9 percent.

5.3 Managing Cycle Time and Capacity

The analysis of cycle time and capacity provides process managers with valuable information about the performance of the process. This information, however, is wasted if managers do not translate it into action. Through cycle time analysis, managers and process designers can find out the cycle time efficiency of the process and discover, for example, that the waiting time in the process is excessive for a desired level of customer service. This section discusses ways to reduce cycle time and strategies to increase capacity.

5.3.1 CYCLE TIME REDUCTION

Process cycle time can be reduced in five fundamental ways.

1. Eliminate activities.
2. Reduce waiting time.
3. Eliminate rework.
4. Perform activities in parallel.
5. Move processing time to a noncritical activity.

The first thing that analysts of business processes should consider is the elimination of activities. As discussed in earlier chapters, most of the activities in a process do not add value to the customer; therefore, they should be considered for elimination. Non-value-adding activities, such as those discussed in Chapter 1, increase the cycle time but are not essential to the process.

  If an activity cannot be eliminated, then eliminating or minimizing the waiting time reduces the activity time. Recall that the activity time is the sum of the processing time and the waiting time. It is worth investigating ways to speed up the processing of jobs at an activity, but larger time reductions are generally easier to achieve when waiting time is eliminated. Waiting time can be reduced, for example, by decreasing batch sizes and set up times. Also, improved job scheduling typically results in less waiting and better utilization of resources.

Example 5.3 shows that rework loops add a significant amount of time to the process cycle time. As shown in that example, the cycle time when the activities are performed "right" the first time, and thus eliminating the need for the rework loop, is 85 percent (or 34/40) of the original cycle time. If the jobs always pass inspection, the inspection activity also can be eliminated, reducing the cycle time to 30 minutes. This represents a 25 percent reduction from the original design.

Changing a process design to perform activities in parallel has an immediate impact on the process cycle time. This was discussed in Chapter 4, where the notion of combining activities is the cornerstone of the process design principle known as case management, as described in Chapter 3.) Mathematically, the reduction of cycle time from a serial process configuration to a parallel process configuration is the difference between the sum of the activity times and the maximum of the activity times. To illustrate, suppose that the "checking" activities in Figure 5.5 were performed in series instead of in parallel. The average cycle time for completing one application becomes:

$$CT = 5 + 14 + 20 + 18 + 15 = 72 \text{ minutes}$$

The cycle time with parallel processing was calculated to be 40 minutes. The difference of 32 minutes also can be calculated as follows.

$$\Delta CT = (14 + 20 + 18) - \max(14, 20, 18) = 52 - 20 = 32$$

Finally, cycle time decreases when some work content (or processing time) is shifted from a critical activity to a noncritical activity. In a process with parallel processing (i.e., with a set of activities performed in parallel), the longest path (in terms of time) is referred to as the critical path. The length of the critical path corresponds to the cycle time of the process.

Example 5.13

Consider, for instance, the activities depicted in Figure 5.5. This process has three paths.

Path	Length
Receive → Check Application → Decide	5 + 14 + 15 = 34 minutes
Receive → Check Credit → Decide	5 + 20 + 15 = 40 minutes
Receive → Check References → Decide	5 + 18 + 15 = 38 minutes

The longest path is the second one with a length of 40 minutes.

Then the critical activities are Receive, Check Credit, and Decide, and the path length of 40 minutes matches the cycle time calculated in Figure 5.5.

Example 5.14

Figure 5.10 depicts a process with six activities. In this process, activities C and D are performed in parallel along with activity E. Assume that the numbers between parentheses are activity times. The process has two paths.

Path	Length
A → B → C → D → F	10 + 20 + 15 + 5 + 10 = 60 minutes
A → B → E → F	10 + 20 + 12 + 10 = 52 minutes

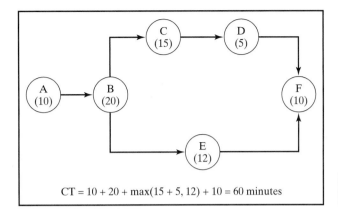

$$CT = 10 + 20 + \max(15 + 5, 12) + 10 = 60 \text{ minutes}$$

FIGURE 5.10 Original Process in Example 5.14

The critical activities in the original process are A, B, C, D, and F. These activities belong to the critical path. In order to reduce cycle time, a redesigned process might move some work from a critical activity to a noncritical activity. In this case, activity E is the only non-critical activity. Suppose it is possible to move 4 minutes of work from activity C to activity E. This change effectively reduces the cycle time by 4 minutes, making both paths critical. That is, both paths of activities in the process now have the same length of 56 minutes; therefore, all the activities in the process have become critical. Note also that in the following calculation of the cycle time, both of the time values compared in the "max" function equal 16 minutes.

$$CT = 10 + 20 + \max(11 + 5, 16) + 10 = 56 \text{ minutes}$$

We next examine ways to increase process capacity.

5.3.2 INCREASING PROCESS CAPACITY

Section 5.2.2 examined the direct relationship between process capacity and the capacity of the bottleneck resource. Given this relationship, it is reasonable to conclude that making the bottleneck resource faster results in an increase of process capacity. Capacity of the process can be increased in two fundamental ways.

- Add resource availability at the bottleneck.
- Reduce the workload at the bottleneck.

Adding resources to the bottleneck might mean additional investment in equipment and labor or additional working hours (i.e., overtime). In other words, the available resources at the bottleneck can be increased with either more workers or with the same workers working more hours.

The approach of reducing workload at the bottleneck is more closely linked to the notion of process redesign. The reduction consists of either shifting activities from the bottleneck to a different resource pool or reducing the time of the activities currently assigned to the bottleneck. Shifting activities from one resource pool to another requires cross training so that workers in a nonbottleneck resource pool can perform new activities.

One must be careful when considering redesign strategies with the goal of reducing cycle time and increasing process capacity. Specifically, the decision must take into consideration the availability of resources and the assignment of activities to each resource pool.

Example 5.15

Assume that five resource types are associated with the process in Figure 5.10. Also assume that each type of resource has only one available unit. Finally, assume that activities A, B, C, and D are assigned to resources R1, R2, R3, and R4, respectively, and that activities E and F are assigned to resource R5. Given these assignments and assuming, for simplicity, that for all activities the processing times equals the activity times in Figure 5.10, the theoretical capacity of the original process can be calculated as shown in Table 5.4.

TABLE 5.4 Capacity of the Original Process

Resource	Unit Load (min.)	Unit Capacity (jobs/min.)	Available Resources (units)	Pool Capacity (jobs/hour)
R1	10	1/10	1	60/10 = 6.0
R2	20	1/20	1	60/20 = 3.0
R3	15	1/15	1	60/15 = 4.0
R4	5	1/5	1	60/5 = 12.0
R5	12 + 10 = 22	1/22	1	60/22 = 2.7

The bottleneck is resource R5 with a capacity of 2.7 jobs per hour, which also becomes the process capacity. The cycle time for this process was calculated to be 60 minutes.

If the process is modified in such a way that 4 minutes of work are transferred from activity C to activity E, then, as shown in Example 5.14, the cycle time is reduced to 56 minutes. Does the process capacity change as a result of this process modification? Table 5.5 shows the process capacity calculations associated with the modified process.

TABLE 5.5 Capacity of the Modified Process

Resource	Unit Load (min.)	Unit Capacity (jobs/min.)	Available Resources (units)	Pool Capacity (jobs/hour)
R1	10	1/10	1	60/10 = 6.0
R2	20	1/20	1	60/20 = 3.0
R3	11	1/11	1	60/11 = 5.4
R4	5	1/5	1	60/5 = 12.0
R5	16 + 10 = 26	1/26	1	60/26 = 2.3

The calculations in Table 5.5 indicate that the process capacity decreases as a result of the decision to transfer units from a critical activity to a noncritical activity associated with the bottleneck resource R5. At first glance, this result seems to contradict Little's law, which specifies that the throughput rate increases when cycle time decreases. In this case, cycle time decreased from 60 minutes to 56 minutes, and the process capacity (measured in units of throughput) decreased from 2.7 jobs/hour to 2.3 jobs/hour.

The change in the level of work-in-process explains this apparent contradiction. Although it is true that a shorter cycle time should increase the throughput rate, this holds only if the work-in-process remains unchanged. In this example, the decision to move processing time from activity C to activity E decreases cycle time and throughput rate, and as a result also decreases the work-in-process.

5.4 Theory of Constraints

Bottlenecks affect the efficiency of processes because they limit throughput, and in many cases they also inhibit the achievement of value-based goals, such as quality, speed, cost, and flexibility. Bottlenecks often are responsible for the differences between what operation managers promise and what they deliver to internal and external customers

(Melnyk and Swink, 2002). Due to the importance of bottlenecks, it is not sufficient to be able to identify their existence. That is, locating the bottlenecks in a process is just part of managing flows; the other part deals with increasing process efficiency despite these limitations. This section introduces a technique for managing bottlenecks that is known as theory of constraints.

Theory of constraints (TOC) provides a broad theoretical framework for managing flows. It emphasizes the need for identifying bottlenecks (or constraints) within a process, the entire firm, or even the business context. For example, an organization's information system represents a constraint if the order-entry function takes longer to prepare an order for release than the transformation process needs to make the product. Other constraints could be associated with resources that perform activities in areas such as marketing, product design and development, or purchasing. All of these constraints limit throughput and, therefore, affect the efficiency of the system.

As mentioned in Chapter 4, TOC draws extensively from the work of Eli Goldratt, an Israeli physicist. TOC leads to an operating philosophy that in some ways is similar to just-in-time[5]. TOC assumes that the goal of a business organization is to make money. To achieve this goal, the company must focus on throughput, inventory, and operating expenses. In order to increase profit, a company must increase throughput and decrease inventory and operating expenses. Then, companies must identify operations policies that translate into actions that move these variables in the right directions. However, these policies have to live within a set of relevant constraints.

Theory of constraints gets its name from the concept that a constraint is anything that prevents a system from achieving higher levels of performance relative to its goal (Vonderembse and White, 1994). Consider the following situations where decisions must be made in constrained settings.

Example 5.16

A company produces products A and B using the same process. The unit profit for product A is $80, and the market demand is 100 units per week. The unit profit for product B is $50, and the market demand is 200 units per week. The process requires 0.4 hours to produce one unit of A and 0.2 hours to produce one unit of B. The process is available 60 hours per week. Because of this constraint, the process is unable to meet the entire demand for both products. Consequently, the company must decide how many products of each type to make. This situation is generally known as the product-mix problem.

If the objective of the company is to maximize total profit, one would be inclined to recommend the largest possible production of A, because this product has the largest profit margin. This production plan can be evaluated as follows. First, calculate the maximum number of units of A that can be produced in 60 hours of work.

$$\text{Units of A} = (60 \text{ hours / week}) / (0.4 \text{ hours / unit}) = 150 \text{ units}$$

Although 150 units can be produced per week, the market demands only 100. Therefore, the production plan would recommend 100 units of A. Because producing 100 units of A requires 40 hours of process time (i.e., 0.4×100), then 20 hours are still available to produce product B. This process time translates into 100 units of product B (i.e., 20/0.2). The total profit associated with this production plan is:

$$\text{Total profit} = \$80 \times 100 + \$50 \times 100 = \$13,000$$

Is this the best production plan? That is, does this production plan maximize weekly profits? To answer this question, first examine an alternative plan. If the company first attempts to meet

---

[5]Originally developed by Toyota, just-in-time (JIT) is now being used by many organizations around the world, including General Motors, Apple Computers, IBM, and others. JIT is mostly known for allowing companies to become more efficient by keeping low levels of inventory. However, JIT is more than just another inventory control system, because its underlying philosophy for managing operations influences all parts of a company.

the demand for product B, then the required process time would be 40 hours (i.e., 200 × 0.2). This would leave 20 hours to produce product A, resulting in 50 units (i.e., 20/0.4). The total profit associated with this plan would be:

$$\text{Total profit} = \$80 \times 50 + \$50 \times 200 = \$14,000$$

The alternative plan increases total profit by $1,000 per week. This example shows that when constraints are present, decisions cannot be made using simplistic rules. In this case, we attempted to solve the problem by simply maximizing the production of the product with the largest profit margin. This solution, however, takes into consideration neither the production constraints nor the market demand constraints.

Example 5.17

A department store chain has hired an advertising firm to determine the types and amounts of advertising it should have for its stores. The three types of advertising available are radio and television commercials and newspaper ads. The retail chain desires to know the number of each type of advertisement it should pursue in order to maximize exposure. It has been estimated that each ad or commercial will reach the potential audience shown in Table 5.6. This table also shows the cost associated with each type of advertisement.

TABLE 5.6 Advertising Data

Type of Advertisement	Exposure (people/ad or commercial)	Cost
Television	20,000	$15,000
Radio	12,000	$6,000
Newspaper	9,000	$4,000

In order to make a decision, the company must consider the following constraints.

1. The budget limit for advertisement is $100,000.
2. The television station has time available for four commercials.
3. The radio station has time available for 10 commercials.
4. The newspaper has space available for seven ads.
5. The advertising agency has time and staff available for producing no more than a total of 15 commercials and/or ads.

The company would like to know how many and what kinds of commercials and ads to produce in order to maximize total exposure. If one follows the simple criterion of choosing advertising by its exposure potential, one would try to maximize TV commercials, then radio commercials, and finally newspaper ads. This would result in four TV commercials ($60,000), six radio commercials ($36,000) and one newspaper ad ($4,000). The cost of the campaign would be $100,000 with an estimated exposure of 161,000 people. This problem, however, can be formulated as an *integer programming*[6] model and optimally solved, for instance, with Microsoft Excel's Solver. The optimal solution to this problem calls for two TV commercials, nine radio commercials, and four newspaper ads for a total cost of $100,000 and a total exposure of 184,000 people.

This example shows, once again, that simplistic solutions to constrained problems can lead to inferior process performance. In this case, a more comprehensive solution method is able to increase by 14 percent the total exposure that can be achieved with a fixed amount of money.

---

[6]Integer programming is an optimization technique that allows decision problems to be modeled as a set of linear equations. There is one equation to model the objective function and one equation for each constraint in the problem. The solution method is based on solving a series of linear programming problems, which essentially allow for the decision variables to take on noninteger values.

Examples 5.16 and 5.17 include constraints associated with production, demand, and capacity. In general, constraints fall into three broad categories.

Resource constraint: A resource within or outside the organization, such as capacity, that limits performance.
Market constraint: A limit in the market demand that is less than the organization's capacity.
Policy constraint: Any policy that limits performance, such as a policy that forbids the use of overtime.

In Examples 5.16 and 5.17, the limit in the process hours and the budget for advertising can be identified as resource constraints. An external resource constraint is the limit on the number of ads or commercials the advertising agency is able to produce for the discount stores. The market constraint in Example 5.16 is characterized by a limit on the weekly demand for each product. One possible policy constraint in Example 5.17 might be to insist on a plan whereby the number of TV commercials is greater than the number of newspaper ads.

TOC proposes a series of steps that can be followed to deal with any type of constraint (Vonderembse and White, 1994).

1. Identify the system's constraints.
2. Determine how to exploit the system constraints.
3. Subordinate everything else to the decisions made in step 2.
4. Elevate the constraints so a higher performance level can be reached.
5. If the constraints are eliminated in step 4, go back to step 1. Do not let inertia become the new constraint.

Example 5.18

We now apply the first three steps of this methodology to a process with nine activities and three resource types. Three types of jobs must be processed, with each job following a different processing path. The routing for each job, the weekly demand, and the estimated profit margins are shown in Table 5.7.

To make the analysis for this example simple, assume that activities 1, 2, and 3 require 10 minutes and that the other activities require 5 minutes of processing for each job. Also, assume that activities 1, 2, and 3 are performed by resource X; activities 4, 5, and 6 are performed by resource Y; and activities 7, 8, and 9 are performed by resource Z. Finally, assume that 2,400 minutes of each resource are available per week.

1. *Identify the system's constraints.* This problem has two types of constraints: a resource constraint and a market constraint. The resource constraint is given by the limit on the processing time per week. The market constraint is given by the limit on the demand for each job. Next, identify which one of these two types of constraints is restricting the performance of the process. Table 5.8 shows the resource utilization calculations if the process were to meet the market demands. That is, these calculations assume that 50 A jobs, 100 B jobs, and 60 C jobs will be processed per week.

   The requirement calculations in Table 5.8 reflect the total time needed by each job type per resource. For example, resource Y performs activities 4, 5, and 6. Because 50 A jobs are routed through activity 4 and the activity time is 5 minutes, this requires $5 \times 50 = 250$

TABLE 5.7 Job Data for Example 5.17

Job	Routing	Demand (units/week)	Profit Margin
A	4, 8, and 9	50	$20
B	1, 2, 3, 5, 6, 7, and 8	100	$75
C	2, 3, 4, 5, 6, 7, 8, and 9	60	$60

TABLE 5.8 Utilization Calculations for Example 5.17

Resource	Requirements (min./week)	Utilization
X	$(30 \times 100) + (20 \times 60) = 4,200$	$4,200/2,400 = 175\%$
Y	$(5 \times 50) + (10 \times 100) + (15 \times 60) = 2,150$	$2,150/2,400 = 90\%$
Z	$(10 \times 50) + (10 \times 100) + (15 \times 60) = 2,400$	$2,400/2,400 = 100\%$

minutes of resource Y per week. Then 100 B jobs are routed through activities 5 and 6, adding $10 \times 100 = 1,000$ minutes to resource Y. Finally, 60 C jobs are routed through activities 4, 5, and 6, resulting in $15 \times 60 = 900$ additional minutes of resource Y. Hence, the process requires 2,150 minutes of resource Y per week. Because 2,400 minutes are available, the utilization of resource Y is $2,150/2,400 = 90$ percent. The utilization of resources X and Z are obtained in the same manner.

In order to meet market demand, resource X is required at more than 100% utilization, so clearly the process is constrained by this resource.

2. *Determine how to exploit the system's constraint.* Next, determine how resource X can be utilized most effectively. Let us consider three different rules to process jobs, and for each rule, calculate the total weekly profit.

   2.1 *Rank jobs based on profit margin.* This rule would recommend processing jobs in the order given by B, C, and A.

   2.2 *Rank jobs based on their profit contribution per direct labor hour.* These contributions are calculated as the ratio of profit and total direct labor. For example, job A has a contribution of $1.33 per direct labor minute, because its profit margin of $20 is divided by the total labor of 15 minutes (i.e., $20/15 = $1.33). Similarly, the contributions of B and C are $1.50 and $1.20, respectively. These calculations yield the processing order of B, A, and C.

   2.3 *Rank jobs based on their contribution per minute of the constraint.* These contributions are calculated as the ratio of profit and direct labor in resource X (i.e., the bottleneck). For example, job B has a contribution of $2.50 per direct labor minute in resource X, because its profit margin of $75 is divided by the total labor of 30 minutes in resource X (i.e., $75/30 = $2.50). Similarly, the contribution of C is $3.00. The contribution of A in this case is irrelevant, because A jobs are not routed through any activities requiring the bottleneck resource X. The rank is then C and B, with A as a "free" job with respect to the constraint.

3. *Subordinate everything else to the decisions made in step 2.* This step involves calculating the number of jobs of each type to be processed, the utilization of each resource, and the total weekly profit. These calculations depend on the ranking rule used in step 2, so the results of using each of the proposed rules are shown as follows.

   3.1 Start by calculating the maximum number of jobs of each type that can be completed using ranking rule 2.1. The maximum number of B jobs is 80 per week, which is the maximum that resource X can complete (i.e., $2,400/30 = 80$). If 80 B jobs are processed, then no C jobs can be processed, because no capacity is left in resource X. However, type A jobs can be processed, because they don't use resource X. These jobs use resources Y and Z. Resource Y does not represent a constraint, because its maximum utilization is 90 percent (as shown in Table 5.8). After processing B jobs, 1,600 minutes are left in resource Z (i.e., $2,400 - 800$). Each A job requires 10 minutes of resource Z, so a maximum of $1,600/10 = 160$ A jobs can be processed. Given that the demand is 50 A jobs per week, the entire demand can be satisfied. The utilization of each resource according to this plan is shown in Table 5.9.

   The total profit of this processing plan is $75 \times 80 + 20 \times 50 = $7,000.

   3.2 The ranking according to rule 2.2 is B, A, and C. Because A does not require resource X, the resulting processing plan is the same as the one for rule 2.1 (see Table 5.9). The total profit is also $7,000.

   3.3 For the ranking determined by rule 2.3, first calculate the maximum number of C jobs that can be processed through the bottleneck. C jobs require 20 minutes of resource X, so a total of 120 C jobs can be processed per week (i.e., $2,400/20 = 120$). This allows for the entire demand of 60 C jobs to be satisfied. Now, subtract the capacity

TABLE 5.9 Utilization for Ranking Rules 2.1 and 2.2

Resource	Requirements (min./week)	Utilization
X	$80 \times 30 = 2,400$	$2,400/2,400 = 100\%$
Y	$(10 \times 80) + (5 \times 50) = 1,050$	$1,050/2,400 = 44\%$
Z	$(10 \times 80) + (10 \times 50) = 1,300$	$1,300/2,400 = 54\%$

TABLE 5.10 Utilization for Ranking Rule 2.3

Resource	Requirements (min./week)	Utilization
X	$(30 \times 40) + (20 \times 60) = 2,400$	$2,400/2,400 = 100\%$
Y	$(5 \times 50) + (10 \times 40) + (15 \times 60) = 1,550$	$1,550/2,400 = 64\%$
Z	$(10 \times 50) + (10 \times 40) + (15 \times 60) = 1,800$	$1,800/2,400 = 75\%$

from the bottleneck and calculate the maximum number of B jobs that can be processed with the remaining capacity. This yields $1,200/30 = 40$ B jobs. Finally, the number of A jobs that can be processed is calculated. A jobs are "free" with respect to resource X but require 10 minutes of processing in resource Z. The updated capacity of resource Z is 1,300 minutes (after subtracting 400 minutes for B jobs and 900 minutes for C jobs); therefore, the entire demand of A jobs can be satisfied. The utilization of the resulting plan is given in Table 5.10.

The total profit of this processing plan is $\$20 \times 50 + \$75 \times 40 + \$60 \times 60 = \$7,600$.

Rule 2.3 yields superior results in constrained processes where the goal is selecting the mix of products or services that maximizes total profit. Therefore, it is not necessary to apply rules 2.1 and 2.2 in these situations, because their limitations have been shown by way of the previous example. The application of rule 2.3 to the production and marketing examples (Examples 5.16 and 5.17) presented earlier in this section is left as exercises.

5.5 Summary

This chapter has discussed two important aspects in the modeling and design of business processes: cycle time analysis and capacity analysis. Cycle time analysis represents the customer perspective because most customers are concerned with the time that they will have to wait until their jobs are completed. Market demands are such that business processes must be able to compete in speed in addition to quality and other dimensions of customer service.

On the other hand, operations managers are concerned with the efficient utilization of resources. Capacity analysis represents this point of view. Competitive processes are effective at balancing customer service and resource utilization. The techniques for managing flow discussed in this chapter are relevant in the search for the right balance.

5.6 References

Anupindi, R., S. Chopra, S. D. Deshmukh, J. A. Van Mieghem, and E. Zemel. 1999. *Managing business process flows.* Upper Saddle River, NJ: Prentice Hall.

Finch, B. J., and R. L. Luebbe. 1995. *Operations management: Competing in a changing environment.* Fort Worth, TX: Dryden Press.

Little, J. D. C. 1961. A proof of the queuing formula $L=\lambda W$. *Operations Research* 9: 383–387.

Melnyk, S., and M. Swink. 2002. *Value-driven operations management: An integrated modular approach.* New York: McGraw Hill/Irwin.

Sterman, J. D. 2000. *Business dynamics: Systems thinking and modeling for a complex world.* Boston: Irwin McGraw-Hill.

Vonderembse, M. A., and G. P. White. 1994. *Operations management: Concepts, methods, and strategies.* Ontario: John Wiley & Sons Canada Ltd.

5.7 Discussion Questions and Exercises

1. Explain in your own words the different types of flows in a process.
2. What is the relationship between work-in-process and the input and output rates over time?
3. A Burger King processes on average 1,200 customers per day (over the course of 15 hours). At any given time, 60 customers are in the store. Customers may be waiting to place an order, placing an order, waiting for the order to be ready, eating, and so on. What is the average time that a customer spends in the store?
4. A branch office of the University Federal Credit Union processes 3,000 loan applications per year. On the average, loan applications are processed in 2 weeks. Assuming 50 weeks per year, how many loan applications can be found in the various stages of processing within the bank at any given time?
5. In Exercise 3, it is mentioned that at any given time, one can find 60 customers in the store. How often can the manager of the store expect that the entire group of 60 customers would be entirely replaced?
6. The process of designing and implementing a Web site for commercial use can be described as follows. First, the customer and the Web design team have an informational meeting for half a business day. If the first meeting is successful, the customer and the Web design team meet again for a full day to work on the storyboard of the site. If the first meeting is not successful, then the process is over, which means the customer will look for another Web designer. After the storyboard is completed, the site design begins; immediately after that, the site is developed. The design of the site typically takes 10 business days. The development of the site requires 2 business days. While the site is being designed and developed, the contents are prepared. It takes 5 business days to complete an initial draft of the contents. After the initial draft is completed, a decision is made to have a marketing team review the initial draft. Experience shows that about 60 percent of the time the marketing review is needed, and 40 percent of the time the final version of the contents is prepared without the marketing review. The marketing review requires 3 business days, and the preparation of the final version requires 4 business days. The contents are then put into the site. This activity is referred to as *building*. (Note that before the building can be done, the development of the site and the contents must be completed.) Building the site takes about 3 business days. After the site is built, a review activity is completed to check that all links and graphics are working correctly. The review activity typically is completed in 1 business day. The final activity is the approval of the site, which is done in half a business day. About 20 percent of the time, the sites are not approved. When a site is rejected, it is sent back to the building activity. When the site is approved, the design process is finished.
   a. Draw a flowchart of this process.
   b. Calculate the cycle time.
7. Consider the process flowchart in Figure 5.11.

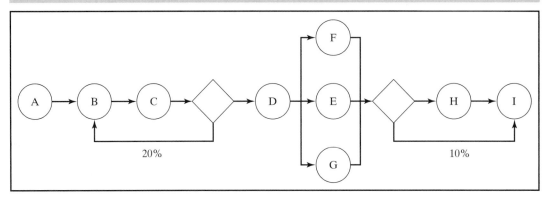

The estimated waiting time and processing time for each activity in the process are shown in Table 5.11. All times are given in minutes.

TABLE 5.11 Time Data for Exercise 7

Activity	Waiting Time (in min.)	Processing Time (in min.)
A	7	3
B	5	8
C	4	2
D	10	5
E	7	2
F	0	3
G	2	5
H	8	9
I	2	8

    a. Calculate the average cycle time for this process.
    b. Calculate the cycle time efficiency.
8. For the process in Exercise 7, assume that the resources in Table 5.12 are needed in each activity.

TABLE 5.12 Resource Assignment for Exercise 8

Activity	Resource Type
A	R1
B	R2
C	R2
D	R2
E	R3
F	R3
G	R4
H	R4
I	R1

Also assume that there are two units of R1, three units of R2, two units of R3, and two units of R4.
    a. Calculate the theoretical process capacity and identify the bottleneck.
    b. If the actual throughput has been observed to be 6 jobs per hour, what is the capacity utilization?
9. For the process flowchart in Figure 5.12, where the numbers between parentheses are the estimated activity times (in minutes), calculate the average cycle time.
10. Assume that the processing times (in minutes) for the activities in Exercise 9 are estimated as shown in Table 5.13. Calculate the cycle time efficiency.

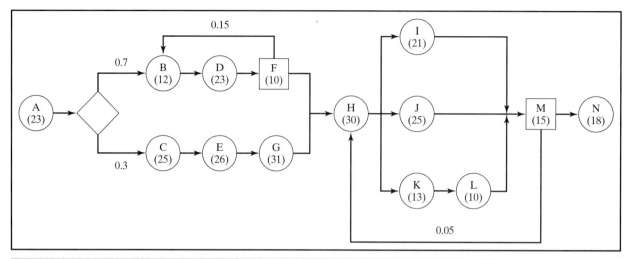

FIGURE 5.12 Flowchart for Exercise 9

TABLE 5.13 Processing Times for Exercise 10

Activity	Processing Time (in min.)
A	13
B	2
C	15
D	13
E	20
F	10
G	28
H	25
I	11
J	15
K	12
L	5
M	5
N	11

11. Assume that four resource types are needed to perform the activities in the process of Exercises 9 and 10. The resource type needed by each activity is shown in Table 5.14.

TABLE 5.14 Resource Assignment for Exercise 11

Resource	Activities
1	A, E, and G
2	B, D, and J
3	C, I, K, and M
4	F, H, L, and N

a. Considering that there are two units of resource 1, two units of resource 2, three units of resource 3, and three units of resource 4, calculate the capacity of the process.

b. If the actual throughput of the process is 2.5 jobs/hour, what is the capacity utilization?

12. Three teams (T1, T2, and T3) work in the process depicted in Figure 5.13, where the numbers in each activity indicate processing times in minutes. Calculate the capacity utilization of the process assuming that the throughput is one job per hour.

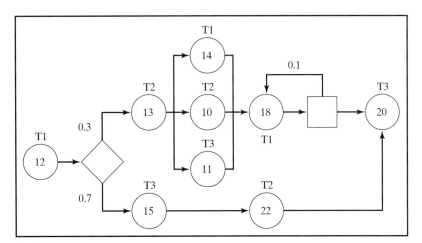

FIGURE 5.13 Flowchart for Exercise 12

13. Consider the business process depicted in Figure 5.14 and the time values (in minutes) in Table 5.15. Use cycle time efficiency to compare this process with a redesigned version where the rework in activity G has been eliminated and activities D, E, and F have been merged into one with processing time of 10 minutes and zero waiting time.

FIGURE 5.14 Flowchart for Exercise 13

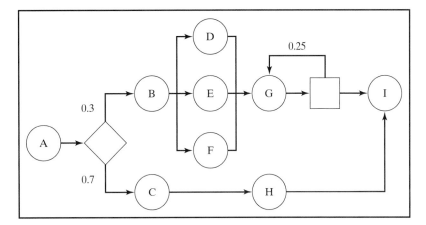

TABLE 5.15 Data for Exercise 13

Job	A	B	C	D	E	F	G	H	I
Activity time (in min.)	12	13	15	14	10	11	18	22	20
Processing time (in min.)	5	4	7	4	6	3	8	12	15

14. Nine people work in the process depicted in Figure 5.15.The numbers next to each activity are processing times in minutes. Table 5.16 shows the assignment of workers to activities.
   a. Calculate the capacity of the process in jobs per hour.
   b. Management is considering adding one worker to the process, but this would increase the operational cost by $23 per hour. Management knows that increasing the process capacity by one job per hour adds $30 per hour to the bottom line. Based on this information, would you recommend adding a worker, and if so, with whom should the new person work?

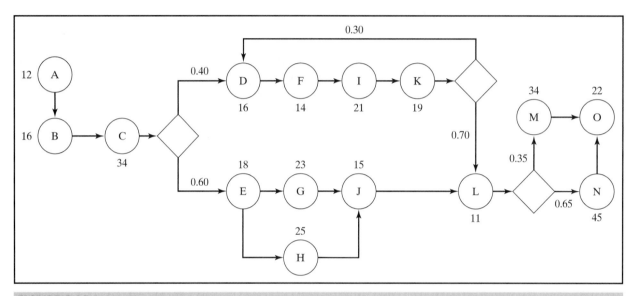

FIGURE 5.15 Flowchart for Exercise 14

TABLE 5.16 Data for Exercise 14

Workers	Activities
David and Steve	A, B, C, and M
Laura	E and J
Debbie, Betty, and John	D, F G, and N
Diane and Gary	I, K, and O
Fred	H and L

15. A reengineering team has studied a process and has developed the flowchart in Figure 5.16. The team also has determined that the expected waiting and processing times (in minutes) corresponding to each activity in the process are as shown in Table 5.17.
   a. Calculate the average cycle time for this process.
   b. Calculate the cycle time efficiency.
16. A process design team is analyzing the capacity of a process. The team has developed the flowchart in Figure 5.17. The numbers between parentheses indicate the processing times in minutes, and the labels above or below each activity indicate the resource type (i.e., R1 = resource 1). The process has one unit of resource R1, two units of resource R2, and three

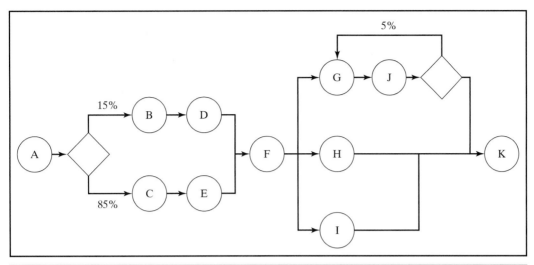

FIGURE 5.16 Flowchart for Exercise 15

TABLE 5.17 Data for Exercise 15

Activity	Waiting Time (in min.)	Processing Time (in min.)
A	20	12
B	15	18
C	5	30
D	12	17
E	3	12
F	5	25
G	8	7
H	5	10
I	15	25
J	5	20
K	4	10

units of resource R3. Assume that a reworked job has the same chance to pass inspection as a regular job.

a. Calculate the theoretical process capacity and identify the bottleneck.
b. If the actual throughput rate of the process is one job per hour, what is the capacity utilization?

FIGURE 5.17 Flowchart for Exercise 16

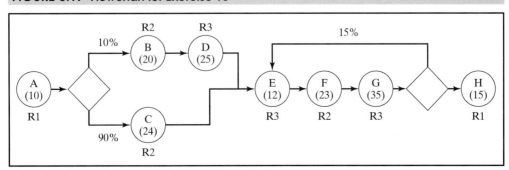

17. Use the theory of constraints and the data in Tables 5.18 and 5.19 to determine how many units of each job type should be completed per week in order to maximize profits. Consider that the availability is 5,500 minutes for resource R1, 3,000 minutes for resource R2, and 8,000 minutes for resource R3.

TABLE 5.18 Routing, Demand, and Profit Data for Exercise 17

Job	Activity Routing	Demand (units per week)	Profit Margin
A	1, 4, 7	80	$10
B	2, 3, 5, 6	100	$15
C	1, 3, 5, 6, 7	120	$20

TABLE 5.19 Processing Times and Resource Assignments for Exercise 17

Activity	Time (in min.)	Resource
1	20	R1
2	12	R2
3	7	R2
4	18	R1
5	9	R3
6	29	R3
7	8	R3

18. An order-fulfillment process has demand for three order types during the next 4 weeks, as shown in Table 5.20. The assignment of activities to workers and processing time for each activity are shown in Table 5.21. All workers have 40 hours per week available to work on this process. Use the TOC principles to find the number of orders of each type that should be processed to maximize total profit.

TABLE 5.20 Data for Exercise 18

Order Type	Activities	Demand	Profit Margin
Basic	1, 2 and 5	150	$125
Special	1, 3, 4 and 6	110	$175
Deluxe	2, 4, 5 and 6	90	$200

TABLE 5.21 Data for Exercise 18

Activity	Processing Time (in min.)	Assignment
1	24	Anne
2	18	Anne
3	25	Meg
4	27	Joe
5	15	Joe
6	14	Meg

CHAPTER 6

Introduction to Queuing and Simulation

The process models analyzed in Chapters 4 and 5 have one thing in common: They assume that activity times and demand are deterministic and constant; that is, that they are known with certainty. In reality, an element of variability will always exist in the time it takes to perform a certain task and in the demand for service. In situations where the variability is small, deterministic models of the type studied in Chapters 4 and 5 might be an adequate way of describing a process. However, in situations with more accentuated variability, these models do not suffice. In fact, the variability itself is often one of the most important characteristics to capture in the model of a process.

Consider, for example, the checkout process at a grocery store where one of the main design issues is to avoid long lines. Customers arrive at the checkout stations with their items so they can pay and leave. Each cashier scans the items, bags them, and collects payment from the customer. The time it takes to service a customer depends on the amount and type of groceries and the form of payment used; therefore, it varies from customer to customer. In addition, the number of customers per time unit that arrive at the cashier's station, meaning the demand for service, is highly uncertain and variable. Applying a deterministic model to describe this process, using only the average service time and the average number of customer arrivals per time unit, fails to capture the variability and explain why queues are forming. This is because the deterministic model assumes that it always takes exactly the same amount of time for a cashier to serve a customer, and that customers arrive at constant intervals. Under these assumptions, it is easy to determine the number of cashiers needed to avoid queues. However, the fact that everyone has waited at a cashier's station indicates that this is too simplistic of a way to describe the complex reality. Variability makes it difficult to match demand and capacity in such a way that queues are avoided.

The focus of this chapter is the incorporation of variability into models of business processes. These types of models, known in the literature as *stochastic models*, enable us to evaluate how the process design decisions affect waiting times, queue lengths, and service levels. An important difference compared to the deterministic models that have been considered so far is that in the stochastic models the waiting time is no longer an input parameter; it is the result of the specified process time and the demand pattern. Because eliminating non-value-adding waiting time is an important objective when designing a new business process (see, for example, Section 1.1), the usefulness of stochastic models in process design is obvious.

The modeling approaches that will be explored in this chapter belong to two distinct groups: *analytical queuing models* stemming from the field of mathematical queuing theory, and *simulation models*, which are in their nature experimental and in this case computer based. Chapters 7 through 10 also address the simulation modeling approach. The reason for considering these two approaches is that they offer different advantages to the process designer. The analytical queuing models express important performance characteristics in mathematical formulae and are convenient to use when the necessary conditions are in place. The drawback is that these conditions can be restrictive with regard to the process structure and the representation of variability in the models. The simulation models are more flexible, but they usually take more time to set up and run, in addition to requiring a computer with the appropriate software. Because the simulation models are experimental, they also require statistical analysis of input and output data before obtaining the appropriate information on performance characteristics sought by the process designer. This chapter investigates the technical aspects of these two modeling approaches. However, before getting into the modeling details, it is important to understand why variability in process parameters is such an important issue from an operational and an economic perspective.

From an *operational perspective*, the main problem with variability in processing times, demands, and capacity is that it leads to an unbalanced use of resources over time, causing the formation of waiting lines. This will be referred to loosely as a capacity-planning problem. The core of this problem is that queues (or waiting lines) can arise at any given time when the demand for service exceeds the resource capacity for providing the service. This means that even if the average demand falls well below the average capacity, high variability will lead to instances when the demand for service exceeds the capacity and a queue starts to form. This explains the formation of waiting lines in the grocery store example. On the other hand, in some instances the capacity to provide service will greatly exceed the demand for service. This causes the queue to decrease. Moreover, if no queue exists at all, the resource providing the service will be idle. At a grocery store, even if a cashier has nothing to do for long periods during the day, the arrival of a customer with a full cart could initiate a queue.

At this point, it is important to recognize that queues concern individuals as well as documents, products, or intangible jobs such as blocks of information sent over the Internet. However, the issues with waiting in line are particularly important in service industries where the queue consists of people waiting for service. The reason is that, as opposed to objects or pieces of information, people usually find waiting frustrating, and they often give an immediate response regarding their dissatisfaction.

From an *economic perspective*, the capacity-planning problem caused by high variability in demand and process times comes down to balancing the cost of having too much capacity on certain occasions against the cost associated with long waiting lines at other times. The cost of delays and waiting can take on many different forms including the following.

- The *social costs* of not providing fast enough care at a hospital.
- The *cost of lost customers* who go elsewhere because of inadequate service.
- The *cost of discounts* because of late deliveries.
- The *cost of goodwill loss* and bad reputation affecting future sales.

- The *cost of idle employees* who have to wait for some task to be completed before they can continue their work.

Ultimately, these costs will affect the organization, even though the impact sometimes might be hard to quantify. The cost of excessive capacity is usually easier to identify. Primarily, it consists of the fixed and variable costs of additional and unused capacity, including increased staffing levels. Returning to the grocery store example, the store must balance the cost of hiring additional cashiers and installing more checkout stations against the cost of lost customers and lower sales revenues due to long queues and waiting times at the checkout stations.

Figure 6.1 depicts the economic tradeoff associated with the capacity-planning problem. The *x*-axis represents the service capacity expressed as the number of jobs per unit of time the system can complete on average[1]. The *y*-axis represents the total costs associated with waiting and providing service. The waiting cost reflects the cost of having too little service capacity, and the service cost reflects the cost of acquiring and maintaining a certain service capacity.

It follows that in order to arrive at design decisions that will minimize the total costs, the first step is to quantify the delay associated with a certain capacity decision. Second, this delay needs to be translated into monetary terms to compare this to the cost of providing a certain service capacity. This chapter investigates models that deal with both of these issues.

Section 6.1 specifies a conceptual model over the basic queuing process and defines what a queuing system is. This section also discusses strategies that are often used in service industries for mitigating the negative effects of making people wait in line. The conceptual model for the basic queuing process serves as a basis for the analytical queuing models investigated in Section 6.2 and for the general understanding of the simulation models in Section 6.3. Finally, a summary and some concluding remarks are provided in Section 6.4.

FIGURE 6.1 Economic Tradeoff of Between Service Capacity and Waiting Times

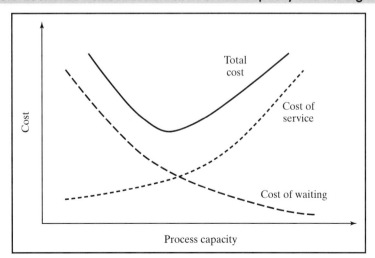

---

[1]See the process capacity calculations in Section 5.2.2.

6.1 Queuing Systems, the Basic Queuing Process, and Queuing Strategies

Queuing processes, queuing systems, and queuing models might appear to be abstract concepts with limited practical applicability, but nothing could be further from the truth. Wherever people go in their daily lives, they encounter simple queuing systems and queuing processes (e.g. at the bank, in the grocery store, or when calling for a taxi, going to the doctor, eating at a restaurant, buying tickets to the theater, or taking the bus). In simple terms, an elementary queuing system consists of a service mechanism with servers providing service and one or more queues of customers or jobs waiting to receive service. The queuing process, on the other hand, describes the operations of the queuing system; that is, how customers arrive at the queuing system and how they proceed through it. The queuing system is an integral part of the queuing process. Noting the subtle distinction between a queuing process and a queuing system will prove useful when discussing detailed modeling issues. However, in practical situations and in higher-level discussions, these two terms are often interchangeable. Going back to the definition of a business process as a network of connected activities and buffers (see Section 1.1), a business process can be interpreted as a network of queuing processes or elementary queuing systems.

To expand the frame of reference regarding queuing systems and to make this concept more concrete, one can look at a number of examples of real-world queuing systems that can be broadly classified as commercial, transportation, business-internal, and social service systems.

Many of the queuing systems we encounter daily are *commercial service systems*, whereby a commercial organization serves external customers. Often the service is a personal interaction between the customer and an employee, but in some cases, the service provider might be a machine. Typically, customers go to a fixed location to seek service. Examples include a dentist's office (where the server is the dentist), banks, checkout stations at supermarkets or other stores, gas stations, and automated teller machines. However, the server also can travel to the customer. Examples include a plumber or cable company technician visiting the customer's home to perform a service.

The class of *transportation service systems* represents situations where vehicles are either customers or servers. Examples where vehicles are customers include cars and trucks waiting at tollbooths, railroad crossings, or traffic lights; trucks or ships waiting to be loaded; and airplanes waiting to access a runway. Situations where vehicles constitute the servers in a queuing system include taxicabs, fire trucks, elevators, buses, trains, and airplanes transporting customers between locations.

In *business-internal service systems*, the customers receiving service are internal to the organization providing the service. This definition includes inspection stations (the server), materials handling systems like conveyor belts, maintenance systems where a technician (the server) is dispatched to repair a broken machine (the customer), and internal service departments like computer support (the server) servicing requests from employees (the customers). It also includes situations where machines in a production facility or a supercomputer in a computing center process jobs.

Finally, many *social service systems* are queuing systems. In the judicial process, for example, the cases awaiting trial are the customers and the judge and jury is the server. Other examples include an emergency room at a hospital, the family doctor making house calls, and waiting lists for organ transplants or student dorm rooms.

This broad classification of queuing systems is not exhaustive and it does have some overlap. Its purpose is just to give a flavor of the wide variety of queuing systems facing the process designer.

A conceptual model of the basic queuing process describes the operation of the queuing systems just mentioned and further explains the subtle distinction between a queuing process and a queuing system. It also will provide the basis for exploring the mathematical queuing models in Section 6.2 and help conceptualize the simulation models in Section 6.3. Following the discussion of the basic queuing process, Section 6.1.2 looks at some pragmatic strategies used to mitigate the negative economic impact of long waiting lines.

6.1.1 THE BASIC QUEUING PROCESS

The basic queuing process describes how customers arrive at and proceed through the queuing system. This means that the basic queuing process describes the operations of a queuing system. The following major elements define a basic queuing process: the calling population, the arrival process, the queue configuration, the queue discipline, and the service mechanism. The elements of the basic queuing process are illustrated in Figure 6.2, which also clarifies the distinction between the basic queuing process and the queuing system.

Customers or jobs from a calling population arrive at one or several queues (buffers) with a certain configuration. The arrival process specifies the rate at which customers arrive and the particular arrival pattern. Service is provided immediately when the designated queue is empty and a server (resource) is available. Otherwise, the customer or job remains in the queue waiting for service.

In service systems in which jobs are actual customers (i.e., people), some may choose not to join the queue when confronted with a potentially long wait. This behavior is referred to as *balking*. Other customers may consider, after joining the queue, that the wait is intolerable and *renege* (i.e., they leave the queue before being served). From a process performance perspective, an important distinction between balking and reneging is that the reneging customers take up space in the queue and the balking customers do not. For example, in a call center, the reneging customers will accrue connection costs as long as they remain in the queue.

FIGURE 6.2 The Basic Queuing Process and the Queuing System

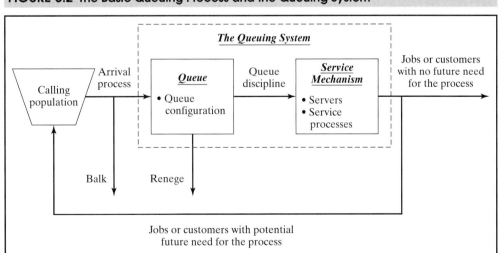

When servers (resources) become available, a job is selected from the queue and the corresponding service (activity) is performed. The policy governing the selection of a job from the queue is known as the *queue discipline*. Finally, the service mechanism can be viewed as a network of service stations where activities are performed. These stations may need one or more resources to perform the activities, and the availability of these resources will result in queues of different lengths.

This description of a queuing process is closely related to the definition of a general business process given in Section 1.1. In fact, as previously mentioned, a general business process can be interpreted as a network of basic queuing processes (or queuing systems).

Due to the importance of the basic queuing process, the remainder of this section is devoted to a further examination of its components.

The Calling Population

The calling population can be characterized as homogeneous (i.e., consisting of only one type of job), or heterogeneous, consisting of different types of jobs. In fact, most queuing processes will have heterogeneous calling populations. For example, the admissions process at a state university has in-state and out-of-state applicants. Because these applications are treated differently, the calling population is not homogeneous. In this case, the calling population is divided into two subpopulations.

The calling population also can be characterized as infinite or finite. In reality, few calling populations are truly infinite. However, in many situations, the calling population can be considered infinite from a modeling perspective. The criterion is that if the population is so large that the arrival process is unaffected by how many customers or jobs are currently in the queuing system (in the queue or being served), the calling population is considered infinite. An example of this is a medium-sized branch office of a bank. All potential customers who might want to visit the bank define the calling population. It is unlikely that the number of customers in the bank would affect the current rate of arrivals. Consequently, the calling population could be considered infinite from a modeling perspective.

In other situations, the population cannot be considered infinite. For example, the mechanics at a motorized army unit are responsible for maintenance and repair of the unit's vehicles. Because the number of vehicles is limited, a large number of broken down vehicles in need of repair implies that fewer functioning vehicles remain that can break down. The arrival process—vehicles breaking down and requiring the mechanic's attention—is most likely dependent on the number of vehicles currently awaiting repair (i.e., in the queuing system). In this case, the model must capture the effect of a finite calling population.

The Arrival Process

The arrival process refers to the temporal and spatial distribution of the demand facing the queuing system. If the queuing process is part of a more general business process, there may be several entry points for which the arrival processes must be studied. The demand for resources in a queuing process that is not directly connected to the entry points to the overall business process is contingent on how the jobs are routed through this process. That is, the path that each type of job follows determines which activities are performed most often and therefore which resources are most needed.

The arrival process is characterized by the distribution of interarrival times, meaning the probability distribution of the times between consecutive arrivals. To determine these distributions in practice, data need to be collected from the real-world system and then statistical methods can be used to analyze the data and estimate the distributions. The approach can be characterized in terms of the following three-step procedure.

1. Collect data by recording the actual arrival times into the process.
2. Calculate the interarrival times for each job type.
3. Perform statistical analysis of the interarrival times to fit a probability distribution.

Specific tools to perform these steps are described in Chapter 9.

The Queue Configuration

The queue configuration refers to the number of queues, their location, their spatial requirements, and their effect on customer behavior. Figure 6.3 shows two commonly used queue configurations: the single-line versus the multiple-line configuration.

For the multiple-line alternative (Figure 6.3a), the arriving job must decide which queue to join. Sometimes the customer, like in the case of a supermarket, makes the decision. However, in other cases this decision is made as a matter of policy or operational rule. For example, requests for technical support in a call center may be routed to the agent with the fewest requests at the time of arrival. In the single-line configuration (Figure 6.3b), all the jobs join the same line. The next job to be processed is selected from the single line.

Some advantages are associated with each of these configurations. These advantages are particularly relevant in settings where the jobs flowing through

FIGURE 6.3 Alternative Queue Configurations

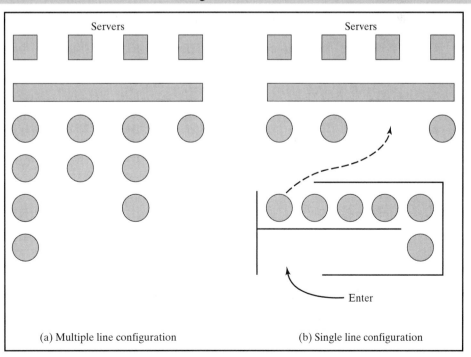

(a) Multiple line configuration   (b) Single line configuration

Source: Adapted from Fitzsimmons and Fitzsimmons, 1998

the process are people. The multiple-line configuration, for instance, has the following advantages.

1. The service provided can be differentiated. The use of express lanes in supermarkets is an example. Shoppers who require a small amount of service can be isolated and processed quickly, thereby avoiding long waits for little service.
2. Labor specialization is possible. For example, drive-in banks assign the more experienced tellers to the commercial lane.
3. The customer has more flexibility. For example, the customer in a grocery store with several check out stations has the option of selecting a particular cashier of preference.
4. Balking behavior may be deterred. When arriving customers see a long, single queue snaked in front of a service, they often interpret this as evidence of a long wait and decide not to join the line.

The following are advantages of the single-line configuration.

1. The arrangement guarantees "fairness" by ensuring that a first-come-first-served rule is applied to all arrivals.
2. Because only a single queue is available, no anxiety is associated with waiting to see if one selected the fastest line.
3. With only one entrance at the rear of the queue, the problem of cutting in is resolved. Often the single line is roped into a snaking pattern, which makes it physically more difficult for customers to leave the queue, thereby discouraging reneging. Reneging occurs when a customer in line leaves the queue before being served, typically because of frustration over the long wait.
4. Privacy is enhanced, because the transaction is conducted with no one standing immediately behind the person being served.
5. This arrangement is more efficient in terms of reducing the average time that customers spend waiting in line.
6. Jockeying is avoided. Jockeying refers to the behavior of switching lines. This occurs when a customer attempts to reduce his or her waiting time by switching lines as the lines become shorter.

The Queue Discipline

The queue discipline is the policy used to select the next job to be served. The most common queue discipline is first-come-first-served (FCFS), also known as first-in-first-out (FIFO). This discipline, however, is not the only possible policy for selecting jobs from a queue. In some cases, it is possible to estimate the processing time of a job in advance. This estimate can then be used to implement a policy whereby the fastest jobs are processed first. This queue discipline is known as the shortest processing time first (SPT) rule, as discussed in Chapter 4. Other well-known disciplines are last-in-first-out (LIFO) and longest processing time first (LPT).

In addition to these rules, queue disciplines based on priority are sometimes implemented. In a medical setting, for example, the procedure known as triage is used to give priority to those patients who would benefit the most from immediate treatment. An important distinction to be made in terms of priority disciplines is that between *nonpreemptive* and *preemptive* priorities. Under a nonpreemptive priority discipline, a customer or job that is currently being served is never sent back to the queue in order to make room for an arriving customer or job with higher priority. In a preemptive discipline, on the other hand, a job that is being served will be thrown back into the queue immediately to make room for an arriving job with higher priority.

The preemptive strategy makes sense, for example, in an emergency room where the treatment of a sprained ankle is interrupted when an ambulance brings in a cardiac arrest patient and the physician must choose between the two. The drawback with the preemptive discipline is that customers with low priorities can experience extremely long waiting times.

The nonpreemptive strategy make sense in situations where interrupting the service before it is finished means that all the work put in is wasted and the service needs to be started from scratch when the job eventually rises in importance again. For example, if a limousine service is driving people to and from an airport, it makes little sense to turn the limousine around in order to pick up a VIP client at the airport just before it reaches the destination of its current passenger.

In many cases in which the customers are individuals, a preemptive strategy can cause severe frustration for low-priority customers. A nonpreemptive approach is often more easily accepted by all parties. Note that queuing disciplines in queuing theory correspond to dispatching rules in sequencing and scheduling (see Section 4.2.6).

The Service Mechanism

The service mechanism is comprised of one or more service facilities, each containing one or more parallel service channels referred to as servers. A job or a customer enters a service facility, where one server provides complete service. In cases where multiple service facilities are set up in series, the job or customer might be served by a sequence of servers. The queuing model must specify the exact number of service facilities, the number of servers in each facility, and possibly the sequence of service facilities a job must pass through before leaving the queuing system. The time spent in a service facility, meaning time in one particular server or service station, is referred to as the service time. The service process refers to the probability distribution of service times associated with a certain server (possibly different across different types of customers or jobs). Often it is assumed that the parallel servers in a given service facility have the same service time distribution. For example, in modeling the parallel tellers in a bank, it is usually reasonable to assume that the service process is the same for all tellers. Statistically, the estimation of the service times can be done in a similar way as the estimation of interarrival times. See Chapter 9.

The design of the service mechanism and queues together with the choice of queuing disciplines result in a certain service capacity associated with the queuing system. For example, the service mechanism may consist of one or more service facilities with one or more servers. How many is a staffing decision that directly affects the ability of the system to meet the demand for service. Adding capacity to the process typically results in decreasing the probability of long queues and, therefore, decreases the average waiting time of jobs in the queue. Often, the arrival process is considered outside the decision maker's control. However, sometimes implementing so-called demand management strategies is an option. This can involve working with promotional campaigns, such as "everyday low prices" at Wal-Mart, to encourage more stable demand patterns over time. These types of activities also go by the name of revenue management.

6.1.2 STRATEGIES FOR MITIGATING THE EFFECTS OF LONG QUEUES

In some situations, it might be unavoidable to have long waiting lines occasionally. Consider, for example, a ski resort. Most people arrive in the morning to buy tickets so they can spend the whole day on the slopes. As a result, lines will form at the ticket offices early in the day, no matter how many ticket offices the resort opens.

A relevant question is how the process designer or process owner might mitigate the negative economic effects of queues or waiting lines that have formed. This is of particular interest in service systems that want to avoid balking and reneging. Commonly used strategies are based on the ideas of concealing the queue, using the customer as a resource, making the wait comfortable, distracting the customer's attention, explaining the reasons for the wait, providing pessimistic estimates of remaining waiting time, and being fair and open about the queuing discipline.

An often-used strategy for minimizing or avoiding lost sales due to long lines is to conceal the queue from arriving customers (Fitzsimmons and Fitzsimmons, 1998). Restaurants achieve this by diverting people to the bar, which in turn has the potential to increase revenues. Amusement parks such as Disneyland require people to pay for their tickets outside the park, where they are unable to observe the waiting lines inside. Casinos "snake" the waiting line for nightclub acts through the slot machine area, in part to hide its true length and in part to foster impulsive gambling.

In some cases, a fruitful approach is to consider the customer as a resource with the potential to be part of the service delivery. For example, a patient might complete a medical history record while waiting for a doctor, thereby saving the physician valuable time. This strategy increases the capacity of the process while minimizing the psychological effects of waiting.

Regardless of other strategies, making the customer's wait comfortable is necessary to avoid reneging and loss of future sales due to displeased and annoyed customers. This can be done in numerous ways, such as by providing complementary drinks at a restaurant or by having a nicely decorated waiting room with interesting reading material in a doctor's office.

Closely related to this idea is distracting the waiting customers' attention, thereby making the wait seem shorter than it is. Airport terminals, for instance, have added public TV monitors, food courts, and shops.

If an unexpected delay occurs, it is important to inform the customer about this as soon as possible, but also to explain the reason for the extra wait. The passengers seated on a jumbo jet will be more understanding if they know that the reason for the delay is faulty radio equipment. Who wants to fly on a plane without a radio? However, if no explanation is given, attitudes tend to be much less forgiving because the customers feel neglected and that they have not been treated with the respect they deserve. Keeping the customers informed is also a key concept in all industries that deliver goods. Consider, for example, the tracking systems that FedEx and other shipping companies offer their customers.

To provide pessimistic estimates of the remaining waiting time is often also a good strategy. If the wait is shorter than predicted, the customer might even leave happy. On the other hand, if the wait is longer than predicted the customers tend to lose trust in the information and in the service.

Finally, it is important to be fair and open about the queuing discipline used. Ambiguous VIP treatment of some customers tends to agitate those left out; for example, think about waiting lines at popular restaurants or nightclubs.

6.2 Analytical Queuing Models

This section will examine how analytical queuing models can be used to describe and analyze the basic queuing process and the performance characteristics of the corresponding queuing system. The mathematical study of queues is referred to as queuing or queuing theory.

The distributions of interarrival and service times largely determine the operational characteristics of queuing systems. After all, considering these distributions instead of just their averages is what distinguishes the stochastic queuing models from the deterministic models in Chapters 4 and 5. In real-world queuing systems, these distributions can take on virtually any form, but they are seldom thought of until the data is analyzed. However, when modeling the queuing system mathematically, one must be specific about the type of distributions being used. When setting up the model, it is important to use distributions that are realistic enough to capture the system's behavior. At the same time, they must be simple enough to produce a tractable mathematical model. Based on these two criteria, the exponential distribution plays an important role in queuing theory. In fact, most results in elementary queuing theory assume exponentially distributed interarrival and service times. Section 6.2.1 discusses the importance and relevance of the exponential distribution, as well as its relation to the Poisson process.

The wide variety of specialized queuing models calls for a way to classify these according to their distinct features. A popular system for classifying queuing models with a single service facility with parallel and identical servers, a single queue and a FIFO queuing discipline, uses a notational framework with the structure $A1/A2/A3/A4/A5$. Attributes $A1$ and $A2$ represent the probability distribution of the interarrival and service times, respectively. Attribute $A3$ denotes the number of parallel servers. Attribute $A4$ indicates the maximum number of jobs allowed in the system at the same time. If there is no limitation, $A4 = \infty$. Finally, attribute $A5$ represents the size of the calling population. If the calling population is infinite, then $A5 = \infty$. Examples of symbols used to represent probability distributions for interarrival and service times—that is, attributes $A1$ and $A2$—include the following.

M = Markovian, meaning the interarrival and service times follow exponential distributions

D = Deterministic, meaning the interarrival and service times are deterministic and constant

G = General, meaning the interarrival times may follow any distribution

Consequently, $M/M/c$ refers to a queuing model with c parallel servers for which the interarrival times and the service times are both exponentially distributed. Omitting attributes $A4$ and $A5$ means that the queue length is unrestricted and the calling population is infinite. In the same fashion, $M/M/c/K$ refers to a model with a limitation of at most K customers or jobs in the system at any given time. $M/M/c/\infty/N$, on the other hand, indicates that the calling population is finite and consists of N jobs or customers.

Exponentially distributed interarrival and service times are assumed for all the queuing models in this chapter. In addition, all the models will have a single service facility with one or more parallel servers, a single queue and a FIFO queuing discipline. It is important to emphasize that the analysis can be extended to preemptive and non-preemptive priority disciplines, see, for example, Hillier and Lieberman (2001). Moreover, there exist results for many other queuing models not assuming exponentially distributed service and interarrival times. Often though, the analysis of these models tends to be much more complex and is beyond the scope of this book.

This exploration of analytical queuing models is organized as follows. Section 6.2.1 discusses the exponential distribution, its relevance, important properties, and its connection to the Poisson process. Section 6.2.2 introduces some notation and terminology used in Sections 6.2.3 through 6.2.8. Important concepts include steady-state analysis and Little's law. Based on the fundamental properties of the exponential distribution and the basic notation introduced in Section 6.2.2, Section 6.2.3 focuses on general birth-and-death processes and their wide applicability in modeling queuing processes. Although a powerful approach, the method for analyzing general birth-and-death processes can be tedious for large models. Therefore, Sections 6.2.4 through 6.2.7

explore some important specialized birth-and-death models with standardized expressions for determining important characteristics of these queuing systems. Finally, Section 6.2.8 illustrates the usefulness of analytical queuing models for making process design-related decisions, particularly by translating important operational characteristic into monetary terms.

6.2.1 THE EXPONENTIAL DISTRIBUTION AND ITS ROLE IN QUEUING THEORY

The exponential distribution has a central role in queuing theory for two reasons. First, empirical studies show that many real-world queuing systems have arrival and service processes that follow exponential distributions. Second, the exponential distribution has some mathematical properties that make it relatively easy to manipulate.

In this section, the exponential distribution is defined and some of its important properties and their implications when used in queuing modeling are discussed. The relationship between the exponential distribution, the Poisson distribution, and the Poisson process is also investigated. This discussion assumes some prior knowledge of basic statistical concepts such as random variables, probability density functions, cumulative distribution functions, mean, variance, and standard deviation. Basic books on statistics contain material related to these topics, some of which are reviewed in Chapter 9.

To provide a formal definition of the exponential distribution, let T be a random (or stochastic) variable representing either interarrival times or service times in a queuing process. T is said to follow an exponential distribution with parameter α if its probability density function (or frequency function), $f_T(t)$, is:

$$f_T(t) = \begin{cases} \alpha e^{-\alpha t} & \text{for } t \geq 0 \\ 0 & \text{for } t < 0 \end{cases}$$

The shape of the density function $f_T(t)$ is depicted in Figure 6.4, where t represents the realized interarrival or service time.

FIGURE 6.4 The Probability Density Function for an Exponentially Distributed Random Variable *T*

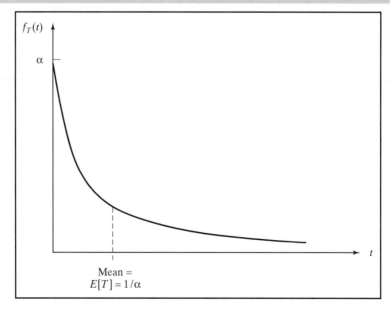

The expression for the corresponding cumulative distribution function, $F_T(t)$, is then

$$F_T(t) = \int_{-\infty}^{t} f_T(x)dx = \int_{0}^{t} \alpha e^{-\alpha x} dx = 1 - e^{-\alpha t}$$

To better understand this expression, recall that per definition $F_T(t) = P(T \le t)$, where $P(T \le t)$ is the probability that the random variable T is less than or equal to t. Consequently, $P(T \le t) = 1 - e^{-\alpha t}$ This also implies that the probability that T is greater than t, $P(T > t)$, can be obtained as $P(T > t) = 1 - P(T \le t) = e^{-\alpha t}$. Finally, it can be concluded that the mean, variance, and standard deviation of the exponentially distributed random variable T, denoted $E(T)$, $\text{Var}(T)$, and σ_T are, respectively:

$$E(T) = \frac{1}{\alpha} \quad \text{Var}(T) = \frac{1}{\alpha^2} \quad \sigma_T = \frac{1}{\alpha}$$

Note that the standard deviation is equal to the mean, which implies that the relative variability is high.

Next, the implications of assuming exponentially distributed interarrival and service times will be examined. Does it make sense to use this distribution? To provide an answer, it is necessary to look at a number of important properties characterizing the exponential distribution, some of which are intuitive and some of which have a more mathematical flavor.

First, from looking at the shape of the density function $f_T(t)$ in Figure 6.4, it can be concluded that it is decreasing in t. (Mathematically, it can be proved that it is *strictly decreasing in t*, which means that $P(0 \le T \le \delta) > P(t \le T \le t + \delta)$ for all positive values of t and δ).

Property 1: The Density Function $f_T(t)$ Is Strictly Decreasing in t.   The implication is that exponentially distributed interarrival and service times are more likely to take on small values. For example, there is always a 63.2 percent chance that the time (service or interarrival) is less than or equal to the mean value $E(T) = 1/\alpha$. At the same time, the long, right-hand tail of the density function $f_T(t)$ indicates that large time values occasionally occur. This means that the exponential distribution also encompasses situations when the time between customer arrivals, or the time it takes to serve a customer, can be very long. Is this a reasonable way of describing interarrival and service times?

For interarrival times, plenty of empirical evidence indicates that the exponential distribution in many situations is a reasonable way of modeling arrival processes of external customers to a service system. For service times, the applicability might sometimes be more questionable, particularly in cases of standardized service operations where all the service times are centered around the mean.

Consider, for example, a machining process of a specific product in a manufacturing setting. Because the machine does exactly the same work on every product, the time spent in the machine is going to deviate only slightly from the mean. In these situations, the exponential distribution does not offer a close approximation of the actual service time distribution. Still, in other situations the specific work performed in servicing different customers is often similar but occasionally deviates dramatically. In these cases, the exponential distribution may be a reasonable choice. Examples of where this might be the case could be a bank teller or a checkout station in a supermarket. Most customers demand the same type of service—a simple deposit or withdrawal, or the scanning of fewer than 15 purchased items. Occasionally, however, a customer requests a service that takes a lot of time to complete. For example, in a bank, a customer's transaction might involve contacting the head office for clearance; in a supermarket, a shopper might bring two full carts to the cashier.

To summarize, the exponential distribution is often a reasonable approximation for interarrival times and of service times in situations where the required work differs across customers. However, its use for describing processing (or service) times in situations with standardized operations performed on similar products or jobs might be questionable.

Property 2: Lack of Memory. Another interesting property of the exponential distribution, which is less intuitive, is its lack of memory. This means that the probability distribution of the remaining service time, or time until the next customer arrives, is always the same. It does not matter how long a time has passed since the service started or since the last customer arrived. Mathematically, this means that $P(T > t + \delta \mid T > \delta) = P(T > t)$ for all positive values of t and δ.

MATHEMATICAL DERIVATION

$$P(T > T + \delta \mid T > \delta) = \frac{P(T > t + \delta, T > \delta)}{P(T > \delta)} = \frac{P(T > t + \delta)}{P(T > \delta)} = \frac{e^{-\alpha(t+\delta)}}{e^{-\alpha\delta}}$$

$$= e^{-\alpha t} = P(T > t)$$

This property is important for the mathematical tractability of the queuing models that will be considered later. However, the main question here is whether this feature seems reasonable for modeling service and interarrival times.

In the context of interarrival times, the implication is that the next customer arrival is completely independent of when the last arrival occurred. In case of external customers arriving to the queuing system from a large calling population, this is a reasonable assumption in most cases. When the queuing system represents an internal subprocess of a larger business process so that the jobs arrive on some kind of schedule, this property is less appropriate. Consider, for example, trucks shipping goods between a central warehouse and a regional distribution center. The trucks leave the central warehouse at approximately 10 A.M. and 1 P.M. and arrive at the regional distribution center around noon and 3 P.M., respectively. In this case, it is not reasonable to assume that the time remaining until the next truck arrives is independent of when the last arrival occurred.

For service times, the lack of memory property implies that the time remaining until the service is completed is independent of the elapsed time since the service began. This may be a realistic assumption if the required service operations differ among customers (or jobs). However, if the service consists of the same collection of standardized operations across all jobs or customers, it is expected that the time elapsed since the service started will help one predict how much time remains before the service is completed. In these cases, the exponential distribution is not an appropriate choice.

The exponential distribution's lack of memory implies another result. Assume as before that T is an exponentially distributed random variable with parameter α, and that it represents the time between two events; that is, the time between two customer arrivals or the duration of a service operation. It can be asserted that no matter how much time has elapsed since the last event, the probability that the next event will occur in the following time increment δ is $\alpha\delta$. Mathematically, this means that $P(T \leq t + \delta \mid T > t) = \alpha\delta$ for all positive values of t and small positive values of δ, or more precisely

$$\lim_{\delta \to 0} \frac{P(T \le t + \delta \mid T > t)}{\delta} = \alpha$$

The result implies that α can be interpreted as the mean rate at which new events occur. his observation will be useful in the analysis of birth-and-death processes in Section 6.2.3.

Property 3: The Minimum of Independent Exponentially Distributed Random Variables Is Exponentially Distributed.   A third property characterizing the exponential distribution is that the minimum of independent exponentially distributed random variables is exponentially distributed. To explain this in more detail, assume that $T_1, T_2, \ldots, T_n$ are n independent, exponentially distributed random variables with parameters $\alpha_1, \alpha_2, \ldots, \alpha_n$ respectively. (Here *independent* means that the distribution of each of these variables is independent of the distributions of all the others.) Furthermore, let T_{min} be the random variable representing the minimum of $T_1, T_2, \ldots, T_n$; that is, $T_{min} = \min\{T_1, T_2, \ldots, T_n\}$. It can be asserted that T_{min} follows an exponential distribution with parameter

$$\alpha = \sum_{i=1}^{n} \alpha_i$$

MATHEMATICAL DERIVATION

$$P(T_{min} > t) = P(T_1 > t, T_2 > t, \ldots, T_n > t) = P(T_1 > t)P(T_2 > t) \ldots P(T_n > t)$$

$$= e^{-\alpha_1 t} e^{-\alpha_2 t} \ldots e^{-\alpha_n t} = e^{-\left(\sum_{i=1}^{n} \alpha_i\right) t}$$

To interpret the result, assume that $T_1, T_2, \ldots, T_n$ represent the remaining service times for n jobs currently being served in n parallel servers operating independently of each other. T_{min} then represents the time remaining until the first of these n jobs has been fully serviced and can leave the service facility. Because T_{min} is exponentially distributed with parameter α, the implication is that currently, when all n servers are occupied, this multiple-server queuing system performs in the same way as a single-server system with service time T_{min}. The result becomes even more transparent if one assumes that the parallel servers are identical. This means that the remaining service times $T_1, T_2, \ldots, T_n$ are exponential with parameter μ, meaning $\mu = \alpha_1 = \alpha_2 = \ldots = \alpha_n$, and consequently T_{min} is exponential with parameter $\alpha = n\mu$. This result is useful in the analysis of multiple-server systems.

In the context of interarrival times, this property implies that with a calling population consisting of n customer types, all displaying exponentially distributed interarrival times but with different parameters $\alpha_1, \alpha_2, \ldots, \alpha_n$, the time between two arrivals is T_{min}. Consequently, the arrival process of undifferentiated customers has interarrival times that are exponentially distributed with parameter

$$\alpha = \sum_{i=1}^{n} \alpha_i$$

Consider, forexample, a highway where connecting traffic arrives via a on-ramp. Assume that just before the on-ramp, the time between consecutive vehicles passing a given point on the highway is exponentially distributed with a parameter $\alpha_1 = 0.5$. Furthermore, assume the time between consecutive vehicles on the ramp is exponentially distributed with parameter $\alpha_2 = 1$. After the two traffic flows have merged (i.e., after the on-ramp), the time between consecutive vehicles passing a point on the highway is exponentially distributed with a parameter $\alpha = \alpha_1 + \alpha_2 = 1.5$.

The Exponential Distribution, the Poisson Distribution, and the Poisson Process.
Consider a simple queuing system, say a bank, and assume that the time T between consecutive customer arrivals is exponentially distributed with parameter λ. An important issue for the bank is to estimate how many customers might arrive during a certain time interval t. As it turns out, this number will be Poisson distributed with a mean value of λt. More precisely, let $X(t)$ represent the number of customers that has arrived by time t ($t \geq 0$). If one starts counting arrivals at time 0, then $X(t)$ is Poisson distributed with mean λt, this is often denoted $X(t) \in Po(\lambda t)$. Moreover, the probability that exactly n customers have arrived by time t is:

$$P(X(t) = n) = \frac{(\lambda t)^n e^{-\lambda t}}{n!} \quad \text{for } n = 0, 1, 2, ..$$

Note that if $n = 0$, the probability that no customers have arrived by time t is $P(X(t) = 0) = e^{-\lambda t}$, which is equivalent to the probability that the arrival time of the first customer is greater than t, i.e., $P(T > 0) = e^{-\lambda t}$.

Every value of t has a corresponding random variable $X(t)$ that represents the cumulative number of customers that have arrived at the bank by time t. Consequently, the arrival process to the bank can be described in terms of this family of random variables $\{X(t); t \geq 0\}$. In general terms, such a family of random variables that evolves over time is referred to as a stochastic or random process. If, as in this case, the times between arrivals are independent, identically distributed, and exponential, $\{X(t); t \geq 0\}$ defines a Poisson process. It follows that for every value of t, $X(t)$ is Poisson distributed with mean λt. An important observation is that because λt is the mean number of arrivals during t time units, the average number of arrivals per time unit, or equivalently, the mean arrival rate, for this Poisson process is λ. This implies that the average time between arrivals is $1/\lambda$. This should come as no surprise because we started with the assumption that the interarrival time T is exponentially distributed with parameter λ, or equivalently with mean $1/\lambda$. To illustrate this simple but sometimes confusing relationship between mean rates and mean times, consider an arrival (or counting) process with interarrival times that are exponentially distributed with a mean of 5 minutes. This means that the arrival process is Poisson and on average, one arrival occurs every 5 minutes. More precisely, the cumulative number of arrivals describes a Poisson process with the arrival rate λ equal to 1/5 jobs per minute, or 12 jobs per hour.

An interesting feature of the Poisson process is that aggregation or disaggregation results in new Poisson processes. Consider a simple queuing system, for example the bank discussed previously, with a calling population consisting of n different customer types, where each customer group displays a Poisson arrival process with arrival rate $\lambda_1, \lambda_2, \ldots, \lambda_n$, respectively. Assuming that all these Poisson processes are independent, the aggregated arrival process, where no distinction is made between customer types, is also a Poisson process but with mean arrival rate $\lambda = \lambda_1 + \lambda_2 + \cdots + \lambda_n$.

To illustrate the usefulness of Poisson process disaggregation, imagine a situation where the aforementioned bank has n different branch offices in the same area and the arrival process to this cluster of branch offices is Poisson with mean arrival rate λ. If every customer has the same probability p_i of choosing branch i, for $i = 1, 2, \ldots, n$ and every arriving customer must go somewhere, $\sum_{i=1}^{n} p_i = 1$, it can be shown that the arrival process to branch office j is Poisson with arrival rate $\lambda_j = p_j\lambda$. Consequently, the total Poisson arrival process has been disaggregated into branch office–specific Poisson arrival processes.

To conclude the discussion thus far, the exponential distribution is a reasonable way of describing interarrival times and service times in many situations. However, as with all modeling assumptions, it is extremely important to verify their validity before using them to model and analyze a particular process design. To investigate the assumption's validity, data on interarrival and service times must be collected and analyzed statistically. (See Chapter 9.) For the remainder of this section on analytical queuing models, it is assumed that the interarrival and service times are exponentially distributed.

6.2.2 TERMINOLOGY, NOTATION, AND LITTLE'S LAW REVISITED

This section introduces some basic notation and terminology that will be used in setting up and analyzing the queuing models to be investigated in Sections 6.2.3 through 6.2.8. A particularly important concept is that of steady-state analysis as opposed to transient analysis. Little's law (introduced in Chapter 5) also will be revisited, and its applicability for obtaining average performance measures will be discussed.

When modeling the operation of a queuing system, the challenge is to capture the variability built into the queuing process. This variability means that some way is needed to describe the different situations or states that the system will face. If one compares the deterministic models discussed in Chapters 4 and 5, the demand, activity times, and capacity were constant and known with certainty, resulting in only one specific situation or state that needs to be analyzed. As it turns out, a mathematically efficient way of describing the different situations facing a queuing system is to focus on the number of customers or jobs currently in the system (i.e., in the queue or in the service facility). Therefore, the state of a queuing system is defined as the number of customers in the system. This is intuitively appealing, because when describing the current status of a queuing system, such as the checkout station in a supermarket, the first thing that comes to mind is how many customers are in that system—both in line and being served. It is important to distinguish between the queue length (number of customers or jobs in the queue) and the number of customers in the queuing system. The former represents the number of customers or jobs waiting to be served. It excludes the customers or jobs currently in the service facility. Defining the state of the system as the total number of customers or jobs in it enables one to model situations where the mean arrival and service rates, and the corresponding exponential distributions, depend on the number of customers currently in the system. For example, tellers might work faster when they see a long line of impatient customers, or balking and reneging behavior might be contingent on the number of customers in the system.

General Notation:

$N(t)$ = The number of customers or jobs in the queuing system (in the queue and service facility) at time t ($t \geq 0$), or equivalently the state of the system at time t

$P_n(t)$ = The probability that exactly n customers are in the queuing system at time $t = P(N(t) = n)$

c = The number of parallel servers in the service facility

λ_n = The mean arrival rate (i.e., the expected number of arrivals per time unit) of customers or jobs when n customers are present in the system (i.e., at state n)

μ_n = The mean service rate (i.e., the expected number of customers or jobs leaving the service facility per time unit) when n customers or jobs are in the system

In cases where λ_n is constant for all n, this constant arrival rate will be denoted with λ. Similarly, in cases where the service facility consists of c identical servers in parallel, each with the same constant service rate, this constant rate will be denoted by μ. This service rate is valid only when the server is busy. Furthermore, note that from property 3 of the exponential distribution discussed in Section 6.2.1, it is known that if k ($k \leq c$) servers are busy, the service rate for the entire service facility at this instance *is* $k\mu$. Consequently, the maximum service rate for the facility when all servers are working is $c\mu$. It follows that under constant arrival and service rates, $1/\lambda$ is the mean interarrival time between customers, and $1/\mu$ is the mean service time at each of the individual servers.

Another queuing characteristic related to λ and μ is the utilization factor, ρ, which describes the expected fraction of time that the service facility is busy. If the arrival rate is λ and the service facility consists of one server with constant service rate μ, then the utilization factor for that server is $\rho = \lambda/\mu$. If c identical servers are in the service facility, the utilization factor for the entire service facility is $\rho = \lambda/c\mu$. The utilization factor can be interpreted as the ratio between the mean demand for capacity per time unit (λ) and the mean service capacity available per time unit ($c\mu$). To illustrate, consider a switchboard operator at a law firm. On average, 20 calls per hour come into the switchboard, and it takes the operator on average 2 minutes to figure out what the customer wants and forward the call to the right person in the firm. This means that the arrival rate is $\lambda = 20$ calls per hour, the service rate is $\mu = 60/2 = 30$ calls per hour, and the utilization factor for the switchboard operator is $\rho = 20/30 = 67$ percent. In other words, on average, the operator is on the phone 67 percent of the time.

As reflected by the general notation, the probabilistic characteristics of the queuing system is in general dependent on the initial state and changes over time. More precisely, the probability of finding n customers or jobs in the system (or equivalently, that the system is in state n) changes over time and depends on how many customers or jobs were in the system initially. When the queuing system displays this behavior, it is said to be in a transient condition or transient state. Fortunately, as time goes by, the probability of finding the system in state n will in most cases stabilize and become independent of the initial state and the time elapsed (i.e., $\lim_{t \to \infty} P_n(t) = P_n$). When this happens, it is said that the system has reached a steady-state condition (or often just that it has reached steady state). Furthermore, the probability distribution $\{P_n; n = 0, 1, 2, \ldots\}$ is referred to as the steady-state state or stationary distribution. Most results in queuing theory are based on analyzing the system when it has reached steady state. This so-called steady-state analysis is also the exclusive focus in this investigation of analytical queuing models. For a given queuing system, Figure 6.5 illustrates the transient and steady-state behavior of the number of customers in the system at time t, $N(t)$. It also depicts the expected number of customers in the system,

$$E[N(t)] = \sum_{n=0}^{\infty} nP_n(t)$$

(Recall that $P_n(t)$ is the probability of n customers in the system at time t, i.e., $P_n(t) = P(N(t) = n)$)

Both $N(t)$ and $E[N(t)]$ change dramatically with the time t for small t values; that is, while the system is in a transient condition. However, as time goes by, their behavior stabilizes and a steady-state condition is reached. Note that per definition, in steady state $P_n(t) = P_n$ for every state $n = 0, 1, 2, \ldots$. Consequently,

$$E[N(t)] = \sum_{n=0}^{\infty} nP_n$$

This implies that as a steady-state condition is approached, the expected number of customers in the system, $E[N(t)]$, should approach a constant value independent of time t. Figure 6.5 shows that this is indeed the case, as t grows large $E[N(t)]$ approaches

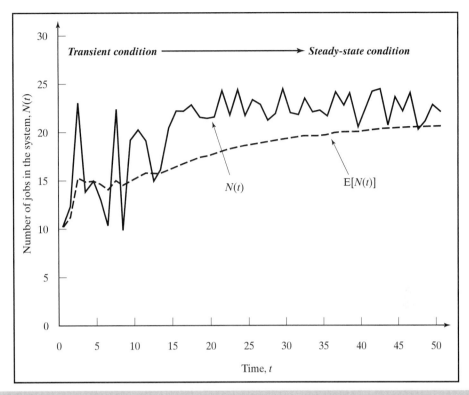

FIGURE 6.5 **Illustration of Transient and Steady-State Conditions for a Given Queuing Process. *N(t)* Is the Number of Customers in the System at Time *t*, and *E(N(t))* Represents the Expected Number of Customers in the System**

21.5 customers. $N(t)$, on the other hand, will not converge to a constant value; it is a random variable for which a steady-state behavior is characterized by a stationary probability distribution, $(P_n, n = 1, 2, 3, \dots)$, independent of the time t.

Due to the focus on steady-state analysis, a relevant question is whether all queuing systems are guaranteed to reach a steady state condition. Furthermore, if this is not the case, how can one know which systems eventually will reach steady state? The answer to the first question is no; there could well be systems where the queue explodes and grows to an infinite size, implying that a steady-state condition is never reached. As for the second question, a sufficient criterion for the system to eventually reach a steady-state condition is that $\rho < 1$. In other words, if the mean capacity demand is less than the mean available service capacity, it is guaranteed that the queue will not explode in size. However, in situations where restrictions are placed on the queue length ($M/M/c/K$ in Section 6.2.6) or the calling population is finite ($M/M/c/\infty/N$ in Section 6.2.7), the queue can never grow to infinity. Consequently, these systems will always reach a steady-state condition even if $\rho > 1$.

For the steady-state analysis that will follow in Sections 6.2.3 through 6.2.7, the following notation will be used.

P_n = The probability of finding exactly n customers or jobs in the system, or equivalently the probability that the system is in state n

L = The expected number of customers or jobs in the system, including the queue and the service facility

L_q = The expected number of customers or jobs in the queue

W = The expected time customers or jobs spend in the system, including waiting time in the queue and time spent in the service facility

W_q = The expected time customers or jobs spend waiting in the queue before they get served

Using the definition of *expected value*, the expected number of customers or jobs in the system can be determined as follows.

$$L = \sum_{n=0}^{\infty} nP_n$$

Furthermore, by recognizing that in a queuing system with c parallel servers, the queue will be empty as long as c or fewer customers are in the system, the expected number of customers in the queue can be obtained as follows.

$$L_q = \sum_{n=c}^{\infty} (n - c)P_n$$

To determine W and W_q, one can turn to an important relationship that is used extensively in steady-state analysis of queuing systems—namely, Little's law, which also was discussed in Chapter 5. In the following, this basic relationship will be recapitulated and it will be shown how it can be extended to a more general situation with state-dependent arrival rates.

Assuming first that the mean arrival rate is constant and independent of the system state, $\lambda_n = \lambda$ for all n, Little's law states that:

$$L = \lambda W \quad \text{and} \quad L_q = \lambda W_q$$

For an intuitive explanation, think of a queuing system as a pipeline where customers arrive at one end, enter the pipeline (the system), work their way through it, and then emerge at the other end and leave. Now consider a customer just before he or she leaves the pipeline (the system), which is such that customers cannot pass one another. Assume that 2 hours have gone by since the customer entered it. All the customers currently in the pipeline must have entered it during these 2 hours, so the current number of customers in the pipeline can be determined by counting how many have arrived during these 2 hours. Little's law builds on the same logic but states the relationships in terms of expected values: The mean number of customers in the system (or the queue) can be obtained as the mean number of arrivals per time unit multiplied by the mean time a customer spends in the system (or the queue).

In case the arrival rate is state dependent, that is, λ_n is not the same for all n, Little's law still applies, but the average arrival rate $\overline{\lambda}$ has to be used instead of λ. The general expressions are then:

$$L = \overline{\lambda} W \quad \text{and} \quad L_q = \overline{\lambda} W_q \quad \text{where} \quad \overline{\lambda} = \sum_{n=0}^{\infty} \lambda_n P_n$$

Note that if $\lambda_n = \lambda$ for all n, it means that $\overline{\lambda} = \lambda$.

Another useful relationship in cases where the service rate at each server in the service facility is state independent and equal to μ is:

$$W = W_q + \frac{1}{\mu}$$

This relationship follows because W_q is the expected time spent in the queue, $1/\mu$ is the expected service time, and W is the expected time spent in the queue and service facility together. An important observation is that by using this expression together with Little's law, it suffices to know $\bar{\lambda}$ and one of the mean performance measures L, L_q, W, or W_q, and all the others can be easily obtained.

6.2.3 BIRTH-AND-DEATH PROCESSES

All the queuing models considered in this chapter are based on the general birth-and-death process. Although the name sounds ominous, in queuing, a birth simply represents the arrival of a customer or job to the queuing system, and a death represents the departure of a fully serviced customer or job from that same system. Still, queuing is just one of many applications for the general birth-and-death process, with one of the first being models of population growth, hence the name.

A birth-and-death process describes probabilistically how the number of customers in the queuing system, $N(t)$, evolves over time. Remember from Section 6.2.2 that $N(t)$ is the state of the system at time t. Focusing on the steady-state behavior, analyzing the birth-and-death process enables one to determine the stationary probability distribution for finding $0, 1, 2 \ldots$ customers in the queuing system. By using the stationary distribution, determining mean performance measures such as the expected number of customers in the system, L, or in the queue, L_q, is straightforward. With Little's law, it is then easy to determine the corresponding average waiting times W and W_q. The stationary distribution also allows for an evaluation of the likelihood of extreme situations to occur; for example, the probability of finding the queuing system empty or the probability that it contains more than a certain number of customers.

In simple terms, the birth-and-death process assumes that births (arrivals) and deaths (departures) occur randomly and independently from each other. However, the average number of births and deaths per time unit might depend on the state of the system (number of customers or jobs in the queuing system). A more precise definition of a birth-and-death process is based on the following four properties.

1. For each state, $N(t) = n; n = 0, 1, 2, \ldots$, the time remaining until the next birth (arrival), T_B, is exponentially distributed with parameter λ_n. (Remember that the state of a queuing system is defined by the number of customers or jobs in that system.)
2. For each state, $N(t) = n; n = 0, 1, 2, \ldots$, the time remaining until the next death (service completion), T_D, is exponentially distributed with parameter μ_n.
3. The time remaining until the next birth, T_B, and the time remaining until the next death, T_D, are mutually independent.
4. For each state, $N(t) = n; n = 1, 2, \ldots$, the next event to occur is either a single birth, $n \rightarrow n + 1$, or a single death, $n \rightarrow n - 1$.

The birth-and-death process can be illustrated graphically in a so-called rate diagram (also referred to as a state diagram). See Figure 6.6. In this diagram, the states (the number of customers in the system) are depicted as numbered circles or nodes, and the transitions

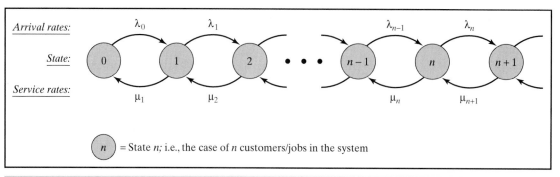

FIGURE 6.6 Rate Diagram Describing a General Birth-and-Death Process

between these states are indicated by arrows or directed arcs. For example, the state when zero customers are in the system is depicted by a node labeled 0. The rate at which the system moves from one state to the next is indicated in connection to the arc in question. Consider, for example, state n. The interarrival times and the service times are exponential with parameters λ_n and μ_n, respectively, so it is known from the properties of the exponential distribution that the mean arrival rate (or birth rate) must be λ_n and the service rate (or death rate) is μ_n. This means that the process moves from state n to state $n-1$ at rate μ_n and from state n to state $n+1$ at rate λ_n. The rate diagram also illustrates the fact that the birth-and-death process by definition allows for transitions involving only one birth or death at a time ($n \rightarrow n+1$ or $n \rightarrow n-1$).

The rate diagram is an excellent tool for describing the queuing process conceptually. However, it is also useful for determining the steady-state probability distribution $\{P_n; n = 0,1,2 \dots\}$ of finding $0,1,2,\dots$ customers in the system. A key observation in this respect is the so-called Rate In = Rate Out Principle, which states that when the birth-and-death process is in a steady-state condition, the expected rate of entering any given state n ($n = 1,2,3,\dots$) is equal to the expected rate of leaving the state. To conceptualize this principle, think of each state n as a water reservoir, where the water level represents the probability P_n. In order for the water level to remain constant (stationary), the average rate of water flowing into the reservoir must equal the average outflow rate.

Rate In = Rate Out Principle. For every state $n = 0, 1, 2, \dots$ the expected rate of entering the state = the expected rate of leaving the state.

MATHEMATICAL DERIVATION OF THE RATE IN = RATE OUT PRINCIPLE

Consider an arbitrary state n and count the number of times the process enters and leaves this state, starting at time 0.

Let

$I_n(t)$ = The number of times the process has entered state n by time $t \geq 0$
$O_n(t)$ = The number of times the process has left state n by time $t \geq 0$

It follows that for any t, the absolute difference between $I_n(t)$ and $O_n(t)$ is 0 or 1:

$$\left| I_n(t) - O_n(t) \right| \leq 1$$

(continued)

Dividing this expression by t and letting $t \to \infty$—that is, by considering what happens to the average number of arrivals and departures at state n in steady-state—the following is obtained.

$$\left| \frac{I_n(t)}{t} - \frac{O_n(t)}{t} \right| \leq \frac{1}{t} \quad \text{and} \quad \lim_{t \to \infty} \left| \frac{I_n(t)}{t} - \frac{O_n(t)}{t} \right| = 0$$

which implies that:

$$\lim_{t \to \infty} \frac{I_n(t)}{t} = \lim_{t \to \infty} \frac{O_n(t)}{t}$$

The Rate In = Rate Out Principle follows, because by definition:

$$\lim_{t \to \infty} \frac{I_n(t)}{t} = \text{Mean rate (average number of times per time unit)}$$
at which the process enters state n = Expected Rate In

$$\lim_{t \to \infty} \frac{O_n(t)}{t} = \text{Mean rate at which the process leaves state} \quad n = \text{Expected Rate Out}$$

The following example illustrates how the rate diagram and the Rate In = Rate Out Principle can be used to determine the stationary distribution for a queuing process.

Example 6.1: Queuing Analysis at TravelCall Inc.

TravelCall Inc. is a small travel agency that only services customers over the phone. Currently, only one travel agent is available to answer incoming customer calls. The switchboard can accommodate two calls on hold in addition to the one currently being answered by the travel agent. Customers who call when the switchboard is full get a busy signal and are turned away. Consequently, at most three customers can be found in the queuing system at any time. The calls arrive to the travel agent according to a Poisson process with a mean rate of nine calls per hour. The calls will be answered in the order they arrive; that is, the queuing discipline is FIFO. On average, it takes the travel agent 6 minutes to service a customer, and the service time follows an exponential distribution. The management of TravelCall wants to determine what the probability is of finding zero, one, two, or three customers in the system. If the probability of finding two or three customers in the system is high, it indicates that maybe the capacity should be increased.

The first observation is that the queuing system represented by TravelCall fits the aforementioned criteria 1 through 4 that define a birth-and-death process. (Using the previously defined framework for classifying queuing models, it also represents an $M/M/1/3$ process). Second, it should be recognized that the objective is to determine the stationary probability distribution $\{P_n, n = 0, 1, 2, 3\}$ describing the probability of finding zero, one, two, or three customers in the system. Now that the system and the objective of the analysis are clear, it is time for some detailed calculations.

The first step in the numerical analysis is to decide on a time unit, and to determine the mean arrival and service rates for each of the states of the system. The arrival rate and the service rate are constant and independent of the number of customers in the system. They are hereafter denoted by λ and μ, respectively. All rates are expressed in number of occurrences per hour. However, it does not matter which time unit is used as long as it is used consistently. From the aforementioned data, it follows that $\lambda = 9$ calls per hour and $\mu = 60/6 = 10$ calls per hour.

Because the number of states the mean arrival rate, and the service rate for each state are known, it is possible to construct the specific rate diagram describing the queuing process. See Figure 6.7. For state 0, the mean rate at which the system moves to state 1 must be λ, because this is the mean rate at which customers arrive to the system. On the other hand, the service rate for state 0 must be zero, because at this state the system is empty and there are no customers who can leave. For state 1, the mean rate at which the system moves to state 2 is still λ,

FIGURE 6.7 Rate Diagram for the Single Server Queuing Process at TravelCall

because the mean arrival rate is unchanged. The service rate is now μ, because this is the mean rate at which the one customer in the system will leave. For state 2, the mean arrival and service rates are the same as in state 1. At state 3, the system is full and no new customers are allowed to enter. Consequently, the arrival rate for state 3 is zero. The service rate, on the other hand, is still μ, because three customers are in the system and the travel agent serves them with a mean service rate of μ customers per time unit.

To determine the probabilities P_0, P_1, P_2, and P_3 for finding zero, one, two, and three customers in the system, use the Rate In = Rate Out Principle applied to each state together with the necessary condition that all probabilities must sum to 1 ($P_0 + P_1 + P_2 + P_3 = 1$).

The equation expressing the Rate In = Rate Out Principle for a given state n is often called the balance equation for state n. Starting with state 0, the balance equation is obtained by recognizing that the expected rate in to state 0 is μ if the system is in state 1 and zero otherwise. See Figure 6.7. Because the probability that the system is in state 1 is P_1, the expected rate into state 0 must be μ times P_1, or μP_1. Note that P_1 can be interpreted as the fraction of the total time that the system spends in state 1. Similarly, the rate out of state 0 is λ if the system is in state 0, and zero otherwise. (See Figure 6.7). Because the probability for the system to be in state 0 is P_0, the expected rate out of state 0 is λP_0. Consequently, we have:

$$\text{Balance equation for state 0: } \mu P_1 = \lambda P_0$$

Using the same logic for state 1, the rate in to state 1 is λ if the system is in state 0 and μ if the system is in state 2, but zero otherwise. (See Figure 6.7). The expected rate into state 1 can then be expressed as $\lambda P_0 + \mu P_2$. On the other hand, the rate out of state 1 is λ, going to state 2, and μ, going to state 0, if the system is in state 1, and zero otherwise. Consequently, the expected rate out of state 1 is $\lambda P_1 + \mu P_1$, and the corresponding balance equation can be expressed as follows.

$$\text{Balance equation for state 1: } \lambda P_0 + \mu P_2 = \lambda P_1 + \mu P_1$$

By proceeding in the same fashion for states 2 and 3, the complete set of balance equations summarized in Table 6.1 is obtained.

The balance equations represent a linear equation system that can be used to express the probabilities P_1, P_2, and P_3 as functions of P_0. (The reason the system of equations does not have a unique solution is that it includes four variables but only three linearly independent equations.) To find the exact values of P_0, P_1, P_2, and P_3, it is necessary to use the condition that their sum must equal 1.

Starting with the balance equation for state 0, one finds that $P_1 = (\lambda/\mu)P_0$. Adding the equation for state 0 to that of state 1 results in $\lambda P_0 + \mu P_2 + \mu P_1 = \lambda P_1 + \mu P_1 + \lambda P_0$, which simplifies

TABLE 6.1 Balance Equations for the Queuing Process at TravelCall

State	*Balance Equations:* *Expected Rate In = Expected Rate Out*
0	$\mu P_1 = \lambda P_0$
1	$\lambda P_0 + \mu P_2 = \lambda P_1 + \mu P_1$
2	$\lambda P_1 + \mu P_3 = \lambda P_2 + \mu P_2$
3	$\lambda P_2 = \mu P_3$

to $\mu P_2 = \lambda P_1$. This means that $P_2 = (\lambda/\mu)P_1$ and using the previous result that $P_1 = (\lambda/\mu)P_0$, one finds that $P_2 = (\lambda/\mu)^2 P_0$. In the same manner, by adding the simplified equation $\mu P_2 = \lambda P_1$ to the balance equation for state 2, one finds that $\lambda P_1 + \mu P_3 + \mu P_2 = \lambda P_2 + \mu P_2 + \lambda P_1$, which simplifies to $\mu P_3 = \lambda P_2$. Note that this equation is identical to the balance equation for state 3, which then becomes redundant. P_3 can now be expressed in P_0 as follows: $P_3 = (\lambda/\mu)P_2 = (\lambda/\mu)^3 P_0$. Using the expressions $P_1 = (\lambda/\mu)P_0$, $P_2 = (\lambda/\mu)^2 P_0$, and $P_3 = (\lambda/\mu)^3 P_0$, together with the condition that $P_0 + P_1 + P_2 + P_3 = 1$, the following is obtained.

$$P_0\left(1 + \frac{\lambda}{\mu} + \frac{\lambda^2}{\mu^2} + \frac{\lambda^3}{\mu^3}\right) = 1 \quad \text{equivalent to} \quad P_0\left(\frac{\mu^3 + \mu^2\lambda + \mu\lambda^2 + \lambda^3}{\mu^3}\right) = 1,$$

which results in

$$P_0 = \frac{\mu^3}{\mu^3 + \mu^2\lambda + \mu\lambda^2 + \lambda^3}$$

Because it is known that $\lambda = 9$ and $\mu = 10$, one can obtain $P_0 = 0.2908$. Because $P_1 = (\lambda/\mu)P_0$, $P_2 = (\lambda/\mu)^2 P_0$, and $P_3 = (\lambda/\mu)^3 P_0$, one also has $P_1 = (9/10)P_0 \approx 0.2617$, $P_2 = (9/10)^2 P_0 \approx 0.2355$, and $P_3 = (9/10)^3 P_0 \approx 0.2120$.

These calculations predict that in steady state, the travel agent will be idle 29 percent of the time (P_0). This also represents the probability that an arbitrary caller does not have to spend time in the queue before talking to an agent. At the same time, it is now known that 21 percent of the time the system is expected to be full (P_3). This means that all new callers get a busy signal, resulting in losses for the agency. Moreover, the probability that a customer who calls in will be put on hold is $P_1 + P_2 = 0.2617 + 0.2355 \approx 0.50$.

Although the explicit costs involved have not been considered, it seems reasonable that TravelCall would like to explore the possibilities of allowing more calls to be put on hold; that is, to allow a longer queue. This way, they can increase the utilization of the travel agent and catch some customers who now take their business elsewhere. Another more drastic option to reduce the number of lost sales might be to hire one more travel agent.

The procedure for determining the stationary distribution of a general birth-and-death process with state-dependent arrival and service rates is analogous to the approach explained in Example 6.1. The balance equations are constructed in the same way, but their appearance is slightly different, as shown in Table 6.2. (See also the corresponding rate diagram in Figure 6.6.)

A complicating factor is that a large state space—one with many states to consider—means that it would be tedious to find a solution following the approach in Example 6.1. For example, to handle the cases of infinite queue lengths, some additional algebraic techniques are needed to obtain the necessary expressions. This is the motivation for studying the specialized models in Sections 6.4 through 6.7, where expressions are available for the

TABLE 6.2 Balance Equations for the General Birth-and-Death Process

State	Balance Equations: Expected Rate In = Expected Rate Out
0	$\mu_1 P_1 = \lambda_0 P_0$
1	$\lambda_0 P_0 + \mu_2 P_2 = \lambda_1 P_1 + \mu_1 P_1$
$\vdots$	$\vdots$
$n-1$	$\lambda_{n-2}P_{n-2} + \mu_n P_n = \lambda_{n-1}P_{n-1} + \mu_{n-1}P_{n-1}$
n	$\lambda_{n-1}P_{n-1} + \mu_{n+1}P_{n+1} = \lambda_n P_n + \mu_n P_n$
$\vdots$	$\vdots$

steady-state probabilities and for certain important performance measures such as average number of customers in the system and queue, as well as the corresponding waiting times. Still, for smaller systems, the general approach offers more flexibility.

As previously mentioned, interesting performance measures for queuing processes are the average number of customers or jobs in the system (L) and in the queue (L_q), as well as the corresponding average waiting times (W and W_q). With the stationary probability distribution $\{P_n; n = 1, 2, 3, ...\}$ available, it is straightforward to obtain all these measures from the definition of expected value and Little's law. (See Section 6.2.2 for the general expressions.) Next is an explanation of how to do this in the context of TravelCall Inc.

Example 6.2: Determining Average Performance Measures at TravelCall

In Example 6.1, the steady-state probability distribution was determined for zero, one, two, and three customers in the queuing system describing the operations at TravelCall. The probabilities were $P_0 = 0.2908, P_1 = 0.2617, P_2 = 0.2355$, and $P_3 = 0.2120$. Although interesting information, TravelCall also wants know what this means in terms of average performance measures.

- The expected number of customers in the system = L.
- The expected number of customers waiting in the queue = L_q.
- The expected time a customer spends in the system = W.
- The expected time a customer spends in the queue before being served = W_q.

Because the probabilities of having zero, one, two, and three customers in the system are known, to calculate L simply apply the definition of an expected value as follows.

$$L = \sum_{n=0}^{\infty} nP_n = (0)P_0 + (1)P_1 + (2)P_2 + P_3$$
$$= 0.2617 + (2)0.2355 + (3)0.2120$$
$$= 1.3687 \approx 1.37 \text{ customers}$$

To calculate L_q, proceed in a similar way but subtract the one customer that is being served in all those situations (states) where one or more customers are in the system. To clarify, when one customer is in the system, this customer is being served by the travel agent so the queue is empty. If two customers are in the system, $n = 2$, then one is being served by the travel agent and one is waiting in the queue. Finally, if three customers are in the system, then two of them are in the queue. The expected number of customers in the queue is obtained in the following way.

$$L_q = \sum_{n=1}^{\infty} (n-1)P_n = (1-1)P_1 + (2-1)P_2 + (3-1)P_3$$
$$= 0.2355 + (2)0.2120 = 0.6595 \approx 0.66 \text{ customers}$$

To determine the mean time spent in the system, W, and the mean time spent in the queue, W_q, use Little's law as discussed in Section 6.2.2.

$$L = \bar{\lambda}W \quad \text{and} \quad L_q = \bar{\lambda}W_q \quad \text{where} \quad \bar{\lambda} = \sum_{n=0}^{\infty} \lambda_n P_n$$

First determine the average arrival rate, which is not λ because when three customers are in the system, no more customers can be accommodated and the arrival rate for state 3 is effectively zero. For all other states, the arrival rate is λ. See Figure 6.7.

$$\bar{\lambda} = \sum_{n=0}^{3} P_n \lambda_n = \lambda P_0 + \lambda P_1 + \lambda P_2 + 0P_3 = \lambda(P_0 + P_1 + P_2)$$
$$= \lambda(1 - P_3) = 9(1 - 0.2120) = 7.0920$$
$$\approx 7.09 \text{ customers per hour}$$

W and W_q can now be obtained from Little's formula.

$$W = \frac{L}{\overline{\lambda}} = \frac{1.3687}{7.0920} \approx 0.1930 \text{ hours} \approx 11.6 \text{ minutes}$$

$$W_q = \frac{L_q}{\overline{\lambda}} = \frac{0.6595}{7.0920} \approx 0.0930 \text{ hours} \approx 5.6 \text{ minutes}$$

Note that $W - W_q = 11.6 - 5.6 = 6$ minutes, which is the expected service time, or $1/\mu$. With these average performance measures, TravelCall is in a better position to decide whether something needs to be done with respect to the system design. The waiting time of 5.6 minutes on the average might not seem long; however, for the customer waiting at the other end of the phone line, this might be perceived as a very long time, and it could lead to reneging (customer leaving the queue before being served; see Section 6.1.1).

Thus far, the examples have assumed that the service facility has a constant mean service rate. To illustrate a more general model, Example 6.3 extends Examples 6.1 and 6.2 to a situation with two travel agents and state-dependent mean service rates. By relating back to the results in Examples 6.1 and 6.2, this example also shows how these types of queuing models can be used for better-informed design decisions.

Example 6.3: TravelCall Inc. Revisited

Based on the queuing analysis performed on the existing process in Examples 6.1 and 6.2, the management of TravelCall is contemplating hiring a second travel agent. However, before proceeding they want to investigate the effects such a design change might have regarding the following.

- The fraction of time, or equivalently, the probability that the system is empty.
- The fraction of time that the system is full and potentially loses customers.
- The probability that a customer gets to talk to a travel agent immediately.
- The probability that a customer will be put on hold.
- The average performance measures L, L_q, W, and W_q.

The second travel agent is presumed to be just as efficient as the existing one, meaning the service time for the new agent is also exponentially distributed with the parameter $\mu = 10$ customers per hour. The customer arrival rate is assumed unaffected; that is, Poisson distributed with mean rate $\lambda = 9$ customers per hour. Moreover, the travel agents work independently of each other and fully service one customer at a time. (In fact, TravelCall will encourage them to work from their homes and thereby reduce the overhead costs for office space, still using a common switchboard though.) As a result, the travel agency can be modeled as a queuing system with two parallel and identical servers. Recall from Section 6.1 that this means the mean service rate for the service facility is 2μ when both servers are busy and μ when only one server is busy. This observation is key in constructing the correct rate diagram shown in Figure 6.8. Starting in state 0, no customers are in the system so the service rate is zero and the arrival rate is λ. In state 1, one customer is in the system, and is currently being served by one of the travel agents at the service rate μ. The arrival rate is unaffected and equals λ. In state 2, two customers are in the system, each being serviced by a travel agent. As discussed previously, the service rate for the service facility with the two parallel agents is then 2μ. The arrival rate is still λ. In state 3, three customers are in the system, one in the queue and two being serviced in parallel. The combined service rate for the two agents

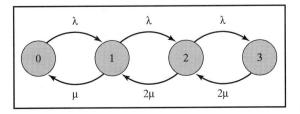

FIGURE 6.8 Rate Diagram for the Two Server Queuing Process at TravelCall

> **TABLE 6.3** Balance Equations for the Two-Server
> Queuing Process at TravelCall
>
> | State | *Balance Equations:*
Expected Rate In = Expected Rate Out |
> | --- | --- |
> | 0 | $\mu P_1 = \lambda P_0$ |
> | 1 | $\lambda P_0 + 2\mu P_2 = \lambda P_1 + \mu P_1$ |
> | 2 | $\lambda P_1 + 2\mu P_3 = \lambda P_2 + 2\mu P_2$ |
> | 3 | $\lambda P_2 = 2\mu P_3$ |

is, therefore, still 2μ. The arrival rate, on the other hand, is zero because the system is full and any new arrivals are turned away.

Based on the rate diagram, the balance equations can be formulated as in Table 6.3, assuring that for each state the expected rate in equals the expected rate out.

Solving the equation system in the same way as described in Example 6.1, one obtains P_1, P_2, and P_3 expressed in P_0: $P_1 = (\lambda/\mu)P_0$, $P_2 = (\lambda^2/2\mu^2)P_0$, $P_3 = (\lambda^3/4\mu^3)P_0$. Using these expressions in conjunction with the condition that the steady-state probabilities must sum to 1; that is, the system must always be in one of the attainable states, $P_0 + P_1 + P_2 + P_3 = 1$, one gets the following.

$$P_0\left(1 + \frac{\lambda}{\mu} + \frac{\lambda^2}{2\mu^2} + \frac{\lambda^3}{4\mu^3}\right) = 1 \quad \text{equivalent to} \quad P_0\left(\frac{4\mu^3 + 4\mu^2\lambda + 2\mu\lambda^2 + \lambda^3}{4\mu^3}\right) = 1,$$

which results in

$$P_0 = \frac{4\mu^3}{4\mu^3 + 4\mu^2\lambda + 2\mu\lambda^2 + \lambda^3}$$

With $\lambda = 9$ and $\mu = 10$, this means $P_0 = (1/2.48725) \approx 0.4021$ and consequently $P_1 = (\lambda/\mu)P_0 = (0.9)P_0 \approx 0.3618$, $P_2 = (\lambda^2/2\mu^2)P_0 = (0.9^2/2)P_0 \approx 0.1628$, and $P_3 = (\lambda^3/4\mu^3)P_0 = (0.9^3/4)P_0 \approx 0.0733$. It can then be concluded that in the new design:

- The fraction of time that the system is empty $= P_0 \approx 40$ percent.
- The fraction of time that the system is full and potentially loses customers $= P_3 \approx$ 7 percent.
- The probability that a customer gets to talk to a travel agent immediately $= P_0 + P_1 \approx$ 76 percent.
- The probability that a customer will be put on hold $= P_2 \approx 16$ percent.

With the steady-state probability distribution in place, the expected number of customers in the system and in the queue, L and L_q, respectively, can be determined. (In comparing the expressions that follow with the general formulae, note that in the present case $c = 2$ and $P_n = 0$ for $n > 3$.)

$$L = \sum_{n=0}^{\infty} nP_n = (0)P_0 + (1)P_1 + (2)P_2 + (3)P_3 = 0.3618 + (2)0.1628 + (3)0.0733 = 0.9073$$

$$\approx 0.91 \text{ customers}$$

$$L_q = \sum_{n=2}^{\infty} (n - 2)P_n = (2 - 2)P_2 + (3 - 2)P_3 = (1)0.0733 \approx 0.07 \text{ customers}$$

TABLE 6.4 Comparison of the Process Performance When There Are Two Travel Agents at TravelCall Instead of One

Performance Characteristic	One Travel Agent	Two Travel Agents
Fraction of time the system is empty	29%	40%
Fraction of time the system is full	21%	7%
Probability that a customer gets immediate access to a travel agent	29%	76%
Probability that a customer will be put on hold	50%	16%
Expected number of customers in the system (L)	1.37 customers	0.91 customers
Expected number of customers in the queue (L_q)	0.66 customers	0.07 customers
Expected time spent in the system (W)	11.6 minutes	6.5 minutes
Expected waiting time in the queue (W_q)	5.6 minutes	0.5 minutes

The expected time in the system, W, and in the queue, W_q, can now be obtained from Little's law.

$$\bar{\lambda} = \sum_{n=0}^{\infty} \lambda_n P_n = \lambda P_0 + \lambda P_1 + \lambda P_2 + 0P_3 = \lambda(P_0 + P_1 + P_2) = 9(0.4021 + 0.3618 + 0.1628)$$
$$= 8.3403 \approx 8.34 \text{ customers per hour}$$
$$W = \frac{L}{\bar{\lambda}} = \frac{0.9073}{8.3403} \approx 0.1088 \text{ hours} \approx 6.5 \text{ minutes}$$
$$W_q = \frac{L_q}{\bar{\lambda}} = \frac{0.0733}{8.3403} \approx 0.0088 \text{ hours} \approx 0.5 \text{ minutes}$$

Table 6.4 contrasts the results obtained for the system with two travel agents with those obtained for the current single-server system evaluated in Examples 6.1 and 6.2.

Hiring a second agent dramatically increases the customer service levels. For example, the probability that a customer will get immediate access to an agent goes up from 29 percent in the single-server system to 76 percent when two travel agents are working the phones. At the same time, the average waiting time on hold decreases from 5.6 minutes in the current single-server process to 0.5 minutes in the new design. Moreover, in terms of potentially lost sales, customers in the two-server system encounter a busy signal only 7 percent of the time compared to 21 percent in the single-server system.

This improved service comes at the expense of lower resource utilization, indicated by the fact that the fraction of time the system is empty goes up from 29 percent in the single-server system to 40 percent in the system with two agents. Hiring the second travel agent also increases the operational costs significantly. In order to make an informed decision whether to pursue the new design, these service costs must be quantified and compared against the expected revenue increase due to the improved customer service. Models dealing with these issues will be examined in Section 6.2.8.

Hiring a second agent is just one possibility for changing the process design. Another option is to allow customers to contact the travel agent via other channels, such as through a Web site or e-mail. In this way, the existing travel agent can work with these requests between phone calls. Most likely, it also will lead to fewer customers calling, implying shorter waiting times for telephone customers and a lower risk of encountering a busy signal. A further analysis of this option is beyond the scope of this example but illustrates the potential advantages of thinking about doing things in new ways. Another example of creative design ideas, which relates to the design principle of treating geographically dispersed resources as if they were centralized, as discussed in Section 3.6.2, is letting the travel agents work from their homes.

Examples 6.1 through 6.3 assume that customers who have the opportunity to enter the queue also will choose to join it. However, some customers, after realizing that they

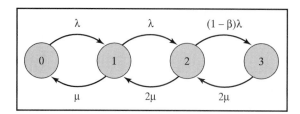

FIGURE 6.9 Rate Diagram for the Two Server Queuing Process at TravelCall if Customers Balk with Probability β, When They Do Not Get Immediate Access to a Travel Agent

will have to wait before getting served, will choose to leave; in other words, they will balk. Balking can be modeled as state-dependent arrival rates using the fact that Poisson processes can be disaggregated into new Poisson processes, as seen in Section 6.2.1. Assume, for example, that customers calling TravelCall in Example 6.3 will hang up with probability β if they don't get immediate access to a travel agent. This means that as soon as both travel agents are busy, the arrival process will be Poisson with mean arrival rate $(1 - \beta)\lambda$ as opposed to a mean arrival rate of λ for the other states. Figure 6.9 shows the corresponding rate diagram. It might be hard to assess an accurate value of β because customers who hang up are not registered. Most likely, a market research effort would have to be launched to explore and better understand customer attitudes.

Given the rate diagram in Figure 6.9, the model with balking can be analyzed using the same approach as in Examples 6.1 through 6.3.

The discussion on balking and state-dependent arrival rates concludes this investigation of the general birth-and-death process. Sections 6.2.4 through 6.2.7 focus on some important birth-and-death processes with specialized structures that are often used in queuing analysis. Their importance stems from their wide applicability and the expressions that make it straightforward to evaluate important performance measures quickly. Still, it is important to remember that all of these models are specialized birth-and-death processes that can be analyzed using the general approach explored in this section.

6.2.4 THE *M/M/*1 MODEL

The *M/M/*1 model is a special case of the general birth-and-death process described in Section 6.2.3. Because of its simplicity, it has found applications in a wide range of areas, and it is one of the most commonly used queuing models. It describes a queuing system with a single server, exponentially distributed service and interarrival times, constant arrival and service rates, an infinite calling population, and no restrictions on the queue length. More precisely, going back to the major elements of the basic queuing process, the model is based on the following assumptions.

- *Calling population*: Jobs arrive from such a large population that it can be considered infinite for modeling purposes. The jobs are independent of each other; that is, the arrival of one job does not influence the arrival of others. Also, the arrival of jobs is not influenced by the system (e.g., there are no appointments).
- *Arrival process*: The interarrival times are exponentially distributed with a constant parameter λ, independent of the number of customers in the system. In other words, the arrival process is Poisson with the mean rate λ, independent of the state of the system.
- *Queue configuration*: A single waiting line is used with no restrictions on length. The model does not consider balking or reneging.
- *Queue discipline*: The queue is managed using a FIFO rule.
- *Service mechanism*: The service facility consists of a single server, whose service times are exponentially distributed with a constant parameter μ, independent of

the number of customers in the system. Consequently, the mean service rate is μ for all states of the system.

The *M/M/1* process can be illustrated by the rate diagram in Figure 6.10. Recall from Section 6.2.3 that in this diagram, the states, that is the number of customers in the system, are depicted as numbered circles or nodes (node 0 indicates state 0 with zero customers in the system), and the transitions between these states are indicated by arrows or directed arcs. Furthermore, the rate at which the system moves from one state to the next is displayed in connection with each arc. As discussed previously, customers or jobs arrive to the system at the mean rate λ, independent of the number of customers currently in the system. Consequently, the rate at which the process moves from state n to state $n + 1$ is λ for all $n = 0, 1, 2, \ldots$. Similarly, the mean service rate at which the server services customers is μ for all states where there is someone to serve; that is, all states except state 0 when the system is empty and the service rate is zero. As a result, the rate at which the process moves from state n to $n - 1$ is μ for all $n = 1, 2, \ldots$.

For the steady-state analysis of the *M/M/1* model, the following notation, first introduced in Section 6.2.2, is used.

P_n = The probability of finding exactly n customers or jobs in the system, or equivalently, the probability that the system is in state n

λ = The mean arrival rate (the mean number of arrivals per time unit); the same for all system states

μ = The mean service rate (the mean number of service completions per time units in a busy server); constant for all relevant system states

ρ = λ/μ = utilization factor

L = The expected number of customers or jobs in the system including the queue and the service facility

L_q = The expected number of customers or jobs in the queue

W = The expected time customers or jobs spend in the system including waiting time in the queue and time spent in the service facility

W_q = The expected time customers or jobs spend waiting in the queue before they get served

A necessary and sufficient condition for the *M/M/1* process to reach steady state—that is, for the existence of a steady-state probability distribution $\{P_n, n = 0, 1, 2, \ldots\}$—is that the mean arrival rate λ is strictly less than the mean service rate μ, or equivalently $\rho < 1$. The analysis and expressions that will be explored in this section therefore assume that $\rho < 1$. If $\rho \geqslant 1$, it means that the average demand for service exceeds the average service capacity and the queue will explode in size.

FIGURE 6.10 Rate Diagram for the *M/M/1* Model

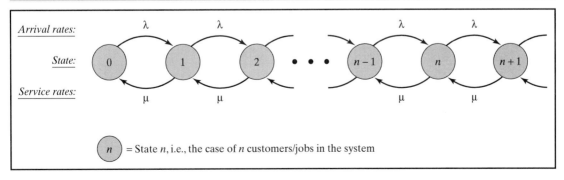

Arrival rates: λ λ λ λ

State: 0   1   2   • • • $n-1$ n $n+1$

Service rates: μ μ μ μ

n = State n, i.e., the case of n customers/jobs in the system

The steady-state operating characteristics of the $M/M/1$ system can be calculated from the following set of expressions. (The expressions can be derived using the general approach for analyzing birth-and-death processes in Section 6.2.3.)

Probability of zero jobs in the system:

$$P_0 = 1 - \rho$$

Probability that the number of jobs in the system is exactly n:

$$P_n = P_0\rho^n = (1-\rho)\rho^n$$

MATHEMATICAL DERIVATION

Using the rate diagram in Figure 6.10, it is straightforward to construct the balance equations for the $M/M/1$ queue using the approach in Section 6.2.3. See also Table 6.2 with $\lambda_n = \lambda$ and $\mu_n = \mu$ for all n. From these equations, it follows that $P_1 = (\lambda/\mu)P_0 = \rho P_0$, $P_2 = \rho^2 P_0, \ldots$ and consequently $P_n = \rho^n P_0$.

To determine P_0, invoke the condition $\sum_{n=0}^{\infty} P_n = 1$, which results in: $P_0 \sum_{n=0}^{\infty} \rho^n = 1$.

Observing that $\sum_{n=0}^{\infty} \rho^n$ is the sum of a geometric series for which it is known that

$\sum_{n=0}^{\infty} \rho^n = \dfrac{1}{1-\rho}$ for any $\rho < 1$, we get $P_0 = 1 - \rho$.

Probability that the number of jobs in the system is k or more:

$$P(n \geq k) = \rho^k$$

Probability that the number of jobs in the system is at least one:

$$P(n \geq 1) = 1 - P_0 = \rho$$

Because $P(n \geq 1)$ also represents the probability that the server is busy, it explains why ρ is known as the utilization factor for the server in this model.

MATHEMATICAL DERIVATION

$$P(n \geq k) = \sum_{n=k}^{\infty} P_n = \sum_{n=k}^{\infty} (1-\rho)\rho^n = (1-\rho)\rho^k \sum_{n=k}^{\infty} \rho^{n-k}$$

$$= (1-\rho)\rho^k \sum_{n=0}^{\infty} \rho^n = (1-\rho)\rho^k \frac{1}{1-\rho} = \rho^k$$

where we use that $\sum_{n=0}^{\infty} \rho^n = \dfrac{1}{1-\rho}$ for any $\rho < 1$.

Mean number of jobs in the system:

$$L = \frac{\rho}{1-\rho} = \frac{\lambda}{\mu - \lambda}$$

MATHEMATICAL DERIVATION

$$L = \sum_{n=0}^{\infty} nP_n = \sum_{n=0}^{\infty} n(1-\rho)\rho^n = (1-\rho)\rho\sum_{n=0}^{\infty} n\rho^{n-1} = (1-\rho)\rho\sum_{n=0}^{\infty} \frac{d}{d\rho}\rho^n$$

$$= (1-\rho)\rho\frac{d}{d\rho}\left(\sum_{n=0}^{\infty}\rho^n\right) = (1-\rho)\rho\frac{d}{d\rho}\left(\frac{1}{(1-\rho)}\right) = (1-\rho)\rho\left(\frac{1}{(1-\rho)^2}\right) = \frac{\rho}{(1-\rho)}$$

where we use that the derivative of x^n is nx^{n-1}, i.e., $\frac{d}{dx}(x^n) = nx^{n-1}$ and the fact

that $\frac{d}{d\rho}\left(\sum_{n=0}^{\infty}\rho^n\right) = \sum_{n=0}^{\infty}\frac{d}{d\rho}(\rho^n) = \sum_{n=0}^{\infty} n\rho^{n-1}$ for $\rho < 1$.

Mean number of jobs in the queue:

$$L_q = L - \rho = \frac{\rho^2}{1-\rho} = \frac{\rho\lambda}{\mu-\lambda}$$

MATHEMATICAL DERIVATION

$$L_q = \sum_{n=1}^{\infty} (n-1)P_n = \sum_{n=0}^{\infty} nP_n - \sum_{n=1}^{\infty} P_n = L - (1-P_0) = L - \rho = \frac{\rho}{1-\rho} - \rho$$

$$= \frac{\rho - (1-\rho)\rho}{1-\rho} = \frac{\rho^2}{1-\rho}$$

where we use $P_0 = 1 - \rho$.

Mean time a job spends in the system:

$$W = \frac{L}{\lambda} = \frac{1}{\mu-\lambda}$$

Mean time a job spends in the queue:

$$W_q = \frac{L_q}{\lambda} = \frac{\rho}{\mu-\lambda}$$

MATHEMATICAL DERIVATION

The expressions follow directly from Little's law, $\rho = (\lambda/\mu)$, and the afore-mentioned expressions for L and L_q.

$$W = \frac{L}{\lambda} = \frac{\rho}{(1-\rho)\lambda} = \frac{\lambda}{\mu\left(1-\frac{\lambda}{\mu}\right)\lambda} = \frac{1}{\mu-\lambda};$$

$$W_q = \frac{L_q}{\lambda} = \frac{\rho^2}{(1-\rho)\lambda} = \frac{\rho}{\mu\left(1-\frac{\lambda}{\mu}\right)} = \frac{\rho}{\mu-\lambda}$$

Example 6.4 illustrates how the previous expressions can be used to analyze a business process that can be modeled as an *M/M/*1 system.

Example 6.4: Policy Requests at an Insurance Company

An insurance company receives an average of 40 requests for new auto policies per week. Through statistical analysis, the company has been able to determine that the time between two consecutive requests arriving to the process is approximately exponentially distributed. A single team handles the requests and is able to complete an average of 50 requests per week. The actual times to complete requests also are considered to follow an exponential distribution. The requests have no particular priority; therefore, they are handled on a first-come-first-served basis. It also can be assumed that requests are not withdrawn.

What is the probability that an arriving request must wait for processing? That is, what is the probability that the team will be busy working on a request when a new request arrives?

Because $\lambda = 40$ and $\mu = 50$, then $\rho = 40/50 = 0.8$, and $P(n \geq 1) = \rho^1 = (0.8)^1 = 0.8$

What is the probability that an arriving request does not have to wait? That is, what is the probability that the arriving request will find the team idle?

$$P_0 = 1 - \rho = 1 - 0.8 = 0.2$$

What is the expected number of requests in the process?

$$L = \frac{\lambda}{\mu - \lambda} = \frac{40}{50 - 40} = 4 \text{ requests}$$

What is the expected number of requests in the queue?

$$L_q = \frac{\rho\lambda}{\mu - \lambda} = \frac{(0.8)(40)}{50 - 40} = 3.2 \text{ requests}$$

What is the average time that a request spends in the process? In other words, what is the average cycle time?

$$W = \frac{1}{\mu - \lambda} = \frac{1}{50 - 40} = 0.1 \text{ weeks} = 0.5 \text{ days} = 4 \text{ hours}$$

(It is assumed that a week has 5 working days and that each day has 8 hours.)
What is the average waiting time?

$$W_q = \frac{\rho}{\mu - \lambda} = \frac{0.8}{50 - 40} = 0.08 \text{ weeks} = 0.4 \text{ days} = 3.2 \text{ hours}$$

From these calculations, it can be predicted that the team will be busy, in the long run, 80 percent of the time. Therefore, 80 percent of the time an arriving request will have to join the queue instead of receiving immediate attention. The average cycle time is estimated to be 4 hours, from which 3.2 hours are expected to be waiting time. This calculation reveals that only 20 percent of a request's cycle time is spent in value-adding activities, and the other 80 percent consists of a non-value-adding waiting time.

Another operating characteristic that can be calculated is the probability that a given number of jobs are in the process (either waiting or being served) at any point in time. This calculation is performed using the equation for P_n, where n is the number of jobs in the process. Figure 6.11 shows a plot of the probability values associated with a range of *n*-values from 0 to 20.

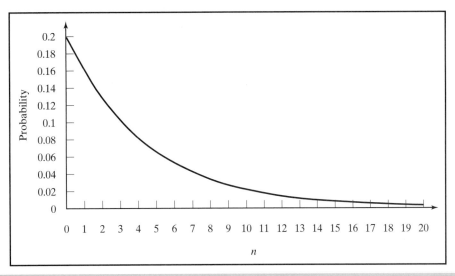

FIGURE 6.11 Probability of *n* Jobs in an *M/M/*1 System with $\rho = 0.8$

Figure 6.11 shows that the probability of finding *n* jobs in the process significantly decreases for $n \geq 10$. In fact, the exact value for the probability of finding 10 jobs or more in the process is $P(n \geq k) = \rho^k = (0.8)^{10} \approx 0.1074$. This means that the probability of finding fewer than 10 jobs in the process is almost 90 percent.

In some processes where space needs to be provided for jobs in the queue, the ability to estimate the probability of the number of jobs in the system is critical. For example, suppose that technical support for a popular piece of software is provided via a toll-free telephone number. The process designer needs to know the expected number of customers that typically would be put on hold to provide the necessary "space" in the telephone system. In the same way, it is important to estimate the waiting time that customers would experience with different levels of staffing.

6.2.5 THE *M/M/c* MODEL

The *M/M/c* model is a generalization of the *M/M/*1 model that allows for multiple parallel servers in the service facility. More precisely, the added feature is that the service facility can consist of *c* identical parallel servers each with a constant service rate, μ and exponentially distributed service times working independently of each other. Still, with exception for the server configuration, the assumptions defining the *M/M/c* model are the same as for the *M/M/*1 model, implying that the *M/M/c* model also represents a birth-and-death process. Figure 6.12 describes the *M/M/c* process in terms of its rate

FIGURE 6.12 Rate Diagram for the *M/M/c* Model

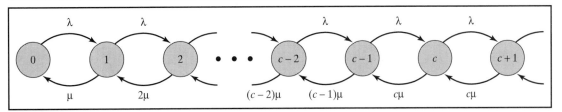

diagram. Note that for state $1, 2, \ldots, c$, all customers or jobs in the system will be under service and the queue will be empty. This means that these states will have $1, 2, \ldots, c$ independent servers working in parallel, each with the service rate μ. From property 3 of the exponential distribution discussed in Section 6.2.1, it can be concluded that the service rates for the service facility in state $0, 1, 2, \ldots, c$ are $0, \mu, 2\mu, \ldots, c\mu$, respectively. For states $c + 1, c + 2, \ldots$, all c servers are busy and the service rate for the service facility is $c\mu$, so the additional customers have to wait in the queue. The arrival rate is independent of the system state and equal to λ.

In order for the *M/M/c* model to reach steady state, the mean arrival rate λ must be less than the mean service rate when all c servers are busy, that is, $c\mu$. Because the utilization factor of the service facility ρ is defined as $\rho = (\lambda/c\mu)$ (see Section 6.2.2), the following relationship must hold in order for the *M/M/c* queue to reach steady state.

$$\rho = \frac{\lambda}{c\mu} < 1$$

In other words, the utilization of the service facility, ρ, must be less than 100 percent for the *M/M/c* system to reach steady state; otherwise, the queue will explode in size and grow infinitely large.

As with the *M/M/1* process, a set of expressions can be identified for evaluating the operating characteristics of this system. See, for example, Hillier and Lieberman (2001). These equations can be derived from the approach used for analyzing the general birth-and-death process, but the algebra poses more of a challenge. Therefore, the mathematical derivations of the following expressions are omitted.

Probability of zero jobs in the system:

$$P_0 = \frac{1}{\displaystyle\sum_{n=0}^{c-1} \frac{(\lambda/\mu)^n}{n!} + \frac{(\lambda/\mu)^c}{c!(1-\rho)}}$$

Probability that all servers are busy:

$$P(n \geq c) = \frac{(\lambda/\mu)^c}{c!(1-\rho)} P_0$$

Probability of exactly n jobs or customers in the system:

$$P_n = \begin{cases} \dfrac{(\lambda/\mu)^n}{n!} P_0 & \text{for } n = 1, 2, \ldots c \\ \dfrac{(\lambda/\mu)^n}{c! \, c^{n-c}} P_0 & \text{for } n = c, c + 1, \ldots; \end{cases}$$

Mean number of jobs in the system:

$$L = \frac{(\lambda/\mu)^c \rho}{c!(1-\rho)^2} P_0 + \frac{\lambda}{\mu}$$

Mean number of jobs in the queue:

$$L_q = \frac{(\lambda/\mu)^c \rho}{c!(1-\rho)^2} \, P_0 = L - \frac{\lambda}{\mu}$$

Note that if the steady-state criteria $\rho < 1$ is violated and $\rho = 1$, L and L_q will become infinite because their expressions include a division with zero.

Mean time a job spends in the system:

$$W = \frac{L}{\lambda} = \frac{L_q}{\lambda} + \frac{1}{\mu}$$

Mean time a job spends in the queue:

$$W_q = \frac{L_q}{\lambda}$$

A useful observation is that if L_q is known, the expressions for W_q, W, and L can be found easily using Little's law and the relationship $W = W_q + (1/\mu)$ discussed in Section 6.2.2. The expressions are: $W_q = (L_q/\lambda)$; $W = W_q + (1/\mu)$ and $L = \lambda W = \lambda(W_q + 1/\mu) = L_q + \lambda/\mu$.

To illustrate how the above formulae can be used to analyze a queuing system with parallel servers, Example 6.5 extends Example 6.4 to a situation with two servers.

Example 6.5: Policy Requests at an Insurance Company Revisited

Suppose the insurance company in Example 6.4 contemplates hiring a second team. However, before making a decision, they want to investigate the effects this will have on several important operating characteristics. A realistic assumption is that the new team will be just as efficient as the existing team, and for modeling purposes they can be treated as parallel servers with identical service rates. Because the only difference from the situation described in Example 6.4 is that the new process will have two independent teams handling the arriving requests, the new process conforms to an *M/M/c* queuing model with $c = 2$.

Recall from Example 6.4 that $\lambda = 40$ requests per week and $\mu = 50$. The new system has two parallel servers, so $c = 2$. The corresponding utilization factor for the service facility is then:

$$\rho = \frac{\lambda}{c\mu} = \frac{40}{2(50)} = 0.4$$

Also note that just as in Example 6.4, $(\lambda/\mu) = 0.8$.

The first question posed by the insurance company concerns the probability that an arriving request must wait for processing. That is, what is the probability that both teams will be busy working on requests when a new request arrives?

To provide an answer, first calculate the probability of zero requests in the system. (Recall that $n! = n(n-1)(n-2)\ldots(2)(1)$ where by definition $0! = 1$).

$$P_0 = \frac{1}{\displaystyle\sum_{n=0}^{c-1} \frac{(\lambda/\mu)^n}{n!} + \frac{(\lambda/\mu)^c}{c!(1-\rho)}} = \frac{1}{\displaystyle\sum_{n=0}^{1} \frac{(0.8)^n}{n!} + \frac{(0.8)^2}{2!(1-0.4)}} = \frac{1}{1.8 + \dfrac{0.64}{1.2}} \approx 0.4286$$

Then for $c = 2$, $P(n \geq c)$ is calculated as follows:

$$P(n \geq c) = \frac{(\lambda/\mu)^c}{c!(1-\rho)} P_0 = \frac{(0.8)^2}{2!(1-0.4)}(0.4286) \approx 0.2286 \approx 0.23$$

A related question concerns the probability that an arriving request gets processed immediately. That is, what is the probability that the arriving request will find at least one team idle?

$$P(n < 2) = P_0 + P_1 = P_0 + \frac{(\lambda/\mu)^1}{1!} P_0$$

$$= 0.4286 + \frac{(0.8)^1}{1!}0.4286 = 0.4286(1 + 0.8) \approx 0.77$$

Note that this probability is the complement of the probability of finding two or more requests in the process. Mathematically, this means that $P(n < 2) = 1 - P(n \geq 2) \approx 1 - 0.23 = 0.77$.

An important operating characteristic is the average work-in-process (WIP), or equivalently: What is the expected number of requests in the process?

$$L = \frac{(\lambda/\mu)^c \rho}{c!(1-\rho)^2} P_0 + \frac{\lambda}{\mu} = \frac{(0.8)^2 0.4}{2!(1-0.4)^2}(0.4286) + 0.8 \approx 0.95 \text{ request}$$

A related performance measure is the expected number of requests in the queue.

$$L_q = L - (\lambda/\mu) = 0.95 - 0.8 = 0.15 \text{ requests}$$

Finally, the time measures W and W_q need to be analyzed. The first question is about the average time that a request spends in the process. In other words, what is the average cycle time W?

$$W = \frac{L}{\lambda} = \frac{L_q}{\lambda} + \frac{1}{\mu} = \frac{0.15}{40} + \frac{1}{50} = 0.02375 \text{ weeks} = 0.11875 \text{ days} = 0.95 \text{ hours}$$

(As before, assume that a week has 5 working days and that each day has 8 hours.)

Second, what is the average waiting time for a job before it is processed? That is, what is the value of W_q?

$$W_q = \frac{L_q}{\lambda} = \frac{0.15}{40} = 0.00375 \text{ weeks} = 0.01875 \text{ days} = 0.15 \text{ hours}$$

To summarize the results, the average utilization of the two teams is $\rho = 40$ percent. The average cycle time is estimated to be 57 minutes (i.e., 0.95 hours), of which only 9 minutes are expected to be waiting time. The cycle time reduction is significant when compared to the 4 hours achieved with a single server. This reduction translates into 84.2 percent (i.e., 48/57) of value-adding activity time and 15.8 percent (i.e., 9/57) of non-value-adding activity time in the two-server system. In the single-server system, only 20 percent of a request's cycle time is spent in value-adding activities, and the other 80 percent consists of non-value-adding waiting time.

The decision about whether to increase the service capacity must be made based on the benefits associated with reducing non-value-adding time (in this case, waiting time) and the cost of achieving the reduction. Going from a one-server system to a configuration with two teams working in parallel reduces total expected cycle time from 4 hours to 0.95 hours. However, at the same time the utilization of the servers drops from 80 percent to 40 percent when the number of servers is increased. To assess this economic tradeoff, the operating characteristics need to be translated into monetary terms, as explored in Section 6.2.8.

Next, two generalizations of the *M/M/c* model will be considered: allowing limitations on the queue length and the size of the calling population.

6.2.6 THE *M/M/c/K* MODEL

The *M/M/c/K* model imposes the restriction that at most *K* customers can be in the *M/M/c* system at the same time. This means that the system is full when *K* customers are in it, and customers arriving during this time are rejected. This type of queuing model is applicable in situations when the queuing system has a limited capacity to harbor customers. Examples include a limitation on the number of beds in a hospital, the size of a switchboard at a call center, the size of the waiting room at a barbershop, the size of a car wash, a computer network, or a parking lot. The *M/M/c/K* model also addresses the balking behavior of customers who choose to go elsewhere if they arrive when *K* customers are already in the system.

Apart from the constraint of no more than *K* customers in the system, the *M/M/c/K* model is based on the same assumptions as the *M/M/c* model: a single queue, exponential service and interarrival times, FIFO queuing discipline, and *c* identical servers in parallel working independently from one another, each with a mean service rate of μ. The difference is that because no more than *K* customers are allowed in the system, the arrival rate is zero for states $K, K + 1, K + 2, \ldots$, but is λ for states $0, 1, 2, \ldots, K - 1$. This is illustrated in the rate diagram for the *M/M/c/K* model in Figure 6.13. It follows that the *M/M/c/K* model is a birth-and-death process with state-dependent service and interarrival rates.

$$\lambda_n = \begin{cases} \lambda & \text{for } n = 0, 1, 2, \ldots K - 1 \\ 0 & \text{for } n \geq K \end{cases} \qquad \mu_n = \begin{cases} n\mu & \text{for } n = 0, 1, 2, \ldots, c \\ c\mu & \text{for } n \geq c \end{cases}$$

The queuing models analyzed in Examples 6.1 through 6.3 fall into the class of *M/M/c/K* models.

An important observation is that the *M/M/c/K* queue is guaranteed to reach steady state even if $\rho = (\lambda/c\mu) \geq 1$. This is so because the queue can never grow infinitely large. As a matter of fact, it can never be larger than $K - c$ customers or jobs (or equivalently, the number of customers in the system cannot exceed *K*, as shown in Figure 6.13). In this model, at most *K* servers can be busy at the same time. Therefore, without loss of generality, the following exposition assumes that $c \leq K$.

As in the case of *M/M/1* and *M/M/c* models, a set of expressions exists for calculating important performance characteristics for the *M/M/c/K* model. Although the approach for analyzing general birth-and-death processes could be used, algebraically it can be tedious for large *K* values. Therefore, the following expressions can be used to characterize the performance of *M/M/c/K* systems. In addition to the assumption that $c \geq K$, the expressions use that $\rho = (\lambda/c\mu)$.

FIGURE 6.13 Rate Diagram for the *M/M/c/K* Model

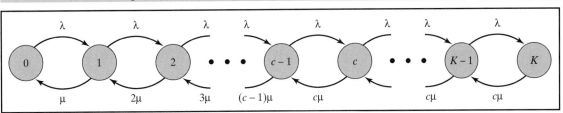

Probability of zero jobs in the system:

$$P_0 = \frac{1}{\sum\limits_{n=0}^{c} \frac{(\lambda/\mu)^n}{n!} + \frac{(\lambda/\mu)^c}{c!} \sum\limits_{n=c+1}^{K} \rho^{n-c}}$$

Probability of exactly n jobs in the system:

$$P_n = \begin{cases} \dfrac{(\lambda/\mu)^n}{n!} P_0 & \text{for } n = 1, 2, \ldots c \\ \dfrac{(\lambda/\mu)^n}{c! \, c^{n-c}} P_0 & \text{for } n = c, c+1, \ldots, K \\ 0 & \text{for } n > K \end{cases}$$

Mean number of jobs in the queue:

$$L_q = \frac{(\lambda/\mu)^c \rho}{c!(1-\rho)^2} P_0 \left(1 - \rho^{K-c} - (K-c)\rho^{K-c}(1-\rho)\right)$$

Note that the expression for L_q is not valid for $\rho = 1$. However, this does not imply that steady state is never reached for $\rho = 1$. It is simply a result of how the expression is derived. The case of $\rho = 1$ can be handled separately, but this special case is not shown here.

Mean number of jobs or customers in the system:

$$L = L_q + \sum_{n=0}^{c-1} nP_n + c\left(1 - \sum_{n=0}^{c-1} P_n\right)$$

Observe that the last two terms in the expression for L represent the expected number of jobs in the service facility. In other words, the expression corresponds to the sum of the average number of jobs in the queue and the average number of jobs in the service facility.

Applying Little's law, it is easy to obtain the expected time spent in the system and in the queue. The average arrival rate in this case is:

$$\bar{\lambda} = \sum_{n=0}^{\infty} \lambda_n P_n = \sum_{n=0}^{K-1} \lambda P_n = \lambda \sum_{n=0}^{K-1} P_n = \lambda(1 - P_K)$$

Mean time a job or a customer spends in the system:

$$W = \frac{L}{\bar{\lambda}} = \frac{L}{\lambda(1 - P_K)}$$

Mean time a job or a customer spends in the queue:

$$W_q = \frac{L_q}{\bar{\lambda}} = \frac{L_q}{\lambda(1 - P_K)}$$

In Example 6.6, the travel agency TravelCall Inc. is used to illustrate how the $M/M/c/K$ model works. Example 6.6 studies the same process as in Example 6.3, but the performance measures are now determined from the expressions of the $M/M/c/K$ model instead of using the general approach investigated in Section 6.2.3. For convenience, the TravelCall process is described again.

Example 6.6: TravelCall Inc. Revisited: A Streamlined Approach

Recall from Example 6.1 that TravelCall Inc. is a small travel agency that services customers over the phone. The agency employs only one travel agent to answer incoming customer calls. However, management is contemplating hiring a second agent and wants to investigate how the system would perform with two agents. It is assumed that these two agents would work independently on separate customers, and that their service rates would be identical. The switchboard accommodates one call on hold in addition to the two routed to the travel agents. Customers who call when the switchboard is full will get a busy signal. Consequently, the maximum number of customers in the queuing system is three. The calls arrive to TravelCall according to a Poisson process with a mean rate of nine calls per hour, and the calls are answered in the order they arrive, so the queuing discipline is FIFO. On average, it takes a travel agent 6 minutes to service a customer, and the service time follows an exponential distribution. The travel agency wants to determine the probability of finding zero, one, two, or three customers in the system, as well as the average performance measures L, L_q, W, and W_q.

The queuing system at TravelCall fits the $M/M/c/K$ model with $c = 2$ and $K = 3$, meaning a two-server system with at most $K = 3$ customers allowed in the system at the same time. Furthermore, the model can be described in terms of the rate diagram in Figure 6.14, which has the same structure as the rate diagram for the general $M/M/c/K$ process in Figure 6.13.

As before, the first step in the numerical analysis is to decide on a time unit and to determine the mean arrival and service rates. All rates will be expressed in number of occurrences per hour. The mean arrival rate when no more than three customers are in the system is $\lambda =$ nine calls per hour and zero otherwise (see Figure 6.14). Furthermore, the mean service rate for each of the two servers is $\mu = 60/6 = 10$ calls per hour. This means that the utilization factor is $\rho = \lambda/c\mu = 9/((2)(10)) = 9/20 = 0.45$.

First, the probability, P_0, that the system is empty is determined.

$$P_0 = \frac{1}{\sum_{n=0}^{k} \dfrac{(\lambda/\mu)^n}{n!} + \dfrac{(\lambda/\mu)^c}{c!} \sum_{n=c+1}^{K} \rho^{n-c}} = \frac{1}{\sum_{n=0}^{2} \dfrac{(0.9)^n}{n!} + \dfrac{(0.9)^2}{2!} \sum_{n=3}^{3} 0.45^{n-2}}$$

$$= \frac{1}{(1 + 0.9 + 0.405) + 0.405(0.45)} = \frac{1}{2.48725} \approx 0.4021$$

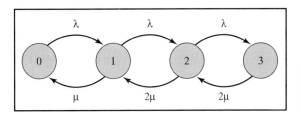

FIGURE 6.14 Rate Diagram for the Two Server Queuing Process at TravelCall.

Then the probabilities P_1, P_2, and P_3 can be obtained using:

$$
P_n = \begin{cases}
\dfrac{(\lambda/\mu)^n}{n!} P_0 & \text{for } n = 1, 2, \ldots c \\[2ex]
\dfrac{(\lambda/\mu)^n}{c!\, c^{n-c}} P_0 & \text{for } n = c, c+1, \ldots, K
\end{cases}
$$

$$
P_1 = \frac{(0.9)^1}{1!} P_0 = \frac{0.9}{2.48725} \approx 0.3618
$$

$$
P_2 = \frac{(0.9)^2}{2!} P_0 = \frac{0.81}{2} P_0 = \frac{0.405}{2.48725} \approx 0.1628
$$

$$
P_3 = \frac{(0.9)^3}{2!\,2} P_0 = \frac{0.729}{4} P_0 = \frac{0.18225}{2.48725} \approx 0.0733
$$

These probability values are the same as those determined in Example 6.3.

The next step is to determine the expected number of customers in the queue, L_q, and in the system, L.

$$
L_q = \frac{(\lambda/\mu)^c \rho}{c!(1-\rho)^2} P_0 \left(1 - \rho^{K-c} - (K-c)\rho^{K-c}(1-\rho)\right) = \frac{(0.9)^2 0.45}{2!(0.55)^2} \cdot \frac{\left(1 - 0.45^1 - (1)0.45^1(0.55)\right)}{2.48725}
$$

$$
= 0.0733 \approx 0.07 \text{ customer}
$$

$$
L = L_q + \sum_{n=0}^{c-1} nP_n + c\left(1 - \sum_{n=0}^{c-1} P_n\right) = L_q + P_1 + 2(1 - P_0 - P_1) = 0.0733 + 0.3618
$$

$$
+ 2(1 - 0.4021 - 0.361) = 0.9073 \approx 0.91 \text{ customer}
$$

Finally, Little's law is used to determine the mean time a customer spends in the system, W, and the mean time he or she spends in the queue, W_q.

$$
W = \frac{L}{\bar{\lambda}} = \frac{L}{\lambda(1-P_K)} = \frac{L}{\lambda(1-P_3)} = \frac{0.9073}{9(1-0.0733)} \approx 0.1088 \text{ hours} \approx 6.5 \text{ minutes}
$$

$$
W_q = \frac{L_q}{\bar{\lambda}} = \frac{L_q}{\lambda(1-P_K)} = \frac{L_q}{\lambda(1-P_3)} = \frac{0.0733}{9(1-0.0733)} \approx 0.0088 \text{ hours} \approx 0.5 \text{ minutes}
$$

A comparison with Example 6.3 verifies that the results are identical.

6.2.7 THE *M/M/c/∞/N* MODEL

The *M/M/c/∞/N* model is another generalization of the basic *M/M/c* model, which deals with the case of a finite calling population of *N* customers or jobs. Apart from this feature, the *M/M/c/∞/N* model is based on the same assumptions as the *M/M/c* model: a single queue, *c* independent, parallel and identical servers, exponentially distributed interarrival and service times, unlimited queue length, and a FIFO queuing discipline.

An important observation in understanding the *M/M/c/∞/N* model is that because the calling population is finite, each of the *N* customers or jobs must be either *in* the queuing system or *outside*, in the calling population. This implies that if *n* customers or jobs are in the system, meaning the queuing system is in state *n*, the remaining *N − n* customers or jobs are found in the calling population. When constructing the model, it is assumed that for each of the customers or jobs currently in the calling population, the time remaining until it arrives to the queuing system is independent and exponentially distributed with parameter λ. As a result, if n ($n <= N$) customers are in the queuing system, the arrivals at this system state occur according to a Poisson process with mean arrival rate $(N - n)\lambda$. (See Section 6.2.1.) To obtain this, let T_j be the time remaining until job $j, j = 1, 2, \ldots, N - n$ in the calling population will arrive to the queue. The time remaining until the next arrival is then $T_{\min} = \min\{T_1, T_2, \ldots T_{N-n}\}$. The conclusion follows because $T_{\min}$ is exponentially distributed with parameter $(N - n)\lambda$. Assuming, as before, that the mean service rate for each server is μ, the $M/M/c/\infty/N$ model can be described by the rate diagram in Figure 6.15. Moreover, because the service and interarrival times are mutually independent and exponentially distributed, the $M/M/c/\infty/N$ model describes a birth-and-death process with state-dependent interarrival and service rates.

$$\lambda_n = \begin{cases} (N - n)\lambda & \text{for } n = 0, 1, 2, \ldots N \\ 0 & \text{for } n \geq N \end{cases} \qquad \mu_n = \begin{cases} n\mu & \text{for } n = 0, 1, 2, \ldots, c \\ c\mu & \text{for } n \geq c \end{cases}$$

Figure 6.15 explicitly illustrates the fact that because only N jobs or customers are in the calling population, the maximum number of jobs or customers in the queuing system is N, which means that the maximum queue length is $N - c$. As a result, the $M/M/c/\infty/N$ model, like the $M/M/c/K$ model, is guaranteed to reach a steady state even if $\rho = (\lambda/c\mu) \geqslant 1$.

A common application area for the $M/M/c/\infty/N$ model is for analyzing machine maintenance or repair processes. These processes are characterized by c service technicians (or teams of service technicians) who are responsible for keeping N machines or service stations operational; that is, to repair them as soon as they break down. The jobs (or customers) in this queuing process are the machines or service stations. Those that are currently in operation are in the calling population, and those that are undergoing repair are in the queuing system. The service technicians or teams of technicians are the servers. For a maintenance process of this sort to be adequately described by an $M/M/c/\infty/N$ model, the time between breakdowns for each individual machine in operation needs to be exponentially distributed with a constant parameter, λ. Furthermore, the c service technicians (or service teams) should work independently from each other on separate machines all displaying exponentially distributed service times with the same service rate μ. Note that if n machines are undergoing repair, then $N - n$ machines are in operation.

To analyze the performance of a given $M/M/c/\infty/N$ system, the general approach in Section 6.2.3 can be used; however, as with the $M/M/c$ and $M/M/c/K$ systems, the algebra can be somewhat tedious for larger systems. As an alternative, the following expressions have been derived to aid in the analysis. See, for example, Hillier and Lieberman (2001). It is assumed that $c \leqslant N$.

FIGURE 6.15 Rate Diagram for the *M/M/c/∞/N* Model

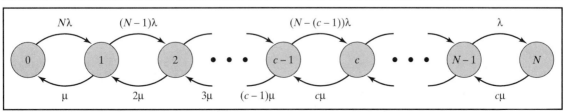

Probability of zero jobs in the system:

$$P_0 = \frac{1}{\sum_{n=0}^{c-1} \frac{N!}{(N-n)!\,n!}\left(\frac{\lambda}{\mu}\right)^n + \sum_{n=c}^{N} \frac{N!}{(N-n)!\,c!\,c^{n-c}}\left(\frac{\lambda}{\mu}\right)^n}$$

Probability of exactly n jobs in the system:

$$P_n = \begin{cases} \dfrac{N!}{(N-n)!\,n!}\left(\dfrac{\lambda}{\mu}\right)^n P_0 & \text{for } n = 0,1,2,\ldots c \\[3mm] \dfrac{N!}{(N-n)!\,c!\,c^{n-c}}\left(\dfrac{\lambda}{\mu}\right)^n P_0 & \text{for } n = c, c+1, \ldots, N \\[3mm] 0 & \text{for } n > N \end{cases}$$

Mean number of jobs or customers in the queue:

$$L_q = \sum_{n=c}^{N} (n - c)P_n$$

Note that this expression is simply the definition of L_q.

Mean number of jobs or customers in the system:

$$L = L_q + \sum_{n=0}^{c-1} nP_n + c\left(1 - \sum_{n=0}^{c-1} P_n\right)$$

Observe that the last two terms in this expression for L represent the expected number of jobs in the service facility. Consequently, the expression simply adds the average number of jobs in the queue to the average number of jobs in the service facility.

To obtain the expected time spent in the system and in the queue, Little's law can be used as discussed in Section 6.2.2. The average arrival rate in this case is:

$$\bar{\lambda} = \sum_{n=0}^{\infty} \lambda_n P_n = \sum_{n=0}^{N} (N-n)\lambda P_n = \lambda\left(N\sum_{n=0}^{N} P_n - \sum_{n=0}^{N} nP_n\right) = \lambda(N - L)$$

Mean time a job or a customer spends in the system:

$$W = \frac{L}{\bar{\lambda}} = \frac{L}{\lambda(N - L)}$$

Mean time a job or a customer spends in the queue:

$$W_q = \frac{L_q}{\bar{\lambda}} = \frac{L_q}{\lambda(N - L)}$$

Remark   The $M/M/c/\infty/N$ model is based on the assumption that the time an individual job or customer spends in the calling population outside the queuing system is exponentially distributed. However, it has been shown (see Bunday and Scraton, 1980) that the expressions for P_0 and P_n (and consequently those for L, L_q, W, and W_q) also hold in more general situations. More precisely, the time that a job or customer spends outside the system is allowed to have any probability distribution as long as this distribution is the same for each job or customer and the average time is $1/\lambda$. Note that these situations fall outside the class of birth-and-death processes into a $G/M/c/\infty/N$ model.

Example 6.7 illustrates the analysis of an $M/M/c/\infty/N$ model in the context of a machine repair process as discussed previously.

Example 6.7: The Machine Repair Process at PaperCo Inc.

PaperCo Inc. is a manufacturer of fine paper. Its most important product is a special, environmentally friendly type of bleached paper used for laser printers and copiers. PaperCo has one production facility consisting of three large paper-milling machines. These machines are expensive and need to be kept operational to the largest extent possible. At the same time, their complexity makes them sensitive to malfunctions. Currently, PaperCo has one repair team on call 24 hours a day, 7 days a week. However, management is contemplating increasing this to two teams and would like a performance analysis of this double-team scenario. They already know the performance of the current process with one team. Each team is configured so that all competencies needed are available within the team, and having two teams working on the same machine provides no advantages. Therefore, it can be assumed that the two teams work independently from one another on different machines. Furthermore, their service times are assumed to be identical and exponentially distributed with a mean of 4 hours. Empirical data show that the time between malfunctions in each of the three machines when they are operating is exponential with a mean of 8 hours. The machines are equally important, so broken-down machines are serviced in a FIFO manner.

PaperCo wants to know the steady-state probabilities that zero, one, two, or three machines are nonoperational. They also want to determine the average time before a machine that breaks down is operational again, as well as how long on average a broken machine has to wait before a service team starts to work on the problem.

The first step in analyzing this problem is to recognize that the PaperCo repair process can be modeled as an $M/M/c/\infty/N$ system with $c = 2$ servers (the service teams) and $N = 3$ jobs in the calling population (the machines). Furthermore, the mean service rate for each of the two teams is $\mu = 1/4 = 0.25$ jobs per hour, and the failure rate for each machine in operation is $\lambda = 1/8 = 0.125$ machines per hour. The rate diagram for the repair process is depicted in Figure 6.16. (See also Figure 6.15 for the general structure.) It should be noted that this problem can be analyzed using the general approach for birth-and-death processes discussed in Section 6.2.3, although a different method is used here.

Using the expressions given previously, one can determine the steady-state probabilities $\{P_n, n = 0, 1, 2, 3\}$ of zero, one, two, and three machines malfunctioning. Note that $N = 3$, $c = 2$, $\lambda = 0.125$, $\mu = 0.25$, and $(\lambda/\mu) = 0.5$.

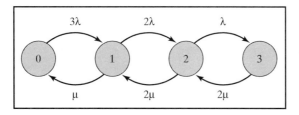

FIGURE 6.16 Rate Diagram for the $M/M/2/\infty/3$ Model Describing the Machine Repair Process at PaperCo

Probability of zero jobs in the system:

$$P_0 = \cfrac{1}{\displaystyle\sum_{n=0}^{c-1} \frac{N!}{(N-n)!\,n!}\left(\frac{\lambda}{\mu}\right)^n + \sum_{n=c}^{N} \frac{N!}{(N-n)!\,c!\,c^{n-c}}\left(\frac{\lambda}{\mu}\right)^n}$$

$$= \cfrac{1}{\left(\dfrac{3!}{3!} + \dfrac{3!}{2!}(0.5)^1\right) + \left(\dfrac{3!}{2!}(0.5)^2 + \dfrac{3!}{2!\,2^1}(0.5)^3\right)}$$

$$= \frac{1}{1 + 1.5 + 0.75 + 0.1875} = \frac{1}{3.4375} \approx 0.2909$$

Probability of exactly n jobs in the system:

$$P_n = \begin{cases} \dfrac{N!}{(N-n)!\,n!}\left(\dfrac{\lambda}{\mu}\right)P_0 & \text{for } n = 0,1,2,\ldots c \\[3mm] \dfrac{N!}{(N-n)!\,c!\,c^{n-c}}\left(\dfrac{\lambda}{\mu}\right)^n P_0 & \text{for } n = c, c+1, \ldots, \\[3mm] 0 & \text{for } n > K \end{cases}$$

$$P_1 = \frac{3!}{(3-1)!\,1!}(0.5)^1 P_0 = \frac{1.5}{3.4375} \approx 0.4364$$

$$P_2 = \frac{3!}{(3-2)!\,2!}(0.5)^2 P_0 = \frac{0.75}{3.4375} \approx 0.2182$$

$$P_3 = \frac{3!}{(3-3)!\,2!\,2^1}(0.5)^3 P_0 = \frac{0.1875}{3.4375} \approx 0.0545$$

$$P_n = 0 \qquad \text{for } n \geq 4$$

Mean number of jobs or customers in the queue:

$$L_q = \sum_{n=c}^{N} (n-c)P_n = (2-2)P_2 + (3-2)P_3 = P_3 = 0.0545 \approx 0.05 \text{ machine}$$

Mean number of jobs or customers in the system:

$$L = L_q + \sum_{n=0}^{c-1} nP_n + c\left(1 - \sum_{n=0}^{c-1} P_n\right) = L_q + (1)P_1 + 2(1 - P_0 - P_1) = 0.0545 + 0.4364$$

$$+ 2(1 - 0.2909 - 0.4364)$$

$$= 1.0363 \approx 1.04 \text{ machine}$$

Little's law can be used to determine the expected downtime for a broken machine, W, and the expected time a broken machine has to wait for a service team, W_q.

$$W = \frac{L}{\bar{\lambda}} = \frac{L}{\lambda(N-L)} = \frac{1.0363}{0.125(3-1.0363)} \approx 4.22 \text{ hours} \approx 4 \text{ hours and } 13.3 \text{ minutes}$$

$$W_q = \frac{L_q}{\bar{\lambda}} = \frac{L_q}{\lambda(N-L)} = \frac{0.0545}{0.125(3-1.0363)} \approx 0.22 \text{ hours} \approx 13.3 \text{ minutes}$$

Consequently, with two service teams all machines are operational 29 percent of the time, two out of three are working 44 percent of the time, two machines are down 22 percent of the time, and 5 percent of the time all three machines are standing still. Moreover, it takes 4 hours and 13 minutes on average from the moment a machine breaks down until it is up and running again, of which 13 minutes is waiting time before a team is available.

It seems that PaperCo needs to do something about this process. Even with two teams, a significant amount of costly downtime is occurring.

6.2.8 QUEUING THEORY AND PROCESS DESIGN

The analytical queuing models studied in Sections 6.2.3 through 6.2.7 have proven useful in analyzing the steady-state behavior of various queuing systems. The analysis focuses on the probability distribution for the number of customers in the queuing system and on the average performance measures, such as the mean queue length and the mean time customers spend in the queue and in the queuing system as a whole. Examples also have been provided of how this type of information can help the process designer better understand the impact that capacity-related decisions have on service to the customers. However, as discussed in the introduction to this chapter, an optimal design decision involves an economic trade-off between the cost of additional capacity and the cost of poor service in terms of long delays. This section explores these issues further, particularly by investigating how waiting costs (or shortage costs) can be used to translate the service performance into monetary terms. Challenges related with appropriately quantifying waiting costs also will be discussed. First, however, the decisions facing the process designer need to be examined.

When designing basic queuing systems such as those in Sections 6.2.3 through 6.2.7—single-queue, parallel-server systems—two design parameters are usually under the decision maker's control.

- The number of parallel servers in the service facility; for example, the number of physicians at a hospital ward, the number of checkout stations in a grocery store, or the number of operators in a call center.
- The service time or speed of individual servers; for example, size and thereby the service time of a repair team, the type of materials handling system (conveyor belts, forklift trucks, and so on) in a production facility, or the speed of an airplane transporting people.

In the context of the models in Section 6.2.3 through 6.2.7, these decisions involve determining c, the number of parallel and identical servers, and μ, the service rate for an individual server (assuming that the service time for individual servers is state independent). Another design parameter that might be under the decision maker's control is K, the maximum number of customers in the system (or equivalently $K-c$ as the maximum queue length). This could involve decisions regarding the number of calls that can be placed on hold at a call center, the size of the waiting area at a restaurant, the number of beds in a hospital, and so on. The effect of increasing K is that more customers fit into the system and fewer customers are denied service, but at the same time the waiting time for those in the system tends to increase. Translating these effects into monetary terms typically requires a somewhat more complex waiting cost structure than when considering changes only in c and μ. The following analysis assumes that $K = \infty$ and focuses on design changes in c and μ, meaning the focus is on designing $M/M/c$ systems.

In addition to the design parameters, c and μ, which relate to the queuing system's available capacity, the process design team sometimes is in a position to affect the demand for capacity through the arrival process. This could involve demand-management initiatives to reduce the variability in the demand pattern, making the arrival process more stable. Note, however, that under the assumption of exponentially distributed arrival times, it is not possible to reduce the demand variability without changing the mean demand. Consequently, the effects of demand management initiatives cannot be properly analyzed using the $M/M/c$ models that have been introduced.

Given the available design parameters, the design team must decide how to set these parameters, meaning the amount and type of capacity to acquire in order to satisfy the customers' service requirements. A fundamental design issue is therefore to quantify these service requirements. The two standard approaches are to specify an acceptable service level or to specify a waiting cost (or shortage cost).

For the service level approach, the decision problem is to minimize the capacity-related costs under the service level constraint; that is, to determine c, μ, and if applicable K, to minimize the expected cost of operating the queuing system given that the service level is met. Different ways of measuring the service level exist, such as the average waiting time, the percentage of customers receiving service immediately, or the percentage of customers waiting less than, say, 5 minutes.

The focus in this section is on the waiting cost approach. In this case, the corresponding decision problem is to determine c or μ to minimize the total cost of waiting and operating the queuing system. To investigate this further, some additional notation needs to be introduced.

WC = Expected waiting cost per time unit for the queuing system
SC = Expected service cost per time unit for operating the queuing system
TC = Expected total cost per time unit for the queuing system = $SC + WC$
C_w = Waiting cost rate = waiting cost per customer and time unit
$C_s(\mu)$ = Service cost per time unit for an individual server with service rate μ

It is worth noting that although a constant waiting cost rate, C_w, is assumed, it is straightforward to extend the analysis to state-dependent waiting cost rates, see, for example, Hillier and Lieberman (2001).

The decision problem can be stated as:

$$\text{Minimize } TC = SC + WC$$

The corresponding cost functions, TC, SC, and WC, are illustrated in Figure 6.17.

Determining *WC*

In order to determine an expression for the expected waiting cost per time unit for the system, WC, note that if n customers are in the system, the waiting cost per time unit is $C_w n$. From the definition of expected value and the steady-state probability distribution for finding n customers in the system, an expression for WC can be found.

$$WC = \sum_{n=0}^{\infty} C_w n P_n = C_w \sum_{n=0}^{\infty} n P_n = C_w L$$

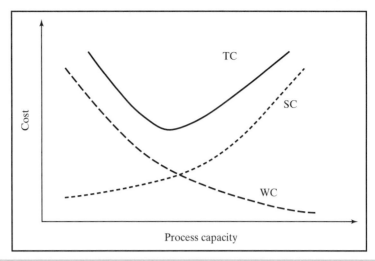

FIGURE 6.17 Schematic Illustration of the Cost Function *TC, SC,* and *WC*

The expected waiting cost per time unit for the queuing system is obtained by multiplying the waiting cost per customer and per time unit with the expected number of customers in the system. This expression assumes that every customer in the queuing system incurs the same waiting cost whether the customer is waiting in the queue or is in the service facility. In cases where only the customers in the queue incur waiting costs, the expression for *WC* is:

$$WC = C_w L_q$$

If not otherwise specified, we will assume that the waiting costs are based on the number of customers in the system and not just those in the queue.

Determining *SC*

The expected service cost per unit of time for the system depends on the number of servers, c, and the speed of these servers. When all c servers are identical with service rates μ, the expected service cost can be expressed as follows.

$$SC = cC_s(\mu)$$

A Decision Model for Designing Queuing Systems

Based on the expressions for *WC* and *SC*, a decision model for determining the values of the design parameters c and μ can be formulated as follows. The objective is to minimize the total costs per time unit for the entire queuing system.

$$\text{Minimize}_{c,\mu} \; TC = SC + WC = cC_s(\mu) + C_w L$$

Examples 6.8 and 6.9 illustrate how the process design team can use this general decision model for optimizing the performance of queuing systems.

Example 6.8: Process Design at CopyCo Inc.—The Option of a Second Machine

CopyCo is a small print shop located near a large university campus. Currently, all jobs involving paper-to-paper copies are carried out on one copy machine. For some time, CopyCo has experienced backlog problems with jobs submitted to the paper-to-paper copier. Management is worried that the long waiting times might be detrimental to future sales, so they are contemplating the acquisition of a second identical copy machine. The current machine is leased at a cost of $50 per day. Other costs for operating the machine, such as labor and electricity, amount to $150 per day. The second copier also would be leased, and it is estimated that it would accrue the same costs as the existing one—$200 per day. Empirically, it has been shown that the service and interarrival times are exponentially distributed. Furthermore, on average, CopyCo receives 95 jobs per day involving paper-to-paper copying, and the mean service time on the current machine is 6 minutes. CopyCo is open 10 hours per day, and the number of jobs that can be in the store at the same time is subject to no immediate space restrictions. The hourly waiting cost per customer is estimated to $5. Management wants to design the paper-to-paper copying process to minimize the total expected costs while considering the option of acquiring a second machine.

First, a suitable queuing model needs to be selected for this situation. It is known that the service and interarrival times are exponentially distributed, and that no restrictions are placed on the queue length. In the case of a single copier, the queuing process at CopyCo fits an $M/M/1$ model. In the case of two identical copiers working in parallel, the appropriate model is an $M/M/2$ model.

Because the objective is to find the design alternative that minimizes the total expected costs, an appropriate decision model is:

$$\text{Minimize}_{c=\{1,2\}} \ TC = SC + WC = cC_s(\mu) + C_w L$$

The only decision variable is the number of servers, $c = 1$ or 2. The service rate μ for each individual server is fixed.

The known cost, demand, and service information is

λ = 95 jobs per day = 95/10 = 9.5 jobs per hour,
μ = 60/6 = 10 jobs per hour,
$C_s(\mu)$ = $200 per day = 200/10 = $20 per hour,
C_w = $5 per customer and hour.

All parameters should be expressed in the same time units, and in this case hours have been chosen.

The only unknown values in this decision model are the expected number of jobs in the system for the single- and double-copier alternatives. Let L_1 be the expected number of jobs in the $M/M/1$ system and L_2 be the expected number of josbs in the $M/M/2$ system. Using the formulae from Sections 6.2.4 and 6.2.5 and the decision model, one gets:

M/M/1 system:

$$\rho = \lambda / \mu = 9.5/10 = 0.95$$
$$L_1 = \frac{\rho}{1-\rho} = \frac{(0.95)}{1-(0.95)} = 19 \text{ jobs}$$
$$TC_1 = SC_1 + WC_1 = 1(20) + 5(19) = \$115 \text{ per hour}$$

M/M/2 system:

$$\rho = \lambda / (2\mu) = 9.5/20 = 0.475$$

$$P_0 = \frac{1}{\sum_{n=0}^{c-1} \frac{(\lambda/\mu)^n}{n!} + \frac{(\lambda/\mu)^c}{c!(1-\rho)}} = \frac{1}{1 + 0.95 + \frac{(0.95)^2}{2!(1-0.475)}} \approx 0.3559$$

$$L_2 = \frac{(\lambda/\mu)^c \rho}{c!(1-\rho)^2} P_0 + \frac{\lambda}{\mu} = \frac{(0.95)^2(0.475)}{2!(1-0.475)^2} 0.3559 + 0.95 \approx 1.23 \text{ jobs}$$

$$TC_2 = SC_2 + WC_2 = 2(20) + 5(1.23) = \$46.15 \text{ per hour}$$

Because the expected total cost is considerably lower with a second copy machine in place $(TC_2 < TC_1)$, it is recommended that the CopyCo management team choose this alternative. This recommendation is made despite the fact that the service costs of operating the two copiers are twice as high as when only one copier is used.

Example 6.9: Process Design at CopyCo Inc.—The Option of a Single Faster Machine

As the management team at CopyCo contacted the leasing company to sign up for a second machine, the sales person informed them about another alternative. A brand new model of their old copier just came on the market. The new model is twice as fast as the old one, which for CopyCo would mean an estimated average service time of 3 minutes. The service times are assumed exponential, and the jobs arriving to the print shop are the same as before. The cost to lease this new model is $150 per day. Operating the new model efficiently will require additional personnel and more electricity, rendering an estimated operating cost of about $250 per day. Consequently, the total service cost of operating the new machine is $400 per day, which is the same as the cost of operating two of the old machines. The question is whether leasing one fast machine is better than leasing two slower copiers.

Because service and interarrival times are exponential and the queue length has no restrictions, the new alternative with one fast copier can be modeled as an $M/M/1$ queue.

From Example 6.8, it is known that

$$\lambda = 95 \text{ jobs per day} = 95/10 = 9.5 \text{ jobs per hour}$$
$$C_w = \$5 \text{ per customer and hour}$$

From the information about the new model of the copy machine, it is known that:

$$\mu_{new} = 60/3 = 20 \text{ jobs per hour}$$
$$C_s(\mu_{new}) = \$250 + \$150 \text{ per day} = 400/10 = \$40 \text{ per hour}$$

Because the objective is to find the design alternative that minimizes the total expected costs, an appropriate decision model is:

$$\underset{c,\mu}{\text{Minimize }} TC = SC + WC = cC_s(\mu) + C_w L$$

The decision variables in this case are the number of servers, $c = 1, 2$, and their individual speed, $\mu = 10$ or 20. However, only two alternatives are being compared: the alternative with two copiers of the old model—$c = 2$ and $\mu = 10$ jobs per hour, and the alternative with one copier of the new model—$c = 1$ and $\mu = 20$ jobs per hour. Furthermore, for the alternative with two copiers of the old model, the expected cost has already been determined in Example 6.8, $TC_2 = \$46.15$ per hour.

For the new alternative with one fast copier, the costs are obtained as follows:

M/M/1 system:

$$\rho = \lambda / \mu_{new} = 9.5 / 20 = 0.475$$
$$L_{new} = \frac{\rho}{1-\rho} = \frac{(0.475)}{1-(0.475)} \approx 0.9048 \text{ jobs}$$
$$TC_{new} = SC_{new} + WC_{new} = 1(40) + 5(0.9048) \approx \$44.52 \text{ per hour}$$

The cost comparison indicates that the alternative with one fast copier of the new model is preferable to the option of leasing two copiers of the old model ($44.52 < $46.15).

Remark. The conclusion in Example 6.9 is a consequence of a more general result regarding single- and multiple-server facilities with the same mean capacity. It can be shown that a queuing system with one fast server with service rate equal to $c\mu$ will always render shorter expected waiting times and fewer customers in the system than a service facility with c parallel servers, each with a service rate of μ. This also implies that the expected total cost TC is lower for the single-server system as long as the service cost SC is such that $C_s(c\mu) \geqslant cC_s(\mu)$.

Thus far, it has been assumed that a relevant waiting cost rate C_w is readily available. Unfortunately, this is not always the case. In fact, finding an appropriate waiting cost rate is often a major challenge in the practical application of decision models based on waiting costs.

Because of the wide variety of queuing situations, there exists no single procedure for estimating the customers' waiting cost rates or waiting cost functions. In fact, the entire waiting cost concept is situation dependent. For example, the waiting costs for long delays at an emergency room are very different from those experienced by customers in a supermarket. Essentially, the waiting cost rate should reflect the monetary impact that a delay of a single customer or job has on the organization where the queuing system in question resides. This implies that first, it is necessary to understand the consequences of time delays for the customers, and to understand customer requirements and behavior. Second, these consequences must be translated into monetary effects for the queuing system or the organization to which it belongs. This has to be done on a case-by-case basis. However, in broad terms, one can distinguish between situations in which the customers are external to the organization and ones in which they are internal. Furthermore, there is typically a difference between profit-maximizing organizations and nonprofit organizations.

In the case of external customers arriving to profit-maximizing organizations, the waiting costs are related primarily to lost profits and bad reputation affecting future sales. For example, long lines at a grocery store might discourage a customer from coming back or from entering the store in the first place. For nonprofit organizations, on the other hand, the waiting costs are typically related to future social costs. In order to estimate these costs, it is necessary to understand how waiting affects the individual customers and society as a whole. For example, what is the cost to society of having long waiting times at an emergency room? Social costs and costs related to lost profits can be hard to quantify in monetary terms. In some cases, it might be easier to estimate an acceptable service level and use the service level approach. Again, in other cases, the costs associated with delays and waiting might be easier to identify. Consider, for example, the drug approval process of a pharmaceutical company, which has a cost associated with its cycle time. If the process requires 1 year to be completed and 80 percent of this time is due to delays, then the cost of waiting is 9.6 months of lost sales. In this case, loss of market share due to late market introduction also should be added to the lost sales cost.

In situations where the arriving customers are internal to the organization where the queuing system resides, it is usually somewhat easier to estimate the waiting costs. The customers (or jobs) in these cases are typically machines or employees of the organization. Therefore, it is often possible to identify the immediate consequences associated with having these customers idle. The main component of the waiting costs associated with this idleness is, in most cases, the lost profit due to the reduced productivity.

Estimating waiting costs is often a challenging task based on customer requirements and the consequences of poor service. However, as discussed in Chapters 1 through 3, gaining an understanding of the customer requirements is at the core of effective business process design.

6.3 Introduction to Simulation

Section 6.2 explored how analytical queuing models offer powerful means for understanding and evaluating queuing processes. However, the use of these analytical models is somewhat restricted by their underlying assumptions. The limitations pertain to the structure of the queuing system, the way variability can be incorporated into the models, and the focus on steady-state analysis. Because many business processes are cross functional and characterized by complex structures and variability patterns, a more flexible modeling tool is needed. Simulation offers this flexibility and represents a powerful approach for analysis and quantitative evaluation of business processes.

In general, to simulate means to mimic reality in some way. Simulation can be done, for example, through physical models such as wind tunnels, simulators where pilots or astronauts train by interacting with a computer in a virtual or artificial reality, or through computer-based models for evaluation of a given technical system or process design. In the latter case, simulation software is used to create a computer model that mimics the behavior of the real-world process.

The rapid development of computer hardware and software in recent years has made computer simulation an effective tool for process modeling and an attractive technique for predicting the performance of alternative process designs. It also helps in optimizing their efficiency. Simulation is useful in this context because business process design is a decision-making problem for which the following is true.

- Developing analytical mathematical models in many cases might be too difficult or perhaps even impossible.
- The performance of a process design typically depends heavily on the ability to cope with variability in interarrival and processing times (implying a need for a modeling tool that can incorporate several random variables).
- The dynamics are often extremely complex.
- The behavior over a period of time must be observed to validate the design.
- The ability to show an animation of the operation is often an important way to stimulate the creativity of the design teams.

Despite its many virtues, simulation is sometimes met by skepticism from practitioners and managers. Much of the reluctance toward using simulation stems from the misconception that simulation is extremely costly and time-consuming. This is despite the many success stories showing that the savings from using simulation to improve process designs has far exceeded its costs. (See Examples 6.10 and 6.11.) In fact, with the advanced modeling tools that are currently available, the model development and experimentation phase might take only a few days or weeks, representing only a small fraction of the overall project development time (Harrell and Tumay, 1995). One of the most resource-consuming efforts that goes into building a valid simulation model is understanding how the process operates. However, as discussed in Chapter 3, this process understanding is a necessity for achieving an effective process design and must be done whether or not simulation is used. Savings from the use of simulation are well documented, as illustrated in Examples 6.10 and 6.11.

Example 6.10: Layout and WIP Investments

A *Fortune* 500 company used simulation for the design of a facility for producing and sorting subassembled components in preparation for the final assembly of a number of different metal products. One of the decisions involved determining the number of containers required to store the subassembled components. It initially was estimated that 3,000 containers were required. However, after a simulation study, it was found that throughput was not significantly affected when the number of containers varied from 2,250 to 3,000. By purchasing 2,250 containers instead of 3,000, savings of $528,375 was expected in the first year, with annual savings thereafter of at least $200,000 from floor space (Law and McComas, 1988).

Example 6.11: Capacity Expansion in Connection with Facility Relocation

When a company decided to relocate to a new facility and expand its production capacity, it needed to analyze the impacts of changes in future demand. The relocation also provided the company with an opportunity to analyze its current production process and to seek improvements before increasing its capacity. Process simulation was used for capacity analysis and process improvement. Outputs from the process simulation were the primary inputs in determining the equipment and work-in-process inventory. The expansion alternatives from the process simulation identified the type and number of each piece of equipment needed to meet future capacity requirements. The queue lengths (average and maximum) were used to estimate the work-in-process inventory that needed to be accommodated at the new facility. Therefore, the facility lay-out design was fashioned along the recommended feasible alternatives and using other outputs from the process simulation, given the prescribed space constraints. The suggested layout design generated a throughput that exceeded the target production goal by 50 percent (Eneyo and Pannirselvam, 1999).

6.3.1 SIMULATION MODELS

Simulation models in general and computer-based models in particular can be classified in three different ways according to their attributes.

- Static or dynamic.
- Deterministic or stochastic.
- Discrete or continuous.

A static model is used when time does not play a role in the actual system. For example, a model of a bridge does not depend on time. A deterministic model is such that the outputs are fully determined after the inputs are known. Take a computer model for calculating the water pressure of a pipe network as an example. The pressure is known once the designer selects the pipe diameters for all the pipe segments. A discrete model considers that individual units (i.e., the transient entities of the system) are important. Most manufacturing, service, and business processes are discrete. Business processes in general are represented as computer-based dynamic, stochastic, and discrete simulation models.

A computer-based simulation model is an abstraction of the actual business process, represented in the computer as a network of connected activities and buffers (or equivalently, a network of basic queuing systems) through which jobs or customers flow. To provide a correct representation of the process, the model also must capture the resources and various inputs needed to perform the activities.

Because process modeling is only one application area for simulation modeling, a more general terminology for describing a simulation model is to refer to it as an abstraction of a system rather than a process. Conceptually, a system is defined as a collection of entities that interact with a common purpose according to sets of laws and policies. Entities are either transient or resident. In the process terminology defined in Chapter 1, transient entities are the jobs that flow through the system, and the resident entities are the buffers, workstations, and resources that make up the process network. Laws are not under the process designer's control. Laws generally are represented by parameters. Sensitivity analysis is the experimentation used to determine the effect of changes in parameter values. Policies, on the other hand, are under the designer's control. A policy typically is implemented by changing input factors. Design is the experimentation used to determine the effect of changes in input factors and system structure.

Example 6.12: An Order-Fulfillment Process

Consider an order-fulfillment process in which customers call a toll-free number to place an order. In this process, the orders are transient entities, and the sales representatives answering phone calls are resident entities. The arrival pattern of phone calls is a law, because it is beyond the process designer's immediate control. The number of sales representatives can be controlled; therefore, it is considered a policy. In a simulation model of this process, the number of sales representatives can be expressed as an input factor so the analyst is able to experiment with different values, meaning that a sensitivity analysis can be carried out and the performance of the process can be tested (as measured, for example, by the cycle time).

In process design, models are used to study the behavior of a process. A process can be modeled symbolically, analytically, or with simulation. Symbolic models (or graphical tools) were introduced in Chapter 4. These models include process activity charts, process diagrams, and flowcharts. Symbolic models are quick and easy to develop, and are easily understood by others. The main disadvantage of symbolic models is that they fail to capture the dynamics of the process. Various analytical models have been investigated in Chapters 4 through 6. Deterministic models were introduced in Chapters 4 and 5, and stochastic models were introduced in Section 6.2. If their underlying assumptions were valid for a system under study, these models would be a convenient way to evaluate quantitatively different process designs. The main disadvantage is that these underlying assumptions are often restrictive. Furthermore, because these tools offer no obvious graphical representation, they might appear abstract to the process designer.

Modern simulation software in a sense combines the descriptive strength of the symbolic models with the quantitative strength of the analytical models. It offers graphical representation of the model through graphical interfaces, as well as graphical illustration of the system dynamics through plots of output data and animation of process operations. At the same time, it enables estimation of quantitative performance measures through statistical analysis of output data. The main disadvantage of simulation is the time spent learning how to use the simulation software and how to interpret the results.

To summarize, the following are some of the main attributes that make simulation powerful.

- Simulation, like analytical modeling, provides a quantitative measure of performance (e.g., resource utilization or average waiting time).
- Simulation, unlike analytical and symbolic models, is able to take into consideration any kind of complex system variation and statistical interdependencies.
- Simulation is capable of uncovering inefficiencies that usually go undetected until the system is in operation.

An interesting distinction between a simulation model and an optimization model is that simulation is a tool for evaluating a given design, and an optimization model is a tool used to search for an optimal solution to a decision problem. That is, a simulation model is by nature descriptive, and an optimization model is by nature prescriptive because it provides an optimal solution prescribing a course of action to the user.

Until recently, simulation software packages could be used only as what-if tools. This means that given a simulation model, the designer would experiment with alternative designs and operating strategies in order to measure system performance. Consequently, in such an environment, the model becomes an experimental tool that is used to find an effective design.

However, modern simulation software packages merge optimization technology with simulation. The optimization consists of an automated search for the best values (near-optimal values) of input factors (the decision variables). This valuable tool allows designers to identify critical input factors that the optimization engine can manipulate to search for the best values. The best values depend on the measure of performance that is obtained after one or several executions of the simulation model. The notion of optimizing simulations will be expanded in Chapter 10.

6.3.2 DISCRETE EVENT SIMULATION

Business processes usually are modeled as computer-based, dynamic, stochastic, and discrete simulation models. The most common way to represent these models in the computer is using discrete-event simulation. In simple terms, discrete-event simulation describes how a system with discrete flow units or jobs evolves over time. Technically, this means that the computer tracks how and when state variables such as queue lengths and resource availabilities change over time. The state-variables change as a result of an event (or discrete event) occurring in the system. A characteristic is that discrete-event models focus only on the time instances when these discrete events occur. This feature allows for significant time compression because it makes it possible to skip through all time segments between events when the state of the system remains unchanged. Therefore, in a short period of time, the computer can simulate a large number of events corresponding to a long real-time span.

To illustrate the mechanics of a discrete-event simulation model, consider an information desk with a single server. Assume that the objective of the simulation is to estimate the average delay of a customer. The simulation then must have the following state variables.

- Status of the server (busy or idle).
- Number of customers in the queue.
- Time of arrival of each person in the queue.

As the simulation runs, two events can change the value of these state variables: the arrival of a customer or the completion of service.

The arrival of a customer either changes the status of the server from idle to busy or increases the number of customers in the queue. The completion of service, on the other hand, either changes the status of the server from busy to idle or decreases the number of customers in the queue.

Because the state variables change only when an event occurs, a discrete-event simulation model examines the dynamics of the system from one event to the next. That is, the simulation moves the "simulation clock" from one event to the next and considers that the system does not change in any way between two consecutive events. For example, if a single customer is waiting in line at a grocery store and the next event is the completion of service of the customer who is currently paying for his groceries, then discrete-event simulation does not keep track of how the customer in the line spends her waiting time. In other words, the simulation keeps track of the time when each event occurs but assumes that nothing happens during the elapsed time between two consecutive events.

Figure 6.18 summarizes the steps associated with a discrete-event simulation. The simulation starts with initializing the current state of the system and an event list. The initial state of the system, for example, might include some jobs in several queues as specified by the analyst. It also could specify, for instance, the availability of some resources in the process. The most common initial state is to consider that no jobs are in the process and that all resources are currently available and ready. The event list indicates the time when the next event will occur. For example, the event list initially might include the time of the first arrival to the process. Other events might be scheduled initially, as specified by the analyst.

Once the initialization step is completed, the clock is advanced to the next event in the event list. The next event is then executed. Three activities are triggered by the execution of an event. First, the current state of the system must be changed. For example, the executed event might be a job arriving to the process. If all the servers are busy,

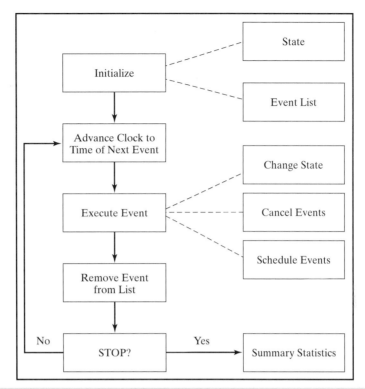

FIGURE 6.18 Discrete-Event Simulation

then the state change consists of adding the arriving job to a queue. Other state changes might require deleting a job from a queue or making a server busy.

The execution of an event might cause the cancellation of other events. For example, if the executed event consists of a machine breakdown, then this event forces the cancellation of the processing of jobs that are waiting for the machine. Finally, the execution of an event may cause the scheduling of future events. For example, if a job arrives and is added to a queue, a future event is also added to the event list indicating the time that the job will start processing.

When an event is executed, the event is removed from the event list. Then the termination criterion is checked. If the criterion indicates that the end of the simulation has been reached, then raw data along with summary statistics are made available to the analyst. On the other hand, if the termination criterion indicates that the simulation has not finished (for example, because more events remain in the event list), then the clock is advanced to the time of the next event.

Example 6.13: Discrete-Events and Simulation Time Line in a Single-Server Process

A single-server queuing process can be represented with a time line on which the time of each event is marked. Assume the following notation.

- t_j = Arrival time of the jth job
- $A_j = t_j - t_{j-1}$ = Time between the arrival of job $j - 1$ and the arrival of job j
- S_j = Service time for job j
- D_j = Delay time for job j
- $c_j = t_j + D_j + S_j$ = Completion time for job j
- e_i = Time of occurrence of event i

Figure 6.19 shows a graphical representation of the events in a single-server process. This example has six events, starting with event 0 and finishing with event 5.

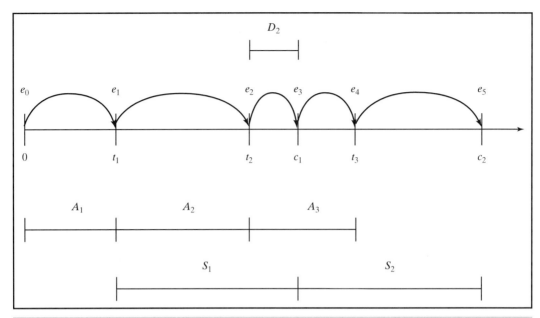

FIGURE 6.19 Events Timeline for a Single Server

Event 0, e_0, is the initialization of the simulation. Event 1, e_1, is the arrival of the first job, with arrival time equal to t_1. The arrival of the second job occurs at time t_2. Because $c_1 > t_2$, the second job is going to experience a delay. The delay D_2 is equal to the difference between c_1 and t_2 ($D_2 = c_1 - t_2$).

In Figure 6.19, the completion time for job 1 is calculated as $c_1 = t_1 + S_1$, because this job does not experience any delay. The last event in this figure, labeled e_5, is the completion time for job 2. In this case, the calculation of the completion time c_2 includes the waiting time D_2 ($c_2 = t_2 + D_2 + S_2$).

6.3.3 SPREADSHEET SIMULATION OF A SINGLE-SERVER PROCESS

It is possible to simulate a single-server process using an electronic spreadsheet program such as Microsoft Excel. The spreadsheet model must be capable of handling the following events.

1. A job arrives.
2. A job waits to be processed if the server is busy.
3. A job is processed.
4. A job leaves the system.

Next, a spreadsheet model will be created with the goal of estimating average waiting time and the percentage of time that the server is busy (the server utilization). To calculate waiting times, the arrival time of each job and its completion time must be known. To calculate idle time, one must know the time when processing starts for the current job and the completion time of the previous job. The following definitions are needed in addition to the variables defined in Example 6.13.

b_j = Time when processing begins for job j
I_j = Idle time between job j and job $j - 1$

It is assumed that for each job, the interarrival time A_j and its service time S_j can be generated using a random generation function. Furthermore, it is assumed that the model being simulated is *M/M/*1. The interarrival and service times can be generated with the Excel functions RAND() and LN() and the following expressions.

$$A_j = -\left(\frac{1}{\lambda}\right) \times \text{LN(RAND())}$$

$$S_j = -\left(\frac{1}{\mu}\right) \times \text{LN(RAND())}$$

In these expressions, μ is the mean arrival rate, and λ is the mean service rate. The Excel formula RAND() generates a random number between 0 and 1. The natural logarithm of the random number is found to transform this number into an exponentially distributed value. The transformation to an exponential distribution is completed when the value is divided by the appropriate mean rate and the negative sign is applied. (See Section 9.4 of Chapter 9 for a detailed explanation of how to generate exponentially distributed random numbers using this transformation.) The following relationships can be established based on the interarrival and service values.

Arrival time of the first job:	$t_1 = A_1$
Arrival time of job j, for $j > 1$:	$t_j = A_j + t_{j-1}$
Starting time of the first job:	$b_1 = t_1$
Starting time of job j, for $j > 1$:	$b_j = \max(t_j, c_{j-1})$
Delay time for job j:	$D_j = b_j - t_j$
Idle time associated with the first job:	$I_1 = t_1$
Idle time associated with job j, for $j > 1$:	$I_j = b_j - c_{j-1}$

Figure 6.20 shows a spreadsheet simulation of the *M/M/*1 model of Example 6.4. Recall that in this process, the arrival rate is 40 requests per week ($\lambda = 40$) and the service rate is 50 requests per week ($\mu = 50$).

The spreadsheet simulation in Figure 6.20 uses the mean arrival rate and the mean service rate to generate interarrival times (D column) and service times (F column), respectively. The model simulates 200 requests and estimates the average waiting time and the server utilization. Note that the true average waiting time in steady state, as calculated using the analytical model, is 3.2 hours. The simulation of 200 requests shown in Figure 6.20 resulted in an estimated value of 3.621 hours. The average waiting time estimate by the simulation model approaches the analytical value as more requests are simulated; that is, as more rows are added to the spreadsheet.

The spreadsheet simulation also estimates the utilization of the server. The estimated value in the simulation shown in Figure 6.20 is 81.4 percent, which is close to the true steady-state value of 80 percent found with the analytical model. This estimate also improves when more requests are added to the simulation. The formulas needed to create the simulation model are shown in Table 6.5.

Table 6.5 shows the formulas for the first request (row 8) and the second request (row 9). All the other requests are modeled after the formulas in row 9. In order to calculate the statistics of interest (i.e., the estimated average waiting time and the estimated utilization), the following formulas are used in cells I3 and I4, respectively.

$$= \text{AVERAGE(H8:H207)} * 40$$
$$= 1 - \text{SUM(I8:I207)/G207}$$

Request	Interarrival Time	Arrival Time	Start Time	Service Time	Completion Time	Waiting Time	Idle Time
1	0.0018	0.0018	0.0018	0.0058	0.0076	0.0000	0.0018
2	0.0205	0.0223	0.0223	0.0234	0.0457	0.0000	0.0147
3	0.0014	0.0237	0.0457	0.0372	0.0829	0.0219	0.0000
4	0.0713	0.0950	0.0950	0.0084	0.1034	0.0000	0.0121
5	0.0148	0.1098	0.1098	0.0067	0.1165	0.0000	0.0064
6	0.0422	0.1520	0.1520	0.0221	0.1740	0.0000	0.0355
7	0.1423	0.2943	0.2943	0.0218	0.3160	0.0000	0.1202
8	0.0502	0.3445	0.3445	0.0194	0.3638	0.0000	0.0284
9	0.0255	0.3699	0.3699	0.0334	0.4033	0.0000	0.0061
10	0.0020	0.3719	0.4033	0.0191	0.4224	0.0314	0.0000
11	0.0094	0.3813	0.4224	0.0130	0.4354	0.0410	0.0000
12	0.0031	0.3844	0.4354	0.0221	0.4574	0.0510	0.0000
13	0.0713	0.4557	0.4574	0.0081	0.4655	0.0017	0.0000
14	0.0450	0.5007	0.5007	0.0095	0.5102	0.0000	0.0351
15	0.0277	0.5284	0.5284	0.0002	0.5286	0.0000	0.0182
16	0.0099	0.5382	0.5382	0.0346	0.5728	0.0000	0.0097
17	0.0772	0.6154	0.6154	0.0056	0.6210	0.0000	0.0426
18	0.0046	0.6199	0.6210	0.0143	0.6353	0.0011	0.0000
19	0.0188	0.6387	0.6387	0.0371	0.6758	0.0000	0.0035
20	0.0127	0.6514	0.6758	0.0097	0.6855	0.0244	0.0000

Single-Server Queuing Simulation

Mean arrival rate 40.000 requests/week   Average waiting time 3.621 hours (Estimated)
Mean service rate 50.000 requests/week   Server utilization 81.4%

FIGURE 6.20 Single-Server Spreadsheet Simulation

TABLE 6.5 Formulas for Spreadsheet Simulation

	C	D	E	F	G	H	I
8	= –(1/\$D\$3) *LN(RAND())	= C8	= D8	= –(1/\$D\$4) *LN(RAND())	= E8 + F8	= E8 – D8	= E8
9	= –(1/\$D\$3) *LN(RAND())	= D8 + C9	= max(G8,D9)	= –(1/\$D\$4) *LN(RAND())	= E9 + F9	= E9 – D9	= E9 – G8

The average waiting time is multiplied by 40 to convert it from weeks to hours. The estimated utilization is based on the percentage of idle time. The percentage of idle time is the sum of the idle times (cells I8 to I207) divided by the completion time of the last job (cell G207). The utilization is then calculated as the complement of the percentage of idle time.

One limitation of performing process-driven simulations on a spreadsheet is that estimates of the number of jobs in the queue cannot be calculated (Evans and Olson, 1998). These statistics are a function of time rather than the number of customers. Because one customer is processed at a time, there is no convenient way of capturing data related to the length of the queue within the spreadsheet model. Another serious limitation of spreadsheets for waiting-line simulation is that behaviors such as balking, reneging, and jockeying are difficult (if not impossible) to include. To handle these extensions, an event-driven simulator such as the one introduced in Chapters 7 and 8 must be used.

6.4 Summary

Variability in the time that it takes to perform certain activities as well as in the demand for these activities is an important concern when designing business processes. This variability causes unbalanced capacity utilization over time. This in turn manifests itself through queues and their associated non-value-adding waiting times. The economic implication is that the process design team is faced with the problem of balancing the cost of acquiring additional capacity against the cost of poor service.

This chapter investigated ways to explicitly incorporate variability in activity times and demand into process models. It explored analytical queuing models stemming from mathematical queuing theory and computer-based, discrete-event simulation models, which are experimental in nature.

Regardless of which of the two modeling approaches is used, the analysis assumes an understanding of the elementary components defining a basic queuing process: the calling population, the arrival process, the queue configuration, the queue discipline, and the service mechanism.

Because even in well-designed processes occasional long queues might be unavoidable, it is important to consider strategies to mitigate the negative economic effects of these potentially long lines. This is particularly relevant in service situations in which the queue consists of people who are sensitive to waiting and might decide to leave. The pros and cons of several strategies that are often used in service industries were discussed, including (1) concealing the queue, (2) using the customer as a resource, (3) making the wait comfortable, (4) keeping the customers informed of the reason for the wait, (5) providing pessimistic estimates of remaining waiting time, and (6) the importance of being fair and open about the queuing discipline used.

The exponential distribution plays a central role in mathematical queuing modeling. A thorough discussion about when using this distribution might be a realistic assumption for modeling service and interarrival times was provided. Of particular interest is to understand the implications of important properties such as a strictly decreasing density function, and lack of memory and its relation to the Poisson process.

The analytical queuing models considered in this chapter all consist of a single queue with a FIFO queuing discipline and a service mechanism with parallel servers. All models assumed exponentially distributed service and interarrival times. This represents an important class of queuing models, which are based on the general birth-and-death process. In the context of a queuing process, a birth represents a customer arrival and a death represents a service completion. In addition to an approach for steady-state analysis of general birth-and-death processes, based on the so-called Rate In = Rate Out Principle and the corresponding balance equations, a number of specialized models also were explored. These models represent important special cases often seen in practice for which important performance characteristics can be obtained from standardized mathematical formulae. The specialized models covered in this chapter were: $M/M/1$, $M/M/c$, $M/M/c/K$, and $M/M/c/\infty/N$.

In order to aid capacity-related design decisions, meaning to balance the costs of additional capacity against the costs of poor service, waiting costs were introduced as a way to translate the effects of queues and waiting time into monetary terms. The corresponding decision model is based on the ability to analyze the behavior of queuing processes quantitatively, particularly in terms of expected number of customers in the system or in the queue. A major challenge in applying these types of decision models pertains to estimating relevant waiting cost rates—the waiting costs per customer and time unit. This task typically requires good understanding of customer requirements and the economic consequences of delays.

In situations where the business process under study violates the assumptions of existing analytical models and new mathematical models may be hard or even possible to derive, an attractive modeling tool is computer-based, discrete-event simulation. This modeling technique allows the representation of processes, people, and technology in a dynamic computer model. The simulation model mimics the operations of a business process, including customer arrivals, truck deliveries, absent workers, or machine breakdowns. A characteristic of discrete-event simulation is that it focuses solely on the instances when discrete events occur and change the state of the simulated process. This allows for considerable compression of time, enabling the analyst to look far into the future. While stepping through the events, the simulation software accumulates data related to the model elements and state variables, including capacity utilization of resources, number of jobs at different workstations, and waiting times in buffers. The performance of the process can then be evaluated through statistical analysis of the collected output data.

To illustrate the principles of discrete-event simulation, the chapter concluded with an exploration of how a single-server queuing process could be simulated in a spreadsheet environment such as Microsoft Excel.

6.5 References

Bunday, B. D., and R. E. Scraton. 1980. The G/M/r machine interference model. *European Journal of Operational Research* 4: 399–402.

Eneyo, E. S., and G. P. Pannirselvam. 1999. Process simulation for facility layout. *IIE Solutions* 31(11): 37–40.

Evans, J. R., and D. L. Olson. 1998. *Introduction to simulation and risk analysis.* Upper Saddle River, NJ: Prentice Hall.

Fitzsimmons, J. A., and M. J. Fitzsimmons. 1998. *Service management: Operations, strategy, and information technology.* New York: Irwin/McGraw-Hill.

Harrell, C., and K. Tumay. 1995. *Simulation made easy: A manager's guide.* Atanta: Engineering and Management Press.

Hillier, F. S., and G. J. Lieberman. 2001. *Introduction to operations research,* 7th edition. New York: McGraw-Hill.

Kleinrock, L. 1975. *Queuing systems—Volume I: Theory.* New York: John Wiley and Sons Inc.

Law, A. M., and M. G. McComas. 1988. How simulation pays off. *Manufacturing Engineering* 100(2): 37–39.

Little, J. D. C. 1961. A proof for the queuing formula $L = \lambda W$. *Operations Research* 9: 383–387.

6.6 Discussion Questions and Exercises

1. Demonstrate that each of the following situations can be represented as a basic queuing process by identifying its components. How would you define the corresponding queuing system?
   a. The checkout stations in a supermarket.
   b. The tollbooth at a road-toll checkpoint.
   c. An auto shop or garage.
   d. An emergency rescue unit.
   e. A plumber.
   f. A bus station.
   g. The materials-handling equipment at a production facility.
2. A mechanic, Bob, requires on average 3 hours to complete a repair. Furthermore, the repair time closely follows an exponential distribution. Bob realizes that by hiring his nephew Bill as an assistant, he can reduce the average repair time to 2 hours. The repair time would still be exponential because the job structure is unchanged. For each repair job, Bob gets paid $220 if he finishes in less than 2 hours and $180 if he cannot. Assume that Bob does not want to decrease his expected payment per repair job. What is the maximum amount per job that Bob would be willing to pay Bill?
3. Purchasing requests arrive to an agent at a rate of six per day. The time between arrivals is exponentially distributed. The agent typically requires 1 hour to process a request. The processing time is also exponentially distributed. Assuming 8-hour working days:

a. What is the cycle time (the average time that a request spends in the process)?
b. What is the work-in-process inventory (the average number of requests in the process)?
c. How often is the WIP entirely replaced with a new set of requests?

4. A small branch office of a local bank has two tellers for which customers line up in a single queue. The customers are being served on a first-come-first-served basis. It has been determined that the steady-state probability distribution for finding exactly n customers in the system, $\{P_n, n = 0, 1, 2 \ldots\}$, is $P_0 = (2/18), P_1 = (5/18), P_2 = (6/18), P_3 = (3/18), P_4 = (1/18), P_5 = (1/18)$, and $P_n = 0$ for $n = 6, 7, \ldots$.
    a. Determine the expected number of customers in the system, L.
    b. Determine the expected number of customers in the queue, L_q.
    c. Determine the expected number of customers in the service facility.
    d. Assuming that the mean arrival rate is six customers per hour, determine the expected time a customer spends in the system, W, and in the queue, W_q.
    e. Determine the expected service time—the expected time a customer spends in the service facility—assuming that the two tellers are identical.

5. It has been concluded that a single-server queuing system with exponentially distributed service and interarrival times can be modeled as a birth-and-death process with state-dependent mean service and arrival rates, μ_n and λ_n, respectively.

$$\mu_n = \begin{cases} n & \text{for } n = 0, 1, 2, 3 \\ 0 & \text{otherwise} \end{cases} \qquad \lambda_n = \begin{cases} 3 - n & \text{for } n = 0, 1, 2, 3 \\ 0 & \text{otherwise} \end{cases}$$

    a. Construct the corresponding rate diagram.
    b. Calculate the stationary probabilities for finding exactly n customers in the system, $\{P_n, n = 0, 1, 2, 3, \ldots\}$.
    c. Determine the expected number of customers in the queuing system, L, and in the queue, L_q. Also determine the expected time a customer spends in the system, W, in the queue, W_q, and in the service facility, W_s.

6. A queuing process is modeled as a birth-and-death process with mean arrival rates $\lambda_0 = 2$, $\lambda_1 = 4, \lambda_2 = 3, \lambda_3 = 1$, and $\lambda_n = 0$ for $n > 3$ and mean service rates $\mu_1 = 2, \mu_2 = 4, \mu_3 = 1$, $\mu_4 = 1$ and $\mu_n = 0$ otherwise.
    a. Construct a rate diagram.
    b. Develop the balance equations and solve them to obtain P_n, $n \geq 0$.
    c. Determine L, L_q, W, and W_q assuming the queuing process has two parallel servers.

7. Consider a birth-and-death process with mean birth rates and death rates, λ_n and μ_n, shown in Table 6.6.
    a. Construct a rate diagram.
    b. Calculate the stationary probabilities for finding the process in state $n, n = 0, 1, 2, 3, \ldots$.
    c. If a queuing process with two identical servers fits this birth-and-death process, what is the mean arrival and service rate for each of the two servers when they are busy serving customers?

8. The mean service and arrival rates for a birth-and-death process describing a queuing system with two parallel servers are given in Table 6.7.
    a. Construct the corresponding rate diagram.
    b. Develop the balance equations and solve them to determine the stationary probabilities for finding n customers in the system $P_n, n = 0, 1, 2, 3, 4, \ldots$.

TABLE 6.6 Birth-and-Death Process for Exercise 7

State (n)	Mean Birthrate (λ_n)	Mean Death Rate (μ_n)
0	2	0
1	2	2
2	2	4
3	0	4

TABLE 6.7 Birth-and-Death Process for Exercise 8

State (n)	Mean Birthrate (λ_n)	Mean Death Rate (μ_n)
0	4	0
1	4	1
2	4	2
3	4	2
4	0	2

    c. Determine the expected number of customers in the system, L, and in the queue, L_q, as well as the expected time spent in the system, W, and in the queue, W_q.

    d. Identify the type of queuing model that corresponds to this birth-and-death process. Use the formulae derived for this queuing model to calculate $P_n, n = 0, 1, 2, 3, 4, \ldots, L$, L_q, W, W_q.

9. A gas station has a single automated car wash. Cars arrive to the gas station according to a Poisson process with an average of 30 cars per hour. One third of the customers also want a car wash, so for every customer there is a 33.33 percent chance it desires a car wash. The mean service rate is 10 cars per hour. Although several different washing programs are available, it is a bit of a stretch to say that the service times follow an exponential distribution. Still, as a first-cut analysis, management has decided to make this assumption and model the queuing system as a birth-and-death process. It has been observed that customers balk from the car wash queue when it increases in length. More precisely, the probability that a customer will balk is $n/3$ for $n = 1, 2, 3$ customers in the car wash system. If more than three customers are in the system, no customers will join the queue.

    a. Construct a rate diagram for this queuing process.

    b. Formulate the balance equations and solve them to determine the steady-state probability distribution for the number of cars in the car wash.

    c. What is the expected utilization of the car wash?

    d. Determine the expected waiting time in line for those customers who join the queue.

10. A small machine shop consists of three sensitive machines that break down frequently but independently from each other. The company has two service technicians on standby to repair the machines as soon as they break down. For each fully functional machine, the breakdown rate is 0.1 times per hour, and the time between breakdowns is exponentially distributed. The service technicians work independently of one another, and due to restricted space around the machines, only one technician at a time can work on a machine. For each technician, the average service rate is 0.2 machines per hour, and the service times follow an exponential distribution.

    The operations manager realizes that this system can be modeled as a birth-and-death process with state-dependent arrival and service rates. He also has figured out what these arrival and service rates are, expressed in $\lambda =$ the machine breakdown rate (the same for all machines) and $\mu =$ the service rate for each of the technicians. Table 6.8 shows a summary of what he has discovered.

    a. Unfortunately, the operations manager lacks training in analyzing queuing systems, and his analysis of the arrival and service rates is not entirely correct. Show the correct service and arrival rates for the system by drawing a state/rate diagram.

TABLE 6.8 Summary Information for Exercise 10

Number of Broken Down Machines	Breakdown Rate (= arrival rate)	Service Rate
0	3λ	0
1	2λ	2μ
2	λ	2μ
3	0	2μ

The operations manager is stubborn and does not admit that he is wrong, so he orders you to continue the analysis based on the arrival rates he has specified.

  b. Construct the state/rate diagram corresponding to the given arrival and service rates. Develop the balance equations and solve them to determine the steady-state probability distribution. What is the probability that all the machines are functioning?

  c. Calculate the expected number of broken machines and the expected time for a machine to be operating again after it has broken down.

11. Consider an *M/M/*2 model. Derive the following expressions by constructing the rate diagram and solving the balance equations.

$$\rho = \lambda / 2\mu$$
$$P_0 = (1-\rho)/(1+\rho)$$
$$P_n = 2\rho^n P_0$$
$$L = 2\rho/1 - \rho^2$$
$$L_q = 2\rho^3 / (1 - \rho^2) = L - 2\rho$$

(Hint: Look at the technique used to derive the corresponding results for the *M/M/*1 queue in Section 6.2.4.)

12. A pharmaceutical company has formed a team to handle FDA applications for approval of new drugs. Requests for applications arrive at a rate of one every year. The arrivals follow a Poisson distribution. On average, the team processes an application in 9 months. The company estimates that the average cost of revenue losses associated with waiting for a new drug to be approved is $100,000 per drug per month. The cost of a team is $50,000 per month.

  a. Estimate the total cost due to revenue losses in the current process.

  b. Should the company add a second team?

13. A telecommunications company receives customer calls at a rate of 25 per hour. The inter-arrival times are exponentially distributed. Each call requires an average of 20 minutes. The times for each call also follow an exponential distribution.

  a. What is the minimum number of customer service agents needed for this process to reach steady state?

  b. Create a plot that shows the expected waiting time in the queue as a function of the number of agents.

  c. The telecommunications company would like to limit the average waiting time in the queue to 2 minutes or less. How many agents should the company hire?

14. A mechanic is responsible for keeping two machines in working order. The time until a working machine breaks down is exponentially distributed with a mean of 12 hours. The mechanic's repair time is exponentially distributed with a mean of 8 hours.

  a. Show that this queuing process is a birth-and-death process by defining the states, $n = 0, 1, 2, 3, \ldots$; specifying the state-dependent mean arrival and service rates, λ_n and μ_n for $n = 0, 1, 2, 3, \ldots$; and constructing the rate diagram. Also specify the criteria defining a birth-and-death process and make sure this process satisfies these criteria.

  b. Specify the balance equations and use them to determine the steady-state probability distribution for finding n customers in the system, P_n, $n = 0, 1, 2, 3, \ldots$.

  c. Use the definitions and Little's law to determine L, L_q, W, and W_q.

  d. Determine the fraction of time that at least one machine is working.

15. Consider the description of problem 14.

  a. Identify an appropriate queuing model that adequately describes the queuing process. Use the corresponding formulae to determine: P_n, $n = 0, 1, 2, 3, \ldots$, L, L_q, W, and W_q.

  b. Determine the fraction of time that the mechanic is busy.

  c. Determine the fraction of time that both machines are operational.

16. A workstation has enough storage space to store three jobs in addition to the one being processed. Excess jobs are routed to another workstation, which is used solely to handle this overflow of jobs from the regular workstation. Jobs arrive to the regular workstation according to a Poisson process with a mean of eight jobs per day. The process time in the

regular workstation is exponentially distributed with a mean of 30 minutes. A workday is comprised of 8 hours.

a. Construct the rate diagram describing this queuing process.
b. Develop the balance equations and use them to determine the steady-state probability distribution for finding n customers in the system $\{P_n, n = 0, 1, 2, 3, \ldots\}$.
c. Identify a specialized queuing model that describes this queuing process and use the corresponding formulae to determine the steady-state probability distribution for finding n customers in the system $\{P_n, n = 0, 1, 2, 3, \ldots\}$. Compare the results to part b.
d. Determine the fraction of time that the storage space at the regular work center is adequate to handle the demand.
e. What is the average number of jobs stored at the regular work center (excluding the job being processed), and what is the average waiting time in line before processing?

17. Plans are being made to open a small gas station in a central location in Springfield. The owner must decide how much space should be provided for waiting cars. This is an important decision because land prices are high. It is assumed that customers (cars) arrive according to a Poisson process with a mean rate of 20 per hour. However, if the waiting area is full, customers will go elsewhere. The time it takes to service one customer is exponentially distributed with a mean of 4 minutes. The gas station will have two gas pumps. Before making a decision about how much land to acquire, the owner wants to analyze the situation further using queuing modeling.

a. Identify an appropriate queuing model to describe this queuing process. Use the corresponding formulae to calculate the fraction of time that sales will be lost for the following options regarding spaces for waiting cars (excluding the ones being served because they are filling gas or paying).
   i. No spaces for waiting cars
   ii. Two spaces for waiting cars
   iii. Four spaces for waiting cars
b. Assuming the gas station is open 24 hours each day, what is the expected number of lost customers per day for alternatives (i), (ii), and (iii) in a? If on average a customer generates a profit of $3 for the owner of the gas station, what is the expected lost profit per day under alternatives (i), (ii), and (iii)?

18. A facility management company has recently acquired a number of new commercial properties within the city of Greenfield. They are faced with the problem of hiring a number of on-call janitors, who are responsible for fixing emergency problems that arise at these different facilities. The question is how many locations to assign to each janitor. The janitors work independently on the properties that they are responsible for serving. When the janitor gets a call from a location other than the one he/she is at, the request is placed in a queue and served on a FIFO basis. When visiting a certain location, the janitor will attend to all matters at this facility. This means that a location that has called for the janitor will not call again even if new matters arise. Therefore, consider a facility that has placed a call to the janitor as "non-operational." If no matters need janitorial attention, the facility is considered fully operational. For each fully operational facility, the times between emergency calls to the janitor are exponentially distributed with a mean of 2.5 hours. The time it takes for the janitor to fix the problems at a location is exponentially distributed with a mean of 20 minutes, including travel time. The facility-management company has determined a service-level criteria, specifying that at least 75 percent of the time the facilities should receive immediate emergency service from a janitor.

a. Identify a queuing model that adequately describes this process of emergency janitorial assistance. Use the corresponding steady-state formulae to determine the largest number of facilities that can be assigned to a janitor without violating the specified service requirement.
b. Given the maximum number of facilities assigned to each janitor in a, what is the expected fraction of time that a janitor is busy with emergency calls? What is the expected number of facilities not fully operational? What is the expected waiting time before a facility gets emergency assistance?

19. A company has a central document-copying service. Arrivals can be assumed to follow the Poisson probability distribution, with a mean rate of 15 per hour. It can be assumed that service times are exponentially distributed. With the present copying equipment, the average service time is 3 minutes. A new machine can be leased that has a mean service time of 2 minutes. The average wage of the people who bring the documents to be copied is $8 an hour.
    a. If the machine can be leased for $5 per hour more than the old machine, should the company replace the old machine?
    b. Suppose the new machine is leased. How much space (e.g., number of chairs) must be provided for people to wait to guarantee that at least 90 percent of the time this space will be sufficient?

20. The manager of a movie theater would like to predict the consequences of adding a second ticket clerk. Data show that arrivals to the theater are Poisson distributed at a rate of 250 per hour, and service times are exponentially distributed with a mean of 12 seconds. The manager has also estimated that losses in concession revenue when customers wait in the ticket line are $1.50 per waiting hour. This revenue is not recovered after the customers enter the theater. Given that it costs $5 per hour to have a ticket clerk, should the manager add a second server?

21. A process has a bottleneck resource that consists of specialized equipment. Jobs arrive to this machine at a rate of 40 per hour (according to a Poisson arrival process). The processing times average 1 minute and are exponentially distributed. Compare the performance (e.g., average cycle time through the bottleneck) of the current process with the following alternatives.
    a. Add a second identical machine in the bottleneck.
    b. Replace the current machine with one that is twice as fast.

22. Most arrivals to a hospital emergency room are not considered emergencies in that the patients can wait to see a doctor until they complete the proper forms. At County Hospital, emergency patients arrive at a rate of six per hour. This process is, to no one's surprise, a Poisson arrival process. It takes the admission clerk approximately 10 minutes to fill out the patient's form. The length of time is not exact and, in fact, follows an exponential distribution. As soon as the form is filled out, the patient is examined. The chief of staff is concerned with the quality of the operations and wants to know the expected performance of the current process. Use queuing theory to evaluate the performance of this process.

23. A fast food chain is opening a new restaurant in a shopping mall. The restaurant needs to hire a cashier and has two prime candidates. Candidate 1 is experienced and fast but demands a higher salary. Candidate 2 is inexperienced and slower but also has more modest salary requests. The question is which one the restaurant manager should choose. Both candidates can be considered to have exponentially distributed service times, candidate 1 with a mean of 1 minute and candidate 2 with a mean of 1.5 minutes. The customers arrive according to a Poisson process with a mean of 30 customers per hour. The waiting cost has been estimated to be $6 per hour for each customer until he or she has been fully served and has paid for the meal. Determine the maximum difference in monthly salary that would justify hiring candidate 1 instead of candidate 2 when the objective for the restaurant manager is to minimize the expected total cost. Assume that a month has 30 workdays and each workday is 8 hours long.

24. Consider a cashier at a grocery store. Customers arrive at this cashier's station according to a Poisson process with a mean of 25 customers per hour. The cashier's service times are exponentially distributed with a mean of 2 minutes. By hiring a person to help the cashier bag the groceries and occasionally assist customers by bringing their groceries to their car, the mean service time for the checkout station can be reduced to 1 minute. The service times are still exponentially distributed. Hiring a cashier's aid would incur a cost of $10 per hour for the store. Furthermore, it has been estimated that the store is facing a waiting cost (lost profit and future lost sales) of $0.10 per minute that a customer spends in line or in the checkout station. The store manager wants to determine whether proceeding to hire a cashier's aid is a good idea or not. The criterion is that the manager wants to minimize the expected total costs. What is your recommendation after analyzing the situation using an appropriate queuing model?

TABLE 6.9 Arrival Rate and Service Times for Exercise 25

Period	Incoming Rate (calls per hour)	Service Time (in min.)
Morning	3.2	8
Afternoon	3.5	10
Evening	7.8	5

25. The arrival and service rates in Table 6.9 pertain to telephone calls to a technical support person in a call center on a typical day. The interarrival times and the service times are exponentially distributed.
    a. Determine the average time the callers wait to have their calls answered for each period.
    b. What should be the capacity of the switchboard so it is capable of handling the demand 95 percent of the time? The capacity of the switchboard is measured as the number of calls that can be placed on hold plus the call that the technical-support person is answering.
26. Truckloads of seasonal merchandise arrive to a distribution center within a 2-week span. Because of this, merchandised-filled trucks waiting to unload have been known to back up for a block at the receiving dock. The increased cost caused by unloading delays including truck rental and idle driver time is of significant concern to the company. The estimated cost of waiting and unloading for truck and driver is $18 per hour. During the 2-week delivery time, the receiving dock is open 16 hours per day, 7 days per week, and can on average unload 35 trucks per hour. The unloading times closely follow an exponential distribution. Full trucks arrive during the time the dock is open at a mean rate of 30 per hour, with interarrival times following an exponential distribution. To help the company get a handle on the problem of lost time while trucks are waiting in line or unloading at the dock, find the following measures of performance.
    a. The average number of trucks in the unloading process.
    b. The average cycle time.
    c. The probability that more than three trucks are in the process at any given time.
    d. The expected total daily cost of having the trucks tied up in the unloading process.
    e. It has been estimated that if the storage area were to be enlarged, the sum of waiting and unloading costs would be cut in half next year. If it costs $9,000 to enlarge the storage area, would it be worth the expense to enlarge it?
27. A case team completes jobs at a rate of two per hour, with actual processing times following an exponential distribution. Jobs arrive at rate of about one every 32 minutes, and the arrival times also are considered exponential. Use queuing theory to answer the following questions.
    a. What is the average cycle time?
    b. What is the cycle time efficiency? (*Hint*: Remember that cycle time includes processing time and waiting time.)
28. The manager of a grocery store is interested in providing good service to the senior citizens who shop in his store. The manager is considering the addition of a separate checkout counter for senior citizens. It is estimated that the senior citizens would arrive at the counter at an average of 30 per hour, with interarrival times following an exponential distribution. It is also estimated that they would be served at a rate of 35 per hour, with exponentially distributed service times.
    a. What is the estimated utilization of the checkout clerk?
    b. What is the estimated average length of the queue?
    c. What is the estimated average waiting time in line?
    d. Assess the performance of this process.
    e. What service rate would be required to have customers average only 8 minutes in the process? (The 8 minutes include waiting and service time.)
    f. For the service rate calculated in part e, what is the probability of having more than four customers in the process?

g. What service rate would be required to have only a 10 percent chance of exceeding four customers in the process?

29. A railroad company paints its own railroad cars as needed. The company is about to make a significant overhaul of the painting operations and needs to decide between two alternative paint shop configurations.

    Alternative 1: Two "wall-to-wall" manually operated paint shops, where the painting is done by hand (one car at a time in each shop). The annual joint operating cost for each shop is estimated at $150,000. In each paint shop, the average painting time is estimated to be 6 hours per car. The painting time closely follows an exponential distribution.

    Alternative 2: An automated paint shop at an annual operating cost of $400,000. In this case, the average paint time for a car is 3 hours and is exponentially distributed.

    Regardless of which paint shop alternative is chosen, the railroad cars in need of painting arrive to the paint shop according to a Poisson process with a mean of one car every 5 hours (the interarrival time is 5 hours). The cost for an idle railroad car is $50 per hour. A car is considered idle as soon as it is not in traffic; consequently, all the time spent in the paint shop is considered idle time. For efficiency reasons, the paint shop operation is run 24 hours a day, 365 days a year for a total of 8,760 hours per year.

    a. What is the utilization of the paint shops in alternative 1 and 2, respectively? What are the probabilities for alternative 1 and 2, respectively, that no railroad cars are in the paint shop system?

    b. Provided the company wants to minimize the total expected cost of the system including operating costs and the opportunity cost of having idle railroad cars, which alternative should the railroad company choose?

30. The chief of staff in the emergency room of problem 22 is considering the computerization of the admissions process. This change will not reduce the 10-minute service time, but it will make it constant. Develop a spreadsheet simulation to compare the performance of the proposed automated process with the performance of the manual existing process. (Simulate 500 patients in each case.)

31. At Letchworth Community College, one person, the registrar, registers students for classes. Students arrive at a rate of 10 per hour (Poisson arrivals), and the registration process takes 5 minutes on the average (exponential distribution). The registrar is paid $5 per hour, and the cost of keeping students waiting is estimated to be $2 for each student for each hour waited (not including service time). Develop a spreadsheet simulation to compare the estimated hourly cost of the following three systems. (Simulate 500 students in each case.)

    a. The current system.

    b. A computerized system that results in a service time of exactly 4 minutes. The computer leasing cost is $7 per hour.

    c. Hiring a more efficient registrar. Service time could be reduced to an average of 3 minutes (exponentially distributed), and the new registrar would be paid $8 per hour.

32. A process manager is considering automating a bottleneck operation. The operation receives between three and nine jobs per hour in a random fashion. The cost of waiting associated with the jobs is estimated at $2.20 per hour. The team's equipment choices are specified in Table 6.10.

    Develop a spreadsheet simulation to compare the estimated hourly cost of the three alternatives. (Simulate 500 jobs in each case.)

TABLE 6.10 Equipment Choices for Exercise 32

Machine	Service Time	Hourly Cost
A	Uniform between 4 and 12 minutes	$12
B	Exponential with an average of 8 minutes	$8
C	Normal with an average of 8 minutes and a standard deviation of 1 minute	$15

Introduction to Extend

This chapter introduces the simulation software called Extend[1]. This tool will be applied to the analysis and design of business processes. The general Extend package is not industry specific, so it can be used to model and simulate discrete-event or continuous systems in a wide variety of settings ranging from production processes to population-growth models. The BPR library within this software was created for the specific purpose of modeling and simulating business processes. This special functionality of Extend is utilized throughout Chapters 7, 8, 9, and 10.

The best way to learn the material discussed in this chapter is in front of a computer. Students should install Extend and open the application to either create the models shown in this chapter or review the models that are distributed in the CD that accompanies this book. For convenience, all the models used for illustration purposes have been included in the CD. The models are named Figurexx.xx.mox; xx.xx is the number that corresponds to the figure number in the book. For instance, the first model that is discussed in this chapter is the one that appears in Figure 7.2, so the corresponding file is Figure07.02.mox.

The development of a simulation model using Extend entails the following steps.

1. Determine the goals of the model.
2. Understand the process to be modeled through the use of basic analysis and design tools, such as flowcharting.
3. Draw a block diagram using the appropriate blocks in the available libraries to represent each element of the model accurately.
4. Specify appropriate parameter values for each block.
5. Define the logic of the model and the appropriate connections between blocks.
6. Validate the model.
7. Add data collection and graphical analysis capabilities.
8. Analyze the output data and draw conclusions.

Before building a model, the analyst must think about what questions the model is supposed to answer. For example, if the goal is to examine the staffing needs of a process, many details that are not related to process capacity can be left out of the model. The level of detail and the scope of the model are directly related to the overall goal of the simulation effort. Because the model will help the analyst predict process performance, a good starting point is to define what constitutes "good" performance. This definition can be used later to enhance the process design via optimization[2].

---

[1]Extend is a trademark of Imagine That, Inc., 6830 Via del Oro, Suite 230, San Jose, CA 95119-1353, USA (imaginethatinc.com). The descriptions in Chapters 7 through 10 are based on Extend v. 6 for Windows. The names of the libraries and menu items in the Macintosh version of Extend are similar to those in Windows.
[2]The use of optimization in the context of discrete-event simulation will be discussed in Chapter 10.

Before modeling processes within the simulator's environment, the analyst needs to understand the process thoroughly. This implies that the analyst knows the activities in the process, the sequence in which they are performed, the resources needed to perform the activities, and the logical relationships among activities. This understanding includes the knowledge of the arrival and service process for each activity. In particular, the analyst must be able to estimate the probability distributions that govern the behavior of arrivals to the process and the time needed to complete each activity. This step usually requires some statistical analysis to determine appropriate probability distributions associated with the processing times in each activity and the time between job arrivals. Typically, data are collected for the processing times in each activity and then a distribution is fitted to the data. Similarly, data are collected to figure out what distribution best represents the arrival pattern. A statistical test, such as the Chi-square, can be used for this purpose, as discussed in Chapter 9. ExpertFit (www.averill-law.com) and Stat::Fit (www.geerms.com) are two software packages that can be used to determine automatically and accurately what probability distribution best represents a set of real-world data. These products are designed to fit continuous and discrete distributions and to provide relative comparisons among distribution types. The use of Stat::Fit is illustrated in Chapter 9.

Extend, like most modern simulation packages, provides a graphical modeling environment. This environment consists of representing the actual process as a block diagram. Modeling in Extend entails the appropriate selection of blocks and their interconnection. Blocks are used to model activities, resources, and the routing of jobs throughout the process. Additional blocks are used to collect data, calculate statistics, and display output graphically with frequency charts, histograms, and line plots. Extend also includes blocks to incorporate activity-based costs in the simulation model, as explained in Chapter 8.

The most basic block diagram of a business process starts with the representation of the activities in the process. Then the conditions that determine the routing of jobs through the process, and if appropriate, a representation of resources, is included. In addition, rules are provided to define the operation of queues and the use of available resources. Finally, data collection and displays of summarized output data are added to the model.

In order to measure performance, the analyst must determine whether additional blocks are needed. If performance is measured by the waiting time in the queues, no additional blocks are necessary because the blocks that model queues collect waiting time data. The same goes for resource blocks and utilization data. However, if the analyst wants to count the number of jobs that are routed through a particular activity during a given simulation, a Count Items block (from the Information submenu of the Discrete Event library) needs to be included in the model. Extend libraries also include blocks that can be used to collect other important data, such as cycle times.

One of the most important aspects of a simulation is the definition and monitoring of resources. As discussed in Chapter 5, resources are needed to perform activities, and resource availability determines process capacity. Therefore, for a simulation model of a business process to be useful, resources must be defined and the resource requirements for each activity must be specified. Extend provides a Labor Pool, in the Resources submenu of the BPR library, that is used to define the attributes of each resource type, including availability and usage. A Labor Pool may represent, for instance, a group of nurses in a hospital. Every time a nurse starts or finishes performing an activity, the number of available nurses is adjusted in the Labor Pool block. These blocks are particularly useful for determining staffing needs based on performance measures such as queue length, waiting time, and resource utilization.

The proper completion of these steps results in a simulation model that describes the actual process (at a level of detail that is consistent with the goals outlined in step 1). Because in all likelihood some mathematical and logical expressions will be used during the modeling effort, it is necessary to check that the syntax employed to write these expressions is indeed correct. Checking the syntax allows the analyst to create a simulation model that is operational. A computer simulation cannot be executed until the syntax is completely correct.

Not all simulation models that run are valid; that is, one can develop a simulation model where jobs arrive, flow through the process, and leave. However, this does not mean that the model represents the actual process accurately. Model validation is an essential step in building simulations. The validation of a model consists of ensuring that the operational rules and logic in the model are an accurate reflection of the real system. Model validation must occur before the simulation results are used to draw conclusions about the behavior of the process.

7.1 Extend Elements

A simulation model in Extend is an interconnected set of blocks. A block performs a specific function, such as simulating an activity, a queue, or a pool of resources. A library is a repository of blocks. In order to use a particular block in a model, the library in which the block resides must be open. The tutorial of Section 7.2 will show how to open libraries. A simple simulation model of a process can be constructed using five basic blocks. (See Figure 7.1.)

- The Executive block from the Discrete Event library is a special block that must be included in all business process simulations. The block controls the timing and passing of events in the model. This block is the heart of a business process simulation and must be placed to the left of all other blocks in the block diagram. (Typically, the Executive block is placed at the upper-left corner of the simulation model.)
- The Import block from the Generators submenu of the BPR library is used to generate items at arrival times specified in the dialogue box. When developing the model, one must determine what items will be generated, for example jobs, customers, purchasing orders, insurance claims, or patients, to name a few.
- The Repository block from the Resources submenu of the BPR library is similar to a holding area that can initially contain a specified number of items. This block can be used to model the "in box" of a clerk. In the dialogue, the number of items

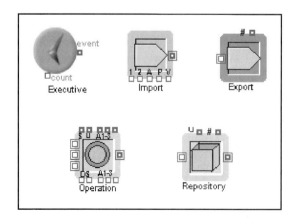

FIGURE 7.1 Basic Extend Blocks

can be specified at the beginning of the simulation, and an attribute and a priority can be added to the items as they leave.

- The Operation block from the Activities submenu of the BPR library has multiple uses; however, its most common use is to simulate an activity. The simulation of an activity is achieved by delaying an item passing through the Operation block by an amount of time that is equivalent to the processing time. The processing time specified in this block is always constant. To add uncertainty to the processing time, an Input Random Number block from the Inputs/Outputs submenu of the Generic library can be added.

- The Export block from the Routing submenu of the BPR library is used to indicate that items leave the process. Because a business process can have several exit points, more than one Export block might be needed in a simulation model.

Figure 7.2 shows these basic elements in a simple credit application process[3]. The block labeled "Apps In" generates the arrival of an application every 10 minutes. The application is placed in the block labeled "In Box" until the reviewer is available. The application stays in the block labeled "Reviewer" for 14 minutes and then is passed to the block named "Apps Done". The In Box block shows the number of applications held in this repository, and the Apps Done block shows the number of completed applications. These numbers are updated during the simulation run. In addition to the blocks, the model in Figure 7.2 contains a text box with a brief description of the model. Extend includes a drawing tool that can be used to add graphics and text to the model to enhance presentation and documentation.

Double-clicking on a block activates its dialogue window, which is used to set the properties of a block. For example, operation blocks are used to model activities in a business process. The basic property of an activity is its processing time. The dialogue window of an Operation block allows one to set the processing time of the activity that the block is modeling. In the lower left corner of every dialog window is a convenient help button. Clicking on this button opens a help window, which explains all the features of this particular block and how to use them.

Typically, additional blocks are needed to model the logic associated with an actual process, as well as to collect output data. A complete simulation model may contain one or more blocks that are not directly related to an activity in the process, but they

FIGURE 7.2 A Simple Credit Application Process

---

[3]This model is in the file Credit App—Step 1 that is distributed with Extend. This file is located in the folder Extend6\Examples\Operations Research\BPR\Credit Application.

help implement some necessary logical conditions, data collection, and reporting. These blocks will be introduced as this discussion moves from simple to more elaborate simulation models.

In simulation models, a path establishes the relationship between any pair of blocks. When more than one path originates from a block, it might be necessary to add a Decision(2) or a Decision(5) block from the Routing submenu of the BPR library. Decision blocks are used to program the logic to route jobs correctly through the process. For example, if a credit approval request can be processed by a group of generalists or by a specialist, the logic that determines where the job should go is implemented in a decision block. Additional blocks for routing are available in the Routing submenu of the Discrete Event library. For instance, the Select DE Output block is ideal for modeling the probabilistic selection of one of two possible paths.

A Repository block (in the Resources submenu of the BPR library) or a Stack block (in the Queues submenu of the BPR library) is needed when the resources required for performing an activity are limited. For example, consider the activity of a patient walking from the reception area to a laboratory in a hospital admissions process. The relevant resource to perform this activity is the hallway that connects the reception area with the laboratory. Because, for all practical purposes, the capacity of the hallway can be considered unlimited, the block used to model this activity (for example, the Transaction block in the BPR library or the Activity Multiple block in the Discrete Event library) does not need to be preceded by a Repository or Stack block. On the other hand, after the patient reaches the laboratory, a Repository or Stack block might be necessary to model the queue that is formed due to the limited number of technicians performing lab tests.

In many business processes, transportation activities such as mailing, e-mailing, or faxing documents are modeled with Activity blocks (Transaction or Activity Multiple blocks allowing for parallel processing) without a preceding Repository or Stack block. This is so because the only interest is in adding the time that it takes for the job to go from one place to another. The combination of a Repository or Stack block and an Activity block (for example the Operation block) is used to model activities such as recording data onto a database or authorizing a transaction, because the resources needed to perform these activities are usually limited. An example of this situation is depicted in Figure 7.2.

7.2 Extend Tutorial: Basic Queuing Model

The basic queuing model consists of one server (e.g., a teller at a bank, an underwriter at an insurance company, and so on). The model also considers that jobs wait in a single line (of unlimited size) and that they are served according to a first-in-first-out (FIFO) discipline[4]. In this tutorial section, a simulation of the basic queuing model will be built following a set of simple steps. Although the resulting model will represent a simple process, the methodology can be extended to model more elaborate systems. Students are strongly encouraged to build the models presented in this tutorial even though it is possible to just load them into Extend from the accompanying CD.

It is assumed that the Extend application has been launched. The main Extend window that appears after the software is loaded is shown in Figure 7.3.

A short description of each button in the toolbar can be obtained by placing the mouse pointer directly on top of each button. The first four buttons (from left to right) correspond to File menu items: New Model (Ctrl + N), Open... (Ctrl + O),

---

[4]This queuing discipline is also known as first-come-first-served (FCFS). The FIFO notation is used in Extend.

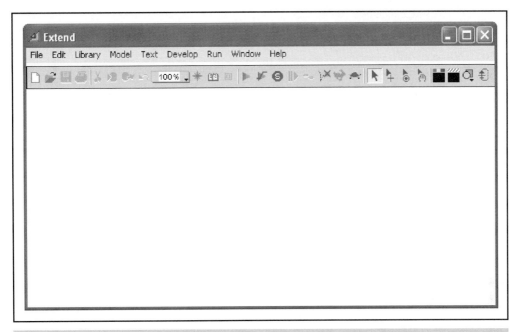

FIGURE 7.3 Main Extend Window

Save (Ctrl + S), and Print (Ctrl + P). The next four buttons correspond to Edit menu items: Cut (Ctrl + X), Copy (Ctrl + C), Paste (Ctrl + P), and Undo (Ctrl + Z). Buttons from the Library, Model, and Run menu follow. Finally, some of the buttons have no equivalent menu items and are part of the Drawing tool of Extend.

Before blocks are added to the simulation model, a new model and the libraries that contain the blocks to be added must be opened. Because the goal is to model business processes, the BPR and the Discrete Event Simulation libraries should always be opened. To do this, choose Open Library from the Library menu (i.e., Library > Open Library . . . [5], or Ctr + L), and then choose BPR from the Libraries folder. Perform this operation again, but this time choose Discrete Event from the Libraries folder. The Libraries folder is one of the folders created during the installation of Extend and is located in the folder where the Extend application resides. After adding these libraries, the items BPR.LRX and DISCRETE EVENT.LIX should appear under the Library menu. A model can now be built using blocks in these libraries, as illustrated in the following example.

Example 7.1

An insurance company receives an average of 40 requests for underwriting per week. Through statistical analysis, the company has been able to determine that the time between two consecutive requests arriving to the process is adequately described by an exponential distribution. A single team handles the requests and is able to complete on average 50 requests per week. The requests have no particular priority; therefore, they are handled on a first-come-first-served basis. It also can be assumed that requests are not withdrawn and that a week consists of 40 working hours.

To model this situation, a time unit needs to be agreed upon for use throughout the simulation model. Suppose *hours* is selected as the time unit. If 40 requests arrive per week, the

---

[5]The notation Menu > Menu Item will be used to indicate the menu item to select. For instance, File > New Model indicates to click on the File menu and then choose the New Model item.

average time between arrivals is 1 hour. If the team is able to complete 50 requests in a week, the average processing time per request is 0.8 hours (i.e., 40/50). Perform the following steps to build an Extend simulation model of this situation.

1. Add the Executive block to the model. Choose the Executive item in the submenu of the Discrete Event library.
2. Add a block to generate request arrivals. Choose the Import block from the Generators submenu of the BPR library. (An alternative is the Generator block from the Generators submenu of the Discrete Event Library.) Double-click on the Import block and change the Distribution to Exponential. Make sure the mean value is 1. Also type "Requests In" in the text box next to the Help button (lower-left corner of the dialogue window). Press OK. The complete dialogue window after performing this step is shown in Figure 7.4.
3. When an Import block is used to generate requests, it must be followed with a Repository or a Stack block because the Import block always pushes items out of the block regardless of whether or not the following block is ready to process them. Add a Repository block to the model to simulate the In Box of the underwriting team. Choose the Repository item from the Resources submenu of the BPR library. Drag the Repository block and place it to the right of the Import block. Double-click on the Repository block and type "In Box" in the text box next to the Help button (lower-left corner of the dialogue window). Do not change any other field, because it is assumed that the In Box is initially empty.
4. Add an Operation block to the model to simulate the underwriting activity. Choose the Operation item from the Activities submenu of the BPR library. Drag the Operation block and place it to the right of the Repository block. Double-click on the Operation block and change the processing time to 0.8. Also type "Underwriting" in the text box next to the Help button (lower-left corner of the dialogue window). No other field needs to be changed to model the current situation.
5. Add an Export block to the model to simulate the completion of a request. Choose the Export item from the Routing submenu of the BPR library. Drag the Export block and place it to the right of the Operation block. Double-click on the Export block and type "Requests Done" in the text box next to the Help button (lower-left corner of the dialogue window).
6. Connect the blocks in the model. Make a connection between the Requests In block and the In Box block. Also make a connection between the In Box block and the top input connector

FIGURE 7.4 Import Dialog Window

FIGURE 7.5 Underwriting Process Model with a Single Team

of the Underwriting block. Finally, make a connection between the Underwriting block and the Requests Done block. To make a connection, make sure that the Main Cursor or Block/Text Layer tool is selected (this is the arrow in the drawing tool); then click on one connector and drag the line to the other connector. The input connectors are on the right-hand side of the blocks, and the output connectors are on the left-hand side. These connectors are used to allow jobs to move from one block to another. Connectors on the bottom of a block are used to input values, and those at the top are used to output results.

The simulation model should look as depicted in Figure 7.5. This figure does not show the Executive block, which is always present in simulation models of business processes.

Before running the simulation, the time units used in the model can be specified. Choose Run > Simulation Setup . . . and change the global time units to hours. Also, change the simulation time to 40 hours, so this process can be observed for one working week. Press OK. Now make sure that Show Animation and Add Connection Line Animation are checked in the Run menu. Then, choose Run > Run Simulation. The number of requests in the In Box is updated as requests go in and out of this Repository block. Also, the Requests Done block shows the number of completed requests. If this model is run more than once, the number of completed requests changes from one run to another. As default, Extend uses a different sequence of random numbers every time a simulation is run. To force Extend to use the same sequence of random numbers every time, a random seed that is different than zero must be specified. Choose Run > Simulation Setup . . . and click on the Random Numbers tab. Change the Random seed value to a number different than zero.

During the simulation, the activity in any block can be monitored by double-clicking on the block to display its dialogue window. For example, run the simulation either by choosing Run > Run Simulation or pressing Ctrl + R and double-clicking on the Underwriting block. In the dialogue window, click on the Results tab and monitor the utilization of the underwriting team. When the simulation is completed, the final utilization value is the average utilization of the underwriting team during the simulated week. The average interarrival time of the request also can be determined by displaying the Results tab of the Requests In block dialogue.

7.3 Basic Data Collection and Statistical Analysis

Extend provides a number of tools for data collection and statistical analysis. The easiest way of collecting and analyzing output data in an Extend model is to add blocks from the Statistics submenu of the Discrete Event library. These blocks can be placed anywhere in the model and do not need to be connected to any other blocks. The blocks in this submenu that are used most commonly in business process simulations are shown in Figure 7.6.

- The Activity Stats block from the Discrete Event library provides a convenient method for collecting data from blocks that have a delay or processing time, such as an Operation block. In the dialogue of this block, one can specify whether statistics are to be reported during the simulation or just at the end. The results also can be copied and pasted to a word processing program, or they can be cloned to the model Notebook.

FIGURE 7.6 Blocks in the Statistics Submenu of the Discrete Event Library

- The Queue Stats block from the Discrete Event library provides a convenient method for collecting data from all queue-type blocks, such as a Stack. The following statistics are calculated in this block: average queue length, maximum queue length, average waiting time, and maximum waiting time.
- The Resource Stats block from the Discrete Event library provides a convenient method for collecting data from all resource-type blocks, such as a Repository or a Labor Pool. The main statistic calculated in this block is the resource utilization.
- The Costs Stats block from the Discrete Event library provides a convenient method for collecting data from all costing blocks, such as an Operation block. The main statistics calculated in this block are cost per item, cost per unit of time, and total cost.
- The Cost by Item block from the Discrete Event library collects data and calculates statistics associated with the cost of every item that passes through the block. The block must be connected to the process model to collect data of the items passing through. In addition to displaying the cost of each item, the dialogue of this block also shows the average cost and the total cost. The A, C, and T connectors can be used to plot the values of the average, current, and total cost, respectively.

Suppose that we are interested in analyzing the statistics associated with the requests that have to wait in the In Box before being processed by the underwriting team. Since we used a Repository block to model the In Box we will not be able to obtain queue data with the Queue Stats block of the Discrete Event library. We can remedy this situation by replacing the Repository block with a Stack block (see Figure 7.7):

- The Stack block from the BPR library is similar to the Repository block. However, you can specify the order in which items are taken from the stack (in the Repository block, they always leave in the order they entered), and you can specify the maximum number of items allowed in the block at a time. Your choices for the queuing discipline are FIFO (first in, first out, like in the Repository block), LIFO (last in, first out) Priority (items with the lowest priority number go first), and Reneging (items leave if the wait is too long).

The modified simulation model is depicted in Figure 7.8.

The modified model can now be run, and the statistics associated with the new In Box block can be analyzed. After running this model with the Random Seed Value of

FIGURE 7.7 Stack Block

FIGURE 7.8 Underwriting Process Model with a Stack Block

1,415, a value that was chosen arbitrarily to make the experiment reproducible, the queue statistics shown in Figure 7.9 are generated. The average wait for the simulated week was 0.3712 hours (or about 22 minutes), and the maximum wait was 1.83 hours. The results show that at no point during the simulation were more than three requests waiting in the In Box of the underwriting team.

The statistics that are relevant to measure the performance of a given process vary according to the context in which the system operates. For instance, in the supermarket industry, the percentage of customers who find a queue length of more than three is preferred to the average waiting time as a measure of customer service.

Although analyzing statistical values at the end of a simulation run is important, these values fail to convey the dynamics of the process during the simulation run. For example, knowing the final average and maximum waiting times does not provide information about the time of the week when requests experience more or less waiting time. Extend includes a Plotter library that can be used to create plots that provide insight on the behavior of the process. For example, a plotter block can be used to generate a Waiting Time vs. Simulation Time plot. The "Plotter, Discrete Event" block can be used for this purpose. (See Figure 7.10.)

- The "Plotter, Discrete Event" block from the Plotter library constructs plots and tables of data for up to four inputs in discrete-event models. The value and the time the value was recorded are shown in the data table for each input. In the dialogue, it

FIGURE 7.9 Queue Statistics for the In Box Block

FIGURE 7.10 Plotter, Discrete Event Block

FIGURE 7.11 Underwriting Process Model with a Plotter Block

is possible to specify whether to plot values only when they change or to plot all values. The Show Instantaneous Length option should be used if an input is attached to the L connector of a Stack block and a report on items that arrive and depart on the same time step (i.e., items that stay zero time in the queue) is desired.

Next, the Plotter library is added to the current Extend model. Choose Library > Open Library . . . and go to the Libraries directory inside the Extend directory. Choose the Plotter library in this directory. Now choose Library > Plotter > Plotter, Discrete Event and connect the w output from the In Box to the top (blue) input of the Discrete Event Plotter. The modified model looks as depicted in Figure 7.11.

After running the simulation and customizing some plot titles, a Waiting Time Versus Simulation Time plot is produced, as shown in Figure 7.12.

The plot in Figure 7.12 discloses that the busiest time for the underwriting team was after 32.5 simulation hours, when the maximum waiting time of 1.83 hours

FIGURE 7.12 Waiting Time Versus Simulation Time

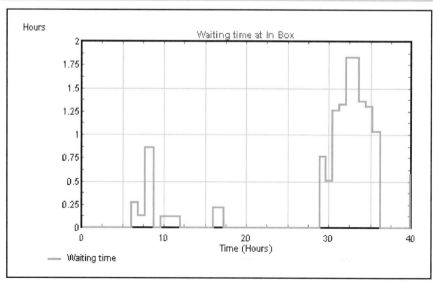

occurred. In a real setting, the analyst must run the simulation model several times, with different random seeds, in order to draw conclusions about the process load at different points of the simulation horizon (i.e., 1 week for the purpose of this illustration). Next, model enhancements are examined and additional blocks are introduced.

7.4 Adding Randomness to Processing Times

Up to now, the models in this chapter have used constant values to represent the time it takes the underwriting team to process a request. The next goal is to have the actual processing times more closely approximate real-world conditions. Random numbers with specified probability distributions are used to simulate the actual processing time in the Underwriting block. These distributions are available in the Input Random Number block. (See Figure 7.13.)

- The Input Random Number block from the Inputs/Outputs submenu of the Generic library generates random numbers based on a catalog of probability distributions. The probability distribution is selected in the Distributions tab of the dialogue window. This tab also is used to set appropriate parameter values for the selected distribution.

For the purpose of this tutorial, it is assumed that the processing time follows an exponential distribution with a mean value of 0.8 hours. The following steps are necessary to add randomness to the processing times.

1. Add an Input Random Number block near the Underwriting block.
2. Connect the output of the Input Random Number block to the D input of the Underwriting block. The D input is the delay time that the Underwriting block will use when the simulation model is executed.
3. In the dialogue of the Input Random Number block, select the Exponential distribution. Set the mean value to 0.8.

The model that represents the current situation in the insurance company now looks as shown in Figure 7.14.

Because the current model uses an exponential distribution with a mean value of 1 hour to model interarrival times and an exponential distribution with a mean of 0.8 hours to model processing times, the model should be able to approximate the theoretical values calculated in Chapter 6 for the same example. The current model is run for 100 weeks (4,000 hours) and queue statistics are collected in the In Box block. (See Figure 7.15.)

The empirical values for the average queue length (2.96 requests) and average waiting time (2.94 hours) in Figure 7.15 are close to the analytical values (3.2 requests and 3.2 hours, respectively) calculated with the M/M/1 model in Chapter 6.

An interesting question regarding the performance of the current underwriting process relates to the percentage of time that the In Box block has more than a specified number of requests. For example, one might wonder what percentage of time the

FIGURE 7.13 Input Random Number Block

FIGURE 7.14 Underwriting Process Model with Random Processing Times

FIGURE 7.15 Queue Statistics for the In Box Block (100-week run)

In Box has more than four requests. A Histogram block from the Plotter library can help answer this question. Choose Library > Plotter > Histogram. Connect the L output from the In Box block to the top (blue) input of the Histogram block. After rerunning the model and adjusting the number of bins to six in the Histogram block dialogue, a histogram based on the frequencies in Table 7.1 is constructed.

The Length column in Table 7.1 represents the length of the queue. That is, out of a total of 7,961 arrival and departure events, 5,639 times (or 71 percent of the time) the In Box was empty. In terms of the original question, it is now known that 90 percent of the time the In Box had four requests or fewer.

In Chapter 6, an analytical queuing model was used to predict that the underwriting team would be busy 80 percent of the time in the long run. In other words, the prediction was made that the utilization of the underwriting team would be 80 percent.

TABLE 7.1 Frequency Table for the In Box Block

Length	No. of Events	Percentage of Events
0	5,639	71.0%
4.4	1,510	19.0%
8.8	584	7.3%
13.2	189	2.3%
17.6	38	0.4%
22	1	0.0%

The simulation model can be used to compare the theoretical results with the empirical values found with the simulation model. Figure 7.16 shows the Results tab of the dialogue window associated with the Underwriting block. The utilization of the underwriting team after 100 simulated weeks is almost exactly 80 percent.

The long-run average utilization of 80 percent is observed after 100 simulated weeks, but the utilization varies throughout the simulation and in particular within the first 10 simulated weeks. Figure 7.17 shows a plot of the average utilization of the underwriting team during the simulation.

The utilization plot can be obtained easily by connecting the u output connector of the Underwriting block to the Discrete Event Plotter. The same plotter can be used to create Figures 7.12 and 7.17. Using the plotter, up to four different data inputs can be turned on and off. A combine plot also can be drawn with two different scales (one for the waiting time and one for the utilization). Figure 7.17 reveals the importance of running a simulation for a sufficiently long time in order to predict the behavior of a process at steady state (after a period, known as warm-up, in which average values have not converged yet). If the simulation were stopped after 40 hours (1 week), a team utilization of 70 percent would have been predicted. Equally important to running simulations for a sufficiently long time is running the model several times. To run a model more than once, choose Run > Simulation Setup ... (Ctrl + Y) and change the number of runs in the Discrete Event tab. Chapter 9 addresses issues associated with terminating and nonterminating processes as well as warm-up periods.

FIGURE 7.16 Dialog Window of the Underwriting Block

FIGURE 7.17 Average Utilization of the Underwriting Team

7.5 Adding a Second Underwriting Team

The original model illustrated a common method in modeling, namely making simple assumptions first and then expanding the model to incorporate additional elements of the actual process. Suppose one would like to predict the effect of adding another underwriting team. To achieve this, the model needs to be expanded by duplicating the Operation block and the Export block as follows.

1. Select the Operation and Export blocks.
2. Move them up to make room for the second underwriting team.
3. Choose Edit > Copy (Ctrl + C).
4. Click below the original two blocks.
5. Choose Edit > Paste (Ctrl + V).
6. Attach the input of the new Operation block to the output of the Stack block.
7. Attach the output of the Random Number block to the D connector of the new Operation block.

The result of performing these operations is shown in Figure 7.18.

After running the model with two underwriting teams, the resulting queue statistics can be compared with those in Figure 7.15 (which correspond to the model with a single underwriting team). Table 7.2 shows the direct comparison.

Adding a team to the underwriting process significantly improves key measures of customer service, such as the maximum waiting time at the In Box block. Therefore, from

FIGURE 7.18 Underwriting Process Model with Two Teams

TABLE 7.2 Queue Statistics for Two Alternatives

Statistic	One Team	Two Teams
Queue length at end of run	17	0
Average queue length	2.960	0.167
Average waiting time	2.937	0.167
Maximum queue length	22	7
Maximum waiting time	17.185	3.728

the point of view of the customer, adding a second underwriting team is undoubtedly beneficial. However, from the point of view of management, the utilization of the teams should be considered before making a final decision about whether or not to add a team. The final average utilization is 49.9 percent for team 1 and 30.8 percent for team 2.

An alternative way of modeling two teams working in parallel uses the Transaction block from the Activities submenu of the BPR library. (See Figure 7.19.) This block can be used to represent several processes that occur in parallel. The maximum number of transactions that can occur at the same time is specified in the dialogue window of this block. The transaction time can be constant, as specified in the dialogue box, or variable by connecting the output of an Input Random Number block to the D input of the Transaction block.

To modify the current model to use the Transaction block, the Operation blocks and one of the Export blocks are deleted. Then the Transaction block is added, and the output from the Stack block to the input of the Transaction block is connected. The output of the Transaction block is also connected to the input of the Export block. Finally, the output of the Input Random Number block is connected to the D connector of the Transaction block. In the dialogue box of the Transaction block, the maximum number of transactions is set to 2. The transaction time also can be set to 0.8 hours, although this is not absolutely necessary because the Input Random Number block will generate the actual transaction times randomly according to an exponential distribution with a mean of 0.8 hours. After these changes, the model looks as depicted in Figure 7.20.

FIGURE 7.19 Transaction Block

FIGURE 7.20 Modeling Multiple Teams with a Transition Block

After running the model with the Random Seed Value set at 1,415, exactly the same queue statistics are obtained as those reported in Table 7.2 under the Two Teams column. The average utilization in the Transaction block is 40.4 percent.

7.6 Adding a Labor Pool

Suppose that before the underwriting activity, a review activity takes place in which 80 percent of the requests are approved and 20 percent are rejected. The underwriting team performs the review activity, which can be assumed to take between 15 and 30 minutes; if the request is approved, the team proceeds with the underwriting activity. If the request is rejected, then the team is free to work on the next request. In order to modify the current model to deal with this situation, the blocks depicted in Figure 7.21 can be used.

- The Merge block from the Routing submenu of the BPR library can be used to combine up to three streams of items into one. This block does not do any processing on the items and does not hold them; it simply combines them into a single stream.
- The Select DE Output block from the Routing submenu of the Discrete Event library allows items in two different paths to be routed according to a variety of conditions. A common way of using this block is to model routing based on a probability value. This is done by checking the Do Not Use Connector box and then selecting the Route Items by Probability option. A probability value associated with the top output should be provided in the dialogue of this block.
- The Labor Pool block from the Resources submenu of the BPR library is used to introduce people as resource items in the model. The initial number of people is specified in the block's dialogue window. The Labor Pool block keeps track of the utilization of the people in the resource pool.
- The Batch block from the Batching submenu of the Discrete Event library is used to batch up to three inputs into a single output. The number of required items from each input is specified in the dialogue window of this block.
- The Unbatch block from the Batching submenu of the Discrete Event library is used to unbatch items that have been batched previously with a Batch block. For example, a Batch block could be used to batch a job with the worker who is going to perform the job. When the worker completes the job, the Unbatch block can be used to separate the worker from the job and return the worker

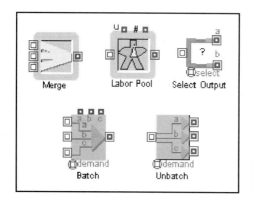

FIGURE 7.21 Additional Blocks from the BPR and Discrete Event Libraries

to a Labor Pool. When using the Batch and Unbatch blocks in this way, one must make sure that the Preserve Uniqueness box is checked in both blocks. Preserve Uniqueness appears in the first tab of the dialogue window of both blocks.

The blocks previously discussed are used to extend the current model as follows.

1. Add a Batch block, a Transaction block, and a Select DE Output block between the In Box block and the Underwriting block. Also add two Unbatch blocks, a Merge block, a Labor Pool block, and an Input Random Number block.
2. Connect the In Box block to the top input of the Batch block (named Batch block). Connect the output of the Labor Pool block (now named Teams block) to the bottom input of the Batch block. Then connect the output of the Batch block to the new Transaction block, now named Review block. Connect the blocks to make the model look like the one depicted in Figure 7.22. The model contains two named connections: Review Done and Underwriting Done. To make these connections, double-click where text is to be added. This opens a text box. Type the desired text and when finished typing, click anywhere else in the model or press Enter. The text box can now be connected to any block connector. Copy and paste the text box to establish the named connection.
3. In the dialogue window of the Batch block, enter a quantity of 1 for the top and the bottom outputs. Check the Preserve Uniqueness box. If one of the two incoming items is not available (such as if a request is waiting to be processed but there is no team ready), the Batch block does not release the batched item until both inputs come into the block.
4. In the dialogue window of the Teams block, set the initial number to 2.
5. The dialogue of the Select DE Output block labeled Approve? is depicted in Figure 7.23. The Do Not Use Select Connector box is checked, the Route Items by Probability option is selected, and the probability of 0.2 for the top output connector is specified.

FIGURE 7.22 Underwriting Process Model with a Review Activity and a Labor Pool

FIGURE 7.23 Dialogue Window for the Block Labeled "Approve?"

6. In the dialogue of the Unbatch blocks, enter a 1 in the Top and Bottom outputs. Also, check the Preserve Uniqueness box. This block separates the team from the request, and the team is sent back to the Labor Pool block.

The Input Random Number blocks in the model in Figure 7.22 are named after the probability distribution they simulate. For example, the Uni(0.25,0.5) block simulates a uniform distribution with parameters 0.25 and 0.5 to represent the number of hours to review a request. This means that in the dialogue of this block, the distribution "Real, uniform" is selected with Min = 0.25 and Max = 0.5. As in previous versions of this model, the Exp(0.8) simulates the exponential distribution with Mean = 0.8. After running the model in Figure 7.22, the following results are obtained.

- The utilization of the underwriting teams is approximately 51 percent.
- No requests are in the In Box at the end of the run, and the maximum number of requests throughout the simulation is seven. The average and maximum waiting times in the In Box are 0.123 and 4.9 hours, respectively.

Also, approximately 21 percent of the requests are rejected (836/3,989). This rejection rate is close to the assumed rejection rate of 20 percent.

7.7 Customizing the Animation

Model development and validation have always been considered key elements in computer simulations, but animation is gaining recognition as an additional key component. Extend offers extensive opportunities for customizing the animation in a model. The Animate Value, Animate Item, and Animate Attribute blocks, all from the Animation library, show customized animation in response to model conditions. Based on choices in their dialogues, these blocks can display input values, show a level that changes between specified minimums and maximums, display text or animate a shape when the input value exceeds a critical value, or change an item's animation icon based on an attribute value. The blocks in this library can be used to develop models with sophisticated animation features, including pictures and movies.

A simple way of customizing the animation in a simulation model consists of changing the appearance of the items in the model. Turn on animation by selecting Run > Show Animation, and make sure that Add Connection Line Animation also is selected in the Run menu. When the simulation is run, Extend's default animation picture, a green circle, will flow along the connection lines between blocks. In the Animate tab of blocks that generate items, such as the Import block named "Requests In" in this model, the animation picture that will represent the items generated by this block can be chosen. In the animation tab of the Requests In block, choose the paper picture to represent the requests as shown in Figure 7.24.

The request generated in the Requests In block will now appear as paper flowing through the model. Make sure that in the Animate tab of blocks that do not generate items but process them, the option Do Not Change Animation Pictures is selected.

The Teams block provides people for the review and underwriting activities. In the Animate tab of this Labor Pool block, choose the person picture to represent the teams. Because of how attributes are merged in the batching activity, the teams will inherit the animation picture of the requests (paper picture) while the two items remain batched. The items recover their original animation after they are unbatched. In the Teams block it is possible to make sure that all items are animated using the person picture by checking the "All Items Passing Through This Block Will Animate the Above Picture" option in the Animate tab, as depicted in Figure 7.25.

FIGURE 7.24 Animate Tab of Requests In Block

FIGURE 7.25 Animate Tab of the Teams Block

The model now shows the paper and person pictures when running the simulation in the animation mode.

7.8 Calculating Costs and Using the Flowchart View

Extend's activity-based costing feature can help in calculating the cost of reviewing and underwriting. In this model, two things contribute to the total cost.

- The teams are paid $46.50 per hour. (Three team members each earn $15.50 per hour.)
- As part of the review activity, a report is generated that costs $25.

In the Cost tab of the Labor Pool block, fill in the cost per hour for the teams and select Resources in the Workers Used As: pop-up menu shown in Figure 7.26.

In the Cost tab of the Transaction block named Review, fill in the cost of the report (Cost per Item), as shown in Figure 7.27.

In the dialogue of both Unbatch blocks, choose the Release Cost Resources option. (See Figure 7.28.)

When the simulation is run, the costs are tracked with each request. To collect the cost data, add a Cost Stats block (from the Statistics submenu of the Discrete Event library) anywhere in the model and Cost by Item blocks (also from the Statistics submenu of the Discrete Event library) after the Unbatch blocks as shown in Figure 7.29.

The average cost per rejected request is approximately $42.21, and the average cost of a completed request is approximately $80.15. These values are given in the dialogue of the Cost by Item blocks at the end of the simulation run. This information provides the basis for setting the value for a possible application fee for this process. From the Cost Stats block, it also is known that the cost of this process is approximately $4,107 per week.

Figure 7.29 shows the simulation model using the classic view of Extend. Instead of this classic view, simulation models can be viewed using flowchart icons. This easy

FIGURE 7.26 Cost Tab of Labor Pool Block

Workers are	resources	
	Cost per hour*	46.5
	Cost per use:	0
	Total cost:	188443.73
*model default		

Define cost of activity (optional):

Cost per hour*	0
Cost per item:	25
Total cost:	99725

FIGURE 7.27 Cost per Request

FIGURE 7.28 Unbatch Block Dialogue

FIGURE 7.29 Underwriting Process Model with Cost Collection Blocks

transformation is done by selecting Model > Change Icon Class > Flow Chart. The result of this change is shown in Figure 7.30.

A flowchart view such as the one shown in Figure 7.30 is particularly helpful in situations in which the simulation model is based on an existing flowchart of a process. The flowchart view allows a direct comparison between the model and the document that was used as the basis for the development of the simulation.

FIGURE 7.30 Flowchart View of the Simulation Model for the Underwriting Process

262

7.9 Summary

This chapter introduced the main discrete-event simulation functionality of Extend. A simple, one-stage process was used to illustrate how to model using block diagrams. The basic concepts discussed in this chapter are sufficient to model and analyze fairly complicated business processes. However, the full functionality of Extend goes beyond what is presented here and makes it possible to tackle almost any situation that might arise in the design of business processes.

7.10 References

Extend v6 User's Guide. 2002. Imagine That, Inc., San Jose, California.

7.11 Discussion Questions and Exercises

1. Consider a single-server queuing system for which the interarrival times are exponentially distributed. A customer who arrives and finds the server busy joins the end of a single queue. Service times of customers at the server are also exponential random variables. Upon completing service for a customer, the server chooses a customer from the queue (if any) in a first-in-first-out (FIFO) manner.
    a. Simulate customer arrivals assuming that the mean interarrival time equals the mean service time (e.g., consider that both of these mean values are equal to 1 minute). Create a plot of number of customers in the queue (*y*-axis) versus simulation time (*x*-axis). Is the system stable? (Hint: Run the simulation long enough [e.g., 10,000 minutes] to be able to determine whether or not the process is stable.)
    b. Consider now that the mean interarrival time is 1 minute and the mean service time is 0.7 minute. Simulate customer arrivals for 5,000 minutes and calculate: (i) the average waiting time in the queue, (ii) the maximum waiting time in the queue, (iii) the maximum queue length, (iv) the proportion of customers having a delay time in excess of 1 minute, and (v) the expected utilization of the server.
2. For the single-server queuing system in exercise 1b, suppose the queue has room for only three customers, and that a customer arriving to find that the queue is full just goes away. (This is called balking.) Simulate this process for 5,000 minutes, and estimate the same quantities as in part b of exercise 1, as well as the expected number of customers who balk.
3. A service facility consists of two servers in series (tandem), each with its own FIFO queue. (See Figure 7.31.) A customer completing service at server 1 proceeds to server 2, and a customer completing service at server 2 leaves the facility. Assume that the interarrival times of customers to server 1 are exponentially distributed with mean of 1 minute. Service times of customers at server 1 are exponentially distributed with a mean of 0.7 minute, and at server 2 they are exponentially distributed with a mean of 0.9 minute.
    a. Run the simulation for 1,000 minutes and estimate for each server the expected average waiting time in the queue for a customer and the expected utilization.
    b. Suppose that there is a travel time from the exit of server 1 to the arrival to queue 2 (or server 2). Assume that this travel time is distributed uniformly between 0 and 2 minutes. Modify the simulation model and run it again to obtain the same performance

FIGURE 7.31 Process with Two Servers in Series

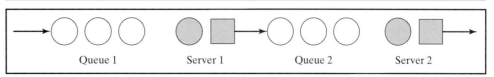

Queue 1   Server 1   Queue 2   Server 2

measures as in part a. (Hint: You can add a Transaction block to simulate this travel time. A uniform distribution can be used to simulate the time.)

c. Suppose that no queuing is allowed for server 2. That is, if a customer completing service at server 1 sees that server 2 is idle, the customer proceeds directly to server 2, as before. However, a customer completing service at server 1 when server 2 is busy with another customer must stay at server 1 until server 2 gets done; this is called blocking. When a customer is blocked from entering server 2, the customer receives no additional service from server 1 but prevents server 1 from taking the first customer, if any, from queue 1. Furthermore, new customers may arrive to queue 1 during a period of blocking. Modify the simulation model and rerun it to obtain the same performance measures as in part a.

4. A bank with five tellers opens its doors at 9 A.M. and closes its doors at 5 P.M., but it operates until all customers in the bank by 5 P.M. have been served. Assume that the interarrival times of customers are exponentially distributed with a mean of 1 minute and that the service times of customers are exponentially distributed with a mean of 4.5 minutes. In the current configuration, each teller has a separate queue. (See Figure 7.32.) An arriving customer joins the shortest queue, choosing the shortest queue furthest to the left in case of ties.

   The bank's management is concerned with operating costs as well as the quality of service currently being provided to customers and is thinking of changing the system to a single queue. In the proposed system, all arriving customers would join a single queue. The first customer in the queue goes to the first available teller. Simulate 5 days of operation of the current and proposed systems and compare their expected performance.

5. *Airline Ticket Counter*—At an airline ticket counter, the current practice is to allow queues to form before each ticket agent. Time between arrivals to the agents is exponentially distributed with a mean of 5 minutes. Customers join the shortest queue at the time of their arrival. The service time for the ticket agents is uniformly distributed between 2 and 10 minutes.

a. Develop an Extend simulation model to determine the minimum number of agents that will result in an average waiting time of 5 minutes or less.

b. The airline has decided to change the procedure involved in processing customers by the ticket agents. A single line is formed and customers are routed to the ticket agent who becomes free next. Modify the simulation model in part a to simulate the process change. Determine the number of agents needed to achieve an average waiting time of 5 minutes or less.

c. Compare the systems in parts a and b in terms of the number of agents needed to achieve a maximum waiting time of 5 minutes.

d. It has been found that a subset of the customers purchasing tickets is taking a long period of time. By separating ticket holders from nonticket holders, management believes that improvements can be made in the processing of customers. The time

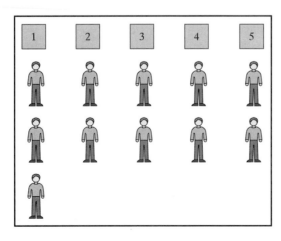

FIGURE 7-32 Teller Configuration (multiple queues)

needed to check in a person is uniformly distributed between 2 and 4 minutes. The time to purchase a ticket is uniformly distributed between 12 and 18 minutes. Assume that 15 percent of the customers will purchase tickets and develop a model to simulate this situation. As before, the time between all arrivals is exponentially distributed with a mean of 5 minutes. Suggest staffing levels for both counters, assuming that the average waiting time should not exceed 5 minutes.

6. *Inventory System*—A large discount store is planning to install a system to control the inventory of a particular video game system. The time between demands for a video game system is exponentially distributed with a mean time of 0.2 weeks. In the case where customers demand the system when it is not in stock, 80 percent will go to another nearby discount store to find it, thereby representing lost sales; the other 20 percent will backorder the video system and wait for the arrival of the next shipment. The store employs a periodic review-reorder point system whereby the inventory status is reviewed every 4 weeks to decide whether an order should be placed. The company policy is to order up to the stock control level of 72 video systems whenever the inventory position, consisting of the systems in stock plus the systems on order minus the ones on backorder, is found to be less than or equal to the reorder point of 18 systems. The procurement lead time (the time from the placement of an order to its receipt) is constant and requires 3 weeks. Develop an Extend model to simulate the inventory policies for a period of 6 years (312 weeks) to obtain statistics on (a) the number of video systems in stock, (b) the inventory position, (c) the safety stock (the number of video systems in stock at the time of receiving a new order), and (d) the number of lost sales. Investigate improvements on this inventory policy by changing the reorder point, the stock control level, and the time between reviews.

7. *Bank Tellers*—Consider a banking system involving two inside tellers and two drive-in tellers. Arrivals to the banking system are either for the drive-in tellers or for the inside tellers. The time between arrivals to the drive-in tellers is exponentially distributed with a mean of 1 minute. The drive-in tellers have limited waiting space. Queuing space is available for only three cars waiting for the first teller and four cars waiting for the second teller. The service time of the first drive-in teller is normally distributed with a mean of 2 minutes and a standard deviation of 0.25. The service time of the second drive-in teller is uniformly distributed between 1 minute and 3 minutes. If a car arrives when the queues of both drive-in tellers are full, the customer balks and seeks service from one of the inside bank tellers. However, the inside bank system opens 1 hour after the drive-in bank, and it takes between 0.5 and 1 minute to park and walk inside the bank. Customers who seek the services of the inside tellers directly arrive through a different process, with the time between arrivals exponentially distributed with a mean of 1.5 minutes. However, they join the same queue as the balkers from the drive-in portion. A single queue is used for both inside tellers. A maximum of seven customers can wait in this single queue. Customers arriving when seven are in the inside queue leave. The service times for the two inside tellers are triangularly distributed between 1 and 4 minutes with a mode of 3 minutes. Simulate the operation of the bank for an 8-hour period (7 hours for the inside tellers). Assess the performance of the current system.

8. *Grocery Store*—You are hired by Safeway to help them build a number of simulation models to better understand the customer flows and queuing processes in a grocery store setting. The pilot project at hand focuses on an off-peak setting where at most two checkouts are open. To better understand the necessary level of detail and the complexities involved, Safeway wants a whole battery of increasingly more realistic and complex models. For each model, Safeway wants to keep track of (i.e., plot) the average cycle time, queue length, and waiting time in the queue. To understand the variability, they also want to see the standard deviation of these three metrics. In addition, they would like to track the maximum waiting time and the maximum number of customers in line. Furthermore, to better understand the system dynamics, plots of the actual queue lengths over time are required features of the model. The off-peak setting is valid for about 4 hours, so it is reasonable to run the simulation for 240 minutes. Furthermore, to facilitate an easier first-cut comparison between the models, a fixed random seed is recommended. Because Safeway plans to use these different models later, it is important that each model sheet has a limit of one model.

a. In the first model, your only interest is the queues building up at the checkout counters. Empirical investigation has indicated that it is reasonable to model the arrival process (to the checkout counters) as a Poisson process with a constant arrival intensity of three customers per minute. The service time in a checkout station is on average 30 seconds per customer and will, in this initial model, be considered constant. Inspired by the successes of a local bank, Safeway wants to model a situation with one single line to both checkout counters. As soon as a checkout is available, the first person in the queue will go to this counter. After the customers have paid for their goods, they immediately leave the store.

b. Upon closer investigation, it is clear that the service time is not constant but rather normally distributed with $\mu = 30$ seconds and $\sigma = 10$ seconds. What is the effect of the additional variability compared to the results in part a?

c. To be able to analyze the effect of different queuing configurations, Safeway wants a model in which each checkout counter has its own queue. When a customer arrives to the checkout point, he or she will choose the shortest line. The customer is not allowed to switch queues after making the initial choice. Can you see any differences in system performance compared to the results in part b?

Modeling and Simulating Business Processes

Chapter 7 introduced the basic elements of Extend and showed how to use them to build a simple queuing model. The model was then expanded to add more than one server and a labor pool. These basic elements can be used to model simple processes, but in some cases they are not sufficient to model realistic business processes consisting of a potentially large set of activities, resource types, and complex job routings and information structures. This chapter explores additional Extend tools with the goal of modeling and simulating business processes found in practice. Recall that the process-flow analysis in Chapter 5 considered that activity times were deterministic (i.e., the times were certain and there was no variation). However, in practical settings, the processing times typically are not deterministic; therefore, process performance must be assessed taking into consideration the variability in the process. In general, three types of variability are relevant in business processes: (1) variation in the arrival of jobs, (2) variation in the processing time of each activity, and (3) variation in the availability of resources. Along with variability, these simulation models will add other realistic elements of business processes that the basic analysis tools of Chapters 4, 5, and 6 cannot easily incorporate.

The best way to learn the material discussed in this chapter is to read it while using Extend and to look at the simulation models found on the CD that accompanies this book. For convenience, all the models used for illustration purposes have been included in the CD. The simulation models in the CD are named Figurexx.xx.mox; xx.xx corresponds to the figure number in the book. For instance, the first model that is discussed in this chapter is the one that appears in Figure 8.2. Its corresponding file is Figure08.02.mox.

8.1 General Modeling Concepts

All simulation models share five general concepts:

- Selection of time units
- Length of a run
- Number of runs
- Model verification
- Model validation

8.1.1 SELECTION OF TIME UNITS

Although Extend allows models to be built with generic time units, it is generally more practical to establish a default time unit. To establish the default time unit in the model, select Run > Simulation Setup. . . and change the global time units in the Time Units tab. The parameter values also can be selected to convert hours into days and days into years on this tab. Once a global time unit is selected, all time-based parameters in the blocks in the model will be set to the selected time unit. The selected global time unit becomes the default time unit throughout the model. Note that it is possible to use other time units within a block. For example, the global time unit might be set to hours, but a processing time for an activity could be given in minutes. Extend will make the right conversions to establish a single time unit during the simulation run. If the global time units are changed from hours to minutes, all parameters set to the default time units also will change from hours to minutes. The default time unit is marked with an asterisk (*) in the dialogue window of a block.

In some cases, it might not be desirable to leave a parameter set to the default time unit, because a global change in the model could introduce an error. For example, suppose the processing time of an activity is 2 hours. If the global time unit is hours and the processing time is set to the default time unit, the model will be correct as long as the global time unit is not changed. However, if the global time unit is changed to days, then the processing time of the activity will be 2 days instead of 2 hours. To avoid this, use a local time unit for the block and set it to 2 hours (without the asterisk), indicating that the time units will not be affected by changes to the global time unit.

8.1.2 LENGTH OF A RUN AND NUMBER OF RUNS

Another important consideration when building a model is the length of a run and the number of runs. The selection of end time and number of runs in the Discrete Event tab of the Simulation Setup dialogue typically depends on the following four factors.

1. Whether the process is terminating (has a natural end point) or nonterminating (has no obvious end point).
2. The period of interest (i.e., the portion of time being modeled).
3. The modeling objectives (e.g., estimating performance or exploring alternative designs).
4. The method in which samples for statistical analysis are obtained (e.g., from running multiple short simulations or analyzing portions of a long one).

Some processes have an obvious termination point. In these terminating processes, there is a point in time when no more useful data will be obtained by running the simulation any longer. Most service processes have a point at which activities end. Setting the end time at 8 hours, for example, can safely simulate a walk-in customer service center that is opened 8 hours per day. Customers will not wait overnight at the queue, so the process is emptied before the beginning of a new day (i.e., the beginning of a new simulation run). Because terminating processes typically do not reach a steady state (see Section 9.5.2), the purpose of the analysis usually is to identify trends and look for changes rather than to obtain long-run statistics, such as average performance. In the customer service center, it would be more relevant to identify peaks and valleys for the activity level than to calculate averages. Basing decisions on average utilization in this case could obscure transient problems caused by multiple periods of understaffing.

Because the initial conditions in terminating processes affect results, it is important for these conditions to be realistic and representative of the actual process. An initial condition for the customer service center example might establish the number of people waiting in line when the doors are opened in the morning. If the actual process starts empty, then no initial conditions need to be set in the simulation model. This might be the case for a movie theater at the beginning of each day. Terminating processes are simulated using multiple runs, whereby each run represents a natural breaking point for the process (e.g., each run might represent a working day). The selection of a given random seed affects the output data obtained from a set of runs. The random seed can be changed in the Random Numbers tab of the Simulation Setup dialogue.

The length of the simulation is usually not an issue when dealing with terminating processes because of their natural end point. For example, the simulation of a bank branch that is open to the customers from 9 A.M. until 4 P.M. could be set to end after 7 hours. However, sometimes a particular period of operation of a terminating process might be of interest; therefore, the starting and ending of the simulation could be adjusted to collect data for this period of interest. In the bank example, a period between 11 A.M. and 2 P.M. might be of interest and therefore simulated a number of times to collect relevant data.

Nonterminating processes do not have a natural or obvious end time. Models of nonterminating processes are often referred to as steady-state processes, because they tend to reach steady state when run for a long period of time. (See Section 9.5.1.) Some service operations such as a 24-hour grocery store, emergency rooms, and special call centers are nonterminating processes. Many business processes are also nonterminating, because the work-in-process remains in the process from one day to the next. For example, an order-fulfillment process that does not complete an order in a given day might finish the processing during the next working day. Hence, business processes that do not "clear out" at the end of a working day can be considered nonterminating. In order to simulate 30 working days of a nonterminating business process, the end time is set to 30*8 = 240 hours, considering 8-hour working days. Thus, a single run of 240 hours of a nonterminating process corresponds to 30 runs of 8 hours of a terminating process. Note that the initial conditions for each day in a nonterminating process depend on the final state of the process at the end of the previous day. On the other hand, the initial conditions at the beginning of each day in a terminating process are typically the same from one run to the next.

One of the important considerations when simulating nonterminating processes is the determination of the warm-up period. This is the period between the beginning of the simulation (when the process is initially empty) and the time when the process operates at a normal or steady-state level. If data are collected during the warm-up period, measures of performance will be biased. A realistic picture of the steady-state performance of a process is obtained when data are collected after the warm-up period. Another way of minimizing the effect of the warm-up period is to run the simulation model for an extended period of time. In this way, the data collected after the warm-up period will "swamp" the bias caused by the initial conditions. To obtain multiple samples for statistical analysis, a nonterminating process can be run several times (with different seeds for the random number generator). As is the case with terminating processes, the greater the number of samples is, the higher the statistical confidence is.

In contrast with terminating processes, determining the length of the run in nonterminating processes can be difficult. Theoretically, a nonterminating process can run indefinitely. In practice, the length of the run is related to the time the process requires to reach steady state. Also, the length of the run should be such that all the events that are possible in a simulation happen at least once. For example, a model might include an event that simulates a machine breaking down; therefore, the length of the run should be such that this event happens at least once so its effects can be analyzed.

8.1.3 MODEL VERIFICATION

Model verification is the process of debugging a model to ensure that every portion operates as expected (i.e., that the model behaves as expected given the logic implemented). One way of verifying that the model is correct is to use an incremental building technique. This means that the model is built in stages and run at each stage to verify that it behaves as expected. Another technique is to reduce the model to a simple case for which the outcome can be easily predicted. This simplification can be obtained as follows.

- Remove all the variability to make the model deterministic.
- Run the deterministic model twice to verify that the same results are obtained.
- For processes with several job types, run the model using one job type at a time.
- Reduce the size of the labor pool (e.g., to one worker).
- Uncouple interacting parts of the model to see how they run on their own.

Other techniques for verification include accounting for all the items in the model and adding animation. After the model is verified, it needs to be validated.

8.1.4 MODEL VALIDATION

Model validation refers to determining whether the model represents the real process accurately. A valid model is a reasonably accurate representation of the real processes that conforms to the model's intended purpose. During validation, the analyst needs to be sure that comparisons against a real process are made using the same metrics (i.e., that measures of performance are calculated in the same manner). Determining whether the model makes sense is often part of validating a model. The analyst also can ask someone familiar with the process to observe the model in operation and approve its behavior. Simulation results also can be compared with historical data to validate a model. If enough historical data are available (for example, arrival and processing times), these data can be used to simulate the past and validate that the model resembles the actual process under the same conditions.

8.2 Items and Values

Within an Extend simulation model, an item is a process element that is being tracked or used. For example, items being tracked (transient entities) could be jobs, telephone calls, patients, or data packets. Items being used (resident entities) could be workers, fax machines, or computers. Items are individual entities and can have unique properties (for example, a rush order versus a normal order) that are specified by their attributes and priorities. An item can only be in one place at a time within the simulation model. Items flow in a process and change states when events occur. For example, a server could change from idle to busy when a customer arrives.

Values provide information about items and the state of the simulated process. Values can be used to generate output data such as the waiting time in a queue or the actual processing time of an activity. These values will be referred to as output values. Output values include statistics such as the average queue length and the average utilization of a resource. There are also state values, which indicate the state of the process. For example, the number of customers waiting in line at a given time indicates the state of the system. Most blocks in Extend include connectors that can be used to track output or state values.

8.2.1 GENERATING ITEMS

The simulation of a business process typically starts with a job entering the process. Arrivals are generally random, because in most situations that don't deal with scheduled appointments, it would be difficult (or even impossible) to predict when the next job will arrive. Most of the time, all the analyst can hope for is to be able to assign a pattern (a probability distribution function) to the time elapsed between one arrival and the next. The Import block from the Generators submenu of the BPR library or the Generator block from the Discrete Event library is the most common method used for generating random arrivals in Extend. The focus here will be on how to use the Import block. The dialogue window of this block contains a pop-up menu with several probability distribution choices. Figure 8.1 shows the dialogue of the Import block set to generate one item every 6 minutes (on average) using an exponential distribution; that is, the interarrival times are exponentially distributed with a mean of 6 minutes.

Other probability distributions (uniform, triangular, or normal) can be used to model the interarrival times with an Import block. The selection of a distribution depends on the business process under study and the outcome of a statistical analysis of input data (as described in Chapter 9). In the Import block dialogue, parameters of the chosen distribution are assigned consecutive numbers. For example, the exponential distribution has only one parameter, the mean; therefore, this parameter is labeled number one (1). The normal distribution has two parameters, the mean and the standard deviation, so the mean is parameter number 1 and the standard deviation is parameter number 2. The connectors labeled 1 and 2 at the bottom of the Import block are used to set the values for the distribution parameters from outside of the block.

In addition to specifying the pattern of interarrival times, one can specify the number of items to be generated per arrival by the Import block. (See the # of Items(V) box in Figure 8.1.) The typical item value V is 1, meaning that one item is generated per arrival. However, suppose a process receives jobs in batches of 10 every 2 hours (with no variation). To model this situation with an Import block, change the Distribution to constant, make the constant value equal to 2, and change the time units to hours. In addition, change the # of items (i.e., the V value) to 10. This means that the Import block will generate an

FIGURE 8.1 Import Block Dialogue Showing Exponential Interarrival Times with Mean of 6 Minutes

item with a V value of 10 every 2 hours. When an item with V = 10 arrives to a resource-type block or a queue, the item is split into 10 individual items with V = 1.

In some practical settings, the rate of arrivals (or the mean time between arrivals) changes during the simulation. For example, the rate of customers arriving to a dry cleaner is larger in the morning and evening than during the day. Changes can be modeled in the interarrival times with an Input Data block from the Inputs/Outputs sub-menu of the Generic library. (See Figure 8.2.)

Suppose that in the dialogue of the Import block, the exponential distribution is chosen to model the time between job arrivals. The mean of the distribution is labeled (1) Mean = in the Import block. When the output of the Input Data block is connected to the 1 input connector of the Import block, the mean of the distribution overriding the value in the Import block dialogue is changed. This allows one to dynamically change the average time between arrivals. Suppose that the time between arrivals at a dry cleaner is 30 seconds between 8 A.M. and 9 A.M. and between 5 P.M. and 6 P.M.; the rest of the day it is 5 minutes. If the simulation model is such that each run represents a 10-hour working day from 8 A.M. until 6 P.M., then the Input Data dialogue in Figure 8.3 can be used to

FIGURE 8.2 Input Data Block Used to Change the First Parameter of the Interarrival Time Distribution in the Import Block

FIGURE 8.3 Input Data Block Dialogue for Dry Cleaner Example model the changes in the mean interarrival time. It is assumed that the Import block uses minutes as the time unit and that the probability distribution is set to exponential.

The dialogue in Figure 8.3 shows that the mean interarrival time is half of a minute (or 30 seconds) during the first and last hour of a 10-hour simulation. The mean interarrival time is 5 minutes the rest of the time. Note that the time units in the Import block must be set to minutes, but the time units in the Input Data block are hours. In other words, the time unit of the Time column in the dialogue of Figure 8.3 is hours, and the time unit in the Y Output column is minutes.

Instead of generating arrivals at random times, some models require the generation of arrivals at specific times. This generation of arrivals is referred to as scheduled arrivals. The Program block (see Figure 8.4) from the Generators submenu of the Discrete Event library can be used to schedule item arrivals to occur at given times. For example, suppose that an order-fulfillment process receives 500 orders per week and almost all of the orders are received on Tuesday. Also suppose that the time unit of the simulation is days and that the model is set up to run for 1 week. Then the arrival times are entered in the Output Time column, and the number of orders is entered in the Value column of the Program block, as shown in Figure 8.4.

FIGURE 8.4 Program Block (and Dialogue Window) Connected to a Stack Block for the Order Fulfillment Example

In the Program block, the actual arrival time is entered in the Output Time column instead of the interarrival time, as done in the Import block. The order-fulfillment example has five arrival events (one for each day of the week), and the item values range from 40 to 300. The table in Figure 8.4 indicates that 40 orders are received on Monday, 300 on Tuesday, and so forth. To avoid "losing" items in the simulation, follow a Program block with a Stack block (from the Queues submenu of the BPR library). Like in the case of the Import block, the Program block generates items with values greater than 1 as a batch of items arriving at the same time. When the batched item goes to the Stack block, it becomes multiple copies of itself. For example, as each order item is input from the Program block to the Stack block, it will become 40, 300, or 50 orders, depending on the given value.

8.2.2 ASSIGNING ATTRIBUTES TO ITEMS

Attributes play an important role in business process simulations. An attribute is a quality or characteristic of an item that stays with it as it moves through a model. Each attribute consists of a name and a numeric value. The name identifies some characteristic of the item (such as OrderType), and a number specifies the value of the attribute (for example, 2). It is possible to define multiple attributes for any item flowing through the simulation model. The easiest way to set item attributes is to use the Import block (although this also can be done in the Operation, Repository, Labor Pool, and Program blocks). The Discrete Event library also has two separate blocks for assigning attributes: Set Attribute and Set Attribute (5). In the Attribute tab of these blocks, it is possible to either select an attribute from the pop-up menu or create a new attribute. After an attribute has been selected or a new one has been created, the value of the attribute is entered in the box labeled Attr. Value =. Extend also provides a way of dynamically changing the values of up to three attributes using the Operation block. However, the dynamic modification of attributes is beyond the scope of this book.

Attributes are commonly used to specify the amount of processing time required, routing instructions, or item types. For example, an Operation block could use attribute values to determine the amount of operation time needed for an item. Attributes are used to specify things like "item needs final check" or "send item unchecked." In this case, depending on the value of the attribute, the item is sent to an Operation block for the final check or the activity is skipped. The use of attributes will be illustrated in the context of routing in Section 8.4. In the Discrete Event library, the Get Attribute block reads the value of a given attribute for every job passing through it. The attribute value is then made available through one of the value connectors of this block. This can be useful in modeling business processes with complex logic and information structures.

8.2.3 PRIORITIZING ITEMS

Priorities are used to specify the importance of an item. When comparing two priority values, Extend assigns top priority to the smallest value (including negative values). Priorities can be set in different ways within an Extend model; however, if the Import block is used to generate arrivals, the easiest is to set the item's priority in the Attributes tab. Also, the Set Priority block in the Discrete Event library assigns priorities to items passing through it. Priorities are useful when the processing of jobs does not have to follow a first-in-first-out discipline. For example, priorities can be used to model a situation in which a worker examines the pending jobs and chooses the most urgent one to be processed next. In Extend, items can have only one priority.

The Stack block in the Queues submenu of the BPR library allows the order in which items will be released from the queue to be set. The default order is first-in-first-out.

FIGURE 8.5 Selection of a Priority Queue in the Queue Tab of a Stack Block

Choosing Priority from the pop-up menu of the Queue tab causes the Stack block to choose the next item based on priority value. (See Figure 8.5.)

For an item to be ranked by priority, other items must be in the group at the same time. In other words, items will be sorted by their priority value in a Stack block only if they have to wait there with other items.

8.3 Queuing

Reducing non-value-added time is one of the most important goals in process design. Quantifying the amount of unplanned delays (such as waiting time) is critical when designing new processes or redesigning existing processes. Statistics such as average and maximum waiting time represent useful information for making decisions with respect to changes in a process under study. In order to collect waiting time and queue length data, queues need to be added to the simulation model. The Stack block in the Queues submenu of the BPR library provides different types of queues or waiting lines.

The Stack block has several predefined queuing disciplines, as shown in Figure 8.5. The FIFO option models a first-in-first-out or first-come-first-served queue. The LIFO option models a last-in-first-out queue. The Priority option checks the items' priorities and picks the item with the highest priority (the smallest priority value) to be released first. If all the items in the queue have the same priority, then a FIFO discipline is used. The Reneging option can be used to specify how long an item will wait before it reneges, or prematurely leaves. An item will wait in the queue in a FIFO order until its renege time (the maximum amount of time the item is allowed to spend in the queue) has elapsed. At that point, it will exit through the lower (renege) output connector.

8.3.1 BLOCKING

Queues are used to avoid blocking. Blocking occurs when an item is finished processing but is prevented from leaving the block because the next activity is not ready to pick it up (or the next resource block is full). Blocking can occur in serial processes where activities are preceded by queues. For example, consider two activities in a serial process, where activity B follows activity A. Suppose this process has two workers, one who performs activity A and one who performs activity B, and the workers don't have an In Box, or queue. If activity A is completed while activity B is still in process, the worker performing activity A is blocked, because that person cannot pass on the item until the other worker completes activity B. Adding a queue to activity B eliminates the blocking problems because completed items go from activity A to the queue from which the worker performing activity B picks them.

8.3.2 BALKING

In service operations, customers sometimes enter a facility, look at the long line, and immediately leave. As discussed in Chapter 6, this is called *balking*. A Decision(2) block from the Routing submenu of the BPR library can be used to model balking. Figure 8.6 shows a process with one queue and balking. Customers are generated at the Import block with an exponentially distributed interarrival time (mean = 1 minute) and go to the Decision(2) block to check on the length of the queue. The length of the queue is passed from the L connector of the Stack block to the Decisio1n(2) block. The current length is used to decide whether the customer will leave or stay. In Figure 8.6, if the length of the queue is five or more, the customer leaves. If the customer leaves, he or she goes to the Export block. If the customer stays, he or she joins the queue (that is, the Stack block) and eventually is served in the Operation block, which has a constant processing time of 1.5 minutes.

The model in Figure 8.6 has two Export blocks to keep track of the number of customers served versus the number of balking customers. The Decision(2) block employs the logic shown in Figure 8.7, which sends customers to the YesPath if QLength is greater than or equal to 5.

In this case, Qlength is the variable name given to the input of the first connector at the bottom of the Decision(2) block. The names Path, YesPath, and NoPath are system variables from Extend.

8.3.3 RENEGING

Another important queuing phenomenon is reneging. Reneging occurs when an item that is already in the queue leaves before it is released for processing. An example of

FIGURE 8.6 **Model of a Single Server with a Queue, Where Customers Balk if the Line Reaches a Specified Number of Customers**

FIGURE 8.7 Dialogue Window of the Decision(2) Block of Figure 8.6

reneging is a caller hanging up before being helped after being put on hold. Figure 8.8 shows a model that simulates this situation. Suppose the customer hangs up if the waiting time reaches 5 minutes. The Import block in Figure 8.8 generates calls with inter-arrival times exponentially distributed with a mean of 3 minutes. It is assumed that the processing time of a call is uniformly distributed between 2 minutes and 5 minutes. (The duration of the call is modeled with an Input Random Number block from the Inputs/Outputs submenu of the Generic library.)

In the model in Figure 8.8, the Stack block (labeled Calls on Hold) is of the reneging type. To set the stack type, Reneging was chosen in the Type of Stack pop-up menu in the Queue tab of the Stack block. The Renege Time is set to 5 minutes, as shown in Figure 8.9.

FIGURE 8.8 Model of a Single Server with a Queue, Where Customers Hang Up After Being on Hold for a Specified Amount of Time

FIGURE 8.9 **Stack Block to Simulate a Reneging Queue with a Reneging Time of 5 Minutes**

In this example, a call waits on hold until one of the two representatives is available to answer the call. The Transaction block (labeled Helping Customers) from the Activities submenu of the BPR library is used to model the two customer service representatives. The maximum number of transactions in the Activity tab of the Transaction block is set to 2. The Stack block uses the waiting time of the calls on hold to decide whether to release a call to the Transaction block through the upper output connector or to the Export block through the lower output connector.

The renege time can be adjusted dynamically using the R input connector of the Stack block. Although this model uses an Export block to count the number of lost calls, this is not necessary because the Stack block keeps track of the number of reneges and displays it in the Results tab. Because items that renege leave the Stack block through the output connector on the lower right, these items can be rerouted back to the original line or to other activities in the process.

8.3.4 PRIORITY QUEUES

As discussed in Section 8.2.3, when a block downstream can accept an item, a priority queue searches through its contents and releases the item with the highest priority (i.e., the item with the smallest priority value). The Stack block can be set to operate as a priority queue by selecting Priority in the Type of Stack pop-up menu.

Consider the following situation. Patients arrive at a hospital admissions counter, and 20 percent of the time they cannot be admitted because they need to fill out additional forms. After they fill out additional forms, they come back to the counter to complete the admissions process. Patients returning to the counter are given higher priority and can go to the front of the line. To model this situation, generate arriving patients and set their priority to 2. This is done in the Import block from the Generators submenu of the BPR library. In the Attributes tab of the Import block, the priority of the items being generated can be set to a value of 2. In this way, priority 1 can be used for patients who return to the line after filling out the additional forms. Figure 8.10 shows a simulation model of this simple admissions process.

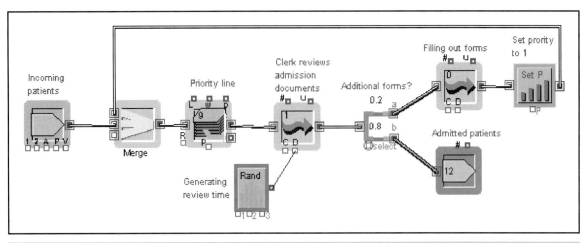

FIGURE 8.10 Admissions Process with a Priority Queue That Allows Patients to Go in Front of the Line After Filling Out Additional Forms

The model in Figure 8.10 shows that a Select DE Output block from the Routing submenu of the Discrete Event library is used to simulate the percentage of patients needing to fill out the additional forms. In the Select Output tab of the dialogue window of the Select DE Output block, the Do Not Use Select Connector box should be checked. Also, Route Items by Probability should be selected, and a probability value of 0.2 should be used for the top output. The dialogue window of the Select DE Output block is the same as the one shown in Figure 7.23.

It is assumed that the clerk gives the forms to the patients, and after a constant time (simulated with the Transaction block labeled Filling Out Additional Forms), the priority of the patients is changed and they are sent back to the queue. The dialogue of the Stack block that models the priority queue is shown in Figure 8.11.

FIGURE 8.11 Dialogue Window of the Stack Block in Figure 8.10

[3] Stack

| Queue | Results | Animate | Comments |

Holds items in a queue until needed.

Type of stack: Priority queue

OK

Cancel

Maximum items allowed = 1000

☐ Stop simulation if maximum is reached

☑ Calculate waiting cost

Help

Default View

The Set Priority block from the Attributes submenu of the Discrete Event library is used to change the priority of the patients from 2 to 1. After the priority is changed, patients who return to the queue have higher priority than patients who just arrived. As mentioned earlier, Extend uses a FIFO queue discipline when all the items in a queue have identical priority values.

8.4 Routing

When modeling business processes, it is common to encounter situations where jobs come from different sources or follow different paths. For example, Figure 8.10 shows that the clerk's line receives newly arriving patients and patients who completed additional paperwork. In other words, the Stack block that simulates the queue receives patients from two different sources: the Import block that simulates the patients arriving to the hospital, and the Transaction block simulating the patients filling out additional forms. The patients coming from these two sources are merged into one stream with the Merge block; however, the patients remain as individual items and retain their unique identity.

The Merge block in the Routing submenu of the BPR library can merge items from up to three separate sources. Another example of merging items from different sources occurs when telephone orders and mail orders are directed to an order-entry department. Also, the Merge block can be used to simulate workers returning to a labor pool from different parts of a process. (Resources and labor pools are discussed in Section 8.7.)

Chapter 5 introduced two types of routing: multiple paths and parallel activities. This chapter will now discuss how to simulate these routing conditions with Extend.

8.4.1 MULTIPLE PATHS

Jobs do not usually arrive, join a queue, get completed in a single step, and leave. If this were true, every process could be simulated with an Import block (to generate arrivals), a Stack block (to simulate a queue), an Operation block (for the service activity), and an Export block (for jobs leaving after the completion of a single activity). Real-world business processes call for routing jobs for processing, checking, approval, and numerous other activities. The simulation models must be capable of routing jobs based on a probability value, logical and tactical decisions, or job characteristics.

Probabilistic routing occurs when a job follows a path a specified percentage of the time. For example, Figure 8.10 shows a model in which 20 percent of the time hospital patients cannot be admitted because they need to fill out an additional form. A rework loop shares this characteristic. That is, after an inspection (or control) activity, jobs are sent back for rework with a specified probability. In Figure 8.10, a Select DE Output block from the Routing submenu of the Discrete Event library was used to model a probabilistic routing with two paths. To model probabilistic routing with up to five possible paths, a Decision(5) block and a Random Input block are needed. Suppose a job follows one of three possible paths (labeled 1, 2, and 3) with probabilities 0.2, 0.3, and 0.5, as shown in Figure 8.12.

This situation is simulated by first generating jobs with an Import block and then adding a Decision(5) block to probabilistically route each job, as illustrated in Figure 8.13.

In the Input Random Number block, an Empirical table is chosen from the Distribution pop-up menu. The values in the Empirical table reflect the probability that a job follows each path, as shown in Table 8.1. Therefore, the path number is probabilistically determined in the Input Random Number block and is sent to the first connector of the Decision(5) block.

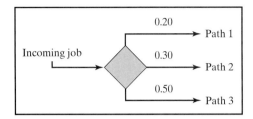

FIGURE 8.12 Example of Probabilistic Routing of an Incoming Job

FIGURE 8.13 An Illustration of Probabilistic Routing with Extend

The Decision(5) block is set to read the path number from the Input Random Number block and use this number to route the current job to one of the three paths. The name of the first connector is specified as PathNum, and the value is used in the routing logic box to force the selection of each path according to the given path number.

    if (PathNum == 1) Path = Path1;
    if (PathNum == 2) Path = Path2;
    if (PathNum == 3) Path = Path3;

Although the default path names Path1, Path2, and Path3 are used in this example, the Decision(5) block allows the path names to be changed to ones that are more descriptive in terms of the process being modeled. Also, the paths in this example simply consist of an Export block that counts the number of jobs routed in each direction. In a real process, the paths would consist of multiple activities and possibly even a merging point later in the process.

In addition to probabilistic routing, business process models often include tactical routing. This type of routing relates to the selection of paths based on a decision that

TABLE 8.1 Empirical Probability Table in Input Random Number Block	
Value	*Probability*
1	0.20
2	0.30
3	0.50

typically depends on the state of the system. For example, suppose one wants to model the checkout lines at a supermarket where customers choose to join the shortest line. Figure 8.14 shows an Extend model of this tactical decision.

The Import block in Figure 8.14 generates the customers arriving to the cashiers. Each cashier is modeled with an Operation block and the independent lines with Stack blocks. The model connects the L (queue length) connector from each Stack block to a Max & Min block from the Math submenu of the Generic library. This block calculates the maximum and the minimum of up to five inputs. The Max and the Min output connectors give the maximum and the minimum values, respectively. The Con connector tells which of the inputs generated the largest or the smallest value. The equation in the Decision(5) block dialogue decides the routing based on the value provided by the Max & Min block:

if(MinQ == 1) Path = Line1;
if(MinQ == 2) Path = Line2;
if(MinQ == 3) Path = Line3;

FIGURE 8.14 Illustration of Tactical Routing with Customers Choosing the Shortest Line

MinQ is the name assigned to the first input connector in the Decision(5) block. The Line1, Line2, and Line3 names are the labels used for each path. If the lines have the same number of customers, the incoming customer joins the first line. This is why even when the cashiers work at the same speed, the first cashier ends up serving more customers than the other two. (See the Export blocks in Figure 8.14.) This could be corrected with additional logic that randomly assigns a customer to a queue when all queues have the same length.

8.4.2 PARALLEL PATHS

Some business processes are designed in such a way that two or more activities are performed in parallel. For example, in an order-fulfillment process, the activities associated with preparing an invoice can be performed while the order is being assembled, as depicted in Figure 8.15.

In Figure 8.15, the order is not shipped until the invoice is ready and the order has been assembled. To model parallel paths with Extend, use the Operation, Reverse block in the Batching submenu of the BPR library. This block separates an incoming item into multiple copies and outputs them one at a time. For each output connector (up to a total of three), the number of copies to be created can be specified. Figure 8.16 shows the Operation, Reverse block along with its dialogue.

The dialogue in Figure 8.16 shows that the Operation, Reverse block is set to create two copies of the input item. One copy will be sent through the top output connector, and the other copy will be sent through the bottom connector. After the activities in each parallel path are completed, an Operations block from the Activities submenu of the BPR library is used to batch the corresponding items into one. This block batches items from up to three inputs into a single item. In the dialogue of this block, it is possible to specify the number of items required from each input to create a single output item. All required inputs must be available before the output item is released. Figure 8.17 shows the dialogue for the Operation block.

Each input connector that is used must have a quantity of items strictly greater than zero specified in the dialogue. Figure 8.17 shows that an item from the top input connector and an item from the bottom input connector are needed to create a single output item.

Figure 8.18 shows the "skeleton" (without timing information) of an Extend model for the order-fulfillment process depicted in Figure 8.15. Orders are generated with the Import block and are sent to the Operation block labeled Receiving Order. The

FIGURE 8.15 Parallel Activities in an Order-Fulfillment Process

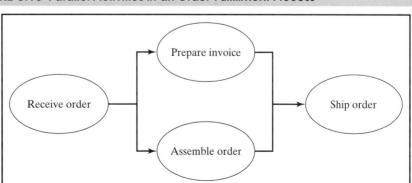

FIGURE 8.16 Operation, Reverse Block and Dialogue Window

FIGURE 8.17 Operation Block That Batches Two Items

Operation, Reverse block creates two copies of the order and sends one to Prepare Invoice and another one to Assemble Order. After both of these activities are completed, the activity Shipping Order is performed.

Parallel paths can consist of more than one activity each. In the model in Figure 8.18, each parallel path consists of one activity, but the same modeling principles applied to paths with multiple activities. That is, an Operation, Reverse block is needed to create copies of the job, and then an Operation block is needed to transform the multiple copies into one.

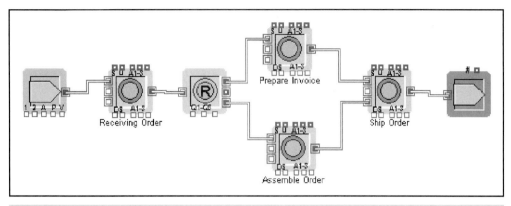

FIGURE 8.18 Extend Model of the Order-Fulfillment Proces in Figure 8.15

8.5 Processing Time

One of the key tasks when creating simulations of business processes is modeling the processing time of activities. In Extend, the Operation block or the Transaction block is used to model activities. The main difference between these two blocks is that the Operation block can process only one item at a time, and the Transaction block can process several items at a time (up to a specified limit). Section 7.5 showed how the Transaction block can be used to model processes where multiple servers perform the same activity.

Activities, such as those modeled with the Operation and Transaction blocks, involve a processing time or delay that represents the amount of time it takes to perform the specified task. The Decision(2) and the Decision(5) blocks also include a processing time that is used to model the time to make a decision. Processing time can be static or vary dynamically depending on model conditions. The time can be random, scheduled based on the time of the day, depend on the item being processed, or be affected by any combination of these factors.

The easiest way of setting the processing time is to choose a value in the dialogue of the corresponding block. This, however, is useful only when the processing time is known and does not change throughout the simulation. In other words, it is useful when the processing time is deterministic and constant. For example, if the task of typing an invoice always takes 5 minutes, the value 5 is entered as the processing time in the dialogue of the activity block. On the other hand, if the processing time is not deterministic and constant, the D connector of activity or decision blocks is used to dynamically change the processing time (as shown in Section 7.4).

When the processing time is fixed (i.e., deterministic and constant) but one wants to have the ability to change it from run to run without having to open the corresponding dialogue, a Slider can be added to the model. A Slider, shown in Figure 8.19, is a control that makes simulation models more user friendly.

To add a Slider, select it from Model > Controls. Then click on the maximum and minimum values to change them appropriately. By default, these values are set to zero and one. Next, the middle output connector is connected to the D connector of an activity or decision block. The processing time can now be set by moving the Slider to the desired level. The Slider in Figure 8.19 sets the processing time for the Operation block at 17 time units.

In some situations, the processing time depends on the time of the day. For example, a worker might take longer to perform a task at the end of the day. The Input Data

FIGURE 8.19 Slider Control

block from the Inputs/Outputs submenu of the Generic library can be used to model this situation. The Input Data block is connected to the D connector of an activity block (e.g., a Transaction block) as illustrated in Figure 8.20, which also shows the dialogue of the Input Data block.

The dialogue in Figure 8.20 shows that the activity is performed in 10 minutes during the first 6 hours of operation and in 12 minutes during the second 6 hours. Note that the time in the Y Output column is given in minutes (because the processing

FIGURE 8.20 Input Data Block to Model Variable Processing Time

FIGURE 8.21 Processing Time Based on the Value of the ProcTime Attribute

time in the Transaction block is set to minutes), but the values in the Time column are given in hours (which is the time unit used as the default for the entire simulation model).

One of the most common ways of modeling processing times is using a probability distribution. Random processing times that follow a known or empirical probability distribution can be simulated with an Input Random Number block from the Inputs/Outputs submenu of the Generic library (as illustrated in Section 7.4). The output of this block is simply connected to the D connector of the activity block, and the processing time is drawn from the specified probability distribution function.

Finally, an attribute can be used to assign the processing time for a job. Section 8.2.2 discussed how to assign attributes to items. An Import block can be used to assign an attribute to an item in such a way that the attribute value represents the processing time. The attribute name is then identified in the dialogue of the activity block, as shown in Figure 8.21.

In the dialogue of Figure 8.21, it is assumed that the processing time was stored in the attribute named ProcTime when the item was generated with the Import block.

8.6 Batching

In many business processes, paperwork and people coming from different sources are temporarily or permanently batched. For example, memos, invoices, and requests might originate from several parts of the process. The batched items move through the process together. For instance, in an office that handles real estate acquisitions, the requests, bids, and real estate analysis come together in an early step and travel as a single item through the rest of the process.

Batching allows multiple items from several sources to be joined as one for simulation purposes. In Section 8.4.2, the Operation block was used to batch items belonging to the same job that were previously split to be processed in parallel paths. Another way of modeling batching with Extend is with the Batch block from the Batching submenu of the Discrete Event library. The Batch block accumulates items from each source to a specified level and then releases a single item that represents the batch. Figure 8.22 shows the Batch block and its dialogue window.

FIGURE 8.22 Batch Block and Dialogue Window

In Figure 8.22, the single item is not produced as the output of the Batch block until an item from the top input connector (a) and an item from the bottom input connector (b) are both available.

Batching is used to accomplish two slightly different tasks: kitting and binding. Kitting occurs when a specified number of items are physically put together and then released as a single item. This is most common when simulating the assembly of different kinds of paperwork into a single package. The batched item may or may not be unbatched at some later point in the process. Typically, the batched item remains that way through the rest of the process. For example, a kit can be formed of an original order, a salesperson's memo, and a release form from the warehouse. This kit is then stored as a single item after the order is shipped.

Binding items is used to reflect situations where one item is required to be associated temporarily with one or more items to flow together through a portion of the process. Items that are batched for this purpose are typically separated from each other later in the simulation. This type of batching or binding is common when simulating labor movement, as shown in Section 7.6. For example, in a customer service process, the customer is coupled with a customer service representative and possibly some paperwork. These items are batched until the service is completed, at which point the customer, the customer service representative, and the paperwork are unbatched so they can follow different paths for the remainder of the process.

When batching workers with paperwork (such as a request or an order), the Preserve Uniqueness box in the Batch block should be checked so that the worker and the paperwork preserve their identity after the unbatching. Suppose a purchasing agent is merged with a purchase order. The purchase order comes into a Batch block as the top input and the purchasing agent comes in as the middle input. Figure 8.23 shows the dialogue of the Batch block with the Preserve Uniqueness box checked. The discussion of a labor pool will be extended in Section 8.7.

FIGURE 8.23 Preserving Uniqueness When Batching a Purchase Order and an Agent

When a worker is batched with another item, such as a request or an order, the binding is temporary and the items are unbatched at some point in the process. The unbatching allows the worker to return to a labor pool and the paperwork to continue the appropriate routing through the rest of the process. The Unbatch block in the Routing submenu of the Discrete Event library is used for unbatching items. When dealing with binding, it is important to unbatch items using the same output connectors used when the items were batched in the Batch block. If this is not done, items could be routed the wrong way. For example, the job could get sent to the labor pool and the worker to the remaining processing steps. Figure 8.24 illustrates how to batch and unbatch correctly. In this figure, a nurse is batched with a patient through the *c* connector of a Batch block and later unbatched and sent back to the labor pool through the *c* connector of the Unbatch block. The number of items that the Unbatch block outputs should be the same as the number of items batched with a Batch block. The Output boxes in the Unbatch block are used to specify the number of items routed through each output connector for every item that enters the block, as shown in Figure 8.25.

In Figure 8.25, it is assumed that the Unbatch block is being used to separate items that are required to preserve their own identity, such as a worker and a document. As discussed in Section 8.4.2, unbatching also can be used to duplicate an item into several clones of itself. We saw that this can be done with the Operation, Reverse block even if the item has not been batched previously; for example, an order that is received is entered into a computer and printed in triplicate. The printout can be unbatched to represent a packing slip, an invoice, and a shipping copy.

8.7 Resources

Most business processes require resources to perform activities. For example, a customer service representative is the resource used to perform the activities associated with assisting customers. In other words, resources are the entities that provide service to the items that enter a simulation model. In Extend, resources can be modeled explicitly using a resource block or implicitly using an activity block. Activity blocks can represent the

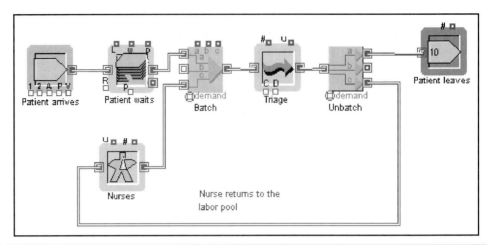

FIGURE 8.24 Model that Batches Patients and Nurses

FIGURE 8.25 Unbatching Items with an Unbatch Block

resource and the activity the resource is performing. For example, in Figure 7.5, an Operation block was used to represent the team and the underwriting activity. Later a labor pool was used as a source of underwriting teams for the model. (See Figure 7.22.)

The explicit modeling of resources provides the flexibility of tying up resources for several activities. For example, suppose a nurse must accompany a patient through several activities in a hospital admissions process. The model can include a Labor Pool block to simulate the availability of nurses. When a nurse leaves the Labor Pool block and is batched with a patient, the nurse returns to the labor pool only after performing all the activities as required by the process. Figure 8.24 shows a simple Extend model that simulates the arrival of patients and a single operation (triage) that requires a nurse. Patients wait in a waiting area (modeled with the Stack block) until the next nurse is available. After the activity is completed, the nurse returns to the Labor Pool block and the patient exits this part of the process through the Export block.

The Discrete Event library of Extend provides an alternative way of modeling resources with three blocks: Resource Pool, Queue Resource Pool, and Release Resource Pool. Although this alternative way has advantages in some situations over the batching procedure explained previously, the modeling of resources with these blocks is beyond the scope of this book.

8.8 Activity-Based Costing

Many companies use activity-based costing (ABC) as the foundation for business process redesign. The ABC concept is that every enterprise consists of resources, activities, and cost objects. Activities are defined by decomposing each business process into individual tasks. Then the cost of all resources consumed by each activity and the cost of all activities consumed by each product or cost object are tracked (Nyamekye, 2000).

Activity-based costing is a method for identifying and tracking the operational costs directly associated with processing jobs. Typically, this approach focuses on some unit of output such as a completed order or service in an attempt to determine its total cost as precisely as possible. The total cost is based on fixed and variable costs of the inputs necessary to produce the specified output. ABC is used to identify, quantify, and analyze the various cost drivers (such as labor, materials, administrative overhead, and rework) and determine which ones are candidates for reduction.

When a simulation modeled is built, the outputs as well as the resources needed to create such outputs are fully identified. Adding ABC to the model entails entering the costing information into the appropriate block dialogues. Blocks that generate items (e.g., the Import block) or resources (e.g., the Labor Pool block) and blocks that process items (e.g., the Operation and Transaction blocks) have tabs in their dialogues for specifying cost data. These tabs allow one to enter variable cost per unit of time and fixed cost per item or use. Figure 8.26 shows the Cost tab of the Import block dialogue.

FIGURE 8.26 Cost Tab of the Import Block

After the cost information has been entered, Extend keeps track of the cost automatically as the items enter the process, flow through the activities in their routing, and exit. When considering ABC in a simulation model, every item is categorized as either a cost accumulator or a resource. Cost accumulators are the items (or jobs) being processed. Jobs accumulate cost as they wait, get processed, or use resources. For example, suppose one wants to determine the cost of receiving crates at a warehouse. As each shipment arrives, a labor resource is required to unpack crates and stock the contents on the appropriate shelves. In this case, crates are being processed; therefore, they become the cost accumulators. A crate accumulates cost while waiting and while being processed. For example, it might take an employee approximately 30 minutes to unpack a crate. Figure 8.27 shows a model where processing time and the hourly wage are used to calculate the cost of this process.

The calculated cost is then added to the accumulated cost for each crate. More cost is added to the accumulated total as a crate flows through the receiving process. In this case, the crates are generated with an Import block and their cost information is established in the Cost tab of this block. Resources do not accumulate cost, but their cost information is used to calculate the cost that is added to the total of the cost accumulator. For example, suppose the hourly wage of the employees unpacking crates is $9.75. When an employee is batched with a crate, the hourly rate along with the processing time (the time required to unpack the crate) is used to add cost to the total associated with the crate. If a given crate requires 25 minutes to be unpacked, the accumulated cost of the crate is increased by $9.75 × (25/60) = $4.06.

As mentioned previously, Extend has two types of costs: the fixed cost (cost per use or per item) and the variable cost (the cost per unit of time). Cost accumulators have their own fixed and variable costs. The Cost tab in Figure 8.26 shows that the variable cost of a crate is $0.15 per hour. This is the rate charge per hour of waiting. Also, a $3.59 docking fee is charged per crate. This is a fixed cost that is charged per item (i.e., per crate) entering the process.

The Cost tab of resource-type blocks (such as a Labor Pool block) allows the cost per unit of time (e.g., an hourly rate) and the cost per use of the resource (i.e., the fixed cost) to be specified. The cost per time unit is used to calculate and assign a time-base cost to the cost accumulator during the time it uses the resource. The cost per use, on

FIGURE 8.27 Model to Accumulate Cost per Unpacked Crate

the other hand, is a one-time cost assigned to the cost accumulator for the use of the resource (a fixed service charge). When using a labor pool to model resources and adding ABC, be sure that the Release Cost Resources option is selected in the Unbatch block. This option is at the bottom of the Unbatch tab. Because the cost accumulators and the resources are batched, the unbatching operation needs to release the resources and modify the accumulation of cost before the items can continue with further processing.

Cost information also can be defined for activities. For instance, within the Cost tab of activity-type blocks (such as an Operation block or a Transaction block), variable and fixed costs can be defined. These cost drivers allow resources to be modeled implicitly (i.e., without a labor pool and the batching method) as done in Figures 7.14 and 7.20.

Cost data are accumulated in two blocks: the Cost by Item block and the Cost Stats block, both from the Statistics submenu of the Discrete Event library. These blocks were introduced in Section 7.3 and used in Section 7.8. Basically, the Cost by Item block collects cost data of items passing through the block. The block must be placed in the model in such a way that the items of interest pass through it at a time when the accumulated cost has the value one wants to track. The Cost Stats collects data for all costing blocks such as an Operation or a Labor Pool block. Figure 8.27 shows the process of receiving and unpacking crates with a Cost Collection block for the crates. The Cost by Item block is placed immediately after the completion of the unpacking activity. Figure 8.28 shows the dialogue of the Cost by Item block after a 40-hour simulation. A total of 79 crates were unpacked during the 40 hours, and the Cost by Item block indicates that the average cost of unpacking a crate is $9.38.

FIGURE 8.28 Dialogue of the Cost by Item Block of the Simulation Model in Figure 8.27

8.9 Cycle Time Analysis

One of the most important measures of process performance is cycle time. In addition to total cycle time (i.e., the time required by an item to go from the beginning to the end of the process), in some cases it might be desirable to calculate the time needed to go from one part of the process to another. In other words, it might be of value to know the cycle time of some process segments in addition to knowing the cycle time for the entire process. In both cases, Extend provides a way of adding cycle time analysis to a simulation model.

The Timer block in the Information submenu of the Discrete Event library is used to calculate the cycle time of individual items. The block is placed at the point where the timing should start. The items enter the block through the input connector. The output connector should send the items out to the rest of the activities in the model. The sensor input is connected to the output of a block that is the ending point for the process or process segment for which the cycle time is being calculated. Figure 8.29 shows a process with two operations and a Timer block before the first operation.

The model has two Stack blocks, where items wait to be processed. The cycle time is measured from the time items arrive and join the first queue to the time the items leave after completing the second operation. The D connector in the Timer block is used to read the individual cycle time values for each item. The Histogram block in the Plotter library is used to create a histogram of the cycle time values for all items. The M connector is used to plot the average cycle time versus the simulation time. This is done using the Plotter Discrete Event block in the Plotter library. Both of these plotters are shown connected to the Timer block in Figure 8.29, and the resulting plots after a 10-hour simulation run are shown in Figure 8.30.

The plots in Figure 8.30 show that the average cycle time seems to be converging to a value between 4.5 and 5 minutes. This needs to be verified through a longer simulation run so that the effects of the warm-up period of the first 150 simulation minutes are minimized. The histogram shows that most of the jobs were completed in 4.3 minutes or less.

FIGURE 8.29 Two Operations in Series with a Timer Block to Measure Cycle Time

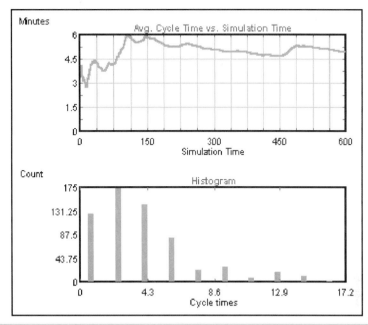

FIGURE 8.30 Histogram of Cycle Time and Average Cycle Time Versus Simulation Time

8.10 Model Documentation and Enhancements

Section 7.7 discussed the use of simple animation within Extend. Other forms of documenting and enhancing a model are adding text, using named connections, adding controls such as a slider or a meter, and displaying results. Text can be added with the Text tool. Also, the Text menu allows the size and font to be modified, and the Color tool allows the text color to be changed. Named connections are helpful because as the model grows, more connecting lines might intersect and make the model less readable. Named connections were introduced in the model in Figure 7.22. The idea is simple: A text box is created with the name of the connection, and then the box is duplicated (Edit > Duplicate) and an output connector is connected to one copy of the text box and the corresponding input connector is connected to the other copy of the text box.

Extend has three special blocks that can be used to add interactive control directly to the model. These blocks can be chosen with the Controls command in the Model menu. These blocks are used to add interactive control directly to the model. They are used to control other blocks and show values during the execution of the simulation. The controls are Slider, Switch, and Meter. A Slider resembles those typical of stereo systems. A Slider is used in Figure 8.19 to set the processing time of an operation. The maximum and minimum are set by selecting the numbers at the top and the bottom of the Slider and typing the desired values. The output of the Slider can be changed by dragging the level indicator up or down. Figure 8.31 shows the Slider connected to an Input Random Number block that is set to generate a random number from an exponential distribution. The Slider is used to change the mean (parameter 1) of the exponential distribution modeled with the Input Random Number block.

The maximum and minimum values also can be output by connecting their corresponding output connector. The middle connector outputs the current level indicated in the Slider's arrow.

FIGURE 8.31 Slider Control to Set the Mean Value of an Exponential Distribution

The Switch control has two inputs and one output and looks like a standard light switch. This control typically is used in connection with blocks that have true-false inputs. The use of this control is beyond the scope of this book, but a detailed description can be found in the Extend user's manual.

The Meter can be used to show values that vary between a specified maximum and minimum. The maximum and minimum values are set through the Meter's dialogue or through the top and bottom connectors. The Meter is useful when one wants to monitor a particular value with known maximum and minimum (e.g., the utilization of a certain resource) and there is no interest in saving these values using a plotter block. Figure 8.32 shows a Meter connected to the utilization output of a Labor Pool block.

This chapter has shown how to use the connectors from blocks such as the Timer and the Stack to display results graphically. The results connectors associated with these blocks are connected to plotters such as the Histogram and the Plotter Discrete Event to create graphical displays during the simulation. Another easy way of displaying results during the execution of the simulation is by cloning. Suppose one wants to display the average waiting time in a Stack block as it is updated during the simulation. Open the dialogue of the Stack block and click on the Results tab. Then click on the Clone Layer tool (see Figure 8.33), highlight the Average Wait text and value box, and drag them to the place in the model where they are to be displayed.

The Clone Layer tool creates a copy of the chosen items and allows them to be placed in the model to enhance documentation and animation.

Chapter 7 and the first 10 sections of this chapter have introduced Extend blocks and functionality that are relevant to building simulation models of business processes. This chapter concludes with two process design cases that make use of many of the concepts that have been discussed so far.

FIGURE 8.32 Meter Connected to the Utilization Output of Labor Pool Block

FIGURE 8.33 Clone Layer Tool

8.11 Process Design Case: Software Support

This section shows how a simulation model can be used to analyze and improve the efficiency of a relatively simple business process. The setting for this process is a call center that handles requests for software support[1].

The manager of a software support organization that provides phone and e-mail help to users wants to use simulation to explain why the productivity of the group is less than he thinks it should be. His goal is to redesign the support processes so that time to completion for problem resolution is reduced. The facilitator working with the manager would like to use this goal to define parameters by which the process can be measured. The facilitator knows that establishing a goal early in a modeling effort will allow her to determine the attributes of the process that will have to be investigated. In addition, this also will help in the task of interviewing process participants.

Before interviewing the process participants, the facilitator asked for any documentation about the process that was available. The documentation of the process and the flowcharts treat phone and e-mail support as separate processes. (See Figure 8.34.) However, the reality is that in addition to reviewing and solving problems that have been submitted in writing, support personnel also have to answer phone calls. In fact, answering the telephone, or real-time response, was given priority over providing e-mail help. The support personnel have suggested to management that one person should handle all the phone calls, and the others should handle problems submitted via e-mail. The request has been ignored, because management has concluded that: (1) There is time to perform both activities, and (2) with three support personnel, if one only takes phone calls, a 33 percent reduction in problem-solving productivity will result.

In an effort to better understand the interaction between the e-mail software support system and the phone call process, the facilitator has collected data and made the following assumptions.

1. Requests for software support arrive at a rate of about 18 per hour (with interarrival times governed by an exponential distribution). Two-thirds of the requests are e-mails and one-third are phone calls.
2. E-mails require an average of 12 minutes each to resolve. It can be assumed that the actual time varies according to a normal distribution with mean of 12 minutes and standard deviation of 2 minutes.

FIGURE 8.34 Documented Software Support Process

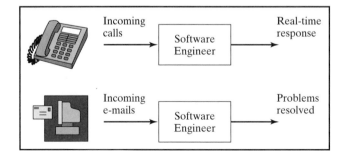

---

[1]Adapted from G. Hansen. 1994. *Automating business process reengineering*, Upper Saddle River, NJ: PTR Prentice Hall.

3. The majority of the phone calls require only 8 minutes to resolve. Specifically, it can be assumed that the time to serve a phone call follows a discrete probability distribution where 50 percent of the calls require 8 minutes, 20 percent require 12 minutes, 20 percent require 17 minutes, and 10 percent require 20 minutes.

Given this information, the manager of the group has concluded that he is correct in his assumption that with a little extra effort, support personnel can handle e-mails as well as phone calls. His logic is the following: 96 e-mails (12 e-mails/hour × 8 hours) at 12 minutes each require 1,152 minutes, and 48 phone calls (6 calls/hour × 8 hours) at an average of 8 minutes each require 384 minutes. That totals 1,536 minutes, or 3 working days of 8 hours and 32 minutes. He reasons that his personnel are professionals and will work the required extra 32 minutes.

8.11.1 MODELING, ANALYSIS, AND RECOMMENDATIONS

First, one should take a closer look at the manager's reasoning. The manager has based his calculations on the assumption that it takes an average of 8 minutes to resolve problems reported by phone. Although half (50 percent) of the calls require 8 minutes, the average call requires 11.8 minutes ($8 \times 0.5 + 12 \times 0.2 + 17 \times 0.2 + 20 \times 0.1$). Furthermore, the probability is fairly large (30 percent) that a phone call will require 17 or more minutes, which more than doubles what the manager is using for his calculations. He also is ignoring the variability of the arrivals of requests for technical support.

The manager is concerned with the group's productivity, which he most likely defines as the ratio of resolved problems to total requests. In addition to this, he would like to reduce the time needed to resolve software problems. Controlling the time to resolve a problem might be difficult, so the reduction in cycle time must come from reductions in waiting time. This is particularly important when handling phone calls because customers are generally irritated when they have to spend a long time on hold.

The process currently in use can be analyzed by modeling the work of one of the support people. To do this, adjust the arrival rates of e-mails and phone calls to represent what a single support person observes. According to the aforementioned arrival rates, the interarrival times are 5 and 10 minutes for e-mails and phone calls, respectively. If three support people are working, each of them experiences interarrival times of 15 and 30 minutes for e-mails and phone calls, respectively.

Figure 8.35 shows a simulation of one support person in the actual process. Two Import blocks are used to model the arrivals of e-mails and phone calls separately. E-mails are set to arrive one every 15 minutes, and phone calls are set to arrive one every 30 minutes. Both interarrival times are set to follow an exponential distribution in the Import blocks. When an e-mail or a phone call is generated with the Import block, the corresponding processing time also is generated with an Input Random Number block and assigned as an attribute. The Input Random Number block for e-mails is set to the Normal distribution with mean 12 and standard deviation of 2 minutes. The Input Random Number block for phone calls is set to an Empirical distribution with values as specified previously. In the Attribute tab of the Import block, create new attributes EmailTime to store the processing time of an e-mail and CallTime to store the processing time of a phone call.

After an e-mail or a phone call is generated, it is sent to a Stack block that is set to use the FIFO queuing discipline. The Operation blocks labeled Resolve model the time it takes to resolve a technical problem reported via mail or with a phone call. The Measurement block from the Attributes submenu of the BPR library is used to read the CallTime attribute of a phone call that is about to be served. (This is a phone call that goes from the Stack block to the Operation block in the Phone Support process.) This time is

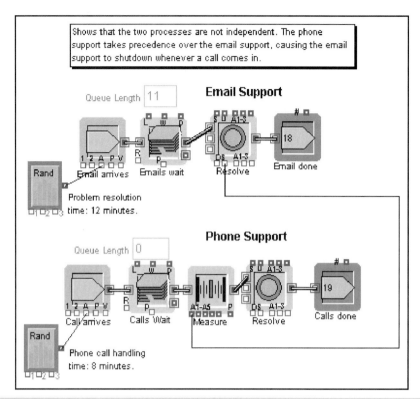

FIGURE 8.35 Simulation Model of Actual Process

then passed to the S connector of the Operation block in the E-Mail Support process. The S connector is used to specify the duration of an Operation shutdown.

The model in Figure 8.35 shows that after one run of 8 hours, the number of e-mails in the queue of one of the support people is 11. No phone calls are waiting to be answered.

The documented process, which is also the implementation proposed by the support personnel, is modeled as shown in Figure 8.36.

In this model, requests are generated and routed independently. Both queues are FIFO, and the Transaction blocks are set to a maximum of two items for the e-mail support and one item for the phone support.

Table 8.2 summarizes the performance of both systems with three software engineers (one to answer phone calls exclusively in the documented process) when simulating 30 days of operation (240 hours of operation). Times are given in minutes.

It is clear that neither the documented process nor the actual process is able to handle the volume of requests with three people. The utilization values show that the volume of work is unreasonably large considering the current level of resources. The average waiting time is somewhat reasonable for phone calls arriving to the actual process due to the priority system that is in place. When a dedicated server is used for phone call requests, the average waiting time explodes to more than 17 hours.

Based on the results in Table 8.2, one may conclude that both processes need additional staff. After simulating both processes with five people (two dedicated to phone calls in the documented process), the summary statistics in Table 8.3 were found over a 30-day run.

The results in Table 8.3 indicate that both processes are now stable. The actual process performs better when considering the maximum waiting time of the phone

FIGURE 8.36 Simulation Model of Documented Process

TABLE 8.2 Performance Comparison with Three Engineers

Measures of Performance		Documented Process		Actual Process	
		Phone Calls	E-Mails	Phone Calls	E-Mails
Waiting Time	Ave.	1,043.9	1,232.2	6.1	2,262.5
	Max.	2,019.3	2,316.9	65.3	3,943.9
Utilization	Ave.	0.99	0.99	0.99	

TABLE 8.3 Performance Comparison with Five Engineers

Measures of Performance		Documented Process		Actual Process	
		Phone Calls	E-Mails	Phone Calls	E-Mails
Waiting Time	Ave.	3.4	8.2	3.5	25.3
	Max.	44.9	80.8	35.5	133.9
Utilization	Ave.	0.58	0.80	0.76	

calls. The documented process works better when considering all the other waiting time values. The manager can now use this information to make a decision regarding the final configuration of the process, and the support people can use this information to show that they need additional help.

8.12 Process Design Case: Hospital Admissions

The admissions process of a hospital is described next[2]. This process has to deal with routing several types of patients and managing several types of resources. The main performance measure of interest is cycle time. Three types of patients are processed by the admissions function, as indicated in Table 8.4.

Service times in the admissions office vary according to patient type as given in Table 8.4. On arrival to admitting, a person waits in line if the two admissions officers are busy. When idle, an admissions officer selects a patient who is to be admitted before those who are only to be preadmitted. From those who are being admitted (Types 1 and 2), Type 1 patients are given higher priority.

Type 1 Process. After filling out various forms in the admitting office, Type 1 patients are taken to their floors by an orderly. Three orderlies are available to escort patients to the nursing units. Patients are not allowed to go to their floor on their own as a matter of policy. If all the orderlies are busy, patients wait in the lobby. After patients have been escorted to a floor, they are considered beyond the admitting process. The travel time between the admitting desk and a floor is uniformly distributed between 3 and 8 minutes. There is an 80 percent probability that the orderly and the patient have to wait 10 minutes at the nursing unit for the arrival of the paperwork from the admitting desk. It takes 3 minutes for the orderly to return to the admitting room.

Type 2 Process. After finishing the paperwork at the admitting office, patients walk to the laboratory for blood and urine tests. These patients are ambulatory and as a result require no escorts. After arriving at the lab, they wait in line at the registration desk. One person is in charge of the registration desk. The service time at the registration desk follows a Gamma distribution with a scale parameter of 2.5, a shape parameter of 1.6, and a location of 1. This service time includes copying information from the admission forms onto lab forms. The lab technicians use the lab forms to perform the indicated tests. After registration, patients go to the lab waiting room until they are called by one of the two lab technicians. The time spent drawing a lab specimen follows an Erlang distribution with a mean of 5 minutes, a *k* value of 2, and a location of 1. After the samples are drawn, patients walk back to the admitting office. Upon return to the admitting office, they are processed as normal Type 1 patients. The travel time between the admitting office and the lab is uniformly distributed between 2 and 5 minutes.

Type 3 Process. These patients follow the same procedure as Type 2 patients. The registration desk in the laboratory does not assign priorities to either Type 2 or Type 3 patients. After the samples are drawn, these patients leave the hospital.

TABLE 8.4 Data for Three Types of Patients

Type	Description	Service Time
1	Those patients who seek admission and have previously completed their preadmission forms and tests	Normal(15, 1.5)
2	Those patients who seek admission but have not completed preadmission	Normal(40, 4)
3	Those patients who are only coming in for preadmission testing and information gathering	Normal(30, 3)

---

[2]Adapted from A. Pristker. 1984. *Introduction to simulation and SLAM II.* New York: Halsted Press.

Arrivals and Office Hours.   The time between arrivals to the admitting office is exponentially distributed with a mean of 15 minutes. Before 10 A.M., the probability of a Type 1 arrival is 90 percent and the probability of a Type 2 arrival is 10 percent. No preadmissions (Type 3) are scheduled until 10 A.M. because of the heavy morning workload in the lab. After 10 A.M., the probability of a Type 1 arrival is 50 percent, and the probabilities are 10 percent and 40 percent for Type 2 and 3 arrivals, respectively. The admitting office is open from 7:00 A.M. until 5:00 P.M. At 4:00 P.M., incoming admissions are sent to the outpatient desk for processing. However, Type 2 patients returning from the lab are accepted until 5:00 P.M., which is when both admitting officers go home and the office is closed.

A graphical representation of the admitting process is shown in Figure 8.37. Travel times are indicated, as well as waiting lines. All queues are infinite and FIFO ranked except where noted. Activity and travel times are given in minutes.

Figure 8.38 shows the Extend simulation model of the current process. In this model, the cycle times are recorded for each patient type using a Timer block. The model also uses four hierarchical blocks. Hierarchical blocks contain process segments and make simulation models more readable. To make a hierarchical block, highlight the process segment and then choose Model > Make Selection Hierarchical.

The first hierarchical block, labeled Arrivals, consists of an Import block and ancillary blocks that model the arrivals of three different types of patients. (See Figure 8.39.) Because the probability of arrivals changes depending on the time of the day, the model uses the System Variable block (set at the Current time) from the Inputs/Outputs submenu of the Generic library to switch between the two Input Random Number blocks labeled Before 10 A.M. and After 10 A.M. The actual switch is performed with a Select Input block from the Decisions submenu of the Generic library. The type of patient value (1, 2, or 3) is entered as a priority in the Import block and then assigned as an attribute. The attribute is used to identify the patient type and to sort the cycle time values in the Timer block properly. The priority is used to sort the patients in the admissions queue.

The current time from an additional System Variable block is used to determine whether a patient has arrived on or before 4 P.M. If the patient arrives after 4 P.M., he or she is sent to the outpatient desk, modeled with an Export block. Otherwise, the patient is routed to the admitting officers through the named connector Con1Out.

FIGURE 8.37 Schematic Representation of the Hospital Admissions Process

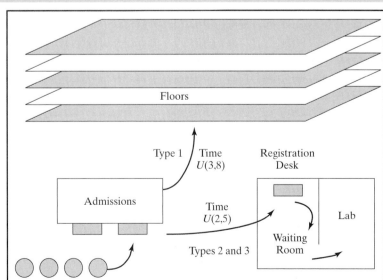

FIGURE 8.38 Extend Model of the Current Admissions Process

Patients arrive every 15 minutes

Arrivals

Arriving patients and type 2 patients returning from the lab are merged

Admitting officers help patients

Orderlies accompany patients to their rooms

Total number of patients served

33

Timer

sensor

Admissions

Rooms

Types 1 and 2

Patients type 2 and 3 go to registration and lab tests

Change priority from type 2 to 1.5

Set P

Reg and Lab

Type 3 patients

Type 2 patients

Type 2 patiens walk back to admissions

Walk back

Activity Stats

Update

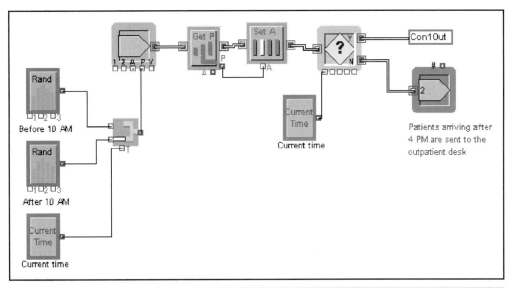

FIGURE 8.39 Arrivals Block from the Admissions Model of Figure 8.38

The Timer block after the Arrivals block is used to record the arrival time of all patients. The sensor of this block is connected to the output of the Merge block at the end of the process. The Merge block at the end joins the flow of the three different types of patients before sending a single stream to the final Export block that counts the total number of patients served.

The second hierarchical block is labeled Admissions and models the activities associated with the admitting officers, as shown in Figure 8.40. Patients form a line until an admitting officer becomes available. The Stack block (labeled Queue) is set to follow a Priority queue discipline, where the highest priority is 1 and the lowest is 3. A labor pool is used to simulate the availability of admitting officers. Three combinations of a Transaction block and an Input Random Number block are used to model the time required at the admissions desk by each patient type. A Decision(5) block from the Routing submenu of the BPR library is used to route patients according to their type. An Unbatch block is used to unbatch officers and patients so the patients can continue their routing through the process and the officers can return to the Labor Pool block. Type 2 and 3 patients are sent to the lab through the named connector Con2Out, and Type 1 patients along with returning Type 2 patients (whose priority value has been changed to 1.5) are sent to the rooms through the named connector Con3Out.

The hierarchical block labeled Reg and Lab consists of the registration and test lab activities, as shown in Figure 8.41. Patients form a line at the registration desk and then wait for a lab technician. After the tests are completed, Type 3 patients leave the process and Type 2 patients return to admissions. When Type 2 patients return to admissions, the model uses a Transaction block to simulate the time to walk back. Also, a Set Priority block from the Attribute submenu of the Discrete Event library is used to change the priority of these patients from 2 to 1.5. The purpose of this change is to identify that these Type 2 patients have already completed the lab tests and are ready to be admitted.

The final hierarchical block is labeled Rooms and consists of the activities related to orderlies taking patients to their rooms, as shown in Figure 8.42. The Batch block is used to batch an orderly and a patient so they walk together to the room, where they might need to wait for paperwork to arrive. After the patient arrives at his or her room, the orderlies walk back to admissions (which is modeled with a path from the Transaction block labeled

FIGURE 8.40 Admissions Block from the Admissions Model of Figure 8.38

FIGURE 8.41 Registration and Lab Block from the Admissions Model of Figure 8.38

307

FIGURE 8.42 Rooms Block from the Admissions Model of Figure 8.38

TABLE 8.5 Cycle Time Statistics for Current Admissions Process			
Statistic	*Type 1*	*Type 2*	*Type 3*
Min	16.18	71.92	28.19
Max	71.29	214.02	295.88
Mean	37.81	114.94	67.33
Std. Dev.	11.60	33.63	39.34

Walk Back to the Labor Pool block). The Unbatch block is used to unbatch orderlies and patients. Patients leave this process segment through the Con1Out named connector.

Table 8.5 summarizes the cycle time information for 10 days of operation of the hospital admissions process. The first column identifies the statistic. The second through the fourth columns identify the cycle time statistical value for each patient type. All values are given in minutes.

Table 8.5 indicates that all patients experience fairly long cycle times. On the average, a patient seeking admission will require approximately 2 hours to complete the process. If the patient has been preadmitted, the average time is about 40 minutes. The time values associated with Type 3 patients are all very long, with a maximum of almost 5 hours. The dispersion of the cycle time values for Type 3 patients is the largest, as indicated by the standard deviation. A frequency distribution of the cycle times for Type 1 patients, shown in Figure 8.43, revels that 75 percent of Type 1 patients experience a cycle time longer than 30 minutes. It is assumed that the hospital would like to minimize the number of Type 1 patients who experience unreasonably long cycle times, because this would discourage future patients from following the preadmission process. In other words, a patient would prefer to seek admission directly as a Type 2 patient instead of going through preadmission first as a Type 3 patient and then returning to be admitted as a Type 1 patient.

It might be possible to decrease the cycle time by adding more staff to the admissions desk, because the admitting officers have the highest average utilization of 64 percent. However, it seems more promising to explore the potential for improvement by redesigning the process instead of taking the simple approach of adding more staff.

FIGURE 8.43 Histogram of Cycle Times for Type 1 Patients

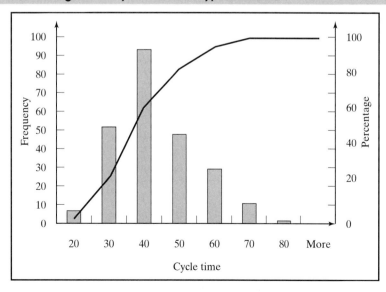

The process design project can begin with the formulation of a vision statement. A vision statement for this process might include a reference to improving service as measured by the cycle time that each patient type experiences: for instance:

> The hospital admissions process will preadmit patients in an average of less than 30 minutes and never more than 45 minutes and admit patients who have been previously preadmitted in an average of less than 15 minutes and never more than 30 minutes.

The case for action in this situation might focus on the need to improve customer service in the highly competitive health care business. The following redesign opportunities are identified.

- All information about a patient can be captured at the admissions desk and distributed to the rest of the hospital via a local area network.
- All paperwork and information gathering can take place during preadmission. Therefore, the service time for Type 1 patients in the admissions desk can be minimized.
- The registration desk at the lab is unnecessary.
- It is unnecessary for patients to wait for paperwork at the nurses' station.
- Type 2 patients could walk from the lab to the lobby to wait for an orderly instead of going back to the admissions desk.

A model of the redesigned process is depicted in Figure 8.44. The features of this model are as follows.

- The lab registration desk has been eliminated, and the person working this desk has been reassigned to the admissions desk. Patients (Types 2 and 3) are instructed to go directly to a lab technician for service. The lab technicians can access all the information about a patient from a computer terminal. The processing time at the lab remains unchanged.
- Preadmission now includes all the paperwork and information gathering necessary to admit a patient. This reduces the service time required by Type 1 patients. It is assumed that their new service time at the admissions desk is normally distributed with a mean of 5 minutes and a standard deviation of 0.5 minutes. Also, the processing times for Type 2 and Type 3 patients are reduced due to more effective (electronic) data handling. Their new processing times at the admissions desk are assumed to be 10 minutes less than the original ones.
- Type 2 patients are not required to go back to the admissions desk after completing the lab tests. Instead, they walk directly from the lab to the lobby, where they wait for an orderly to take them to their floor.
- Patients do not have to wait for paperwork at the nurses' station. All information is available through the local area network.

Table 8.6 summarizes the results of simulating 10 days of operation of the redesigned process. The cycle time statistics show the improvement achieved with the redesigned process.

The new process is better than the original in terms of the specified (technical) measure of performance. The cycle time statistics approximate the goals specified in the vision statement. Although average max and min values are informative, a better picture of the current situation is obtained with a cumulative frequency percentage chart. Table 8.7 shows the cumulative frequency associated with the cycle times of Type 1 patients. Note that fewer than 2 percent of the Type 1 patients experience more than 14 minutes of cycle time under the new design.

FIGURE 8.44 Extend Model of the Redesigned Admissions Process

311

TABLE 8.6 Cycle Time Statistics for Redesigned Process

Statistic	Type 1	Type 2	Type 3
Min	7.53	31.43	17.54
Max	15.88	61.36	40.20
Mean	10.45	43.29	25.86
Std. Dev.	1.68	6.29	4.57

TABLE 8.7 Frequency Distribution of Cycle Times for Type 1 Patients

Cycle Time	Frequency	Cumulative (%)
10	105	44.49%
12	81	78.81%
14	47	98.73%
16	3	100.00%
18	0	100.00%

A common managerial concern is the trade-off between customer service and the cost of installing the new local area network. One possible cost-savings strategy is to reduce the staff by operating with two admissions officers as in the original system. The cycle time statistics must be recomputed to figure out how close they are to the numerical goals specified in the vision statement.

8.13 Summary

This chapter introduced a number of modeling concepts to take advantage of the power of discrete-event simulation. Focus was placed on Extend features that are linked directly with the modeling of business processes. The chapter showed how to translate static representation of processes (flowcharts) into dynamic simulation models. In particular, it showed how to model multiple and parallel paths, priority queues, blocking, balking, and reneging. Another main goal of this chapter was to show how to conduct cycle time analysis using the Timer block to collect cycle time data. This analysis is an expansion of the one conducted in Chapter 5, where the processing times were considered deterministic. The Labor Pool block was used to perform capacity analysis and identify bottlenecks. This also represents an extension of the analysis introduced in Chapter 5 for the deterministic case.

The chapter concludes with two case studies that illustrate how simulation can be used to improve processes. The exercises that follow in Section 8.15 reinforce the modeling concepts and Extend features introduced in this and the previous chapter. Therefore, it is a good idea to be familiar with the material in both chapters before attempting to work on some of the more elaborate problems, such as those labeled as projects.

8.14 References

Imagine That Inc. 2003. *Extend User's Guide,* version 6. www.imaginethatinc.com.

Nyamekye, K. 2000. New tool for business process re-engineering. *IIE Solutions* 32(3): 36–41.

8.15 Discussion Questions and Exercises

1. *Measuring Cycle Times of Different Types of Jobs* — Three types of jobs arrive to a process at a rate of four jobs per hour. The interarrival times are exponentially distributed. The arrivals are not equally likely for each job type. Typically, 40 percent of the jobs are type I, 35 percent are type II, and 25 percent are type III. It can be assumed that all of the processing times are exponentially distributed; however, the mean times depend on the job type. Table 8.8 shows the mean processing time for the activities associated with each job type. (All times are given in minutes.)

   A flowchart of the process is depicted in Figure 8.45. Note that type I jobs are routed through activities B and C, and job types II and III are routed through activities D and E.

   The percentage of rework also depends on the job type. About 5 percent of the type I jobs are reworked, about 4 percent of the type II jobs are reworked, and about 6 percent of the type III jobs are reworked. In terms of resources, the process has three types of workers. Five superworkers can handle any job; therefore, managers employ them to work on activities A, F, or G. Three type I specialists can handle only type I jobs; therefore, management employs them to work on activities B and C. Finally, three type II and III specialists can handle only type II and type III jobs; therefore, management employs them to work on activities D and E.
   a. Develop a simulation model for this process.
   b. Run the simulation for 250 hours to generate approximately 1,000 job arrivals and collect data on cycle times for each job type separately.
   c. Assess the performance of the process based on your analysis in part b.
2. *Investigating the Effect of Pooling Resources* — Three types of jobs arrive to a process at a rate that randomly varies between two and five jobs per hour; that is, the interarrival times

TABLE 8.8 **Mean Processing Times for Three Different Job Types**

| | Job Type | | |
Activity	I	II	III
A	15	20	35
B	34		
C	12		
D		9	14
E		45	24
F	25	18	22
G	14	27	12

FIGURE 8.45 Measuring Cycle Times of Different Types of Jobs

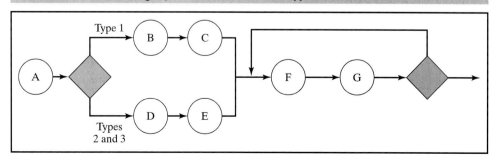

are governed by a uniform distribution with mean equal to three and a half jobs per hour. The process is currently configured in a way such that each arrival is sent to a team of specialists according to the type of job. Each team consists of three members. A team performs three activities in order to complete each job, and any team member can work on any of the three activities (A, B, or C). Figure 8.46 shows a flowchart of the process.

The arrivals are not equally likely for each job type. Typically, 30 percent of the jobs are type 1, 35 percent are type 2, and 35 percent are type 3. Processing times (in minutes) associated with the activities depend on the job type and are summarized in Table 8.9.

Management is concerned with the current performance of the process and is considering cross training the teams so team members can work on any job type.

a. Develop a simulation model of this process that can be used to model one day of operation; that is, one run of the model will consist of 8 hours of operation.

b. Use your model to assess performance with the following measures: cycle times, resource utilization, and overtime (the time needed to finish all jobs after the process closes). Simulate 10 days of operation to collect data for your analysis.

c. Assume that the teams are cross trained and that all nine people can perform any of the activities in the process. Compare this design with the original process using the measures in part b.

3. *Investigating the Effect of Rework Rates*—A proposed business process consists of five serial workstations. One caseworker is positioned in each workstation. The processing times at each workstation are exponentially distributed with mean values of 11, 10, 11, 11, and 12 minutes, respectively. The interarrival times are uniformly distributed between 13 and 15 minutes. The workstations have an unlimited queuing capacity, and it is assumed that the downstream transfer time is negligible. The unique aspect of this process is that between workstations 2 and 5, it is possible that the job will need to be reprocessed by the workstation immediately preceding the current one. For example, after workstation 3, it is possible that the job will be sent back to the queue in workstation 2. When this occurs, the transfer requires 3 minutes. The probability of rework remains the same regardless of the number of times a job is sent back for reprocessing. The rework probability is considered to be the same for all workstations and is currently estimated to be between 5 percent and 10 percent.

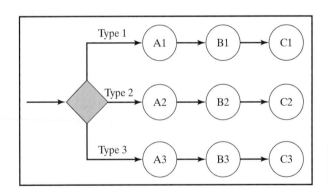

FIGURE 8.46 Investigating the Effect of Pooling Resources

TABLE 8.9 Probability Distributions for Processing Times

Activity	Distribution	Job Type 1	2	3
A	Exponential	28	20	40
B	Normal	(34, 5)	(38, 7)	(21, 3)
C	Lognormal	(19, 3.5)	(28, 2.3)	(17, 3.1)

(Mean, Standard Deviation)

    a. Develop a simulation model of this process that is capable of running 10,000 minutes of operation.

    b. Run 10,000 minutes of operation for rework probabilities of 5 percent, 6 percent, 7 percent, 8 percent, 9 percent, and 10 percent. Collect cycle time data for each run.

    c. Construct a plot of the average cycle time (y-axis) versus the rework probability (x-axis). Also construct a plot of the maximum cycle time versus the rework probability.

    d. Assume that the processing times are constant. Rerun the simulation six times with the rework probabilities in part b.

    e. Construct plots of average cycle time and maximum cycle time versus the rework probability. Compare these plots with the ones obtained in part c.

4. *Assessing Process Performance*—The process of insuring a property consists of four main activities: review and distribution, underwriting, rating, and policy writing. Four clerks, three underwriting teams, eight raters, and five writers perform these activities in sequence. The time to perform each activity is exponentially distributed with an average of 40 minutes, 30 minutes, 70 minutes, and 55 minutes, respectively. On the average, a total of 40 requests per day are received. Interarrival times are exponentially distributed. A flowchart of the process is depicted in Figure 8.47.

    a. Develop a simulation model of this process. The model should simulate 10 days of operation. Assume that work-in-process at the end of each day becomes the beginning work-in-process for the next day.

    b. Add data collection to calculate the following measures: resource utilization, waiting time, length of the queues, work-in-process at the end of each day, and average daily throughput (given in requests per day).

    c. Assess the performance of the process with the data collected in part b.

5. *Variable Resource Availability*—Travelers arrive at the main entrance door of an airline terminal according to an exponential interarrival time distribution with a mean of 1.6 minutes. The travel time from the entrance to the check-in is distributed uniformly between 2 and 3 minutes. At the check-in counter, travelers wait in a single line until one of five agents is available to serve them. The check-in time follows a normal distribution with a mean of 7 minutes and a standard deviation of 2 minutes. Upon completion of their check-in, travelers walk to their gates.

    a. Create a simulation model of the check-in process.

    b. Run the simulation for 16 hours and collect cycle time and cycle time efficiency for each traveler. Plot a frequency distribution of these values. Create a line plot of the cycle time versus the clock and the cycle time efficiency versus the clock. Also analyze queue information.

    c. Assume that the 16 hours are divided into two 8-hour shifts. Agent breaks are staggered, starting at 90 minutes into each shift. Each agent is given one 15-minute break. Agent lunch breaks (30 minutes) are also staggered, starting 3.5 hours into each shift. Compare the results of this model to the results without agent breaks. Use cycle time and queue data to make the comparison.

6. *Multiple Queues*—The order-fulfillment process of an entrepreneurial catalog business operates as follows. Orders arrive with exponential interarrival times with a mean of 10 minutes. A single clerk accepts and checks the orders and processes payment. These activities require a random time that is uniformly distributed between 8 and 10 minutes. Upon completion of these activities, orders are assigned randomly to one of two stock persons, who retrieve the

FIGURE 8.47 Assessing Process Performance

orders from the warehouse. The time to retrieve an order randomly varies between 16 and 20 minutes. The stock persons retrieve only their assigned orders.

a. Develop a simulation model that is capable of running 5,000 minutes of this process.

b. Assess the performance of the process using measures such as cycle time, queue statistics, and resource utilization.

c. A manager points out that the assignment of orders should not be made at random. Instead, the manager suggests that the next order should be assigned to the stock person with the shortest queue. He also suggests breaking ties arbitrarily. Follow these recommendations and change your model accordingly. Compare the performance of this process with the original.

d. A bright young "reengineer" recommends that the company eliminate the assignment of an order to a specific stock person and allow both stock persons to select their next order from a single queue. Modify your model to simulate this suggestion. Compare the performance with the previous two configurations.

7. *Priority Queues*—A business process consists of six activities, as shown in the flowchart of Figure 8.48. The activity times are normally distributed with mean values of 15, 10, 8, 8, 13, and 7, respectively, for activities A through F. Similarly, the standard deviations are 3, 2.5, 2, 3, 3.5, and 2.

Jobs arrive every 10 minutes on the average, with actual interarrival times following an exponential distribution. Caseworkers process the jobs. Two caseworkers can perform activities A and B. Five caseworkers can perform activities C, D, E, and F. Activity C requires two caseworkers per job, and the other activities require only one caseworker per job.

When jobs arrive, they are assigned a due time, which is calculated as follows.

$$\text{Due time} = \text{arrival time} + \text{random number between 30 and 50}$$

a. Develop a simulation model for this process.

b. Simulate the arrival of 200 jobs (i.e., simulate the process for approximately 2,000 minutes), and collect data on the tardiness for each completed job. (Hint: Consider using the Max & Min block from the Math submenu of the Generic library to calculate tardiness. This block calculates the maximum and minimum value of up to five inputs.)

c. Change the queues so jobs with the earliest completion time are given priority. Compare the process performance with the process that uses a FIFO queuing discipline. (Note that Priority queues can be used to model a priority queuing discipline. Because the item with the smallest priority value is processed first, consider assigning the due date as priority in the Import block and then choose Priority in the Stack block that simulates the queue.)

8. Figure 8.49 shows the flowchart of a business process that receives an average of one job every 10 minutes with a standard deviation of 2.5 minutes. The actual interarrival times approximately follow a normal distribution. The processing times are exponentially distributed with the mean values (in minutes) shown in Table 8.10. Three teams work in this process. The teams are assigned to activities as shown in Table 8.11.

a. Create a simulation model of this process.

b. Simulate the process for 10 working days, where each working day consists of 8 hours.

FIGURE 8.48 Priority Queues

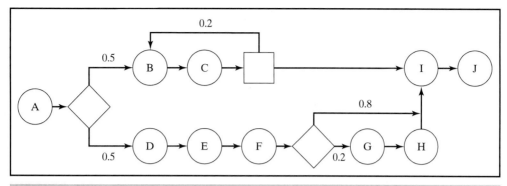

FIGURE 8.49 Flowchart for Exercise 8

TABLE 8.10 Mean Values for Exercise 8

	A	B	C	D	E	F	G	H	I	J
Mean time	6	3	10	2	6	4	5	10	9	2

TABLE 8.11 Activity Assignments for Exercise 8

Team	*Activities*	*Number of Team Members*
1	A, B, and C	2
2	D, E, and F	2
3	G, H, I, and J	2

    c. Assess the performance of the process considering waiting times, the utilization of the teams, and the work-in-process (WIP) at the end of the 10-day period.

    d. Add cycle time data collection and evaluate process performance considering the distribution of cycle times.

9. Refer to the grocery store described in problem 8 in Chapter 7 to answer the following questions.

    a. To make the model more realistic, Safeway also wants to include the time customers spend in the store walking around and picking up their groceries. Empirical investigation has shown that there are basically two types of customers, and they need to be treated somewhat differently.

    Type 1: The light shopper who buys only a few items (fewer than 15)

- About 60 percent of the customers arriving to the store.
- The shopping time follows a triangular distribution with a most likely value of 5 minutes, a minimum value of 2 minutes, and a maximum value of 8 minutes.
- The service times for these customers at the checkout counter are exponentially distributed with a mean of 15 seconds.

    Type 2: The heavy shopper who buys several items (more than 15)

- Represents about 40 percent of the arriving customers.
- The shopping time is triangularly distributed with a most likely value of 10 minutes, a minimum value of 5 minutes, and a maximum value of 15 minutes.
- The service times for these customers at the checkout counter are exponentially distributed with a mean of 52 seconds.

    The total arrival process to the store is still a Poisson process with a mean of three customers per minute. As for the queue configuration, Safeway feels that the setup in b with one line for each checkout is better for psychological reasons; one long line might deter customers from entering the store.

Modify the simulation model developed for problem 8 in Chapter 7 to incorporate the realistic elements described previously. Analyze the performance of the current process using the performance measures discussed in problem 8 of Chapter 7 as well as the following additional measures:

- The time spent shopping (average and standard deviation).
- The number of customers (average and standard deviation).
- The separate cycle times for heavy and light shoppers (average and standard deviation).

b. To improve the service for the light shoppers, Safeway is thinking about dedicating one of the checkout counters to this customer group. In other words, only light shoppers are allowed to use checkout 1. The other checkout (checkout 2) will handle heavy and light shoppers. However, empirical interviews indicate that no light shopper will choose the regular lane unless at least two more shoppers are waiting in line at the express lane. How does this design change affect the cycle times for the two customer groups and for the average customer?

8.16 Modeling, Simulation, and Design Projects

8.16.1 CREDIT APPLICATIONS

The management of a mortgage company has decided with limited information that the company can save money if it reduces its staff. Before downsizing, management asks you to model the credit application process to provide reassurance that service will not be severely affected by the reduction in staff.

The mortgage company currently employs three loan agents, two of whom perform an initial review of credit applications and a third who performs a second review of the applications that fail the initial review. The second review is performed as an attempt to correct the deficiencies by contacting the originating party. The process has the following characteristics.

- Approximately four to eight credit applications (and most likely six) arrive every hour.
- It takes 12 to 16 minutes to complete the first review.
- About 20 percent of the applications fail the first review.
- It takes 25 to 35 minutes to complete the second review.
- About 50 percent of the applications fail the second review.

Your task is to compare the performance of the current process with the performance of the process using two loan agents. For the downsized process, management wants the two remaining loan agents to work in either of the two reviewing steps; that is, the loan agents are not assigned to the first or second review step, but rather they are to perform initial or second reviews as needed.

Questions

1. Create a simulation model of the current process. Use the triangular distribution to model the arrivals of credit applications and the uniform distribution for the reviewing times.
2. Simulate the process for 5 working days (40 hours), and collect the following data: utilization of loan agents, waiting time, and cycle time.
3. Modify the model to simulate the downsized process. Repeat question 2 for the new model. Compare the performance of the two processes by analyzing the data collected during the simulation runs.

8.16.2 X-RAY PROCESS[3]

The Valley of Hope Hospital wishes to improve the service level in its X-ray operation. Patients have identified the total required time as the major service level issue in this process.

---

[3]Adapted from R. Anupindi, S. Chopra, S. D. Deshmukh, J. A. Van Mieghem, and E. Zemel. 1999. *Managing business process flows.* Upper Saddle River, NJ: Prentice Hall.

Management, on the other hand, is concerned with utilization of available resources. Management has created a process improvement team to study this problem. The process might be redesigned as a result of the team's recommendations.

The team has identified as the entry point to the process the instant a patient leaves the physician's office en route to the X-ray lab. The exit point has been defined as the instant at which the patient and the completed X ray enter the physician's office. The team has identified 12 activities in the current process, as shown in Table 8.12. The times are given in minutes. Figure 8.50 shows a flowchart of the process. Further study reveals the information in Table 8.13 concerning resource usage in the X-ray process.

The team also has analyzed the arrival and service times in the process and has determined the following. The interarrival time is exponentially distributed with a mean time of 8 minutes. The times associated with transportation activities can be considered constant. All other activity times are exponentially distributed.

TABLE 8.12 Activities in the X-Ray Process

Activity	Description	Type	Time
1	Patient leaves physician's office with instructions.	Start	—
2	Patient walks to the lab.	Transportation	7
3	Receptionist receives from the patient the insurance information, completes a claim form, and sends the form.	Business value added	6
4	X-ray technician fills out a standard form based on information supplied by the physician.	Business value added	5
5	Patient undresses and prepares for X rays.	Value added	3
6	X-ray technician takes the required X rays.	Value added	5
7	Dark room technician develops the X rays.	Value added	12
8	An X-ray technician and a dark room technician check X rays for clarity.	Inspection	3
9	If X rays are not clear, then repeat steps 6, 7, and 8. (Historically, the probability of rejecting X rays has been 25 percent.)	Decision	—
10	Patient walks back to physician's office.	Transportation	7
11	Messenger transfers X rays to physician.	Transportation	10
12	Patient and X rays enter physician's office.	End	—

FIGURE 8.50 Flowchart for X-Ray Process

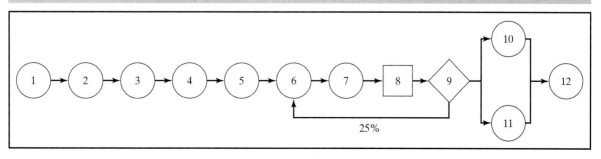

TABLE 8.13 Resource Data for X-Ray Process

Resource	Activities	No. of Units Available	Hourly Salary
Receptionist	3	1	$12
X-ray technician	4, 6, and 8	4	$25
X-ray lab	6 and 8	2	
Dark room technician	7 and 8	3	$20
Dark room	7	2	
Changing room	5	2	
Messenger	11	2	$8

Questions

1. Develop a simulation model of this process.
2. Simulate 10 days of operation and compute the cycle time and resource utilization statistics. Assume a working day has 8 hours.
3. Assess the performance of the process using the values calculated in question 2.
4. The hospital is willing to allocate up to $2,000 per day for labor associated with the X-ray process. The hourly salaries for each labor resource are shown in Table 8.13. Management also is considering adding two more facilities, which can be a combination of X-ray labs, dark rooms, or changing rooms. Find the best configuration for the current process, assuming that management would like to minimize the maximum cycle time. The number of facilities of each type and the corresponding staffing levels define a configuration.

8.16.3 ADOPTION PROCESS IN A HUMANE SOCIETY

The purpose of this project is to redesign the pet adoption process of a Humane Society. One of the main goals of the project is the development of a simulation model of the process. The adoptions department of the Humane Society would like to use this model as a tool for evaluating the effect of proposed changes to the current pet adoption process. Management considers that the model significantly reduces the risks associated with this redesign project, because a number of what-if scenarios can be tested before implementing any changes. Furthermore, management believes that the model can help them obtain buy-in from the employees directly involved in the process.

The modeling process consists of the following steps.
1. Flowcharting and analysis of the current process.
2. Simulation modeling and validation.
3. Performance analysis of the current process.
4. Discussion of different options for redesigning the current process.
5. Development of several scenarios.
6. Modeling and testing of scenarios.
7. Selection of final proposed process.

A task force is created to understand the current process. After several meetings of the task force, the current process is summarized as follows.

Patrons arrive to the Humane Society and look for a place to park. The arrival rate is about 10 patrons per hour, and the interarrival times follow an exponential distribution. If a patron finds the parking lot full, he or she leaves. If the parking lot is not full, the patron parks the car and enters the building (between 2 and 5 uniformly distributed minutes). Patrons then walk through the kennels (between 10 and 45 uniformly distributed minutes) and may decide to leave if they don't find a suitable pet. About 15 percent of patrons leave at this point. If a patron finds a suitable pet, then he or she finds out what to do next to start the adoption process (between 1 and 5 uniformly distributed minutes). Patrons then count the number of people in the waiting area. (This includes people filling out the sign-in form and people waiting for a counselor.) If a patron finds fewer than 10 people in the waiting area, then he or she proceeds to sign in. If 10 people or more are in the waiting area, the patron leaves with a 70 percent probability. It takes a patron Normal(5,1) minutes to fill out the sign-in form. After signing in, patrons wait to be called to the counter to meet with a counselor. Counseling takes between 10 and 60 minutes, and 20 percent of the time patrons also must talk to a supervisor after counseling, an activity that takes Normal(15,2) minutes. After finishing counseling (or talking to the supervisor), patrons decide to stay and continue with the adoption process or leave. About 35 percent of the patrons leave at this stage of the adoption process. If a patron decides to stay, he or she must wait for a kennel technician. After a brief conversation with a kennel technician (between 2 and 5 uniformly distributed minutes), the patron and the technician visit the animals and explore options (between 5 and 45 uniformly distributed minutes). After visiting the animals, about 15 percent of the patrons decide to leave. Those who stay work with the technician to check on holds, which takes Normal(15, 3) minutes. This is necessary because some of the animals are held for people who have visited them at the Humane Society and currently are considering adoption. If there are holds (10 percent of the time), the patron is asked to return later. If there are no holds, the patron receives instructions from the kennel technician, Normal(10,2) minutes, and walks (between 1 and 2 uniformly distributed minutes) to meet with a counselor. A counselor and the patron fill out the adoption contract (between 10 and 45 uniformly distributed minutes). After the contract is signed, the health of the animal is checked (5 exponentially distributed minutes). After the health check is complete, the patron walks to the car with his or her pet and leaves (between 2 and 5 uniformly distributed minutes).

Note: A processing time given as a range of numbers is assumed to follow a uniform distribution. For example, if the time is between 10 and 45 minutes, the actual time follows a uniform distribution with a minimum value of 10 minutes and a maximum value of 45 minutes. Also, a processing time of Normal(15,3) minutes means that the actual time follows a normal distribution with a mean of 15 minutes and a standard deviation of 3 minutes.

The current process operates 10 hours per day and utilizes the following resources:

> 30 parking spaces
> 8 counselors
> 1 supervisor
> 5 kennel technicians
> 1 veterinarian

It is assumed that the process is empty when the doors open every morning. Also, the doors are closed after 10 hours, but personnel stay until the last patron leaves the building. Working time beyond 10 hours is considered overtime.

PART I

1. Draw a flowchart of the current process.
2. Create a simulation model of the current process.
3. Run 30 days of operation (using 55 for the Random Seed Number).
4. Analyze the performance of the system according to cycle time, resource utilization, ratio of number of adoptions per number of arrivals, and daily overtime.

The report for Part I of this project consists of an executive summary with the objectives and main findings. The supporting materials should include a flowchart of the current process, a printout of the simulation model (i.e., an annotated task network), and the following charts and tables:

- A frequency distribution of the cycle times observed during the 30-day simulation.
- A table of daily resource utilization with five columns, one for each resource, and 30 rows, one for each day. Three additional rows should contain the minimum, the average, and the maximum utilization for each resource type.
- A table with 30 rows, one for each day, and two columns, one for the daily ratio of number of adoptions per number of arrivals and one for the daily overtime. Three

additional rows should contain the minimum, the average, and the maximum overtime and the adoption ratio.

PART II

1. Discuss different options for redesigning the current process. For example, consider eliminating activities or performing some activities in parallel.
2. Develop a redesign scenario.
3. Model a redesigned process.
4. Predict the performance of the redesigned process in terms of cycle time, resource utilization, ratio of adoptions to patron arrivals, and daily overtime.

The report for Part II of this project consists of an executive summary with objectives, methodology, main findings, and recommendations. The supporting materials should be the same as in the report for Part I.

8.16.4 INTERNET ORDERING PROCESS

The management of a software company wants to study the performance of the company's Web order processing. The interarrival times of orders are exponentially distributed with a mean of 7 minutes. The orders arrive in the form of e-mail. Upon arrival, a clerk looks for the buyer's name in the company's database. The time required to look for a name in the database is uniformly distributed between 20 and 45 seconds. If the buyer is not in the database, the clerk enters the buyer's information, which includes name, address, phone number, and e-mail address. The time required to enter the buyer's information in the database is uniformly distributed between 10 and 30 seconds. Approximately 60 percent of the time, the buyer's name is not in the database. Some orders are for an upgrade of the software, and the others are from first-time buyers. For all practical purposes, it takes no time to figure out whether an order is for an upgrade or from a first-time buyer. Approximately 30 percent of the orders are for upgrades. If the order is for an upgrade, then the clerk simply enters a code in the electronic purchase order (PO), created when the buyer's name was entered or found in the database. (This code is later e-mailed to the customer, so he or she can download an upgrade from the company's Web site.) Entering the code requires an exponentially distributed time with a mean of 2 minutes, because the clerk needs to verify the customer's current software version and platform. After entering the code, the electronic PO goes to accounting.

When the order is from a first-time buyer, the clerk checks whether the buyer wants the CD version with printed documentation or whether he or she prefers to download the software from the company's Web site. This requires an exponentially distributed time with a mean of 1 minute because sometimes this information has been misplaced. About 70 percent of the buyers prefer the CD version. When the CD version is preferred, the clerk needs to retrieve it from the storage room. This activity requires a normally distributed time with a mean of 5 minutes and a standard deviation of 1. The clerk then prepares the software for shipping, which takes between 3 and 6 minutes (uniform distribution). If the buyer prefers to download the software, the clerk enters an appropriate code in the electronic PO. Entering the code requires an exponentially distributed time with a mean of 1 minute, because a computer program sometimes is slow at generating a license for each customer.

Purchase orders for upgrades and first-time buyers go to accounting after a clerk has either entered a code for downloading or prepared the CD version for shipping. Accounting personnel charge the purchase to a credit card (Exponential distribution with a mean of 2 minutes) and prepare the invoice (Normal distribution with a mean of 1 minute and a standard deviation of 12 seconds). Finally, the accounting personnel mail the software or e-mail the access code with the invoice. This activity requires a uniformly distributed time between 45 and 90 seconds.

Currently, the company employs two people for this process: one clerk for the initial processing and one person in charge of the accounting. However, management is considering adding one person to the process and would like to use simulation to determine where to add this new employee to obtain the maximum customer service benefit.

Questions

1. The first task is to understand this process, so you should develop a flowchart. This chart should be the first exhibit in your written report.
2. Using the flowchart as a guideline, develop a simulation model of this process. Because only two resource types are in this process (the clerks and the accounting personnel), your model should have only two queues. Include an exhibit consisting of the simulation model.
3. Set the random seed value to 34 in the Simulation Setup of the Run menu. Run the model for 15 working days and collect the waiting time at the queues, cycle time, resource utilization, and work-in-process. (A working day consists of 8 hours.)
4. Discuss the performance of the current process based on the collected data. Include the following exhibits to support your arguments: queue statistics, line graphs of resource utilization, a histogram of cycle times, and the WIP value at the end of the 15 days.
5. Identify the bottleneck and add the new employee to the bottleneck. Compare the utilization of clerks and accounting personnel before and after adding the new employee. Also compare the frequency distribution of cycle times before and after adding the new employee. Include line graphs for the utilization of resources after adding the new employee and a histogram of cycle times.

8.16.5 AN ASSEMBLY FACTORY

The LeedsSim factory is a traditional assembly facility working as a subcontractor to the telecommunications industry. Their main product is a specialized switchboard cabinet used in the third-generation network base stations. The company has been successful on the sales side, and with the 3G expansion taking off in Europe, the orders are piling up. Unfortunately, the operations department has had some problems with reaching the desired (and necessary) productivity levels. Therefore, they have decided to seek your help to create a simulation model of the involved processes as a first step to analyze and improve the process design.

To find the right level of detail in the model description, they want to start with a simple model and then successively add more details until a suitable model with the right level of complexity is obtained. The simulation should be run over a 1-month (4-week) period of 8-hour workdays. A schematic flowchart of the manufacturing process is shown in Figure 8.51.

After the cabinets are completed and inspected, the finished cabinets leave the factory. It is noteworthy that each workstation can handle only one item at a time. Workstations 1 through 4 cannot store items. Each cabinet that is made requires one unit each of five sorts of components/raw materials delivered to the inbound storage area. Workstation 1 requires one unit each of raw

FIGURE 8.51 Flowchart of the Production Process

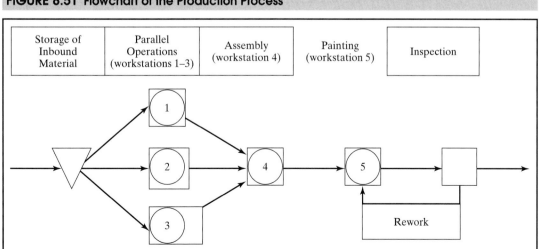

TABLE 8.14 Estimated Processing and Inspection Times		
Processing Unit	*Processing Time Distribution*	*Parameter Values (hours)*
Workstation 1	Triangular	Max = 3; Min = 1.5; Most likely = 2
Workstation 2	Triangular	Max = 3; Min = 1.5; Most likely = 2
Workstation 3	Triangular	Max = 3; Min = 1.5; Most likely = 2
Workstation 4	Triangular	Max = 4; Min = 2; Most likely = 3
Workstation 5	Triangular	Max = 6; Min = 3; Most likely = 4
Inspection	Exponential	$\mu = 2$

materials 1 and 2, workstation 2 requires one unit of raw material 3, and workstation 3 requires one unit each of raw materials 4 and 5. Table 8.14 specifies the estimated processing times in workstations 1 through 5, as well as the estimated inspection time.

The performance measure that LeedsSim is most interested in is the number of cabinets produced in 1 month. However, they also want to keep track of the following.

- The work-in-process levels—the total as well as at different parts of the workshop, including inbound storage (the maximum, the mean, and the standard deviation).
- The cycle time, measured from the instant a component arrives to the storage area until a finished cabinet leaves the factory (both the mean and standard deviation). (Hint: Note that all components for a particular cabinet have the same cycle time.)
- Utilizations of workstations and equipment such as the forklift truck.

Questions

1. The raw material arrives by truck once every week on Monday morning. Each shipment contains 15 units each of the five necessary components. The internal logistics within the factory are such that the transportation times for the incomplete cabinets can be neglected. However, to transport the fully assembled cabinet to and from the paint shop, a special type of forklift truck is needed. The transportation time from the assembly line to the paint shop is exponentially distributed with a mean of 45 minutes, which includes the travel time for the truck to get from its parking area to the assembly line. The transportation time between the paint shop and the inspection station at the loading dock is normally distributed with a mean of 60 minutes and a standard deviation of 15 minutes, including the travel time for the truck to get from its parking area to the paint shop. After delivery, the forklift truck always returns to the strategically located parking area to get new instructions. The travel time, without load, back from the inspection station as well as the paint shop is 20 minutes (constant). One forklift truck is available at the moment. For this first model, assume that all painted cabinets pass inspection so no rework occurs.
   a. Run the simulation once with random seed = 5.
      How many cabinets are being produced?
      How is the WIP situation?
      What does a plot over the storage inventory levels tell us?
      Where is the bottleneck?
   b. Run the simulation 15 times with different random seeds.
      How many cabinets are being produced on average?
      What is the standard deviation?
      How is the WIP situation?
      Where is the bottleneck?
         (Hint to collect the data and analyze it efficiently: Use the Resource, Activity, and Queue statistics blocks, check Append New Updates, and click on Confidence Interval. For the number of units produced, use a Mean and Variance block, connect it to the exit block, and check the dialogue options Calculate for Multiple Simulations, and Use Number of Inputs-1.)

2. In reality, only 75 percent of the painted cabinets pass the inspection. If a cabinet fails the inspection, it needs to be transported back to the paint shop to be repainted. The transportation time (including travel time for the truck to get to the inspection site) is the same as in the opposite direction (normally distributed with a mean of 60 minutes and a standard deviation of 15 minutes). The forklift truck will always go back to the parking area after a completed mission. The travel time without load from the paint shop to the parking area is constantly 20 minutes. When arriving to the paint shop, repainting has higher priority than the ordinary paint jobs and follows an exponential distribution with a mean of 2 hours. Inspecting the reworked cabinets is no different from inspecting nonreworked cabinets. How does the introduction of these features affect the performance measures?

   a. Run the simulation once with random seed = 5.
      How many cabinets are being produced?
      How is the WIP situation?
      Where is the bottleneck?

   b. Run the simulation 15 times with different random seeds.
      How many cabinets are being produced on average?
      What is the standard deviation?
      How is the WIP situation?
      Where is the bottleneck?

3. Based on your understanding of the process, suggest a few design changes and try them out. What is your recommendation to LeedsSim regarding how to improve their operations?

4. In this model, we have started to collect statistics and count units produced from time 0, meaning we assume the system is empty when we start. It would be more accurate to run the system for a warm-up period, say 1 week, before starting to collect data. Implement this and see the difference. Does it change your conclusions?

CHAPTER

Input and Output Data Analysis

Data analysis is a key element of computer simulation. Without analysis of input data, a simulation model cannot be built and validated properly. Likewise, without appropriate analysis of simulation output data, valid conclusions cannot be drawn and sound recommendations cannot be made. In other words, without input data analysis, there is no simulation model, and without output data analysis, a simulation model is worthless.

Input data analysis is needed because business processes are rarely deterministic. Factors such as arrival rates and processing times affect the performance of a process, and they are typically nondeterministic (i.e., stochastic). For instance, the time elapsed between the arrival of one job and the next generally follows a nondeterministic pattern that needs to be studied and understood in order to build a simulation model that accurately represents the real process. In addition, building a simulation model of a process entails the re-creation of the random elements in the real process. Therefore, three main activities are associated with the input data necessary for building a valid simulation model.

1. Analysis of input data.
2. Random number generation.
3. Generation of random variates.

The first part of this chapter is devoted to these three activities. Input data are analyzed to uncover patterns such as those associated with interarrival times or processing times. After the analysis is performed, the patterns are mimicked using a stream of random numbers. The stream of random numbers is generated using procedures that are based on starting the sequence in a so-called seed value. Because the patterns observed in the real process may be diverse (e.g., a pattern of interarrival times might be better approximated with an Exponential distribution, and a pattern of processing times might follow a Uniform distribution), some random numbers need to be transformed in a way such that the observed patterns can be approximated during the execution of the simulation model. This transformation is referred to as the generation of random variates.

The second part of the chapter is devoted to the analysis of output data. One of the main goals of this analysis is to determine the characteristics of key measures of performance such as cycle time or throughput for given input conditions such as changes in resource availability or demand volume. This can be used to either understand the behavior of an existing process or to predict the behavior of a suggested process. Another important goal associated with the analysis of output data is to be able to compare the results from several simulated scenarios and determine the conditions under which the process is expected to perform efficiently.

326

9.1 Dealing with Randomness

One option for mimicking the randomness of a real process is to collect a sufficient amount of data from the process and then use the data as the input values for the simulation model. For example, in a simulation of a call center, it might be possible to record call data for several days of operation and then use these data to run the simulation model. Relevant data in this case might be the time between the arrival of calls, the pattern of call routings within the center, and the time to complete a call.

However, this approach has several shortcomings. First, field data (also called real data) typically are limited in quantity because in most processes, the collection of data is expensive. Therefore, the length of the simulation would be limited to the amount of available data. Second, field data are not available for processes that are not currently in operation. However, an important role of simulation is to aid in the design of processes in situations where an existing process is not available. Field data can be used on a proposed redesign of an existing process, but it is likely that the problem of not having enough data to draw meaningful conclusions would be encountered. Third, the lack of several scenarios represented by field data would prevent one from performing sensitivity analysis to disclose the behavior of the process under a variety of conditions. Finally, real data may not include extreme values that might exist but that do not appear in the data set collected. Probability distribution functions include these extreme values in the tails.

Although field data are not useful for gaining a full understanding of the behavior of a process, they are useful for model validation. Validating a model entails checking that the model behaves like the actual process when both are subject to exactly the same data patterns. In the call center example, one should expect that given all relevant data patterns (e.g., the actual interarrival times for the calls during a given period of time), the model would produce the same values for the performance measures (e.g., average waiting time) as observed in the actual call center. Model validation is necessary before the model can be used for analysis and prediction. A valid model also can be used for buy-in with the process stakeholders; that is, if the process stakeholders are convinced that the model does represent the actual process, then they are more likely to accept recommendations that are drawn from testing design alternatives using the computer simulation.

Due to these limitations, simulation models are typically built to run with artificially generated data. These artificial data are generated according to a set of specifications in order to imitate the pattern observed in the real data; that is, the specifications are such that the characteristics of the artificially generated data are essentially the same as those of the real data. The procedure for creating representative artificial data is as follows.

1. A sufficient amount of field data is collected to serve as a representative sample of the population. The collection of the data must observe the rules for sampling a population so the resulting sample is statistically valid.
2. Statistical analysis of the sample is performed in order to characterize the underlying probability distribution of the population from which the sample was taken. The analysis must be such that the probability distribution function is identified and the appropriate values of the associated parameters are determined. In other words, the population must be fully characterized by a probability distribution after the analysis is completed.
3. A mechanism is devised to generate an unlimited number of random variates from the probability distribution identified in step 2.

The analyst performs step 1 by direct observation of the process or by gathering data using historical records including those stored in databases. Some software packages provide distribution-fitting tools to perform step 2. These tools compare the characteristics

FIGURE 9.1 Distribution Fitting Tab in the Input Random Number Block of Extend

of the sample data to theoretical probability distributions. The analyst can choose the probability distribution based on how well each of the tested distributions fits the empirical distribution drawn from the sample data. Extend includes a built-in tool for fitting distributions to filed data called Stat::Fit. The link to this distribution-fitting software is established using the Input Random Number block of the Generic library. Figure 9.1 shows the distribution-fitting tab of the dialogue for this block. The use of Stat::Fit is illustrated later in this chapter. Examples of other popular distribution-fitting software are BestFit and ExpertFit.

Finally, most simulation software packages (including Extend) provide a tool for performing the third step. These tools are designed to give users the ability to choose the generation of random variates from an extensive catalog of theoretical probability distributions (such as Exponential, Normal, Gamma, and so on).

9.2 Characterizing the Probability Distribution of Field Data

A probability distribution function (PDF)—or if the data values are continuous, a probability density function—is a model to represent the random patterns in field data. A probability distribution is a mathematical function that assigns a probability value to a given value or range of values for a random variable. The processing time, for instance, is a random variable in most business processes.

Researchers have empirically determined that many random phenomena in practice can be characterized using a fairly small number of probability distribution and density functions. This small number of PDFs seems to be sufficient to represent the most commonly observed patterns occurring in systems with randomness. This observation has encouraged mathematicians to create a set of PDF structures that can be used to represent each of the most commonly observed random phenomena. The structures are referred as theoretical distribution functions. Although the structures are referred to as theoretical in nature, they are inspired by patterns observed in real systems. Some of the best-known distributions are Uniform, Triangular, Normal, Exponential, Binomial, Poisson, Erlang, Weibull, Beta, and Gamma. The structures of these distributions are well established, and guidelines exist to match a given distribution to specific applications. Figure 9.2 shows the shape of some well-known probability distribution functions.

To facilitate the generation of random variates, it is necessary to identify a PDF that can represent the random patterns associated with a real business process appropriately. It is also desirable to employ a known theoretical PDF if one can be identified as a good approximation of the field data. At this stage of the analysis, several PDFs must be considered while applying statistical methods (such as the goodness-of-fit test) to assess how well the theoretical distributions represent the population from which the sample data were taken.

A simple method for identifying a suitable theoretical probability distribution function is the graphical analysis of the data using a frequency chart or histogram.

FIGURE 9.2 Shapes of Well-Known Probability Distribution Functions

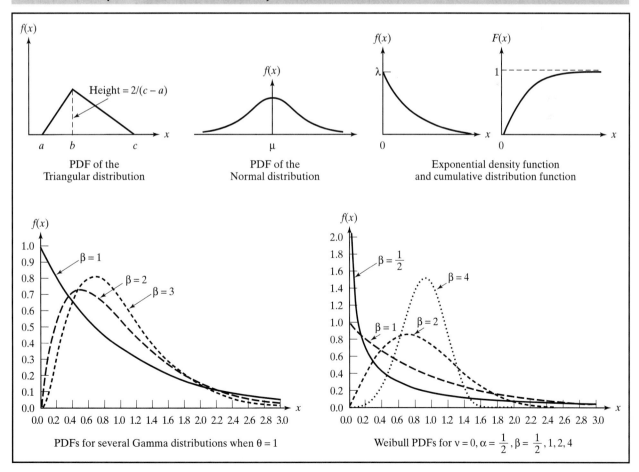

PDF of the
Triangular distribution

PDF of the
Normal distribution

Exponential density function
and cumulative distribution function

PDFs for several Gamma distributions when $\theta = 1$

Weibull PDFs for $v = 0, \alpha = \frac{1}{2}, \beta = \frac{1}{2}, 1, 2, 4$

Histograms are created by dividing the range of the sample data into a number of bins or intervals (also called cells) of equal width. Although no precise formula exists to calculate the best number of bins for each situation, it is generally accepted that the number of bins typically does not exceed 15. The square root of the number of observations in the sample also has been suggested as a good value for the number of bins. The bins must be defined in such a way that no overlap between bins exists. For example, the following three ranges are valid, nonoverlapping bins for building a histogram with sample data of a random variable x.

$$0 \leq x < 10$$
$$10 \leq x < 20$$
$$20 \leq x < 30$$

After the bins have been defined, frequencies are calculated by counting the number of sample values that fall into each range. Therefore, the frequency value represents the number of occurrences of the random variable values within the range defined by the lower and upper bound of each bin. In addition to the absolute frequency values, relative frequencies can be calculated by dividing the absolute frequency of each bin by the total number of observations in the sample. The relative frequency of a bin can be considered an estimate of the probability that the random variable takes on a value that falls within the bounds that define the bin. This estimation process makes histograms approach the shape of the underlying distribution for the population. Because the number of bins and their corresponding width affect the shape, the selection of these values is critical to the goal of identifying a suitable PDF for the random variable of interest. The shape of the histogram is then compared to the shape of theoretical distribution functions (such as those shown in Figure 9.2), and a list of candidate PDFs is constructed to perform the goodness-of-fit tests. The following example shows the construction of a histogram using Microsoft Excel.

Example 9.1

Suppose the 60 data points in Table 9.1 represent the time in minutes between arrivals of claims to an insurance agent.

The characterization of the data set starts with the following statistics.

Minimum = 6
Maximum = 411
Sample Mean = 104.55
Sample Standard Deviation = 93.32

TABLE 9.1 Interarrival Times

13	294	134	16	107	87
242	164	82	32	84	411
204	83	89	77	23	16
21	55	27	8	34	71
6	315	280	166	323	61
172	18	118	52	135	52
29	72	95	150	219	58
7	153	72	299	66	221
22	70	108	115	85	15
53	114	55	25	38	60

Bin	Frequency
TABLE 9.2 Frequency Distribution for Interarrival Times	
0–59	23
60–119	20
120–179	7
180–239	3
240–299	4
300–359	2
360–419	1

Setting the bin width at 60 minutes, Excel's Data Analysis tool can be used to build a histogram. The resulting histogram consists of seven bins with the ranges and frequencies given in Table 9.2.

Note that in Excel's Data Analysis tool, it is necessary to provide the Bin Range, which corresponds to the upper bounds of the bins in Table 9.2; that is, the Bin Range is a column of the spreadsheet that contains the upper bound values for each bin in the histogram (e.g., 59, 119, 179, and so on). After that data and the bin ranges have been specified, the histogram in Figure 9.3 is produced.

The next step of the analysis consists of testing the goodness of fit of theoretical probability distribution functions that are candidates for approximating the distribution represented by a frequency histogram of the sample data, such as the one shown in Figure 9.3.

9.2.1 GOODNESS-OF-FIT TESTS

Before describing the goodness-of-fit tests, it is important to note that these tests cannot prove the hypothesis that the sample data follow a particular theoretical distribution. In other words, the tests cannot be used to conclude, for instance, that the sample data in Example 9.1 are data points from an Exponential distribution with a mean of 100 minutes. What the tests can do is rule out some candidate distributions and possibly conclude that one or more theoretical distributions are a good fit for the sample data. Therefore, the

FIGURE 9.3 Histogram of Sample Interarrival Times

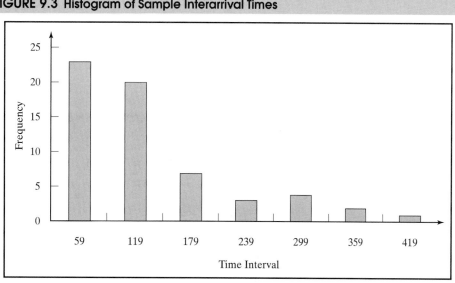

tested hypothesis is that a given number of data points are independent samples from a theoretical probability distribution. If the hypothesis is rejected, then it can be concluded that the theoretical distribution is not a good fit for the sample data. If the hypothesis cannot be rejected, then the conclusion is that the candidate theoretical distribution is a good fit for the sample data. Failure to reject the hypothesis does not mean that the hypothesis can be accepted, and several candidate theoretical distribution functions might be considered a good fit if the tests fail to reject the hypothesis.

The tests are based on detecting differences between the pattern of the sample data and the pattern of the candidate theoretical distribution. When the sample is small, the tests are capable of detecting only large differences, making them unreliable. When the sample is large, the tests tend to be sensitive to small differences between the sample data and the theoretical distribution. In this case, the tests might recommend rejecting the hypothesis of goodness of fit even if the fit could be considered close by other means, such as a visual examination of the frequency histogram. The rest of this section is devoted to the description of two of the most popular goodness-of-fit tests. The tests are described and illustrated with numerical examples.

The Chi-Square Test

The chi-square test is probably the most commonly used goodness-of-fit test. Its name is related to the use of the Chi-square distribution to test the significance of the statistic that measures the differences between the frequency distribution from the sample data and the theoretical distribution being tested. The procedure starts with building a histogram. The lower and upper bounds for each bin in the histogram can be used to calculate the probability that the random variable x takes on a value within a given bin. Suppose the lower bound of the ith bin is l_i and the upper bound is u_i. Also suppose that the theoretical distribution under consideration is the Exponential distribution with a mean of $1/\mu$, a PDF denoted $f(x)$ and a CDF denoted $F(x)$. Then the probability associated with the ith bin, pi, is calculated as $F(u_i)-F(l_i)$, or equivalently, as the area under $f(x)$ over the interval $l_i<=x<=u_i$ as shown in Figure 9.4.

FIGURE 9.4 Probability Calculation of an Exponential Distribution

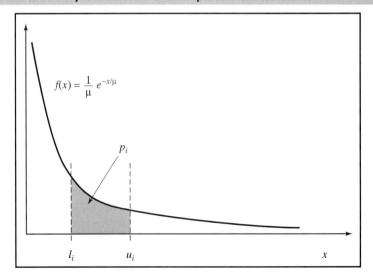

$$f(x) = \frac{1}{\mu} e^{-x/\mu}$$

p_i

l_i u_i x

The probability values for the most common theoretical probability distribution functions are available in tables. These tables can be found in most statistics books, and a few are included in the Appendix of this book. Alternatively, probabilities can be computed easily using spreadsheet software such as Microsoft Excel. Suppose the lower bound of a bin is in cell A1 of a spreadsheet, and the upper bound is in cell A2. Also suppose the PDF being tested is the Exponential distribution with a mean of $1/\lambda$ (where λ is the estimated arrival rate of jobs to a given process). Then the probability that the random variable x takes on a value within the range [A1, A2] defined by a particular bin can be found using the following Excel expression.

$$= \text{EXPONDIST}(A2, \lambda, \text{TRUE}) - \text{EXPODIST}(A1, \lambda, \text{TRUE})$$

The form of the Excel function that returns the probability values for the Exponential distribution is:

$$= \text{EXPONDIST}(x\text{-value, rate, TRUE or FALSE})$$

The first argument is a value of the random variable x. The second argument is the rate (e.g., λ for arrivals or μ for service) of the Exponential distribution under consideration. The third argument indicates whether the function should return the distribution's density value or the cumulative probability associated with the given value of x. The aforementioned expression means that the cumulative probability value up to the lower bound (given in cell A1 of the spreadsheet) is subtracted from the cumulative probability value up to the upper bound (given in cell A2 of the spreadsheet). The statistical functions in Excel include the calculation of probability values for several well-known theoretical distributions in addition to the Exponential, as indicated in Table 9.3.

TABLE 9.3 Excel Functions for Some Well-Known Theoretical Probability Distribution Functions

Theoretical Probability Distribution	Excel Function	Argument Description
Beta	BETADIST(x, α, β, A, B)	α and β = shape parameters A and B = optional minimum and maximum values
Exponential	EXPONDIST(x, λ, TRUE)	λ = mean rate value TRUE = returns the cumulative probability value
Gamma	GAMMADIST(x, α, β, TRUE)	α = shape and β = scale TRUE = returns the cumulative probability value
Normal	NORMDIST(x, μ, σ, TRUE)	μ = mean s = standard deviation TRUE = returns the cumulative probability value
Weibull	WEIBULL(x, α, β, TRUE)	α = shape and β = scale TRUE = returns the cumulative probability value

The Excel functions in Table 9.3 return the cumulative probability value up to the value of x. Note that the default range for the Beta distribution is from 0 to 1, but the distribution can be relocated and its range can be adjusted with the appropriate specification of the values for A and B. After the probability values p_i for each bin i have been calculated, the test statistic is computed in the following way,

$$\chi^2 = \sum_{i=1}^{N} \frac{(O_i - np_i)^2}{np_i}$$

where n is the total number of observations in the sample, O_i is the number of observations in bin i, and N is the number of bins. The product np_i represents the expected frequency for bin i. The statistic compares the theoretical expected frequency with the actual frequency, and the deviation is squared. The value of the χ^2 statistic is compared with the value of the Chi-square distribution with N-k-1 degrees of freedom, where k is the number of estimated parameters in the theoretical distribution being tested (using N-1 degrees of freedom is sometimes suggested as a conservative estimate, see Law and Kelton, 2000). For example, the Exponential distribution has one parameter, the mean, and the Normal distribution has two parameters, the mean and the standard deviation, that may need estimation. The test assumes that the parameters are estimated using the observations in the sample. The hypothesis that the sample data come from the candidate theoretical distribution cannot be rejected if the value of the test statistic does not exceed the chi-square value for a given level of significance. Chi-square values for the most common significance levels (0.01 and 0.05) can be found in the Appendix of this book. Spreadsheet software such as Excel also can be used to find chi-square values. The comparison for a significance level of 5 percent can be done as follows.

Do not reject the hypothesis if $\chi^2 \leq$ CHIINV$(0.05, N$-k-1$)$

The chi-square test requires that the expected frequency in each bin exceeds 5; that is, the test requires $np_i > 5$ for all bins. If the requirement is not satisfied for a given bin, the bin must be combined with an adjacent bin. The value of N represents the number of bins after any merging is done to meet the specified requirement.

Clearly, the results of the chi-square test depend on the histogram and the number and size of the bins used. Because the initial histogram is often built intuitively, the results may vary depending on the person performing the test. In a sense, the histogram must capture the "true" grouping of the data for the test to be reliable. Regardless of this shortcoming, the chi-square goodness-of-fit test is popular and often gives reliable results. The precision (or strength) of the test is improved if the bins are chosen so that the probability of finding an observation in a given bin is the same for all bins. A common approach is to reconstruct the histogram accordingly, before performing the chi-square test. It should be noted that other tests exist (such as the Kolmogorov-Smirnov test) that are applied directly to the sample data without the need for constructing a histogram first. At the same time, some of these tests are better suited for continuous distributions and tend to be unreliable for discrete data. The applicability of a test depends on each situation. The following is an illustration of the chi-square test.

Example 9.2

Consider the interarrival time data in Example 9.1. The shape of the histogram along with the fact that the sample mean is almost equal to the sample standard deviation indicates that the Exponential distribution might be a good fit. The Exponential distribution is fully characterized by the mean value (because the standard deviation is equal to the mean). The sample mean of

TABLE 9.4 Chi-Square Test Calculations

Bin	Observed Frequency (O_i)	Expected Frequency (np_i)	$\dfrac{(O_i - np_i)^2}{np_i}$
0–59	23	25.88	0.32
60–119	20	14.58	2.01
120–179	7	8.21	0.18
180–239	3	4.63	0.02
240–299	4	2.61	
300–359	2	1.47	
360–∞	1	0.83	
Totals	60		2.54

104.55 is used as an estimate of the true but unknown population mean. Table 9.4 shows the calculations necessary to perform the chi-square test on the interarrival time data.

The expected frequency in bins 4 to 7 is less than 5, so these bins are combined and the statistic is calculated using the sum of the observed frequencies compared to the sum of the expected frequencies in the combined bins. The total number of valid bins is then reduced to four, and the degree of freedom for the associated Chi-square distribution is $N - k - 1 = 4 - 1 - 1 = 2$. The level of significance for the test is set at 5 percent. Because $\chi^2 = 2.54$ is less than the chi-square value CHIINV(0.05,2) = 5.99, the hypothesis that the sample data come from the Exponential distribution with a mean of 104.55 cannot be rejected. In other words, the test indicates that the Exponential distribution provides a reasonable fit for the field data.

The Kolmogorov-Smirnov Test

The Kolmogorov-Smirnov (KS) is another frequently used goodness-of-fit test. One advantage of this test over the chi-square test is that it does not require a histogram of the field data. A second advantage of the KS test is that it gives fairly reliable results even when dealing with small data samples. On the other hand, the major disadvantage of the KS test is that it applies only to continuous distributions.

In theory, all the parameters of the candidate distribution should be known in order to apply the KS test (as originally proposed). This is another major disadvantage of this test because the parameter values typically are not known and analysts can only hope to estimate them using field data. This limitation has been overcome in a modified version of the test, which allows the estimation of the parameters using the field data. Unfortunately, this modified form of the KS test is reliable only when testing the goodness of fit of the Normal, Exponential, or Weibull distribution. However, in practice the KS test is applied to other continuous distributions and even discrete data. The results of these tests tend to reject the hypothesis more often than desired, eliminating some PDFs from consideration when in fact they could be a good fit for the field data.

The KS test starts with an empirical cumulative distribution of the field data. This empirical distribution is compared with the cumulative probability distribution of a theoretical PDF. Suppose that $x_1, \ldots, x_n$ are the values of the sample data ordered from the smallest to the largest. The empirical probability distribution has the following form.

$$F_n(x) = \frac{\text{number of } x_i \leq x}{n}$$

Then, the function is such that $F_n(x_i) = i/n$ for $i = 1, \ldots, n$. The test is based on measuring the largest absolute deviation between the theoretical and the empirical cumulative probability distribution functions for every given value of x. The calculated deviation is compared to a tabulated KS value (see Table 9.5) to determine whether or not the deviation can be due to randomness; in this case, one would not reject the hypothesis that the sample data come from the candidate distribution. The test consists of the following steps.

1. Order the sample data from smallest to largest value.
2. Compute D^+ and D^- using the theoretical cumulative distribution function $\hat{F}(x)$.

$$D^+ = \max_{1 \le i \le n}\left[\frac{i}{n} - \hat{F}(x_i)\right]$$

$$D^- = \max_{1 \le i \le n}\left[\hat{F}(x_i) - \frac{i-1}{n}\right]$$

3. Calculate $D = \max(D^-, D^+)$.
4. Find the KS value for the specified level of significance and the sample size n.
5. If the critical KS value is greater than or equal to D, then the hypothesis that the field data come from the theoretical distribution is not rejected.

TABLE 9.5 Kolmogorov-Smirnov Critical Values

Degrees of Freedom (n)	$D_{0.10}$	$D_{0.05}$	$D_{0.01}$
1	0.950	0.975	0.995
2	0.776	0.842	0.929
3	0.642	0.708	0.828
4	0.564	0.624	0.733
5	0.510	0.565	0.669
6	0.470	0.521	0.618
7	0.438	0.486	0.577
8	0.411	0.457	0.543
9	0.388	0.432	0.514
10	0.368	0.410	0.490
11	0.352	0.391	0.468
12	0.338	0.375	0.450
13	0.325	0.361	0.433
14	0.314	0.349	0.418
15	0.304	0.338	0.404
16	0.295	0.328	0.392
17	0.286	0.318	0.381
18	0.278	0.309	0.371
19	0.272	0.301	0.363
20	0.264	0.294	0.356
25	0.240	0.270	0.320
30	0.220	0.240	0.290
35	0.210	0.230	0.270
Over 35	$\dfrac{1.22}{\sqrt{n}}$	$\dfrac{1.36}{\sqrt{n}}$	$\dfrac{1.63}{\sqrt{n}}$

TABLE 9.6 Calculations for KS Test

i	x_i	$\hat{F}(x_i)$	i/n	D^+	$D-$
1	0.05	0.0079	0.1	0.0921	0.0079
2	0.20	0.0313	0.2	0.1687	−0.0687
3	1.40	0.1997	0.3	0.1003	−0.0003
4	3.10	0.3894	0.4	0.0106	0.0894
5	5.30	0.5697	0.5	−0.0697	0.1697
6	7.00	0.6717	0.6	−0.0717	0.1717
7	9.10	0.7649	0.7	−0.0649	0.1649
8	10.90	0.8235	0.8	−0.0235	0.1235
9	12.10	0.8542	0.9	0.0458	0.0542
10	13.70	0.8869	1	0.1131	−0.0131
			Totals	0.1687	0.1717

The following example illustrates the application of the KS test.

Example 9.3

This example uses the KS test to determine whether the Exponential distribution is a good fit for 10 interarrival times (in minutes) collected in a service operation: 3.10, 0.20, 12.1, 1.4, 0.05, 7, 10.9, 13.7, 5.3, and 9.1. Table 9.6 shows the calculations needed to compute that value of the D statistic.

Note that the x_i values in Table 9.6 are ordered and that the theoretical cumulative distribution function values are calculated as follows.

$$\hat{F}(x_i) = 1 - e^{-x_i/6.285}$$

where 6.285 is the average time between arrivals calculated from the sample data. Because $D^+ = 0.1687$ and $D^- = 0.1717$, then $D = 0.1717$. The critical KS value for a significance level of 0.05 and a sample size of 10 is 0.410. (See Table 9.5.) The KS test indicates that the hypothesis that the underlying probability distribution of the field data is exponential with a mean of 6.285 minutes cannot be rejected.

Although no precise recipes can be followed to choose the best goodness-of-fit test for a given situation, the experts agree that for large samples (i.e., samples with more than 30 observations) of discrete values, the chi-square test is more appropriate than the KS test. For smaller samples of a continuous random variable, the KS test is recommended. However, the KS test has been applied successfully to discrete probability distributions, so it cannot be ruled out completely when dealing with discrete data.

9.2.2 USING STAT::FIT TO FIT A DISTRIBUTION

Stat::Fit is a distribution-fitting package that is bundled with Extend and that can be used to model empirical data with a probability distribution function. To access Stat::Fit, open the dialogue window of an Input Random Number block of the Inputs/Outputs submenu of the Generic library. The Stat::Fit button is located under the Distribution Fitting tab. The Stat::Fit software is launched after clicking on the Open Stat::Fit button.

The main Stat::Fit window is shown in Figure 9.5. Data files can be imported into the software with the File > Open . . . function. Alternatively, the data can be input by typing values in the empty table that appears when the Stat::Fit is called from Extend. The data shown in Figure 9.5 correspond to the interarrival times of Table 9.1.

The fastest way of fitting a distribution is to select the Auto Fit function, which is shown in the toolbar of Figure 9.5. After clicking on the Auto Fit button, the dialogue in Figure 9.6 appears. In this case, an unbounded continuous distribution (such as the Exponential) has been chosen to fit.

FIGURE 9.5 Stat::Fit Window Showing Table 9.1 Data

FIGURE 9.6 Auto Fit Dialogue Window

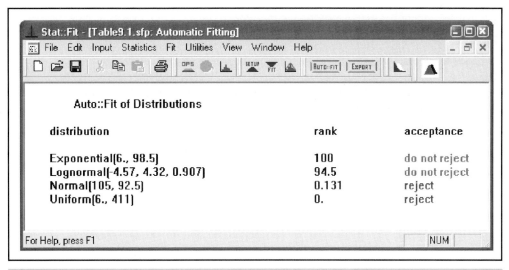

FIGURE 9.7 Auto Fit Results

The results of the Auto Fit are shown in Figure 9.7. Stat::Fit tried to fit four different continuous distributions, and the Exponential distribution with a mean value of 98.5 was ranked the highest. The Lognormal distribution also is considered a good fit, but the Uniform and the Normal distributions are not.

The fitted distribution can be plotted to provide visual confirmation that these are good models for the input data. The plot of the input data and the fitted distribution is shown in Figure 9.8. This plot is constructed by the Graph Fit tool in the toolbar of Stat::Fit.

Instead of using the Auto::Fit function, it is possible to test the goodness of fit of a particular distribution, just as was done by hand in the previous subsection. To do this, open the Fit > Setup . . . dialogue, then select the distribution(s) to be tested in the Distributions tab and the tests to be performed in the Calculations tab. After choosing the Exponential distribution in the Distributions tab and the chi-square and KS tests in the Calculations tab, the results shown in Figure 9.9 were obtained. Note that the chi-square value calculated by Stat::Fit matches the one obtained in Table 9.4.

The results of the distribution fitting performed with Stat::Fit can be exported to Extend. To do this, open the dialogue File > Export > Export Fit or click on the Export button in the toolbar. Pick Extend under the application window and then choose the desired distribution. Next, click OK and go back to Extend. The Input Random Number block from which Stat::Fit was invoked will show the fitted distribution in the Distributions tab.

9.2.3 CHOOSING A DISTRIBUTION IN THE ABSENCE OF SAMPLE DATA

When using simulation for process design, it is possible (and even likely) to be in a situation where field data are not available. When this situation arises, it is necessary to take advantage of the expert knowledge of the people involved in the process under consideration. For example, the analyst could ask a clerk to estimate the length of a given activity in the process. The clerk could say, for instance, that the activity requires "anywhere between 5 and 10 minutes." The analyst can translate this estimate into the use of a Uniform (or Rectangular) distribution with parameters 5 and 10 for the simulation model.

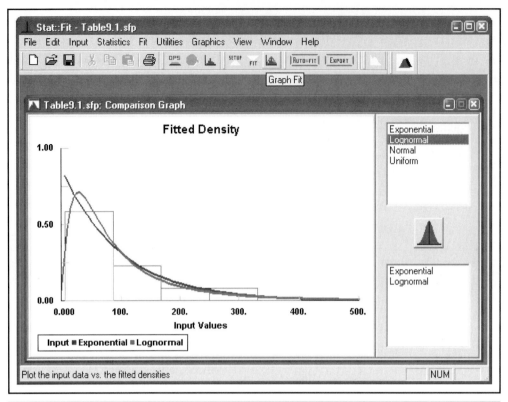

FIGURE 9.8 Plot of the Input Data and the Fitted Probability Density Functions

Sometimes process workers are able to be more precise about the duration of a given activity. For instance, a caseworker might say: "This activity requires between 10 and 30 minutes, but most of the time it can be completed in 25 minutes." This statement can be used to model the activity time as a Triangular distribution with parameters (10, 25, 30), where $a = 10$ is the minimum, $b = 30$ is the maximum, and $c = 25$ is the mode. The additional piece of information (the most likely value of 25 minutes) allows the use of a probability distribution that reduces the variability in the simulation model when compared to the Uniform distribution with parameters 10 and 30.

If the analyst is able to obtain three estimates representing the minimum, the maximum, and the most likely value, a generalization of the Triangular distribution also can be used. This generalization is known as the Beta distribution. The Beta distribution is determined by two shape parameters, α and β. Given these parameters the corresponding mean, μ, and mode, c, are obtained with the following mathematical expressions.

$$\mu = a + \frac{\alpha(b - a)}{\alpha + \beta} \qquad \text{and} \qquad c = a + \frac{(\alpha - 1)(b - a)}{\alpha + \beta - 2}$$

If an estimate $\bar{x}$ of the true mean μ is available, along with an estimate of the mode c, the following relationships can be used to obtain the values of the α and β parameters for the Beta distribution.

FIGURE 9.9 Goodness-of-Fit Tests Results

$$\alpha = \frac{(\bar{x} - a)(2c - a - b)}{(c - \bar{x})(b - a)}$$

$$\beta = \frac{\alpha(b - \bar{x})}{\bar{x} - a}$$

The Beta distribution has some interesting properties. For example, the Beta distribution with parameters (1,1) is the same as the Uniform distribution with parameters

(0,1). A beta random variable x in the interval from 0 to 1 can be rescaled and relocated to obtain a beta random variable in the interval between A and B with the transformation:

$$A + (B - A)\, x$$

Also, the Beta distribution with parameters (1,2) is a left triangle, and the Beta distribution with parameters (2,1) is a right triangle. The selection of the parameter values for the Beta distribution can change the shape of the distribution drastically. For example, when $\bar{x}$ is greater than c, the parameter values α and β calculated as shown previously result in a Beta distribution that is skewed to the right. Otherwise, the resulting Beta distribution is skewed to the left. A beta random variable can be modeled in Extend with an Input Random Number block from the Inputs/Outputs submenu of the Generic library. Figure 9.10 shows the dialogue screen for the Input Random Number block when the Beta distribution is chosen from the Distribution menu. The Shape1 parameter is α, the Shape2 parameter is β, and the Maximum and Location parameters are B and A, as specified previously.

Example 9.4

Suppose an analyst would like to use the Beta distribution to simulate the processing time of an activity. No field data are available for a goodness-of-fit test, but the analyst was told that the most likely processing time is 18.6 minutes, with a minimum of 10 minutes and a maximum of 20 minutes. It is also known that the average time is 17.8 minutes. With this information, the analyst can estimate the value of the shape parameters as follows.

FIGURE 9.10 Beta Distribution Modeled with the Input Random Number Block

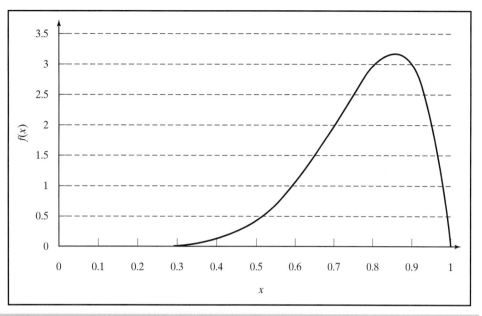

FIGURE 9.11 Beta Distribution with $\alpha = 7$ and $\beta = 2$

$$\alpha = \frac{(17.8 - 10)(2 \times 18.6 - 10 - 15)}{(18.6 - 17.8)(20 - 10)} \approx 7$$

$$\beta = \frac{7(20 - 17.8)}{17.8 - 10} \approx 2$$

The shape of the Beta distribution with $\alpha = 7$ and $\beta = 2$ is shown in Figure 9.11.

Note that the x values in Figure 9.11 range from 0 to 1. To obtain processing times in the range from 10 to 20 minutes, simply use the transformation $10 + (20 - 10)x$.

9.3 Random Number Generators

Random numbers are needed to create computer simulations of business processes. The generation of random numbers is an important element in the development of simulation software such as Extend. The random number generators typically are hidden from the user of the simulation software, so it might seem that these numbers are generated magically and that there should be no concern regarding how they were obtained. However, random number generation is one of the most fundamental elements in computer based simulation techniques. For the conceptual understanding of this type of simulation methods, it is therefore imperative to address a few basic issues related to random number generators.

Computer software uses a numerical technique called pseudo-random number generation to generate random numbers. The word *pseudo-random* indicates that the stream of numbers generated using numerical techniques results in a dependency of the random numbers. In other words, numerical techniques generate numbers that are not completely independent from one another. Because the numbers are interlinked by the formulas used with a numerical technique, the quality of the stream of random numbers depends on how well the interdependency is hidden from the tests that are used to show that the stream of numbers is indeed random. Consider, for example, a simple but poor numerical technique for generating random numbers. The technique is known as the mid-square procedure.

1. Select an *n*-digit integer, called the seed.
2. Find the square of the number. If the number of digits of the resulting value is less than 2*n*, append leading zeros to the left of the number to make it 2*n* digits long.
3. Take the middle *n* digits of the number found in step 2.
4. Place a decimal point before the first digit of the number found in step 3. The resulting fractional number is the random number generated with this method.
5. Use the number found in step 3 to repeat the process from step 2.

Example 9.5

Create a stream of five four-digit random numbers in the range from 0 to 1 using the mid-square procedure, starting with the seed value 4, 151.

Table 9.7 shows the stream of random numbers generated from the given seed. Note that the mid-square procedure can fail to generate random numbers if the seed is such that the square of the current number creates a pattern of a few numbers that repeat indefinitely. For example, if the seed 1,100 is used, the method generates the sequence 0.2100, 0.4100, 0.8100, 0.6100 and repeats this sequence indefinitely. The seed value of 5,500 always generates the same "random" number—0.2500. Try it!

TABLE 9.7 Random Number Generation with Mid-Square Procedure

No.	Square of Current Number	Random Number
1	$(4151)^2 = 17230801$	0.2308
2	$(2308)^2 = 05326864$	0.3268
3	$(3268)^2 = 10679824$	0.6798
4	$(6798)^2 = 46212804$	0.2128
5	$(2128)^2 = 04528384$	0.5283

Random number generators in simulation software are based on a more sophisticated set of relationships that provide a long stream of random numbers before the sequence of values repeats. One popular procedure is the so-called linear congruential method. The mathematical relationship used to generate pseudo-random numbers is:

$$Z_i = (aZ_{i-1} + c) \bmod m$$
$$r_i = Z_i / m$$

The Z values are integer values with Z_0 being the seed. The *r*-values are the random numbers in the range from 0 to 1. The mod operator indicates that Z_i is the remainder of the division of the quantity between parentheses by the value of *m*. The parameter values *a*, *c*, and *m* as well as the seed are nonnegative integers satisfying $0 < m, a < m, c < m,$ and $Z_0 < m$.

Example 9.6

Create a stream of five four-digit random numbers in the range from 0 to 1 using the linear congruential method with parameters $a = 23, c = 7, m = 34,$ and a seed of 20.

$Z_1 = (20 \times 23 + 7) \bmod 34 = 25$ $r_1 = 25/34 = 0.7353$
$Z_2 = (25 \times 23 + 7) \bmod 34 = 4$ $r_2 = 4/34 = 0.1176$
$Z_3 = (4 \times 23 + 7) \bmod 34 = 31$ $r_3 = 31/34 = 0.9118$
$Z_4 = (31 \times 23 + 7) \bmod 34 = 6$ $r_4 = 6/34 = 0.1765$
$Z_5 = (6 \times 23 + 7) \bmod 34 = 9$ $r_5 = 9/34 = 0.2647$

The linear congruential method may degenerate if the parameter values are not chosen carefully. For example, if the parameter *m* is changed to 24 in Example 9.6, the sequence of random numbers degenerates in such a way that 0.8333 and 0.4583 repeat indefinitely.

Numerical methods for generating pseudo-random numbers are subjected to a series of tests that measure their quality. High-quality generators are expected to create random numbers that are uniform and independent. The goodness-of-fit test can be used to check uniformity. The runs test typically is used to check dependency.

9.3.1 THE RUNS TEST

The runs test is used to detect dependency among values in a data set represented as a sequence of numbers. A run is a succession of an increasing or decreasing pattern in the sequence. The length of the run is given by the number of data points within one pattern before the pattern changes. Typically, the plus (+) sign is used to indicate a pattern of increasing numbers, and a minus ($-$) sign indicates a pattern of decreasing numbers. For example, the sequence 1, 7, 8, 6, 5, 3, 4, 10, 12, 15 has three runs:

$$+ + - - - + + + +$$

First is an increasing pattern that changes when the sequence goes from 8 to 6. The decreasing pattern continues until the sequence goes from 3 to 4, from which the increasing pattern continues until the end of the sequence. Note that any sequence of n numbers cannot have more than $n - 1$ runs and less than 1 run.

The runs test is based on comparing the expected number of runs in a true random sequence and the number of runs observed in the data set. If R is the number of runs in a true random sequence of n numbers, then the expected value and the standard deviation of R have been shown to be:

$$\mu_R = \frac{2n - 1}{3} \quad \text{and} \quad \sigma_R = \frac{16n - 29}{90}$$

Also, it has been shown that the distribution of R is Normal for $n > 20$. The runs test has the following form.

H_0 : The sequence of numbers is independent
H_A : The sequence of numbers is not independent

The following statistic is used to test this hypothesis:

$$Z = \frac{R - \mu_R}{\sigma_R}$$

where R is the number of runs in the data set with μ_R and σ_R computed as shown previously. The null hypothesis is not rejected at the α level of significance if the following relationship holds.

$$-Z_{\alpha/2} \le Z \le Z_{\alpha/2}$$

In other words, if the Z statistic falls outside the range specified by the level of significance, the hypothesis that the numbers in the sequence are independent is rejected.

Example 9.7

Consider the following sequence of 22 numbers. Perform the runs test to determine, with a 95 percent confidence level, whether or not the numbers in the sequence (ordered by rows) are independent.

30	34	21	89	81	8	94	67	58	19	18
22	37	33	88	56	67	77	36	27	67	90

The following represents the runs in the sequence.

$$+ - + - - + - - - - + + - + - + + - - + +$$

Then, the number of runs R, the expected number of runs μ_R, and the standard deviation of the number of runs σ_R are:

$$R = 13$$

$$\mu_R = \frac{2 \times 22 - 1}{3} = 14.33$$

$$\sigma_R = \frac{16 \times 22 - 29}{90} = 3.58$$

The Z statistic is calculated as follows.

$$Z = \frac{13 - 14.33}{3.58} = -0.37$$

The critical value can be found from the Normal distribution tables (see the Appendix) or with the following Microsoft Excel function.

$$Z_{\alpha/2} = \text{NORMSINV}(0.975) = 1.96$$

Because Z is within the interval defined by $-Z_{\alpha/2}$ and $Z_{\alpha/2}$, the null hypothesis, which states that the numbers in the sequence are independent, is not rejected.

9.4 Generation of Random Variates

The previous section showed two methods for generating random numbers uniformly distributed between 0 and 1. However, in most simulation models it is necessary to generate random numbers from probability distributions other than the Uniform (or Rectangular) distribution. Chapter 6, section 6.3.3 showed how a function transformation can be used to generate variates from the Exponential distribution. This technique is known as the inverse transformation technique. The technique takes advantage of the fact that cumulative distribution functions (CDFs) are defined in the range between 0 and 1. In addition, the CDF values corresponding to the values of the random variable are uniformly distributed, regardless of the probability distribution of the random variable. Mathematically, this is expressed as follows:

$$F(x) = r$$

where $F(x)$ is the cumulative distribution function of the random variable x, and r is a random number uniformly distributed between 0 and 1. If the CDF is known, then random variates of the random variable x can be found with the following inverse transformation.

$$x = F^{-1}(r)$$

Example 9.8
Use the uniform random numbers generated in Example 9.6 to generate variates of an exponentially distributed random variable with a mean of 10 minutes. The Exponential cumulative distribution function has the following form.

$$F(x) = 1 - e^{-\mu x}$$

Applying the inverse transformation, the following is obtained.

$$r = 1 - e^{-\mu x}$$
$$-\mu x = \ln(1 - r)$$
$$x = -\frac{1}{\mu}\ln(1 - r) = -\frac{1}{\mu}\ln(r)$$

Note that if r is a random variable uniformly distributed between 0 and 1, then $1 - r$ is also a random variable uniformly distributed between 0 and 1. Therefore, random variates of the Exponential distribution with mean value of 10 can be generated as follows.

$r_1 = 0.7353$	$x_1 = -10 \times \ln(0.7353) = 3.075$
$r_2 = 0.1176$	$x_2 = -10 \times \ln(0.1176) = 21.405$
$r_3 = 0.9118$	$x_3 = -10 \times \ln(0.9118) = 0.923$
$r_4 = 0.1765$	$x_4 = -10 \times \ln(0.1765) = 17.344$
$r_5 = 0.2647$	$x_5 = -10 \times \ln(0.2647) = 13.292$

Although the inverse transformation technique is a good method for generating random variates, there are some distributions for which the inverse of the CDF does not have a closed analytical form. For example, random variates of the Normal distribution cannot be obtained with a direct application of the inverse transformation technique. The technique can be applied using an approximation that takes advantage of the central limit theorem.

Fortunately, simulation software provides an automated way of generating random variates of the most popular theoretical distributions. In Extend, the Input Random Number block from the Inputs/Outputs submenu of the Generic library is used for the purpose of generating random variates from a catalog of well-known probability distribution functions. As shown in Figure 9.10, one simply selects the probability distribution from the drop-down menu and then enters the appropriate parameter values.

Occasionally, it is necessary to simulate processes for which some of the uncertainty is due to random variables with discrete probability distributions of an arbitrary form. For example, the transportation time from a distribution center to a customer could be specified as being 2 days 20 percent of time, 3 days 50 percent of the time, and 4 days 30 percent of the time. This distribution of times is clearly an arbitrary discrete probability distribution function. Table 9.8 shows the cumulative distribution function associated with the transportation times.

The inverse transformation technique can be used to generate random variates of an arbitrary discrete distribution function. Once again, a uniformly distributed random variable r is used. The transformation associated with the probability distribution in Table 9.8 is given in Table 9.9.

Example 9.9

Use the uniform random numbers generated in Example 9.6 to generate variates of the arbitrary discrete probability distribution function in Table 9.8. When the inverse transformation in

TABLE 9.8 Arbitrary Discrete PDF and CDF

Number of Days x	Probability p(x)	Cumulative Probability P(x)
2	0.20	0.20
3	0.50	0.70
4	0.30	1.00

TABLE 9.9 Inverse Transformation for an Arbitrary Discrete PDF

Uniform Random Number Range	Random Variate
$0.00 \leq r < 0.20$	2
$0.20 \leq r < 0.70$	3
$0.70 \leq r \leq 1.00$	4

Table 9.9 is applied to the uniform random numbers generated in Example 9.6, the following random variates are generated.

$r_1 = 0.7353$	$x_1 = 4$
$r_2 = 0.1176$	$x_2 = 2$
$r_3 = 0.9118$	$x_3 = 4$
$r_4 = 0.1765$	$x_4 = 2$
$r_5 = 0.2647$	$x_5 = 3$

Extend provides an easy way of generating random variates from arbitrary discrete probability distribution functions. The Input Random Number block from the Inputs/Outputs submenu of the Generic library provides this functionality. Figure 9.12 shows the dialogue of the Input Random Number block when the Empirical Table is chosen from the Distribution menu and the Empirical Values option is set to Discrete.

The Input Random Number block also provides the functionality to generate random variates from an arbitrary continuous distribution. Suppose that instead of the

FIGURE 9.12 An Arbitrary Discrete PDF Modeled with Extend discrete probability distribution in Table 9.8, one would like to use a continuous probability distribution of the following form.

$$f(x) = 0.2 \qquad\qquad 1 \le x < 2$$
$$f(x) = 0.5 \qquad\qquad 2 \le x < 3$$
$$f(x) = 0.3 \qquad\qquad 3 \le x < 4$$

The inverse transformation technique could be applied using integral calculus to find the inverse of the cumulative distribution function. In Extend, however, this arbitrary continuous distribution can be modeled easily with the Input Random Number block. The Empirical Table is chosen from the Distribution menu and then the Stepped option is used for the Empirical values. Figure 9.13 shows the dialogue for this Extend block along with the corresponding plot of the arbitrary continuous distribution.

Note that the first value in the Empirical Table of Figure 9.13 corresponds to the lower bound of the first range in the arbitrary continuous distribution (which is 1 in this case). The bounds of the subsequent ranges are given in order until the upper bound of the last range is reached (which is 4 in this case). Also note that the last two probability values are the same, indicating the end of the PDF.

9.5 Analysis of Simulation Output Data

The previous sections have addressed the issues associated with the modeling of process uncertainty using discrete-event simulation. The stochastic behavior of the output of a process is due to inputs (e.g., the uncertainty in the arrival of jobs) and internal elements (e.g., the uncertainty of processing times, the routing of jobs in the process, or the availability of resources). Hence, the output of a simulation model also should be treated as a set of random variables. For example, the waiting time of jobs is a random variable that depends on the inputs to the simulation model as well as the model's internal elements. Other random variables that are outputs of process simulations are cycle time and work-in-process.

The goal of this section is to discuss some basic concepts of statistical analysis of data obtained from running a process simulation. In the context of business process design, simulation studies are performed for the following reasons.

1. To estimate the characteristics (e.g., mean and standard deviation) of output variables (e.g., cycle time) given some input conditions and values of key parameter settings. This estimation helps one understand the behavior of an existing business process or predict the behavior of a proposed process design.
2. To compare the characteristics (e.g., minimum and maximum) of output variables (e.g., resource utilization) given some input conditions and values of key parameter settings. These comparisons help one choose the best design out of a set of alternative process configurations. Also, the comparisons can be used to determine the best operating conditions for a proposed process design.

Statistical analysis of simulation output is necessary in order to draw valid conclusions about the behavior of a process. When performing statistical analysis, one must deal with the issues related to sampling and sample sizes. These issues cannot be ignored, because valid conclusions cannot be drawn from a single simulation run of arbitrary length. To illustrate the danger of ignoring proper statistical sampling techniques, consider the following example.

Example 9.10

A simulation model has been built to estimate the number of insurance policies that are in process at the end of a working day in an underwriting department. After running the simulation model

FIGURE 9.13 An Arbitrary Continuous PDF Modeled with Extend

one time, the WIP is estimated at 20 policies at the end of the day. However, making decisions based on this estimate would be a terrible mistake. First of all, this estimate is based on a single run that represents a day of operation starting with an empty process. In other words, the WIP is zero at the beginning of the simulation. If 30 days of operation are simulated by running the model 30 times, the wrong assumption would be made that the WIP is always zero at the beginning of each day. It would be assumed that the policies that were in process at the end of one day would disappear by the beginning of the next business day. What needs to be done is to run the simulation model for $30 \times 8 = 240$ hours and record the WIP at the end of each 8-hour period. After running this simulation, one would observe that the WIP at the end of the first day is 20, but the WIP at the end of the 30th day is 154 insurance policies. This might indicate that the process is not stable and that the WIP will keep increasing with the number of simulated days. This is confirmed by a simulation run of 300 days that results in a final WIP of 1,487 insurance policies.

The previous example illustrates the importance of choosing an appropriate value for the simulation length. Clearly in this example, simulating 10 days of operation was not enough to determine whether or not the current process configuration is indeed stable. The example also addresses the difference between a terminating and a nonterminating process. Figure 9.14 shows the types of statistical analysis associated with simulation models for terminating and nonterminating processes.

The following two subsections comment on the differences between the analyses that are appropriate for each of these simulation types.

9.5.1 NONTERMINATING PROCESSES

A nonterminating process is one whose operation does not end naturally within a practical time horizon. Many business processes are nonterminating. For example, order fulfillment, credit approval, and policy underwriting are nonterminating processes. These processes are correctly viewed as nonterminating, because the ending condition of the previous day is the beginning condition of the current day. Other systems such as traffic and telecommunications networks are clearly nonterminating because their operation is not divided into discrete units of time (such as working days). Most nonterminating processes eventually reach a steady state—a condition in which the process state distribution does no longer change with time and is no longer affected by the initial state in which the simulation was started. Example 9.10 is an illustration of a nonterminating process that doesn't reach a steady state. Typically, nonterminating processes go through a transient period before reaching a steady state. An output variable, such as the utilization of a resource, exhibits a transient

FIGURE 9.14 Analysis of Output Data According to Simulation Characteristics

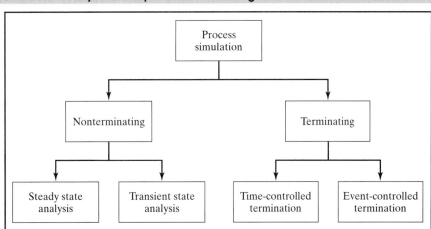

period at the beginning of a simulation before reaching a steady state that represents the long-term condition for the given resource.

Determining the end of a transient period is an essential part of studying the steady-state behavior of a process. The data collected during a transient period belong to a different statistical population than data collected during a steady state. Mixing data from a transient period with data from the steady state results in unreliable estimates of key output statistics. Therefore, the steady-state analysis should be performed with data collected after the end of the transient period.

Some statistical techniques have been used to determine the end of the transient period. For example, the runs test has been applied for this purpose. A simple way of finding the transition between the transient period and a steady state is to examine a line plot of the output variable of interest. Figure 9.15 shows the cycle time values from a simulation of a given process. The figure also shows the cumulative average cycle time. Note that the running average has a smoother pattern of change, which makes it easier to identify underlying changes in the process behavior.

In the line graph depicted in Figure 9.15, a change in the cycle times can be identified at simulation time 15. After detecting the length of the transient period using a pilot run, additional runs can be made with instructions to the software to start data collection after the so-called warm-up period has ended. In Extend, this is done by connecting a Program block from the Generators submenu of the Discrete Event library and a Clear Statistics block from the Statistics submenu of the Generic library, as shown in Figure 9.16.

The blocks shown in Figure 9.16 clear the statistics computed during the warm-up period. If the warm-up period, for instance, is 15 minutes, then the Program block is set to generate an item with a value of 1 at time 15, as shown in Figure 9.17.

FIGURE 9.15 Line Plot of Cycle Times and Average Cycle Time

Program Block   Clear Statistics
Block

FIGURE 9.16 Warm-Up Period Modeling with Extend

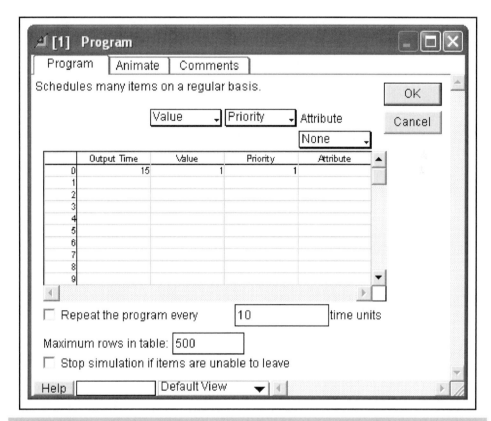

FIGURE 9.17 Program Block Scheduled to Generate an Item at Time 15

The item generated by the Program block is passed to the Clear Statistics block. The Clear Statistics block is set to clear the statistics in all the blocks that calculate them, as shown in Figure 9.18.

The initial conditions of the process generally affect the steady-state analysis. However, the effect of the initial conditions decreases with the length of the simulation. For simulation of an existing process, it is possible to use average values to create an initial condition for the simulation. For example, average values can be used to initialize the queues in a process in such a way that when the simulation starts, the process is not empty.

9.5.2 TERMINATING PROCESSES

A terminating process is one that typically starts from an empty state and ends also at an empty state. The termination of the process happens after a certain amount of time has elapsed. For example, the pet adoption process of a Humane Society

FIGURE 9.18 Clear Statistics Block Dialogue

(described in Chapter 8) starts at an empty state in the morning and closes after 8 hours of operation.

The state of a terminating process is empty when it closes. Terminating processes might or might not reach a steady state. Many terminating processes might not even have a steady state. To find out whether or not a terminating process has a steady state, a simulation model of the process can be executed beyond the natural termination of the process. For example, the pet adoption process mentioned previously could be simulated for 100 continuous hours to determine whether or not the process reaches a steady state. The steady-state behavior of a terminating process could be used to estimate critical measures of performance and make decisions about the configuration of such a process.

The estimation of performance for terminating processes is generally achieved with statistical analysis of multiple independent runs. In this case, the length of each run is determined by the natural termination of the process. The number of runs is set to collect enough data to perform statistical analysis that allows the analyst to draw valid conclusions about the performance of the process.

The amount of data available after a single run of a terminating process depends on the output variable under study. For example, suppose a simulation model of the aforementioned pet adoption process is run once and that 40 adoptions are completed. At the end of the run, a data set consisting of 40 observations is available for output variables such as cycle time and cycle time efficiency (because these values can be recorded for each completed adoption). On the other hand, there will be only a single observation of output variables such as daily throughput rate and overtime. In this case, a meaningful sample is taken, executing the simulation for a number of independent runs. Each run starts with the same initial conditions, but the runs use a different stream of random numbers. The Discrete Event tab of the Simulation Setup in the Run menu of Extend allows the number of runs for a single execution of the simulation model to be set. When more than one run is specified, the execution does not stop until all runs are completed. One run follows the next one, and the stream of random numbers is not reinitialized. Instead, each run uses a different section of the stream of random numbers that is seeded as specified in the Random Numbers tab of the Simulation Setup.

This method results in samples of random variables for which only one observation can be obtained per run. The samples consist of independent observations of the random variable. In addition, it is valid to assume that the observations are identically distributed. These properties make the application of traditional statistical methods for estimation and hypothesis testing a robust approach to analyze output simulation data.

Example 9.11

A project consists of seven activities with duration and precedence relationships given in Table 9.10.

The duration of each activity is a random variable as specified in Table 9.10. An activity can be started only after all preceding activities are completed. One of the main goals of project management is to estimate the duration of the project. When the duration of the activities in the project is uncertain, project managers often rely on a methodology called PERT (Project Evaluation and Review Technique) to obtain an estimate of the expected completion time and its associated standard deviation. PERT calculations assume that the activity times are distributed according to a Beta distribution. A minimum, a maximum, and a most likely value for the duration of each activity are used to perform the analysis. The advantage of using simulation in this context is that one does not have to assume that the activity times are beta distributed. An Extend model of this project is shown in Figure 9.19.

TABLE 9.10 Project Activities with Random Duration

Activity	Duration (days)	Immediate Predecessor
A	Uniform(2, 6)	None
B	Uniform(2, 17)	None
C	Exponential(7)	A and B
D	Normal(8, 2)	B
E	Normal(4, 1)	C and D
F	Beta(7, 2, 3, 9)	D
G	Exponential(5)	E and F

FIGURE 9.19 Extend Model of a Project with Seven Activities

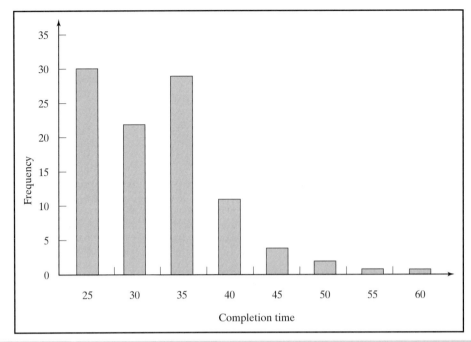

FIGURE 9.20 Histogram over Completion Times

Note that the simulation model in Figure 9.19 uses a Timer block to calculate the completion time of the project. Then this value is passed to the File Output block from the Inputs/Outputs submenu of the Generic library. This block creates a file of all the data that are passed to it. The activities are modeled as hierarchical blocks containing an Input Random Number block from the Generic library and an Operation block from the BPR library. The simulation is executed 100 times, and the completion times are recorded in a file. Note that in this simulation, the sample can be collected by executing the model once with 100 arrivals generated with the Import block. A histogram over the sample data is shown in Figure 9.20.

The histogram in Figure 9.20 (constructed by importing the output file to Excel) shows that about 80 percent of the time, the project is completed within 35 days. The expected completion time is 29.8 days with a standard deviation of 7.6 days. In addition to calculating simple statistics, these sample data can be used to estimate confidence intervals, to calculate an appropriate sample size for a specified interval precision, and to test hypotheses, as presented in the following sections.

9.5.3 CONFIDENCE INTERVALS

Statistical estimation of characteristics (e.g., the mean) of a population is typically done in two ways: point estimates and confidence intervals. Point estimates are obtained by calculating statistics from a sample of the population. For example, the sample mean is an estimate of the true but unknown population mean. The average waiting time in a queue calculated from simulation output is a point estimate of the true but unknown mean of the population of all waiting times for the queue. Confidence intervals expand this analysis by expressing the estimates as intervals instead of single values. The intervals might or might not contain the true value of the parameter; however, a so-called confidence level represents the accuracy of the estimation. If two intervals have the same confidence level, the narrower of the two is preferred. Similarly, if two intervals have the same width, the one with a higher confidence level is preferred. Typically, the analyst chooses a desired confidence level and constructs an appropriate interval according to this selection.

The sample size and the standard deviation are the main factors that affect the width of a confidence interval. For a given confidence level, the following relationships hold.

- The larger the sample size is, the narrower the confidence interval is.
- The smaller the standard deviation is, the narrower the confidence interval is.

The first relationship generally is used to approach the estimation problem from the point of view of determining the sample size that will satisfy a set of requirements for the confidence interval. In other words, the analyst can specify a level of confidence and a desired width for the confidence interval first and then use this to determine a sample size.

Confidence Interval for a Population Mean

Mean values are often the focus of statistical analysis of simulation output. Average cycle time, average waiting time, average length of a queue, and average resource utilization are just a few examples of average values that are used to measure process performance. The most widely reported statistics associated with simulation output are the mean and the standard deviation. Suppose the values of an output variable are represented by $x_1, x_2, \ldots, x_n$ (where n is the number of observations in the sample). The mean and the variance are estimated as follows.

$$\bar{x} = \frac{x_1 + x_2 + \ldots + x_n}{n}$$

$$s^2 = \frac{\sum_{i=1}^{n} (x_i - \bar{x})^2}{n - 1}$$

If the random variables are independent and identically distributed, the distribution of the sample mean $\bar{x}$ is Normal for a sufficiently large sample size (an often used rule of thumb is 30 observations or more). This is a result from the central limit theorem, which states that for a sufficiently large sample size, the distribution of the sample mean follows a Normal distribution regardless of the distribution of the individual observations, as long as they are independent and identically distributed. The random variable Z is defined as follows.

$$Z = \frac{\bar{x} - \mu}{\sigma_{\bar{x}}}$$

This random variable follows a standard normal distribution, meaning a Normal distribution with a mean of 0 and a standard deviation of 1. The population mean is represented by μ, and $\sigma_{\bar{x}} = \sigma/\sqrt{n}$ is the standard deviation of distribution of the sample mean. In this case, μ and σ are true but unknown parameters from the population. The mean value μ is the parameter that is to be estimated. If the population standard deviation σ is not known (as is typically the case), then it is possible to use the sample standard deviation s as a reasonable approximation as long as the sample size is large (at least 30).

At a confidence level of $1 - \alpha$, a symmetrical confidence interval can be constructed from the following probability statement.

$$P\{-Z_{\alpha/2} \leq Z \leq Z_{\alpha/2}\} = 1 - \alpha$$

Then substitute the Z variable and solve for μ to obtain the confidence interval.

$$\bar{x} - \frac{Z_{\alpha/2}\sigma}{\sqrt{n}} \leq \mu \leq \bar{x} + \frac{Z_{\alpha/2}\sigma}{\sqrt{n}}$$

When the sample size is fewer than 30 observations, the use of the Normal distribution, as implied by the Central Limit Theorem, can be questionable. Instead of the Normal distribution, the Student t distribution can be employed in the following way.

$$\bar{x} - \frac{t_{n-1,\alpha/2}s}{\sqrt{n}} \leq \mu \leq \bar{x} + \frac{t_{n-1,\alpha/2}s}{\sqrt{n}}$$

This confidence interval based on the Student t distribution is exact only if the observed x-values are normally distributed. However, it is often used as an approximation when this condition is not satisfied. If we compare the critical values for the standard normal distribution with those obtained with the Student t distribution for a given confidence level, $1 - \alpha$, then $t_{n-1,\alpha/2}$ is strictly greater than $Z_{\alpha/2}$. Consequently, using the Student t distribution produces a wider confidence interval. This is why the Student t produces confidence intervals that are closer to the desired confidence level $1 - \alpha$ when the sample size n is small. We also know that as the sample size becomes larger $t_{n-1,\alpha/2}$ approaches $Z_{\alpha/2}$. The critical values for the standard Normal distribution and the Student t distribution can be found in the Appendix. Alternatively, these values also can be found using the following Microsoft Excel functions.

$$Z_{\alpha/2} = \text{NORMSINV}(1 - \alpha / 2)$$
$$t_{n-1,\alpha/2} = \text{TINV}(\alpha, n - 1)$$

Example 9.12

Table 9.11 shows 50 observations of the cycle time for a given business process. Construct a 95 percent confidence interval to estimate the true but unknown value of the mean cycle time for this process.

The point estimates for the mean and the standard deviation are $\bar{x} = 7.418$ and $s = 1.565$. The Z-value for a 95 percent confidence level is $Z_{0.975} = 1.96$. Then, the 95 percent confidence interval for the population mean is:

$$7.418 - \frac{(1.96)(1.565)}{\sqrt{50}} \leq \mu \leq 7.418 + \frac{(1.96)(1.565)}{\sqrt{50}}$$
$$6.98 \leq \mu \leq 7.85$$

TABLE 9.11 Sample Cycle Times

6.8	6.3	6.5	5.1	5.3	8.9	5.9	8.2	10.0	8.7
8.8	9.7	9.6	9.5	9.6	7.4	7.5	6.4	5.2	6.5
7.5	5.9	5.3	9.3	9.2	7.1	9.2	7.2	7.0	6.0
5.5	6.3	8.0	7.8	5.5	7.4	8.0	10.0	5.4	8.4
5.3	9.6	8.6	7.5	9.3	6.6	6.1	8.9	5.0	6.1

In Extend, the blocks Queue Stats, Activity Stats, Resource Stats, and Cost Stats from the Statistics submenu of the Discrete Event library automatically construct confidence intervals. Figure 9.21 shows the dialogue of a Queue Stats block after 20 runs of a simulated process.

The block in Figure 9.21 has recorded statistics of single Stack block labeled In Box. Because these data come from 20 independent runs, they can be used to set confidence intervals. The result of clicking on the Confidence Interval button of the Queue Stats block is shown in Figure 9.22. Using the data in Figure 9.21, one can verify that Extend constructed the confidence intervals using the equation with the t distribution as presented previously.

Confidence Interval for a Population Proportion

Some output variables from a process simulation are proportions. For example, in pet adoption processes, directors of operations of Humane Societies are interested in estimating the proportion of patrons who adopt a pet to the total of patrons who initiate the process. The percentage of jobs going through a specialized operation and the percentage of jobs requiring rework are two more examples of output variables that represent proportions. In general, a proportion is a value representing the percentage of one type of outcome (often referred to as *success*) in a number of trials.

The true but unknown probability of success is denoted by p. Therefore, the probability of failure is $1 - p$. The resulting random variable takes on two values: zero with probability $1 - p$ and 1 with probability p. A random variable of this kind follows a Bernoulli distribution, for which the mean value is p and the variance is $p(1 - p)$. In a sample of n observations, the ratio of the number of successes to the total number of

FIGURE 9.21 Queue Stats Block After 10 Runs

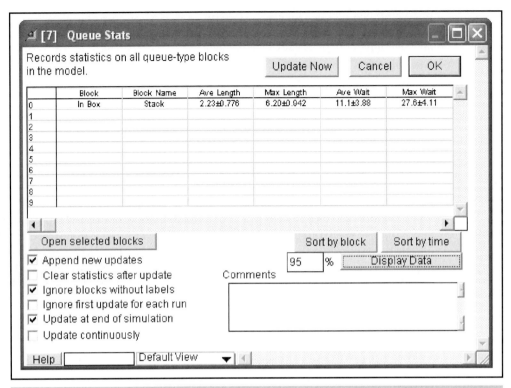

FIGURE 9.22 Confidence Intervals Calculated with the Queue Stats Block

trials $\bar{p}$ is a point estimate of p. The distribution of the $\bar{p}$ statistic is approximately Normal for n larger than 10 and both $np > 5$ and $n(1 - p) > 5$. A $(1 - \alpha)$ percent confidence interval for p can be constructed from the following probability statement.

$$P\left\{-Z_{\alpha/2} \leq \frac{\bar{p} - p}{\sqrt{p(1 - p)/n}} \leq Z_{\alpha/2}\right\} = 1 - \alpha$$

Note that the probability statement requires the knowledge of p to be able to calculate the standard deviation. Because p is the parameter to be estimated, $\bar{p}$ can be used to approximate p for the calculation of the standard deviation when the sample size is sufficiently large. Substituting p with $\bar{p}$ in the denominator and rearranging the elements of the probability statement gives the following confidence interval for a proportion.

$$\bar{p} - Z_{\alpha/2}\sqrt{\bar{p}(1 - \bar{p})/n} \leq p \leq \bar{p} + Z_{\alpha/2}\sqrt{\bar{p}(1 - \bar{p})/n}$$

Example 9.13

Consider the cycle time data in Table 9.11. Suppose the proportion p of interest is the percentage of jobs whose cycle time is greater than 7. Suppose also that the goal is to construct a 99 percent confidence interval for p. Table 9.11 shows 28 observations with cycle time greater than 7; therefore, $\bar{p} = 0.56$. The resulting confidence interval is as follows.

$$0.56 - 2.576\sqrt{0.56(1 - 0.56)/50} \leq p \leq 0.56 + 2.576\sqrt{0.56(1 - 0.56)/50}$$
$$0.379 \leq p \leq 0.741$$

Note that as in the case of the confidence interval for a population mean, the interval width is reduced as the number of observations in the sample is increased. The value of 2.576 in the aforementioned calculation is the Z value (obtained from Excel) that yields a cumulative probability of 0.995 in a standard Normal distribution.

9.5.4 SAMPLE SIZE CALCULATION

The previous section assumed that the sample size was a given value. In practice, however, one of the key issues in statistical analysis of simulation output is the determination of an appropriate sample size. The sample size is either related to the length of the simulation or the number of simulation runs, depending on the model. The theory of statistics includes what is known as the law of large numbers, which refers to the property that statistics calculated using large samples from independent random variables are nearly exact estimates of the population parameters. Today's simulation software coupled with the power of state-of-the-art computer hardware makes it possible to perform many lengthy simulation runs within a reasonable amount of time. Nevertheless, the question of what can be considered a reasonably large sample size still remains. The answer depends on the variation of the random variable of interest.

An important issue in determining an appropriate sample size is the desired precision level. The analyst must set a desired width of the confidence interval and also specify a level of confidence. With this in place the equations derived in the previous section can be solved to determine the corresponding sample size. It is interesting to point out that the sample size cannot be determined before the simulation model is run a few times because an estimate of the standard deviation is needed to determine the sample size. So in practice, a provisional sample size is used for an initial run that can yield enough data to estimate the standard deviation. The resulting estimate is used to derive an appropriate sample size that in turn yields the necessary data for constructing the desired confidence interval.

Suppose the goal is to construct a confidence interval with a total width of $2d$, where d is half of the interval's width. The confidence interval for a population mean can be expressed as follows.

$$\bar{x} - d \leq \mu \leq \bar{x} + d$$

Comparing this inequality with the one derived in the previous section, one can write:

$$d = \frac{Z_{\alpha/2}\sigma}{\sqrt{n}}$$

Because the true standard deviation is generally not known, the sample standard deviation s can be used to estimate it. The following equation is used to solve for the sample size.

$$n = \left(\frac{Z_{\alpha/2}s}{d}\right)^2$$

The resulting sample size value guarantees a $(1 - \alpha)$ percent confidence interval of width $2d$ as long as the sample standard deviation represents a good estimate of the population standard deviation.

Example 9.14

Consider once again the cycle time data in Table 9.11. The confidence interval constructed in Example 9.12 with these data has a total width of 0.868 (i.e., $2d = 0.868$ or $d = 0.434$). Suppose one wants to construct a confidence interval with the same confidence level of 95 percent but with a total width of 0.6 (i.e., $2d = 0.6$ or $d = 0.3$). Calculate the sample size needed to achieve the desired precision level.

$$n = \left(\frac{1.96 \times 1.565}{0.3} \right)^2 \approx 104.54 \approx 105$$

A similar calculation can be made to find the sample size necessary to construct a confidence interval of a given precision for a population proportion. Again assume that the analyst desires a $(1 - \alpha)$ percent confidence interval with a total width of $2d$. The confidence interval can be expressed as follows.

$$\bar{p} - d \leq p \leq \bar{p} + d$$

where

$$d = Z_{\alpha/2} \sqrt{\bar{p}(1 - \bar{p}) / n}$$

Solving for the sample size n, one obtains the following.

$$n = \frac{(Z_{\alpha/2})^2 \bar{p}(1 - \bar{p})}{d^2}$$

Note that in this calculation, it is also necessary to execute a preliminary simulation run to be able to estimate the true proportion p with the sample proportion $\bar{p}$. Because an estimated value is being used to calculate the sample size, the accuracy of the calculation depends on the accuracy of the estimate obtained after the preliminary run. A more conservative approach is to use the maximum standard deviation value instead of the one calculated with the available $\bar{p}$. The maximum standard deviation of 0.25 occurs when $p = 0.5$. Therefore, a conservative and accurate sample size calculation for constructing a confidence interval on a proportion is:

$$n = \frac{(Z_{\alpha/2})^2}{4d^2}$$

The advantage of using this equation is that it does not depend on any population parameters; therefore, the sample size can be calculated without performing a preliminary simulation run.

Example 9.15

Consider Example 9.13. Calculate a sample size needed to construct a 99 percent confidence interval with a total width of 0.2. Use the formula that considers maximum standard deviation of the population.

$$n = \frac{(2.576)^2}{4 \times (0.1)^2} \approx 165.89 \approx 166$$

9.5.5 Hypothesis Testing

The previous sections addressed several issues associated with statistical estimation. However, sometimes it is important to not only estimate the value of a parameter but to test whether a parameter is equal to a critical value. Similarly, it might be interesting to test whether there is a difference between two parameters, such as the means of two design alternatives of the same process. The statistical background used to set up and perform tests of hypotheses is the same one used to establish confidence intervals. In particular, it is assumed that the sample means are normally distributed.

A hypothesis states a certain relationship about an unknown population parameter that might or might not be true. This relationship is known as the null hypothesis (denoted by H_0). Because the test is based on estimated values, it is possible to commit errors. When the null hypothesis is true and the test rejects it, it is said to have committed a type I error. A type II error occurs when the test fails to reject a false null hypothesis. The level of significance of the test is denoted by α and is interpreted as the maximum risk associated with committing a type I error. The confidence level of the test is $1 - \alpha$.

Suppose $\bar{x}$ is the mean and s is the standard deviation estimated from a sample of n observations. Also suppose that we would like to test the following hypothesis.

$$H_0 : \mu = a$$
$$H_A : \mu \neq a$$

Then, the null hypothesis is rejected (with a significance level of α) if the following relationship does not hold.

$$-Z_{\alpha/2} \leq \frac{\bar{x} - a}{s / \sqrt{n}} \leq Z_{\alpha/2}$$

This is a so-called two-tail test on a population mean. The two related one-tail tests are shown in Table 9.12.

In addition to testing if a population mean is equal, greater than, or less than a given value, it is sometimes desirable to be able to compare the difference between two means. This is particularly useful in the context of process design, where it might be necessary to show that a new design is better than an existing design in terms of a key output variable. Suppose μ_1 is the population mean of a new process design and that its value is estimated with $\bar{x}_1$. Suppose also that μ_2 is the population mean of the existing process design and its value is estimated with $\bar{x}_2$. Then the following two-tail test can be formulated.

$$H_0 : \mu_1 - \mu_2 = a$$
$$H_A : \mu_1 - \mu_2 \neq a$$

TABLE 9.12 One-Tail Hypothesis Test on One Mean

Hypothesis Test	*Reject Null Hypothesis if . . .*
$H_0 : \mu \geq a$ $H_A : \mu < a$	$\dfrac{\bar{x} - a}{s / \sqrt{n}} < -Z_\alpha$
$H_0 : \mu \leq a$ $H_A : \mu > a$	$\dfrac{\bar{x} - a}{s / \sqrt{n}} < -Z_\alpha$

TABLE 9.13 One-Tail Hypothesis Test on the Differences Between Two Means

Hypothesis Test	*Reject Null Hypothesis If ...*
$H_0 : \mu_1 - \mu_2 \geq a$ $H_A : \mu_1 - \mu_2 < a$	$\dfrac{\bar{x}_1 - \bar{x}_2 - a}{\sqrt{\dfrac{s_1^2}{n_1} + \dfrac{s_2^2}{n_2}}} < -Z_\alpha$
$H_0 : \mu_1 - \mu_2 \leq a$ $H_A : \mu_1 - \mu_2 > a$	$\dfrac{\bar{x}_1 - \bar{x}_2 - a}{\sqrt{\dfrac{s_1^2}{n_1} + \dfrac{s_2^2}{n_2}}} > Z_\alpha$

The null hypothesis is rejected (with a significance level of α) if the following relationship does not hold:

$$-Z_{\alpha/2} \leq \frac{\bar{x}_1 - \bar{x}_2 - a}{\sqrt{\dfrac{s_1^2}{n_1} + \dfrac{s_2^2}{n_2}}} \leq Z_{\alpha/2}$$

where n_1 and n_2 are the sample sizes for each population, respectively. Also, s_1 and s_2 are the sample standard deviations for the populations. One-tail tests similar to those in Table 9.12 can be formulated for the difference between two means, as shown in Table 9.13.

Example 9.16

Consider the cycle time data in Table 9.11. A new design has been proposed for the process, and a computer simulation prototype has been built. The cycle times in Table 9.14 were obtained from running the simulation model of the proposed process design.

Does the mean cycle time in the proposed process represent an improvement over the mean cycle time of the existing process? To find out, one can test the null hypothesis $\mu_1 - \mu_2 \geq 0$, where μ_1 is the true but unknown mean cycle time for the existing process and μ_2 is the true but unknown mean cycle time for the proposed process. Comparing with the expressions in Table 9.13 this corresponds to a one-tail test with $a = 0$. Assume that a significance level of 5 percent will be used for this test.

Using the sample data, calculate $\bar{x}_1 = 7.418$, $\bar{x}_2 = 6.586$, $s_1^2 = 2.450$, and $s_2^2 = 7.981$. The test score is then calculated as follows.

TABLE 9.14 Cycle Times for a Proposed New Process Design

2.7	10.5	5.7	9.5	3.3	8.8	7.1	11.8	5.5	7.6
5.8	5.5	4.0	2.8	5.1	6.1	3.5	2.8	11.3	6.1
8.9	11.5	2.2	7.2	7.7	7.9	5.5	5.6	4.2	7.7
9.5	2.7	6.1	7.8	4.2	8.8	3.9	11.0	8.3	8.6
11.3	2.2	8.8	7.5	2.0	3.9	9.8	2.9	8.2	7.9

$$Z = \frac{7.418 - 6.586}{\sqrt{\dfrac{2.450}{50} + \dfrac{7.981}{50}}} = 1.82$$

From the Normal distribution table in the Appendix, one can obtain $Z_{0.05} = 1.645$. Because $Z > Z_{0.05}$, the null hypothesis can be rejected. This conclusion is reached at the confidence level of 95 percent.

The Data Analysis Toolpack of Microsoft Excel provides a tool for performing hypothesis testing directly on an electronic spreadsheet. Assume that the data in Table 9.11 are copied onto an Excel spreadsheet in the range A1:A50. Also assume that the data in Table 9.14 are copied onto the same Excel spreadsheet in the range B1:B50. Select the Data Analysis item in the Tools menu. Then select *t*-Test: Two-Sample Assuming Unequal Variances. Note that at this point one cannot choose the *Z* test, because this test assumes that the variances are known. The estimates of the variance could be entered in the corresponding text boxes; however, it is preferable to let Excel calculate the variances and use the *t* statistic. (Recall that the values of the *t* distribution with more than 30 degrees of freedom are similar to the values of the standard Normal distribution.) Figure 9.23 shows the completed dialogue for the selected *t* test. Table 9.15 shows the results of the *t*-test.

The *t* statistic of 1.822 is identical to the *Z* statistic that was used before. The *t* critical one-tail value of 1.665 is similar to $Z_{0.05} = 1.645$. The one-tail test shows the rejection of the null hypothesis. It also shows that the null hypothesis would not be rejected at a significance level of 3.6 percent (see the $P(T \le t)$ one-tail value in Table 9.15). The two-tail test shows that the null hypothesis $\mu_1 - \mu_2 = 0$ cannot be rejected because the *t* statistic (1.822) falls within the range $(-1.992, 1.992)$. The two-tail null hypothesis would be rejected at a level of significance of 7.2 percent (as specified by the two-tail *p*-value in Table 9.15).

FIGURE 9.23 Excel Dialogue for a t Test of the Difference Between Two Population Means

TABLE 9.15 *t*-Test: Two-Sample Assuming Unequal Variances

	Variable 1	*Variable 2*
Mean	7.418	6.586
Variance	2.450	7.981
Observations	50	50
Hypothesized mean difference	0	
Degrees of freedom	76	
t Stat	1.822	
P(T ≤ *t*) one-tail	0.036	
t Critical one-tail	1.665	
P(T ≤ *t*) two-tail	0.072	
t Critical two-tail	1.992	

9.6 Summary

This chapter presented some basic statistical analysis tools for input and output simulation data. On the input side, it was shown how goodness-of-fit tests can be employed to determine suitable distributions for random variables such as interarrival times and processing times. The chapter also explored the mechanics involved in the generation of uniformly distributed random numbers and random variates from well-known distributions.

On the output side, the focus was placed on the problem of estimation and hypothesis testing. These tools are necessary to be able to draw valid conclusions with respect to the performance of business processes.

9.7 References

Khoshnevis, B. 1994. *Discrete systems simulation.* New York: McGraw-Hill.

Law, A. M., and W. D. Kelton. 2000. *Simulation modeling and analysis,* 3rd edition. Boston: McGraw-Hill.

9.8 Exercises

1. Use the chi-square goodness-of-fit test and a significance level of 0.1 to test the set of interarrival times in Table 9.16 for possible fit to the Exponential distribution.
2. Use the chi-square goodness-of-fit test and a significance level of 0.05 to test the set of service times in Table 9.17 for possible fit to the Normal distribution.
3. An analyst is interested in determining whether the Weibull distribution with parameters $\alpha = 6$ and $\beta = 10$ is a good fit to the data set in Table 9.18. Use Microsoft Excel to perform a chi-square goodness-of-fit test to help the analyst make a decision.

TABLE 9.16 Interarrival Times for Exercise 1

1.9	5.3	1.1	4.7	17.8	44.3
9.0	18.9	114.2	47.3	47.1	11.2
60.1	38.6	107.6	56.4	10.0	31.4
58.6	5.5	11.8	62.4	24.3	0.9
44.5	115.8	2.0	50.3	21.1	2.6

TABLE 9.17 Service Times for Exercise 2

8.9	13.6	21.6	20.8	19.9	20.6
21.0	27.7	10.0	27.7	13.1	25.5
22.7	33.9	14.5	29.0	9.9	26.8
18.7	17.3	14.1	29.0	14.2	24.3
31.2	25.3	27.3	23.4	18.4	20.0

TABLE 9.18 Data Set for Exercise 3

11.14	11.11	8.24	7.52	9.53	10.85
6.10	7.13	9.83	12.23	9.97	8.05
11.18	7.62	10.41	9.33	7.41	7.48
6.81	9.03	9.09	8.62	10.23	9.87
8.46	10.87	8.52	9.74	9.60	9.40
10.30	10.95	8.09	11.45	10.45	6.99
9.74	7.66	8.30	6.11	5.08	12.38
11.77	9.52	9.52	6.59	10.32	4.19
5.69	11.09	11.31	9.18	8.19	9.07
8.51	9.39	10.00	10.10	9.10	12.00

4. Use the Kolmogorov-Smirnov test to examine under the significance level of 0.01 whether the observations in Table 9.19 are random numbers uniformly distributed between 0 and 1.
5. Apply the Kolmogorov-Smirnov test to the data in Exercise 1.
6. Apply the Kolmogorov-Smirnov test to the data in Exercise 2.
7. Consider the data in Exercise 4. Perform the runs test to determine with a 95 percent confidence level whether or not the numbers in the sequence (ordered by rows) are independent.
8. The data set in Table 9.20 consists of cycle times of jobs in a given process. Perform the runs test to determine with a 99 percent confidence level whether or not the cycle times (ordered by columns) are independent.
9. Starting with a seed of 3,461, generate 10 four-digit random numbers using the mid-square method.
10. Use the linear congruential method with parameters $Z_0 = 79, a = 56214, c = 17$, and $m = 999$ to generate 10 three-digit random numbers.
11. Perform the following tests on the numbers generated in Exercise 10.
    a. Test for randomness using Kolmogorov-Smirnov with a significance level of 0.05.
    b. Test for independence using the runs test with a 0.05 level of significance.

TABLE 9.19 Data Set for Exercise 4

0.385	0.855	0.309	0.597	0.713	0.660
0.137	0.396	0.238	0.657	0.583	0.194

TABLE 9.20 Cycle Times for Exercise 8

10.76	18.73	10.55	8.17	17.42	15.22
8.54	13.09	13.53	14.30	12.32	10.75
12.52	25.10	18.23	14.71	13.23	8.22
10.19	20.39	12.80	36.53	14.14	11.34
13.35	13.88	11.06	29.41	14.78	10.97

TABLE 9.21 Probability Distribution for Exercise 12

Value	Probability
5	0.12
6	0.28
7	0.27
8	0.33

TABLE 9.22 WIP Data for Exercise 14

26	31	27	29	27
28	28	27	28	26
28	27	31	32	24
25	25	29	28	28
27	26	23	30	25
31	26	25	27	30
29	25	30	30	27
27	26	25	23	27

12. Use the data in Exercise 4 to generate random variates from the discrete probability distribution function in Table 9.21.

13. Use the data in Exercise 4 to generate random variates from an Exponential distribution with a mean of 25.

14. The data set in Table 9.22 represents the work-in-process (WIP) at the end of a day for a 40-day simulation of a given business process. Find a 99 percent confidence interval for the mean WIP.

15. An analyst has suggested a new design for the process in Exercise 14. A simulation of the proposed process yielded the WIP values in Table 9.23. Test the hypothesis that the new process has a mean WIP that is less than the average of the old process. Assume a 5 percent significance level.

16. With a preliminary simulation of 10 days of operation of an emergency room, an analyst found the results, shown in Table 9.24, in terms of the average number of patients waiting. Suppose the analyst would like to estimate the average number of patients waiting with a 95 percent confidence interval whose total width is four patients. Calculate the number of times the model must be run to be able to construct the desired confidence interval.

17. (Adapted from Khoshnevis, 1994) The management of a major ski resort wants to simulate the rental program during the high season. The resort has two types of customers: people who pay cash and people who use a credit card. The interarrival times of these customers is exponentially distributed with means of 130 seconds and 60 seconds, respectively. After

TABLE 9.23 WIP Data for Exercise 15

25	21	21	24	27
24	23	25	26	24
25	26	29	24	23
26	24	26	24	28
28	17	21	26	26
26	27	26	22	23
25	29	25	19	20
27	22	22	25	25

TABLE 9.24 Data for Exercise 16

Day (run number)	Average No. of Patients	Day (run number)	Average No. of Patients
1	23	6	19
2	45	7	32
3	12	8	8
4	21	9	14
5	31	10	5

arrival, customers must fill out a waiver form. The time taken to fill out the waiver form is normally distributed with a mean of 60 and a standard deviation of 20 seconds.

After filling out the form, customers get in line to pay. Time to pay depends on the method of payment. The time required to pay in cash is uniformly distributed between 30 and 45 seconds; the time required to pay by credit card is uniformly distributed between 90 and 120 seconds.

Three types of rental equipment—boots, skis, and poles—are rented in that order in frequency. Not everyone rents all three types of equipment because some people already have some of the equipment. After paying, 80 percent of the people rent boots, 10 percent go directly to skis, and the rest only rent poles. At the boot counter, an employee takes a normally distributed time with a mean of 90 and a standard deviation of 5 seconds to obtain the boots for each customer. The time to try the boots is uniformly distributed between 60 and 240 seconds. About 20 percent of the people need a different size boot; the rest go to get their skis.

At the ski rental counter, everyone waits until a resort employee is free to obtain the right size ski, which takes a uniformly distributed time between 45 and 75 seconds. Twenty percent of these people need their bindings adjusted. The binding-adjustment process is exponentially distributed with a mean of 180 seconds. (The binding-adjustment process is considered separately in terms of staffing.) Seventy percent of the people go on to get poles; the rest leave. Ninety percent of the people who get their bindings adjusted go on to get poles, and the rest leave. At the station where the poles are rented, service is normally distributed with a mean of 60 and a standard deviation of 10 seconds.

a. Assume that one employee is located in each service station (one at the cash register, one at the boots counter, one at the skis counter, and one at the poles). Simulate this process for 60 days and collect the daily average cycle time. Set a 95 percent confidence interval with the data collected during the simulation.

b. Test the hypothesis (using a 5 percent significance level) that a difference in the mean cycle time results when one employee is added to the boots counter.

c. Test the hypothesis (using a 5 percent significance level) that a difference in the mean cycle time results when one employee is added to the ski counter.

d. Test the hypothesis (using a 5 percent significance level) that a difference in the mean cycle time results when two employees are added, one to the boots counter and one to the ski counter.

18. The management of a mortgage company has decided, with limited information, that the company can save money if it reduces its staff size. Before downsizing, management asks you to model the credit application process to provide reassurance that service will not be severely affected by the reduction in staff.

The mortgage company currently employs three loan agents, two of whom perform an initial review of credit applications and a third who performs a second review of the applications that fail the initial review. The second review is performed in an attempt to correct the deficiencies by contacting the originating party. The process has the following characteristics.

- Approximately four to eight credit applications (and most likely six) arrive every hour.
- It takes 12 to 16 minutes to complete the first review.
- About 20 percent of the applications fail the first review.

- It takes 25 to 35 minutes to complete the second review.
- About 50 percent of the applications fail the second review.

    Your task is to compare the performance of the current process with the performance of the process with two loan agents. For the downsized process, management wants the two remaining loan agents to work in either of the two reviewing steps. That is, the loan agents are not assigned to the first or second review step, but rather they perform initial or second reviews as needed.

a. Create a simulation model of the current process. Use the Triangular distribution to model the arrivals of credit applications and the Rectangular distribution for the reviewing times.

b. Simulate the process for 45 working days. (A working day is 8 hours of operation.) For each day, collect the average utilization of loan agents and the average cycle time.

c. Modify the model to simulate the downsized process. Repeat part b for the new model.

d. Use the runs test to determine whether the utilization average values are independent at a significance level of 0.05. Perform the same test for the cycle time averages. If the observations are independent, then perform a test of hypotheses to determine whether the overall mean utilization has changed from the current to the proposed process. Perform the same test for the overall average cycle time.

C A S E S

Simulation Project: Improving the X-Ray Process at County Hospital

County Hospital wishes to improve the service level of its regular X-ray operation, which runs from 8 A.M. to 8 P.M. Patients have identified the total required time as their main concern with this process. Management, on the other hand, is concerned with utilization of available resources. Management has created a process-improvement team to study this problem. The process might be redesigned as a result of the team's recommendations.

The team has defined the entry point to the X-ray process to be the instant a patient leaves the physician's office en route to the X-ray lab. The exit point has been defined as the instant at which the patient and the completed X-ray enter the physician's office.

Broadly speaking, two types of patients arrive to the X-ray process: emergency and nonemergency patients (priority levels 1 and 2, respectively). The emergency patients arrive according to a Poisson process with a mean of four patients per hour. The nonemergency patients are registered as they enter, and a sample of the arrival time data is provided in Table 9.25. Until now, no attempt has been made to further analyze this data, so there is no insight into what the arrival process looks like.

The team has identified 12 activities in the current X-ray process (see Table 9.26), which is the same irrespective of the patient type. The only differences between patient categories are the activity times and their distributions, specified in Table 9.27.

The patient priority levels determine the service order of all the X-ray activities. Emergency patients (priority 1) come first at the expense of nonemergency patients (priority 2). However, after service is started, it will never be interrupted to benefit a high-priority patient.

The resource data for the X-ray process is specified in Table 9.28. The orderlies will always take one patient back from the X-ray lab when they have dropped one off. Assume that the transportation time back from the X-ray lab is exactly the same as the transportation time to the X-ray lab. If no patient is ready to go back, the orderly will wait for 5 minutes; if no patient becomes available during this time, the orderly will return to the ward without a patient. The time for an orderly to walk back without a patient is always 5 minutes. The orderlies will never go and pick up a patient at the X-ray area without bringing another patient with them from the ward.

PART I: ANALYZING THE CURRENT PROCESS DESIGN

1. Draw a flowchart of the current X-ray process.
2. Develop a simulation model of this process.

   - The model requires analysis of input data regarding the arrival process of nonemergency patients.
   - *Modeling Hint:* For batching and unbatching, use the blocks Batch and Unbatch from the Discrete Event library with the option Preserve Uniqueness checked.
   - *Modeling Hint:* Build the model incrementally based on your flowchart. Do not try to put everything together at once and then test whether it works. The key is to use individual, small steps.
   - As a first check that everything works as it is supposed to, it is often useful to run a shorter simulation with animation. Use different symbols for different types of items, such as different types of labor and different types of jobs.

3. As a first-cut analysis, run a 1-day simulation with the random seed set at 100, using

TABLE 9.25 Sample Arrival Times of Nonemergency Patients

Patient No.	Time of Arrival (in min. from time 0)	Patient No.	Time of Arrival (in min. from time 0)
1	6.30	31	197.89
2	10.13	32	205.50
3	17.07	33	215.42
4	17.09	34	219.95
5	23.94	35	223.50
6	26.06	36	233.33
7	27.65	37	234.89
8	29.21	38	239.20
9	41.65	39	244.29
10	44.69	40	247.29
11	49.79	41	249.90
12	60.07	42	250.25
13	70.34	43	256.34
14	70.73	44	257.90
15	74.32	45	268.97
16	84.59	46	276.82
17	91.77	47	280.43
18	95.78	48	281.94
19	98.20	49	293.23
20	117.24	50	293.57
21	122.85	51	299.79
22	130.58	52	303.75
23	137.46	53	306.58
24	139.76	54	308.13
25	142.52	55	314.06
26	150.70	56	322.84
27	151.95	57	326.51
28	154.74	58	338.21
29	157.48	59	339.91
30	193.25	60	365.79

the correct activity time distributions. Look at the average cycle time, the throughput rate, the resource, the queue, and the activity statistics. What are the problems in this process?

4. Simulate 30 days of operation and compute the cycle time and daily throughput (average and standard deviation). Also compute the activity and resource utilization statistics and queue statistics with 95 percent confidence intervals. (Use the Statistics blocks in the Discrete Event library of Extend.)

Assume that any patients remaining in the system at the end of the day will be taken care of by the night shift. Every morning, the system is assumed to be empty. Are there any surprises when you compare these results with the ones in question 3?

5. Assess the performance of the process using the values calculated in question 4. Where is the bottleneck? What is the problem area in terms of reducing the cycle time and increasing the throughput rate?

TABLE 9.26 Activities in the Current X-Ray Process

Activity	Description	Type
1	Patient leaves physician's office with instructions.	Start of the X-ray process
2	Patient is taken to the lab by an orderly, on foot, in wheelchair, or lying in bed.	Transportation
3	The patient is left in the waiting area outside the X-ray lab in anticipation of an X-ray technician.	Waiting
4	An X-ray technician fills out a standard form based on information supplied by the physician and the patient (done outside the X-ray lab). The technician then leaves the patient, who queues up in front of the X-ray labs.	Business value-adding
5	The patient enters the X-ray lab, undresses, and an X-ray technician takes the required X-rays (all done in the X-ray lab).	Value-adding
6	A darkroom technician develops the X-rays. (Assume that the patient and the X-ray technician accompany the X-rays.)	Value-adding
7	The darkroom technician and the X-ray technician check the X-rays for clarity. (Assume that the patient accompanies his/her X-rays.)	Inspection
8	If X-rays are not clear, the patient returns to the waiting room in anticipation of repeating steps 5, 6, and 7. Historically, the probability of rejecting X-rays has been 25%. If the X-rays are acceptable, the patient proceeds to activity 9 and the X-rays are put in the outbox, where eventually the messenger service will pick them up.	Decision
9	Patient waits for an orderly to take him/her back to the physician's office.	Waiting
10	Patient is taken back to the physician's office by an orderly	Transportation
11	A messenger service transfers the X-rays to the physician's office in batches of five jobs.	Transportation
12	Patient and X-ray enter physician's office together.	End

PART II: SUGGEST AND EVALUATE A NEW PROCESS DESIGN

6. Based on your insight about the current operations, identify a plausible way of reducing the average cycle time by redesigning the process. For example: What happens if the X-ray technician no longer has to stay with the patient while the X-rays are developed? What if the messenger batch size changes? Is the messenger service necessary? What if more personnel are hired? What type of personnel would be most useful?

TABLE 9.27 Resource Data for X-Ray Process

Resource	Activities	No. of Units Available
Orderlies	2 and 10	3
X-ray technician	4, 5, 6, and 7	3
X-ray lab	5	2
Darkroom technician	6 and 7	2
Darkroom	6	1

TABLE 9.28 Activity Times for X-Ray Process

Activity	Patient Type	Activity Time Distribution	Parameter Values (in min.)
1	All types	Not Applicable	Not Applicable
2	Emergency patients	Uniform	Max = 9, Min = 5
	Nonemergency patients	Uniform	Max = 12, Min = 5
3	All types	Not Applicable	Not Applicable
4	All types	Uniform	Max = 6, Min = 4
5	Emergency patients	Normal	$\mu = 9, \sigma = 4$
	Nonemergency patients	Normal	$\mu = 11, \sigma = 4$
6	All types	Normal	$\mu = 12, \sigma = 5$
7	All types	Constant	Value = 2
8	All types	Constant	Value = 0
9	All types	Not Applicable	Not Applicable
10	Emergency patients	Uniform	Max = 9, Min = 5
	Nonemergency patients	Uniform	Max = 12, Min = 5
11	All types	Uniform	Max = 7, Min = 3
12	All types	Not Applicable	Not Applicable

7. Investigate the performance of the redesigned process in terms of the cycle time and the daily throughput. Also look at the resource and activity utilization statistics and queue statistics with 95 percent confidence intervals as before. What are your conclusions? Is the new design significantly better than the old process with regards to the cycle time and throughput? Are any drawbacks obvious?

10

Optimizing Business Process Performance

After a simulation model has been developed to represent an existing or proposed business process, one might want to find the configuration that is best (according to some performance measure) among a set of possible choices. For simple processes, finding the best configuration might be easy. In the queuing example in Section 7.2 in Chapter 7, the system can be simulated with one underwriting team, and measures of performance (e.g., percentage of requests that wait for more than 10 minutes) can be calculated. Then the simulation can be run again with two underwriting teams, and the new values can be calculated. Finally, a decision about the optimal number of underwriting teams can be made by calculating the marginal increase in service compared to the marginal increase in cost.

When processes are complex and the configuration depends on a number of strategic choices, the trial-and-error approach can be applied with only limited success. Consider, for example, a supermarket with nine cash registers. Suppose the manager wants to find the optimal staffing level in a 10-hour period; that is, the manager would like to determine how many cash registers to open during each period in order to optimize the checkout process according to a specified measure of service. At the same time, the manager might be faced with budget constraints that prevent overstaffing the system. With a simulation model of the supermarket and a quantifiable definition of the performance criterion, an optimizer (such as Extend's Evolutionary Optimizer) can be invoked to search for the best configuration (as determined by a set of values for input factors to the simulation model). Optimizers are designed to search for configurations that meet the user's constraints while maximizing or minimizing the value of an objective function. The number of possible configurations in this case is large ($9^{10} \approx 3.5$ billion), rendering the enumeration of all possible combinations impractical.

This chapter is devoted to exploring how process performance can be optimized when a simulation model is available. The use of Extend's Evolutionary Optimizer, which has the ability to search for optimal values of the input parameters of simulation models, is introduced.

10.1 Introduction to Optimization by Evolutionary Computation

In most simulation models, some variables can be controlled, such as the ratio of generalists to specialists in a credit application process or the processing priority rules in an insurance underwriting process. These control variables are called decision

375

variables. Finding the optimal values for these decision variables is an important goal of decision making.

Obtaining these optimal values generally requires that one search in an iterative or ad hoc fashion. This involves running a simulation for an initial set of values, analyzing the results, changing one or more values, re-running the simulation, and repeating this process until a satisfactory solution is found. This process can be tedious and time-consuming even for small models, and it is often not clear how to adjust the values from one simulation to the next.

A more rigorous method would enumerate all possible alternatives systematically. Although this approach would guarantee an optimal solution (i.e., the values for the decision variables that achieve the best outcome), it has limited application. Suppose a simulation model depends on only two decision variables. If each variable has 10 possible values, trying each combination requires 100 simulations (10^2 alternatives). If each simulation were short (e.g., 2 seconds), then the entire process would be completed in approximately 3 minutes of computer time.

However, if instead of two variables the model depends on six, then trying all combinations would require 1 million simulations (10^6 alternatives), or approximately 23 days of computer time. A complete enumeration could easily take weeks, months, or even years to carry out.

Optimizers based on evolutionary computation—such as Extend's Evolutionary Optimizer, Evolver[1], and OptQuest[2]—overcome the limitations of ad hoc and enumerative methods by searching intelligently for optimal solutions to simulation models. An optimization problem can be described in the optimizer's interface, and then it can search for the optimal solution given a predefined objective (i.e., a measure of process performance). In almost all cases, these optimizers will find an optimal or near-optimal solution among large sets of possible alternatives efficiently, even when exploring only a small fraction of them.

The idea of applying the biological principle of natural evolution to artificial systems was introduced in the early 1970s. Usually grouped under the term *evolutionary algorithms* or *evolutionary computation*, one finds the domains of genetic algorithms, evolution strategies, evolutionary programming, genetic programming, and scatter search. Evolutionary algorithms have been applied successfully to numerous problems from different domains, including optimization, machine learning, economics, social systems, ecology, population genetics, studies of evolution, and learning.

An evolutionary algorithm is an iterative procedure that consists of a constant-size population of individuals, each one represented by a finite string of symbols, known as the genome, encoding a possible solution in a given problem space. This space, referred to as the search space, comprises all possible solutions to the problem at hand. Generally speaking, genetic algorithms are applied to spaces that are too large to be searched exhaustively (such as those in combinatorial optimization).

The standard evolutionary algorithms proceed as follows: An initial population of individuals is generated at random or heuristically. At every evolutionary step, known as a generation, the individuals in the current population are decoded and evaluated according to some predefined quality criterion, referred to as the fitness, or fitness function. To form a new population (the next generation), individuals are selected according to their fitness. Many selection procedures are currently in use, one of the simplest being Holland's original fitness-proportionate selection, in which

---

[1]Evolver is a trademark of Palisade Corporation, Newfield, NY (www.palisade.com).
[2]OptQuest is a trademark of OptTek Systems Inc., Boulder, CO (www.opttek.com).

individuals are selected with a probability proportional to their relative fitness. This ensures that the expected number of times an individual is chosen is approximately proportional to its relative performance in the population. Thus, high-fitness ("good") individuals stand a better chance of "reproducing," and low-fitness ones are more likely to disappear.

Genetically inspired operators are used to introduce new individuals into the population (i.e., to generate new points in the search space). The best known of such operators are crossover and mutation. Crossover is performed with a given probability between two selected individuals, called parents, by exchanging parts of their genomes (encoding) to form two new individuals called offspring; in its simplest form, substrings are exchanged after a randomly selected crossover point. This operator tends to enable the evolutionary process to move toward promising regions of the search space. The mutation operator is introduced to prevent premature convergence to local optima by randomly sampling new points in the search space. Mutation entails flipping bits at random with some (small) probability. Evolutionary algorithms are stochastic iterative processes that are not guaranteed to converge to the optimal solution; the termination condition can be specified as some fixed, maximal number of generations or as the attainment of an acceptable fitness level for the best individual.

As noted, the problem with optimization algorithms based on evolutionary computation stems from the inability to tell when the optimal solution has been found, or even if the optimal solution has been simulated. A good approach within Extend is to allow the optimization to continue for an "adequate" amount of time and check to see if the population of solutions converges. After that, the user could try the optimization procedure several times to make sure the answers from several optimization runs agree or are close.

10.2 Optimizing Processes

Traditional search methods work well when finding local solutions around a given starting point or when model data are precisely known. However, these methods fail when searching for global solutions to real-world problems that contain a significant amount of uncertainty, as in the case of most business processes. Recent developments in optimization have produced efficient search methods, such as those based on evolutionary computation, capable of finding optimal solutions to complex problems involving elements of uncertainty.

The Evolutionary Optimizer incorporates metaheuristics to guide its search algorithm toward improved solutions. *Metaheuristics* is the term used to describe a family of optimization approaches that includes genetic algorithms, simulated annealing, tabu search, and others (including hybrids). The particular approach embedded in the evolutionary optimizer uses the evolutionary computation paradigm outlined in the previous section. Because this technique does not use the hill-climbing approach of simple optimizers, it typically does not get trapped in local optimal solutions, and it does not get thrown off course by noisy (uncertain) model data.

After an optimization problem is described (by selecting decision variables and the objective, and possibly by imposing constraints), the evolutionary optimizer runs the simulation to evaluate the output for different sets of decision variable values. The evolutionary optimizer uses the outputs of the current and previous runs to determine a new set of values for the decision variables to evaluate. This is an iterative process that successively generates new sets of values and runs the simulation to measure their performance (in terms of maximizing profits or minimizing costs, for example).

Not all of these values improve the objective, but over time this search provides a trajectory to the best solutions. The search process continues until the evolutionary optimizer reaches some termination criteria, specified in the Optimizer Parameters tab of the Evolutionary Optimizer block from the Optimization submenu of the Generic library.

When optimizing the performance of a business process, analysts are faced with many difficult decisions; such decisions include staffing or operational policies and might involve thousands or millions of potential alternatives. As mentioned previously, considering and evaluating each of the alternatives would be impractical or perhaps impossible. A simulation model can provide valuable assistance in analyzing decisions and finding good solutions. Simulation models capture the most important features of a problem and present them in a form that is easy to interpret. Models often provide insights that intuition alone cannot provide. In order to optimize a simulation model, one must formulate an optimization model, which is a model that seeks to maximize or minimize some quantity, such as profit or cost. Optimization models consist of three major elements: decision variables, constraints, and an objective.

- *Decision variables:* Quantities that the decision maker can control; for example, the number of people to employ, the number of dollars to allocate among different resources, or the operational rule to use from a set of alternatives. Decision variables are selected from the dialogues of blocks such as the Labor Pool block. If a decision is important in the context of a given process, this decision must be linked to a value that appears in the dialogue of a block used in the simulation model. The optimization model can be formulated in terms of the decision variables that are selected (by cloning the variable, as explained later). The values of the decision variables selected change with each trial simulation until the best value for each is found during the optimization run.
- *Constraints:* Relationships among decision variables that restrict the values of the decision variables. For example, a constraint might ensure that the total amount of money allocated among various resources cannot exceed a specified amount, or that at least a specified minimum number of nurses are assigned to the emergency room of a hospital at a given time. Constraints restrict the possible values for the decision variables. For example, if the total annual labor budget for a process with two resources (labeled R1 and R2) is $500,000, the following constraint could be added to the optimization model.

$$20,000 \times R1 + 10,000 \times R2 \leq 500,000$$

Here, it is assumed that each R1 resource costs $20,000 per year, and each R2 resource costs $10,000 per year. It also is assumed that R1 and R2 are initial values in separate Labor Pool blocks and that they have been cloned to be added to the Evolutionary Optimizer block. Given this constraint, combinations of values for the two resource variables whose sum is $500,000 or less are considered during the optimization run.

Not all optimization models need constraints; however, those that do must deal with the distinction between a feasible and an infeasible solution. A feasible solution is one that satisfies all constraints. An optimization model is infeasible when no combination of values of the decision variables can satisfy the set of constraints. Note that a solution (i.e., a single set of values for the decision variables) can be infeasible if it fails to satisfy the problem constraints, but this doesn't imply that the problem or model itself is infeasible. For example, suppose that in a business process with two resource types, R1 and R2, one insists on finding an optimal configuration that meets the following constraints.

$$R1 + R2 \leq 4$$
$$R1 + R2 \geq 5$$

Clearly, no combination will make the sum of the units of R1 and the units of R2 no more than 4 and at the same time greater than or equal to 5. Infeasible problems can be made feasible by fixing the inconsistencies of the relationships modeled by the constraints. For a constrained problem, the optimal solution is the best solution that satisfies all constraints.

- *Objective:* A mathematical representation of the optimization model's objective, such as maximizing profit or minimizing cost, in terms of the decision variables. Each optimization model has one objective function that represents the model's goal mathematically. The optimizer's job is to find the optimal value of the objective by selecting different values for the decision variables. When model data are uncertain and can only be described using probability distributions, the objective itself will have some probability distribution for any set of decision variables. This probability distribution can be found by performing statistical analysis on the values of the output variable of interest. For example, a plotter can be used to create a frequency distribution of cycle time values if these values are used to calculate the objective function.

A conceptualization of an optimization model is shown in Figure 10.1. The solution to an optimization model provides a set of values for the decision variables that optimizes (maximizes or minimizes) the associated objective (e.g., a measure of process performance). If the world were simple and the future were predictable, all data in an optimization model would be constant (making the model deterministic), and techniques such as linear and nonlinear programming could be used to find optimal solutions.

However, a deterministic optimization model can't capture all the relevant intricacies of a practical decision environment. When model data are uncertain and can only be described probabilistically, the objective will be a random variable that follows an unknown probability distribution for any chosen set of decision variables. An optimization model with uncertainty has several additional elements including the following.

FIGURE 10.1 Conceptualization of an Optimization Model

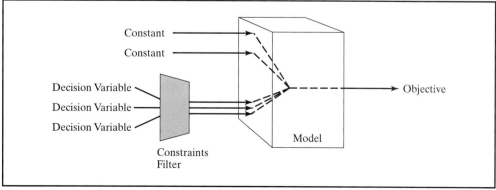

- *Assumptions:* Capture the uncertainty of model data using probability distributions. Assumptions are modeled primarily by choosing appropriate probability distributions in Input Random Number or Import blocks.
- *Output Variables:* Capture values of interest such as waiting time, cycle time, and resource utilization. Output variables typically are represented by frequency distributions.
- *Output Statistics:* Summary values of an output variable, such as the mean, standard deviation, or variance. The optimization can be controlled by maximizing, minimizing, or restricting output statistics, such as the average waiting time or the maximum queue length.
- *Requirements:* Relationships among output variables. Requirements are basically constraints that involve output variables. The Evolutionary Optimizer does not allow the user to set requirements, but other optimizers such as OptQuest do.

Figure 10.2 shows a conceptualization of an optimization model with uncertainty. This figure shows that instead of constant data, the assumptions turn the calculation of the objective function into a stochastic evaluation. For example, if average processing times are used to calculate the cycle time of a process, the result is a deterministic model that uses constant values to estimate performance. However, if probability distributions are used to estimate processing times, then the cycle time calculation becomes a stochastic evaluation performed with a simulator.

The steps for adding optimization to an Extend simulation are as follow.

1. Open an existing simulation model or develop one for which to optimize performance by changing the values of some decision variables.
2. Open the Optimization library by clicking on the Library menu, selecting the Open Library command, and then selecting the Generic library.
3. Place an Evolutionary Optimizer block on the model by clicking on the Optimization submenu of the Generic library and selecting the Evolutionary Optimizer.
4. Define a cost or profit equation (also called the objective function) to optimize.
5. Determine which parameters are needed for that equation.
6. Drag the needed variables onto the closed Evolutionary Optimizer block on the model.
7. Set the limits for the chosen decision variables in the Optimizer's Variables table (within the Set Cost tab).

FIGURE 10.2 Conceptualization of an Optimization Model with Uncertainity

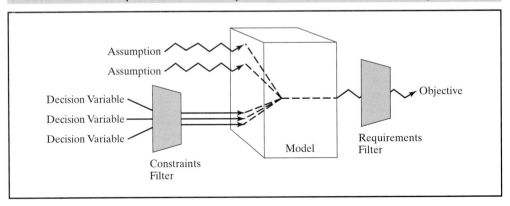

8. Write the profit or cost equation in the Optimizer's dialogue.
9. Add appropriate constraint equations in the Constraints tab.
10. Set the optimizer defaults for either a random or nonrandom model.
11. Click on the Results tab, and then click on the New Run button.

The following tutorial illustrates these steps.

10.3 Process Optimization Tutorial

A business process consists of 10 activities as illustrated in the flowchart in Figure 10.3. Four resource types perform these activities: clerks, agents, technicians, and supervisors. As shown in Figure 10.3, some activities require more than one resource type; for example, a technician and a supervisor perform activity F.

The process manager would like to minimize cycle time but would not like to add resources in a way that such resources would become underutilized. Therefore, the process manager also would like to set limits on the number of resources of each type and an overall limit on the total number of resources. The manager's optimization problem can be summarized as follows.

Minimize   Average cycle time
Subject to   Clerks + Technicians + Supervisors + Agents ≤ 12
             $1 \leq$ Clerks ≤ 10
             $1 \leq$ Technicians ≤ 10
             $2 \leq$ Supervisors ≤ 5
             $1 \leq$ Agents ≤ 10

Figure 10.4 shows an Extend simulation model of the process depicted in Figure 10.3. The model uses hierarchical blocks to simulate groups of activities. The hierarchical blocks contain the Stack, Batch, Unbatch, Transaction, Merge, and Decision blocks that are necessary to model the flow of jobs and resources in the process. The model uses four labor pools, one for each resource type. The labor pools are labeled Clerks, Technicians,

FIGURE 10.3 **Business Process with Multiple Resource Types**

FIGURE 10.4 Extend Model of Process in Figure 10.3 with an Evolutionary Optimizer Block

Supervisors, and Agents. Only three out of the four labor pools are shown in Figure 10.4, because the pool of agents is within the H, I, and J hierarchical block.

For the purpose of this tutorial, assume that the simulation model has been built already and that optimization is to be added. The first step consists of adding the Evolutionary Optimizer block to the model. This block is in the Optimization submenu of the Generic library. After the block has been inserted in the simulation model, the optimization problem needs to be modeled. The optimization model consists of four decision variables, the objective function, and one constraint. Therefore, the next step is to add the decision variables to the Evolutionary Optimizer block. The variables are added with the clone layer tool. (See Figure 10.5.)

The clone layer tool clones dialogue items and allows the cloned items to be placed in other parts of the model. For example, the utilization rate of a labor pool can be cloned and placed next to the Labor Pool block. When the model is run, changes in the utilization rate of the labor pool can be seen without opening the block dialogue. The clone tool is used to create a copy of the initial value for each labor pool in the model. The dialogue of the Labor Pool that models the supervisors is shown in Figure 10.6.

To clone the initial value of the available supervisors and add it as a decision variable in the Evolutionary Optimizer block, select the Clone Layer tool and click-drag the Initial Value item to the Evolutionary Optimizer block. Do the cloning four times to add the initial value of supervisors, clerks, agents, and technicians as decision variables in the Evolutionary Optimizer block. Next, add the average cycle time to the Evolutionary Optimizer block to be able to formulate the objective function. The average cycle time is calculated in the Timer block. (See dialogue in Figure 10.7.)

To add the average cycle time to the Evolutionary Optimizer dialogue, select the Clone Layer tool and click-drag the Average Delay time item. Next, add the bounds

FIGURE 10.5 Clone Tool in the Extend Toolbar

FIGURE 10.6 Labor Pool Block Dialogue for Supervisors

FIGURE 10.7 Timer Block Dialogue

on the decision variables and formulate the objective function. This is done in the Evolutionary Optimizer block dialogue. The bounds are added in the Min Limit and Max Limit columns of the Set Cost tab. No bounds are associated with the average cycle time, because this variable holds an output value from the simulation model and not a decision variable. Descriptive names can be given to the variables by clicking on the corresponding row of the Equation Var column. These names cannot contain spaces or special characters, but they can contain underscores. The objective function has the form MinCost = Avg_Cycle_Time; to indicate the desire to minimize

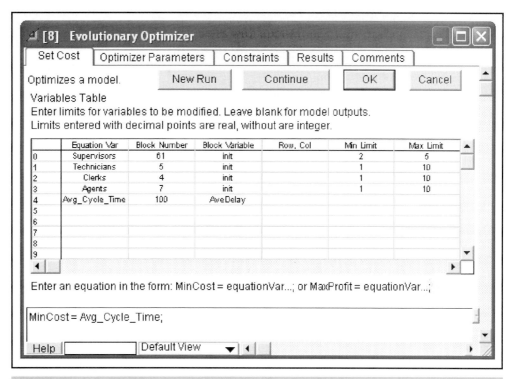

FIGURE 10.8 Set Cost tab of the Evolutionary Optimizer Block Dialogue

the value of Avg_Cycle_Time (average cycle time.) The completed dialogue is shown in Figure 10.8.

To complete the formulation, the constraint that restricts the total number of workers to no more than 12 needs to be added. Constraints are added in the Constraints tab of the Evolutionary Optimizer dialogue. Extend has two types of constraints: constraints on individual variables and global constraints. A global constraint is a relationship that involves more than one decision variable. Therefore, the constraint that limits the number of total workers in the process is a global constraint. Figure 10.9 shows the Constraints tab of the Evolutionary Optimizer block.

FIGURE 10.9 Global Constraint to Model Limit in the Total Number of Workers

FIGURE 10.10 Parameter Settings for the Evolutionary Optimizer

To formulate a global constraint in Extend, choose Global Constraint from the drop-down menu and use the Reject system variable to establish the appropriate logic. For example, in Figure 10.9, Extend is instructed to reject solutions for which the sum of the variables Supervisors, Technicians, Clerks, and Agents exceeds 12.

The optimization model is now completed, and the search for the optimal values for the decision variables can begin. The search is controlled by a set of parameter values. Extend provides a fair amount of flexibility in terms of setting these values for particular optimization problems. Fortunately, Extend includes two default parameter settings for models with random elements (such as those used for business process design). The parameter settings are labeled Quicker Defaults, Random Model and Better Defaults, Random Model, as shown in Figure 10.10.

The Quicker Defaults are meant for optimization runs where reasonably good solutions are desired within a short amount of computer time. For better solutions, Better Defaults is used; however, the computational time increases. After selecting either the Quicker or the Better defaults, click on the New Run button to begin the search. During the search, Extend displays the Results tab and the Optimization Value plot. The Results tab (Figure 10.11) shows the population of solutions ordered from best to worst. These results were found using the Quicker Defaults.

FIGURE 10.11 Results Tab Showing Ordered Population

	Supervisors	Technicians	Clerks	Agents	Avg_Cycle_Time	MinCost
0	4	1	3	4		52.9621528475
1	4	1	3	4		53.99746079
2	4	1	3	4		54.0358345691
3	4	1	3	4		54.1042293139
4	4	1	3	4		54.1265870618
5	4	1	3	4		54.320716679
6	4	1	3	4		54.5965376515
7	4	1	3	4		55.0688691632
8	4	1	3	4		55.3377167507
9	4	1	2	4		55.6748812157

FIGURE 10.12 Optimization Value Plot

The solutions in Figure 10.11 are all the same except for the last one; however, because they were obtained in different simulation runs, the average cycle time values are not all the same. Given that the last solution employs a total of only 11 employees, it would be worthwhile to test both solutions (i.e., with 2 and 3 clerks) by performing longer runs several times and testing for significant differences between the two staffing levels. The statistical tests discussed in Chapter 9 can be used to determine whether a significant reduction in average cycle time is achieved when the process employs 3 clerks instead of 2.

The Optimization Value plot (see Figure 10.12) shows the search trajectory; that is, the objective function value of the best solution found during the current optimization run. Because the problem is to minimize the average cycle time, the trajectory shows a downward trend as the optimization search progresses. This plot also shows the convergence rate, which is a value between 0 percent and 100 percent that indicates the similarity of the objective function values of the best and worst solutions in the population.

The Optimization Value plot in Figure 10.12 has two scales in the *y*-axis. The first scale (on the left) refers to the objective function value, that is, the average cycle time in this case. The second scale (on the right) refers to the convergence. The plot shows that the population converged (with a convergence value of 95.61 percent) after 51 generations.

10.4 Alternative Optimization Models

In the tutorial of the previous section, it was assumed that the process manager was interested in minimizing the average cycle time subject to some limits in the number of individual resources and an overall limit on the total amount of resources. This is just one optimization model among several possible variations. For example, the manager might wish to minimize the average cycle time subject to a budget constraint. In this case, the global constraint would limit the amount of money instead of the number of people. Because the simulation model of this example is set up for one working week, it would be possible to try to optimize performance subject to a weekly labor cost budget. Suppose the budget is $8,500 and the weekly salaries are $500 for a clerk, $650 for a technician, $700 for an agent, and $790 for a supervisor. The resulting constraint would be:

$$500 \times \text{Clerks} + 650 \times \text{Technicians} + 790 \times \text{Supervisors} + 700 \times \text{Agents} \leq 8,500$$

Now suppose the manager is as concerned with minimizing the average cycle time while maintaining a reasonable level of resource utilization. Ideally, the manager would like to use a constraint that rejects solutions in which the utilization of the resources does not satisfy a desired minimum level. However, Extend does not allow setting constraints on output variables—that is, variables that hold output values, such as average cycle time or resource utilization. Therefore, in order to achieve the desired balance between customer service (modeled as an average cycle time minimization) and resource utilization, the objective function needs to be reformulated. Because it is desirable to minimize the average cycle time and also to maximize the minimum utilization, a possible objective function is:

$$\text{Minimize} = \frac{\text{Average cycle time}}{\text{Minimum utilization}}$$

If two solutions exist with approximately the same average cycle time, then the objective function will give preference to the solution that has the larger minimum utilization. The minimum utilization is given by the resource that is utilized the least.

10.5 Summary

This chapter introduced the notion of optimizing simulations. In recent years, this has been a relevant and exciting research topic. Coupling metaheuristic optimizers and simulation modeling has resulted in powerful tools for designing effective business processes.

After an introduction to metaheuristic optimization, a tutorial was presented that shows how to set up optimization models using the Evolutionary Optimizer block within Extend. The Clone Layer tool is needed to create a connection between the variables in the simulation model and the variables used for optimization in the Evolutionary Optimizer. The Evolutionary Optimizer is fairly simple to use; however, one must keep in mind that any metaheuristic optimizer can converge to a suboptimal solution, particularly if it is not run long enough. Extend recommends that at least 100 generations are used, and the model should be run several times with convergence to the same or near solution. Finally, longer confirmation runs should be performed with the proposed solution before that solution is put into practice.

10.6 References

Imagine That Inc. 2003. *Extend User's Guide,* Version 6. www.imaginethatinc.com.

10.7 PROCESS MODELING AND SIMULATION PROJECTS

This chapter concludes with two small simulation-optimization projects. The goals of the projects are to create a simulation model of the process and to apply the Evolutionary Optimizer block to optimize key input parameters to the model.

10.7.1 STAFFING A PROCESS WITH MULTIPLE JOB TYPES

A process is designed to handle three types of jobs. Jobs arrive about every 10 minutes, with interarrival times following an Exponential distribution. About 60 percent of the jobs are type 1, about 30 percent of the jobs are type 2, and about 10 percent of the jobs are type 3. The process consists of 10 activities (labeled A to J), and each job is routed according to its type, as shown in Table 10.1.

The activity times depend on each job type. The probability distribution of times and the resource (employee) type needed to perform each activity are fixed for all job types. Table 10.2 summarizes the time and resource data associated with each activity.

Currently, four Type-I employees are employed, and they are paid $1,250 per week. Five Type-II employees each earn $750 per week. Finally, two Type-III employees each earn $500 per week. A cost is associated with cycle times greater than 80 minutes. In particular, if the cycle time for a type-1 job is greater than 80 minutes, a $10 late fee must be paid. The late fees for type-2 and 3 jobs are $200 and $300, respectively.

1. Create a simulation model of this process that will run for 5 days of 10 working hours.
2. Considering that the payroll for this process cannot exceed $10,000 per week, find the staffing levels for each employee type that minimize total late fees. Analyze the frequency distribution of cycle times.

TABLE 10.1 Job Routing

Job	Routing
1	A, B, D, F, H, I, and J
2	B, C, D, E, G, H, and J
3	A, C, E, G, H, and I

TABLE 10.2 Process Time Data

Activity	Employee Type	Probability Distribution	Parameters per Job Type 1	Parameters per Job Type 2	Parameters per Job Type 3
A	I	Exponential	10		17
B	II	Normal	(8, 1)	(10, 2)	
C	I	Normal		(8, 2)	(10, 3)
D	III	Gamma	(5, 0.5)	(7, 2)	
E	II	Rectangular		(3, 5)	(6, 9)
F	III	Exponential	12		
G	III	Exponential		7	9
H	I	Rectangular	(10, 15)	(12, 21)	(8, 12)
I	III	Gamma	(4, 1)		(10, 3)
J	I	Normal	(10, 1)	(9, 1)	

Exponential: Mean
Normal: (Mean, Standard deviation)
Gamma: (Scale, Shape) with Location = 0
Rectangular: (Min, Max)

3. A consultant has suggested that a priority system should be used for this process. Specifically, she suggests changing the priority rule in the queues from FIFO to a system where type-3 jobs have highest priority, followed by type-2 jobs, and finally type-1 jobs. Would this change improve the performance of the process?
4. If the objective were to minimize total cost (payroll plus late fees), would you expect the solution for question 2 to be the best? Use the Evolutionary Optimizer to find the best staffing allocation.

10.7.2 LOAN APPLICATIONS

The following description is for a loan application approval process. Loan amounts tend to be large; therefore, some require several days to be reviewed and approved. When a loan is approved, the loan company begins to collect interest. The company's profit is based on the interest it collects, so it is imperative that processing time be reduced to a minimum.

1. Loan applications are sent into a main office by loan officers at a random rate of five per day. It is not possible to predict exactly how many will arrive every day, but the interarrival time is believed to be exponentially distributed. A clerk checks the loan applications for completeness. This check takes about 48 minutes (a time that is also exponentially distributed). After the application passes the initial check, it is forwarded, using interoffice mail, to a processing team. Interoffice mail takes 0.5 days 50 percent of the time, 1 day 25 percent of the time, 1.5 days 12.5 percent of the time, and 2 days 12.5 percent of the time. The time required to process an application by a single person follows a Triangular distribution with a minimum of 1 day, a most likely time of 1.5 days, and a maximum of 2 days. (A day consists of 8 working hours.) Determine the most efficient staffing levels at the initial check and at the processing task.
2. Consider now that loan applications are broken into five types based on their dollar value. The percentages of each type are shown in Table 10.3 along with their corresponding processing time distribution (actual dollar values are not important at this point, and time is given in 8-hour days).

   Three labor pools for processing loan applications are formed under the current process. The application types that can be handled by each pool are shown in Table 10.4.

   Determine the most efficient staffing levels at the initial check and at the processing task. The staffing levels at the processing task must be given by number of employees in each processing pool.

TABLE 10.3 Job Data

Type	Percentage	Probability Distribution
1	5	Exponential (3.5)
2	15	Exponential (2.75)
3	20	Triangular (2.5, 3.25, 4)
4	25	Triangular (2, 2.375, 2.75)
5	35	Triangular (1, 1.5, 2)

TABLE 10.4 Labor Pool Data

Pool	Type(s)
1	1
2	2
3	3, 4, 5

3. The clerks at the initial check may find that some applications have not been filled in correctly or are missing some information. Historically, 95 percent of type-1 applications are correct, 92 percent of type 2 are correct, 90 percent of type 3 are correct, 85 percent of type 4 are correct, and 80 percent of type 5 are correct. When an application is missing information or has incorrect information, it is sent back to the originator, a process that takes 1 day 25 percent of the time, 2 days 50 percent of the time, and 3 days 25 percent of the time. The number of working days includes the time required to send the application back to the field office, the time required for the loan officer to correct the application, and the time required to send it into the main office again. Find efficient staffing levels for this process.

4. It has been discovered that applications that contain errors are simply put back into the processors' stacks after they have been corrected. Management suggests that the processors handle those applications at a higher priority. Should rework be treated at a higher priority by the processors?

5. A committee has proposed the use of an expert work flow automation system that will eliminate all problems with applications; implement Electronic Data Interchange (EDI); and reduce processing time for type-1 applications by 30 percent, type-2 applications by 33 percent, type-3 applications by 40 percent, type-4 applications by 60 percent, and type-5 applications by 75 percent. Top management has concluded that productivity must be factored into the labor cost calculations, and has decided that cost is determined by the following formula.

$$\text{Labor cost} = (\text{number of workers} \\ \times \text{ the time worked} \\ \times \text{ daily labor rate}) \\ / \text{ utilization}$$

Labor rates for loan processors depend upon the loan type they process. Rates are as follows: type-1 loan processors receive \$350 per day, type 2 receive \$200 per day, type 3 receive \$175 per day, type 4 receive \$150 per day, and type 5 receive \$100 per day. How much should management be willing to pay for the new technology, given the opportunities for staff reduction?

Process Benchmarking with Data Envelopment Analysis

Data envelopment analysis (DEA), introduced by Charnes, Cooper, and Rhodes (1978), is a linear programming method for calculating relative efficiencies of a set of organizations that possess some common functional elements but whose efficiency may vary due to internal differences. One main difference, for instance, might be the management style employed in each organization. In DEA, organizations are referred to as decision-making units (DMUs).

DEA has generated a fair amount of interest in the academic world and among practitioners because it has been applied successfully to assess the efficiency of various organizations in the public and private sectors. The popularity of the technique is evident by the increasing number of articles in scientific journals and the popular press. A search of DEA on the Internet results in hundreds of pages that make reference to this methodology[1]. Recently, DEA has been used as a tool for benchmarking. This chapter discusses the application of DEA to business process benchmarking. When data envelopment analysis is used for benchmarking processes, the process becomes the decision-making unit. Therefore, the terms *DMU* and *process* are used interchangeably throughout this chapter.

DEA considers a process as a black box and analyzes inputs and outputs to determine relative efficiencies. The black-box model (or transformation model) is depicted in Figure 11.1 (see also Section 1.1.2 and Figure 1.1), where possible inputs to and outputs from a process are as follows.

Inputs

- Full-time equivalent (FTE) employees
- Office space
- Regular hours
- Overtime hours
- Operating expenses
- Number of computers
- Number of telephone lines

---

[1] www.csv.warwick.ac.uk/~bsrlu/dea/dea1.htm is one of the most complete DEA pages on the Internet.

FIGURE 11.1 Black Box Model of a Process

Outputs

- Cycle time
- Cycle time efficiency
- Throughput rate
- Capacity utilization
- Customer rating
- On-time deliveries

Using the black-box approach, the efficiency of a process can be calculated with a simple ratio when there is a single input and a single output.

$$\text{Efficiency} = \frac{\text{Output}}{\text{Input}}$$

However, when a process uses multiple inputs and produces multiple outputs, it becomes more difficult to evaluate its efficiency.

Example 11.1

Suppose labor cost and throughput rate are considered a single input and output of a business process, respectively. The efficiency of two processes, say A and B, can be obtained easily as shown in Table 11.1.

Clearly, process A is more efficient than process B, because A is able to complete 0.75 jobs for every dollar spent in labor, but B can complete only 0.733 jobs per dollar. However, the manager of process B might not agree with this assessment, because that manager might argue that efficiency is more directly affected by office space than it is by direct labor costs. The efficiency assessment in this case might be as shown in Table 11.2.

The new assessment shows that process B is more efficient than process A when office space is considered the single input to this process. More realistically, both inputs should be used to compare the efficiency of processes A and B.

TABLE 11.1 Efficiency Calculation Based on Direct Labor Costs

Process	Labor Cost ($/week)	Throughput (jobs/week)	Efficiency (jobs/$)
A	$2,000	1,500	0.750
B	$1,500	1,100	0.733

TABLE 11.2 Efficiency Calculation Based on Office Space

Process	Office Area (ft²)	Throughput (jobs/week)	Efficiency (jobs/ft²)
A	10,000	1,500	0.15
B	6,900	1,100	0.16

The DEA approach offers a variety of models in which multiple inputs and outputs can be used to compare the efficiency of two or more processes. This chapter is limited in scope to the ratio model, which is based on the following definition of *efficiency*.

$$\text{Efficiency} = \frac{\text{Weighted sum of outputs}}{\text{Weighted sum of inputs}}$$

Suppose this definition is used to compare the efficiency of the processes in Example 11.1 by considering that the labor cost is twice as important as the cost of office space. In this case, the efficiency of each process can be calculated as follows.

$$\text{Efficiency (Process A)} = \frac{1,500}{2,000 \times 2 + 10,000 \times 1} = 0.107$$

$$\text{Efficiency (Process B)} = \frac{1,100}{1,500 \times 2 + 6,900 \times 1} = 0.111$$

The chosen weights make process B more efficient than process A, but the manager of process A could certainly argue that a different set of weights might change the outcome of the analysis. The manager's argument is valid, because the weights were chosen arbitrarily. Even if the weights were chosen prudently, it would be almost impossible to build consensus about these values among all process owners. This is why DEA models are based on the premise that each process should be able to pick its own "best" set of weights. However, the weight values must satisfy the following conditions.

- All weights in the chosen set should be strictly greater than 0.
- The set of weights cannot make any process more than 100 percent efficient.

Suppose the owner of process A in Example 11.1 chooses a weight of 0.25 for labor cost and 0.1 for office area. This set of weights makes process A 100 percent efficient.

$$\text{Efficiency (Process A)} = \frac{1,500}{2,000 \times 0.25 + 10,000 \times 0.1} = 1$$

However, the set of weights is not "legal" when used to compare the efficiency of process A with the efficiency of process B, because the weights result in an efficiency value for process B that is more than 100 percent.

$$\text{Efficiency (Process B)} = \frac{1,100}{1,500 \times 0.25 + 6,900 \times 0.1} = 1.033$$

As seen in this example, the weight values can be "legal" or "illegal," depending on the processes that are being compared. Also, the efficiency of one process depends on the performance of the other processes that are included in the set. In other words, DEA is a tool for evaluating the relative efficiency of decision-making units; therefore, no conclusions can be drawn regarding the absolute efficiency of a process when applying this technique.

Typical statistical methods are characterized as central tendency approaches because they evaluate processes relative to the performance of an average process. In contrast, DEA is an extreme point method that compares each process with only the "best" processes.

A fundamental assumption in an extreme point method is that if a given process A is capable of producing *Out*(A) units of output with *In*(A) units of input, then other processes also should be able to do the same if they were to operate efficiently. Similarly, if process B is capable of producing $Out(B)$ units of output with $In(B)$ units of input, then other processes also should be capable of the same production efficiency. DEA is based on the premise that processes A, B, and others can be combined to form a composite process with composite inputs and composite outputs. Because this composite process does not necessarily exist, it typically is called a virtual process.

The heart of the analysis lies in finding the best virtual process for each real process. If the virtual process is better than the real process by either making more output with the same input or making the same output with less input, then the real process is declared inefficient. The procedure of finding the best virtual process is based on formulating a linear program. Hence, analyzing the efficiency of n processes consists of solving a set of n linear programming problems.

11.1 Graphical Analysis of the Ratio Model

Before describing the linear programming formulation of the ratio model, the ratio model will be examined for the case of a single input and two outputs. This special case can be studied and solved on a two-dimensional graph.

Example 11.2

Suppose one would like to compare the relative efficiency of six processes (labeled A to F) according to their use of a single input (labor hours) and two outputs (throughput rate and customer service rating). The relevant data values are shown in Table 11.3. (For the sake of this illustration, do not consider the relative magnitudes and/or the units of the data values.)

The ratio model can be used to find out which processes are relatively inefficient and also how the inefficient processes could become efficient. In order to answer these questions, first calculate two different ratios: (1) the ratio of throughput with respect to labor and (2) the ratio

TABLE 11.3 Input and Output Data for Example 11.2

Process	*Labor*	*Throughput*	*Rating*
A	10	10	10
B	15	30	12
C	12	36	6
D	22	25	16
E	14	31	8
F	18	27	7

TABLE 11.4 Independent Efficiency Calculations

Process	$x = \dfrac{\textit{Throughput}}{\textit{Labor}}$	$y = \dfrac{\textit{Customer Rating}}{\textit{Labor}}$
A	1	1
B	2	0.8
C	3	0.5
D	1.136	0.727
E	2.214	0.571
F	1.5	0.389

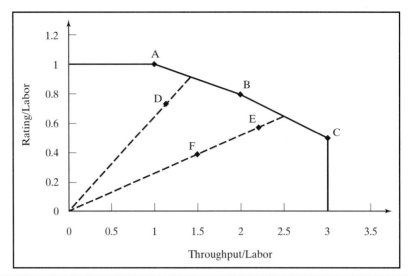

FIGURE 11.2 Efficient Frontier for Example 9.2

of customer rating with respect to labor. Table 11.4 shows the values of the independent efficiency ratios, where the first ratio is labeled *x* and the second ratio is labeled *y*.

The x and y values are used in Table 11.4 to plot the relative position of each process in a two-dimensional coordinate system. The resulting graph is shown in Figure 11.2.

Figure 11.2 shows the efficient frontier of this benchmarking problem. Processes that lie on the efficient frontier are nondominated, but not all nondominated processes are efficient. A nondominated process is such that no other process can be at least as efficient in all the different performance measures and strictly more efficient in at least one performance measure. The nondominated processes that are in the outer envelope of the graph define the efficient frontier. Under this definition, processes A, B, and C characterize the efficient frontier in Figure 11.2. These also are called the relatively efficient processes. Note that A is better than B and C in terms of the y-ratio, but it is inferior to both of those processes in terms of the x-ratio. Also note that E is a nondominated process that is not efficient, because it does not lie on the efficient frontier.

This graphical analysis has helped answer the question about the relative efficiency of the processes. A, B, and C are relatively efficient processes, and D, E, and F are relatively inefficient. The term *relatively* efficient or inefficient is used because the efficiency depends on the processes that are used to perform the analysis. In order to clarify this issue, suppose a process G is added with $x = 2.5$ and $y = 1$. This addition makes process B relatively inefficient, because the revised envelope moves farther up (i.e., in the direction of the positive y values) relative to the original processes. In the absence of such a process, B is relatively efficient.

11.1.1 EFFICIENCY CALCULATION

Relatively efficient processes (i.e., those on the efficient frontier) are considered to have 100 percent efficiency under the ratio model. What is the relative efficiency value of a process that is relatively inefficient? To answer this question, analyze the situation depicted in Figure 11.3.

This figure shows a relatively inefficient process P0 with coordinates (x_0, y_0) and relatively efficient processes P1 and P2 with coordinates (x_1, y_1) and (x_2, y_2), where $x = \dfrac{\text{output1}}{\text{input}}$ and $y = \dfrac{\text{output2}}{\text{input}}$. Because processes P1 and P2 are relatively efficient,

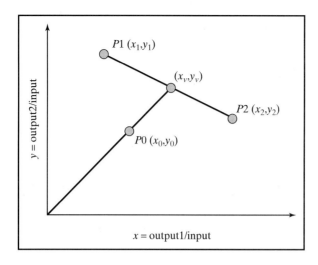

FIGURE 11.3 Projection of a Relatively Inefficient Process

their efficiency value is 100 percent. Also, because the line going from the origin to process P0 intersects the line from process P1 to process P2, these two processes are known as the peer group (or reference set) of process P0.

The efficiency associated with process P0 is less than 100 percent, because this process is not on the efficient frontier. The efficiency of process P0 is the distance from the origin to the (x_0, y_0) point divided by the distance between the origin and the virtual process with coordinates (x_v, y_v). To calculate the efficiency of process P0, it is necessary to first calculate the coordinates of the virtual (and efficient) process. This can be done using the following equations.

$$a = \frac{y_2 - y_1}{x_2 - x_1}$$

$$b = \frac{x_2 y_1 - x_1 y_2}{x_2 - x_1}$$

$$x_v = \frac{b}{\dfrac{y_0}{x_0} - a}$$

$$y_v = ax_v + b$$

Then the efficiency of process P0 is given by:

$$E_0 = \sqrt{\frac{x_0^2 + y_0^2}{x_v^2 + y_v^2}}$$

To illustrate the use of these equations, consider process D in Tables 11.3 and 11.4 and Figure 11.2. This process is relatively inefficient, and its peer group consists of processes A and B. First, the coordinates of the virtual process corresponding to the real process D can be calculated.

$$a = \frac{y_B - y_A}{x_B - x_A} = \frac{0.8 - 1}{2 - 1} = -0.2$$

$$b = \frac{x_B y_A - x_A y_B}{x_B - x_A} = \frac{2 \times 1 - 1 \times 0.8}{2 - 1} = 1.2$$

$$x_V = \frac{b}{\dfrac{y_D}{x_D} - a} = \frac{1.2}{\dfrac{0.727}{1.136} + 0.2} = 1.428$$

$$y_V = ax_V + b = -0.2 \times 1.428 + 1.2 = 0.914$$

The coordinates of the efficient virtual process allow the calculation of the relative efficiency of process D.

$$E_0 = \sqrt{\frac{x_D^2 + y_D^2}{x_V^2 + y_V^2}} = \sqrt{\frac{1.136^2 + 0.727^2}{1.428^2 + 0.914^2}} = \sqrt{\frac{1.819}{2.875}} = 0.795$$

The relative efficiency of process D is 79.5 percent. Process D can become relatively efficient by moving toward the efficient frontier. The movement does not have to be along the line defined by the current position of process D and the origin; in other words, process D does not have to become the virtual process that was defined to measure its relative efficiency. Because process D can become efficient by moving toward the efficiency frontier, process D can become efficient in an infinite number of ways. These multiple possibilities involve a combination of using less input to produce more output or producing more output with the same input.

This analysis shows that DEA is not only able to identify relatively inefficient units, but it also is capable of setting targets for these units so they become relatively efficient. When used in the context of benchmarking processes, DEA identifies the best practice processes and also gives the inefficient processes numerical targets to achieve efficiency relative to their peers.

One can calculate a set of targets for process D in Example 11.2, first based on fixing the labor hours and then fixing the throughput and customer ratings. If the labor hours remain fixed, then process D must increase its output to the following values in order to move to the efficient frontier.

$$\text{Throughput} = x_V \times \text{labor} = 1.428 \times 22 = 31.4$$
$$\text{Rating} = y_V \times \text{labor} = 0.914 \times 22 = 20.1$$

This means that if throughput is increased from 25 to 31.4, customer ratings are increased from 16 to 20.1, and the labor hours remain at 22, process D becomes relatively efficient by moving to the coordinates of its corresponding virtual process on the efficient frontier. The process also can move to the coordinates of the virtual process by using fewer resources to produce the same output. The new input can be calculated as follows.

$$\text{Labor} = \frac{\text{Throughput} + \text{Customer ratings}}{x_V + y_V} = \frac{25 + 16}{1.428 + 0.914} = 17.5$$

Therefore, process D becomes relatively efficient if it reduces its input from 22 to 17.5.

11.2 Linear Programming Formulation of the Ratio Model

The ratio model introduced in the previous section is based on the idea of measuring the efficiency of a process by comparing it to a hypothetical process that is a weighted linear combination of other processes. Relative efficiency was measured as the weighted sum of outputs divided by the weighted sum of inputs.

The main assumption in the previous illustrations was that this measure of efficiency requires a common set of weights to be applied across all processes. This assumption immediately raises the question of how such an agreed-upon common set of weights can be obtained. Two kinds of difficulties can arise in obtaining a common set of weights. First, it might simply be difficult to value the inputs or outputs. For example, different processes might choose to organize their operations differsently so that the relative values of the different outputs are legitimately different. This perhaps becomes clearer if one considers an attempt to compare the relative efficiency of schools with achievements in music and sports among the outputs. Some schools might legitimately value achievements in sports or music differently to other schools. Therefore, a measure of efficiency that requires a single common set of weights is unsatisfactory.

The DEA model recognizes the legitimacy of the argument that processes might value inputs and outputs differently and therefore adopts different weights to measure efficiency. The model allows each process to adopt a set of weights, which shows it in the most favorable light in comparison to the other processes.

The DEA ratio model, in particular, is formulated as a sequence of linear programs (one for each process) with the following characteristics.

Maximize the efficiency of one process
Subject to the efficiency of all processes ≤ 1

The variables in the model are the weights assigned to each input and output. A linear programming formulation of the ratio model that finds the best set of weights for a given process p is:

$$\text{Maximize} \quad \sum_{j=1}^{q} out(j,p) \times wout(j)$$

Subject to

$$\sum_{i=1}^{m} in(i,k) \times win(i) = 1$$

$$\sum_{j=1}^{q} out(j,k) \times wout(j) - \sum_{i=1}^{m} in(i,k) \times win(i) \leq 0 \qquad \text{for } k = 1,\dots,n$$

$$wout(j) \geq 0.0001 \qquad\qquad\qquad\qquad\qquad \text{for } j = 1,\dots,q$$

$$win(i) \geq 0.0001 \qquad\qquad\qquad\qquad\qquad\; \text{for } i = 1,\dots,m$$

The decision variables in this model are:

$wout(j)$ = the weight assigned to output j
$win(i)$ = the weight assigned to input i

Because there are m inputs and q outputs, the linear program consists of $m + q$ variables. The data are given by the following.

$out(j,k)$ = the amount of output j produced by process k
$in(i,k)$ = the amount of input i used by process k

The linear programming model finds the set of weights that maximizes the weighted output for process p. This maximization is subject to forcing the weighted input for process p to be equal to 1. The efficiency of all units also is restricted to be less than or equal to 1. Therefore, process p will be efficient if a set of weights is found such that the weighted output also is equal to 1. Because all weights must be strictly greater than 0, the last two sets of constraints in the model force the weights to be at least 0.0001.

Using the data in Table 11.3, the linear programming model can be formulated and used to calculate the relative efficiency of process D.

$$\text{Maximize} \quad 25 \times wout(1) + 16 \times wout(2)$$

$$
\begin{aligned}
\text{Subject to} \quad & 22 \times win = 1 \\
& 10 \times wout(1) + 10 \times wout(2) - 10 \times win \leq 0 \\
& 30 \times wout(1) + 12 \times wout(2) - 15 \times win \leq 0 \\
& 36 \times wout(1) + 6 \times wout(2) - 12 \times win \leq 0 \\
& 25 \times wout(1) + 16 \times wout(2) - 22 \times win \leq 0 \\
& 31 \times wout(1) + 8 \times wout(2) - 14 \times win \leq 0 \\
& 27 \times wout(1) + 7 \times wout(2) - 18 \times win \leq 0 \\
& wout(1), \ wout(2), \ win \geq 0
\end{aligned}
$$

In the formulation of the DEA model for process D, this process is allowed to choose values for the weight variables that will make its efficiency calculation as large as possible. However, these values cannot be 0 and cannot make another process more than 100 percent efficient. The constraint that forces the efficiency of process A to be less than or equal to 1:

$$10 \times wout(1) + 10 \times wout(2) - 10 \times win \leq 0$$

is equivalent to:

$$\frac{10 \times wout(1) + 10 \times wout(2)}{10 \times win} \leq 1$$

However, a linear constraint is the standard form for formulating restrictions in a linear programming model.

From solving this problem graphically, it is known that no values for $wout(1)$, $wout(2)$, and win can make process D 100 percent efficient without violating at least one of the constraints. (If this is not convincing, give it a try.)

For benchmarking problems with processes that use several inputs and outputs, the DEA models typically are solved using specialized software. These packages provide a friendly way of capturing the problem data, and they automate the task of solving the linear programming problem for each process.

11.3 Excel Add-In for Data Envelopment Analysis

This section describes an add-in to Microsoft Excel that can be used to perform data envelopment analysis. The DEA solver consists of two files: dea.xla and deasolve.dll[2]. Perform the following steps in order to install the add-in for Microsoft Excel.

1. Create a new folder on the hard drive. For example, create the new folder dea inside the Program Files directory.
2. Copy the files dea.xla and deasolve.dll onto the dea folder that was just created.
3. Open the Microsoft Excel application and select Add-Ins. . . from the Tools menu.
4. Click on the Browse. . . button and change the directory to the dea folder. Select dea.xla and press OK.
5. The Data Envelopment Analysis tool should appear in the list of add-ins. Make sure that the box next to the DEA Add-In is checked and press OK.

The DEA add-in is now available under the Tools menu. The DEA Add-In has two options: New Model and Run Model. The use of the DEA Add-In is illustrated with the data from Example 11.2. (See Table 11.3.) This illustration will start with the creation of a new DEA model as illustrated in Figure 11.4.

The New Model option of the DEA Add-In opens a dialogue window where the following data must be entered.

- Name of the model
- Number of decision-making units (or processes)
- Number of input factors
- Number of output factors

The completed dialogue window for this example appears in Figure 11.5.

After pressing OK on the New Model dialogue window, the DEA Add-In creates two new worksheets: Example.Input and Example.Output. The model data are entered

FIGURE 11.4 Creating a New DEA Model

---

[2]These files are located in the Excel directory of the CD accompanying this book.

FIGURE 11.5 New Model Dialogue Window

in the corresponding cells for each worksheet. The labels of each table can be modified to fit the description of the current model. Figure 11.6 shows the completed Output sheet for this example. The Input sheet is filled out similarly.

After the Input and Output worksheets have been filled out, the Run Model option of the DEA Add-In can be selected. The Run Model dialogue window appears, displaying the following analysis options.

Efficiency: This output consists of a table displaying the efficiency of each decision-making unit (or process in this case) along with the peer group for relatively inefficient processes. A relatively efficient process has no peer group. By default, this is the only output that the DEA Add-In produces.

Best Practice: This is a table that ranks decision-making units according to their average efficiency. It also displays the weight values associated with each input and output. The average efficiency is obtained by applying the weight values to each decision-making unit. The rationale is that the best practice units are relatively efficient regardless of the set of weights used to measure their performance.

FIGURE 11.6 Completed Example: Output Worksheet

The best practice calculations can be used to detect processes that are relatively efficient only due to an uncharacteristic set of weight values.

Targets: For each relatively inefficient process, this worksheet displays a set of target input and output values that can make the process relatively efficient. As mentioned before, theoretically, an infinite number of target values can turn a relatively inefficient process into a relatively efficient process. In practice, however, certain values cannot be changed easily. For example, if the location of a process is an input in the analysis, changing this value might not be feasible in practice. More sophisticated analysis can be performed to find target values for some inputs or outputs within specified value ranges while keeping values for other inputs and outputs fixed.

Virtual Outputs: This option creates a worksheet and a chart. The worksheet shows the total weighted output for each process. The total weighted output is 100 for relatively efficient processes. The total output for other processes is equal to their efficiency value. The virtual value for output j and process k is calculated as follows.

$$out(j, k) \times wout(j, k)$$

where $out(j,k)$ is the value for output j corresponding to process k from the Output worksheet, and $wout(j,k)$ is the weight for output j of process k from the Best Practice worksheet. The Virtual Output chart graphically shows the contribution of each output to the total output of each process. The processes in the chart are ordered by their corresponding efficiency values.

Duals[3]: This information is relevant only to relatively inefficient processes. The dual values for relatively efficient processes are 0. For the relatively inefficient processes, the dual values that are not 0 correspond to the constraints associated with a peer process. The dual values are used to create a virtual process for a relatively inefficient process. The values in the Target worksheet correspond to the virtual process created with the dual values. Below, we show this calculation using the data from Example 11.2.

After checking all the boxes in the Run Model dialogue window and pressing OK, the DEA Add-In creates six new worksheets:

- Example.Efficiency
- Example.Best Practice
- Example.Target
- Example.Virtual Outputs
- Example.VO Chart
- Example.Dual

Figure 11.7 shows the table in the Example.Efficiency worksheet. As was shown graphically in Figure 11.2, processes A, B, and C are relatively efficient, and the other three processes are relatively inefficient. In Section 11.1.1, the relative efficiency of

---

[3]This terminology comes from linear programming, where duality theory roughly establishes that for each primal model with n variables and m constraints, there exists a dual model with m variables and n constraints. The dual variables of the ratio model give the necessary information to create a virtual process for a relatively inefficient process. When the real process is relatively efficient, no virtual process can be more efficient than the real one; therefore, the dual values are equal to 0.

FIGURE 11.7 Efficiency Worksheet

process D was calculated as 0.795, a value that the DEA Add-In finds by solving the linear programming formulation of the ratio model. Figure 11.2 shows that processes A and B are the peer group of process D, and the DEA Add-In confirms this finding. Likewise, the peer group for processes E and F is confirmed as consisting of processes B and C.

Figure 11.8 shows the table in the Example.Best Practice worksheet. This table shows that process B is robust in terms of its relative efficiency. Regardless of the set of weights, process B yields a relative efficiency equal to 1. If the efficiency of process B is calculated using its chosen weights, 100 percent efficiency is obtained.

$$\text{Efficiency} = \frac{30 \times 1.42857 + 12 \times 4.76190}{15 \times 6.66667} = 1$$

FIGURE 11.8 Best Practice Worksheet

In the same way, it can be easily verified that the efficiency of process B is still 1 if any of the set of weights preferred by other processes are used.

Process C has the next-best average efficiency. This process has a relative efficiency of 1 when using its preferred set of weights (8.33333 for labor, 1.78571 for throughput, and 5.95238 for customer ratings). Its average efficiency is not equal to 1 because for some other set of weights, process C is not 100 percent efficient. For example, when applying the set of weights preferred by process A to process C, the following efficiency value is obtained.

$$\text{Efficiency} = \frac{36 \times 1.66667 + 6 \times 8.33333}{12 \times 10} = 0.9166$$

Process B not only has the best average efficiency but also appears in all the peer groups for relatively inefficient processes. (See Figure 11.7.) Process C appears in two out of three peer groups, and process A appears in one.

Figure 11.9 shows the target values for the relatively inefficient processes. These targets are calculated using the dual values in the Example.Dual worksheet.

Consider process D. The peer group for this process consists of processes A and B. The corresponding dual values for these processes are 1.0 and 0.5 (given in the Example.Dual worksheet not shown here). A weighted combination of processes A and B creates the virtual process that corresponds to the real process D. The input and outputs for the virtual process are as follows.

Labor = dual(A) × labor(A) + dual(B) × labor(B) = 1 × 10 + 0.5 × 15 = 17.5
Throughout = 1 × 10 + 0.5 × 30 = 25
Ratings = 1 × 10 + 0.5 × 12 = 16

The resulting target for process D is the input-oriented target calculated in Section 11.1.1.

FIGURE 11.9 Target Worksheet

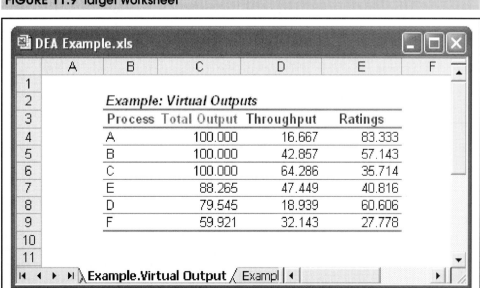

Process	Total Output	Throughput	Ratings
A	100.000	16.667	83.333
B	100.000	42.857	57.143
C	100.000	64.286	35.714
E	88.265	47.449	40.816
D	79.545	18.939	60.606
F	59.921	32.143	27.778

FIGURE 11.10 Virtual Output Worksheet

Figures 11.10 and 11.11 show the Virtual Output worksheet and the associated chart. The table consists of one column for the total weighted output and one column for the contribution of each output to the total. There is one row for each process in the set. The total weighted output is simply the numerator of the efficiency calculation in the ratio model. In other words, the total output for a process is the sum of the products of each output times its corresponding weight. The output values are given in the Example.Output worksheet, and the weight values are contained in the Example.Best Practice worksheet.

The weighted throughput and ratings values for process B are calculated as follows.

$$\text{Weighted throughput} = 1.42857 \times 30 = 42.857$$
$$\text{Weighted customer rating} = 4.76190 \times 12 = 57.143$$

The bars in the virtual output chart of Figure 11.11 represent the total output for each process. The processes are ordered from maximum to minimum total output. It already has been determined that process B is not only relatively efficient but also represents the best practice process. This process has a balanced total output with almost equal contribution from throughput and customer ratings. In contrast, process A, which is also relatively efficient, obtains most (83.3 percent) of its output from customer ratings. This unbalanced output results in a lower best-practice ranking for process A.

11.4 DEA in Practice

The benefits of applying DEA are well documented. Sherman and Ladino (1995) report their experiences with the application of DEA in a bank. The analysis resulted in a significant improvement in branch productivity and profits while maintaining service quality. The analysis identified more than $6 million of annual expense savings not identifiable with traditional financial and operating ratio analysis. The DEA models were used to compare branches objectively to identify the best-practice branches (those on the efficient frontier), the less-productive

FIGURE 11.11 Virtual Output Chart

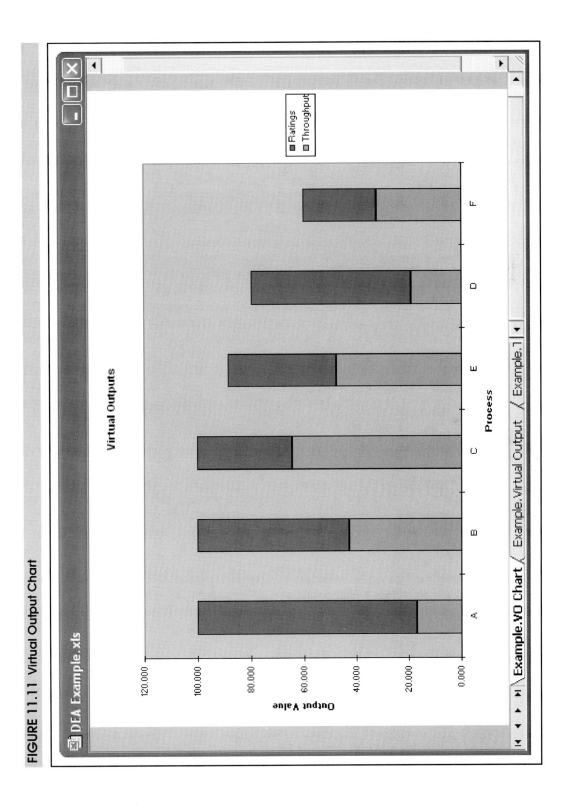

407

branches, and the changes that the less-productive branches needed to make to reach the best-practice level and to improve productivity.

The model used inputs such as number of customer service tellers, office square footage, and total expenses (excluding personnel and rent). The outputs that were considered included number of deposits, withdrawals, loans, new accounts, bank checks, and travelers checks. Out of the 33 branches, the analysis identified that 10 were relatively efficient. The peer groups for the relatively inefficient branches were used to identify the operating characteristics that made the less-productive branches more costly to operate.

11.5 Summary

This book first looked at the issues of process design from a conceptual, high-level view in the first three chapters. Chapter 4 began the move from a high-level to a low-level, detailed examination of processes and flows. This detailed examination led readers through deterministic models for cycle time and capacity analysis in Chapter 5, stochastic queuing models in Chapter 6, and the use of computer simulation for modeling business processes in Section 6.3 and Chapters 7, 8, and 9. Chapter 10 began the ascent to a higher-level view of a process by treating simulation models as black boxes. In the black-box view, the internal details of the simulation model were not of concern; instead, the focus was on finding effective values for input parameters, where effectiveness was measured by retrieving relevant output from the simulation model. Finally, Chapter 11 continued the ascent to an even higher-level view that not only treats a process as a black box but also measures effectiveness with a static set of input and output values. Data envelopment analysis, the technique used in this final chapter, is not concerned with the dynamics of the process but rather with the effective transformation of a chosen set of inputs into outputs.

Data envelopment analysis (DEA) is not well known, even though the technique was introduced more than 25 years ago and is based on mathematical models that originated in the 1950s. This chapter is an attempt to bring DEA to the forefront of the benchmarking techniques. The exploration of DEA as a benchmarking tool goes beyond the ratio model presented in this chapter. Other models have been developed already, and ongoing research continues to uncover innovative ways of applying DEA.

11.6 References

Charnes, A., W. W. Cooper, and E. Rhodes. 1978. Measuring the efficiency of decision making units. *European Journal of Operational Research* 2(6): 429–444.

Emrouznejad, Ali. 1995–2001. Ali Emrouznejad's DEA HomePage. Warwick Business School, Coventry CV4 7AL, UK (www.deazone.com).

Sherman, H. D., and G. Ladino. 1995. Managing bank productivity using data envelopment analysis. *Interfaces* 25(2): 60–73.

11.7 Discussion Questions and Exercises

1. Use the graphical approach to data envelopment analysis and the data in Table 11.5 to determine the efficiency of each process.
2. One major concern with the DEA approach is that with a judicious choice of weights, a high proportion of processes in the set will turn out to be efficient and DEA will thus have little discriminatory power. Can this happen when a process has the highest ratio of one of the outputs to one of the inputs, considering all the processes in the analysis? Why or why not?

TABLE 11.5 Data for Exercise 1

Process	Input	Output 1	Output 2
A	15	90	66
B	20	45	130
C	30	87	147
D	15	75	90
E	30	150	120
F	10	75	40

3. Do you think it is possible for a process to appear efficient simply because of its pattern of inputs and outputs and not because of any inherent efficiency? Give a numerical example to illustrate this issue.

4. In some applications of DEA, it has been suggested to impose limits on the weight values for all the processes; that is, the application considers that each weight must be between some specified bounds. Under which circumstances would it be necessary to impose such a range?

5. Consider the linear programming model for process D shown in Section 11.2. The manager of process D has suggested the use of the following weight values: $wout(1) = 0.4$, $wout(2) = 0.75$, and $win = 1$. The manager argues that if each process is allowed to choose weights in order to maximize its efficiency, he should be allowed to use these values, which clearly show that process D is relatively efficient. What is wrong with the manager's reasoning?

6. *Warehouse Efficiency:* A distribution system for a large grocery chain consists of 25 warehouses. The director of logistics and transportation would like to evaluate the relative efficiency of each warehouse. Warehouses have a fleet of trucks to deliver grocery items to a set of stores within their region. The director has identified five input factors and four output factors than can be used to evaluate the relative efficiency of the warehouses. The input factors are number of trucks, full-time-equivalent employees, warehouse size, operating expenses, and average number of overtime hours per week. The manager of each warehouse uses overtime hours to pay drivers so delivery routes can be completed. The output factors are number of deliveries, percentage of on-time deliveries, truck utilization, and customer ratings. Truck utilization is the percentage of time that a truck is actually delivering goods, which excludes traveling time when the truck is empty. This output measure encourages an efficient use of the fleet by employing routes that minimize total travel time. Store managers within each region give customer ratings to their supplying warehouses (10 is a perfect score). Table 11.6 shows data relevant to this analysis.

   a. Use data envelopment analysis to identify the relatively efficient warehouses.

   b. Find the set of less-productive warehouses and identify the percentage of excess resources used by each warehouse in this set.

   c. Identify the reference set (or peer group) for each inefficient warehouse.

   d. The director is concerned with the fact that some warehouses might appear relatively efficient by ignoring within their weighing structure all but very small subsets of their inputs and outputs. The director wants to be sure that relative efficiency is not simply the consequence of a totally unrealistic weighing structure. He would like you to construct a cross-efficiency matrix to determine efficient operating practices. (See Table 11.7.) This matrix conveys information on how a warehouse's relative efficiency is rated by other warehouses. The entry in cell (i, j) shows the relative efficiency of warehouse j with the DEA weights that are optimal for the warehouse i. Then the average efficiency in each column is computed to get a measure of how the warehouse associated with the column is rated by the rest of the warehouses. A high average efficiency identifies good operating practices. The director believes this procedure can effectively discriminate between a warehouse that is a self-evaluator and one that is an evaluator of other warehouses.

TABLE 11.6 Data for Exercise 6

No.	No. of Trucks	FTE Employees	Warehouse Size	Operating Expenses	Driver Overtime	On-time Deliveries (%)	Number of Deliveries	Truck Utilization	Customer Rating
1	10	19	9,828	10,995	7	97	232	0.662	8.10
2	16	25	15,485	14,459	15	84	370	0.627	6.37
3	11	17	11,625	10,505	8	87	333	0.872	5.20
4	14	33	13,221	16,750	14	99	265	0.532	8.69
5	10	21	10,643	10,990	9	81	211	0.569	9.43
6	19	44	19,312	19,389	16	97	588	0.937	5.05
7	14	30	13,373	18,410	13	94	309	0.650	7.71
8	19	31	18,405	17,820	17	90	420	0.628	9.25
9	20	40	20,782	27,519	16	77	388	0.539	8.25
10	20	37	19,183	21,748	17	90	436	0.644	9.38
11	19	40	18,878	20,842	15	75	568	0.836	5.82
12	16	28	16,661	20,969	16	80	408	0.708	8.93
13	12	26	12,763	14,226	10	97	318	0.807	7.79
14	18	34	17,025	17,279	18	89	441	0.685	5.53
15	11	23	10,178	11,723	10	91	339	0.859	8.77
16	10	23	9,239	8,673	9	96	302	0.887	9.57
17	20	49	20,103	25,258	19	82	575	0.871	6.19
18	18	37	17,262	19,160	14	91	450	0.744	9.01
19	12	18	12,033	11,131	8	71	352	0.888	8.39
20	18	39	17,326	23,390	13	90	532	0.837	7.26
21	14	24	14,555	16,996	13	86	383	0.821	6.01
22	19	45	18,719	22,281	19	91	548	0.865	5.51
23	19	31	19,776	20,774	15	78	480	0.713	5.03
24	11	25	11,690	11,306	7	76	236	0.578	6.47
25	15	35	14,471	13,861	13	94	343	0.674	5.31

TABLE 11.7 Efficiency Matrix Template

Warehouse (i)	Warehouse (j)		
	1	2	...
1	1		
2		1	
...			1
Average			

e. The director also would like to set targets for those warehouses that have been identified as inefficient. Can you recommend some targets for the relatively inefficient warehouses?

f. The director is preparing a presentation to discuss the results of this analysis with the warehouse managers. What output data or exhibits would you recommend the director use for this presentation?

Appendix

Statistical Tables

Chi-Square Distribution Table

n	$\chi^2_{0.995}$	$\chi^2_{0.99}$	$\chi^2_{0.975}$	$\chi^2_{0.95}$	$\chi^2_{0.90}$
1	7.88	6.63	5.02	3.84	2.71
2	10.60	9.21	7.38	5.99	4.61
3	12.84	11.34	9.35	7.81	6.25
4	14.86	13.28	11.14	9.49	7.78
5	16.75	15.09	12.83	11.07	9.24
6	18.55	16.81	14.45	12.59	10.64
7	20.28	18.48	16.01	14.07	12.02
8	21.95	20.09	17.53	15.51	13.36
9	23.59	21.67	19.02	16.92	14.68
10	25.19	23.21	20.48	18.31	15.99
11	26.76	24.73	21.92	19.68	17.28
12	28.30	26.22	23.34	21.03	18.55
13	29.82	27.69	24.74	22.36	19.81
14	31.32	29.14	26.12	23.68	21.06
15	32.80	30.58	27.49	25.00	22.31
16	34.27	32.00	28.85	26.30	23.54
17	35.72	33.41	30.19	27.59	24.77
18	37.16	34.81	31.53	28.87	25.99
19	38.58	36.19	32.85	30.14	27.20
20	40.00	37.57	34.17	31.41	28.41
21	41.40	38.93	35.48	32.67	29.62
22	42.80	40.29	36.78	33.92	30.81
23	44.18	41.64	38.08	35.17	32.01
24	45.56	42.98	39.36	36.42	33.20
25	46.93	44.31	40.65	37.65	34.38
26	48.29	45.64	41.92	38.89	35.56
27	49.65	46.96	43.19	40.11	36.74
28	50.99	48.28	44.46	41.34	37.92
29	52.34	49.59	45.72	42.56	39.09
30	53.67	50.89	46.98	43.77	40.26
40	66.77	63.69	59.34	55.76	51.81
50	79.49	76.15	71.42	67.50	63.17
60	91.95	88.38	83.30	79.08	74.40
70	104.21	100.43	95.02	90.53	85.53
80	116.32	112.33	106.63	101.88	96.58
90	128.30	124.12	118.14	113.15	107.57
100	140.17	135.81	129.56	124.34	118.50

Normal Distribution Table

Z	0.00	0.01	0.02	0.03	0.04	0.05	0.06	0.07	0.08	0.09
0.0	0.5000	0.5040	0.5080	0.5120	0.5160	0.5199	0.5239	0.5279	0.5319	0.5359
0.1	0.5398	0.5438	0.5478	0.5517	0.5557	0.5596	0.5636	0.5675	0.5714	0.5753
0.2	0.5793	0.5832	0.5871	0.5910	0.5948	0.5987	0.6026	0.6064	0.6103	0.6141
0.3	0.6179	0.6217	0.6255	0.6293	0.6331	0.6368	0.6406	0.6443	0.6480	0.6517
0.4	0.6554	0.6591	0.6628	0.6664	0.6700	0.6736	0.6772	0.6808	0.6844	0.6879
0.5	0.6915	0.6950	0.6985	0.7019	0.7054	0.7088	0.7123	0.7157	0.7190	0.7224
0.6	0.7257	0.7291	0.7324	0.7357	0.7389	0.7422	0.7454	0.7486	0.7517	0.7549
0.7	0.7580	0.7611	0.7642	0.7673	0.7704	0.7734	0.7764	0.7794	0.7823	0.7852
0.8	0.7881	0.7910	0.7939	0.7967	0.7995	0.8023	0.8051	0.8078	0.8106	0.8133
0.9	0.8159	0.8186	0.8212	0.8238	0.8264	0.8289	0.8315	0.8340	0.8365	0.8389
1.0	0.8413	0.8438	0.8461	0.8485	0.8508	0.8531	0.8554	0.8577	0.8599	0.8621
1.1	0.8643	0.8665	0.8686	0.8708	0.8729	0.8749	0.8770	0.8790	0.8810	0.8830
1.2	0.8849	0.8869	0.8888	0.8907	0.8925	0.8944	0.8962	0.8980	0.8997	0.9015
1.3	0.9032	0.9049	0.9066	0.9082	0.9099	0.9115	0.9131	0.9147	0.9162	0.9177
1.4	0.9192	0.9207	0.9222	0.9236	0.9251	0.9265	0.9279	0.9292	0.9306	0.9319
1.5	0.9332	0.9345	0.9357	0.9370	0.9382	0.9394	0.9406	0.9418	0.9429	0.9441
1.6	0.9452	0.9463	0.9474	0.9484	0.9495	0.9505	0.9515	0.9525	0.9535	0.9545
1.7	0.9554	0.9564	0.9573	0.9582	0.9591	0.9599	0.9608	0.9616	0.9625	0.9633
1.8	0.9641	0.9649	0.9656	0.9664	0.9671	0.9678	0.9686	0.9693	0.9699	0.9706
1.9	0.9713	0.9719	0.9726	0.9732	0.9738	0.9744	0.9750	0.9756	0.9761	0.9767
2.0	0.9772	0.9778	0.9783	0.9788	0.9793	0.9798	0.9803	0.9808	0.9812	0.9817
2.1	0.9821	0.9826	0.9830	0.9834	0.9838	0.9842	0.9846	0.9850	0.9854	0.9857
2.2	0.9861	0.9864	0.9868	0.9871	0.9875	0.9878	0.9881	0.9884	0.9887	0.9890
2.3	0.9893	0.9896	0.9898	0.9901	0.9904	0.9906	0.9909	0.9911	0.9913	0.9916
2.4	0.9918	0.9920	0.9922	0.9925	0.9927	0.9929	0.9931	0.9932	0.9934	0.9936
2.5	0.9938	0.9940	0.9941	0.9943	0.9945	0.9946	0.9948	0.9949	0.9951	0.9952
2.6	0.9953	0.9955	0.9956	0.9957	0.9959	0.9960	0.9961	0.9962	0.9963	0.9964
2.7	0.9965	0.9966	0.9967	0.9968	0.9969	0.9970	0.9971	0.9972	0.9973	0.9974
2.8	0.9974	0.9975	0.9976	0.9977	0.9977	0.9978	0.9979	0.9979	0.9980	0.9981
2.9	0.9981	0.9982	0.9982	0.9983	0.9984	0.9984	0.9985	0.9985	0.9986	0.9986
3.0	0.9987	0.9987	0.9987	0.9988	0.9988	0.9989	0.9989	0.9989	0.9990	0.9990
3.1	0.9990	0.9991	0.9991	0.9991	0.9992	0.9992	0.9992	0.9992	0.9993	0.9993
3.2	0.9993	0.9993	0.9994	0.9994	0.9994	0.9994	0.9994	0.9995	0.9995	0.9995
3.3	0.9995	0.9995	0.9995	0.9996	0.9996	0.9996	0.9996	0.9996	0.9996	0.9997
3.4	0.9997	0.9997	0.9997	0.9997	0.9997	0.9997	0.9997	0.9997	0.9997	0.9998
3.5	0.9998	0.9998	0.9998	0.9998	0.9998	0.9998	0.9998	0.9998	0.9998	0.9998

Student *t* Distribution Table

n	$t_{0.995}$	$t_{0.99}$	$t_{0.975}$	$t_{0.95}$	$t_{0.90}$
1	63.656	31.821	12.706	6.314	3.078
2	9.925	6.965	4.303	2.920	1.886
3	5.841	4.541	3.182	2.353	1.638
4	4.604	3.747	2.776	2.132	1.533
5	4.032	3.365	2.571	2.015	1.476
6	3.707	3.143	2.447	1.943	1.440
7	3.499	2.998	2.365	1.895	1.415
8	3.355	2.896	2.306	1.860	1.397
9	3.250	2.821	2.262	1.833	1.383
10	3.169	2.764	2.228	1.812	1.372
11	3.106	2.718	2.201	1.796	1.363
12	3.055	2.681	2.179	1.782	1.356
13	3.012	2.650	2.160	1.771	1.350
14	2.977	2.624	2.145	1.761	1.345
15	2.947	2.602	2.131	1.753	1.341
16	2.921	2.583	2.120	1.746	1.337
17	2.898	2.567	2.110	1.740	1.333
18	2.878	2.552	2.101	1.734	1.330
19	2.861	2.539	2.093	1.729	1.328
20	2.845	2.528	2.086	1.725	1.325
21	2.831	2.518	2.080	1.721	1.323
22	2.819	2.508	2.074	1.717	1.321
23	2.807	2.500	2.069	1.714	1.319
24	2.797	2.492	2.064	1.711	1.318
25	2.787	2.485	2.060	1.708	1.316
26	2.779	2.479	2.056	1.706	1.315
27	2.771	2.473	2.052	1.703	1.314
28	2.763	2.467	2.048	1.701	1.313
29	2.756	2.462	2.045	1.699	1.311
30	2.750	2.457	2.042	1.697	1.310
∞	2.576	2.326	1.960	1.645	1.282

Index